THE MADISONS

Oil portraits of James and Dolley Madison painted by Joseph Wood in March 1817 just as Madison was retiring from the Presidency. He was 66, his wife almost 49. This book would stress ripeness. To quote Eliza Lee to whom the Wood portraits were presented: "The likeness of your dear husband almost breathes, . . .

in short it is *himself*. Your likeness, my dear friend, is not satisfactory *to me*. To a common observer it is . . . instantly recognized—but I lament the absence of that expression of your eyes which speaks *from* and *to* the heart. . . ." The reader can put back the light. *(Courtesy of the Virginia Historical Society)*

THE
MADISONS

A Biography

❧ · ❧

VIRGINIA MOORE

McGRAW-HILL BOOK COMPANY

New York   St. Louis   San Francisco

Auckland   Bogotá   Düsseldorf   Johannesburg   London   Madrid

Mexico   Montreal   New Delhi   Panama   Paris   São Paulo

Singapore   Sydney   Tokyo   Toronto

Thomas Quinn and Michael Hennelly were the editors of this book. Christine Aulicino was the designer. Frank Bellantoni and Thomas Kowalczyk supervised the production. It was set in Baskerville by University Graphics, Inc.

Printed and bound by Kingsport Press.

Library of Congress Cataloging in Publication Data

Moore, Virginia
    The Madisons.

     Bibliography: p.
     Includes index.
     1. Madison, James, Pres. U.S., 1751–1836.
2. Madison, Dolley Payne Todd, 1768–1849. 3. President
—United States—Biography. 4. Presidents—United
States—Wives—Biography. I. Title.
E342.M6   973.5'1'0922 [B]   78-17958
ISBN 0-07-042903-0

2 3 4 5 6 7 8 9 KPKP 7 9 4 3 2 1 0 8 9

In memory of my first philosophy teacher
Mary Williamson of Hollins

Contents

Cast of the Main Characters

JAMES MADISON: Chief architect of the Constitution and Fourth President of the United States—scholar, farmer, statesman—whom strangers found stiff but intimates delightful.

DOLLEY PAYNE (TODD) MADISON: Madison's greatest good fortune and America's most popular First Lady, a Quaker who kicked over some traces, but who was more than a stereotype of charm and hospitality, being a woman of substance.

JOHN PAYNE TODD, called Payne: Dolley's son, whom Madison raised as his own, a promising youth, a man who did his best to break their hearts.

ANNA PAYNE CUTTS: Dolley's "sister-child" who gave the Madisons much joy, to say nothing of two loved nieces (Dolley and Mary) and four loved nephews (Walter, Thomas, Madison and Dick).

LUCY PAYNE (WASHINGTON) TODD: Dolley's most ebullient sister, a "great belle" with an ever-moving clapper.

ELIZA COLLINS LEE: Dolley's earliest and lifelong friend—the "little mouse."

DONALD ROBERTSON: The schoolmaster of whom Madison said, "all that I know I owe to that man."

DR. JOHN WITHERSPOON: President and chief lecturer at the college at Princeton, who influenced greatly Madison's philosophy.

WILLIAM BRADFORD: The young Madison's bosom friend.

GEORGE MASON: An old hand at statesmanship who learned something from the novice Madison.

EDMUND RANDOLPH: Madison's friend and Washington's Secretary of State who possessed and lost, through others' malice and his own misjudgment, almost everything.

PATRICK HENRY: Dolley's cousin and Madison's *bête noir.*

JOHN JAY: The treaty-maker whom Madison the forgiving found it hard to forgive.

THOMAS JEFFERSON: For fifty years Madison's collaborator and closest friend—between them no shadow ever fell.

JOHN RANDOLPH of Roanoke: Eloquent raver.

MELLIMELLI: Tunisian Ambassador Extraordinary rigged out in five gold-and-silver-weighted burnooses and a plaster-of-Paris turban.

SARAH (SALLY) COLES STEVENSON: Dolley's gypsy-attractive young cousin and frequent White House guest.

EDWARD (NED) COLES: Dolley's cousin and Madison's White House secretary.

PHOEBE MORRIS: The blond girl whom Dolley wanted for her daughter-in-law and Payne turned down—but death didn't.

BRITISH MINISTER ANTHONY AND MRS. MERRY: A couple who developed scruples against "eating soup" with President Jefferson.

FRENCH MINISTER LOUIS MARIE AND MME. TURREAU: "The butcher" and his likeable, crass, put-upon wife.

SPANISH MINISTER CARLOS MARTINEZ, MARQUIS DE CASA YRUJO: A diplomat who cut quite a figure—also Madison; and who went off to Madrid in umbrage with his wife the gorgeous Sally McKean of Philadelphia (destined to end up fat, wearing eyeglasses, and cynical).

ELIZABETH (BETSEY) PATTERSON: The risqué beauty who married Napoleon's youngest brother Jerome and became, when discarded, the disillusioned (and slightly catty) little "Duchess of Baltimore."

PHILIP FRENEAU: Wielder of a political and sometimes wicked pen.

GEORGE WASHINGTON: Commander-in-Chief and first President who called Madison "my special friend" until, politically, they drifted apart.

THE MARQUIS DE LAFAYETTE: A Frenchman who helped America win its Revolution and returned forty years later in triumph and a red wig.

ALEXANDER HAMILTON: First Madison's friend, later a political foe whom he always esteemed as honest.

AARON BURR: A friend whom the Madisons lived to shun as a traitor to his country.

JAMES MONROE: Friend, antagonist, then (again and thankfully) friend, who became (after a painful delay) Madison's Secretary of State.

ALBERT GALLATIN: President Madison's Swiss-born invaluable Secretary of the Treasury, whom the Federalists sneered at as "the foreigner."

JOHN ARMSTRONG: Madison's Secretary of War, who almost did in Washington City.

JOHN CALHOUN: An honorable troublemaker.

HENRY CLAY: Madison's wide-mouthed ally.

DANIEL WEBSTER: A brilliance.

BRITISH MINISTER AUGUSTUS FOSTER: A decent man who ate too many dinners with the Federalists.

FRENCH MINISTER LOUIS SÉRURIER: A diplomat who admired Americans, most of all Madison.

ADMIRAL SIR ALEXANDER COCHRANE, ADMIRAL SIR GEORGE COCKBURN AND GENERAL ROBERT ROSS: Britishers who, in the War of 1812, fought the United States with no holds barred.

ANDREW JACKSON: Wild-haired victor at the Battle of New Orleans whose Presidential policies, afterward, appalled the Madisons.

NICHOLAS TRIST: Rector Madison's liaison at the University of Virginia, then the aging Madison's political disciple.

ANNIE PAYNE: Dolley's laughing niece, child of her brother John, who became a kind of adopted daughter at Montpelier.

SAWNEY, SUKEY, PAUL JENNINGS: Three of the Madisons' servants.

NAPOLEON BONAPARTE: Conqueror of Europe.

Preface

A BOOK MUST STAND ON ITS OWN FEET. In a very real sense prefaces are superfluous. But let me say a few words.

I have tried to put blood back into the veins of James Madison, not just the politician, but the man, the whole man; and into Dolley Madison who was much more than the stereotype of charm and hospitality usually depicted. Neither was flawless, but each was an extraordinary, developing human being. And I was interested in something no writer had ever traced: their reciprocal relationship.

Like many biographers of people long dead (Madison 143 years, Dolley only thirteen years less) I could wish that the primary sources in some areas were fuller; also that certain journals, such as the one Dolley planned to start, had been written and lay on my desk; and that certain other evidence, such as the packet of love letters from Madison to Dolley which General Ross stole from the White House, had not perished. Still, it is surprising how much a careful piecing together of sources can reveal about this "least known of the founding fathers" and his delightful wife.

Commentators have stressed that Madison stood for freedom and union. Yes—but so did all the early American patriots. I was searching for what made Madison unique.

When Jefferson lay dying he wrote his closest friend, "Take care of me when dead." Madison did. But by one of the ironies of history Madison himself left no peer to defend him against the neglect and misconstruction which followed on the heels of the tremendous reputation he enjoyed at the time of his death in 1836: a reversal explainable by—among other factors—convictions about the Union which, at the approach of the Civil War, alienated his own state of Virginia. Moreover, unlike Jefferson, Madison left no child or grandchild to stand watch at the gate; only a wastrel stepson who scattered most of his personal papers and his splendid library.

I have taken advantage of much hitherto unknown, and some known but unused, material, such as information from collateral descendants living and dead, including Mary E. E. Cutts's experience-wise memoir; and a collection of Catherine Mitchill's letters only recently made available at the Library of Congress. Also a great many known but only partially used, though very rich, sources, such as Anne Royall's interview with Dolley at fifty, reminiscences of the famous English sociologist Harriet Martineau, and—most important, a little-mined lode of pure gold— memorabilia from the estate of Dolley's great-grandnephew John B. Kunkel.

Friends have chided me for my choice of subject and for giving it so many years. What can I say? America needs her great ones. They are relevant.

V. M.

Cliffside
Scottsville, Virginia

Acknowledgments

MY SINCERE THANKS to the staffs of the many institutions where I have done research for this book. I would like to mention in particular Dorothy Eaton, formerly specialist in early American history in the Manuscript Division at the Library of Congress, who, when I first became interested in the Madisons, offered useful suggestions; also Susan Marcell of the University of Virginia's Alderman Library who more than once came to the rescue with cheerfulness and generosity.

I also acknowledge with gratitude the help of many individuals unconnected with institutions; among them, Dr. John A. Washington of Harewood, a direct descendant of Dolley's sister Lucy, who years ago, with his wife Margaret, delighted me with family information while showing me their fine old stone house; Marian Dupont Scott, owner of Montpelier, whose secretary, Chester Hazard, showed me the mansion and its grounds and gardens; Norine Campbell, who kindly took me through Scotchtown before it was open to the public; the late Eleanor Fox Pearson, President of the Dolley Madison Memorial Association who—while we rocked on her porch—shared her considerable knowledge about Dolley Madison's birthplace, then arranged for me to have the great privilege of studying for a week or so the rich Kunkel collection of manuscripts while it was in the Guilford College library under lock and key, still uncataloged; the officers of the Greensboro Historical Museum which now owns the collection, together with much Madison memorabilia acquired from the same source (I recently had the pleasure of reexamining them); Minnie Hite Moody of Atlanta, Georgia, and Granville, Ohio, who opened up for me a treasure of Hite material, including a family history by her cousin Judge H. P. Baker and a letter about the Madisons' honeymoon in the Shenandoah Valley; Mrs. James Madison Cutts III and other members of the Cutts family who have shared with me interesting family lore; and Susie Blair and Mary Dee Stokes who helped me proofread.

Two people perused parts of an early draft of this book: Professor Richard E. Ellis, a specialist in early American history, then at the University of Virginia, and Francis Duke, a retired professor. I appreciate the benefit of their wise comments.

All Madison biographers coming after the late Irving Brant owe him, of necessity, a debt of gratitude for having hewed out paths of research through areas largely ignored by earlier biographers who, in the words of the *Encyclopaedia Britannica,* wrote "little more than histories of the period." I most gratefully acknowledge my own debt.

Finally, a word of thanks to the countless people who have made available, for scholarly purposes, source material connected directly or indirectly with James and Dolley Madison by generous gifts to institutions, and by permission to make microfilm copies. At the head of the list stand Mrs. George B. Cutts of Wellesley, Massachusetts, and Charles M. Storey of Boston, owners of the invaluable Cutts collection now on microfilm at the Library of Congress; also John W. Stenhouse of Washington, D. C., owner of some Morris-Nourse letters on microfilm at the University of Virginia.

THE MADISONS

⊷ I ⊶

MARRIAGE
OF OPPOSITES

THE MARRIAGE TOOK PLACE on September 15, 1794, in the big stone house at Harewood. The groom was forty-three, the bride twenty-six; the groom an intellectual, the bride a woman who ran largely on her feelings ; the groom a bachelor, the bride a widow with a little boy two and a half years old. At a glance the only thing they had in common was a height of 5 feet 6. To cap the dissimilarities the groom was an Episcopalian, the bride a "birth Quaker" raised on the Book of Discipline—one who knew as she fastened her satin wedding gown spidered over with lace (her first had been more severe) that by marrying "out of unity before a hireling priest" she would be asking to be disowned by the Society of Friends.

Her sister Lucy had been disowned. It had made no difference that her young husband was George Steptoe Washington, nephew of the President. And it would make no difference whatsoever that Dolley Payne Todd's choice was the distinguished James Madison, a man who, at twenty-five, had been elected to Virginia's first Constitutional Convention and contributed significantly to Virginia's Bill of Rights by getting religious tolerance changed to religious freedom; who had served in the State's first Assembly, then on Governor Patrick Henry's and Governor Thomas Jefferson's Privy Council, before staying the maximum term (actually more) in the Continental Congress, where he grew famous for the power and clarity of his mind. Most important, he had served brilliantly in the Convention of 1787, in Philadelphia, where his Virginia Plan, modified somewhat during four hot months plagued by flies, had

1

become the backbone of the United States Constitution. At his marriage he had now for five years served as majority leader in the first United States House of Representatives.

Upstairs a subdued bride, downstairs an excited groom: it was as if, under the dynamism of a ripening event, they had exchanged temperaments.

Dolley set a wreath of white flowers on her almost black hair and was ready. Probably, as was customary at country weddings, a fortepiano or harpsichord or fiddle had struck up. White satin slippers crossed the upper hall. Slowly they descended the stair. When Dolley came into view, the little knot of kinsmen and friends waiting in the drawing room saw—if they turned their heads slightly—a slim lady with a dazzling complexion and deep blue eyes. Dolley was not beautiful, if beauty means perfect proportions, but all her life would be seen as beautiful.

Madison was waiting by the greenish marble fireplace. He had decked himself out in a costume braving a richly embroidered waistcoat and a marvelous jabot of Mechlin lace. His head might have belonged to some Roman senator: strong nose, ample forehead, and (to judge by a portrait painted by Charles Willson Peale two years earlier) intense, living eyes. If the occasion had brought back an old shyness, he was also keyed up and had been all day. Excitement always put a flush on his cheeks. Near him, in vestments, stood his cousin-by-marriage the Rev. Alexander Balmaine.

When Dolley had taken her place at Madison's side, the rector began to read the wedding service from the Episcopal Prayer Book. For Dolley time had stopped.

"Dearly beloved," the Rev. Mr. Balmaine intoned, "we are gathered together here in the sight of God to join together this man and this woman. . . . I require and charge you both as ye shall answer at the dreadful day of judgment. . . ."

The words went on. It was happening. Nothing could stop it.

"Wilt thou have this woman . . . ?"

"I will," Madison said, and Dolley knew she was approaching the point of no return.

DOLLEY PAYNE WAS BORN on June 20, 1768, in a two-room log house at the New Garden Quaker settlement near present day Guilford College in North Carolina.

She came from what is known as good Virginia stock. Her maternal grandmother was Lucy Winston of an old Hanover County Welsh-derived Quaker family renowned for eloquence and musical ability. Lucy had married and converted Williams (not William) Coles, fresh out of Ireland. Her sister Mary Ann was the wife of a well-known Richmond merchant, John Coles, her sister Sarah the mother of Patrick Henry. Dolley's mother Mary Coles Payne—Molly—was sixteen when she married a member of the Established Church, handsome, tall, twenty-year-old John Payne of a prominent family in adjoining Goochland County, and went to live on a 200-acre farm on Little Bird Creek. Expelled from the Cedar Creek Meeting for marrying "out of unity," Molly converted her husband and—accompanied by him—found her way back into the fold.

As Dissenters from the Established Church of England, Quakers had had a rough time in the Colony of Virginia. Lovers of peace, they were—ironically—denounced as troublemakers; indeed, an early Virginia law forbade ship captains to deposit any more of these "turbulent" people on the Colony's shores. Quakers were still persecuted, though in some neighborhoods more than in others. John's Goochland kin—Paynes, Flemings, Woodsons—were far from pleased with a turncoat who, among other things, refused to tithe or have his children baptized or fight Indians; they were probably ashamed of their renegade. The situation soured, and in 1765 the young John Paynes, with their little son Walter, moved to North Carolina to pioneer on a tract given to them by John's father Colonel Josias Payne, burgess and large landowner. John kept acquiring land until he held some 280 acres. Two children were born there: William Temple, called Temple, and Dolley. The name is Dolley on the birth certificate, not Dorothy or Dorothea; *Dolley*.

It was a rugged life, and Dolley was only ten months old when she rode a wagon back through wild country to Molly's old home, Coles Hill, near Hanover Courthouse. Molly's father gave them the 176-acre "school 'farm," and John bought 73 additional acres. Later, under circumstances not entirely clear, he moved his growing family 10 miles away to the great tobacco plantation Scotchtown.

Patrick Henry had owned it from 1771 to 1778. That year Wilson Miles Cary (later Governor) of the many seats bought it as a refuge from the Revolution then raging. The British were marauding all too close to his family home Ceeley's on the Chesapeake. Besides, Federalist troops had taken it over for a smallpox camp. But Cary stayed at Scotchtown little, if at all, and apparently rented it to John Payne or hired him as overseer or rented the plantation. (A census gives the number of slaves on its 960 acres as eighty.) Since Cary owned Scotchtown until 1787, four years after the Paynes left Hanover, and no deed exists to show that John ever owned Scotchtown, there is no other way to explain Dolley's fond attachment to and vivid memory of Scotchtown as her Virginia home. Most likely she lived there from the age of ten to fifteen. That John Payne should have preferred tenancy to ownership during the Revolutionary War makes sense. Because Quakers refused to sign the Oath or serve as regulars or militiamen during the Revolution, their property was subject to confiscation. It was safer not to own any.

Scotchtown was a huge old clapboard house with a hip roof and enormous chimneys. It had an above-ground basement of many rooms, a main floor with eight rooms divided by a great hall entered at either end through a big heavy walnut door, and an attic ideal for children's games on a rainy afternoon. Dolley would always remember the white marble figures supporting Scotchtown's black marble mantels.

Outdoors there were bushes of glossy English boxwood, and a brood of buildings clucked around the courtyard of the main house like young quail around the mother: summer kitchen, office, storehouse, washhouse, ashhouse, forge, and tannery. Below a slope running down to the New Found River stood thirty cabins and a flour mill.

The Paynes's family life centered around nearby brick Cedar Creek Meeting House. John Payne in his homespun, shad-bellied black coat, square-toed shoes, and broadbrim, and Molly in grey linsey-woolsey or muslin and a little white cap, were soon made elders, and Papa—now a clerk—gained the further distinction of being "Public Friend" and "Publisher of Truth." Six Payne children went to school in the Meeting Room where Papa often spoke, under inspiration, to a congregation in which the sexes were strictly segregated. As Dolley walked through the woods to her lessons, nature offered all the amusements her elders forbade: theater, county fair, dancing. She could watch yellow butterflies like flowers of Scotch broom fluttering. Pine needles cushioned her feet, and leaves cast interesting shadows. But those big black floppy buzzards—what were they looking for?

As she grew older, she heard talk about things she didn't understand: Stamp Act, Continental Congress, Bunker Hill. Neighbors were shouldering flintlocks and marching off to battle. Some of Papa's kin were majors in the Goochland militia, and his Uncle Tarleton Fleming was the second-in-command: Lieutenant Colonel. But Papa said war was wrong and kept on cultivating tobacco. For his religion he could stand taunts and gibes—imprisonment if need be.

In time Dolley could see how differently from other folks her Quakers dressed and lived and thought. Grandmother Payne, born Anna Fleming of Rock Castle, wore silk dresses and jewelry. Grandfather Josias Payne and Great-uncle John—burgesses—wore fine braided jackets and tricorns, and laughed and gamed and rode horses hard.

Once Grandmother Payne gave Dolley a forbidden, wonderful "bauble" which she wore around her neck in a little chamois bag under her clothes, her terror and her delight. No one knew about it except the children's black nurse Mother Amy, and she wouldn't tell. One day when Dolley was on her way to school, the string broke, and though she combed the leaves, searching, searching, she never found what conscience told her she never should have possessed.

But one vanity her pious mother abetted, or permitted on doctor's orders to prevent a delicate skin from peeling. In strong sunlight Dolley wore a little white linen mask and white linen gloves.

Sitting on a hard bench, the little girl in ankle-length grey muslin could understand why the Colonies didn't want King George III any more. They weren't free; they felt stifled. The reading, writing, and arithmetic for which Papa paid 30 shillings a year kept her shut up for long hours. The reading didn't sing like poetry; it was mostly from the Book of Discipline.

Dolley saw the Quaker coin's two sides, yes and no. Quakers said no to insincerity and "parade," their chief diversion being the Monthly and Quarterly Meetings, when vehicles trundled in from afar, and they felt the fire of a heightened fellowship. Their great yes was to the "inner light." If one stayed very still and "centered down," they said, something mysterious happened or could happen inside; a door opened. The Society's founder George Fox had called the experience an "opening," a "pure opening." It strengthened you to bear difficult things.

There were plenty to bear. Though the Virginia Declaration of Rights granted religious freedom in 1776—thanks largely to a man named James Madison—and Madison's "Remonstrance" had helped to implement the clause, the War had come along to make new and terrible problems of allegiance. Never mind, Papa and Mama said, "We can do all things through Christ which strengtheneth us."

Even abolish slavery. The Cedar Creek Meeting had branded slavery a sin and said steps must be taken against it. Dolley's parents had charge of the book recording manumissions. Though here in Virginia the freeing of slaves was illegal, John and Molly believed that there was a higher law, that to own a human being corrupted the owner no less than the owned.

Papa felt trapped. How raise tobacco without black labor or support his family elsewhere? He had learned no profession and was ignorant of commerce. Sometimes during the spring of 1781 he and Mama talked about Philadelphia, the city of brotherly love, stronghold of their Society, where Walter had gone at seventeen (perhaps to escape conscription). But they could not consider moving in wartime: Cornwallis and Lafayette were playing hide-and-seek across Virginia.

As eldest daughter, now nearly thirteen, Dolley helped with the younger children, Isaac, Lucy, Anna, and baby Mary. Inevitably she was of two minds about the possibility of Philadelphia: reluctant to leave home and friends, curious to see the great world.

The Revolution kept intruding. Friends and relatives died, and there were rumors of defeats and victories, and Papa was in trouble because he would neither fight in a war nor pay taxes for one. General Cornwallis began scorching a path closer at hand. On June 3—it was frightening—he marched his main army past Scotchtown. Then the Paynes heard that Colonel Banastre Tarleton had raided the great Goochland plantations along the James, including Rock Castle, where he tore the Tarleton coat of arms off the wall. What humiliation for Papa's Fleming kin with their Tarleton blood—the whole tribe of Goochland Tarletons. And when redcoats stalked ex-Governor Jefferson at Monticello, he had sent his wife and daughters down the mountain to Enniscorthy, home of Mama's double first cousin John Coles II. The war pressed so close it could be taken personally.

The British surrender at Yorktown opened a gate into the future. Even Quakers celebrated. Virginia had become a free and sovereign state linked to twelve free and sovereign states. The immensity of the nation taxed Dolley's very good imagination.

When Walter was about to sail for England, Mama took a stagecoach to Philadelphia to say good-bye. The city was a revelation. While staying with a Quaker family, the Drinkers, she did some reconnoitering and came home enthusiastic. Yes, why not move to Penn's town? And so it was decided. But the great migration must be postponed until after the birth of Molly's eighth child.

The following year Papa and Mama gave each slave a manumission paper proclaiming his God-given freedom. At last they were ready to take six older children and baby John, widowed Grandmother Coles, and Mother Amy, now a wage earner, and go north.

An undated letter from Dolley—the earliest extant—was written in late June 1783 to a Virginia friend, Judith Richardson, near Rocky Hills. "I cannot think I am never more to see thee my Dr Judith." Because she and her family are about to "embark for Philadelphia" (apparently going by water), she is very busy. It is a great disappointment not to visit Judith and Nancy Morris, as planned, to bring them her affection and explain "the laws of my destiny." Try to come with Nancy, she urges; it is the last opportunity. There have been several farewell "frolics," and if Judith can attend, they will have one more. "Adieu my D^r. May the smiles of Fortune be equal to thy Merit. . . ."

(Dolley would be faithful. In 1800—married—she would send "affectionate love" to all the Richardsons and invite Judith to Montpelier.)

There was acute excitement in packing and traveling hundreds of miles. It was a mighty upheaval. None of the details have been recorded, but on July 9, 1783, the Payne family arrived at the Drinker home in Philadelphia. Dolley had just turned fifteen.

Philadelphia, with its 30,000 inhabitants, was the largest city in the United States. For Dolley it was sheer bedazzlement: brick houses, elegant carriages, ships on the Schuylkill and Delaware, a hospital, a theater, a lending library, the Indian Queen with its fashionable clientele, and the great bronze liberty bell at Independence Hall; the whole place saturated with history. And not all history lay in the past; it was happening now. Dolley could walk past William Penn's house and Betsy Ross's upholstery shop—ah, that first American flag—and see where the Continental Congress was meeting. One who knew her at this time would recall, some fifty years later, that "she came upon our cold hearts in Philadelphia, suddenly and unexpectedly, with all the delightful influences of a summer sun from the sweet South in the month of May."

If Philadelphia was unbelievably large, there Mr. John Payne's house, two stories and an attic, was unbelievably small. The house sat hard against a footpath with not one sprig of grass, a far cry from Scotchtown and the woods of Hanover County.

The next seven years were whited over with starch. Papa ran his modest business on the ground floor, front. A little sister named Philadelphia had died soon after birth. Isaac and Temple were developing young men's troubles. But the family had found new friends as well as problems, and often at the Pine Street Meeting House the voice of inspiration was Papa's.

Unfortunately he had no talent for the new trade; his starch crumbled. The family retreated from house to house to come to rest at last—or so they hoped—at number 231 New Street. After their years of Virginia largess, they felt the bite of poverty. Living costs were rising crazily—beef 13 pence a pound! The money which Papa had brought to Philadelphia had depreciated and melted. He was caught between the pincers of inflation and a failing business. Mother Amy was hard put to feed the family. And the parents felt a mounting sense of disgrace as the Society went on disowning their children: Walter for a cause not recorded, Isaac for immorality, Temple for joining the United States Navy.

Then—it was incredible—the Society ejected Papa himself, Publisher of Truth, for the offense of bankruptcy. It felled him. Amid the raw cries of street vendors—"New quill pens!" "Fresh peaches!"—he sat hunched in his room like a man sent to the stocks and whipping post. He did not criticize the Society. He never criticized the Society—only himself. He rallied enough to join the "free Quakers," who made fewer strictures. But he was still crushed and melancholy.

Mama rallied from the shock of the disaster, and when Temple and Isaac went to Norfolk to seek their fortunes, she pressed the remainder of the family into smaller quarters to make room for congressional boarders. Mother Amy fried more chicken and baked more cornbread, and in spite of the brooding man upstairs, the house stirred with new possibilities.

The nation also was renewing itself. Now that it had a Constitution and its capital had moved back to Philadelphia, the town was in ferment. Dolley knew President Washington's cream-colored coach with its flowers and cupids and liveried postillions, and could recognize many of the notables among sumptuously garbed guests going in and out of the Indian Queen. She enjoyed taking part, however obscurely, in the great experiment of this nation unique on the earth.

Her mother permitted seemly diversions such as picnics at the Drinkers' farm in Frankfort. Sweet-tempered and gay, she was popular with young and old. Sometimes Quaker friends rode over from Maryland on horseback, their grey clothes stuffed into saddlebags. Sometimes Dolley visited friends at their tavern in Haddonfield. When Mrs. Creighton took her into Trenton to shop, a girl starved for beauty enjoyed running her fingers through fine fabrics. Her best friend was a small demure girl with large eyes named Elizabeth Collins and called Eliza or Betsey.

No, Dolley told John Todd when he proposed, she would never marry. But she felt grateful to the young lawyer for loyalty to her father during his humiliation. John persisted. Papa called him a good man, and time passed, and then John Todd, twenty-six, and Dolley Payne, twenty-one, published their banns, and on a snowy day, January 7, 1790—with Eliza Collins and Anthony Morris as attendants—they stood up in Meeting, hand-in-hand, and without any intermediary "hireling priest" pledged themselves man and wife. Eighty witnesses signed the register before the two families withdrew to the bride's home for a quiet wedding supper.

The next three years were as crowded as a Saturday market. The Todds had set up housekeeping on Chestnut Street. When John prospered, they bought a handsome brick larger house at Fourth and Walnut and some better furniture, including a newfangled sideboard, and started to keep a horse and chaise. On February 29, 1792, Dolley gave birth to a son, and her father had the pleasure of seeing little John Payne Todd—his namesake—before his death (the final one) and burial "without parade."

Molly Payne met grief as she had met poverty and disgrace: with courage. Though her genteel boardinghouse was popular with senators, a deranged currency made support so hard it was a relief when Dolley took lighthearted, blond Anna into her home as sister, child, and companion.

For some time Senator Aaron Burr had been growing in favor as a family friend. The polished letters which he received from his nine-year-old daughter Theodosia and showed around convinced Dolley that he had a genius for raising children. He was often asked for advice.

But no counseling could help Mrs. Payne very much the summer of 1793, when fifteen-year-old Lucy eloped with a college student, the President's nephew, and was disowned by the Society for marrying "out of unity." On the death of his brother Ferdinand, George Steptoe Washington had succeeded to Harewood, the estate of his deceased father Samuel Washington. Harewood was near Charles Town in what was then Virginia but would someday be West Virginia. Mama sustained this shock too. Young George was upright; Dolley had a devoted Quaker husband; Anna had a haven; and Isaac and Temple were doing well in Norfolk. With just Mary and John, her youngest, at home she could manage.

That fall yellow fever struck Philadelphia. The city had suffered this plague before, but never on such a scale. The vehicles of horrified citizens pouring out of the city choked the roads. Still weak from the birth of a second son, Dolley was carried on a litter to the resort Gray's Ferry, where she languished with her mother and children while her husband returned to Philadelphia to labor among the stricken. Nothing seemed to help: quinine, mercury, jalap. In their ignorance of the means of contagion people still on their legs were mountains of suspicion. They walked in the middle of the street, refused to shake hands with anybody, burned tar, sprinkled their clothes with vinegar, and fortified their nostrils against infection and the reek of death with sweet and rank perfumes. The 4,000 dead included John Todd's parents. But the scourge was abating.

On October 24, when John felt fever racing through his veins, he rushed back to Gray's Ferry—"I must see her once more!" —and died in Dolley's arms. Baby Temple died the same day, and Dolley barely pulled through. Afterward she was more than ever passionately attached to little Payne. He was her world.

The weary Molly now yielded to the young Washingtons' plea that she and eleven-year-old Mary and ten-year-old John come to live with them at Harewood. Though she had Payne and her thirteen-year-old sister, Dolley felt lonely for her mother. Fortunately John had taken care of her in his will: "Item. I give and devise all my estate, real and personal, to the dear wife of my bosom. . . ."

Seven months later spring was bursting along the boughs when Dolley began to take a little renewed interest in life beyond her door. Men stationed themselves in the street to see her pass. "Really, Dolley," Eliza said smiling, "thee must hide thy face, there are so many staring."

One day Dolley wrote Eliza a slightly frantic note, "Thou must come to me. Aaron Burr says that the great little Madison has asked to be brought to see me this evening."

(Whether or not she had met Madison earlier is purely speculative. He had left Philadelphia just after she came there and returned after her marriage to John Todd, and though they had some mutual friends, they could easily have missed each other.)

Dolley did not wear Quaker grey at the meeting with Burr and Madison. She wore, amid candlelight and probably gleaming silver, a gown the color of crushed mulberries.

Other meetings followed, and soon a cautious man threw caution to the winds. He asked Dolley to marry him. She said it was too soon after her husband's death to think about remarrying.

He kept pressing his case. Public events were asking for his attention: General Wayne's offensive against the Indians in Ohio; western Pennsylvania's refusal to pay a federal tax on the whiskey it distilled, drank, and used as currency; new bills before the House of Representatives. But his mind kept running to Fourth and Walnut. It was more than her face and gift of understanding. A quality impossible to define set her apart. She was the woman he wished to live and die with.

Among other suitors, Madison stood out. Not only had he worked for the "free exercise of religion according to the dictates of conscience"; he was known to have had a strong hand in the Constitution. Dolley looked at his firm, sensitive mouth and direct, slate-blue eyes. It was a good face.

She was no great judge of intellect, but could appreciate character. If a little short for a man, morally he towered.

On the other hand, she wanted to keep her Quaker way of life and avoid hurting a mother who had been hurt too much. But was it not the part of wisdom to give her son, and incidentally herself, a protector as wise and kind as James Madison? The seventeen-year age difference was not insuperable, but what about her inferior education? What if she came to bore a man of his attainments? Thus the arguments rocked back and forth.

One day Martha Washington, Lucy's aunt by marriage, summoned Dolley to ask, "Are you engaged to James Madison?" "No," stammered Dolley, "I think not." "Well, if you are, don't be ashamed, be proud. He'll make a husband all the better for those seventeen extra years"—not understanding where the difficulty lay. "Between him and the General there's great esteem and friendship." They wanted to see Dolley happy.

News spread that Congressman Madison was in love with the pretty Quaker widow, and Congressman Isaac Coles of Halifax, Dolley's cousin and Madison's friend, did what he could as a go-between; also his wife, Catherine. But Dolley's great confidante, as always, was Eliza Collins, now engaged, "out of unity," to Richard Bland Lee. Many of the Pine Street Friends frowned upon both young women for keeping company with outsiders. They thought Dolley should be devoting herself to the memory of her late husband and seeing to it that John Todd's money would stay within the fold. Members called upon the tempted one to warn and advise.

No, she told Madison, she couldn't give him an answer before Congress's adjournment in June. She had rented her house and was about to gather up Anna and Payne and catch a stagecoach to Hanover to ponder.

At times her dilemma seemed to grow. She liked and esteemed Madison. But was that enough? Everything else aside, they were very different kinds of people, he a thinker, she a "feeler." Would the contrast create problems? How measure it against the fact that he would probably make a thoughtful, loving father for little Payne and set a high example? What should be the determining consideration?

In May and June, at Aunt Lucy and Uncle Isaac Winston's plantation Auburn, not far from Scotchtown, she wrestled with the problem, then came down with malaria. While Madison, at Montpelier, looked in vain for a letter, her body ached, her ears rang.

Catherine Coles wrote to say that poor Madison thought so constantly about her during the day, by evening he had lost his tongue. In a little fantasy of her own Catherine imagined him starting up out of a dream, calling on Dolley to cool a flame before it consumed him. She spoke of him as a man *in extremis*. The most substantial thing she had to transmit was a message from Madison delivered with "sparkling eyes": he hoped Dolley would be callous to other suitors. Catherine reported on three other enamored gentlemen, and said that Madison had rented the house vacated by the Monroes when they sailed for Europe. "Do you like it?"

At Montpelier a patient marooned man waited impatiently. Time stretched out. It was good to see his family again, and there was plenty to do, including translating for a French houseguest who spoke not a word of English. But while July and August crept by, Madison was not really there; he was in Hanover.

At last he received Dolley's destiny-settling letter—now lost—written at a Fredericksburg inn where she was changing stagecoaches for Harewood. Yes, after a proper interval she would marry him. And she hoped (he already had an open invitation) he would meet her at Lucy's.

Whether or not she told Madison, she was also writing her Philadelphia lawyer William W. Wilkins, a suitor whom she had converted into a "brother," to ask his advice as to the disposal of her estate. What part should be dowry, what part reserved for Payne?

Madison was elated by her acceptance. But he was perceptive enough to see that her letter lacked the fine ring of conviction, and he asked himself if she had said yes only because she could not quite say no.

The surviving fragment of his August 18 reply not only shows the gist of Dolley's letter but also tells a great deal about Madison's reaction.

> Your precious favor. . . . I cannot express . . . the joy it gave me. The delay in hearing of your leaving Hanover . . . the only satisfactory proof of your recovery had filled me with extreme . . . inquietude, and . . . that welcome event was endeared by the style in which it was conveyed. I hope you will never have another *deliberation*. . . . If the sentiments of my heart can guarantee those of yours . . . there can never be a cause for it.

Unfortunately the houseguest Antoine's grave illness would delay his departure for Harewood; it would be dangerous to leave the man without a translator. This unexpected obstacle was mortifying. He would join her as soon as possible.

A week or so later he made a flying trip to see Jefferson before setting out for Harewood. The road led through the Blue Ridge and lower (upper on the map) Shenandoah Valley. At times the virgin forest gave way to second-stand timber or lonely fields of grain. Horses' hooves astonished the silence. Rough roads shook up his brand new $400 coach. The slave Sam, acting as outrider, shouted warnings. "Tree down!" "Stump!" "Bog!" "Rocks ahead!" For Madison, politics had blown away like chaff. He was on his way to his wedding.

Or so he hoped. For why should Dolley remarry amid the ordeal of censure by unfriendly Friends? Besides, in Philadelphia his own days would be too crowded with congressional duties to permit many carefree hours. They needed some tranquility together before the storm. As he bumped along, Madison honed his argument to a bright cutting edge. A political persuader of no mean ability must now persuade one lady that happiness should be seized at once, with both hands.

The September 1794 weather, recorded in an old almanac, stayed high and serene. Summer had scorched, and winter would freeze, but meanwhile the days—typically—were almost classical; they had measure and equilibrium. Equinoctial rains held back, and what the sun had lost in strength it gained in subtlety, in radiance. The driver on the box flourished his whip. Distant mountains were like elderly statesmen pondering the Bill of Rights.

Often on his way to Warm Springs, Madison had ridden through this fine rolling country, but today every turn of the wheels was bringing him closer to Dolley.

He knew Harewood's story. It was part of George Washington's. After surveying Lord Fairfax's vast domain, Major Washington had so praised Berkeley County that his half-brother Lawrence had bought up a large acreage. When Lawrence died, his four brothers had inherited it. On Harewood, Samuel had built a mansion of rock quarried from a spectacular blue-grey limestone ridge running through the estate (the hauler being paid an acre of land per team per day).

Two miles . . . one mile . . . half a mile. . . . Suddenly on top of a knoll, Madison saw a grove of honey locusts. Below lay the outcropping of limestone; above, its apotheosis, the Harewood mansion.

If the welcome was typically Virginian, people ran out of doors to meet him: not only Dolley and the servants but also Harewood's tall young master George; his gay-hearted wife Lucy, and sister Harriet; his mother-in-law Molly Payne; and her three youngest children—all bent on sweeping up James Madison, the neat-figured, strong-featured, restrained gentleman getting out of his carriage.

In eighteenth-century Virginia country houses, strangers were met courteously, friends welcomed warmly, prospective bridegrooms hailed as princes. This particular one was widely respected, and Harewood "that could withstand an attack of artillery" offered him strength for strength: its great hall with a staircase like Mount Vernon's but broader and with lower risers, its elegantly paneled drawing room with watered-silk walls and a fine marble mantel (one of two which Lafayette had presented to General Washington), its dining room dominated by a portrait of the flamboyant dead Colonel Samuel Washington. The house was Madison's, the welcomers were implying. Had he enjoyed his trip? And he may have been treated to some of the pleasantries reserved for engaged men.

When at last he was alone with Dolley, he slipped onto her fourth finger a guinea-gold ring set with a cluster of eight rose diamonds and urged her to marry him not later but at once.

Soon the whole family knew about his plea. Lucy and George could understand a man in a hurry. At fifteen and—was it twenty?—they had rather rushed things; after meeting on an ice pond, had, so to speak, joined hands and kept skating. But Dolley's mother saw the matter differently. When Dolley married Madison, she would be the sixth member of a family of ten to be cast out by the Society. Molly had more or less adjusted to the idea that her eldest daughter was promised to an Episcopalian. After all, Madison was a good and distinguished man who had helped Quakers. But why compound an offense to the Society by cutting short the customary year of mourning by six or seven weeks? On the other hand, Madison's argument was hard to refute, and Payne did need a father fast, and there was a hope that, after her marriage, Dolley could convert her husband, as her mother had converted her father, and her grandmother her grandfather. It would bring him into, and her back into, the fold. (Madison did not know that Dolley, even more unsure about marrying John Todd, had kept him waiting three years.)

While the marriage date hung fire, an observer might have wondered whether Dolley was less in love with Madison than he with her, if indeed she was in love at all.

The days of indecision were filled with some of the diversions of Virginia country life: riding, hunting, gaming, jesting, drinking coffee or cherry shrub or something stronger in the summerhouse, and eating gargantuan dinners served from covered dishes by black people running relays from an outdoor kitchen. But behind the conviviality stood the question "When?" Having reached the door of a second marriage, hand on knob, Dolley still hesitated.

William Wilkin's reply lay in her hand. Calling her Julia (because she had said she wished that were her name?), he wrote stodgily that he approved of Madison as a man who combined public with private virtues. Then he skidded off the subject to defend his own attachment. "That I have not been insensible to your charms ought not, I think, to be regarded as a fault—few persons in a similar situation would not have felt their irresistible influence, but none . . . could have mingled in their emotions more true respect and fraternal affection." Self-cleared, he answered her question about a financial settlement. The "eyes of the world," including those Friends who had "opened their mouths to censure and condemn," were upon her. He felt sure that Mr. Madison, a man of "genteel though not large property," would not wish for her entire estate, and he suggested that after trustees had paid off the $350 mortgage on her house, plus interest, the rents thereafter be used for Payne's support and education, the property to go to him at twenty-one. Some might call the bequest "unreasonably great," Wilkins added, but those who knew Julia would look for something no less bountiful and "maternally affectionate."

"Affectionate" is a weak word for what Dolley felt for Payne. She worshipped the little boy, and during these days of open engagement and secret misgivings could not but—under difficult circumstances—study Madison as a prospective foster father. She watched him sober and laughing, sipping coffee or a julep while unlimbering a dry, attractive humor; she watched him grow tall in the saddle as the men rode out; she watched him morning and afternoon and at the broadcasting of stars. She was feeling out his quality by what he said and left unsaid, did and disdained to do. Yes, he ought to make a good stepfather for this child with his father's face and her own blue eyes.

Thus Dolley was swept forward. She established a trust for Payne and announced that, whatever happened, he would be brought up a Quaker, for, even if cast out, she would still be a Quaker by conviction. Some things about the Society baffled her; she could not understand why it condemned what seemed to her harmless beauty and gaiety or how it could have ejected her poor father. But she loved its emphasis on conscience and a spiritual seeing. No, nothing could shake her beliefs.

So she set a date six weeks short of the anniversary of John Todd's death, Thursday, September 15. James, delighted, gave her as a wedding gift a necklace and earrings of carved gems representing scenes from Roman history.

Plans went forward. Invitations were sent to Madison's sister Nelly and her husband Major Isaac Hite, who lived near Strasburg, and also to some nearby Lees. People farther away would not be able to get there.

The Rev. Alexander Balmaine of Winchester, a Revolutionary chaplain who had married Madison's cousin Lucy Taylor, was alerted. And there was whispering behind closed doors and the flash of needles.

On the fifteenth the sun rose not quite as usual, and Dolley sat down to write Eliza Collins Lee, now honeymooning at Warm Springs.

"September the 16th," she wrote, confusing her own wedding date. She has delayed answering Eliza's last letter because of a recurrence of the old "excessive weakness" of her eyes, but now, as proof of their long and never interrupted friendship, she has "stolen away" from the family to confide that in the course of this day she will give her hand to "the man . . . I most admire."

Not the one she loves; the one she most admires. "In this union I have everything that is soothing and grateful in prospect, and my little Payne will have a generous and kind protector"—and she had, perhaps, told Eliza more than she had ever made clear to herself. The rest of the letter dwells on Payne. "A settlement of all my real property, with a considerable addition of money, is made upon him with Mr. Madison's full approbation. . . . You are . . . acquainted with the unmerited censure of my enemies on the subject"—which suggests some degree of anxiety. The letter ends "Adieu! adieu!" She is not sure they can visit Eliza and her husband before returning to Philadelphia—meaning at new-built Sully in Loudoun County. "Mama, Madison, Lucy, George, Anna and Harriet join in best love. . . ."

Thus Dolley came to the crucial hour, and put on her white dress and crown of white flowers, and descended the staircase at Harewood, and took her place beside James Madison, and heard him say "I will."

The Rev. Mr. Balmaine had turned toward her. All eyes were upon her; the event was upon her. There was no going back.

"Wilt thou have this man . . . ?"

Somehow she gathered strength to say "I will," and a gold band buckled round her life.

Afterward there was a supper and a lighthearted celebration. Everyone had kissed the bride and congratulated the groom and could start all over again, and more music was in order—such songs as "Possum in de Gum Tree" and "Money Musk." Jemmy Madison, it is recorded, was so recklessly happy he let young ladies cut up his wonderful Mechlin lace jabot for souvenirs.

Then a strange thing happened. At the height of the merrymaking Dolley slipped upstairs and sat down at a desk to add a postscript to her morning letter to Eliza signed "Dolley Payne Todd."

"Evening," she wrote, and then four words: "Dolley Madison! Alas! Alas!"

❧ II ❧

HONEYMOON

JAMES AND DOLLEY MADISON spent the first few days of their honeymoon in the little one-room stone cottage in the yard at Harewood. But their privacy was hardly complete. Because little Payne had always slept with his mother, he continued to do so.

On the fifth day the couple started south to visit Madison's sister Nelly. Again they were not alone. A child who could have stayed with his grandmother and aunts went along, as did young Anna Payne and Harriet Washington. The ladies tucked in full skirts and stepped up. Then the carriage was bowling along the pike.

Though Madison would have preferred to take Dolley home to Montpelier, the longer trip would have been too exhausting before the still longer one to Philadelphia. Major Isaac Hite's place was a compromise. Far gone in pregnancy, Nelly Hite had not dared drive 30 bumpy miles to the wedding.

Madison could have explained about the Shenandoah Valley— "Daughter of the Stars"—for he knew it well. Indians had once planted it in maize. Before the Revolution this road running its length was called the King's Highway, now the Great Road.

If the carriage grew stuffy and Payne fidgety, if dust gushed through cracks or talk stumbled, there were splendid changing views of the mountains and a certain excitement in the journey.

Twenty miles from Harewood, Winchester rose up out of the valley. They spent the night with Cousin Lucy and the Rev. Mr. Balmaine before continuing on. Now two slowly rising ranges were drawing closer. This region was where Major Hite's grandfather, Baron Jost Heydt, had settled fifty-four European families and fought the land claims of Lord Fairfax.

Madison had a still closer connection. His grandfather's brother John

18

had raised his family here in the Valley. It was too beautiful to leave, but Aunt Fanny—his father's sister—had made the mistake of moving to South Carolina, where she and most of her children had been murdered by Seminole, her husband Jacob Hite disjointed alive, and her daughter Eleanor stolen away. This tragedy was part of a great body of Madison lore.

Off to the left, now, there rose a knoblike outpost of the Massamutten Mountains. They were getting closer to Old Hall.

The Hites gave them a hearty welcome. In taking Dolley's measure, they liked what they saw, and she was equally pleased with her discoveries.

Isaac Hite—"our Major" hereabouts—had a nicely oversized mouth and a forehead as broad as one of his wheat fields. Years ago he had ridden down to William and Mary College in Tidewater with a bathtub painted with water lilies tied to his saddle to become the first elected member of Phi Beta Kappa. As aide-de-camp to General Muhlenburg during the Revolution, he had had one of his fingers shot off, and at Yorktown had watched the British drop their arms as they filed past. When, finally, his sweetheart Nelly Madison married him at Montpelier, he had whirled her off in a yellow honeymoon coach with liveried postillions astride a tandem team.

If the Major was solid, his wife was small and delicate and—except in the middle where she was now melon-shaped—slim.

According to Hite tradition, Madison carried Dolley over the threshold.

Their week's visit was long enough for many pleasant things: walking in the gardens; calling on Hite relatives at the great log house on the river, Long Meadows, where Isaac had grown up; playing with Payne and the Hites' little son and daughter (the son had been named James Madison Hite); and talking, talking.

After the details of the wedding and the Madisons' plans had been reported, the triumphs and troubles of the new nation called for a thorough discussion between two men who had long been friends. Among other things they talked about Pennsylvania's whiskey rebellion, "Mad Anthony" Wayne's defeat of an Indian coalition at Fallen Timbers, and Great Britain's nasty habit of seizing American ships and cargoes and impressing American sailors into her navy. Also—in this connection— they discussed the great question: Would Envoy John Jay be able to wrest from George III a treaty protecting neutral rights on the high seas?

In time, inevitably, the discussion came to the ever-growing polariza- tion of the two political parties: the pro-British Federalist party, of which

Jay was a member, and the pro-French Democrat-Republican party to which Madison and Hite belonged. Here Madison could hardly have avoided stating one of his deepest convictions: that political parties formed around principles were more justified, healthier, than factions formed around selfish interests, since mere interests were hostile to the rights of others.

As the men talked, the women were free to listen or not listen. Though Dolley was impressed with her husband's knowledge, political talk made her feel ignorant, for the great world of public business was one in which she had never moved. She could understand better when Isaac and James—Nelly called him Jemmy—discussed wheat, corn, or tobacco. It brought back things she had learned at Scotchtown.

How much, at Old Hall, others were allowed to look after Payne is not known, but a letter preserved by the Hite family burns with exasperation: "Then there was *that child,* who would have nothing else but to sleep in their bed with them, as he had every night since they had been man and wife."

The Hites told their guests about the elegant new house they were planning to construct, to be called Belle Grove after the house on the Rappahannock where Nelly Conway Madison—Nelly and Jemmy's mother—had been raised. It would be 40 by 120 feet, with 2-foot-thick walls, capstones ordered from England, and the finest paneling in the Valley. Madison said yes, he'd be glad to ask Jefferson to look over the drawings.

Meanwhile he and Dolley went on discovering each other. Whenever Nelly or the girls or someone else minded the three children, they had time and leisure to exchange longer confidences. Though Dolley had married knowing the gist of his early life, there were countless details to be filled in. Once James's congenital reserve went down, stories came forth— little human facts to please a young woman who, however poorly educated, was intelligent, warmhearted, and responsive. She very much wanted to know about his childhood and education, partly for her new husband's sake, partly for Payne's—the "precious child" they would bring up together.

JAMES MADISON was born at midnight at the estate Belle Grove in King. George County, Virginia, on March 16 (new style), 1751.

The first male of his line in the Colony of Virginia—five generations earlier—was John Maddison of Gloucester County, a "ship carpenter" or boatwright, presumably a builder of Chesapeake-cruising sloops and river freighters. In 1653 he patented 600 acres on the Mattaponi. Under the headright system a man could patent 50 acres for every immigrant he brought from Europe, which means that he had raised $72 apiece passage fee (a large sum in those days) for twelve persons. Soon he had acquired 1,300 fertile acres. His son John climbed farther up the ladder, becoming a three-county tobacco planter, sheriff, and magistrate. John's three sons by Isabel Todd dropped a "d" from the name Maddison; pioneers have no time for fiddle-faddle.

One of the sons, Ambrose, fell in love with Frances Taylor, daughter of James Taylor, one of the "Knights of the Golden Horseshoe" who in 1716 accompanied Governor Alexander Spotswood across the Blue Ridge Mountains and caught the white man's first glimpse of the Shenandoah Valley. Magnificent! In his enthusiasm over the piedmont, Squire Taylor patented and hewed out a 13,500-acre tract for himself and his descendants: a fateful decision.

In 1721 Ambrose married his sweetheart, and on the birth of the first James, father of the future President, received as dowry some 2,240 acres in what would become Orange County. Ambrose himself patented 2,000 acres, then bought 3,333 more.

He and his slaves cleared whole forests to make fields. Great trees came crashing down. By 1729 he was able to bring his wife and child out to a house in a lonely land stalked by bears, wolves, and wild cats. Fortunately Frances' sister and her husband settled nearby, and her brother James Taylor Jr. took up a homestead called Bloomsbury just an hour or so away by horseback.

For the Herculean tasks in what was then frontier, Ambrose had a will of iron. But he died young, lay down in the earth he had plowed, and his thirty-two-year-old widow and nine-year-old son took on the heavy responsibilities of pioneering.

Frances Taylor Madison, mother of two daughters and a son, was no ordinary woman. Working fifteen slaves, she labored to improve a 5,000-acre estate destined for her son (her other holdings lay in the Blue Ridge); raised, cured, and shipped tobacco; and organized, among other things, wool carding, weaving, shoemaking, candle molding, nail hammering, pit sawing. Devout as well as intelligent, she asked her London agents to send her religious tracts; and amid the rigors of farm management educated her son, the first James Madison. He was a man before he was a boy.

One of the youth's duties was delivering hogsheads of tobacco at the Conway warehouse 9 miles below Fredericksburg. Afterward, a canter down the Rappahannock brought him to Belle Grove, the only home his friend Francis Conway Jr. could remember. Within a year of the death of Francis's father, his mother Rebecca Catlett Conway had married John Moore and brought her son and the baby Nelly to this plantation. In time there were a half brother William and half sister Jane. The house where they all grew up stood so close to the river that if they pitched a stone out a window, they could hear it splash.

One day James's eyes sank into Nelly's. It decided something not unrelated to the not-yet-born United States. When they married in 1749, the young man was twenty-one, the girl seventeen.

Their first child, James Madison Jr., was not robust. The godparents who gathered for his baptism a few weeks after his birth—his grandmother and stepgrandfather Moore, two Catlett aunts, and an uncle—could not have dreamed that the baby whom the Rev. William Davis was signing with a cross was destined to be called the father of a constitution unique on earth and the fourth President of the nation it set on course. In the bishopless Colony of Virginia where Confirmation was impossible, Baptism alone made a child a member of the Established Church, the Anglican Church. But this meant nothing to him as his parents carried him home to Orange County.

James Madison would never claim aristocracy. But the Conway family, generally, holds that the first Virginia Conway was Edwin, a collateral descendant of Sir Edward Conway, Baron of Ragley, who helped the Earl of Essex sack Cadiz in 1596 and was a descendant of Robert the Bruce. This is Madison's characteristically modest note on his forebears: "In both the paternal and maternal line . . . they were planters and among the respectable, though not the most opulent, class."

The farm on which Jemmy grew up was a world in itself. Here in the heart of the "Old Dominion" (Charles II claimed "England, Scotland, Ireland and Virginia" on his coins) Jemmy trailed his father around the countryside, looking, listening, touching, tasting, smelling. From the beginning he went to school to nature, and only later to his indomitable grandmother Frances Taylor Madison. During those first years he learned that if sunlight and rain fell on seeds, they put out shoots, leaves, flowers, and fruit—a wonder past reckoning. A devotion to the rich reddish Orange County soil, born now, would in time help make him a good farmer.

In eighteenth-century Virginia, tobacco was king. The boy came to know well its hairy leaves and pale flowers and the long process of drying and curing. But his father the Squire showed himself ahead of his time by sowing more and more wheat. The boy watched its delicate stalks swaying in the least shift of air before it was cut and its chaff winnowed away at the Madison Mill on the Rapidan.

In a vast county as yet undivided, the boy's father had not a little power. Though Squire Madison had been heir to thousands of acres, he had struggled, on his own, to a position of authority. By the time Jemmy turned eight, this taciturn planter was Justice of the King's Peace and Presiding Magistrate of Orange County, which made him County Lieutenant, Colonel in the field, and head of the King's militia in Orange—all this in a period when the Presiding Magistrate of a county really ran it, being answerable only to the Colony's Acting Governor William Gooch. In other words, Colonel Madison was the county's first citizen.

Jemmy was respectful not only toward his father but also toward his capable mother and redoubtable grandmother. It was the latter, mainly, who taught him to read, write, and cipher and then led him into the greener fields of geography, history, and literature. Elders saw that his mind shot far.

Squire Madison, a vestryman of the Brick Church some 4 miles away, led daily family prayers and Bible readings, and on Sundays, when there were services, ordered his carriage hitched up. James and his two brothers, Francis and Ambrose, learned the catechism with their ABC's and were permitted to receive the Bread and Wine.

Jemmy was both serious and fun-loving. He read books, played games, and ran over the farm with his brothers and a drove of little black boys from the cabins in the Walnut Grove.

The treat was Court Day. Once a month, after Court had adjourned, there reigned a carnival spirit. The crowd exchanged news and gossip; drank cider, beer, and rum; indulged in horseplay; argued; joshed; and in some cases flirted. Sometimes contests were organized, with drums beating out the challenges. Contestants wrestled for silver buckles, or fiddled for a harness, or raced three-legged for a beaver hat. Ballad singers were guaranteed "liquor sufficient to clear the wind-pipes." A favorite entertainer was the juggler who balanced a tumbler of water on his head while catching balls.

Thus Jemmy—bright as a new copper—inhabited three worlds: nature, books, and people. Observing his honesty, ability, and hunger for knowledge, his parents felt easy about primogeniture. That law would not thrust their hard-won property into unworthy or weak hands.

Nelly's and James Madison Sr.'s portraits by Charles Peale Polk, though painted in 1799, record lifelong proportions. The gentleman in knee breeches has a thin, intelligent, proud face with the slightly long upper lip he bequeathed to his eldest son. The lady wearing a dainty fichu and bonnet is ramrod-straight, with a gentle expression and pretty arms and hands. She appears—time would disprove it—as frail as a bird.

Jemmy was about eight when Colonel Madison finished building his growing family a larger home on the next hill, the first brick house in the region. Though its lumber, nails, and bricks were doubtless made on the place, its window glass and brass fittings had to be ordered from Alexandria, Baltimore, Philadelphia, or London. Years later, Madison would remember how he himself carried over some of the lighter-weight furniture.

Though the first known written use of the name Montpelier (or Montpellier) is dated 1781, the plantation may well have received its name now, in honor of handsomer quarters.

The view from the new porch was splendid: ninety undulating miles of that fold of the Appalachians known as the Blue Ridge. It loomed and receded, changing its aspect according to season, hour, and weather, its characteristic color a true cerulean.

Two pillars of Jemmy's life toppled. When he was nine, Grandmother Rebecca Catlett Conway Moore died, and when he was eleven, Grandmother Frances Taylor Madison also disappeared out of sight and sound. Their deaths were great losses.

And signaled other changes. Anxious that Jemmy be well educated, Colonel Madison shipped him off to Mr. Donald Robertson, a scholarly Scotch schoolmaster in King and Queen County who enjoyed an excellent clientele. Five Taylor cousins were enrolled.

Though at first, like all shy boarding pupils, Jemmy would have liked to run home, he made friends and was soon digesting the classical education of the times. At twelve he had Greek and Latin and was reading Cornelius Nepos; by thirteen, Virgil, Horace, Ovid, Sallust, Terence, and Justinian's *Institutes*. His Spanish and French had a burr straight from Edinburgh. No matter; he was reading Cervantes and Montaigne. While running a gauntlet of intellectual disciplines—geometry, algebra, world history—he made good use of a library containing, among other books, Aesop's *Fables*, Thomas à Kempis's *Imitation of Christ*, Smollett's *History of England*, Montesquieu's *Spirit of the Laws*, and a file of *Spectator* papers.

The Spectator gave him a literary model. "When I was at an age which will soon be yours," the elderly Madison would write an eleven-year-old nephew, "a book fell into my hands which I read . . . with particular advantage . . . the *Spectator*." He added that he recommended Joseph

Addison as a first-rate author whose writing consisted of natural though not obvious sentiments. Urbane and rather stiff, that eighteenth-century favorite was not the happiest model. By his choice, Madison was simply proving himself to be a child of his period.

In 1765 Jamie (as Mr. Robertson called him) heard expressions of anger against the Stamp Act. Though Parliament repealed the duty, it declared that Britain had a *right* to bind her Colonies by whatever laws she chose. Jamie pricked up his ears. The world was not as peaceful as his home and school.

Betweentimes—his diffidence having worn off—he rollicked with the boys. An entry in Mr. Robertson's Account Book concerns a loss which might have resulted from some prank: "To Mr. Jamie's hat . . . 17s.6d."

There is extant a 122-page copybook headed "James Madison His Book of Logick" and dated 1766 when he was fifteen. "Logick or Dialectick," it begins, "is the art of reasoning: that is, of discovering truth or error, and demonstrating them to yourself or others by discourse." The distinction between natural and formal logic is likened to that between wild and cultivated land. The contents lean on Locke and Watts while showing knowledge of Euclid, Plato, Aristotle, Fontenelle on the plurality of worlds, and Cartesian astronomy. As for the writing, it appears to be a polishing of class notes. Because of the difficulty of some of the ideas, the date on the copybook has been questioned. But at fifteen James Madison was mentally sharp; he could reason.

The last fourteen pages are given over to drawings. The sun in Jemmy's sketch of the Copernican system has a human face, its corona a full shock of human hair. Along the planets' orbits he has written their sizes and relative distances from the sun.

The copybook's criticism of Locke's distinction between matter's primary and secondary properties follows Berkeley. The "I" of the passage seems to be that of Mr. Robertson, who saw spirit, not matter, as basic to the universe, but it was probably also Jamie's. The well-liked schoolmaster's thinking influenced his pupil's.

In 1767 Jamie left the school, and not too happily. As a man he would say of Mr. Robertson, his teacher for the five formative years between eleven and sixteen: "All I have been in life I owe largely to that man."

Colonel Madison had withdrawn his son because the new rector of the Brick Church, the Rev. Thomas Martin, who was living at Montpelier, had agreed to tutor the older children: Nelly, seven; Ambrose, twelve; Francis, fourteen; and James, sixteen. (William, five, and Sarah, three, were still too young for school.) As a graduate of the College of New

Jersey at Princeton, Mr. Martin was qualified to prepare a youth for college.

The two were congenial. In discussing history, politics, and religion, they forgot the nine-year age difference. Later Mr. Martin's recommendation of his alma mater carried weight. Why, after all, should every young Virginian go to William and Mary in Williamsburg? Just now that college was at low ebb, some of its professors charged with negligence and drunkenness. The presidency of the College of New Jersey had passed to a celebrated Presbyterian cleric fresh from Scotland, Dr. John Witherspoon. Moreover, unlike Virginia, New Jersey had no state-church hookup, and the climate was better.

Meanwhile the Colonies' relations with Britain had been worsening. By ceding huge French lands in America to Britain, the 1763 Treaty of Paris had increased Britain's sense of empire while decreasing the Colonies' sense of dependence, a dangerous imbalance. After the repeal of the Stamp Act, new duties on glass, paper, wine, and tea enraged the Colonies. They were not alone in their indignation. The great William Pitt had said that taxation without representation was tyranny. The situation offended the sense of justice of Colonel Madison, Presiding Magistrate and County Lieutenant of Orange, "Commander of the Plantations." And it offended his firstborn.

While Jemmy was moving from sixteen to eighteen years old, John Dickinson's *Letters from a Farmer* spoke out ringingly against the Townshend Acts, and something in the youth answered the call to patriotism. More and more he was identifying with a raw new world having its own particular conditions, possibilities, and needs; more and more thinking of himself not as a Briton but as a Virginian and an American. George III's peacetime garrisons, here, and writs of assistance increased his sense of outrage.

It was as if everything were conspiring to bend Jemmy toward sobersidedness: sedate parents, dead serious teachers, and the political situation, to say nothing of the "age of enlightenment's" ideal of reason. With a fine mind, he found it easy to believe that reason could solve almost any problem. He did not worry that its exaltation might cause an imbalance as great as any glorification of feeling.

His life-style was thus far removed from that of the fops in velvet jackets and tricorns plastered under the brims with white feathers, who galloped from plantation to town to spa looking for titillation and often drinking themselves blind.

A brown, neatly written, twenty-four-page commonplace book stuffed with quotations and summaries bears the date "Dec. 24, 1759," when he was eight, evidently the year it was given to him, perhaps as a birthday gift. Obviously the contents were set down much later, probably during the two years of Mr. Martin's tutoring. Earlier or later he would have had far less leisure for such a time-consuming enterprise. In contrast to the "Book of Logick," this notebook mirrors a preoccupation with problems of conduct and a taste for epigrammatic thoughts on the business of life.

For example, he quotes the Cardinal de Retz's *Memoirs* on such subjects as prudence, flattery, and the ability to hold one's tongue ("a grave air hides many defects"). A typical entry: "A man shows himself greater by being capable [of] owning a fault than by being incapable of committing it." From Montaigne he copied "A man should not delight in praises that are not his due. . . ." From the Abbé du Bos's *Critical Reflections* he took to heart this warning: "Nothing makes one say and commit so many silly things as the desire to appear witty." And there is a quotation which he may have chosen because of a dawning suspicion that the object of life should be wholeness: "In great affairs the head signifies nothing without the heart." *Nothing without the heart.* He copied passages from Homer, Simonides, Antipater, and that great admiration of the eighteenth century, Alexander Pope.

Thus the notebook is a window opening on young James Madison's mind not long before he packed some saddlebags and rode off on a high adventure. His companions were the Rev. Thomas Martin, the rector's brother Alexander, and black Sawney. It was midsummer as Jemmy set out for the College of New Jersey.

Fredericksburg, Alexandria, Baltimore, Philadelphia: often the road was little more than a stump-studded trail winding through woods. They took their horses across rivers on poled ferries.

His arrival at Nassau Hall was like beaching on a new continent. There stood the four-story stone building with a cupola about which he had heard so much, the largest in the Colonies, and next to it, on the right, Dr. Witherspoon's house. Sore from a week in the saddle, the travelers dismounted.

Jemmy was soon initiated into college life. Three youths occupied each 20-foot-square room. The student body ate in a dining hall presided over by a steward. The Prayer Hall was used for more than services; it was the general meeting place. The students came from New England, New

York, Pennsylvania, and the South. In former years they had flapped about in academic robes, Scotch style. Now, for easier movement, the rule had been relaxed, but woe to any maverick who entered Prayer Hall not wearing his cap and gown.

Jemmy "cut his own wood for exercise."

Dr. Witherspoon, like Mr. Robertson, had studied at the University of Edinburgh. There the resemblance seemed to stop. President Witherspoon was a doughty religious warrior. Long before leaving Scotland last year (bringing the college 300 books), he had won considerable fame with a satirical pamphlet called *Ecclesiastical Characteristics* that excoriated lax clergymen. It had turned his church upside down.

This burly individualist's thunderous voice could send students fleeing in terror, but he could also be tender. One thing he insisted upon: clear English. Writers and orators should keep their mouths shut until they had something to say and stop when they had said it; trimmings were a waste of time. And already he was an American patriot who called George III a scoundrel and stung his students into passionate involvement.

There was a small but efficient faculty. Each of the three lower classes had a special tutor. The President himself taught the senior class and sometimes lectured to the student body.

On arriving in late July Jemmy had asked for advanced standing on the ground that he had covered some college-level courses under Mr. Martin. He was told that his grades on the freshman examinations at the end of September would determine his standing, and he wrote Mr. Martin on August 10, "I am perfectly pleased with my present situation."

While cramming for exams he joined eleven other student patriots in the newly founded American Whig Society. It would help to shape him, as he it.

The summer of '69 was so dry it destroyed his father's tobacco. The leaves withered. Then a hurricane battered the entire East Coast. Princeton was swaying under terrible winds while James took his examinations. He did well and was admitted to the Rev. James Thompson's sophomore class.

October, like April, was a vacation month sandwiched between two 21-week semesters. It is not known whether or not he spent it at Princeton. Afterward, in the full swing of college, he had no complaint about the hard academic pace. But in writing to his father—"Honor'd Sir"—he mentioned an age-old trouble: the buying of trifles consumed a "much greater sum than one would suppose."

He was going more deeply into philosophy now. The man they called the "old doctor" (Witherspoon was forty-seven) argued sternly against the matter-denying thesis of Bishop Berkeley, whom Robertson had so admired. When the president sacked Instructor Periam for following Berkeley, the basic nature of the disagreement struck home to young Madison. He saw that truth was not always self-apparent; first-class minds could clash. This intellectual quarrel challenged him to clarify his own thinking, to face and compare ideas and examine his own self. What was the nature of reality?

Dr. Witherspoon often quoted Montesquieu's *Spirit of the Laws.* Jemmy was listening with great attention. The clues to right government lay in man himself? Yes, said the old doctor, one had only to look into one's heart and ask, "What am I—basically what?" Simply by reason of what they were, people had certain God-given rights not granted *nor grantable* by kings.

According to Princeton tradition Jemmy Madison excelled in metaphysical discussion. Sometimes the arguments in which he took part ran so late into the night that Dr. Witherspoon had to shout, "To bed, lads, to bed!" But young Madison was a student after the old curmudgeon's heart: clear-minded, intense, unsparing.

About this time Dr. Witherspoon saw Philadelphia scientist David Rittenhouse's half-finished, amazing mechanical model of the solar system and ordered it for the college. Let the youths of Nassau Hall relate themselves to the universe.

Meanwhile the political situation was ripening. In March 1770 the "flying machine"—express stagecoach—brought news of the Boston Massacre. So British soldiers had shot down American citizens!

The April vacation came just in time. Now the wound-up spring of Jemmy's nature could be released; he could relax.

That summer Nassau Hall suffered and enjoyed a religious revival. Some students wept for their sins. One youth was unable to walk out of Prayer Hall; he had to be supported.

Converts formed the Cliosophic Literary Society, named after Clio, the muse of history. Though not necessarily less religious, the Whigs taunted the Clios about their "enthusiasm," meaning extreme emotionalism. In effect they were championing a balance of head and heart. Tension between the rival clubs grew. The Whigs called the Clios the most insulting term they could think up: "Tories." Antagonists meeting in Jacob Hyer's tavern on Main Street "at the sign of Hudibras" hurled sourserious epithets.

Actually the whole school was Whig in the sense of being anti-British and pro-American. When New York merchants asked Philadelphia merchants to cooperate in breaking an agreement to buy nothing from England, Jemmy was one of many students who felt outraged. Marching onto campus in caps and gowns, they cheered a "hangman" who threw the New Yorkers' letter onto a bonfire while a bell tolled. Damned traitors!

In July Jemmy asked his father for an advance of next year's allowance of half joes, and though he sent his "Neck and rists" measurements, he asked his mother not to ruffle his shirts until he came home on vacation in October. His letter roundly condemned the New York merchants' "base conduct." "With my love to all the family. . . ."

The September 1770 commencement was a feast of patriotism. Twenty-two graduates proudly stood up wearing defiant suits of American cloth. There was a Latin debate: "Resolved that subjects are bound and obliged by the law of nature to resist their king if he treats them cruelly or ignores the law of the state, and to defend their liberty"— Locke's justification of the Revolution of 1688. Then, six years ahead of the Declaration of Independence, Nassau Hall stole a little of its thunder by proving syllogistically that by the law of nature all men are equal. Sitting on the rostrum was the Royal Governor of New Jersey—Benjamin Franklin's son. He was startled and not pleased.

In October Jemmy carried his burning patriotism home. There was the usual influx of friends and relatives; they stopped by and often stayed for dinner and sometimes for the night. Cousin Frank Taylor described the Madisons' cotton sheets as chilly. In general these people had mastered the art of enjoying life. And many noted that college was maturing Colonel Madison's eldest son. The trees were in their autumn glory when he rode a horse back to Princeton.

During his second year Jemmy Madison and a friend named Joe Ross crammed—by permission of Dr. Witherspoon—their junior and senior years into one. The pace was grueling.

The ordinary regime was strenuous enough. At five o'clock in the morning a bell dragged everyone out of bed. At six the faculty and students assembled in the Hall for prayers and Scripture reading. There was then an hour of study before anyone got his breakfast of porridge and either coffee or tea. At nine, classes began; followed by a study period. At one o'clock the students washed down a plain dinner with a little cider or small beer. On infrequent lucky days they ate pie. After dinner came a free hour; from three to five, classes and study. A bell summoned them to evening prayer and the singing of psalms. After supper they were again sent back to their books. At nine the steward checked their rooms to see that everyone was either asleep or studying.

With double assignments Jemmy had to study far into the night. For weeks on end, he has said, he averaged only five hours of sleep. It was an intellectually exciting but hard winter.

Once when a Frenchman visited Nassau Hall, Jemmy was fetched to interpret. He understood the guest well enough but when he undertook to translate the English reply into French, he met a blank stare. He might as well have been talking (he liked to tell this story) Kickapoo.

With spring a "paper war" broke out between the Whigs and Clios, each group trying to sink the other with lampoons: a merry game. According to Princeton tradition Jemmy's roommate Samuel Smith belonged to the enemy camp. The best Whig poetasters were Hugh Brackenridge and Philip Freneau. But Jemmy made third place. To have one's abusive verse read out to the entire student body was a triumph for oneself and one's team.

Three examples of Jemmy's doggerel show a broad, fumbling, Smollettlike ribald humor. So raw were his verses, they must have fetched boisterous applause. These sophomoric satires shocked Madison's first biographer, William C. Rives, to a point where he hid them and pretended they did not exist.

A few samples will suffice. One broadside throws the Clios' founder, "Great Allen," into a brothel.

> The lecherous rascal there will find
> A place just suited to his mind,
> May whore & pimp & drink & swear,
> Nor more the garb of Christian wear. . . .

"A Poem against the Tories" is another diatribe of dubious taste:

> Come, noble Whigs, disdain these sons
> Of screech owls, monkeys & baboons . . .
> Untill this tribe of dunces find
> The baseness of their grovelling mind
> And skulk within their dens together
> Where each one's stench will kill his brother.

Jemmy guys the Clios' poet laureate Sam Spring unmercifully by sending him on an "aerial journey" to find the muse Clio and try to steal a much-needed "spark of wit." But the gods attack him as an interloper, Apollo smashing his jaw, Euterpe swatting him with a greasy dishrag, Urania pitching a chamber pot, and Clio herself castrating him to improve his voice. She warns him not to compete with Whigs in poetry—it would be imprudent.

> Your nature's bounds you then will pass
> And be transformed into an ass.

From a serious standpoint Jemmy's performance was execrable, but the versifying was a lark. Ever since the Middle Ages, college students have let off steam with crude, crazy horseplay, the buffoonery of young gentlemen struggling into manhood.

Jemmy knew he had no gift for poetry. Still, a few lines in his hudibrastics hint that had he tried for subtler effects, he might have learned to write verse not really good but passable:

> That very dream in which, they say,
> His soul broke loose from mortal clay. . . .

And again,

> Soon as the lamp of day was gone
> And evening shades o'erspread the lawn,
> Tired from the business of the day
> Down on the tender grass I lay.

At Nassau Hall scathing word fights were not all that went on *ex curriculum.* Philip Fithian would describe how students jostled with each other in dark entries, banged doors and ran off, strewed doorways with greasy feathers to make their friends' feet slip, rang the big bell at midnight, burned curse-John for the stink, darted mirrors onto townspeople, lighted squibs written with gunpowder on the floors of timorous boys, ogled women with telescopes, and (where was Dr. Witherspoon?) paraded "bad women." The eighteenth century is not famous for purity.

Ashbel Green would say of the frenzied "paper contentions": "Those who write can do little besides write, and everybody else . . . can scarcely think, hear or talk anything else than the war." Though meant in fun, the jibes sometimes got so badly out of hand that they caused "lasting alienations."

Why did Jemmy Madison try to combine satirical writing with his overburden of academic work? One can only say that popularity for an essentially shy young man can be sweet.

The doggerel and other evidence confound Henry Cabot Lodge's contention in *Historical and Political Essays* that Madison was "dry and serious to the last degree . . . a defect which seems to have been common to the men of that day," that he was sedate beyond "redeeming" and so utterly destitute of humor he "seems never to have had any boyhood or youth." Nonsense.

Between "paper contentions," increasingly, Princeton was a political hotbed. The King's new Prime Minister, Lord North, was reviled as a rogue and a scoundrel.

Young Madison's patriotism found fresh nourishment in Dr. Witherspoon's class in moral philosophy. Indeed, his whole previous education seemed but a prelude to this exposition of Dr. Witherspoon's convictions in all their sweep. And the experience came just when he could use it. A greater maturity—James turned twenty in March 1771—was pushing back the horizons of his mind.

"An inquiry," says the course's syllabus, "into the nature and grounds of moral obligation by reason as distinct from revelation." The pious doctor saw no conflict between these two means of acquiring knowledge. "If the Scripture is true," he held, "the discoveries of reason cannot be *contrary* to it." The class presented the nature of man as a "compound of body and spirit," and Dr. Witherspoon held that it was precisely *this nature* which should determine ethics in the private sector and politics in the public: the standard, the touchstone. Man, though created pure, and certainly immortal, he argued, had fallen to a state of mingled good and evil. Man's higher self wrestled with his lower self and spoke forth in what the old doctor called that "transcript of God's moral excellence," conscience.

Fundamentals settled, he moved on to the question of one's duty to God and man. "Love to others, sincere and active, is the sum of our duty," he said with great earnestness. He was trying to build foundations for lives.

Given Madison's temperament, caliber, and potential, Dr. Witherspoon's lectures and the discussions they spawned could not but cause intense inward excitement. The class moved on to talk about the way truth promotes goodness; about man's passions, selfish and benevolent; about his higher faculties: his appreciation, in the arts, of the harmony which is right proportion; about the benefits of prayer ("Prayer," said Dr. Witherspoon, "has as real an influence in procuring the blessing as ploughing and sowing in procuring the crop."); and, again, about the rights belonging to "natural liberty." Society was depicted as a compact by which people "deliver up or abridge some part of their natural rights in order to have the strength of the united body." Private property was called essential, or at least highly useful, since it made people more industrious and responsible.

When the course reached politics, the students were invited to consider three main types of government: the monarchical, whose danger was tyranny; the aristocratic, whose danger was oppression of the lower classes; and the democratic, whose danger was victimization by ferocious factions. Democracy's great advantage came out clearly: by discovering many otherwise lost talents, it brought into action all the human powers.

To Madison the course was meat and drink. Never mind that his academic load was brutally overtaxing and that the strain was increasing; there was satisfaction in getting down to fundamentals.

The fact that the antimaterialistic "Scottish School" rather than the reigning philosophy of David Hume (which Witherspoon detested) was expounded to him clearly and forcefully during his twenty-first year was a key to what he would become.

In many respects it contradicted the current French and English "enlightenment": contradicted Locke in that it spoke up for the innate ideas he threw out, and contradicted Hume in that it opposed his skepticism. Reason was not considered man's highest faculty; intuition was. Basing itself solidly on a conception of man as having a higher as well as lower self, the Scottish School taught that one is capable of two kinds of observation: that of matter by means of his five physical senses, and that of invisible realities, starting with the operations of his own mind, by means of an inner, if latent, sense or eye *common to all men*.

Because that school is known as the "common sense philosophy," it has often been taken as empirical and pragmatic, and some Madison commentators have so interpreted it. (Webster's dictionary: "Common sense: Sound, ordinary sense.") But this is not at all the term's meaning as applied in the Scottish School then; the meaning is practically the opposite. Common sense, far from being horse sense or down-to-earth sense, is, as stated earlier, a spiritual sense or intuition. (Webster: "Intuition: The power of knowing . . . without recourse to inference or reasoning; innate . . . knowledge.") Anti-Locke, anti-Hume, in a way anti-Enlightenment, but Christian, this school vindicated the "still small voice."

Those who assume that because Madison read Locke, Hume, Voltaire, and Diderot he accepted their philosophy have not taken his pulse. Of course he studied them; every real searcher after truth tests personal convictions by exposing them to the toughest opposition possible. But there is evidence that Madison's lifelong viewpoint was established when Dr. Witherspoon's instruction in moral philosophy met something in his own makeup (William James would say temperament) which predisposed him in that direction.

In the middle of Madison's crucial senior year, Nassau Hall received the Rittenhouse orrery purchased a year ago. It caused a furor of excitement among the students, and would indirectly (the evidence comes later) influence the Constitution of the United States.

Today that planetarium hangs on a Princeton University wall, but when delivered in April 1771, its frame and side panels stood upright on wooden legs. The 4-foot-square face was a blue heaven of stars rimmed by the zodiac. As Dr. Witherspoon turned a crank, ivory globes—Mercury, Venus, Earth, Mars, Jupiter, and Saturn—circled a brass sun whose corona consisted of jagged brass teeth. A dial ticked off a cosmic dance of days, months, years, and centuries. The orrery was a system of balances, a mighty frame of reference capable of expanding a vigorous mind like young James Madison's.

Seniors were allowed to work the drive shaft which sent planets plowing the field of stars. Jemmy had that heady experience. And he saw the implication: without equipoise the universe would fly asunder; it would plunge into chaos. He stood before the contraption fascinated: James Madison on the edge of manhood.

While he stares at the orrery, we can study him. At the age of twenty he had hay-colored hair cut in bangs, skin pale from obstinate overstudy, and eyes with a certain intensity. (Because one eye was nearsighted, the other farsighted, he would never be able to shave himself in a mirror.) Though he did not share the great height of such future friends and foes as Washington, Jefferson, Marshall, Monroe, or John Randolph of Roanoke, his shortness has been exaggerated. He was 5 feet 6, the exact height of fellow student Aaron Burr, and he would outstrip the as yet unborn Napoleon by several inches. Though he cracked jokes among intimates and could laugh with the boys, his usual expression was serious. But the calm was more mask than face. Shy, he was under the necessity of proving himself just one of the boys. Exposed to the idea that balance is fundamental, he could not avoid knowing that he himself was somewhat lopsided.

There seems to be a strong possibility that just at this time Madison fell in love with a pretty Philadelphia girl and became engaged. If so, he could have met her during a vacation spent visiting a Philadelphia college-mate, perhaps his close friend William Bradford; and if so (again), it must have been hard to manage a romance while carrying a double academic load—unacademic thoughts would at times, inevitably, disrupt. Marrying upon graduation, that is at twenty-one, would not have been considered unusual; his brother Francis married at nineteen. But the pretty Philadel-phian, if she existed, changed her mind.

The evidence is a notation fastened to the back of a copy of an ivory miniature of Madison painted by Charles Willson Peale—a picture painted in 1783, say a number of commentators, to be exchanged for a matching one (as was customary) of Catherine Floyd. But there are serious difficulties with this theory. The two miniatures do not match in size or framing, and Madison's, unlike Kitty's, was made to hold hair. Also, Kitty's is engraved with the date "1782," the year before the Floyd-Madison engagement. Moreover, Madison looks like a somewhat callow twenty-one-year-old, not like a thirty-two-year-old man within four years of becoming Father of the Constitution.

The documentary evidence on time-yellowed paper is believed to have been written by Mary Madison McGuire, a descendant of Madison's sister Nelly Hite. Here is the notation:

> James Madison Junior, Montpelier. While President Madison was attending Princeton College, aged 20–1, family tradition says, his heart was captured by a pretty Philadelphian, who accepted his offer of heart and hand. He had the *miniature* painted for her on ivory by the celebrated miniature artist *Peale,* and set in a heavy gold locket according to the fashion of his day. Alas! the fair one proved false and returned the locket. It was an unpleasant reminder of his disappointment, so he sent it to his sister Nelly who [later] gave it to her only daughter Nelly,

and so forth. The chain of ownership can be traced in detail right down to the Leeds family, which recently, in the person of William M. Leeds, presented the miniature to the Library of Congress. Though made for a locket, says the notation, the locket was later converted into a brooch. One might add that Madison's favorite sister Nelly was in a position to know and transmit the truth; though relatives sometimes get family history wrong, they can also get it right.*

*The question of attribution is explored a little further in the "Notes."

Madison passed his senior examinations in September 1771, then collapsed. Obviously, if a jilting were added to overwork, his illness would be still easier to understand, and one could guess that Dr. Witherspoon, who had a great affection for him, knew the circumstances when he excused this exceptional student from the commencement ceremonies.

Though the entire school knew about Jemmy's absence, that is not to say it knew the cause and nature of his ailment. The fact that so outstanding a scholar had not sat among his fellows on the great day must have caused considerable talk.

Among the eleven seniors receiving diplomas, Hugh Henry Brackenridge was the bright particular star. His Latin oration, delivered in an atmosphere of high patriotism, was followed by a metrical dialogue written in "Miltonic" style by himself and Philip Freneau: "The Rising Glory of America." It speaks of the Indians encountered by the first white settlers as being

> Unstable as the sea, wild as the winds,
> Cruel as death and treacherous as hell. . . .

But America was moving toward something better:

> 'Tis but the morning of the world with us
> And science yet but sheds her orient rays. . . .

Madison did not go home in October. He could not. In a third-person autobiographical sketch dictated to Payne Todd in 1830, he says he stayed on at Princeton for graduate studies because his health was "too infirm for a journey home." Unfortunately his letter to his father on the subject has been lost or destroyed.

A later one, that of October 9, sounds studiously offhand, as if he were resolved not to worry the family. He says he's glad his mother has been safely delivered of a son [Reuben] and hopes his father's rheumatism has let up. The bill of exchange is "very acceptable." If he comes home next spring, he'll need "a few Half-Jos" for a horse. If it has been decided that he is to stay longer (it seems clear that he was trying to find out), they could send the cloth—homespun—for his new coat. Apparently he had warmed to the idea of a year of graduate study. Though he loved his family, Princeton offered the companionship of congenial friends, a library of 2,000 books, and stimulating challenges.

That winter Dr. Witherspoon taught him Hebrew and theology.

Madison was trying to decide whether or not he was fitted for the life of a clergyman. Sam Spring and Brackenridge were staying on, and Tutor Smith's mind was an anvil on which to strike the iron of his own.

Having more leisure now, he could give more time to the arts, and he himself has said that at this period he was "captivated much" by poetry, wit, criticism, romances, and plays, supposedly by such popular authors as Milton, Pope, Fielding, Smollett, Pascal, Montaigne, Molière, Racine, and Congreve. He enjoyed sharing these pleasures with his best friend: tall, blond William Bradford.

March brought another religious revival. It resurrected the Whigs' scorn of the Clios' emotionalism. Why were some of the most devout students such roués? Was there a connection? Amid much mock-serious doggerel, an anonymous Whig poured vitriol on a Clio's affair with the coachman's daughter. His health improved, young Madison was in the thick of the literary foray.

Then Colonel Madison decided that in April his eldest son and namesake should come home. It had proved impossible to find a tutor for the younger children, and Jemmy could fill in.

With some reluctance Madison left the college where he had gained knowledge, friends, and a radical patriotism. He left it as a revolutionary—though that was not the word used at the time. A year later alumnus Billey Bradford would write: "I leave Nassau Hall with the same regret that a fond son would feel who parts with an indulgent mother to tempt the dangers of the sea"—a tribute which might have been written by Jemmy Madison when, just past his twenty-first birthday, he said good-bye to Princeton and rode south.

He stopped in Philadelphia to visit Bradford. This largest town in the Colonies could in some respects boast of a tolerance which Virginia lacked. Pennsylvania had no established church; its people were free to live by their consciences; they could be Quakers, Anglicans, skeptics, or whatever, no questions asked. Madison heard and probably joined discussions around a table at Will's Coffee House, owned by Billey's printer-father. Then he continued his journey.

Unfortunately he had not been home long when old symptoms returned or new ones developed; he became the victim of strange attacks. Years later his brother-in-law J. C. Payne would describe them as "of the nature of epilepsy," words which he scratched out to write in their place "of a character and effect which suspended his power of action," which he inked out to substitute "the feebleness of his health." This scaling down aside, the first phrasing does come closer to Madison's own testimony, given elsewhere, that he suffered from "a constitutional liability to sudden attacks somewhat resembling epilepsy and suspending the intellectual functions."

One biographer thinks that a 1753 list of drugs for epilepsy found among the elder Madison's papers may mean that Jemmy had epilepsy as early as the age of two. But in that case would his parents have sent him far away to school at eleven? Or let him, in his teens, take eight- and ten-day trips on horseback? Or let him combine two academic years into one? As for Colonel Madison's list, a planter with a large family and a hundred slaves would have to try to arm himself with nostrums for any emergency.

Brant's theory that Jemmy suffered from epileptoid hysteria, a functional ailment of the nerves which sometimes develops after puberty from physical injury or psychic trauma, seems more probable. Overstudy could cause such a condition, or the anguish of rejection could, and the combination makes a strong case.

That summer Jemmy was sent to Warm Springs, not far from Harper's Ferry, to take the waters. It was a pleasant little spa where the guests lived in log huts, dipped into a pine-screened pool, and drank gallons of mineral water. In the evening they strolled or played cards or just sat around talking about anything but politics. That subject was off-bounds. George Washington had recovered from rheumatic fever there, and Jemmy had high hopes.

By autumn Billey Bradford kept his promise to write. He hated to leave Princeton, being in love with his Nassau Hall "chains," and he didn't expect happiness outside—"hope is a flatterer." His plan is to go back this winter to study history and morality, and he quotes in Greek—misquotes—the Delphic motto meaning "know thyself." He supposes Jemmy has heard about "poor Joe's death."

Jemmy had not. He was shocked. Joe Ross!

He wrote back in a kind of old-man gloom. He hopes Billey will shun the follies which beset a "first entrance on the Theatre of Life." They shouldn't become so involved in worldly matters as to forget to enroll their names in the "annals of heaven." He is "dull and infirm" and no longer expects a long healthy life, indeed has little spirit for what is useless after a person has "exchanged time for eternity." Billey's plan to study history and ethics is fine, but he hopes his friend will season those subjects with a little divinity. "Like the philosopher's stone in the hands of a good man" it will turn everything into a substance more precious than gold. He further advises Billey to avoid "impertinent fops" who breed like flies. Teaching his brothers and sisters doesn't take too much time. He counts on Billey for literary news. Some college talk follows. "Yr. Sincere and affecte friend."

Madison brooded over Joe Ross's death. Together they had worked hard. Could the price of a passionate will to know be so high?

In November he received a bantering letter from Philip Freneau. It was good medicine. That wag had taught school on Long Island for just thirteen days—"Long Island I have bid adieu with all its brutish brainless crew." Now he is teaching in Maryland. He regrets having been out of touch.

In March Bradford wrote again. "You alarm me by what you tell me about your health." Jemmy must have hurt his constitution while at Princeton with "too close an application to study; but I hope . . . you . . . will yet enjoy many days as you seem designed by Providence for extensive usefulness." And Billey quotes Dr. Witherspoon's prayer, "Spare useful lives." He values the fire of friendship but not the "smoke," flattery, and he wishes for Jemmy's company and conversation. "Write soon."

By the time Jemmy answered he had been home an entire year and could say, "My health is a little better." He ascribes the improvement to "more activity and less study"—to much walking and horseback riding in the clean air of "our mountains." Thereafter his letters brightened steadily.

Four pages of notes on the New Testament probably belong to this year. A later confidant, William C. Rives, says that while reading philosophy and literature he carried on "exhaustive theological studies." Certainly he now had the leisure for Bible study, and there is much evidence pointing to a growing concern for ultimates.

His notes follow closely William Burkitt's *Expository Notes . . . on the New Testament,* his pagination corresponding with that of the 1765 edition which Colonel Madison had ordered from his Liverpool agent in 1770. A few of the subjects covered: the Holy Spirit, humility, the need for an *informed* conscience, the "fall and death" of flattery, and self-serving "carnal" politicians.

His choice of what to copy from Burkitt's notes on Matthew, also, is not without significance. On Matthew 3:10, for instance: "Sins of omission as damnable as sins of commission." And again: "Soul[s] die not with the body."

Cutting away from Burkitt, Madison copied some proverbs of Solomon which appealed to him—arraignments of sluggards, talebearers, liars, the anger-prone, the proud, and the contentious.

Rives printed some extracts now lost. The commentary on Acts 17:8–

13, for example, calls the Bereans' daily searching of the Scriptures a "noble example." For Acts 9:6, a passage in which Jesus tells Paul, "*Arise* and *go* into the city and it shall be told what thou shall *do*," the commentary runs: "It is not the *talking* but the *walking* and *working* person that is the true Christian." Another entry explains God's omniscience not as compelling but permitting—an affirmation of free will.

Since Madison's study of the Scripture was purely voluntary and was undertaken when he thought he might be following Joe Ross into death, the selections from Burkitt suggest the climate of the young man's thoughts at this important time.

Senator Rives says that after college Madison "explored the whole history and evidences of Christianity on every side through clouds of witnesses and champions for and against, from the Fathers and school-men down to the infidel philosophers of the eighteenth century," and I have found nothing to contradict this testimony.

Madison's study of deists and atheists (to repeat) seems to have been the endeavor of a man who scorned to believe anything by default, who knew that convictions must be put to the test of the opposition's most trenchant arguments.

On April 28, 1772, he agreed with Billey about the unpleasantness of flattery. "I confess I have not the face to perform ceremony in person and I equally detest it on paper, though Tully says It can't blush. Friends, like all truth, delight in plainness and simplicity. . . ." He was speaking with vigor and balance. It was as if, forced by illness, he had taken into himself more deeply the lesson of the Rittenhouse orrery.

Bradford's letter book contains copies of thirty-one letters, twenty-four of which—a dozen from each young man—would be written during the next two years. This correspondence affords intimate glimpses into Madison's thoughts during his young manhood.

Subjects are discussed with easy familiarity. Bradford asks for a list of books and mails some pamphlets. Madison says a Princeton friend has described Bradford as "very sedate and philosophic" and adds, "I am so myself." He hopes to visit Philadelphia in the spring.

Bradford, who is trying to choose between the law, trade, and the ministry—though he feels unsuited to the pulpit—asks for advice. Madison recommends the law, while hoping his friend will keep "the most sublime of all sciences," the ministry, "obliquely in view" (which tells something about himself). "I have sometimes thought there could not be a stronger testimony in favor of religion . . . than for men who occupy the most honorable and gainful departments and are rising in reputation and wealth publickly to declare their unsatisfactoriness by becoming fervent advocates in the Cause of Christ." He'd like to see Billey offer this kind of testimony—"more striking than a 'cloud of witnesses.'" Starting to study Blackstone, Billey says yes, he intends to keep up his interest in divinity while studying law. And he agrees on the necessity to defend as well as believe in the Christian religion. The two young men saw eye to eye.

After more than a year of home study, Madison himself bought law books in order to "read law occasionally." The principles and modes of government were "too important to be disregarded by an inquisitive mind." What was the Pennsylvania law on religious toleration? Was an ecclesiastical establishment absolutely necessary? Wasn't it harmful? The reviews to which he subscribed were so "loose in their principles," they were "enemies to serious religion." He would soon be putting his brother William into school at Princeton. "I need not say how far the desire of seeing you and others is a powerful inducement" to make the trip.

In December 1773 news of the Boston Tea Party shook Montpelier. Three months earlier Jemmy had told Billey he did not meddle in politics. But he admired these Bostonians who acted out their conviction. Jemmy Madison could no longer stay above the gathering storm.

As Presiding Magistrate of Orange County, James Madison Sr. had a tremendous decision to make. Having long upheld the King's law, he now had to decide whether or not—on the ground of a higher law—to oppose it. Without doubt father and son talked over the issue. Jemmy could not but remember Dr. Witherspoon's statement in the course on moral philosophy that men could never—*never*—consent to be puppets. At Montpelier, now, there was forged a bond with the American patriots of Boston and elsewhere. Philadelphians, with Billey's father at their head, had warned Captain Ayres of the *Polly* that if he didn't take his cargo of tea back down the Delaware, he would soon wear a handsome coat of tar and feathers. "I congratulate you on your heroic proceedings," Jemmy wrote Billey excitedly, and he had made the leap which most patriots would make only later. Sometimes, he said, it was necessary to defend liberty and property by force of arms.

But this new preoccupation did not wean Jemmy away from his concern over religious intolerance. "Ecclesiastical establishments tend to great ignorance and corruption," he wrote Billey. The history of tyranny makes one "fall more in love with liberty." His affection for belles lettres is abating, and his law studies bear "sour fruit." He would like to give his time to something more substantial—and he veers back to religion in Virginia. "I have indeed as good an atmosphere at home as the climate will allow" but can't brag about the "state and liberty of my country." Sad to say, poverty, luxury, pride, ignorance, and knavery thrive among the clergy; also vice among the laity. The thought roused a passion. The "diabolical hell-conceived principle of persecution rages among some," he wrote angrily. It vexes him terribly. The next county has jailed some Baptists. He has "squabbled and scolded, abused and ridiculed" so long and vainly, he can only beg Billey to pray for liberty of conscience everywhere.

Young Madison was no longer a recluse; he was beginning to fight for his convictions.

Various "Nassovians" stopped off to see him, and he kept up with others by letter. When Brackenridge fell ill, "I confess if he were gone," he wrote, "I should almost say with the poet"—with Milton—"that his country could furnish such a pomp for death no more." As for the Cliosophic Dod, a father before he was a husband, the world should be peopled, but not with bastards. "Who could have thought the old monk had been so lecherous?"

His letter looped back again to the question of conscience, that "characteristic of a free people"; he could not let the subject alone. Being dependent on the Crown, the Anglican clergy, he thought, would oppose the right—a shameful thing. "Religious bondage shackles and debilitates the mind and unfits it for every noble enterprise. . . ."

Early in May Jemmy Madison visited the Bradfords in Philadelphia, then took his twelve-year-old brother William on to Princeton, where he saw Dr. Witherspoon, young friends and old sights, and—again—the planets slowly circling the sun on the Rittenhouse orrery.

Leaving Willie in the grammar school, he sailed up the Hudson River to Albany, New York, seeing en route farms worked without benefit of slaves. Slavery: it was on his conscience. Could he escape being involved in so nefarious a practice?

This strenuous two-month trip north is proof positive that the old ailment was either cured or in benign suspension.

During his absence from Virginia the situation there altered considerably. Lord Dunmore—off fighting Indians—had dissolved the Virginia Assembly, then kept it dissolved, and now angry burgesses in rump session were inviting other Colonies to send delegates to a Continental Congress. (Since all the Colonies were on the Eastern seaboard, it might have been called a Federation Congress.)

Jemmy Madison reacted sharply. "Would it not be advisable as soon as possible," he wrote a year before the outbreak of the Revolution, "to begin our defense . . . ?" But private opinions, he went on, must give way before the Congress's judgment. He was pleased that Virginia's seven delegates were all "glowing patriots."

In September, while the federation's Congress was gathering in Philadelphia, he acquired his first property. He paid his parents £30 for a 200-acre farm, Black Level, the boundaries of which began at "three small pines and a red oak." As a freeholder he could now vote and, if the occasion arose, hold office. Perhaps it was with that possibility in mind that he sent for Priestley's pamphlet on government and reread Locke, Harrington, and Montesquieu. He believed that in this crisis, public-spirited citizens must prepare themselves to serve in any way they could.

According to Bradford, who had got it from a librarian, delegates to the Continental Congress read such authors as Vattel, Locke, Barlemqui, and Montesquieu and "debate . . . like philosophers," and Jemmy reported back that here in his province the Congress's proceedings were universally approved. "A spirit of liberty and patriotism animates all degrees and denominations of men." Counties were forming independent military companies. "If America and Britain should come to hostile rupture—"

In December Jemmy's father boldly organized the Orange County Committee of Public Safety with Jemmy as his right hand, and the company got down to the business of raising troops and stockpiling arms and ammunition for defense "in case of a sudden invasion"—preparation for "extreme events." Jemmy was sure that by spring thousands of "well trained high-spirited men" would be equipped, at their own expense, with muskets, powder horns, and shot pouches, ready to meet any danger. Quakers were refusing to sign the Continental agreement designed to flush out disloyal "loyalists," but really they seemed to him "too honest and simple" for sinister plans. "*Vive, vale, et cetare*"—be happy, farewell, and so forth.

Bradford, once so proud of Pennsylvania, now berated it for holding back. "*Your* province seems to take the lead." And again, bitterly, "It is happy for us that we have Boston in the front and Virginia in the rear to defend us. . . . We are placed where cowards ought to be placed, in the middle."

As its first act the Orange committee made a bonfire of some seditious Tory pamphlets seized from the Rev. John Wingate, rector of the Brick Church.

When Lord Dunmore smuggled gunpowder from Williamsburg's magazine to the man-of-war *Fowey*, Patrick Henry's minutemen forced him to pay for it. Young Madison was in the party that rode to offer

Henry the Orange committee's warm congratulations. They caught him at Port Royal (just across the river from Belle Grove), en route to the Second Continental Congress. Henry met Madison personally, for at a later date he delivered a letter from him to Billey in Philadelphia.

Jemmy was in such good health, these days, he did not catch the dysentery which ravaged the family, carrying off little Elizabeth and Reuben and some slaves.

The least boastful of people boasted about the Orange Militia's zeal and marksmanship: "The strength of this Colony will lie chiefly in the rifle-men of the upland counties." Though far from being among the best, Jemmy wrote, he himself wouldn't often miss "a target the bigness of a man's face at . . . 100 yards." The shortage of powder, here as elsewhere, was the problem. "But we have a good cause and great courage. . . ." He was pleased that George Washington had been appointed Commander in Chief. And when he heard that a neighboring preacher had refused to fast or pray on the date set aside by Congress for that purpose, he was so outraged, he advised "new canonicals"—tar and feathers. So General Washington had cordoned off Boston! Bunker Hill would be avenged!

In October 1775 James Madison Jr. was commissioned a full colonel in the Orange County Militia. The order was signed by Edmund Pendleton and six other distinguished Virginians. Because under stress of battle his old "sudden attacks . . . suspending the intellectual functions" might return to endanger not only himself but also others, this fine horseman, good shot, and passionate patriot could not volunteer to join the regulars.

In April 1776 freeholders at Orange Courthouse stepped forward, one by one, for a voice vote: "Jeames Madison Jr." "Jeames Madison Jr." It was thus that young Madison and Major William Moore were elected delegates to the Convention called to frame the first Virginia constitution.

Madison was twenty-five years old.

Eleven days later he and his thirty-six-year-old half uncle rode down to Williamsburg through flowering dogwood. Madison was riding toward his first public office, toward the start of a career in public service which would last forty years—more truly sixty, meaning to the end of his life. Everything up to this time had been, in a very real sense, education for the coming train of events.

WHATEVER PART of her husband's life story Dolley heard during long leisurely honeymoon days at the Hites', it soon mixed with a ringing in her ears. The malaria suffered at the Winstons' had returned. She was racked by chills and fever.

A servant galloped to Winchester to fetch Dr. Baldwin, who ordered a "decisive" use of Peruvian cinchona, containing quinine and usually called "the bark." No one suspected the mosquitoes flitting through unscreened windows. When at last Dolley got back on her feet, wan but otherwise herself, the Madisons told Anna and Harriet (notorious for untidiness) it was time to pack.

The visit ended under a cloud. Madison would write his father (tardily, so absorbed was he in a delightful woman) that their departure was "embittered by the loss sustained the preceding night" by Nelly—Isaac Hite's letter would explain. A descendant has interpreted: "This mishap must have been the birth of one of several stillborn infants. . . . There were several such babies. . . . Isaac and Nelly had been married nine years and had only two children out of a rather continuous brood."

They said their reluctant farewells. Then again, horses' hooves were beating a tattoo on the Long Grey Trail.

Back at Harewood Dolley had a slight relapse into malaria, and Madison finally pinched off time to write his father and apologize for keeping Sam so long. "I found him indispensable for a variety of little services. . . ." After some references to the wedding and the visit to Old Hall, Madison continued in his somewhat formal eighteenth-century "Addisonian" style. In eight or ten days they would set out for Philadelphia. "Your daughter-in-law begs you and my mother to accept her best and most respectful affections, which she means to express herself by an early opportunity, and would be happy to correspond with Fanny"—a message sure to please a family still marveling that its bachelor had finally taken a wife.

The last days at Harewood were a further reprieve. Surrounded by loving people, Madison loosened up. His once ice-clogged streams could complete the melting process and run free. Little blue flowers were beginning to star roadsides, trees turning, the air lighter and finer. And there came a day when the Harewood family watched a carriage head north. It grew smaller and smaller in the distance. Master Payne, Miss Anna Payne, and Mr. and Mrs. James Madison were on their way to Philadelphia.

The road was barbarous with beauty as they crossed the Potomac at Harper's Ferry, amid tumbling rocks, and thundered across Maryland. It was a rough wayward trip. Slowly, on ruts, tree stumps, and merciless stream beds, Madison's new coach was shaking itself to pieces. Payne cried, dust rose, rain fell. Congressman Madison, whose hobby was cabinetmaking, put his skill to use. By tying together some broken parts, he managed to limp into Philadelphia.

Meanwhile something had happened. Only gradually does fruit ripen. Now it was not the ring on Dolley's finger which bound and freed her, nor any bodily talent, nor her husband's potential as a stepfather. It was love, binder together of worlds. She was no longer "Dolley Madison, alas, alas," but Dolley Madison, thank God.

❧ III ❧

"INNOCENCY WITH HER OPEN FACE"

THE DAY AFTER CHRISTMAS 1794 the Pine Street Meeting expelled Dolley Payne Madison for having "disregarded the wholesome order of our discipline in the accomplishment of her marriage to a person not in membership with us, before a hireling priest."

She had awaited this event a little as French ladies in tumbrels awaited the guillotine. But the blade had fallen and she was not destroyed. Though the Quakers had rejected her, she had not rejected the Quakers, and still considered herself one of them. Wasn't the test inward? Nor was she resentful. Her fellow members had done their duty as they saw it.

The Madisons were furnishing their rented house with pieces from Dolley's leased former home, china from Montpelier, and some new purchases. The Monroes had promised to shop around in Paris for rugs, draperies, and a bed—the possessions of murdered and bankrupt aristocrats sold cheap. When James returned to Montpelier, they could take their bargains along.

Madison's threat of retirement bothered Jefferson. Though he had wished the couple "joys perpetual," he preferred them to be experienced in Philadelphia. From Monticello he wrote Madison apprehensively. "Hold on, then, my dear friend, that we may not shipwreck. . . . I do not see, in the minds of those with whom I converse, a greater affliction than the fear of your retirement, but this must not be except to a more splendid and . . . officious post," meaning the Presidency. "There I would rejoice to see you." The plea not to quit the ship was a little ironical, since Jefferson himself had, as Secretary of State, done exactly that. But there is an explanation for this seeming inconsistency.

48

Between October 30, when Jefferson congratulated the Madisons, and December 28, when he begged his friend not to retire, a great deal had happened politically. Returning from putting down the whiskey rebellion without bloodshed, President George Washington had reported his success with understandable pride. But some earlier mistakes had alerted the party called Republican. First, he had taken along the father of the hated excise, Alexander Hamilton, then left him in charge. Second, in his annual message to Congress, he had spoken stingingly of "self-created" societies—the multiplying pro-French Democratic Societies on which he had been angrily blaming the rebellion.

To Jefferson and Madison it confirmed their growing suspicion that Washington had now definitely abandoned his old above-party neutrality to go over to the Federalist side of the political fence. Since when, they asked each other, had citizens forfeited the right to "self-create" any group they pleased? This was a free country, was it not? Would the old alliance with France now be repudiated in favor of Great Britain? Risking, for the sake of principle, his long friendship with Washington, Congressman Madison gave all Federalists (let the shoe fit whom it would) a historic answer: Opinions could never be the objects of legislation, and censorial power lay not with the government but with the people. Now an "essential and constitutional right of the citizen," he wrote Jefferson, had been repelled.

Party lines were tightening.

Madison was quick to acknowledge that in many respects Washington was acting with wisdom and tact. For example, when frontiersmen taken during the late insurrection were herded through Philadelphia with "INSURGENT" stuck in their caps, and Hamilton was demanding death for two ringleaders, the President very sensibly thought it was enough to have proved that federal law would be enforced, and he pardoned them. Hamilton was not pleased. He had written Rufus King: "Without rigor everywhere, our tranquility is likely to be of very short duration, and the next storm will be infinitely worse." Madison rejoiced when Washington ignored Hamilton's recommendation for a standing army, calling it the "business of despotism."

He and other Republicans suspected that Hamilton wanted an army in order to use it against France in a way which would win himself glory and the Presidency.

It was this increased party warfare which made Jefferson so anxious to keep Madison in Philadelphia, and the thought hit him that he might enlist Dolley as an ally. His letter of December 28 goes on: "Present me respectfully to Mrs. Madison, and pray her to keep you where you are for her own satisfaction and the public good. . . ."—not realizing that Dolley preferred what James preferred.

Just after Christmas she received word of two deaths. Her favorite brother, Temple, a bachelor and navy ensign, was living in Isaac's house in Norfolk when illness took him off. Soon afterward an offended man killed Isaac with a pistol. Sorrowful letters groped back and forth between Philadelphia and Harewood.

In February 1795 Payne turned three years old. According to Dolley's great-niece Mary Kunkel, grounding on family sources, the child was as dear to his stepfather as if born to him, this "princely child," son of an "idolized wife." Indeed, so "pure and unselfish" was Madison in this relation, says Mrs. Kunkel, tears wet the eyes of the woman sitting opposite. The boy was running around the house, now, learning the ways of the world by asking questions. He romped with "Papa" and was petted by Mama, and some wondered if he was being spoiled just a little.

To sixteen-year-old Anna, too, Madison was like a father. Physically the sisters stood in contrast, Dolley with the rather Irish look of some of the Coleses, Anna with the Welsh fairness of the Winstons, her pale blue eyes ringed around by so much white that the family teased her with the nickname "white eyes."

Dolley was a natural-born homemaker. As eldest girl in her father's family she had been trained to be efficient domestically, and as the daughter of a failing starch maker, then wife of a struggling lawyer, she had learned to cook everything from corn oysters to strawberry roll.

Some of her recipes have survived. For croquettes: chop leftover meat up fine; season with onion, mace, or nutmeg; roll into balls; dip into beaten egg; coat with crumbs; and fry. Another favorite was crab omelet garnished with parsley and thyme. Also sour-cream ginger cake. She made lip salve by first boiling hog's lard, wax, and alkanet root in a tin pot until the mixture reached a fine red color; then straining and adding lemon. Rubbed onto lips or cheeks, this ointment worked better than red silk soaked in alcohol.

Whereas the Todds' household had been strictly Quaker, the Madisons' was "neo-Quaker," a compromise between James's and Dolley's backgrounds. They were beginning to influence each other, she him, he her, their lives an exchange, a reciprocity.

They were hoping for a troop of offspring. Payne needed brothers and sisters, Dolley was highly maternal, and Madison enjoyed children.

How interesting to speculate what kinds of sons and daughters could be achieved by collaboration.

The mutual explorations included Dolley's slow introduction to the political world which was Jemmy's eminent domain. Some things she learned by direct instruction, some by reading, some by a kind of osmosis when exposed to politicians of different stripes.

At times Madison brought home specific problems. Intelligent though untrained, Dolley felt the national issues swirling about her. If she and Jemmy were part of a larger household, if the United States was, as he said, the greatest experiment in government ever undertaken in this world, she must try to understand his position.

It was a middle position. Having, when the Union was dangerously weak, stressed union, Madison had now dropped back to the political place natural to him, one midway between Hamilton and Jefferson but closer to Jefferson. He was thus a democrat, which was to say in 1795 a Republican (the title would switch meanings after the Civil War)—but a moderate democrat who believed in a representative government which would bring (since men's abilities differ) the wisest to the top, for it was they upon whom the nation must depend—who else?—for steering a straight course through turbulent waters. He tried to explain such matters to Dolley.

Philadelphia's most important social events were President Washington's Wednesday levees for gentlemen only and Martha Washington's teas, open to both sexes, at which she served plum cake. On the latter occasions Washington left off his sword to mingle in the crowd, chatting amiably with ladies dressed to the nines. He wore a black velvet suit and diamond buckles.

Dolley's own style was slowly changing. More and more she was leaving off her fichu to circle her beautiful throat with a necklace. It was pleasant to be able to please both James and herself. The little Quaker girl starved for beauty was beginning to make up for old lacks. A portrait painted soon after her marriage shows three roses stuck in her headgear.

The Madisons entertained without furbelows. It had to be that way; prices had risen 50 percent in one year. But having more and more people at her table gave Dolley no anxiety; she was by nature a social creature. Guests enjoyed the fact that the Madisons were so different. They were really foils for each other: a woman all or largely heart, a man all or largely lucid mind.

John Francis Mercer wrote to congratulate Madison on his marriage and becoming a Mason. "I hold a lodge on your road; pray let me sometimes take your hand." Mrs. Mercer hopes to welcome "the fair prophetess who has converted you to the true faith." But only half of this applied. According to Madison's own testimony, he never joined the Masons, though he may well have once contemplated doing so.

Though Dolley accompanied her husband to church, she did not—could not—take Communion. He, on his part, had now a greater incentive to study the Society of Friends' founder, the mystic George Fox. The Todd library, now Dolley's, could hardly have failed to include, along with Fox's writing, those of his followers Robert Barclay and William Penn. Years later when Jefferson asked Madison to recommend some books on philosophy and religion, his list would include Barclay's *Apologies for Quakers,* Penn's *Counterfeit Christianity Detected, A Key Opening the Way to Every Capacity,* and—a lovely title which describes the childlike side of Dolley Madison—*Innocency with Her Open Face.* Much in Quakerism appealed to Madison. If narrow in some respects, it had in abundance a quality of sincerity he prized. Thus it was that though he and Dolley came from different religious backgrounds, religion, far from being a barrier, proved, as they talked over ultimates, a great bond. Dolley's niece Mary Cutts, who knew "Uncle" thoroughly, would write, "Mr. Madison, though no sectarian, was a religious man. He attended the Episcopal Church and had that religion of the Bible and of the heart so visible throughout his . . . life."

In their talks the name John Witherspoon was bound to come up. But sadness now interfused Madison's admiration. The old doctor, that great moral influence on his life, had died last year at the age of seventy-two. Dolley would never meet him.

A ship's captain had reported that in London, last November, John Jay had negotiated a commercial treaty. There followed a long silence, with conjecture growing. At last Hamilton resigned and went back to his New York law practice. Madison had become too suspicious of his long-term political goals to consider the departure a loss for the Cabinet. When Congress adjourned in March, there was still no news about Jay's Treaty. As the family prepared to drive to Montpelier for the summer, Madison was anxious about its terms; he was restless. No word? No inkling?

If at this juncture Dolley was striving to understand better her husband's attitude toward Great Britain and related problems, she needed to understand better his political career up to this point, or at least up to the framing of the Constitution. His doings in the present House of

Representatives were widely known. But, however imposing, the list was only a skeleton one until fleshed out by warm detailed reminiscences.

Madison had been confiding the sequence to Dolley piecemeal. Now the fragments were beginning to fall together into a meaningful whole.

THE FIRST PERIOD of Madison's public life—1776 to 1787—began on the road to Williamsburg. Though the woods were beautiful with dogwood, it rained and rained. At last Madison and his half uncle William Moore reached the capital, tied their horses, and walked along the ribbon of mud which was Duke of Gloucester Street.

Raleigh Tavern boiled with delegates, the male sleeping quarters as crowded as a box of herring. Tom Paine's pamphlet *Common Sense* had blown up a storm. Men were born to be free, it said; to hell with tyranny. In the dining room men raised mugs of West Indian rum. "Your health, sir! Victory to General Washington, sir!" Dammit, there was no turning back! Delegates who knew their Grotius, Vattel, and Locke argued about the "law of nature," about the "rights of human nature"—natural rights, meaning those belonging to man by reason of what he *is,* God-given rights, inalienable. The crux lay in the question "What is man?" What is his inner constitution? his potential? They felt the excitement of ideas, of getting down to fundamentals. In the morning the smell of brewing coffee and frying bacon penetrated the air. They rose, dressed, ate, and strode off to the new brick Capitol with its double-deck porch—some moderates, but most of them radicals—here where Lord Dunmore had prorogued the Assembly. Thank God he had no power over this Convention.

The first thing the 112 delegates did was to pass a Declaration of Independence. The air crackled; they knew that in Great Britain they were traitors to be hanged by the neck until dead. Then they instructed Virginia's delegates to the Continental Congress to propose that all thirteen Colonies, acting together, boldly, irrevocably, make a similar Declaration.

One evening three young men, Henry Tazewell, Edmund Randolph, and James Madison, fell into a crowd surging out to Waller's Grove. There Virginia's Declaration of Independence was read out, strong and clear, to drawn-up soldiery. Afterward each utterance in a round of toasts was followed by a discharge of now firearms, now cannon, and always loud cheering. The mood was one of defiance and celebration. Britain was sending 45,000 redcoats? Let her—justice was on their side.

James Madison, a young man capable of large conceptions, felt the future running toward him.

The next day Purdie's *Gazette* bore a new masthead: " . . . United we stand, divided we fall." The delegates marched to Bruton Church to hear Dr. Price preach on the text "Hearken ye, all Judah! Be not afraid or dismayed. . . . The battle is not yours but God's."

Madison was appointed to the committee charged with framing a Declaration of Rights and Virginia's first constitution. Chairman George Mason, delayed by gout, arrived limping and was immediately a power to reckon with: a stout gentleman with fine hazel eyes under bushy brows, by turns courteous and irascible. He wrote most of the Bill of Rights. But the center and nerve of the article on religion came from Madison—an extraordinary fact, since in political experience (not theory) the young man was as green as the Williamsburg common.

After Mason's article granting "religious toleration" to dissenters from the Established Church had passed the Convention, Madison—with his springy step—walked the streets of Williamsburg, peering into windows—the potter's, the cobbler's, the candlemaker's—but thinking of something else; he was troubled. Religious toleration was a concession, a condescension; it violated man's God-given right of conscience. He had said as much to Bradford two years ago. Why was he not speaking up strongly for what he believed? So he did speak up to friends and in committee, and he wrote out a substitute article and was successful in getting it passed. The heart of his revision read "All men are equally entitled"—have a *right*—"to enjoy the free exercise of religion, according to the dictates of conscience." But disestablishment of the Anglican Church, which he thought would follow logically and quicken religion, was going too far and too fast for other members of the Convention. For that fruit of his revision he must bide his time.

The amendment which passed would have powerful repercussions in other states and, ultimately, the Constitution. This solid achievement was Madison's first public act.

Edmund Randolph, with whom he set up a lasting friendship, has left a description of Madison at the Convention of 1776: "His diffidence went hand in hand with his morals, which repelled vice, however fashionable. In Convention debate his lips were never unsealed except to some member who happened to sit near him; and [anyone] who had once partaken of the rich banquet did not fail to wish to sit daily within reach. . . ." He was "not inflated by flattery"; he just kept "throwing out . . . jewels. . . ."

Seeking an influential sponsor, Madison had enlisted Patrick Henry. But he had reservations about the firebrand. Even while he "thrilled with the ecstasies of Henry's eloquence," Randolph says, he detected faults in his reasoning. The man he really admired was Edmund Pendleton, his father's attorney, now President of the Convention. What presence and dignity, what power of conciliation!

And then the Convention had done its work, elected Patrick Henry Governor, and broken up. Madison was jogging home when he heard that the die had been shaken and cast; the Colonies had declared their independence from tyrannous Great Britain.

The great bronze liberty bell sent the sound of its ringing all the way to Montpelier. The two James Madisons, father and son, caught the contagion of excitement. To them the Declaration of Independence was dangerous, inevitable, excellent.

September saw Madison back in Williamsburg. According to Virginia's new constitution, every man elected to the Convention was a delegate to the Virginia Assembly until the spring polls. It was a pleasant winter. His cousin James Madison (people confused the two), back from his ordination in England, was again teaching at the College of William and Mary, and made good company.

In the Assembly Madison was appointed to several committees. The one on religion sat him down beside red-haired Thomas Jefferson. Their meeting was like a conjunction of planets. The consequences would last fifty years and beyond. But the relationship began as quietly as the seed of a tree. They met—the tall gangling man from Albemarle and the short, sturdy, ruddy-faced one from Orange—and worked together for certain changes; no more. The question before the committee was legislation to make the religious freedom granted by the Virginia Bill of Rights stick. Petitions for disestablishment—the bird Madison had shot at but failed to bring down—were pouring in from Baptists, Presbyterians, Quakers, even Anglicans. Compulsory tithing, they said, was a tax on conscience. There followed a severe struggle. But the State was still not ripe for a break. The most that could be procured, for now, was a suspension of church taxes. Better half a loaf than no bread at all.

The task of revising Virginia's code of law belonged to older men with legal experience—Madison was too young, too new, and not a member of the bar. But he watched with tremendous interest as Jefferson (his senior by eight years), Thomas Ludwell, and George Wythe set their hands to the task.

Meanwhile General Washington's Continental Army had melted down from 18,000 to 4,000. It posed a desperate problem: how to replace deserters. Then it seemed by reports (communications were bad) that the British had invaded Princeton and seized the College of New Jersey for headquarters and barracks. Madison was apprehensive. Redcoats in the Prayer Hall? In his old room? Perhaps harming the Rittenhouse orrery? Then suddenly Washington won much-needed victories at Trenton and Princeton, and now Continental troops were occupying Nassau Hall. Ironically, it was not the British but the Americans who—in their zest for acquiring souvenirs—stole wheels off the orrery. When Washington retired to Morristown, they left it in shambles.

In the spring of 1777 Madison ran for election and lost. But the Cato in him said he had done right to refuse to honor the old custom of treating voters to free gin and rum. Should public office be bought? Some voters called him stingy; others said he was more suited to the pulpit than the hustings.

The time gained by the rebuff at the polls he spent studying, besides law, the constitutions of federations all the way back to Greece's Amphic-tyonic League, asking in each case, what were its strengths, what brought it to ruin? Appointed an Orange County justice, he declined the honor; he just kept on helping his father oversee the collecting of provender, weaving of blankets, and making of weapons for the Continental Army.

Father and son were drawn closer by their patriotic concerns. They were troubled about the stalemate. Then suddenly Howe appeared on the Chesapeake and began marching toward Philadelphia. It was bitter news that Washington had failed to stop him at Brandywine. The Continental Congress fled to York. It took high faith to believe that the less numerous, less experienced American army would win the war, but the Madisons had faith.

In October, as if to reward it, the elegant British General Burgoyne—"gentleman Jack"—surrendered an army of 5,000 at Saratoga, New York: a great decisive battle. It kept Britain from cutting off the Hudson Valley and seizing New England, and persuaded France to come out openly as America's ally. The family at Montpelier was jubilant.

That November the Virginia Assembly, balloting with tickets dropped into a glass, elected James Madison Jr. to the eight-man Privy Council (Council of State) set up to curb the Governor. Without its consent he could do nothing. Madison had until January to prepare.

It was probably now, soon after his appointment, that he received a letter from his old Princeton tutor and friend, Samuel Stanhope Smith, rejoicing that the country had, in spite of all Madison's modesty, recognized his merits. And Smith asked a favor: that Madison criticize a 1,000-word essay on the slippery subject of free will. Smith would not be posing metaphysical questions, he wrote, if he did not know his friend's taste for them. His basic argument: Free will is an inherent power. We can will to act a certain way because some desire (affection, interest), turning into a motive, so inclines us. Fortunately, through our power over ideas, that is, our ability to call up images conducive to virtue or vice, we can influence our desires, therefore our motives, therefore our actions—a fact of prime importance in matters of morality. Did his friend agree?

Madison's lost reply, apparently delayed until summer (Smith's comment is dated September 15), took a form which, in spite of objections to Smith's terms or logic or whatever, caused his friend to say that *"practically you seem to be one of [free will's] disciples."*

Out of his free will then, let us say, Madison accepted the appointment to the Governor's Privy Council, and on January 14, 1778, he was sworn in and took his seat in one of the high-backed chairs around the Council table. The talk was grim as Governor Patrick Henry's steel-rimmed spectacles slid slowly down a long nose. For three months Washington's troops had been suffering cold and hunger at Valley Forge.

Madison would call the Council the grave of all useful talents. But the Assembly had put him into the right place at the right time. Lucid and well informed, though without rhetorical power, he had landed where his special abilities would show and count. Up the long political staircase he had taken another step.

His cousin of the same name, ordained and now president of William and Mary, invited him to stay at his own handsome brick house and eat at the faculty table. It made for stimulating company. Hard put to show his appreciation of such largess, the guest asked his father to send a load of Montpelier's dried fruits.

And now Orange County, without any rum persuasion, voted him back into the Assembly. It was too late; the election had to be voided.

The Privy Council found time to send George Rogers Clark to conquer the "Great Northwest" and stop British-instigated Indian raids. But its main task was feeding, clothing, arming, and paying Virginia

---

*Because I cannot agree with those who think Madison denied free will and because his viewpoint in this matter is crucial to his character and lifework—and to our understanding—I go into the Smith-Madison exchange more fully in the "Notes."

troops. It was buying up bacon and beef (not with money—the State had none—but with promises) and collecting secondhand boots for the soldiers von Steuben was drilling at Valley Forge. Bloody footprints made snow there the color, as well as texture, of watermelon.

Jemmy had little time, these days, to write Billey Bradford, now deputy muster-master of the Continental Army. But he did get off a hasty letter rejoicing that France had accepted Pennsylvania's Dr. Benjamin Franklin as ambassador (really minister) of the "13 independent States of America."

France, indispensable ally, was sending ships, supplies, troops. And again Lafayette's sword gleamed in American sunlight.

When in June the British evacuated Philadelphia and began harrying the Virginia coast, they came uncomfortably near the Council of State, and during the "sick-season" the Privy Council fled Williamsburg. Madison had a brief respite at Warm Springs.

Then again the Council was sitting around its oval table. Its records for the winter of 1778–1779 would be destroyed by Benedict Arnold, but we know that, emboldened by the group's intimacy, Madison was at last unsheathing the rapier of his mind. More relaxed now, he joked about Virginia's eight governors and one councillor. Actually the spread of authority among nine people threatened a paralysis which only the common dangers of war averted. He brooded over this fact. Wasn't the central government similarly shackled by the absence of any real executive?

Britain's southern campaign quickened. Savannah fell, and General Washington again warned that without supplies his army would starve and break up. Yet many States refused to meet requisitions. There was regional selfishness, and Congress had no power to compel. The Privy Council sent Washington the little extras he had asked for: wine, rum, sugar—a pitiful consolation. Madison wished he could carry a cartouche and load a flintlock. He was proud of Ambrose, former lieutenant paymaster of the 3d Virginia Regiment, now captain of a company guarding Hessian prisoners near Charlottesville. Things looked bad. But how defeat men fighting for a great principle?

The Revolution stumbled along financially, helped by the keen-edged talents of Robert Morris. Virginia was almost bankrupt.

One day Councillor Madison's conical "Cromwellian" hat was stolen from the Rev. Mr. Madison's front hall through a window. Because the Embargo had emptied the hatter's shop, and no gentleman would be caught outdoors uncovered, he stayed shut up two days. Finally, a French dealer in snuff condescended to sell him—at an exorbitant price—a "coarse" hat with a crown so small and a brim so broad, for the rest of the session it afforded his friends much merriment. Fortunately the councillor could laugh at himself.

In the meantime Patrick Henry, deprived of an audience for his golden rhetoric, felt as if he were choking to death, and he was not sorry when, near the tail end of 1779, Thomas Jefferson replaced him as Governor.

Though Jefferson and Madison had met three years ago, this marks the true beginning of an intimate, highly consequential friendship. Thrown more closely together, they rediscovered a community of interests, admired each other increasingly, and cemented a bond.

At William and Mary, where Madison was staying and Jefferson was welcomed as a distinguished alumnus, they sat around after dinner, over wine, discussing State problems, farm problems, world history, the law, Greek and Roman literature, war events, and the bright cause of freedom. The eight-year age difference—Jefferson was thirty-six, Madison twenty-eight—made no difference. But Jefferson's longer political experience, authorship of the Declaration of Independence, and prominence in the effort to revise.Virginia's laws and courts started the relationship off with a certain superiority on his part. Madison looked up to him, and this first attitude would never quite wear off. Not that Jefferson ever wanted subordination; on the contrary, he soon recognized and acknowledged his peer.

Many pleasant hours later—in December—the Virginia Assembly appointed Madison to the Second Continental Congress. Though Jefferson hated to lose his companion and clearest-minded privy councillor, he knew how desperately a Congress at low ebb needed first-class minds.

For Madison it was the next step on the political staircase leading—where?

Before going home for an interlude he asked his father to send the college 600 pounds of flour and, for a certain Mr. Norton, "2 Bear Skins to cover the foot of his chariot"; entered Willey at the College of William and Mary (where the lad would soon be debating "whether polygamy is the dictate of nature or not"); and bought part of Lord Dunmore's library at auction. Then it was time to swing his leg over a horse's saddle. Perhaps he rode the mount "of strong make" which he had advertised as "strayed or stolen from the Common . . . sorrel . . . with a hanging mane and switch tail," white feet, and a "few saddle spots."

That winter at Montpelier snow piled up and drifted; he could not get out. He used the weather's gift of time to study congressional problems and to write an essay on the nature of money. Prices were soaring crazily; paper money was plunging. His 3,500-word article boldly attacked the theories of established authorities such as Montesquieu and Hume. He denied that the value of money was regulated by quantity. No, money lost value, he said, only by the underproduction of commodities, the weakening of public credit, and its resultant unredeemability—an original analysis not without interest today.

Then black Billy drove him to Philadelphia in a two-wheel chaise over vile roads in almost continual rain. The trip took twelve days. En route he turned twenty-nine.

Madison was reimpressed by Philadelphia—40,000 people!—center of the confederation's loose form of government.

After two days at the Indian Queen, he moved to the boarding place at Fifth and Market run by Mrs. Mary House and her daughter Eliza Trist. It was just the "bray of an ass" from the statehouse where Congress met.

On March 20, 1780, James Madison was sworn into the Continental Congress without any fanfare, although—considering his subsequent career—a trumpet salute might not have been inappropriate.

Now he was working for all thirteen states in a government that was steadily weakening. Last September the Congress had forfeited still more of its old power—never very great—by giving up its money-printing prerogative to states increasingly jealous of the central government and each other. Congress had little taxing power and no executive; it could make requisitions but not enforce them. For the first time Madison was seeing from the inside, and in some consternation, its helplessness, its dilemma.

Put on the Board of Admiralty of a little five-ship navy, he signed a demand that the American flag be at all times guarded from insult; and in June, before resigning, he created the first navy seal: thirteen red and white bars above an anchor on a sea-blue ground. The motto was *Sustentans et sustentatus.*

The Congress and the country were struggling against depression over the surrender of Charleston. Lafayette, who had reported a French fleet on its way, went on stubbornly fighting and hoping. At least the British plan to seize the Northeast had failed, and Washington, acting boldly, had not exactly lost the strange battle of Monmouth; he had just not quite won. And there was Wayne's capture of Stony Point to bolster sagging spirits.

The Congress had been served by many brilliant Virginians—among them Peyton Randolph, Washington, Wythe, Pendleton, Henry, and Jefferson—before the Virginia delegation dried up. Now those who had heard about Madison's keen mind looked to him for leadership. But during debate after debate he could not find his tongue.

It was six months before he rose to his feet, but by then he was so well known for privately expressed wisdom, colleagues leaned forward to catch his low voice. The burden of many of his speeches: strengthen the federal government, otherwise the Union would splinter into politically weak and economically unviable fragments, the prey of foreign powers; lay imposts to keep the new nation solvent; fight hard for free navigation of the Mississippi; nurture in every way possible the vital French alliance. During nearly four years in Congress his support of these key issues would never waver.

Writing Jefferson, he lamented the Union's critical situation. Its treasury was empty, its credit exhausted, its army living on free quarter. Moreover, Congress distrusted the people, the people Congress. There was a "defect of adequate statesmen." Without vigorous remedies, he concluded, "we are undone."

Savage inflation had put his own finances into jeopardy. During his whole time in Congress he received not a penny of salary, though state law allowed $20 a day and expenses, and it was costing him about $6,000 a month for room and board, liquor, fruit, laundry, firewood, barbering, and the care of his horses. Colonel Madison remitted what he could. The rest had to be borrowed from a kindly Jew—"little Hayme"—who lent without pressing for repayment.

While Philadelphia waited for French reinforcements, it was splashed with the bright blue uniforms of French volunteers and dazzled by the stout, splendidly dressed French minister, the Chevalier de la Luzerne. His weekly dinners were served on gold-encrusted china, and his elegant, dissipated balls were the season's high lights. "Oh, my dear!" wrote Mrs. Theodorick Bland of Virginia in an ecstatic letter, "such a swarm of French . . . marquises, counts, viscounts, barons and chevaliers!"

There was more democratic entertainment. Crowds mobbed the plays given at the College of Philadelphia. In the hurly-burly, people climbed over others' heads. Once the wife of a Chief Justice grabbed and pulled a gentleman's queue, then broke a fan over his head. A lady lost her false curls and could not find them. Another lost her shoes but kept on going. "Oh, Fanny!" cried Martha Bland to her sister-in-law. "What would I give to have you . . . at some of those scenes of high life below stairs."

This giddy, pretty Mrs. Bland scorned Madison as "a gloomy stiff creature; they say he is clever in Congress, but out of it the most unsocial creature in existence." But then she found the whole Virginia delegation dull except her own vainglorious husband. Joseph Jones with his "sable" complexion looked like a Presbyterian priest, and Meriwether Smith wore the "grimace of a baboon."

Others had a different opinion of Madison. After sitting next to him at dinner, the Marquis de Chastellux spoke of his great enjoyment. And the Blands' cousin Tom Shippen said flatly, "Madison is charming."

The key to the contradiction lies in a comment made years later by Margaret Bayard Smith. She observed that Madison's conversation was "so rich in sentiments and facts, so enlivened by anecdotes and epigrammatic remarks, so frank and confidential . . . on men and measures that it had an interest and charm" few people achieved. Yet, oddly enough, in the presence of a strange or indifferent person, the man turned stiff and mute. The gushing of a Martha Bland stopped him cold.

By mid-July eight French ships of the line, three frigates, and two "bumketchers" carrying the Count de Rochambeau and 5,000 French regulars lay off Providence, Rhode Island. They had been instructed to honor and obey George Washington as a marshal of France.

When Rochambeau wrote Congress, Madison drafted a reply. The French-American coalition would be perfected, he said, when they won, jointly, the "glory of triumphing over a restless and powerful enemy to the rights of Mankind." August turned very hot. Mosquitoes and flies stung legs through silk stockings as a jumpy Congress decided it preferred plainer diction. "The wather," wrote John Folsom of New Hampshire, "hase bin so hot that when out of Congress we have had full imployment to find air enough to breathe in."

The news was bad: at Camden, South Carolina, the raw American militia had run from battle. Shocked, Madison prophesied that shame would make the defeated men fight harder. And there fell the still heavier blow of General Benedict Arnold's treason. Madison recoiled in horror. The blackguard; find him and shoot him.

It was now that Madison made his first venture into foreign affairs by drafting a letter to Minister to Spain John Jay stating reasons why the Union claimed all the land east of the Mississippi which the Treaty of Paris had ceded to Britain. He also advocated free use—this was vital—of the Mississippi River and one or more of its ports. His skillful arguments would have convinced anyone except a Bourbon King who cared not a whit about state charters or the "general good of mankind."

State charters. Six of the thirteen States had undefined western boundaries, and Virginia claimed the whole Northwest Territory. In 1776 Maryland had protested that "the back lands . . . if secured by the blood and treasure of all, ought . . . to be considered as a common stock to be parceled out by Congress into free, convenient and independent governments." In 1780—though twelve states had signed—Maryland was still refusing to put the Articles of Confederation into effect by its own signing. No, that state said, not until "swollen" sister states had disgorged their western lands. Most Virginians balked at dismantling their "empire." By her charter, roared Benjamin Harris in Congress, "Virginia owns to the South Sea." Nobody—nobody—could "pare away" Virginia. But Madison held that Virginia should make large sacrifices for the sake of the Union.

Meanwhile how thwart voracious land companies—the Illinois-Wabash, the Indiana, the Transylvania, the Vandalia? All of them were out to make millions through western speculation. Madison would have none of it. Now and always he studiously avoided any conflict of interest while holding public office.

Then one day a British fleet disembarked 2,000 more troops for use in the South. But on an escarpment of the Blue Ridge, 900 North Carolina militiamen beat back a superior British force. The battle of King's Mountain redeemed the shameful rout at Camden. Madison's prediction had come true.

He had been pleased when his old philosophy teacher Dr. John Witherspoon returned to Congress. The "old doctor" had grown older—but how familiar he looked in his black academic gown. The two sometimes discussed political problems and morality in government. Not that they always saw eye to eye. For instance, when Commissioner Benjamin Franklin's integrity was attacked, they had taken opposite sides: Madison for, Witherspoon against. But they respected each other. That was the great thing.

For a long time it had been eminently clear that the Articles of Confederation must be ratified to strengthen, if only a little, the hand of Congress. That meant mollifying the holdout, Maryland, by cession of the frontier lands. Stung by the urgency of the arguments of Joseph Jones and James Madison, Virginia offered to give up the Great Northwest on condition that the land be sold for the public benefit. To her surprise there were quibbles. Land companies with deeds from Indian tribes wanted no obstacle to their dream of private enrichment. But though this problem would drag on, Maryland signed. On March 1, 1781, Congress celebrated ratification by ringing bells, firing guns, and shooting off gorgeous fireworks. Madison had hope. Yes, the Articles were miserably inadequate, but perhaps they could be made halfway effective by broad interpretations: "implied powers."

About this time two mutinying regiments were heading toward Congress to vent their grievances: starvation rations, no pay at all, and no discharge at the time promised. To make matters worse, Benedict Arnold had started brutal depredations along the Chesapeake Bay. "For God's sake, my countrymen," cried Timothy Standfast in the *Gazette,* "rouse from your lethargy . . . !"

They roused. They defeated Tarleton at Cowpens in South Carolina but were defeated at Guilford Courthouse. Appalled by his stunning loss of troops there, Cornwallis retreated to Virginia and began a fox-and-geese chase with young General Lafayette, back and forth across the state. Getting news of this, Madison worried about Virginia's shortage of guns and ammunition. And was Montpelier safe?

One of the victims of galloping inflation, Madison's father was selling land to raise money. He was also urging Orange County to complete its quota of forty-two army outfits—one cannot say uniforms. Each soldier got a pair of overalls, two shirts, two pairs of socks and shoes, and a hat or cap. Though the weather was still cold, nothing was said about coats. Madison Junior rose often in Congress to debate measures for the relief of ragged, hungry, ill-armed, exhausted troops. In imagination he slogged along muddy roads, shivering.

Twenty-four-year-old Lafayette dodged, feinted, and harassed Cornwallis with his 7,000 or so troops, avoiding battle. He wasn't even strong enough to get himself beaten, he wrote Washington. What was holding up reinforcement by Wayne? "The boy cannot escape me," sneered the veteran Cornwallis. But when Wayne joined Lafayette's cavalry at Culpeper, it moved off rapidly—singeing Orange—to save the "magazine of the Southern States" stored in Old Albemarle Courthouse. Taking a shortcut, Lafayette seized a superb position on the Mechunk in front of Scott's Landing and turned Tarleton's legion. The British fled. The pursuer had become the pursued.

Congress hoped this was the beginning of the end. It was. Lafayette's success marked the redcoats' furthest advance. As Madison wrote a friend, Cornwallis retreated to Richmond and thence "precipitately to Williamsburg." Actually it was a steady retreat all the way to Yorktown. Madison goes on to describe British "barbarity." "They have acted . . . like desperate bands of robbers and buccaneers. . . . Rapes, murders . . . not protection and the distribution of justice. . . ."

He was writing in July. In September Washington and Rochambeau rode south to join Lafayette; Madison thrilled to see 3,000 Continentals and their French allies as they marched through Philadelphia to martial music. Nothing, he said, could match that spectacle. The pomp of arms was glorious. French officers, instructed to "salute Congress as a crowned head, and its President as the first prince of the blood," let fall, as they passed, their flags and the tips of their swords, and congressmen uncovered their heads. The troops bivouacked on the common.

The Chevalier de la Luzerne gave a great dinner for eighty officers and dignitaries, including Madison. Only Washington was absent. Having failed to obtain money with which to pay his troops, he had hastened down the road after them to make sure they did not mutiny. He wished the money to come, he sent word back to Robert Morris, "on the wings of speed." But Congress was helpless. It could not enforce its requisitions.

During the banquet, a courier galloped up. Twenty-eight French ships had sailed into the Chesapeake with 3,000 more troops. It was superb news.

As the days and weeks passed, Philadelphia's tension increased. But Cornwallis was "irretrievably lost." Madison wrote those words on October 2, 1781, the day the last British earthworks fell at Yorktown. So the long struggle was over. Exulting, Congress voted the messenger who brought news of the British surrender a thoroughbred horse and a richly embossed sword.

Madison would hear the details later: 7,000 British troops had waited in vain for General Clinton to reinforce them. French and American ships cut their supplies; Lafayette, Washington, and Rochambeau formed a semicircular trap, then attacked their seven redoubts, wave upon furious wave. Now, if ever, freedom must be won. The dead stared up at the sky, the living straight ahead, while blood soaked the ground and reddened the Chesapeake. On the seventh day of the siege Cornwallis tried to sneak across the river. He was stopped by a terrible storm. On October 19, 1781, the British ran up the white flag of surrender.

Philadelphia went out of its mind with joy. Artillery roared. Marching to church, Congress gave thanks to God Almighty, and that night even Quakers set candles of thanksgiving in their windows. Madison's elation was not to be put into words. It was the greatest he had ever known in his thirty years of life.

But if the military war had ended, the war to consolidate the Union was just beginning, and he knew it.

The next four months brought him close to a tall, craggy man with an iron jaw in a comparatively small head and an unassailable character, George Washington, twenty years his senior. When the Commander in Chief came to Philadelphia for several months in the fall of 1781 to help solve postwar military problems, the two men set up a friendship. Part of the bond was the great love each felt for the young struggling confederation.

They discussed its problems, including its bankruptcy. How could it pay the bankers of France and Holland, and also the Continental Army? Impossible, yet honor required it. Even their State of Virginia had failed to meet requisitions. And how curb this growing speculation and inflation or handle interstate commerce?

The two talked over their friend Robert Morris. It seemed outrageous that this man who had financed the Revolution almost single-handedly—negotiating loans, often using his personal credit and sometimes cash from his own pocket—should now, because he had made a large fortune, be accused of dishonesty by people who had no proof at all. Neither Washington nor Madison believed him to be corrupt. He simply had mercantile genius. ("My charity . . . cannot invent an excuse for the prepense malice," Madison would write, "with which the character and services of this gentleman are murdered.") The two men were delighted when, cleared by Congress, Morris was appointed Superintendent of Finance.

As the months passed, George Washington—himself a restrained man—recognized the power behind the quiet exterior of James Madison, a sustained passion of the mind. And he could see that under a slight stiffness, as of formal garments, there beat a heart in certain ways lonely. The General's handshake, when he left, was massive.

It was true that Madison's life had a monotony. Every day he walked a block to the statehouse and focused his mind on the confederation's business; then he came home tired and, like as not, after dinner, disappeared behind a book. Though the household was congenial, something was missing from his life, and he knew it. His three brothers were all married. Was he to live out his life alone?

When Jefferson arrived at the House-Trist establishment in the fall of '82, he doubted it. He himself had just been through a bad period—a "stupor of mind"—following the death of his wife Martha last spring, but now after six months he had agreed to accept what he had formerly turned down: a place on a Peace Commission to Paris. It was while waiting with his eldest daughter Martha at Mrs. House's for his ship to sail that he noticed how much interest his friend Madison was showing in the second of Delegate William Floyd's three motherless daughters, Catherine. Mrs. House, the Trists, and other boarders—the "family"—had noticed too, for while the Floyds were home at Mastic, New York, on vacation, Kitty had grown from a child into an attractive young woman. So now the whole family was watching its bachelor watch Kitty as she played the harp, and teasing him a little. When they extolled his virtues to Kitty, she agreed.

Madison was not so engrossed in Kitty that he neglected "Long Tom." The two friends were often together, deep in conversation. Madison was making suggestions for Jefferson's "Notes on Virginia," Jefferson taking notes on Madison's record of congressional debates.

Nor were Madison's duties neglected. At the moment he was composing a list of 500 titles for a library—his own idea—which would give Congress books appropriate for consultation. He was also working with Alexander Hamilton, a comparatively new recruit to the Congress, on the old stubborn problem of how to pay and discharge the army. Should the soldiers be given full pay for six years or half pay for life? And should at least some troops be retained for a peacetime army?

Late in January 1783 Jefferson and "Patsy" left for Baltimore. But their ship was blocked by ice and British cruisers, and then word arrived that King George III was at last ready to declare his thirteen former colonies independent states. Jefferson returned to Philadelphia wondering if he would ever see Paris. When the provisional peace treaty arrived, Madison summed up Congress's viewpoint: "On the whole extremely liberal."

"Peace! peace!" rang through the town of Philadelphia. Then there was further rejoicing. The British, French, and Spaniards had signed a general peace. A warring world had gone quiet.

At a celebration ball attended by Madison, Jefferson, and the Floyds, young girls refused to dance with the British officer who had brought the formal announcement across the Atlantic; he was frozen out. Luzerne intervened on his behalf. The redcoat smiled, the ladies repented, a minuet struck up, and now at last the war was over. Unfortunately Madison had never learned to dance.

Congress's peace proclamation said, "We . . . require all the governors to cause this our proclamation to be made public." *Require?* The governors were furious. Virginia's wrote Madison that such words "excited a jealousy" of Congress's *high powers*. Madison rued this attitude. When would the thirteen states understand that they formed a nation?

With the problem of restoring public credit growing ever more pressing, Madison wrote out a revenue plan which he hoped would put the central government in firm control. National bankruptcy, he said, could be staved off only by impost—land and poll taxes. Negroes should count three-fifths as much as free men (a compromise between other proposals) because they were less productive. Interest on the national debt should be paid off as soon as possible, the principal gradually through increased commerce and the sale of western lands. In a somewhat mangled form, Congress adopted this scheme.

To get the public to accept his plan Madison, as head of a committee, wrote an anonymous, masterly "Address to the States." The fruits of the Revolution, he urged, must not be thrown away. "Let it be remembered . . . that it has ever been the pride and boast of America that the rights for which she contended were the rights of human nature"—in other words, he went back to a basic. Through "justice, good faith, honor, gratitude" the cause of liberty would gain "dignity and lustre" and set an example for the whole of mankind. It was the "last and fairest experiment in favor of the rights of human nature."

Congress adopted the address unanimously and ordered it printed as a pamphlet. Madison did not tell even his family the name of the author. The omission was characteristic.

George Washington liked the proposal so much that he put out a supporting circular. Now is the time of choice, it said. Would the new nation be "respectable and prosperous or contemptible and miserable"?

The Virginia Assembly, which Madison had hoped would set an example of swift acceptance, postponed debate until October. But spring had burgeoned, Kitty was charming, and he must decide about knee buckles and stock and whether to wear his buff jacket or the blue.

On his way to Monticello Jefferson wrote Madison with some tact and mostly in cipher: "Be pleased to make my compliments affectionately to the gentlemen and ladies. I desire them to Miss Kit[t]y particularly. Do you know that the raillery you sometimes experienced from our family strengthened by my own observation gave me hopes there was some foundation for it. I wished it to be so as it would give me a neighbor whose worth I rate high, and . . . render you happier than you can possibly be in a single state. I often made it the subject of conversation, more, exhortation, with her and was able to convince myself that she possessed every sentiment in your favor which you could wish."

Madison used cipher too. "Your inference . . . was not groundless. Before you left us I had sufficiently ascertained her sentiments. . . . Most preliminary arrangements . . . will be postponed until the end of . . . Congress." Betweentimes he would probably visit Virginia. Jefferson's interest in his happiness was "pleasing proof that the dispositions which I feel are reciprocal." The letter was Addisonially stiff, but from the heart.

Jefferson wrote quickly, "I rejoice at the information that Miss K. and yourself concur in sentiments." Stiff also, but no less from the heart.

When at the end of April the Floyd family left for the north, Madison accompanied his fiancée as far as New Brunswick, New Jersey, a distance of 60 miles. It took two days. With the father's blessing the couple was planning a November wedding. They would live at Montpelier. Kitty had just turned sixteen, Madison thirty-two.

The Virginia Assembly was urging him to stay on in Congress until May 1784. This was counting his three-year term not from his appointment but from the adoption of the Articles of Confederation, which had set the length of the maximum consecutive term. No, he said firmly, he had other plans.

A widespread opinion of him, as he prepared to leave Philadelphia, is set forth in the words of the Chevalier de la Luzerne to the French government: "James Madison Junior—of a sound and just mind. A man of learning who desires to do good works and to improve himself, and who is not overly ambitious. Of honest principles; zealous, without going to excess, for the honor of the thirteen states. . . . He is regarded as the man of the soundest judgment in Congress."

Chargé d'Affaires Louis Otto added some thoughts. Madison was a person whom, to appraise fairly, one "must study for a long time," Otto said. He had turned down the presidency of the Congress and "may one day be governor of his state, if his modesty permits him to accept that office."

Three hundred mutinous troops surrounded the statehouse and got drunk on "spiritous drink" from a nearby "tippling house"—Madison's words—"liberally served out." The soldiers had vowed not to let any congressman leave until their grievances had been redressed, but at the three o'clock adjournment they sullenly parted ranks.

That night Congress heard conflicting reports. The troops planned to rob a bank. No, they were penitent. No, they would kidnap congressmen for indemnity. Angry, Congress asked why the Pennsylvania Council had furnished no protection against hoodlums, and it finally sent word that, having been insulted, it was moving to Princeton.

Madison spent three days in a loved but now horribly overcrowded village where he could find no desk space and then returned to Philadelphia. That summer, though the Flying Machine took only a day from Philadelphia to Princeton, he seldom made the journey. He needed his papers for an important writing project, he said, and a place to spread them out.

The work was going smoothly when in July Kitty broke their engagement, sealing her letter—was it symbol or lack of wax?—with a dab of rye dough. Hoping to reverse her reversal he asked for a meeting in New York. She said no—and to Edmund Randolph, Madison mentioned a "disappointment." In a letter to Jefferson he opened up a little more.

The crucial passage was so thoroughly inked out later, it can be read only in spots. " . . . The necessity of my visiting . . . N. Jy no longer exists," but there seems to be no need to trouble Jefferson with the details. There is a reference to Kitty's "profession of indifference at what has happened." He hopes for a "more propitious turn of fate."

Jefferson offered sympathy. "I sincerely lament the misadventure . . . from whatever cause. . . . Should it be final . . . the world still presents the same and many other resources of happiness, and you possess many within yourself." His advice was "firmness of mind" and keeping busy. "No event has been more contrary to my expectations."

The truth was that Kitty (encouraged, says the Floyd family, by an older friend) preferred a nineteen-year-old medical student, William Clarkson, who had "hung round her at the harpsichord."

Madison endured as best he could the disappointment and inevitable gossip caused by this second jilting. Fortunately his laid-out writing project kept him well occupied with shaping ideas and paragraphs. But he was a man and must have asked himself with some emotion what he lacked that he should again be first accepted, then rejected. Was he too bookish and dry for any young woman able to attract other types?

It is hard to gauge the degree of his involvement: how much he just believed he ought to marry and have children, how much he desired to marry *Kitty*.

In August he returned to Princeton with two main objectives: to get Virginia's land cession past Congress at long last, and to beat back those who favored New York, Philadelphia, Trenton, or Annapolis, instead of the shores of the Potomac, for the permanent capital of the United States. In the jam-packed town he and Joseph Jones were put into one bed in a room so small—not 10 feet square—he was "obliged to write in a position that scarcely admits the use of any of my limbs."

Wondering if he might not, after all, spend the winter in Philadelphia, he asked Jefferson to meet him at the Alexandria races. He did not sound heartbroken.

September found him still plotting strategy to bring the capital to the Potomac. He and his Southerners countered the opposition by saying, yes, seven states could secure Trenton, but it would take nine to vote money for new buildings, and they refused to appropriate one penny. How about two alternately used permanent seats, Trenton and George Town, the capital, meanwhile, to be divided between Trenton and Annapolis? The scheme worked. The plotters' sole intention was to keep a gate open. A decade later their strange maneuver would achieve their goal.

On September 17 and October 8 Billey Bradford's family organ, the *Pennsylvania Journal,* printed anonymous articles: "The North American," Numbers 1 and 2. The authorship has been a matter of controversy. Did Madison write them?

Probably. Nothing else explains the important summer writing job mentioned to Jefferson. The subject of the articles was the one heaviest on his mind, and the pieces perfectly mirror many of his known convictions. Also, he seemed to hint at an author's role when, on sending Jefferson the first number, he wrote that he was leaving the authorship to his friend's conjecture. Moreover, the essays have a close relation to his "Address to the States," written a few months earlier. Though the style is more emotional, that difference can be explained.

"At an era so awful and so critical," the author says, "it is the design of this address . . . to investigate and to expose with freedom the real situation of these states, and in anticipating evil and misfortune to suggest their remedy." Constructively *expose with freedom*. He analyzes the situation. The basic cause of dissension is that "separate sovereignties" refuse to pull together financially and otherwise. Pushed by ambition, each is guilty of sectional selfishness. This loosens the Union's "Gordian knot" and invites intervention by a foreign power. Through discrimination against American shipping, Great Britain exploits the states' inability to "act as a nation." Despots hate any "vindication of the rights of mankind." The overwhelming need is to establish a Union strong enough to take its place among the nations of the earth. Immense problems loom. But beyond the darkness there shines a light.

The "North American" articles end with a peroration: "Liberty! Thou emanation from the all-beauteous and celestial mind! To Americans thou hast committed guardianship of the darling rights of mankind. . . . The band of patriots who are here thy votaries . . . will instill this holy truth into . . . their children, and teach them to hold it sacred, even as the divine aphorisms of religion: that the safety of America will be found"—his central theme—"in her *union.*"

There is plenty of evidence that Madison, the dedicated patriot, was no stranger to passion; he just kept it under clamps, and this summer of his jilting he must have felt a great inward pressure which, like steam, sought a vent. How could he use it better than on the future welfare of the Union which, during his years in the Continental Congress, he had seen increasingly jeopardized? Anonymity would permit a reticent man to let go. A few changes in word usage, whether originated by himself or suggested by the Bradfords, would complete his disguise.

But why should he never remove his mask for anyone—never— unless for Jefferson in some lost letter or else face-to-face? In the light of Madison's whole political story, the reason seems clear.

With the States courting disaster by refusing to renounce preroga- tives, he was even now searching for the "shared sovereignty" formula which later, in his blueprint for the federal Constitution, would prove to be the solution for conflicting claims, needs, viewpoints. Meanwhile the need was for effective, not just nominal, union. How jolt people into awareness of the fearful alternatives?

Only by loudly acclaiming nationalism. State rights were able, for now, to take care of themselves. Though Madison was a man powerfully drawn toward center, he could in this crisis adopt the ploy of the bar- gainer who, willing to sell for $7, asks $10 because he knows that whatever he asks, the buyer will cut it down. In other words, Madison schemed to strike a balance: the ancient game known to every horse trader. For the good of his country this man of single purpose could, if he must, play a game of strategy. But never thereafter would he be able to reveal his authorship for the simple reason that neither Virginia nor the nation could be counted upon to understand the imperatives of that crucial hour and the importance of timing. His political enemies, if they knew, would not withhold a charge of inconsistency to what, given his deeper objectives and the situation, was profoundly consistent.

The above explanation is not embarrassed by the passage about his seeing, during the Revolution, snow tracks made by bloody feet. This nonevent—or seeming nonevent, for Madison could have gone on some mission to Valley Forge without any reference to it surviving—fits into the pattern of deliberate disguise. And of course, at the least, he had seen such footprints with the eye of the imagination.

Granted it is not a hundred percent certain that Madison wrote the two "North American" articles, the probability seems very great indeed that they mark a shrewd step in his campaign to save the Union while yet preserving the States' identities: a crowning service at the end of 3½ years in the Continental Congress.

His last day was October 25, 1783. He and Jefferson drove south in serene weather to the new temporary capital, Annapolis. After dropping his friend there, Madison went on to Gunston Hall in torrential rain.

That night he discovered that the old curmudgeon George Mason was less opposed to taxation and Virginia's cession of the Northwest than expected, and ripe for a revision of the Virginia constitution. "His heterodoxy lay chiefly in being too little impressed," Madison reported in dismay, "with either the necessity or proper means of preserving the confederacy."

Then on through veils of rain. The roads were bogs, the rivers overflooded. It took nine more days to get home.

The welcome at Montpelier after his nearly four-year absence must have rocked the house. His parents, three brothers and their wives, sister Nelly (about to marry), sister Sarah (nearing twenty), Fanny (twelve), uncles, aunts, and cousins greeted him with love and pride. A Taylor cousin's diary speaks of dinners and a dance at Colonel Madison's, with some guests staying all night. On such occasions gentlemen drank sweetened rum, ladies sangaree.

A bitter winter folded down around Montpelier. Madison spent most of his days reading. Sometimes at night he played whist for small stakes. Trunks containing fifty-six volumes of Buffon's natural history were snowbound in Fredericksburg. He reviewed Coke on Littleton, and by spring was studying in ever greater depth the problems of self-government as illustrated by past confederacies. The study was absorbing. With history reinforcing the lessons of experience, he was convinced that sooner or later the United States must frame a new constitution.

And he was pondering the cost in taxes of Virginia's dependence upon out-of-state importers. Why not build up her own ports? On the Potomac, foreign vessels—because Maryland's boundary was the river's southern shore—flouted Virginia law with impunity. How could they correct this injustice?

Jefferson had proposed that Madison buy a little house on 140 acres near Monticello. Soon Monroe would be living in the neighborhood too. "What would I not give [if] you would fall into the circle." Madison liked the idea of such good company; he was mulling it over.

That spring he and Tom Paine and Billey Bradford were elected to the American Philosophical Society. It was good company.

"Wild geese flying N.ward," he wrote on April 1 in a meteorological

journal; and again, "Blue hyacinths bloom." Though he had no thermometer or barometer, he had joined Jefferson in keeping weather records,
with nature observations. Many people urged him to reenter the Virginia
Assembly. He wrote Edmund Randolph that though such a course would
be noxious to his plan to read law, one of the circumstances which
reconciled him was the thought of being near a "living [legal] oracle."

After Orange elected him, Willie drove him to Richmond in a sulky.
There he sold some dried tobacco, then took his seat. The Assembly had
long been split into two factions led by arch enemies, Patrick Henry and
Richard Henry Lee. The tension forced Madison almost at once into the
heat of battle.

If Madison wished, Jefferson wrote Eliza Trist, he could be elected
Governor of Virginia. She replied in some consternation, "He deserves
everything that can be done for him, but . . . I think it rather too great a
sacrifice. . . . He has a soul replete with gentleness, humanity and every
social virtue." Some newspaper "wretch" might attack him. Madison was
too amiable to "bear up against a torrent of abuse." But she overstressed
his vulnerability. Madison had borne stress with equanimity and was
coming to Richmond prepared, if need be, to endure more.

He put up at the tavern of the Neopolitan Mr. Formicola. Guests
were thrown helter-skelter into four large rooms. A German traveler
named Schoepf has reported, "Every evening our inn was full. Generals,
colonels, captains, senators, assemblymen, judges, doctors, clerks and
crowds of gentlemen of every weight and caliber and every line of dress
sat all together about the fire, drinking, smoking, singing, and talking
ribaldry. . . . The indelicate custom of having so many beds together in
one room is the more surprising since elsewhere in America there is much
store set by decorum and neatness."

Herr Schoepf was astonished by a capital having mud streets. What a
tumult outdoors. "One could almost fancy it was an Arabian village the
whole day long, saddled horses at every turn, and a swarming of riders,
. . . for a horse must be mounted if only to fetch a prize of snuff from
across the way." The doorkeeper at the small Assembly House kept
shouting the names of members. The anteroom was a beehive too—" here
they amust themselves zealously with talk of horse races, runaway slaves,
yesterday's play, politics or, it may be, with trafficking."

Madison was put on five committees, including those on religion, the
courts, and commerce.

The committee on religion was soon fighting Patrick Henry's bill for a
tax to support religion. The committee on justice, of which Madison was

chairman, undertook to reform the court system. The commerce committee, which Madison also chaired, worked to build up Virginia's seaports,
chiefly Norfolk and Alexandria.

Madison's main purpose in re-entering the Assembly after an eight-
year absence had been to promote new grants of power to Congress. For
one thing, it must have teeth in collecting revenues. He knew that nothing
less (the burden of the "North American" articles) could save the Union.
Things were badly out of kilter. He also hoped to put through as much as
possible of the revised Virginia legal code drafted five years ago by Wythe,
Pendleton, and—more particularly—Jefferson. And he wanted to
encourage the rewriting of Virginia's constitution of 1776.

At first Madison and Henry worked together amicably to squeeze
past the Legislature a bill authorizing an amendment to the Articles of
Confederation which would base money quotas not on land valuation but
on population, and promising to comply with requisitions. But the alliance
was too good to last.

Henry ruined the effect by putting through a one-year tax postponement. How could Virginia pay her debts as promised? Madison felt the extreme irony. "We shall make a strange figure, after our declarations . . . ,"
he wrote his father, "if we wholly omit the means of fulfilling them."

Fighting back, he got the moratorium shortened by three months and
the tax money specifically assigned to Congress. And he pushed through
some levies. No, he said, he was against Virginia printing its own
unfunded, unbacked *fiat* money, *fictitious* money. Look at the rapid
depreciation brought on by that practice in other states!

Then he pressed for printing the revised code of Virginia and paying
the revisors $500 apiece, got only 500 copies, and wrote Jefferson in
disgust, "A frivolous economy."

His difficulties had not ended. Henry was violently opposing his
recommendation for a revision of the Virginia constitution.

The only things the two men could agree on, these days, were for the
Assembly to give Tom Paine a farm for *Common Sense* and commission a
marble statue of George Washington. Madison's overlong one-sentence
inscription called the General an "immortal example of true glory."

Near adjournment, Madison moved that the Assembly appoint four
commissioners to meet with a delegation from Maryland to arrange for
joint control of the Potomac. One of those named was himself.

Then Patrick Henry struck a match to dry powder by offering two
bills: one for a tax to support religion, the other for the incorporation of
the Episcopal clergy.

Madison understood the intent. The tithing thrown out the front door was to be sneaked in through the back, and the clergy was to be given life tenures which even misbehavior could not break. Having himself introduced religious liberty into the Virginia Bill of Rights, Madison was prepared to fight for it. But Henry got the debate postponed until fall. Frustrated, Madison went home for the summer vacation.

On July 8 he hand-printed on his meteorological chart the single word "Clear," and five days later, "Flying clouds," then "Sawyers or cherry-dorries first heard."

He had answered Jefferson's invitation to settle near Monticello by saying, "I cannot altogether renounce the prospect, still less . . . embrace it." He knew how deeply attached he was to his lifelong home, Montpelier. This summer the chinch bug, despoiler of wheat, was engrossing his attention almost as much as ancient confederacies. But he was not giving up his long-planned "ramble into the Eastern States"—meaning New England. Before he left, his father deeded over to him—"in consideration of paternal affection and of five shillings"—560 acres of land. It was a parting present.

In Baltimore he ran into the Marquis de Lafayette and his aide, the Chevalier de Caraman. They were on their way to Fort Stanwix in New York State to attend a treaty signing with the Six Nations. Urged to come along, Madison decided to go at least as far as New York City. It was a royal progress. People were jamming the roads to cheer Lafayette.

As they rode, Madison tried to enlist the Frenchman on America's side in the dispute with Spain over free navigation of the Mississippi. Upon the outcome, he firmly believed, hinged the value of the vast Northwest Territory which he was counting on to reduce the war debt and send the slaves back to Africa. Could France act as mediator? Lafayette promised to write the Count de Vergennes.

In New York the Marquis was lionized. Gentlemen huzzahed, and fashionable ladies with "tremendous crap'd heads" flocked around him. It was all fascinating. Madison renounced New England.

With Lafayette he rode a barge up the Hudson River in halcyon weather. What sights—hulking green bluffs, ruined forts, lordly homes. At West Point they met wind and rain, followed by a calm, then a hurricane.

At last they crossed Albany's sandbars and met the French chargé d'affaires Francois de Barbé-Marbois.

Traveling by phaeton, then horseback, the four men and their servants reached the village of Niskayuna. They entered a hall where a hundred "shakers" had been segregated by sex. A speaker was excoriating marriage on the ground that the Saviour had not indulged. Some of the congregation went into convulsions of ecstasy and wept, though they were oddly capable of conversing with their visitors.

Riding on, the little party agreed on a division of labor: Madison directed; Caraman was in charge of lodgings; Marbois did the cooking (his specialty was soup); Lafayette tended the horses. They were carrying rations of cornmeal, tea, and chocolate. Entering the rich Mohawk Valley, they saw more and more Indians. White pioneers were living behind stockades. The roads were so bad, the phaeton had to be abandoned. The travelers tied their horses and camped, rolled up in cloaks and rugs, in a thick forest. The weather had turned very cold, but Lafayette was so hot-blooded, he wore only a gummed taffeta raincoat stuck with bits off the French newspaper in which it had come wrapped; friends had only to draw near to read the *Journal de Paris.* Indian boys, picked up along the way, roasted chickens on a spit. If one of them reversed it—considered unlucky—the others pulled his hair and beat him. When Madison saw its black loam, he decided that the Mohawk Valley had a fine future.

At Fort Stanwix—now Fort Schuyler—they found one of two cabins filled with trinkets for bargaining. The wretched other one, called the "barracks," was waiting for the American commissioners. A missionary loaned them the barracks for a night, while Indians built them a bark shack. They decided to forge ahead 18 miles to visit the Oneida Nation.

The trip was rough. The horses sank into marsh, were pulled out, and sank again. It rained, and they got lost. Their Indian guides re-oriented themselves by the moss and browned bark on the north side of trees. Altogether they opened five kegs of "breasts of milk." It increased their incentive.

A French-speaking guide told them he was Nicholas Jordan, cap-tured during the Seven Years' War and saved from cannibalism by a chief's daughter. As dowry she had brought a house, a garden, a gun, a cow, 12 scalps, and 700 needles and pins. Unfortunately she was always drunk.

When they reached the Oneida, they were fed fruit and fresh salmon, and Madison recognized Chief Grasshopper, who had visited Congress three years ago. Grasshopper welcomed his guests in a Bavarian hunting costume which Minister Luzerne had received from the Bavarian king and passed on. That night masked bucks kept sneaking off from their war dances to the kegs of brandy, then announced to their exhausted guests that they would dance all night. It took Lafayette's charm and ingenuity to get the fearful decision reversed. Later beribboned squaws, having failed to interest the masters as "temporary wives," went off with the servants. The party fought its way back to Fort Stanwix in three-below-zero weather.

Lafayette—"Kayewla"—helped negotiations. The Six Nations admired him extravagantly; the braves caressed him with their hands. "The Commissioners were eclipsed," wrote Madison. Thanks largely to a speech by Kayewla, the Indians renounced all territory from Buffalo to the Mississippi in return for a worthless guarantee of other lands, and the treaty was signed. The three Frenchmen and Madison left to shoot the Mohawk River. Their horses were waiting at Schenectady.

How brilliant the foliage. At Albany, Marbois and Madison bade Lafayette farewell before descending the Hudson faster than they had come up it.

From Philadelphia, Madison wrote Jefferson in code: "The time I have . . . passed with the M[arquis] has given me a thorough insi[gh]t into his character. With great natural frankness . . . he unit[e]s much address with very considerable talents and a strong thirst of praise and popularity. . . . I take him to be as amiable a man as vanity can admit and as sincere an American as any Frenchman can be."

The Virginia Assembly fined Madison for being two weeks late. But he had had a high adventure: one of the happiest experiences of his life.

That fall, first George Washington, then Lafayette, visited the Assembly. Madison wrote the official welcome for the Marquis and got the order for a still unexecuted Lafayette bust doubled. The result was Houdon's famous marble statues.

The following August he would somewhat revise his assessment of the Frenchman. On closer inspection, he told Jefferson, the man improved. Though his foibles remained, his good traits shone forth more brightly. If Lafayette was ambitious, it was "not for . . . the homage which fear renders to power" but rather for the "praise which virtue dedicates to merit." He had a warm nature, and his affection for the United States was unquestionable. Short only of hurting the "essential interests of France," he would remain zealous for America.

After that, Madison kept remembering the richness of the Mohawk Valley. No, he wouldn't mind owning a piece of it.

The Assembly was seeing a revival of the religious issue in the midst of other legislation which was now, in Madison's phrase, "on the anvil." He himself had introduced a bill to establish a circuit court system (Courts of Assize) and was pushing for national imposts and for bills to clean out the

Potomac and James riverbeds for better navigation. But the fight engaging him most deeply was the old one over freedom of conscience. Patrick Henry continued to press for his "moderate tax or contribution" to support Christianity. In the interest of that very Christianity Madison opposed it strongly. In postwar Virginia a tax to support the Christian religion would inevitably help, most, the Protestant Episcopal Church. He had nothing against that church; it was his own. But he was against nominal Christianity and believed that the genuine article could thrive only if voluntary through spiritual means. Besides, how unjust to force Presbyterians, Baptists, and Quakers to support, in any way, shape, or form, tenets in which they did not believe.

The debate raged on. Nations fall when religion decays, thundered Henry. Rising, Madison said flatly that the Assembly had no power to enact the proposed law; it violated the Virginia Bill of Rights. The question was not at all "Is religion necessary?" but "Are religious establishments necessary?" No, he said; that way religion was corrupted. When had the Christian religion flourished most? Was it not during early Christianity and the Reformation, when it had no public support whatsoever? His plea did not kill assessment; it simply caused a rewriting of the bill to give state support to *all* religions. This was not what Madison had worked for at all.

He and Jefferson were tired of Assemblyman Henry acting as a perennial stumbling block. "What we have to do, I think," wrote Jefferson, "is devot[ed]ly to pray for his death." Madison's solution was a little kinder: reelect him Governor. When indeed reelected, Henry had ten days in which to put through his religious tax. But he chose to leave for home while the support for Madison's position was growing. Fearing defeat, some advocates of the bill changed its label to make it more palatable. It was now "for teachers of the Christian religion." Since the schooling of children was largely in the hands of the clergy, this was a camouflage and dodge. Observing the cleverness, Madison decided to play for time. Understanding his friend's pure motives in this fight, Edmund Randolph called him seriously yet teasingly "patron of the Protestant Episcopal Church."

After adjournment, Madison spent two winter weeks studying law in Attorney General Randolph's office and then continued his study at home. But spring brought distractions. "March 12 fair," he wrote on his chart. "Garden peas first sown." And soon he saw the first "crow black birds," then the first martins. "April 22," he wrote with pleasure, "asparagus at dinner."

A lonely man for all his family, friends, and successes, he was still groping for his right path. But one thing stood clear. He would like—being bothered on moral grounds—"to depend as little as possible on the labor slaves." But how to do it? In the wretched institution of slavery he felt trapped.

It was warming to receive a letter from Lafayette, who called him "my friend as my heart reckons but few men. . . . I know you, I esteem you, and love you." He was about to sail for France—please write often.

Jefferson sent an invitation from Paris to spend half a year there, expense-free except for passage, clothes, and theater. No, Madison answered reluctantly, the ocean crossing might revive his old falling sickness. As for settling near Monticello, he still couldn't embrace the idea "absolutely."

Meanwhile he was writing a powerful anonymous tract against any tax of any nature on religion.

In June of '85 he sent it to George Nicholas, and in one day 150 of "our most respectable freeholders" endorsed it with their signatures. Breaking the anonymity, George Mason got this *Memorial and Remonstrance by his Excellency James Madison* printed in Alexandria as a broadside. It spread fast.

In July James Monroe wrote him buoyantly, "What say you to a trip to the Indian treaty . . . on the Ohio?" Or would he prefer to see New York, Boston, Lake George? Choosing Boston, Madison arrived in Philadelphia—only to find there had been some misunderstanding. Monroe had left for the Ohio. So he visited New York by himself and started home. He stopped off at Mount Vernon, where he and George Washington spent two rainy days enthusiastically discussing plans for making the Potomac and James Rivers more navigable and pondering together the state of the Union. Madison asked the General what he thought about speculation in the Mohawk Valley. Fine, said Washington; he was investing there himself.

Back in Richmond that fall, Madison found that his *Remonstrance,* circulated during the summer, had been garnering more signatures. Indeed, petitions for genuine religious freedom, not its shadow, were overwhelming the Assembly. The idea of a religious tax was (Madison's word) "crushed."

His *Remonstrance* advances fifteen arguments against a religious tax. Religious freedom he calls "a right toward man, a duty toward the Creator." Lest more rights be filched, he says, it is "proper to take alarm at the first experiment on our liberties." The proposed bill would weaken confidence in Christianity's "innate excellence"; yes, in God himself. Far from spreading the "precious gift" of Christianity's "light of revelation"—far from aiding truth—state support would corrupt and handicap; it would prove a "spiritual tyranny" differing from the Inquisition only in degree. In logic the Legislature must either destroy all fundamental rights or "leave this particular right untouched and sacred." Madison's *Remonstrance* has been called "one of the truly epoch-making documents in the history of American Church-State separation." And it triumphed. The climate had changed; the Assembly did not even bother to vote down Henry's bill. It was dead.

Buoyed by victory in this matter, Madison pushed through Jefferson's 1779 wording of a bill for religious freedom. Since Madison himself had put religious freedom into the Virginia Declaration of Rights nine years ago, and fought for such freedom all the way through to his famous *Remonstrance,* he might, appropriately, have phrased the bill himself. But his old habit of caring less for credit than for the deed made him quite happy to use Jefferson's wording.

That fall of 1785 James Madison struggled for the enactment of legislation concerned with Virginia's district of Kentucky, the Mississippi, payment of the British debt, slavery, and the incorporation of the James River Company. He was working like a titan to put through as many as possible of the 118 bills of the Jefferson-Wythe-Pendleton revised code. Eventually forty-three would pass into law. This seemed to him too few, but Jefferson, knowing the difficulties, was pleased and grateful. Those forty-three included the most important. Meanwhile Madison kept pounding on the need to prevent chaos by amending the Articles of Confederation. For one thing, it was absolutely necessary for the federal government to gain control over trade and commerce. Interstate disputes could so easily lead to war and foreign intervention, thus destroying the Union. Did the states want standing armies? Did they want to scuttle the ideals of the Revolution? "Congress," he had written Jefferson in deep concern, "has kept the Vessel from sinking, but . . . [only] by standing constantly at the pump. . . ."

In this connection he persuaded the Assembly to send five Virginia commissioners to meet with delegates from other states to solve joint commercial problems. One of those named to the Annapolis Convention was himself.

At this time Madison and Monroe had just bought, at a dollar and a half an acre, 900 acres in the Mohawk Valley. Inflation and a poor tobacco crop had made money so tight, Madison had been forced to borrow his share of the down payment from Monroe. Would the speculation pay off? And—far more important—would the Annapolis Convention lead to a desperately needed stronger central government?

On his way to Annapolis, Madison wrote his favorite brother, Ambrose, that nothing could "bear a worse aspect than our federal affairs. . . . [N]o money comes into the public treasury, trade is on a wretched footing, and the states running mad after paper money." And he reported talk of a convention to amend the Articles of Confederation.

Amend? If the amending were as radical as study and experience had taught him was necessary, it would mean swift, sharp, thorough change, a rewriting—a new constitution. But was the nation ripe for such a step? That was the problem.

In Annapolis he and two other commissioners sat around George Mann's inn (a shilling a night) drinking wine, porter, and punch while waiting. A week later twelve federal-minded commissioners had gathered, but unfortunately only Delaware, New Jersey, and Virginia had quorums, and Massachusetts had sent no delegate at all. The little group decided it was too small to act. And, anyway, should not the regulation of commerce become part of a larger project—revision of the whole federal system, a sweeping revision?

Alexander Hamilton of New York wrote Congress for permission. But Randolph objected that his letter was so violent it would scare people off. "You had better yield to this man," warned Madison, knowing his influence, "otherwise all Virginia will oppose." So Hamilton wrote a letter such as Madison might have written, gently, tactfully, carefully concealing twelve men's high hope for a new constitution. The New Jersey deputies who had come empowered to consider commercial regulations "and other important matters," the letter said, had moved for an expansion; and to make commercial regulations work, "other parts of the system might have to be adjusted." The commissioners recommended that a convention be called in Philadelphia the second Monday in May 1787.

When Madison returned to Richmond, a different trouble was brewing, serious trouble.

Foreign Secretary John Jay had changed his mind about asking for free navigation of the Mississippi—one of Madison's darling hopes—and was negotiating a treaty with Spain abandoning all claims for twenty-five years in exchange for a Spanish market for fish from Jay's home region. Madison saw it as a disgraceful sellout.

Then Shays' Rebellion broke out in Massachusetts. Farmers were protesting violently against such abuses as bankrupting taxes, mortgages at 40 percent, and the jailing of small debtors and seizing of their property. Most Americans, seeing them as dangerous rascals destroying public order, put a higher value on federal power.

The chance to strengthen that power was approaching. When Virginia voted to send seven delegates to the Philadelphia Convention, Madison thought first of George Washington. Without the General's permission he placed that name at the head of the list, then strove to win him over. He himself had already been chosen.

Patrick Henry "smelt a rat."

Eager to fight Jay on the Mississippi issue, Madison accepted reappointment to the Continental Congress and persuaded the Assembly to instruct all its delegates to fight tooth and nail (anything less would "undermine . . . our repose and our Union itself") for free navigation.

On February 9, 1787, his stagecoach arrived in New York. It had traveled "from Princeton to Paulus' Hook," he wrote Mrs. Trist, with "a northeast snowstorm incessantly in our teeth." In Federal Hall the delegates soon got the Mississippi matter in hand. Only three "fish states" voted to sacrifice the Father of Waters.

Meanwhile Madison was working on a paper headed "Vices of the Political System of the United States." The vices as he saw them included flouting federal requisitions, encroaching on federal authority, refusing to pull together for the common good, and being unwilling to give the federal government the executive powers it required if it was to be effective. The *people* had never ratified the Articles of Confederation, he pointed out; only legislatures. Madison's basic thesis: what the country needed was a new, strong, binding federal constitution.

He had talked enough with Washington, Hamilton, and others to be sure they shared his conviction.

Already he was beginning to formulate, in his mind if not on paper, and in growing detail, the kind of constitution he would choose if the solution to the problem were left to him: preparation for a momentous event.

THE STORY of Madison's political life up to the framing of the Constitution became known to Dolley sooner or later, and probably sooner. She must have pieced together the fragments as her husband confided them to her during the first months of their marriage. She was always a good listener—it was part of her charm—and now everything pertaining to Jemmy, big things and little, interested her tremendously. She had entered with enthusiasm upon a long slow education (for which she felt inadequate) in politics.

One consequence of her involvement was sharing her husband's sadness over his growing estrangement from a man whose character they both greatly admired: George Washington. Fourteen years of close friendship—she knew what the cooling of that relationship had cost Jemmy, and how it had cut him. Her own pain was sharper because the General was Lucy's uncle by marriage.

On the other hand, how could Jemmy fail to react when Hamilton called the Republicans "Jacobins," and Washington—scrapping his avowed above-party neutrality—obviously agreed? The European conflict had widened ideological differences. There were those who believed more and those who believed far less in men's capacity to govern themselves.

With lines tightening, Dolley continued to be a very popular hostess among politicians of all stripes. Guests understood the genuineness of her interest in people. They felt as if, having come in out of the cold, they were warming their hands at a fire. Though she was now (against Quaker custom) serving and sipping wine, the stimulant was hardly needed.

Sometimes she acted as a sort of buffer state between great powers. When the Federalist Samuel Dexter wrote to ask Madison why a man of his talents and integrity had shifted his position, Dolley issued an invitation to Sunday dinner, served excellent food, and gave her husband just the right ambience in which to deny that he had changed his principles— tactics perhaps, not principles. Mr. Dexter capitulated.

One frequent dinner topic was the question of whether or not the President would accept a third term. Because it seemed highly unlikely, Jefferson and Madison had taken to assigning each other to the helm of the "political bark." Each firmly declined the honor. Jefferson said his rheumatism was so bad, his friend's idea was "forever closed." Madison said no, politics were getting too rough; he had resolved to retire.

Another topic was the sale of vast acreage around the Yazoo River in western Georgia (now northern Mississippi and Alabama). Working in collusion with land companies for huge profits, the Georgia Legislature had created a very ugly scandal.

Then suddenly at dinner tables and on street corners people were talking about the rumor that John Jay had finished negotiating a treaty in London. On what terms? "I suspect that Jay has been betrayed by his anxiety to couple us with England," wrote Madison out of the depths of his distrust, "and to avoid returning with his finger in his mouth."

The treaty terms were still hidden when, upon the congressional adjournment in March 1795, six months after his marriage, Madison prepared to take his little family to Montpelier. But Dolley and Anna came down with pleurisy, and by the time they had recovered, rain was pouring down. Waiting for drier roads, Madison had the pleasure of spending more time with his wife. At last the carriage had crossed the Susquehanna on the ferry and was pounding south. They were drawing closer and closer to Orange Courthouse. Madison could point out old familiar landmarks. Then there at the top of a long, slow hill stood a brick house.

"James!" "Master Jemmy's home!" Though cries of welcome had greeted him many times in the past, this spring they had a special urgency. A famous member of the family—their longtime bachelor—was bringing home his bride.

Jemmy's parents and brothers and sisters saw that he had chosen well. Dolley was pretty and openhearted. She had a quality hard to define. Perhaps the word which came closest was "innocence."

~ IV ~

JAY'S TREATY
AND
THE CONSTITUTION

IT MIGHT HAVE BEEN a perfect vacation. For half a year Madison had looked forward to introducing Dolley to Montpelier, and he did indeed enjoy presenting his bride to kinsmen and friends, watching her fall in love with his old home, and initiating her into the familiar details of the farm.

But their six months out of Philadelphia were clouded by apprehension over Jay's Treaty. The uncertainty of the treaty terms kept coming back to plague him. How was that pro-British Federalist Jay handling so vital a mission?

Dolley was too sensitive not to feel, at times, the knife-edge of her husband's anxiety.

The house had the attractive solidity of the Madison clan: stout walls; carved staircase; a living room where, of an evening, Fanny played pretty tunes on the pianoforte while the family sat around on much-used, comfortable furniture with touches of elegance, listening.

Dolley could understand better, now, why Jemmy maintained so much reserve in public; his father had the same trait. The "old Colonel" and "young Colonel" did not share that slightly long upper lip for nothing. The father's reticence had been fostered by heavy early farm responsibilities and, later, by his position as magistrate and county lieutenant; the son's by the example of a father he greatly esteemed and by his own experience in office-holding.

But in the bosom of the family both men peeled off that husk of gravity. A minuet tonight? The heir apparent—though he did not dance—was ready for merriment, the lord of the manor sympathetic. Strike up the fiddles.

Nelly Madison had her own formalities. Dolley saw that this small quiet mother of seven living children (five were dead) had also bequeathed something of herself to her firstborn. A little stiff in certain ways, she had a power of love and concern. Her children were devoted to her.

The Madisons' circle included people far removed from Quaker austerity. Dolley was not unprepared. She had seen the life-style of the Paynes, Flemings, and Coleses, and she had visited Harewood and some of the most convivial homes in Philadelphia. Indeed, her own household had, for a year now, been veering in a very liberal direction. Moreover, her temperament delighted in the pith, verve, and freedom of Orange County's way of life. If a gold-laced tricorn turned up at the door, she was dazzled. If ladies in mobcaps chattered about chokecherry "giam" or the latest fashion in ribbons, she joined the excitement. If someone thrust a hot poker into persimmon beer to make flip, she shared in the laughter.

But no diversion made her forget her child. Unfortunately there were people who were ready and willing to help her indulge Payne—people who, meaning well, acted less than wisely. Payne was a handsome, intelligent little fellow, young enough (just three now) for some adults to find streaks of naughtiness cute or unimportant—weren't all little boys mischievous at times? Dolley could always tell herself that any disciplinary problem was temporary; the remedy was brothers and sisters.

She knew how much James's children would mean to the elder Madisons. Though Francis and William were breeding up large families of boys and girls, and Ambrose, Nelly, and Sarah had made good starts at furnishing grandchildren, the offspring of a firstborn, especially in those days of primogeniture, had a special significance.

As spring advanced, farm activities quickened. Rising early, the family scattered to various chores. Besides looking after his own 560 acres, Jemmy was helping his increasingly rheumatic father supervise the cultivation of tobacco (though this crop was being phased out), as well as grain, hemp, and soil-rebuilding red clover. They were working toward a seven-year rotation of crops. To the sharepoint of least resistance on the plow Jefferson had so cleverly invented, the "young Colonel" attached his colter directly: a further improvement. And he was busy trying out all sorts of nonindigenous plants: New England sugar maples, French cork oaks,

Timur rice, Kentucky coffee beans, Gulf Coast pecans. Though his preferred fertilizer was manure, he used any kind of organic matter—from rotted sawdust to sweepings from haylofts. After a rainfall he strolled through wheat fields looking for black rot. He was more and more fascinated by agriculture.

Dolley, too, loved growing things. Before the dew had dried, she was off to the garden. Though a little black boy toted tools and water, she liked to put the seeds into the ground herself, and it was exciting to watch the rounding of a radish, the pleating of a gillyflower. Spring was a procession of tulips, iris, peonies, tiger lilies, nasturtiums. "Gather ye little Knobs quickly," says an old recipe for nasturtium salad, "after ye Blossoms are off." Her favorite flower was the oleander. Pricked by thorns, she brought basketfuls of roses into the house. And she wrote fanciful little secret verses—some have survived—about nature.

A love of poetry and novels pulled her toward the library. In college Madison (as he had once written Bradford) had loved literature. Now, while emphasizing political and philosophical books, he was not immune to letting Dolley draw him back into the works of such eighteenth-century authors as Defoe, Johnson, Goldsmith, Pope. His sharp mind could appreciate Jonathan Swift's satires. Dolley was of a nature to love more emotional authors, such as Richardson, Gray, and Burns. It seems that neither of the Madisons knew Blake, unless they somehow procured the English edition of his *Songs of Innocence*—the quality which Dolley herself exemplified. There was as yet no American edition.

The black folk on the plantation had their own kind of guilelessness. The younger James Madison so hated slavery, he could not bring himself to use the word. Dolley saw his struggle; as a child she had witnessed a similar one in her parents. Jemmy's father shared it to a degree and took pains to see that the black members of his "family" were taught to read, write, and cipher, as well as to work inside or out or practice a craft. He housed, dressed, fed, and doctored them decently, treating them not as chattels but as human beings. But among the Madison clan it was James Junior who went the furthest in his thinking. He said slavery was demoralizing the nation. He did not believe that emancipation, under present conditions, would benefit black people much, if at all; freed slaves were at too great a disadvantage in a white man's society. What he hoped for was a national plan to stake them and send them back to Africa. Meanwhile he treated his black overseer, Sawney, and his white overseer, Mordecai, with an even hand. In Dolley's eyes it did him honor.

The Rev. Philip Slaughter has called the social life of this period around Orange Courthouse "animated." "These people," naming dozens, "seem to have had a gay time—dining parties of twenty-five to thirty from house to house; quilting parties winding up with a dance; balls at Sanford's, Bell's or Alcock's hotel in the winter, varied with hare, fox, and wolf hunting, especially when Major Willis and Hay Taliaferro came up with twenty hounds. In the summer they had fish-fries and barbecues." At balls, though she did not dance, Dolley caught the spirit of revelry just by watching.

Thus the summer passed. Loving people, birds, beasts, and plants, Dolley was never bored on this farm which had been Jemmy's home practically from birth. How noble the distant Appalachians. Even from hour to hour they changed color and shape; sometimes, so magical was the light, they seemed to be suspended in midair or to float like waterfowl.

One day or another in their early life together Madison asked Dolley about the Quaker phrase "inner light." He was told what she had heard from childhood and in some degree experienced: that it was the spirit within, in its different manifestations, and that it was not to be reached (this to a man of intellect) intellectually. There at Montpelier they had times of quiet and leisure in which they discussed such things.

But good talk came up hard against the peril of Jay's Treaty. It was now in President Washington's hands. He had summoned the Senate— whose consent was necessary for treaty signing—to a special session on June 8. In leaking the terms to Madison, Senator Butler remarked that he considered the secret "much safer with you than . . . many to whom confided." Madison saw that his fears had been outstripped. These provisions were disgraceful.

Britain agreed to evacuate her seven Northwest forts—but she had promised that in the Treaty of Paris. She enlarged her list of American exports considered contraband—whereas the need was for the opposite. She would permit only very small, 70-ton, vessels to trade with her West Indian islands—but where was the advantage? This minimal concession was practically worthless; it was granted, of course, only to hurt France. Even worse was her arrogant prohibition against the export of the Deep South's principal crops: coffee, sugar, cocoa, molasses, and cotton—the last increasingly important, indeed vital. The rest was silence. The treaty provided no compensation for slaves taken during the Revolution nor (worst of all) any guarantee—the main object of Jay's mission—that Britain would stop seizing American ships and forcing American seamen into British service. Madison was furious. All gain for England, all loss for the United States! Seeing the treaty as betrayal, he blamed Hamilton as well as Jay, for it was Hamilton who pulled the strings in the Federalist party. He was not wrong here. By constantly telling British Minister Hammond that, whatever she did to the United States, Britain need fear no retaliation, Hamilton had encouraged bolder demands.

The Senate advised the President to ratify all the articles except the one authorizing a mere trickle of trade with the West Indies; that one should be renegotiated. Now the question was, Would Washington sign?

The public roar of protest against the treaty was bipartisan. Better no treaty than one so trade-destroying, unfair, humiliating.

In July Madison took his wife, stepson, and sister-in-law, through scenery burnt by drought, for their first visit to Monticello. Climbing the rough road up to Jefferson's home, the phaeton lurched and swayed. Then out of green foliage leaped a red brick mansion. A tall, thin, gangling gentleman with greying foxy hair and freckles shook hands and presented his daughters to his old friend's new family. Welcome!

Though in 1795 Monticello had not achieved its final form, it was an impressive house. Count François Jean de Chastellux, who saw it at this stage, spoke of "a large lofty salon, topped by a library and flanked by two one-storey wings. . . ." Jefferson loved tearing down to build up. Dolley, who had a strong aesthetic sense, admired the proportions.

The visit passed pleasantly. They sat in the big hall or in the salon or on the tree-shaded lawn, the men conversing while the ladies listened or put in a word or strolled off by themselves. Long separated, Jefferson and Madison had a new and compelling subject to thrash out: Jay's Treaty. They rued it equally, hated it equally. To them it spelled sheer calamity, for it scrapped the Republicans' policy of trade retaliation, usurped a congressional *legislative* function, and—by accepting high crimes on the sea—dishonored the nation.

Meanwhile Jefferson was sizing up Dolley. "Should it be final," he had written Madison twelve years ago, after Kitty's jilting, "the world presents . . . many other resources of happiness. . . ." But he could hardly have foreseen a Madisonian future with so open a face, so pretty a figure, and such curls, sense, and sensibility.

Dolley and his daughter Martha—fairly close in age—got on well together, and Patsy's two children romped with Payne.

At meals Jefferson, whose sense of humor was not strong, enjoyed Madison's drollery. Out the long dining room windows laughter floated. (It was through one of them that Madison, once, having tilted his chair too far, fell out backward.) When the conversation shifted to farming, Jefferson listened intently, for he considered Madison "the best farmer in the world." Then again politics. What was Hamilton's game now? The two old friends returned, full circle, to Jay's Treaty.

They discussed Washington's successor. Who could wear the hat of that monolithic man? Madison nominated Jefferson. Jefferson nominated Madison. But on one thing they agreed. The listing ship of state must be righted; Republicans must seize the helm and steer her safely into port.

It was hard for the two men to tear themselves apart, but one day gravel crunched as down the little mountain plunged Madison's coach-and-four.

Fifteen miles, and the Madisons arrived at Enniscorthy, home of fifty-year-old, horse-loving, expansive John Coles II, his doe-eyed wife Rebecca, and ten children. They could not have guessed during the pleasant visit that nine-year-old Edward and six-year-old Sally would grow up to play prominent roles in their lives.

Then on they drove, past Scott's Landing, past Point of Forks, to visit Dolley's Payne, Fleming, and Winston relatives in Goochland and Hanover Counties. They particularly enjoyed Judge Isaac Winston III of Auburn, his wife Lucy, and their six children. Having sheltered Dolley during her "deliberation" the summer of '94, that family had a kind of vested interest in her marriage.

There were three Hanover houses closely connected with Dolley's early life to show James: her grandparents' Coles Hill on the Pamunkey, the adjoining School Farm where she had lived awhile, and Scotchtown, with its boxwood, many windows, and elegant mantels. From there it was only a short drive to Cedar Creek Meeting House, where Papa had served as "Public Friend" and Dolley had learned her ABC's. Then the dog days—"sickly season"—hurried the little party home to higher ground.

The rest of the summer, whenever her husband looked abstracted, Dolley could guess what bothered him. Disturbing talk about Jay's "ruinous bargain" kept arriving in leather pouches.

Federalists argued that rejection of the treaty might trigger what to them represented the ultimate business disaster: war with Great Britain. Newspaper articles by Curtius (Noah Webster) and, more particularly, Camillus (Hamilton) pounded on that theme. Jefferson begged Madison to wage a pen war against Hamilton, that "colossus," that "host within himself." But Madison thought it best to fight Jay's Treaty in Congress in case—God forbid—Washington signed the treaty.

He considered the "war with Britain" threat groundless. Why should Britain, hard-pressed by France and seeing Napoleon grow steadily stronger, risk a pointless conflict with her best supplier of raw materials and best customer for manufactured articles? It made no sense. It was ridiculous. Rejection would not bring war with Britain, he figured, but acceptance might well precipitate a war with America's fine Revolutionary partner. Jay's Treaty would abrogate the old 1778 treaty with France and set up a virtual alliance with France's archenemy; it would make Britain the "most favored nation," thus enraging France to the point of striking back. If so, who could blame her? Madison called Jay's Treaty an unconscionable reversal of foreign policy.

Amid such thoughts he received word that the hated Order in Council which the British had been relaxing had now been revived in the harshest form. Not just contraband but American ships were again being seized. So this was what they could expect under Jay's Treaty! The news fed public anger. Several towns burned Jay in effigy. In Orange it was reported that even Hamilton had advised the President to sign the treaty but hold back delivery until that Provision Order was revoked. Unfortunately it seemed that Secretary of War Pickering, his crony Secretary of the Treasury Wolcott, and Attorney General Bradford wanted a milder course: protest, but sign and deliver at once.

The President balked. He decided not to sign at all as long as the wretched order was in force. Secretary of State Randolph (as Madison would hear) suggested that reopening negotiations would give the United States an opportunity to clarify and perhaps modify other oppressive points. The President asked for a memorandum to that effect and then, without signing, went off to Mount Vernon for a needed vacation. Indeed, he might never have signed but for Edmund Randolph's terrible disgrace.

The news reaching Montpelier was not to be believed. Madison's mind reeled, and Dolley felt her husband's consternation vicariously. Summoned, the President had hastened back to Philadelphia. Secretary Randolph had resigned. Immediately thereafter Washington ratified Jay's Treaty.

Madison did not preserve the letters he wrote and received at this time on this subject, but they can be imagined. Randolph accused of soliciting a bribe! Randolph, former Governor of Virginia, former Attorney General, and—until his eclipse on August 12—Secretary of State, Washington's friend and his, brought down!

THE FULL STORY would come out piece by piece.

Sour-faced Secretary Timothy Pickering and stout, devious Secretary Oliver Wolcott Jr. had long hated Randolph as a Republican whom they suspected of being an undercover "Jacobin" trying to push—or ease—the nation into war with Great Britain. Moreover, they were personally jealous of him. Recently, for instance, Randolph had been told the treaty terms ahead of themselves and then kept abreast, as they were not, of the President's thinking on the subject. When they saw how, Randolph-advised, Washington was shying away from their own advice that he sign at once, regardless, they had decided to destroy the Secretary of State, if they could, with a document they now held in their possession—to "save our country," in Wolcott's words to Hamilton.

The weapon was a dispatch in a series from French Minister Fauchet to the French government which the British had intercepted on the high seas last fall and passed to Minister Hammond as perhaps "useful in the King's service." Hammond had given it to Wolcott, and it had been translated—in a crucial passage mistranslated—by Pickering. They were delighted to find it well tailored to their malicious purpose.

Banding together, Pickering, Wolcott, and Attorney General Bradford had summoned the President back to town for an urgent reason not to be divulged on paper. Mystified, Washington came posthaste, drank a glass of wine with his Cabinet and, calling the letter writer Pickering aside, asked for an explanation. "That man," said Pickering, pointing to Randolph through an open door, "is a traitor," and he showed the President Fauchet's Dispatch Number 10.

Washington withstood the shock as best he could. That any Cabinet member should have discussed American foreign policy with a foreign official was to him inconceivable. (He did not know that Jefferson had often done so with the French, and Hamilton with the British.) And soliciting a bribe!

The President spent an agonizing night. Had Randolph sold out to a foreign government? Was he a man with a price? Washington remembered the dastardly treason of his erstwhile friend Benedict Arnold. The situation was horrifying.

Though he meant to give Randolph a chance to exonerate himself, his trust in the only Republican in his Cabinet had been severely shaken; and now, as never before, he suspected France also. Thus Britain looked better by contrast. And was not indecision about Jay's Treaty—so the President argued in his mind—endangering the nation? The next morning he told the startled Randolph he would sign the treaty, and did.

Then he and Pickering and Wolcott laid a trap. Washington loathed doing this—it involved some hypocrisy—but how else could he determine, for sure, Randolph's guilt or innocence?

At a Cabinet meeting Washington handed Fauchet's dispatch to

Randolph and asked for comment. While the Secretary read, the others watched his face for signs of guilt. There were none. Looking up, Randolph calmly denied that he had ever spoken with Fauchet improperly or taken or solicited a French bribe. When on request he had stepped out of the room, Pickering and Wolcott were forced to admit that he had shown no telltale agitation, and Washington silently thanked God his friend had passed the test. But when called back, Randolph, insulted and livid, shouted his resignation and plunged out of the room. The three left behind reached a verdict of guilty.

A hullabaloo followed. Randolph told the press he would explain his resignation in an appeal to the American people. This was where matters stood when the Madisons reached town in early November and heard more scuttlebutt.

Randolph's "Vindication" appeared a month later. It contained a clarifying passage from one of Fauchet's earlier dispatches and a ringing exoneration from that Minister. Convinced that Britain had fomented the Whiskey Rebellion in order to divide and weaken the nation, if not cause a civil war, Randolph wrote, he had told Fauchet that proof lay in the hands of four New York flour dealers who dared not testify for fear their British debts would be used to destroy them. Would France care to loosen their tongues with loans for use in paying those debts? The money could be counted as advances for future deliveries of flour to France. As for the anger which had caused so quick a condemnation of himself, Randolph called it the reaction of an honorable man falsely accused.

His defense might have turned the tide but for the mistake of fighting injustice with injustice. In trying to extricate himself, he implied that ·Washington was slipping mentally and charged him with trying to destroy the Republican party—in other words, with dealing knowingly in lies. The public could not stand to see the old hero besmirched. Also, a certain self-vaunting and self-pity in the "Vindication" rebounded; it seemed unmanly. When Randolph lost, his party lost with him, and heavily. There was a surge toward Federalism.

Madison stated his judgment with great sadness, for though he had sometimes deplored the weaknesses mixed with Randolph's strengths, he had loved the man ever since their meeting in Williamsburg, in 1776—so long ago—on his first day in office. "His greatest enemies," Madison wrote Jefferson, "will not easily persuade themselves that he was under a corrupt influence of France, and his best friend can't save him from the self-condemnation of his political career as explained by himself."

Dolley grieved too. She liked the tall man with fine, fertile, dark eyes.

Randolph, smiling and gallant, had often broken bread with the Madisons. Now, like Jemmy, Dolley suffered Randolph's anguish.

The Randolph scandal was not Madison's only regret. This fall William Bradford—Billey of the old days—had suddenly died; Washington had gone over more completely to Federalism; there was a total loss of civility between the two political parties; and the Cabinet was packed solid with Hamilton's henchmen. "Through what official interstice," Madison wrote Jefferson, "can a ray of republican truths penetrate to the President?"

Street corner debates were increasingly vitriolic. Rampant factionalism threatened his and the nation's future. Senator Butler wrote, "There is a vile underhand game playing with a view of injuring unspotted characters. In this an attempt is making to implicate you."

But the most important question was how to wipe out Jay's Treaty. Was there any way? Signed by Washington, it was now en route to Great Britain to be countersigned. On its return it would become the law of the land.

Madison believed it could be foiled. Though the Senate had a Federalist majority, the House had a Republican majority whose members were eager to adopt the plan of action he was pondering day and night. His conclusion as to what could be done rested squarely on his interpretation of the Constitution. It could not have been arrived at without a review of that great document, its meaning, its essence, without his going over the Convention of 1787 as it lived on, burningly, in his memory. Short of his marriage to Dolley, it was the most important event in his life.

THE QUESTION FROM THE BEGINNING had been power. How apportion it? Who should wield it? How prevent abuses and hold it faithful to its proper task of protecting the people?

For years before the Convention of 1787 Madison had mused upon the anatomy of power. During his long study of ancient confederacies, and during the experiences leading up to his writing "Vices of the Political System," the subject had stayed primary and vivid, and certainly it dominated his thoughts the day he wrote Edmund Pendleton that the difficulties to be faced in framing a constitution were so great they "would inspire despair" if the alternative—he meant anarchy—was "less formidable." In his pre-Convention correspondence with Randolph and Washington, too, this basic question weighed upon him, and it was the heaviest part of his luggage when he arrived in Philadelphia on May 3, well ahead of the

Convention's scheduled opening. For government is power, it is force, it is coercion. As Madison tooled his blueprint for the constitution he hoped to see adopted and, later, when the Virginia and Pennsylvania delegates were dining together regularly for discussion, while waiting for a quorum, power was the large, if hidden, question mark.

The Convention opened on May 25. At once George Washington—that Vesuvius of a man—was chosen to preside in the high-backed chair on the dais. Eleven years ago here in this paneled room in the statehouse, long the meeting place of the Continental Congress and thus well known to Madison, the Declaration of Independence had been signed, and here, it was hoped, another great document would come forth.

The delegates sat in a roped-off area facing Washington, at tables covered with green baize. Because Madison had resolved to keep a full record of the proceedings, he chose a seat down front and in the middle. He could hear every word.

There were notable absences. Jefferson, Jay, and Adams were abroad, for example, and Patrick Henry had smelled that rat. But it was a distinguished company which had gathered to wrestle with the problem of power. The first question it gave rise to was in every mind: How much power should the states retain? How much relinquish to the central government?

There was a general conviction that the government's power of coercion must be kept within metes and bounds. No delegate had thought more deeply about this touchy subject than Madison.

He saw clearly—as he waited for the Convention to get under way—that, whether serving or terrorizing man, government had always cut down on the individual's area of self-decision and self-management. But government by consent through representatives cut down far less than other forms of government. In England a degree of power had come to the people by royal grant. But—along with Washington, Jefferson, Adams, and others—Madison believed that free men possessed certain rights not theirs by concession or indulgence, but by birthright: inalienable, ungrantable rights for which they need thank no one short of God. But why, if created free, should man be coerced at all? Why government? The answer for Madison lay in the nature of a human being.

Man was not, or not yet, perfect. The coercions of government were designed to keep imperfect beings from worse coercions, inner or outer. The great need was to organize government in such a way as to preserve maximum freedom while protecting citizens from harms caused by their own passions and wrong motives. Unfortunately power as such had no moral sense. Only those wielding it could bring in moral values. Out of ambition, callousness, and greed it could be fearfully misused. So fences must be built; walls.

In weighing the strengths and weaknesses of human nature Madison realized the dangers, for government, of miscalculation. A government founded on falsity would fail. It must be built on the rock of the truth about man, and the truth was that man had a double nature, good and bad. The faculties belonging to his higher self—conscience, judgment, sense of justice, power of love, the ability to rise above selfish considerations, and free will—these were the traits which made self-government possible. On the other hand, proclivities belonging to his lower nature— such as hate, greed, selfishness, and violence (marks of his moral fragility)—made imperative the curb of at least some laws to force into line offenders against the rights of others, rights belonging to every human being simply because he is a human being. Let government go as far as necessary, was Madison's viewpoint, but not one inch further.

Madison's profound belief in men's equality under the law did not blind him to the obvious fact that individual abilities are highly unequal, the line here being not horizontal but vertical, a ladder, a hierarchy. This seemed too obvious to talk about and certainly impossible to legislate about. It was a reason why Madison thought a constitution should set up limits, restrictions, checks, and balances; it was why governmental decision making should be put, as far as possible, into the most capable hands. As a classicist, Madison knew Plato's *Republic,* but knew also that the philosopher-kings Plato recommended were—practically speaking—not to be found.

Their places must be taken by free citizens using their freedom responsibly. That was the only way to achieve the justice which the Greeks called the highest virtue and Christians saw as an expression of the love they called the highest virtue.

Justice: a balancing, a rectitude, a standard of moral suitability, a potential belonging to man as God's image and likeness—the thing toward which, in his life in society, man must strive. Man would never be fully free while pushed from without by authority, or from within by instinct, habit, passions. And growth in freedom could never be easy. But what else could foster the true ends of life? What else could lead to wholeness? A wise parent removes outer restraints as fast as a child proves he can, by self-discipline, handle responsibilities. In somewhat the same way, government should, as far as possible, treat citizens as adults. Choice, free will: God's great, hazardous gift to man. Madison knew that people are not honest, fair, temperate, kind, by chance or by law but only by choice, and that without power of choice there could be no praise and no blame.

The higher self making man capable of self-government, what was it? As a Bible student, Madison saw it as an immortal element, as spirit. The root of freedom lay in the spirit.

That such convictions lay behind Madison's political thinking is a fact which unfolds with his life, or so it seems to me—nothing else explains. Though he never wrote down these strong persuasions in so many words, they shine forth from what he said and did. The cumulative evidence is overwhelming.

In the winter of 1795, while he brooded over the Constitution's relationship to Jay's Treaty, the background of all his .constitutional thinking—his conception of man, his musings on power—necessarily came back to mind. It was the glass through which he watched in memory the crucial events of that hot summer eight years ago during the framing of the Constitution.

GOVERNOR RANDOLPH'S RICH VOICE droned on. The Virginia Plan which he was reading took most of the day. The delegates were rather tense. They recognized the occasion as historical. On the outcome of the deliberations now starting hung America's future. A three-armed government was being proposed: legislative, executive, and judiciary branches: a high-powered government upon which the States could not encroach. A Congress with two houses would have the power to "legislate in all cases to which the separate states are incompetent." When Randolph had finished, Charles Pinckney of South Carolina read an oligarchic plan of his own. It was now too late for discussion. The Convention adjourned.

The next day the delegates formed themselves into a Committee of the Whole to debate questions and take nonbinding test votes. At this point in the British Commons a mace symbolizing the Crown would have been lowered. But Washington merely yielded his "throne" to a substitute and came and sat at the Virginia table.

Gouverneur Morris had protested that the Virginia Plan's opening resolution was misleading in that it called for revising the Articles of Confederation when, plainly, the other fourteen resolutions would scrap the Articles in favor of a radically new, truly national government. Actually the first resolution had been a sop for Governor Randolph, who feared the word "national." Caucusing, the Virginians now amended that resolution to call forthrightly for a "national government consisting of a *supreme* legislative, executive and judicial": undoubtedly Madison's original wording. "Supreme." Elbridge Gerry of Massachusetts stood up. Did gentlemen propose to abolish state governments? No, answered Randolph, that was not the intention. Next came the question of the difference between a federal government and a national government. Gouverneur Morris explained that a federal one rested on good faith, a national one on force, on compulsion; Madison added that a confederation operated on states, a nation directly on individual citizens. The Convention had now reached the central problem of power.

Some states, long assured of their sovereignty, clung to it. Madison pointed out the pressing need for a change. The States would gain more than they would lose: unity, prosperity, safety from external enemies, internal quiet. Indeed, so acutely did he see the necessity of true nationhood as opposed to the confederation he had watched grow weaker and weaker, he believed that the federal government should be given veto power over any state law whatsoever. (Only gradually would he come to see that supremacy of federal law as upheld by a supreme judiciary would accomplish the purpose less abrasively.)

The debate moved on. A two-house legislature proved to be acceptable, and though small states bent on equality fought it, the idea of popular election for the lower house made some headway. George Mason and James Wilson defended it eloquently, and Madison called it "essential to . . . free government." But how elect the upper house? The question raised such a ruckus, it was postponed; the Convention moved on to a discussion of the executive.

Then on June 6 it looped back to the problem of the lower house. Couldn't so much democracy lead to mobocracy? Look at Shays' Rebellion, someone said. Madison again insisted that, in a free government, direct election of at least one house was a "clear principle"; the "great fabric . . . should rest on the solid foundation of the people themselves." Yes, there were dangers in human nature, but—here he introduced a novel idea—multiplicity of interests was good; it provided a network of restraints against the tyranny of the majority. Contending parties balanced each other out. "Enlarge the sphere." This speech has been called the most important of the Convention.

On June 7 John Dickinson of Delaware used a Princetonian metaphor in a convention which contained nine Princeton men, six of whom had attended the college after Dr. Witherspoon's purchase of the Rittenhouse orrery. "Let our central government be like the sun," he said, "and the states the planets, repelled yet attracted, and the whole moving regularly and harmoniously in their separate orbits."

That Madison had already pondered this analogy is strongly suggested by an undated manuscript which internal evidence places between 1784 and 1791, and which probably predated this Convention. It begins: "The planetary system . . . is regulated by fixed laws and presents . . . a scene of order and proportion. From analogy we conclude that the whole universe, if it were equally understood, would . . . exhibit . . . a like arrangement." Madison saw much the same plan in nature. "Order and symmetry equally appear in the great outlines and in the most minute features. . . ." He kept returning to "the great law of proportion."

If the Constitution was to endure, he was convinced that it must honor that universal law. How else *work?* Freedom and authority, those opposites, were like the centrifugal (out-flying) and the centripetal (in-pulling) forces that, by balancing each other out, held the planets in their orbits. The planets neither crashed into the sun nor hurtled off to certain destruction. Counterpoise: it was the secret of the universe.

The very day after Dickinson likened the national government to the sun and the states to the planets, Madison, in seconding Charles Pinckney's motion that the federal government be given veto power over state laws, harked back to the same peerless relation. " . . . This prerogative of the General Government," he said, " is the great pervading principle that must control the centrifugal tendency of the States; which, without it, will continually fly out of their proper orbits, and destroy the order and harmony of the political system." James Wilson agreed. But the small states opposed so broad a veto power.

That evening, delegates strolling in the serpentine gardens behind the statehouse or conversing at the Black Horse or Indian Queen felt easier. A powerful metaphor had thrown light.

But the public—barred from any knowledge of the proceedings by the rule of secrecy—could only wonder, fear, hope, guess, and feel frustrated as they stared at the statehouse's truncated steeple.

Now the Convention returned to congressional elections, and the issue between small states fearing to be overwhelmed and large states favoring representation by population broke out in fury. New Jersey, cried William Paterson of New Jersey, rejected a union in which she would be "swallowed up." Throw the states into hotchpot! Make them all one size! James Wilson, ruddy and in spectacles, faced this small man with a big nose and neat wig. Pennsylvania, he said, his voice ringing out, wanted equality of individuals, not states. Hotchpot? Nonsense. It was impracticable. "If no state will part with any of its sovereignty, it is in vain to talk of a national government." The heat was awful, fly stings irritating, the mood rancorous. The Convention had reached an impasse. The question of proportional representation was postponed until Monday. Would a quiet weekend help?

The flaming antinationalist Luther Martin of Maryland arrived, and the problem of how to count slaves—if representation were proportioned to population—raised its head. Should slaves be counted fully, not at all, or according to the present 3/5 ratio used for requisitions on states? The decision would greatly affect the weight of certain states in the national councils. And should congressional powers be indefinite and open, or enumerated? It was going to be a long hot summer.

Washington, who had told John Jay that he feared the "monster" sovereignty—state sovereignty—would take over and make the country weak at home and contemptible abroad, still attended Mrs. Bingham's fashionable parties but was enjoying them less. What would be the upshot of all this wrangling? He sent home for his umbrella and "blew Coat with the Cremson collar."

Monday morning Connecticut's Roger Sherman of the homespun suit and mind proposed a compromise. Why not a proportional vote in the House and an equal voice in the Senate—counting only free citizens? Elbridge Gerry seconded the idea of the "honest angel" with the sharp nose. "Blacks are property," he said, "and are used to the southward as horses and cattle to the northward." Why then shouldn't horses and cattle—scathingly—"have the right of representation"? Southerners like Washington, Mason, and Madison who hated slavery felt the keen blade.

Franklin tried for conciliation. "We are sent here to *consult,* not to contend. . . ." And why should large states want to swallow up small states? What advantage? The fear was groundless. But Sherman's "Great Compromise" was struck down. The Committee of the Whole voted, 6 to 5, for proportional representation in both House and Senate. The heat was now so oppressive, delegates loosened their stocks. They were ready to take the binding official vote on all the amended Virginia Resolves—nineteen.

But Paterson asked for a day's recess so that the small states could finish preparing a purely federal plan. He was so fraught with contained anger, he looked taller than his height of 5 feet 2 (4 inches shorter than Madison).

On June 15 he presented the New Jersey Plan, and it was referred to the Committee of the Whole for point-by-point comparison with the Virginia Plan. "Resolved, that the Articles of Confederation ought to be revised, corrected and enlarged," it began—the Virginia Plan's opening resolve as worded to soothe Randolph before it was changed to come out boldly for true nationhood. The state-sovereignty-advocating New Jersey Plan was federal in the sense of the 1780s, not national.

A battle cry had sounded.

James Wilson patiently and ably compared New Jersey's plan with Virginia's. The former called for a Congress with one branch instead of two, and with powers derived from the states only—each state having one vote—instead of from the people so that, conceivably, a minority of the general population could seize power from the majority. Congress would thus be a body with very limited powers, helpless against state laws. New Jersey's plan called, also, for a plural instead of single executive, and— unlike Virginia's plan—it would establish no federal courts below the Supreme Court. The slight figure in the black lawyer's robes said the Convention had no power to do more or differently. True, the Convention could settle nothing, Wilson replied, but could propose anything. And he did not believe the people would find nationhood obnoxious. "Will a citizen of *Delaware* be degraded by becoming a citizen of the *United States?*" Randolph suggested that they had reached the last moment for decision. Failure could only lead to despair.

There followed a weekend of furious thinking.

Monday morning, June 18, Alexander Hamilton addressed the Convention. He was a youngish man (thirty-two), like Madison not tall (5 feet 7), auburn-haired, high-colored, and curiously commanding. For six hours he outlined the high-handed government which his admiration for the British way had led him to favor. At the opposite extreme from New Jersey's Plan, Hamilton's would reduce states to little more than counties. Its main features: a President chosen for life who would appoint state governors and wield absolute veto power over the acts of Congress; senators with life tenure; a lower house composed of congressmen elected by the people for short terms (a sop). "Men love power," he said cynically. Actually the surviving notes for his speech are still bolder, going so far as to say that the advantage of a hereditary monarch was his incorruptibility by reason of great power. Why should he take risks to gain more? And Hamilton flatly contradicted Madison by saying that a republic was unworkable in so large a country. Remember the failure of the Amphictyonic League.

But a nation is not a league, Madison must have been muttering in silence while everyone sat stunned. What audacity! raw courage! gall! The Convention adjourned.

The next day Madison—as if Hamilton's ideas were beneath consideration—rose to attack the New Jersey Plan. Could it stop states from taking advantage of each other? Stop internal disorders? Stop the machinations of foreign powers? Enforce treaties? Indeed, could the nation survive at all under so loose a compact? What would happen if the stubbornness of small states prevented reform? It was a powerful, devastating speech.

When Madison sat down, Rufus King put the crucial question to the Committee of the Whole: Was the Virginia Plan to be preferred above New Jersey's? Yes—by a vote of 7 to 3. Madison had given the New Jersey Plan the *coup de grâce.* The revised Virginia Plan was re-reported.

The next day George Washington resumed the chair on which was painted a sun. Was it rising or setting? The delegates were again in full Convention.

Its first act was conciliatory. It expunged the word "national" from the first resolution, substituting "the Government of the United States." And the Convention launched into the Great Debate.

The battle lasted a month and grew bloody. John Lansing of New York called the plan wrongheaded and unattainable. George Mason asked if militiamen would march from state to state collecting taxes. Luther Martin made a long wild defense of state sovereignty, and delegates wondered if he was on the bottle again. Others spoke of the need for closing all doors against the possibility of corruption. And so it went. Madison knew that the central challenge was to build on principles and—though time and a growing population were bound to bring changes—reduce variables.

Through all the discussions ran a scarlet thread of apprehension, now visible, now concealed. What to do about the basic problems sundering the Convention: whether there should be equal or unequal representation in the Senate, and whether senators should be popularly elected or appointed by state legislatures. The Constitution, and with it the Union, could smash on these rocks. Madison thought it unfair for states with large populations to have the same number of senators (one? two? three?) as states with very small populations. If the large states banded together, shouted Luther Martin, small ones could do the same! Madison stood up to ask which was more of a threat, a strong union or weak selfish neighbors. And *why* should Virginia, Pennsylvania, and Massachusetts combine? They had no common interests, their staple products being, respectively, tobacco, flour, fish; no connection. Actually—look at England and France—they were much more likely to be rivals. The real divisions were between sections with diverse interests; the greatest (he was being perceptive and prophetic) between the North and the South.

Benjamin Franklin, calling for prayer, suggested a Convention chaplain, but others feared to alarm the public with the smell of controversy, and Hamilton did not think the Convention needed "foreign aid." William Few of Georgia has called this day, June 28, an "awful and critical moment." What could break the deadlock?

Connecticut called again for Sherman's compromise, and Dr. Franklin tried again to play the role of peacemaker. "When a broad table is to be made and the plank edges don't fit," he said with homely eloquence, "the artist takes a little from both and makes a good joint." But Jonathan Dayton, unmollified, branded Virginia's "large-state plan" an "amphibious monster," and Gunning Bedford snapped, "They insist . . . they never will hurt or injure the lesser states. *I do not, gentlemen, trust you!*" If the large states dissolved the confederation, the small ones would "find some foreign ally of more honor and good faith" who would "take them by the hand."

This allusion shocked most of the delegates. They had known all along the danger of foreign meddling, *but to court it!* Britain? France? Spain?

On July 2 the question was put: Should states of all sizes have equal representation and say in the Senate? The vote was 5 to 5, with Georgia divided: an impasse. In desperation the Convention set up a committee composed of one person from each state and gave it three days to deliberate before the Convention would meet again after the Fourth of July.

Thanks to the secrecy rule, the country had no inkling of the deadlock. A scene illustrates the tightness of the lid. Someone dropped a page of notes. "Gentlemen! I must entreat gentlemen to be more careful," said Washington sternly and threw the paper on the table. "Let him who owns it take it!" The terrified owner dared not go forward.

The Fourth of July was celebrated with cannonading, bells, parades, toasts. That night, in the windows of the town, candles and lanterns burned brightly.

The next morning the crisis committee recommended compromise. And again there was skirmishing. "We were on the verge of dissolution," Luther Martin would write later, "scarce held together by the strength of a hair." Five days later New York's other two delegates, Yates and Lansing, departed like Alexander Hamilton. But Mason swore he'd bury his bones in Philadelphia rather than quit without a solution, and Washington, who looked gloomier than at Valley Forge, wrote, " . . . I almost despair. . . ."

The argument veered to the Western lands with their growing populations; flatboats riding the rivers were carrying thousands of people and their wagons, horses, cattle, and household goods to new homes. Land companies such as the Vandalia, Grand Illinois, Wabash, and New Wales had bought cheap and were selling high. What states would be carved out of those vast open spaces? The Rev. Manasseh Cutler, founder of the Ohio Company, arrived fresh from the triumph of obtaining new concessions from the Continental Congress: a grant of some 5 million acres at about 9 cents an acre. Under folds of fat and a black velvet suit with silver buckles, he beamed his way into wide favor. Though Madison detested big speculators, he joined some delegates who were questioning the superlobbyist at the Indian Queen, and he enjoyed riding out early one morning with Cutler and a group of fellow delegates to Gray's Ferry Tavern, high above the Schuylkill River, for breakfast.

Admit states beyond the Appalachians on equal terms with the original states? No, said Morris of Pennsylvania; they would drain off wealth. Wilson leaped up to say that by oppressing the Colonies Britain had lost them; by being less than fair, the East would lose the West. Madison, too, recognized the moral issue. Westerners would not and should not submit to a Union which degraded them. Morris had spoken up for loyalty between North and South but jealousy of the West. Did the gentleman determine character by the points of the compass? In Madison's opinion, the Western states should be equals and brothers. Mason agreed. If slighted, he warned, Westerners could either refuse to unite or quickly revolt. In his notes Madison crossed out someone's reference to "a separate people" as if to kill forever the idea of disunion.

At last the heat broke and the question was put. Because there was no other way to get a Constitution—no earthly way—Sherman's compromise passed.

To offset, for the smaller states, proportional representation in the House (one congressman for every 40,000 inhabitants), each state, whatever its size, was to have two senators. Thus was a thorny problem settled. Years later Madison would write that the most *"threatening contest"* at the Convention was not, as some had supposed, the degree of power to be granted the central government but, rather, "the rule by which the States should be represented and vote" in Congress. That was the crux.

A related question was whether Congress's powers should be indefinite or enumerated. Madison said enumerated. Though he wanted a strong national government, he did not want it rampant. A centripetal force must be balanced by the centrifugal; there was the sun and there were the planets.

It was now that the federal negative, for which Madison had spoken up, was rejected, 8 to 3.

On July 19 the *Pennsylvania Packet* said it had heard that the Convention's unanimity was so great, someone had proposed naming its meeting room Unanimity Hall. That was the day the delegates started wrangling over the Presidency. (How address the President?—a peripheral question not affecting the Constitution. His Highness? Madison, who had called the people the "fountain of all power," thought "Mr. President" was quite enough. What greater dignity could there be? It was decided.)

A week later (the Convention had now been in session two months) a Committee of Detail started to try to make order out of the twenty-two passed resolutions. The work took eleven days, during which Washington went off to see his old cantonment at Valley Forge and to fish for trout and perch. Madison enjoyed this break in his wearisome note-taking, and perhaps on August 4 went to the Opera House with some of his fellows to see a comic opera called *The Padlock* and a "comic lecture" on "the generous American."

When the committee's work had been printed and distributed, new arguments consumed five more weeks. August had never seemed so long and dusty. Frogs complained in the creeks. In Market Street stalls the cabbages and lettuce wilted. Then Madison came down with bilious fever. For a week his notes went from voluminous to skimpy. But he did not miss a single day.

More decisions were made. Opposers of the old three-fifths rule for counting slaves were mollified by an 1808 cutoff date for new importations. Treason was defined; rules for patents, copyrights, and citizenship were established; plans for a permanent army and a permanent national capital made; and so forth.

But by what method should the proposed Constitution be ratified? Madison ruled out state legislatures. How could they change the instrument which gave them their existence? No, only the people assembled in special conventions could ratify it. His view won. Then the delegates had to decide how many states could throw the Constitution into gear. Thirteen? Seven? Too few could not be allowed to stop the majority from "consulting their safety." They agreed on nine.

To everyone's dismay Edmund Randolph called for a second Convention in which states could make further emendations before final drafting. Worn-out delegates, including Madison, hotly opposed this idea. Jeopardize success with "insuperable obstacles"? No. Randolph asked grimly if he were expected to sign a plan he believed would "end in tyranny"—well, he refused. If elected to the Virginia Convention, he wanted to be free to use his best judgment.

The Committee of Style and Arrangement consisted of college president William S. Johnson, Alexander Hamilton, Rufus King, Gouverneur Morris, and James Madison. Johnson was chairman, Morris polisher-amanuensis. Madison, judging by the style, drafted the accompanying letter to the President of the Continental Congress. "Sir, we have now the honor to submit" a Constitution, it begins, and goes on to note that individuals forming a society "must give up a share of liberty to preserve the rest."

There it stood, the word "share." No one had yet said "shared sovereignty" because an absolutely new concept was still seeking its terminology—but a step had been taken toward that illuminating central phrase. The Constitution so heralded began forthrightly: *"We the People of the United States"* (the people from whom, as Madison had been stressing, flowed all power), *"in Order to form a more perfect Union, establish Justice, insure domestic Tranquility, provide for the common Defence, promote the general Welfare, and secure the Blessings of Liberty . . . do ordain and establish this Constitution. . . ."*

There followed seven Articles condensed from twenty-three. Number VI used an old Magna Carta phrase as key: "This Constitution . . . shall be the supreme Law of the Land."

On September 12 the Convention fell on the new wording to tear it and rend it. Two-thirds instead of three-fourths of Congress should have the power to veto the President's veto, it decided. And what about trial by jury? Mason said the plan should start with a bill of rights: It was the first time such a thing had been mentioned. "It would give great quiet to the people." A chorus of objections. Sherman argued that the state declarations were enough. Hamilton called it impracticable. Later, outside the Convention, Noah Webster would lampoon by sarcasm. Why not add a clause to the Constitution: " . . . Congress shall never restrain any inhabitant from eating and drinking at seasonable times, or prevent his lying on his left side in a long winter's night. . . ." Thus Mason's motion lost, 10 to 0. The delegates regarded the Constitution itself as a bill of rights.

The motion for a second Constitutional Convention failed, as did Madison's attempt to insert into the document a power to establish a national university (for which he had worked in the Continental Congress). It was time for the Constitution to be engrossed.

Monday, September 17, dawned chilly. There was a smell of autumn. Thirty-eight of the fifty-five delegates who had attended took their seats with a sense of a great, imminent, destiny-shaped and destiny-shaping act. The Constitution, beautifully inscribed on parchment, was recited aloud by a clerk.

James Wilson then read a statement by old feeble Ben Franklin. Though he did not approve of the whole Constitution, he said, he had lived long enough to know he wasn't always right. Really the near-perfection of the Constitution as proposed would astonish their enemies. "Thus I consent, Sir, to the Constitution because I expect no better and because I am not sure it is not the best." He suggested that the delegates sign by the unanimous consent of the *States* present, thus committing no one individually. George Washington broke a monumental silence to back this proposal, and it passed.

It was just past three o'clock in the afternoon when Chairman Washington signed his name. Starting with New Hampshire and moving southward to Georgia, the delegates, one by one, picked up the pen and signed. Four opponents had gone home, and ten supporters were absent (though John Dickinson had authorized a friend to add his signature). At the end Franklin wept.

Meanwhile Virginia had split. George Mason had already pulled out, his acrimony whetted. ("Col. Mason," Madison would write Jefferson, "left . . . in an exceedingly ill humor indeed.") The Virginians who joined Washington in signing were Judge John Blair and James Madison.

As the Georgians were finishing up, Franklin, looking toward Washington's chair with the painted sun cut by a horizon, mused aloud that though all summer he had been unsure, he knew now that the sun was *rising*.

For Madison the hour was a grand climax. Having labored long for this culmination, he felt its overwhelming dignity and was—with a few reservations—elated. William Pierce of Georgia has described him as he emerged from the four-month struggle exhausted. His note-taking had "almost killed" him. " . . . Every person seems to acknowledge his greatness. He blends together the profound politician with the scholar. In the management of every great question he evidently took the lead . . . a most agreeable, eloquent and convincing speaker. . . . In a most eminent degree he always comes forward the best informed man. . . . A gentleman of great modesty. . . ." And William Blount of North Carolina has added that in the Convention, Virginia took the lead and Madison led Virginia.

While the Convention struggled with the prime problem, power, Madison had from first to last championed the Greeks' golden mean— balance. To the question, "Can state sovereignty be reconciled with aggregate sovereignty, or should all be packed featureless into one great monolith?" he had answered with the other Signers, Let there be a divided sovereignty, a shared sovereignty, a two-way pull making for equilibrium, for stability with movement; let each state, like each sun-circling planet, be free yet bound.

No one who attended the Convention ever denied that Madison had been the chief architect of the Constitution. Not only was the Virginia Plan his child; during the Convention he had answered foreseen and unforeseen arguments brilliantly and again and again clarified key issues. Though other men, particularly James Wilson, Roger Sherman, Gouverneur Morris, had played vital, constructive roles, and he himself would in 1827—out of his lifelong incredible modesty—discount the title "Father of the Constitution," by all the evidence he was just that, exactly that.

This is true even though his hope of a federal veto over state laws had been overridden. After the Convention he would write Jefferson that he had espoused the proposal because he thought it the most workable way to prevent encroachment on the central government (he would live to see the opposite), to break the tyranny of majorities, and thus to guarantee stability. But this letter to Jefferson was a temporary reaction. It does not represent his thoughts as they finally shook down. An unmistakably genuine enthusiasm would ring through his future references to the Constitution. For he knew that the supremacy clause which he had supported and the Supreme Judiciary which he had helped set up could go very far toward guaranteeing defense of minorities, and stability and justice; indeed, that the power to prevent passage of a state law contravening a national one, instead of the power to wipe it out later ("stifle in the birth" as he put it) was in fact not so different in effect, only more (his word) "convenient." And the truth remained that the enormous strengthening of the central government which, after watching the helplessness of the Continental Congress, he had worked for long and hard had been accomplished. Moreoever, a tremendous number of ideas which he had originated and proposed, arguing masterfully, had been adopted and now formed the backbone of the Constitution. He knew also that, in the Convention, nothing more or different could have been passed than did pass. As he wrote Jefferson in this same letter, in view of "the diversity of human opinions," it was "impossible to consider the degree of concord which ultimately prevailed as less than a miracle."

After four long grueling months the Convention, that miracle worker, was dissolving. Delegates dining at the City Tavern for the last time had a heady sense of having finished, as Washington said, a "momentous work."

Part of Madison's mind was jubilant, part wary. Having refused to despair at the beginning of the Convention, he refused now—heading back to the Continental Congress—to minimize the difficulties of ratification.

When the Constitution was published, many people objected to it, saying, Instead of amending the Articles of Confederation, the Convention has killed that charter—this new plan looks like the consolidation of an empire.

To further an understanding of what had been done and why, and to increase the likelihood of ratification, Madison joined Alexander Hamilton and John Jay (who soon dropped out because of illness) in writing a series of articles, printed in two New York newspapers, on the proposed Constitution.

Brilliantly written, they were widely copied and would become, in time, for the whole world, the classic exposition of the theory and practice of republican government. Though Madison wrote only twenty-nine essays (Numbers 10, 14, 18 through 20, 37 through 58, 62, and 63), his contributions include the most powerful, central, and fundamental ones. They clarify and amplify the highly original ideas which he had offered to the Constitutional Convention; they apply to conditions on the American continent lessons learned from his in-depth study of constitutional history. Number 10 deals authoritatively with faction as a group "actuated by some common impulse or passion or interest adverse to the rights of other citizens," powerful because "sown in the nature of man himself." Number 14 says the claws of a faction can be clipped in a republic based on elected representatives, *provided the sphere is large enough*—a position contrary to that of Montesquieu, Locke, Hume, and even Dr. Witherspoon (whose syllabus stated, "If [the subjects are] very numerous, the principles of government cannot exert their force over the whole. The Roman Empire fell by its own weight."). Numbers 18, 19, 20, noting that "experience is the oracle of truth," analyze earlier confederations to find out why they fell. Madison's conclusion: governments over governments breed disorder; it is essential that the authority be exercised over individuals. Numbers 37, 38, and 39 discuss the incoherence of the objections raised against the plan, and praise the triumph of republican principles in this government of a "mixed character"—"neither wholly federal nor wholly national." Number 40 outlines the powers of the Convention; Numbers 41, 42, and 43 examine the powers conferred by the Constitution; Number 44 notes the limitations of power; Number 45 enumerates federal powers; Number 46 talks about the relative power of state and nation (the states, Madison says, having nothing to fear, since they have the advantage in defeating encroachments); Numbers 47, 48, and 49 deal with the interrelation between governmental departments; 50 appeals to the people; 51 considers interdepartmental checks and balances whereby ambition is "made to counteract ambition"; 52 through 58 discuss various aspects of the House of Representatives, including power of the purse; 62 and 63 concern aspects of the Senate. Jay wrote the next paper. Then— since Madison had to leave for the Virginia Ratification Convention— Hamilton picked up the pen and finished the series.

POWER OF THE PURSE, that mighty power. In 1795 Madison's purpose in reviewing the Constitution and *Federalist Papers* was to refresh his mind as to this House prerogative designed to offset the Senate's special role with respect to high appointments and treaty making.

The *Federalist* discussion of this House prerogative occurs in Madison's own Number 58: "Notwithstanding the equal authority which will subsist between the two houses on all legislative subjects, except the originating of money bills [which belongs to the House], it cannot be doubted that the House . . . , when supported by the more powerful States . . . will have no small advantage. . . . The House of Representatives cannot only refuse but they alone can propose, the [money] supplies requisite for the support of government. They, in a word, hold the purse—that powerful instrument. . . . This . . . may, in fact, be regarded as the most complete and effectual weapon with which any constitution can arm the immediate representatives of the people for obtaining a redress of every grievance." *Every.* Whenever in the British House of Commons "the engine of a money bill" was used, Number 58 goes on, it had triumphed, and however firm the American President or Senators might be in a matter involving money, they would be no match for an organized, patriotic House.

Thus in the constitutional crisis caused by Jay's Treaty, Madison and other members of the House had what they needed to defeat it. They could fight with great assurance of winning *provided they held together and did not give in.*

❧ V ❧

DEFEAT

MADISON'S BACKWARD LOOKING included the state ratification conventions which followed the framing of the Constitution—in particular the one which he attended and suffered through and which in a way was crucial: Virginia's. For he always maintained that the meanings embedded in the Constitution went back to the interpretations of the ratifiers: that their understanding was of the essence.

These reminiscences as passed on to Dolley in Philadelphia in the first years of their marriage did not interfere with their life together; woven together, they were all of a piece: one cloth.

On returning from Orange in November 1795, the Madisons had moved into a three-story house on Spruce Street. Each floor had three rooms and three front windows. Dolley's life had now subtly changed. During their six months at Montpelier she and Anna had slipped into the more easygoing, laughing Virginia manner. Dolley encouraged her sister's growing interest in parties and beaux. Both thought it no small matter that the new dress trains were looped with bobbin and that hats turned up on each side and that Mrs. Bingham tied hers with a long purple ribbon. Dolley wanted sixteen-year-old Anna to enjoy the social whirl she herself had missed. Though still a Quaker in her heart, she could not persuade herself—it had always been hard—that a little light-hearted diversion was wicked. Also, in relation to her husband, she was like Ruth: "Whither thou goest I will go." At evening gatherings she went so far as to try the fashionable décolletage. She was moving ever closer to high style, which in the 1790s meant French style. Waistlines were pushing up, round-toed slippers were tied at the ankle with ribbons, and ladies made a great to-do over fans, parasols, muffs. They wore bangs.

About this time James Peale painted Dolley with little wispy bangs escaping from under a sheer white cap above dreamy eyes. A breastpin festooned with four gold loops anchors her fichu. James loved the picture so much that, as an old man, he would insist on keeping it near him.

But after New Year's 1796 there was less gaiety in the house, more tension. James was preparing for a fight in the House, and Dolley felt involved. Not that she understood politics very well yet. Much of it baffled her, but she was an earnest scholar, observing, asking questions, studying related convolutions and oddities. The Republicans were not only girding for a constitutional showdown; they were more and more embarrassed by Georgia's corrupt sale of the vast Yazoo lands, a few of them being up to their necks in that bog. And Dolley longed to help.

Though devoted to her husband's party, she did not select dinner guests on a partisan basis. She liked to bring together diverse people and put them at ease with themselves and each other. The amiable Mrs. Madison, they called her, adding that the lady was not unintelligent, not at all. Now that was a sight—a Quaker serving wine!

The Madisons went out to dinner frequently, though not or not much to the Washingtons', for—very quietly—the political rift was widening. Madison's proposal for reprisals against the British had helped it along, as had the President's growing hatred of the "Jacobin" Democratic Societies and, now, Madison's stated opposition to Jay's Treaty. No longer did Washington confide in Madison or ask his advice. The Madisons were deeply sorry about the estrangement. But one must live by one's conscience.

Writing the House's reply to the President's message about Jay's Treaty, Madison held his fire. The issue must be handled tactfully. But when fellow Republicans refused to endorse any move not "compatible with our national honor," he insisted on a rewording still more inclusive: not "compatible . . . with our Constitution and great commercial interests." That was the stone in his slingshot. Now the House must wait until the President asked for an appropriation—until the target stepped into the open.

Meanwhile the bloody excesses of the French Revolution had been halted by a young general named Napoleon Bonaparte. Madison wanted to believe that France, having outlived her madness, would develop a true republicanism. He had no faith in great obdurate Britain that had used its colonies and then a free nation so shabbily. Britain just might have to be taught a lesson.

Amid such ruminations, the Madisons welcomed Mrs. Payne and

Lucy and Mary. After John Adams—the short, stocky, famous Federalist—had dined with them on Spruce Street, he wrote Abigail enthusiastically: "Mrs. Madison is a fine woman, and her two sisters equally so." The Madisons' domestic life could hardly have been happier.

Meanwhile James continued to ponder the Virginia Ratification Convention which, like the Constitution, had an intimate connection with his looming fight in the House. So much had been at stake, it remained vivid.

ON JUNE 2, 1788, the Virginia Ratification Convention opened in the Academy of Arts and Sciences on Shockoe Hill in Richmond. After writing his part of the *Federalist Papers,* Madison had come home from the Continental Congress on the very eve of the election of delegates, conferred with John Leland, a Baptist minister who had been fearing that the Constitution would destroy religious liberty, spoken briefly at the Orange polling place, and won.

Now, two months later, he looked around the Convention. Though he had been corresponding with Edmund Randolph, he still had not learned on which side the handsome Governor would fetch up. But he saw some allies in the coming fight for ratification. For example, there was short, fat, incisive George Nicholas (how Madison had laughed at a cartoon depicting George as a "plum pudding with legs"), his Princeton friend "Light Horse" Harry Lee, and Judge James Innes. He also saw at a glance some powerful foes, chief among them Patrick Henry and Colonel George Mason. Henry sat jiggling his spectacles. Mason looked formidable, scowling there in a black silk mourning suit. Fourteen pistol-packing Kentuckians looked as if they might—in case things went against them—shoot it out.

Recently someone (people were asking if it was Madison) had written the *Chronicle* to warn that rejection of the Constitution would lead to thirteen sovereign States, or to several confederacies, or to a union so weak, foreigners could insult it at will.

Old, white-haired, crippled, elegant Chairman Edmund Pendleton pounded his gavel, and George Mason, racked by gout, demanded that the proposed Constitution be considered clause by clause. That suited Madison perfectly. Henry was no man for details; he liked to sweep his audience along on a flood of feeling. The Convention went at once into a Committee of the Whole, and the fireworks started. The American Demosthenes played on known fears. "We, the people," he quoted scoffingly. Why not "We the States"? He answered himself: Because the framers were out for consolidation. The word suggested a great solid featureless block.

When Randolph stood up, Madison was still wondering which way the tree would fall. Yes, the Governor said, in Philadelphia he had refused to sign the Constitution, holding out for amendments, but he saw nothing against a Bill of Rights inserted *after* ratification. Now Madison breathed more easily.

Angry, George Mason broke the clause-by-clause rule he had proposed by attacking federal taxing power, and Madison rose to say quietly that he would abide by the rules and wait for the tax clause to come up before saying why he took issue. The proposed government was of a mixed nature, he went on, and elaborated the point. Then he broke off until a "more convenient time" and went back to his lodgings with bilious fever. That night he forced himself to write a report to Washington. Though the opposition had cut a lame figure, he said, it did seem to have Kentucky. It was playing on local interests and prejudices.

Henry took advantage of his chief antagonist's absence by sharpening his attack. Light Horse Harry asked him to leave off oratory and stick to facts. Rhetorical or not, Henry's three-hour harangue was brilliantly effective. The Constitution menaced the Virginia Bill of Rights, he said: rights of conscience, trial by jury, liberty of the press—"all." Eight states had ratified. But if twelve states and a half had ratified, "I would with manly firmness . . . reject it." They were proposing a king. Despotism could follow, a "galling yoke." Federal taxing power would bring in federal sheriffs. "But, sir, I mean not to breathe the spirit or utter the language of secession"—thereby uttering it.

The next day Randolph answered sturdily that the Union was the "rock of our salvation."

Madison came back handsomely arrayed in "blue and buff." His illness had been temporary. Basically this short well-proportioned man was now in fine physical health, robust, muscular, ruddy. His debating voice had never had great strength, but he was now at the peak of his powers and—having put off an old timidity—had learned to speak out with great self-possession, his hat in his hand, his notes in his hat, swaying gently with a seesaw motion, a man concerned with only one thing: the truth. "Eloquence," John Marshall, who was present, would testify, "has been defined to be the art of persuasion. If it includes persuading by convincing, Mr. Madison was the most eloquent man I ever heard."

Others on Madison's side spoke well, but it was largely Madison's thinking as voiced by himself and as echoed by men he had taught through words, articles, and letters which wore down the opposition. Listeners heard a simple, devastating logic. *What* dangers? he asked Henry. *No,* despotism was usually invited in, not by the tyranny of rulers, as alleged, but by the people's own violence. *No,* Americans had not been in a state of perfect tranquility as alleged; if so, would complaints have run back and forth across the continent? *No,* the new Constitution would not jeopardize American rights on the Mississippi (the Kentuckians were straining their ears)—quite the contrary. George Nichols supported Madison at length, toughly, wittily, adroitly. But Bushrod Washington knew to whom belonged the palm. Writing his Uncle George he said, "Mr. Madison followed with such force and reasoning and a display of such irresistible truths that opposition seemed to have quitted the field. However," he added, knowing the power of Patrick Henry's golden opposing tongue, "I am not so sanguine. . . ."

During the next two and a half weeks Madison hammered away at the woeful inefficiency of the Articles of Confederation. Ancient and modern confederacies had, without exception, bred anarchy. A weak union could not command respect from other nations; why make treaties with a federation against which any member could turn at any time? As for complying with federal requisitions, look at the record.

One day Henry lost his head and cried that Virginia and Carolina could exist separately from the rest of America. A shock wave passed through the room. Republicanism was not compatible with so large a country, he said, thus contradicting Madison's belief that the larger the democracy the better. And how about a constitution partly national, partly federal, Henry went on. The most fatal Britain-copying yoke of consolidation was to be pressed down on their necks. He then criticized Randolph strongly, who rose to protest. "I disdain his aspersions and his insinuations," said the Governor, " . . . and if our friendship must fall—let it fall like Lucifer, never to rise again."

The debate was getting out of hand. Tempers flared, pulses quickened. So much hung on the outcome. It could powerfully affect the future. "Our only chance of success," Hamilton wrote Madison, "depends on you." The New Yorker was not forgetting the other Virginia debaters; he simply knew that the real antagonists were James Madison and Patrick Henry, logic versus a kind of shamanism.

The absence of a Bill of Rights, shouted Henry, was dangerous in the extreme. It would expose Virginia to armed power. He was answered forthrightly: Why dissolve the Union for lack of a Bill of Rights which could be added by amendment?

Mason protested 1808 as a cutoff date for stopping the importation of slaves—it was too late—while inconsistently complaining that, by the new plan, Congress could tax slavery out of existence. "They'll free your niggers!" shouted Henry, and everybody laughed.

The raising up of bogeys accompanied horrendous accusations.

Madison chose to dwell upon the States' solemn alternatives: unite or splinter. Any amendments would have to be considered by the States that had already ratified. He had once thought that a Bill of Rights guaranteeing what had never been threatened was superfluous, but if it would allay anxiety, he approved. This statement deprived his adversaries of much ammunition.

A ferocious storm attacked the wooden academy. The air darkened, doors slammed, windows rattled. It seemed somehow fitting. The meeting adjourned under great tension.

On the day of decision Attorney General James Innes up-hoisted his huge bulk to say that though he had hoped to hear some reasoned arguments against the proposed Constitution, its opponents had offered only chimeras. Amendments at this time were obviously out of the question. It was quite impossible to bind citizens of any state by things they knew nothing about. His seat rocked when he sat down.

On June 25 ratification was put to a vote. Virginia passed the Constitution 89 to 79. She thought she was the ninth state and, as such, was throwing the new order into gear, but New Hampshire had beaten her to ninth place by five days. Still, her "yes" was a landmark. Without the largest of the States the Union could hardly have survived. Most people gave credit for Virginia's ratification to James Madison.

Unfortunately his victory was bought at the price of Patrick Henry's unwearying malice.

It did not cast Madison down. For one thing, Princeton was preparing to award him a doctorate of law degree. Dr. Witherspoon's letter said that the faculty was proud to honor a son who had done them all "so much honor."

Pulling strings that fall, Henry succeeded in keeping Madison out of the Senate. An appointment by the Legislature (the method then in effect), he cried, would deluge the land with "rivulets of blood." It was not the revenge he thought it was, for Madison had already written Randolph that he preferred the House as being nearer the people. Henry now concentrated on keeping Madison out of the House, where membership was by popular election. He went so far as to piece together a congressional district joining Madison's loyal Orange constituency to seven counties known to be opposed to the Constitution, therefore to Mr. Madison, and he even—in November—charged that Madison was against all amendments (a Bill of Rights) and had ceased to be a "friend to the rights of conscience." To meet the slander, Madison's friends prepared a pamphlet quoting from his letters. No, he said, it would look too much like electioneering.

Before going back to Montpelier from the Continental Congress, Madison paid a long visit to George Washington. Orange constituents were wild with worry about the upcoming first national election. Where was Madison? Why so tardy? Madison and James Monroe (Henry's candidate) spoke at Culpeper Courthouse, which was considered crucial, on Court Day; then for two weeks they traveled around together like a friendly debating team.

One Sunday, standing deep in snow at the Hebron Lutheran Church, they listened to a sermon and some fiddling before presenting rival political views. That night Madison rode 12 miles in such bitter cold to find a bed, he suffered a severe frostbite. It left a small permanent scar on the left side of his nose.

On election day a crowd of men stood around Orange Courthouse slapping each other on the shoulder. They were praising James Madison, the winner. He was their man and he had made it.

James P. Brissot de Warville reports in his *New Travels in the United States* that at this period Madison was not only "celebrated in America" but also "well known," through Jefferson, in Europe. "Though still young he has rendered the greatest service to . . . liberty and humanity"—and Brissot mentions his "immense labors" in the Constitutional Convention and the Virginia Ratification Convention.

MADISON'S RECALLING of those conventions—in order to get everything in clear focus before fighting Jay's Treaty—could hardly stop with his election to the United States Congress set up by the Constitution. His eight years in the House were a highly pertinent continuation. It was all one stream of experience, one process of elucidation. Memory kept going.

On April 23, 1789, President-elect George Washington (having borrowed £600 for the trip) arrived in New York by barge. He was met by a delirium of gun salutes, parades, and cheering. A week later he stepped onto a festively draped balcony overlooking Broad Street and, under a magnificent spread eagle, laid his hand on a Bible. "I do solemnly swear that I will . . . preserve, protect and defend the Constitution of the United States." (Madison had written most of Washington's Inaugural Address, and he would write the House's response and the President's reply to the House: a man immersed in a country he saw as the "hope of the human race.")

Now it could get down to business.

There were problems aplenty. For example, the Continental Congress had left the new government overwhelming debts, and there was as yet no machinery for collecting taxes. The federal judiciary had not been set up. Solutions must be improvised.

Many people looked upon the Constitution as just an experiment. As mentioned, Madison himself had had his moments of doubt before rallying strongly. Washington called the new government a hopeful one; John Adams thought he might outlast it; and Alexander Hamilton openly disparaged it. "A frail and worthless fabric." Though Madison recognized the dangers, the principle of balance on which the plan had been founded gave him—after he had had time to mull it over sufficiently—great faith in its workability. By consciously taking into account the strength and fallibility of human beings, the framers had, he thought, copied the counterpoise embedded in the universe.

The controversy as to the proper title for the President continued. John Adams favored "His Highness the President of the United States of America and Protector of the Liberties of the Same," and the Senate was warming to it. Not Madison. He found it ridiculous. The President would not gain an iota of power, he wrote Jefferson, if loaded with all the titles of Europe and Asia. He was for "Mr. President." Congress finally agreed.

With the passion of a lonely man he flung himself into the work of the House of Representatives. He backed various imposts. How, otherwise, pay twelve government clerks and the national debt? When someone moved for a tax of $10 a head on slaves, he agreed. Slavery was immoral, and he hoped that by expressing "a national disapprobation" of the trade Congress could help destroy what he called a weakening imbecility.

He also argued for a navy and a school for seamen. And on June 8 he proposed ten amendments—guaranteeing freedom of religion, speech, the press, assembly, and so forth—to be incorporated into the Constitution as a Bill of Rights. Most significantly, the powers which the charter neither delegated nor prohibited to the States were, therein, reserved to the States.

In his supporting speech Madison repeated that the greatest danger to liberty sprang not from Congress—though it needed controls—but the people themselves. A tyrannous majority could oppress a minority. He was saying in effect, "Watch yourselves."

Controversy arose over the question of the separation of church and state and also over the issue of congressional powers. St. George Tucker of South Carolina wished to forestall a loose construction of the Constitution through stricter wording. Madison opposed this straitjacket. The Bill of Rights passed substantially as written, to be ratified by the States in December 1791.

These days James Madison, Republican leader of the House of Representatives, often found himself locking horns with the leading Federalist, Fisher Ames of Massachusetts, the delegate most nearly his intellectual peer.

Meanwhile he was discussing the classics with Mrs. Henrietta Colden. His friends at Mrs. Dorothy Ellis's boardinghouse on Maiden Lane wondered if it was a match. He was nearing forty—high time he took a wife. The poor devil must be lonely.

Fisher Ames saw Congressman Madison as a man of "sense, reading, address and integrity" who considered Virginia the land of promise. "His language is very pure, perspicuous and to the point." Madison's chief political adversary probed for a weak spot. "Pardon me if I add that I think him a little too much of a book politician." But Fisher conceded that Madison was "our first man."

Having since 1782 worked to locate the national capital on the Potomac, midway between the North and the South, Madison suspected a maneuver to put it on the Susquehanna. How counter such a scheme? The resolution he sponsored named neither state nor river; it just said the capital should be "as nearly central" as permitted a convenient outlet to the Atlantic and way of passage to the Western territory. When this resolution failed, he tried to block an overhasty decision and play for time. It would prove to be a good stratagem.

In selecting a Cabinet, Washington used Madison as his chief adviser. As a member of Congress serving in an office created during his tenure, Madison himself was prevented—by a law which he himself had urged— from becoming what Washington wanted to make him: Secretary of State. It was ironical. Washington asked him if the returning Jefferson would accept that position. Madison said he hoped so. With his endorsement Alexander Hamilton was made Secretary of the Treasury; General Henry Knox, Secretary of War; Edmund Randolph, Attorney General; and John Jay, Chief Justice of the United States.

Senator Maclay, who, like some others, was jealous of Madison's influence on the President, accused Madison of paying "court to the President whom, I am told, he already affects to govern."

Madison's relationship with Hamilton at this time was entirely easy. The two old friends enjoyed getting together for talk and amusement. Years later an old lady would remember that as a girl she had seen them "talk together in the summer and then turn and laugh, and play with a monkey that was climbing in a neighbor's yard." In October, when he was preparing to go home, Madison sent Hamilton a farewell note along with a loaned book. " . . . Send me your thoughts on . . . an addition to our revenue," Hamilton wrote back. Also on proper ways to reduce the public debt—"may I ask [this] of your friendship . . . ?" After suggesting reduction of the debt by sale of the vacant Western lands, Madison signed his letter "with affectionate regard." Little did he anticipate what was about to happen.

Hamilton's "Report on Public Credit" shocked him. It proposed that Congress redeem for the *holders*—in most cases not the original soldier and sailor owners—the 6 percent certificates representing a quarter of the national debt; also that the federal government assume the States' war debts *in gross*. Both propositions severely offended Madison's sense of justice. He felt duty-bound to launch, in the House, the stiffest sort of opposition.

The certificates had been forced upon war veterans and suppliers, he argued, in lieu of cash. Naturally the present holders would like to be paid in full, but was that fair to those patriots who had been forced to sell to speculators at rates as low as a tenth of the certificates' face value? Hamilton replied that the highly desirable result of paying speculators would be to weld the most reliable citizens to the government. Madison listened coldly. What was this but class favoritism? A move toward a stratified society with special privileges for the rich? Aristocracy? No, he said. Compromise. Give some compensation to the original owners; the present holders would still make a tidy profit. He could not believe that America should erect monuments of gratitude, not to the men who had saved the nation's liberties, but to those who had enriched themselves thereby; no court of equity would judge otherwise.

The trouble was that many in and out of Congress were both friends of Hamilton and hot, greedy speculators. They were not pleased with James Madison; they were not pleased at all.

As for federal assumption of the States' war debts, Madison thought that in all fairness there should be adjustments. Virginia and some other states had already paid off millions of dollars of their war debts. Treat them the same as states which had paid off not one penny? Inequitable.

Madison knew that by arguing against Hamilton's two rather popular proposals he was risking his leadership in the House. The vote on the redemption of certificates did indeed go against his view, and the issue of soldiers' pay was even more abrasive. But Madison's resolute stand also stirred up admiration and support. For example, the *Pennsylvania Gazette* wrote indignantly:

> A soldier's pay is rags and fame,
> A wooden leg—a deathless name.
> To Specs, both in and out of Cong,
> The four and six percents belong.

Madison's struggle was not a personal one against Hamilton; it was strictly a matter of principle. He wished he could talk it over with Jefferson.

The Secretary of State's trip north was delayed by his daughter Martha's marriage to her cousin Thomas Mann Randolph. When in March Jefferson finally reached New York, Hamilton's assumption-of-debts bill was short just one vote in the Senate and only a few votes in the House. Meeting Jefferson on Broadway, Hamilton walked him up and down the street while making an impassioned plea. If his assumption bill failed, he argued, the United States would lose so much European credit, it might disintegrate. Wouldn't Jefferson try to influence some of his friends in its favor (meaning the controller of the Virginia delegation, James Madison)? Come to dinner tomorrow, said Jefferson; he would invite a friend or two. He invited only Madison, and, according to his *Anas,* stayed entirely out of the discussion. Hamilton made his appeal. Yes, said Madison, he was aware that New Englanders had sworn to block funding of the national debt until the assumption bill passed; they had even hinted at secession. Actually, three days earlier Madison, seeing that New England's position made compromise inevitable, had written Monroe, "The assumption still hangs over us. . . . I suspect that it will yet be unavoidable to admit the evil in some qualified shape." So now he counterproposed. If Hamilton would modify his bill so as to deliver votes for moving the capital first to Philadelphia and then, in 1800, to the Potomac, he would muster (while allowing himself the pleasure of voting "no") enough votes to pass the assumption bill. A bargain was struck.

Did Jefferson break with Hamilton and carry Madison with him? This is a recurring canard. The opposite is true. On seeing Hamilton's "Report on Public Credit," Madison broke with his old friend, out of the moral necessities of his nature, while Jefferson was still at Monticello and ignorant of the issue. When Jefferson reached New York, the lines had already been drawn in two important matters between Hamiltonians and Madisonians, which is to say between the emerging Federalist and Republican (Democrat-Republican) parties.* That is a fact. Though the Constitution made no provision for political parties, they were (as Madison would come to see) inevitable.

In the fall of 1790 Madison and Jefferson drove to Virginia in the latter's phaeton. Young Thomas Lee Shippen, who accompanied them from the Eastern shore to George Town, found their companionship exhilarating. "I never knew two men more agreeable." While waiting for the ferry to take them across the Chesapeake, they "talked and dined and strolled and rowed . . . in boats, and feasted upon delicious crabs." At Annapolis they sat for three hours on top of the statehouse steeple looking at the sights before dining on turtle at Mann's Inn. Further on, they cheerfully fended off an assault of "mosquitoes, gnats, flies and bugs." At Bladensburg they breakfasted at a very good house operated by an old black woman. (General and Mrs. Washington had just left.) One thing they discussed was France's overthrow of the old regime. Jefferson, who had seen the first bloodshed in Paris, was enthusiastic. Weren't the French revolutionists fighting for the rights of man? Early one morning the two friends rode out from George Town with a cavalcade of thirteen to look over the site of the future capital. It was beautiful. The air seemed full of potentialities. It was bracing. Shippen left "those charming men Jefferson and Madison" reluctantly as they took off for Mount Vernon.

At Montpelier Jefferson borrowed fresh horses and a servant.

Madison now settled back into farm life. Reelected without opposition, he conferred with his two overseers, black Sawney of "Sawney's" and

---

*A few words about a confusing nomenclature. The party names of 1790, "Federalist" and "Republican," have been likened to "Tory" and "Whig." It is more accurate to note an analogy between the Federalists and conservative Whigs, and between the Republicans and radical Whigs—though some historians question even this relationship. Earlier those men, including Madison, who had supported the new Constitution, were often called "Federalists" simply because they saw the necessity of saving the Union by strengthening the federal government with a stronger written constitution. Between 1787 and 1789, opponents of the Constitution were often called "anti-Federalists" (e.g., Patrick Henry). Neither term was a party name, for there were as yet no real parties. In early 1790, when parties did form, the division, at least at first, was over fiscal policies. The "monarchical," "aristocratic," more-class-conscious, British-favoring *Federalists*—at whose center stood the manufacturing, commercial, seafaring Northeasterners led by Hamilton—faced head-on the more democratic, French-favoring *Republicans* (or Democrat-Republicans, as they are sometimes called), at whose core were agricultural Southerners led by Madison and Jefferson. If one confuses the first loosely called "Federalists" with the later party Federalists, one can make grievous errors. They are not the same.

white Mordecai Collins of "Broad Meadows," while waiting to return to Congress. His instructions to Mordecai: treat the slaves "with all the humanity and kindness consistent with their necessary subordination and work." Never in his life would he strike a slave, or allow an overseer to do so.

Horseback riding around New York had put Madison into fine shape, and at Montpelier he thoroughly enjoyed his outdoor work: building stables and meadow dams, experimenting with red clover, setting out apple trees, and, in one field, substituting potatoes for tobacco.

After the first hard frosts in November, he joined Jefferson to ride north to the new ten-year temporary capital, Philadelphia, which he knew well. As formerly they lodged at Mrs. House's, and Madison began work on another speech for President Washington to deliver to Congress. But this time the President had enlisted Hamilton's help too.

Though Madison's friendship with Hamilton had been hurt by their differences over redemption and assumption, neither one of them, during the controversy, had dealt in personalities. Honest men can disagree and still respect each other.

Then in December 1790 Hamilton proposed that Congress establish a national bank like the Bank of England. He said it would help national money transactions and (his old argument) bind reliable men (wealthy ones?) to the government. The Senate passed the bank bill, and the House was warming to it.

But Madison, Jefferson, and Senator Monroe looked upon it with jaundiced eyes. The Constitution did not give Congress the power to establish a national bank, they said. Was it "necessary" in the sense of the Constitution's "general welfare" clause? No—and Congress must not be allowed to seize a dangerous degree of power. A national bank would create a monopoly, strengthen an avaricious money class, and encourage an imperialism which the signers of the Constitution had never intended.

By now, of course, Madison had told Jefferson and Monroe about Hamilton's speech in the Constitutional Convention: that Hamilton had called Britain's monarchy the best government in the world; that, aware of America's distaste for such a regime, he had outlined a compromise aristocracy with the President and senators elected for life and the States all but extinguished; that later, moreover, Hamilton had said he foresaw the evils of the American system curing people of their absurd fondness for the democracy he called "mobocracy." The three friends discussing the matter at Mrs. House's wondered if Hamilton, through his position as Secretary of the Treasury (the most powerful of the departments because of the country's acute fiscal problems), was trying to edge and "administer" the government over into a form resembling Great Britain's. It would appear so.

On the floor of the House, Madison called the bank plan unconstitutional because—though convenient—it was certainly not necessary. He said that creating a national bank would be a usurpation of power. Fisher Ames rose to refute him, crying that the bank was necessary for the regulation of trade, public credit, and national defense. At this signal Federalists and Republicans—now definite parties—began to battle together in the House. Democrat-Republican Madison's side lost.

When the President asked his Cabinet to examine the bank's constitutionality, Jefferson and Randolph went beyond Madison in their denunciations, whereupon Washington asked Madison to help him write a veto message. But on reading Hamilton's rebuttal, Washington changed his view and signed.

It has been said that Madison changed from a champion of implied powers to a strict constructionist. No; he had never been a nationalist or states' righter in the usual sense; by principle and temperament he was always a centrist, neither as far right (in modern parlance) as Hamilton nor as far left as Jefferson. He was always absolutely convinced of the need in government, as in everything else, for a firm pivot or fulcrum. During this first period of the new government he leaned sometimes toward strong nationalism, sometimes toward decentralization, depending on what, at the time, needed stressing in order to redress the balance beam.

This way of working suggests that, as a classical scholar, Madison was influenced to some degree by Aristotle's *Politics* and *Nichomachean Ethics,* both of which stress the importance in all human endeavor of the golden mean.

His great anxiety, these days, was over the growing alliance between government and mercantile wealth. Whereas Hamilton believed in a governing class, Madison and Jefferson thought of the great American experiment as not exclusive but inclusive; that was its glory. Both were peace-loving men genuinely afraid that if they failed to fight Hamilton tooth and nail the country would fall prey to organized, predatory wealth. Fenno's *Gazette of the United States* was now tigerishly supporting Hamilton's scheme. Why not counter such partisanship with a rival newspaper?

As they talked it over, their feelings were heightened by two circumstances. John Beckley, Clerk of the House, had reported some overheard biting Federalist criticisms. And Thomas Paine's pamphlet *The Rights of*

Man, excoriating Britain for practicing tyranny while praising France for defending freedom, had arrived from Europe. It startled the public almost as much as his *Common Sense* in the year 1776. When it was reprinted in May, a note from Jefferson which he had not meant for publication served as an introduction. Hamiltonians—who understood on whom Jefferson had trained his guns—were infuriated by a reference therein to political heresies. Jefferson had now, willy-nilly, publicly taken sides with the ever bloodier French Revolution.

After Congress adjourned, Madison went to New York to enlist the help of his old collegemate Philip Freneau in founding the long-talked-about Republican paper to offset Fenno's anti-Republican vituperations. Earlier the State Department had offered Freneau a part-time, $250-a-year clerk's job translating foreign languages and been turned down. Perhaps, now, journalism combined with that clerkship could earn him a decent living while he helped republicanism. Freneau said yes.

In May 1791 Jefferson and Madison journeyed through New England in search of "health, recreation, and [the satisfaction of] their curiosity" about the region's flora.

Federalists would charge that they were politicking—that their horticultural studies were only a pretext for carrying on secret machinations in New York and Albany with the aim of setting up a coalition of Virginia and New York "whigs." It is a shaky theory. Since the Livingston-Clinton-Burr group in New York was anti-Hamilton, it would have been natural to seek out those three men for a discussion, but if meetings happened at all they must have been very incidental, for Jefferson was in New York only two days, and he and Madison spent only a few hours in Governor Clinton's Albany.

Their congeniality made all discussions a pleasure, and there was much to talk about. As the carriage rolled along, Madison no doubt told Jefferson how, when the Bank of the United States shares were sold in New York, he had seen the wildest speculation, gambling, and stockjobbing—it was shameful. Packets and express coaches rushed south to buy up depreciated securities. Though he had already written Jefferson about the government's "pretorian band" of crooked brokers—what "daring depravity"—he could now furnish sordid details. The two men blamed the whole wretched situation on Alexander Hamilton.

It was pleasanter to talk about L'Enfant's plan for the new capital which Washington had just shown them, or about the great westward surge of settlers. In the march of empire, covered wagons were moving over mountains and plains, boats plunging down great rivers.

In beautiful Lake George they caught salmon and speckled trout, but on Lake Champlain they were turned back by head winds. After crossing the Sound to visit Long Island's Unquachog Indians, they bought eighty maple trees (which would not survive transplanting). They were like brothers.

On their return, Jefferson stopped two days, Madison two months, in New York. Madison's long lingering in that city caused some whispering. Matchmakers said he was "fascinated" by Mrs. Colden. He reached Philadelphia in time to accompany Jefferson to Virginia. This time there was a great deal of talk about the capture of Louis XVI and Marie Antoinette as they tried to escape; Beckley's discovery that some articles which "squinted at monarchy" were not by John Adams, as supposed, but by John Quincy Adams; the sharpening of factional barbs, most of them aimed at Jefferson, but some hitting Madison; the changed atmosphere of Martha Washington's teas with plum cake. So they were now "filthy democrats"! How painful to see Federalists refusing to greet old friends of the opposite party.

After their vacations Damon and Pythias drove back to Philadelphia, taking pretty young Maria Jefferson. They stopped at Mount Vernon for a visit before driving on to George Town with the Washingtons. It was thrilling to watch the first sales of lots in the 10-mile-square District of Columbia. An acre now cost twenty times as much as the government had paid so recently.

The winter of 1791–1792 Madison wrote a series of anonymous articles for Freneau's *National Gazette*. A geometrically increasing population must in time, he said, outstrip the food supply. And he warned Americans to stand sentinel over their rights—a republic must defend liberty against power, and power against license. He observed that governments are run either by force or by corruption or—the best way—by the people's reasoned will. The invention of the last form was "the glory of America." His articles ran from January to April 1792, and the final one declared that all real friends of the Union stood for liberty, the authority of the people in a republican system. Down with public debt, usurpation, monarchy.

He was striking directly at Hamilton.

Why had he decided to deal this blow? The answer has to do with a deepening estrangement. Last month—March—Madison, on introducing a bill for better protection of the Western frontiers, had said that the decision as to the mode of raising expeditionary supplies belonged not to the Secretary of the Treasury but to the House of Representatives.

Furious, Hamilton had attacked the Congressman in a letter to their mutual friend Edward Carrington of Virginia. Madison had known well, Hamilton wrote, that if his point were won, the Secretary of the Treasury would resign. "My overthrow was anticipated. . . . Mr. Madison boldly led his troops." Hamilton went on to say that his opinion of Madison had dropped; the man's character now seemed "peculiarly artificial and complicated." Hereafter he would treat him as a political enemy. Jefferson was even worse, a man of "profound ambition and violent passions." The letter was a 6,000-word outpouring of fierce resentment.

Hearing about it, Madison had become convinced that Hamilton was bent on organizing a Federalist cabal against himself and Jefferson. By discrediting them in their native state, did Hamilton hope to destroy republicanism in the nation at large? Jefferson and Madison had conferred on the new turn of events. Would Hamilton hang himself with his own rope? He was brilliant, he was powerful. But in New York bankruptcies were increasing. And Hamilton's Treasury assistant, William Duer, promoter of the Scioto Land Company and king of speculators, had been packed off to debtor's prison. All this contributed to Madison's willingness to hit out at Hamilton in his *National Gazette* articles.

Yet one issue found all three men on the same side. They were all begging Washington not to keep his threat to retire at the end of one term. But the President was sick of the quarrels between his Secretary of the Treasury and Secretary of State. They kept the Cabinet in turmoil. Patience, counseled Madison, urging one more sacrifice. There the matter hung fire.

In September, in a resumption of his *National Gazette* articles, Madison for the first time used, publicly, the expression "Republican party." The numerically weak Anti-Republicans catering to money interests, he said, exploited any prejudice to divide Republicans. A dialogue ended this way:

> *Anti-Republican.* . . . I denounce you to the Government as an accomplice of atheism and anarchy.
> *Republican.* And I forbear to denounce you to the people, though a blasphemer of their rights and an idolator of tyranny— Liberty disdains to persecute.

Meanwhile Hamilton, using different pseudonyms, had launched a vituperative newspaper campaign against Jefferson in Fenno's *Gazette*. His underlying motivation seems to have been confessed in a half-crossed-out section of a never-published article found later among his papers: "Mr. Jefferson fears in Mr. Hamilton a formidable rival in the competition for the presidential chair at a future period" and thus thought it necessary to get rid of "the more popular Secretary of the Treasury."

After reading Hamilton's calumnies, Madison rode to Monticello, where he, Jefferson, and Monroe decided on a proper retort. The opening article would quote some of Jefferson's letters to Madison from Paris.

Jefferson himself delivered that first article to the *American Daily Advertiser* in Philadelphia before sending Washington a disavowal written in simulated bewilderment. On arriving in town, he said, he had found excerpts from his letters in the newspapers. Presumably they had been submitted by the "gentleman possessed of the originals." Nothing had been told him in advance, and his copies were still under lock and key.

This seems, among other things, disingenuous.

Hamilton—under his indefatigable aliases—fell to printing self-serving, mutilated extracts from Jefferson's letters to himself. The quarrel was growing rough.

As gauge of Madison's status at this time, here is an estimate of him by Fisher Ames, his adversary in the House, written after Washington's reelection: "Virginia moves in a solid column, and the discipline of the party is as severe as the Prussian. Deserters are not spared. Madison has become a desperate party leader. . . ." Though exaggerated, it is a tribute of sorts.

In December 1792 there came news of the storming of the Tuileries. France was now a republic. James "Adisson," like "Jean Hamilton" and "George Masingthon," received notices that the French National Assembly had made him an honorary citizen. Unlike the other two, Madison accepted. France was a sister republic. How do otherwise? Not that he approved of the pro-French hysteria. It was too extreme.

For three months storms kept out all ships. Then in April America heard that the Paris Commune had lopped off the heads of the King and Queen and many royalists before declaring war on Great Britain.

The ensuing war finished polarizing the United States. The political parties caused by domestic controversies, such as that over the national bank, now focused on foreign affairs. Thousands took one side or the other, often violently. The Federalists, strong in the commercial, sea-smelling Northeast, stuck with Britain; the Democrat-Republicans, who were especially strong in the agrarian South, stuck with France.

Jefferson, to whom the French Revolution was a sacred cause, grew vehemently partisan. Others without his five years in Paris and friendship with French revolutionaries like Lafayette became equally Francophile and cheered when France shucked off her king. If there were bloody massacres in France, ran the reasoning, well, they were temporary; the ideals of the Revolution were still spendid: liberty, equality, fraternity. Madison tended to feel this way too.

On Britain's side were some Americans who, right through the Revolution, had remained Tories at heart; also some Northeastern shipbuilders and traders who, with Dutch credit now cut off, looked to England for loans; and people who, having backed Hamilton on redemption, assumption, and a national bank, now followed his leadership more or less blindly.

From his Princeton days Madison had been a passionate believer in republicanism. Though revolutionary excesses repelled him, they could not change his basic allegiance. He was strongly against a stratified society, and though he greatly admired certain aspects of the British government (no one knew better than he what the American Constitution owed to it), a monarchy with a privileged class was anathema.

The crucial question was this: What position should the United States take toward the war in Europe? The treaty of 1778 made America an ally of France, duty-bound to defend the French West Indies. But how defend them without a navy? Hamilton argued for a declaration of neutrality on the ground that the French King's death released America from its treaty, while Jefferson protested that such a repudiation and reversal would be a great unmerited gift to England; France was still France—*no!* Madison agreed.

On April 22, 1793, Washington's proclamation of neutrality committed the United States to a "conduct friendly and impartial." Madison was taken aback. "It wounds the national honour. . . ."

Meanwhile Citizen Edmond Genêt, minister plenipotentiary from the Paris Commune, had arrived in Charleston. Without bothering to present his credentials to the President, he proceeded to privateer from American ports; he gave Americans French commissions, recruited troops to conquer Florida and Louisiana, and cockily organized Jacobin Clubs. When Hamilton refused to advance installments on America's war debts, Genêt, furious, rode north to put the government in its place. It was a triumphal progress. But Jefferson and Madison had frozen with revulsion—the idiot would "sink the Republican interest"! They were relieved when Washington requested Genêt's recall. Robespierre agreed to trade Gouverneur

Morris. (Preferring to keep his head, Genêt never sailed. Instead he married the daughter of Governor Clinton of New York and settled down to farm.)

Sick of the two parties' poisoned political atmosphere, Jefferson resolved to go home to his daughters, new granddaughter, and the joys of farming. Washington, who despaired of replacing his two gifted quarrelers, begged Jefferson to stay on until January, when Hamilton too would be resigning from the Cabinet. It was agreed, and all three left on vacation.

But soon Jefferson was writing Madison in alarm about some Hamiltonian articles signed "Pacificus." "For God's sake, my dear sir," he begged, "take up your pen . . . and cut him to pieces. . . ." As "Helvidius," Madison assumed the "most grating" task of his life.

In the fall of 1793 Philadelphia was struck by an epidemic of yellow fever. Thousands died. This reign of terror stopped business and disrupted Congress. Jefferson wrote Madison—held at Montpelier by the critical illness of his brother Ambrose—about inhabitants flying from scenes of horror, but he somewhat clouded his very real bravery with an ungenerosity bred of intense political animosity. "Hamilton is ill of the fever, as is said; he had two physicians . . . ; his family thinks him in danger, and he puts himself so by his excessive alarm. . . . A man as timid as he is on water, as timid on horseback, as timid in sickness, would be a phenomenon if the courage of which he had the reputation in military matters were genuine"—this though Hamilton's valor in and out of war was unimpeachable.

In October Madison, grieved by Ambrose's death, set off on horseback to meet Monroe in Fredericksburg, where they bought an antiquated carriage which they hoped, against all probability, would last out their trip to Philadelphia.

That autumn of 1793 Britain issued a brutal Order in Council: she would seize all neutral ships taking provisions to French colonies or bringing back Caribbean products. Owing to the high rewards offered for merchant prizes, this directive was soon being carried out with a vengeance. Yankee brigs and schooners were caught, condemned, and stripped to their gunwales, and their seamen forced into the British Navy. The burden of proof that they were not carrying contraband fell on the skippers, who never won.

Even Federalist shipowners and traders fumed over such injustice, and disenchantment with Britain increased when she announced that she was keeping the Western forts which she had agreed to give up. The

United States laid a thirty-day retaliatory embargo and talked seriously about war. Indeed, Hamilton's pro-British party might have foundered and gone under at this time but for strong counterirritants. The Terror under Danton and Marat was alienating many Francophiles, and Thomas Paine's just published pro-French *Age of Reason* brought an angry reaction by attacking the Bible. Thus each political party stood more or less firm in its allegiances.

When Jefferson resigned at the end of the year, Edmund Randolph succeeded him—with Madison's approval—as Secretary of State, and Madison's college friend William Bradford replaced Randolph as Attorney General. To what extent, if at all, Bradford's federalism had alienated him from Madison is not known. In any case Hamilton, freed of Jefferson, changed his mind about resigning, and his influence over the President markedly increased. Indeed, Washington, who had sincerely tried to stay above party differences, was now widely accounted a Federalist.

Madison had long advocated reciprocal trade rules. If a nation had no commercial treaty with the United States, raise its tonnage tax, he said, and if it made port restrictions, retaliate in kind. Such ideas of equity were embodied in "Mr. Madison's Resolutions" as presented to the House early in January 1794. During the debate which followed he declared that the free trade he believed in would require global freedom. Britain bought far less than what she sold to the United States, whereas France bought seven times as much; the imbalance counseled a policy of tit for tat. War with Britain? Nonsense, he said. It would result only if Britain had predetermined it all along.

In Congress Madison was as quiet as the eye of a tornado: moving but unmoved. Jefferson had packed up and gone home. Some Republicans asked forlornly or indignantly why he had resigned just when the situation worsened and left Hamilton to increase his influence over the President. Madison was too loyal for reproaches; he just missed his friend and more than ever felt the loneliness of his bachelorhood.

Politically, senators like James Monroe and Aaron Burr and representatives like Giles and Page stood with Madison shoulder to shoulder. Still, partywise, Madison was doing double duty. Sometimes he spoke all day on the floor of the House of Representatives. Make it to Britain's interest to be just, he pleaded. One of his Resolutions passed, but the vote on the others was postponed. Federalists used the setback to pillory him. Short, dignified, good-looking, and brilliant, this carrier of a banner stubbornly stood his ground.

The thirty-day embargo was replaced by a nonimportation act which made Britain suspend her hated Order in Council. Hamilton (hoping he himself would be tapped) persuaded Washington to send Britain a minister extraordinary to negotiate, among other things, ship and trade agreements. Washington pondered the appointment. Hamilton? Jefferson? Madison? Jay? He settled on Chief Justice John Jay.

The appointment of this arch-Federalist filled Madison with acute foreboding.

He was now working on *Political Observations,* a 10,000-word pamphlet defending his recent Resolutions. The way Federalists kept invoking Washington's name, he said, aroused "suspicion that those who drew most heavily on that fund were hastening fastest to bankruptcy of their own." He was polishing his text when he heard that the President was hoping to make him Minister to France. The answer must be thanks but no.

He made the decision about the time a young Quaker widow named Dolley Payne Todd wrote her friend Elizabeth Collins a slightly frantic note:

> Thou must come to me. Aaron Burr says that the great little Madison has asked to be brought to see me this evening.

THAT WAS TWO YEARS AGO—and for a year and a half Madison and his wife had been growing ever closer. Now as the winter of 1796 wore on and they waited for the constitutional crisis caused by Jay's Treaty to break wide open, Dolley was a constant source of strength.

On March 3, 1796, the President sent the House—tardily, for its information only—Jay's Treaty as ratified by himself and the Senate. An able new member, Edward Livingston, immediately moved that the House ask for Jay's instructions and reports. The motion passed overwhelmingly. Did not the House have a right to judge any treaty overlapping its legislative duties? No! shouted Federalists. The House had no treaty power; it could not repeal, only accept. The debate waxed hotter. Federalists were saying in effect, Open the purse strings. Republicans were answering that by regulating trade the treaty encroached upon the House's constitutional powers; therefore the House could reject it and withhold implementation. How else could the people's *direct* representatives (senators being then appointed by state legislatures) protect the people's interests?

On the fourth day of a stormy debate James Madison rose. Yes, taken literally, he conceded, legislative and treaty-making powers clashed. But

Congress had many nonlegislative functions. It regulated commerce, borrowed money, raised armies, and declared war—all of which were involved in treaty making. He outlined several ways to construe the relationship. To him the least plausible was to consider the Senate's treaty power total and uncurbable. He believed that in all legislative matters Congress's two powers were—must be—cooperative. Only this interpretation made good sense. The House was no rubber stamp; it had right of sanction. How could it be otherwise in a government of checks and balances? Jay's Treaty had the effect of legislation. It would take the whole Congress to endorse it.

But Washington—as Hamilton advised—refused to give the House the treaty papers, the implication being that it was grabbing for power. Madison suspected that the harsh answer was Hamilton's, that the President was little more than a mouthpiece.

The House reacted violently. True, the treaty-making power was vested in the President and the Senate, but the *lawmaking* prerogative belonged equally to the Senate and the House. By a vote of 57 to 35 the House roundly asserted its right to reject. The only question was whether or not it would exercise that right.

They were harking back to *The Federalist*—to Number 58.

The controversy raged through April. Madison and new Congressman Albert Gallatin (a former senator), having analyzed the situation with brilliant clarity, declared the treaty bad from start to finish. There was no reciprocity, Madison said; worst of all was the treaty's assault on neutral rights. The President had declared that seizing American ships and stealing American sailors violated the nation's declared neutrality. Then how could the nation accept a treaty *licensing* those practices? How accept commercial vassalage? Reject the treaty! Seek more tolerable terms! Nonsense, no war would result. Britain had enough trouble on her hands without attacking her best customer.

Logically, Madison's lucid analysis and passionate plea were unassailable. The slight man with the formidable brain seemed to be carrying all before him. Old political hands prophesied a victory by twenty votes.

Under the stress of controversy Fisher Ames became rudely personal. Madison was "devoid of sincerity and fairness"; he had disgraced himself (Hamilton's tack). He and his colleagues were soiling the nation's honor, inciting war, insulting the President.

Rising, Gallatin poured scorn on the imagined dangers and exaggerated fears which had begotten the monstrous, indefensible treaty now being defended.

But bankers and merchants fought back by every available means. They circularized the nation, worked assiduously and cunningly on influential people, petitioned, and were "sounding the tocsin for foreign wars and domestic convulsions." As a result, some Republicans began to wobble.

Fisher Ames's dramatic—melodramatic—final speech was deadly. He rang the changes on the horrendous consequences of rejecting the treaty; he foresaw attacks from mighty Great Britain accompanied by teeming hordes of red Indians—"we light the savage fires, we bind the victims. . . ." Could a young nation survive such turmoil? No!

This exercise in demagoguery finished crumbling the opposition. A money bill supporting Jay's Treaty passed the House by a narrow margin: 51 to 48.

Madison stared at the debris of an edifice he had worked long and hard to build up. A debacle. "Before some were ripe for the arrangements," he wrote Monroe, "others were rotten." What burned him most was the setback for right principles and the people. It was wormwood and gall. "The progress of this business throughout," he wrote Jefferson in disgust, "has been to me the most worrying and vexatious that I ever encountered, and the more so as the causes lay in the unsteadiness, the follies, the perverseness, and the defections among our friends more than in the strength or dexterity or malice of our opponents." Would the political wounds ever heal?

The Madisonian party lost the May elections, and in Congress Madison could no longer be called Majority Leader. Moreover, as he had predicted, France, seeing that Jay's Treaty discriminated against her and that the United States was now practically allied with Great Britain, turned bitterly hostile. Madison mourned that a crisis which should have strengthened republicanism had weakened it.

In his desert of failed hopes, Dolley was an oasis. She understood perfectly his decision to get out of politics. After their summer vacation at Montpelier he would come back to Washington for a lame-duck session, then at the close of his fourth two-year term, quit the House of Representatives permanently, irrevocably. How beautiful to spend the rest of his life farming!

Not that he was reconciled to seeing Alexander Hamilton's pro-British ideas triumph. God forbid. But just as he had done yeoman duty while Jefferson retired, now Jefferson could get himself elected President or Vice President and take responsibility—stand duty—while *he* retired.

He was pushing hard, in every way he could, for Jefferson's nomination for President, and had the faith to believe that by the time Jefferson had to retire permanently, other and younger friends of France and defenders of republicanism would have been raised up. He did not ask Jefferson if he wanted the nomination for fear he would echo Washington's "I would rather work for my bread with a spade."

The Federalists ran John Adams for President and Thomas Pinckney for Vice President; the Republicans, Jefferson and Burr. When Jefferson demurred, mentioning Madison's fine grasp of the philosophy of government, the retiring Congressman who had done so much to strengthen the Republican party talked about the wonderful drawing power of Jefferson.

That summer the Madisons crossed the Susquehanna at Havre de Grace en route to Montpelier. If Payne was naughty, they could bribe him with a pony; if Anna missed the riding parties, musicales, and other frolics of the Sally McKean set, they could talk about Orange dances and barbecues. Rain, dust, jouncing, "creepers" in crowded inns—nothing cast them down; they had an appointment with their high ground. At George Town—across Rock Creek—they saw a few streets of the future capital. Most of the District of Columbia was a wilderness of azaleas.

At Montpelier they saw old friends, sights, and customs. Again Dolley walked to the garden in a big straw hat and James puttered at his hobby of cabinetmaking. He became once again his sciatica-ridden father's strong right arm. As usual he looked to red clover to replace the soil's leached minerals. Finding no clover seed, he tried timothy and was delighted with the results. When he came home tired, Dolley met him at the door with a cool drink, and he was sure he lived better than a king. How fine that he had refused to seek or accept reelection to Congress.

But he was not without interest in political news. An American vessel had been seized by a French privateer—bad business; Washington was recalling Monroe from Paris—bad; the tide of preelection bitterness was washing higher—regrettable. Able to stand back and see the field as a whole, he knew that good men could differ as to what dangers threatened and the best way to avoid them. Undoubtedly Washington, too, desired, a unified nation; they just disagreed about the way to achieve it, and about Alexander Hamilton. Meanwhile, both parties were charging treason; each declaring that if the other won, the country would sink: chaos-come-again.

A deputation came to Montpelier to urge Madison to accept unanimous election as Governor of Virginia. No, he said, nothing must stand in the way of complete retirement next spring, of a life given over to farming, books, and more time with the sweetest wife in the world. It was Dolley's nature to be happy. He hoped to make her happier.

Late in September Madison received a newspaper copy of Washington's Farewell Address. Four years ago he himself had written a 1,200-word draft. Though Hamilton had done some reshaping, that draft was still recognizable in the first twelve paragraphs. To them Hamilton had attached some of Washington's ideas and a great many of his own; Madison recognized his fine West Indian hand. That the President's mind could have been "wrought up" (as Madison put it) to voice the party politics therein came as a shock. Republicans must keep their heads while resting upon their oars.

Madison stayed on the fringes of the election while John Beckley managed the Republican campaign from Philadelphia. Hamilton was so angry about losing the Federalist nomination to John Adams (who was more popular with the people) he was secretly pulling strings to get Pinckney elected President—Pinckney because he would be more pliable than Adams. The Secretary of the Treasury was risking his prestige in an effort to manipulate the electoral college. As for Jefferson's chances, Madison knew his friend might win first place, second place, or no place at all. *Was* it the best system to have each elector cast votes for two candidates, the man with the second largest total becoming Vice President? (That system would be scrapped later.) Thinking about possibilities, Madison advised Jefferson that, if he got only the second spot, he should seize the opportunity to go back to Philadelphia and work for their mutual ideals. They couldn't forget the good of the country; they couldn't just give up.

Hamilton! Madison loathed the man's notion that people could be moved only by selfish interests or external force. Was his inability to understand republicanism the result of his having had no part in America's two centuries of frontier life? And was he hoping for some crisis (war with France? civil war?) that he could twist to his own wrong purpose? He was brilliant—no question—and his financial measures, though they certainly fostered speculation, had proved successful; and, of course, the triumph of Jay's Treaty was largely his. But, please God, Jefferson would be elected President, and Hamilton's oligarchic schemes be trodden down.

When James, Dolley, Payne, Anna, and James's sister Fanny rode into Philadelphia over frozen mud, in November 1796, there was a bad housing shortage. They stored some furniture, including the brine-soaked pieces Monroe had shipped from Paris, and stuffed themselves into a bandbox. With crucial vote counting going on, such inconveniences seemed trivial.

Adams was elected President; Jefferson, Vice President.

When the latter wrote to congratulate the former, he sandwiched in some remarks which Madison—when asked for his opinion—vetoed. No, Jefferson shouldn't say he was happy to leave to others the "sublime delights of riding in the storm"; better "sound sleep and a warm berth below." How would that sound to supporters?

During the final weeks before his retirement from the House, Madison sponsored a bill for the establishment of a national university. Washington pledged some of his Potomac Canal stock. It was their last cooperation. But the bill failed 37 to 36.

Madison felt that for some time he had been sliding downhill. Around the major disaster of failing to cancel Jay's Treaty clustered other defeats. The Federalists were riding high in the saddle, and many citizens, recognizing a virtual alliance with Britain, expected war with France. Wasn't it for this that Hamilton wanted to build up the army? Washington would almost certainly, before quitting office, receive the push required to "screw [him] up" to declaring war.

Then it was rumored that the new President's first act would be to send three peace envoys to France and that Hamilton, seeing Adams's determination, had advised the appointment of Cabot, Pinckney, and (to please the French) Madison—"yet I would not trust him alone lest his Gallicism work amiss."

Madison denied Gallicism. Yes, he admired the precision of many French minds, and liked such Frenchmen as Lafayette and Marbois and believed that their instinct for freedom made them brothers. How wonderful that shout in the Assembly: "The declaration of rights is the constitution of the world!" In spite of the Reign of Terror, he still believed that France's essential sanity would win out. But "Gallicist," "Francophile," "Anglophobe"—he refused such epithets. British blood flowed in his veins, and no one appreciated more than he the evolution of the British parliamentary system. But right now Great Britain was treating the United States most unjustly. To a proud nation it was an insult. American shopkeepers and speculators, afraid of economic harm from the French Revolution, were joining die-hard Tories? Not many. Madison believed that most Americans knew where the values lay.

The Madisons attended John Adams's inauguration in the Senate

Chamber. There stood the stocky new President in his pearl-grey suit; there the formidable ex-President in black velvet; there, behind Washington, loose-jointed Jefferson in a bright blue coat worn over a crimson vest.

Later, in front of the Indian Queen, where he had gone to pay his respects to his successor, General Washington stood looking at the "immense crowd" which had followed him, and "no man ever saw him so deeply moved." The Madisons were also greatly affected; old attachments were not easily broken.

When the Washingtons had left town in their cream-colored coach drawn by six blooded mares, Madison gave his reply to President Adams about the peace envoy appointment. No, unfortunately he could not undertake a sea voyage. It might stir up an old malady. Moreover, he had an obligation to stay within call of his aging parents, and did earnestly wish to retire. Adams was relieved. Offering Madison the post had stirred up a hornet's nest. "Are we forever going to be overawed and directed by party passions?" he had asked the new Cabinet. Secretary of the Treasury Wolcott had answered for all: "Mr. President, we are ready to resign."

The Madisons were packing for good. At last the wind had dried the road bogs; nailrods, clover seed, eighteen chairs, and sixteen pieces of luggage had been shipped by water; and Mordecai Collins was in town with extra horses for hauling furniture. James and Dolley planned a roundabout return to Montpelier. They would take six weeks to go by way of Harper's Ferry, Warm Springs, Harewood, and Belle Grove (the fine house which Major Hite and Nelly had had on the drawing boards when James and Dolley honeymooned at Old Hall two and a half years ago). A sentimental journey.

James Madison drove toward Harper's Ferry a free man, happy in his private life but not happy about the way his public career was ending. Twenty-one years of public service—three of Shakespeare's famous sevens—yet what was the upshot? Defeat.

After his first public office he had had the setback of not being reelected to the Virginia Assembly, but almost at once there had come the appointment to the Governor's Privy Council, and for two decades a straight run of good fortune. He had been a power in the Continental Congress, the chief actor in the Constitutional Convention, a vital contributor to *The Federalist,* the lodestar of the Virginia Ratification Convention, and (in spite of Patrick Henry) for eight years the Republican leader in the House of Representatives, with some trouble from Hamilton and Ames, but nothing crucial until Jay's Treaty.

That sudden failure. It was not that his whole career had collapsed.

He had not gone to the wall, been utterly beaten, and lost everything. But in an effort to protect the country he loved from dark consequences he had been rebuffed. Given his concern, code of honor, and sensitivity, he could not but feel it greatly. Though he had never been a credit seeker, he did not enjoy personal discredit. Rebuffed, unhorsed. Never had he worked harder than to destroy Jay's Treaty. The House had been with him; then the House—or too much of it—had deserted him. The Federalists had seized the initiative. Now, a year after the disaster, party warfare had increased. He just hoped—as he left Congress forever—that he could get the taste of failure out of his mouth.

Dolley did not agree that he had failed in connection with Jay's Treaty or anything else. She saw him as having given the last drop of his blood. In her eyes he was a man morally triumphant—the only real greatness. Having him she lacked nothing except his child.

❧ VI ❧

TIRELESS
RETIREMENT

THE MADISONS REACHED MONTPELIER in time to see the white notched petals of the dogwood. This was a different kind of homecoming. It is one thing to visit, quite another to bring all one's possessions with the intention of staying.

They began almost at once to make and collect such building materials as boards, beams, bricks, nails, and lime for cement. The present eight-room house, supplemented by outbuildings, was to be enlarged by a row of smaller rooms along the back and dressed up with a handsome Doric portico.

In the midst of a great bustle they received startling, yet not wholly unexpected news. Indignant over the United States' permissive policy toward Great Britain, the French Directory had issued stern rules for the seizing of American ships, and already President Adams had delivered a warlike message to Congress. Madison blamed the peril directly on Jay's Treaty.

Vice President Jefferson wrote him about the victories of "that extraordinary man Bonaparte," whom he expected to help the United States by securing, by force of arms, a European peace. Madison had his doubts. At church his Episcopalians were praying God to grant the President of the United States wisdom and strength to know and to do His will, but Madison thought President Adams should help God help the country by using a little common sense.

Actually John Adams was slowly altering his federalism. Hamilton's scheming to elect Pinckney by maneuvering the electoral college had

142

soured him. It threw Jefferson's fairer dealing into high relief and brought closer two long-estranged friends. Hearing about the rapprochement, Madison hoped Jefferson could act as a brake on the passionate, vain but honest old patriot who was now President.

But when on July 11 Jefferson stopped off at Montpelier, he shook his head. Nothing and no one, he declared, could cure John Adams of the folly of his pride. Though the President had the prestige of a great career and less belligerence than his Cabinet (really Hamilton's) and though he often displayed sound judgment, how the man preened! How he doted on the trappings of monarchy! Disgusting.

While Jefferson and Madison talked about farming, architecture, science, philosophy, always there loomed this question: How could they save the republican principles for which they had both fought long and hard? When Jefferson left Madison this time (his account book says, "Mr. Madison's valet .25"), the problem traveled with one and stayed with the other.

Strangely, Jefferson had not told Madison about the uproar over a letter to Philip Mazzei, the Albemarle neighbor who, during the Revolution, had been sent to Tuscany to borrow money for the State. Translation from English into Italian, then into French and back into English, had warped the meaning. Jefferson had written Mazzei that an Anglo-monarchical party including the executive and judiciary branches of the government, and most of the legislative branch, having bartered liberty for the discarded *forms* of the British monarchy, now desired its *substance*. "It would give you a fever were I to name to you the apostates who have gone over to these heresies, men who were Samsons in the field and Solomons in the council, but who have had their heads shorn by the harlot England." By changing "forms" (such things as a pompous inauguration, levees, and celebration of the President's birthday) to "form" (meaning plan of government), the translator had twisted the letter to an entirely different meaning. Jefferson now asked Madison by post how he could explain this distortion publicly. Wouldn't it offend George Washington who had inaugurated these alien *forms*?

Though Monroe had advised avowal and defense, Madison disagreed. Any reply might breed fresh dilemmas. Inevitably, multitudes would rally to Washington's support; Jefferson stood to lose more than he could gain. And there the matter rested.

The dog days came, and when the elder Madisons went off to Healing Springs, James and Dolley again took charge. Afterward they had their fling. They went off to visit Monticello, Enniscorthy, and some

Goochland and Hanover kin, returning in the splendor of October for a second visit with Jefferson. It was good to get home. But by December they were again in Richmond. Rough roads did not deter; the Madisons could take a battering.

As the months passed, six-year-old Payne seemed to be showing more willfulness. Where was that needed brother or sister? Lucy Washington had a son now; the dying Francis Madison had left a brood of nine children; and the William Madisons and Thomas Macons were busy procreating. One day James and Dolley went to see the Macons' fourth son crowing in his cradle. Were the springs of life, for them, locked? They had been married three years.

In retirement Madison found that his emancipation from politics was less than complete. Still concerned with the problem of how to save constitutional government, he carried on a large political correspondence. Military preparations struck him as ominous. For war with America's old comrade-in-arms, France?

Montpelier's country Christmas seemed nicer than Christmases in Philadelphia. Whereas Dolley's Quakers omitted the holiday as "heathen," Madison's family made a great to-do. Payne's eyes shone like bayberry candles. The fact that Dr. Robert H. Rose was courting Fanny added excitement.

Their wedding took place at Montpelier. Then the twenty-two-year-old bride was driven off to her husband's 900-acre plantation, Buffalo Meadows. The house was quieter. All the Squire's children had married.

Workmen were stuffing the four wooden cases for the portico pillars with brick and cement. But when the mixture set, how hoist them upright? They were heavy—as heavy as the news that France, refused equal treatment, was seizing it by unauthorized (in contrast to Britain's "authorized") plunderings on the high seas.

Madison thought over the three ways the United States could counter the threat: keep off the Atlantic, declare war, or (a compromise) fight back by arming and convoying merchant ships. The last way was current policy. To what sinkhole, asked Madison in anger, had John Jay, Hamilton, Pickering, and Wolcott consigned the nation? As for President Adams, he was a "perfect Quixote."

But many of the Madisons' contacts were warmly human. For instance, in February James, recalling the failure of last year's crop, sent Monroe two bushels of potatoes to "furnish the seed for your garden" at Highlands. "Mrs. Madison insists on adding for Mrs. Monroe a few pickles and preserves, with half a dozen bottles of gooseberries and a bag of dried cherries. . . . We both wish we could substitute something more worthy of acceptance."

The spring of 1798 was loud with hammers and saws. Negroes were trundling wheelbarrows, nailing laths, mixing mortar. Acting as his own architect, Madison drew, measured, planned strategies, directed slaves, totted up costs.

Seeing the results, Minister Augustus Foster would marvel. "Mr. Madison himself superintended the building, which he had executed by the hands of common workmen to whom he prescribed the proportions. . . . Good and massive Doric . . . executed by a proprietor without the assistance of an architect, and of very ordinary materials."

It was characteristic of Madison that he chose the plainest of the three great Greek styles. By the time new leaves unfurled their little flags, the pillars were almost ready to be launched into place. Madison asked Jefferson please to send him from Philadelphia 190 French windowpanes and eight brass door hinges.

That April Ambrose's widow Frances died of tuberculosis, leaving a daughter, Nelly. Montpelier opened its arms to the lonely young girl. She would fill the vacancy left by Fanny.

Within three short months the homestead had seen a marriage and a death. No birth, unless one counted the spring.

A mail pouch brought news that the Federalists had pushed bills through Congress to deport suspect foreigners and gag the press: the Alien and Sedition Acts. But freedom of the press was basic to republicanism and its ultimate safeguard, cried Madison. Before copying Robespierre, the Tories should remember the briefness of his triumph and his permanent infamy. Also a half-war with France had begun. How else interpret a law for the capture of French privateers and, while feeding Britain, the starving out of France's dominions?

And what was this monstrous land tax coming just when the power to pay had been destroyed? Old John Adams was a calamity. "He is verifying completely," Madison wrote Jefferson, "the last feature in the character drawn of him by Dr. F[ranklin], however his title may stand for the two first, 'Always an honest man, often a wise one, but sometimes wholly out of his senses.'"

Worse, Adams's hand was being strengthened against France by the "XYZ scandal." Agents of Talleyrand had tried to squeeze a $250,000 bribe out of some American envoys. A cynical, wicked, stupid business, groaned Madison. Couldn't the French fox see that such tricks only widened the breach between the two nations?

That summer Adams's Sedition Act was put to use. Instead of prosecuting Hamilton for sedition, as it had cause to do, the Administration imprisoned a democratic Congressman for charging the President—in a letter written before the act—with greed, thirst for adulation, and a grasping for power. Reading about the trial, Jefferson and Madison decided that the Federalists were plotting to destroy the Republican party in the elections of 1798 and 1800. Already they were terrorizing newspapers. At any cost they must be thwarted.

With such thoughts, Madison went about his farm duties. Down in the Walnut Grove, he wrote his parents at Healing Springs, Simon was complaining, Ralph recovering from dysentery, Joseph worsening.

The next time Jefferson stopped by Montpelier, he and Madison planned some Resolutions against the Alien and Sedition Acts, to be introduced in state legislatures with no names attached: their reply to the Federalist drive toward monolithic power. They worked out no details, simply agreed on the principle that it was a state's duty to oppose any unconstitutional federal law. A gauntlet was being picked up. If they could not fight from center, they would fight from periphery. In spite of his plan to stay out of politics, Madison felt bound to fight. The future of the nation was at stake. An October visit to Monticello strengthened the entente.

There he read a rough draft of Jefferson's Resolutions, earmarked for the Kentucky Legislature. Wilson C. Nicholas of Warren had shown a copy to a visitor, John Breckenridge, who had promptly nominated his state for the honor of presentation. From the beginning Madison's Resolutions had been intended for the Virginia Assembly.

Meanwhile Madison's carpenters were trying to hoist the Doric pillars into position: a superhuman job. They failed, and he sent to Monticello for a skilled stonefitter.

In the fall by-elections—thanks to the XYZ affair—his "French Party" lost more ground to the "British Party." It was another warning that republicanism stood in jeopardy. The situation looked so grim, Madison was deeply troubled. The Kentucky and Virginia Resolutions seemed more than ever necessary. So in December he took Dolley and made a whirlwind trip to Hanover to arrange for Cousin John Taylor of Caroline to present his Resolutions (already endorsed by a Republican caucus) to the Virginia Assembly.

Later, Madison received word that on December 24 his anonymous Resolutions had passed the Assembly by a vote of 100 to 63. It was a kind of Christmas present.

After pledging to defend the Constitution and uphold the Union, the Resolutions declared that the powers of the federal government were limited by the compact which created them. If other powers were usurped, the states were duty-bound to "interpose for arresting the progress of the evil," that is, to express their objections in an effort to rouse public opinion. Specifically the Resolutions protested the Alien and Sedition Acts. No such powers had been delegated, ran Madison's argument. The acts subverted principles of free government; in fact, the Sedition Act claimed a power which the·Constitution expressly forbade. Virginia urged other states to join her in declaring the acts unconstitutional and to help preserve the "authorities, rights and liberties reserved to the states respectively, or to the people."

The Kentucky Resolutions were more radical. It is no small difference that whereas Madison's held that to correct federal infringements the *legislature* had a right to assert the power of the *states as a group,* Jefferson's declared that *each state could unilaterally judge both infraction and mode of redress;* in other words, each state could declare a federal law null and void. Before he knew that Virginia had adopted his Resolutions, Madison had written Jefferson anxiously about this dangerous gap between their two conceptions. "Have you ever considered thoroughly the distinction between the power of the *state* and that of the *legislature* on questions related to the federal pact? On the supposition that the former is clearly the ultimate judge of infractions, it does not follow that the latter is the legitimate organ, especially as a convention was the organ by which the compact was made." His question: Shouldn't the Assembly, while protesting usurpation, avoid a charge of usurpation on its own part?

This is an example of how, on certain kinds of issues, as Adrienne Koch says in her able *Jefferson and Madison: The Great Collaboration,* Madison's logic "cut deeper . . . than Jefferson's did."

Whatever their differences, the two friends struck hard against the Adams administration. But the other States would refuse endorsement, and there was some sharp criticism.

Hamilton called for action against the mad Southerners. The United States should station a federal justice of the peace in every county, he declared, keep its army on a permanent war footing, and pass a law making libelous criticism of a federal officer seditious; in other words, *teach* those democrats.

Such counterblows glanced off. Jefferson was soon writing Madison happily that more and more citizens showed signs of preferring reason to disgusting blackguardism. He urged his friend to promote the republican cause with weekly articles. (Why he did not take on the chore himself is not clear.)

Six friends put pressure on Madison to come back to the Virginia Assembly, stressing a crying, enormous need (as if he did not know) for wise measures while state republicanism girded for the fray. Patrick Henry, erstwhile arch-democrat now supporting the Alien and Sedition Acts, was out to discredit the Virginia and Kentucky Resolutions. George Washington (of all people) was pushing Henry for the Assembly. "Consider that Virginia is the hope of Republicans throughout the Union," John Taylor of Caroline wrote Madison. " . . . If you will not save yourself or your friends—yet save your country."

It was a powerful plea. The situation was so raw, certain hounded Southern Republicans seemed to stand in physical danger. Madison pondered. Reentry into the political life he had renounced—reentry on the state level—would be a sacrifice. For a clean conscience he would pay the high price of losing a pleasant country retreat with Dolley. But how could he refuse? How be indifferent when the greatest experiment on earth in free government was faltering and in peril? When he talked it over with Dolley she understood that he must do what he must do. He agreed to stand for election to the Virginia Assembly.

Meanwhile Payne, now an attractive child going on seven, was running all over the farm. He loved to fool around the Grove with the black people and to play tricks. When he was difficult, Dolley tried, but not very hard, to discipline him. She made excuses. He was so little. She and James had been married four and a half years—were they never to have a child? Lucy had borne a second son (the first died), Samuel Walter Washington, and all over the nation women were conceiving. Well, give her and Payne's Papa a little more time.

Madison was almost equally proud of Payne. One can take the measure of his attitude in the fragment by Mary Kunkel already mentioned, which goes on to speak about the "unadulterated love" which not only the doting mother but also "this father" exhibited all during Payne's childhood in "every act and service of parental guidance."

That spring of 1799, while plows were turning up Montpelier's red soil, Madison gave away Dolley's youngest sister in marriage to Congressman J. G. Jackson, twenty-five and considered a catch. Mother Molly, young John, Lucy, and George drove over from Harewood for the grand occasion, and there was talk and laughter and sense of beginnings.

A graver note soon sounded. Madison and Jefferson had agreed that in Virginia's democratic struggle the chief antagonist was now Patrick

Henry, more eloquence than brains. True, he had turned down high positions: senator, Secretary of State, Chief Justice, envoy to France. But in their view he was still a barefaced opportunist, tacking with the wind. For the sake of principle, he must be challenged to a showdown.

Suddenly, on June 6, 1799, at sixty-three, Henry died at Red Hill, and Jefferson and Madison, so lately arming to fight what they considered his baneful influence, fell to recalling how, thirty-five years ago, his spirited resistance to the Stamp Act had electrified the House of Burgesses—"Give me liberty or give me death!" For a time they forgot that he had opposed the Constitution as a threat to republican liberties, then inconsistently supported those real threats to liberties, the Alien and Sedition Acts. For a time they forgot that at his death he was trying to do in the Virginia Resolutions which defended the states' rights which he had once, with flaming gorgeous rhetoric, defended. This backtracking idol of the people with a powerful, delightful Celtic tongue in his head had served five times as Governor of Virginia—five. Better to recall his strengths, his talents. In Dolley the death of this first-cousin-once-removed stirred personal memories. Up to the age of ten she had visited Henry and his family at Scotchtown, the estate which had become her home. Now all three—Jefferson, Madison, Dolley—sat stunned. It seemed impossible that the great firebrand had been doused. But every democrat in the State was walking more confidently.

That summer Montpelier's 60-foot portico finally got its four columns. There they stood tall and straight. Walking down the drive, James and Dolley turned to look back, astonished and pleased, at their noble Doric façade. James Madison, classicist, now owned a bit of Greece—the Greece of Socrates whose prayer in the *Phaedrus* he well understood: "Give me beauty in the inward soul, and may the outward and inward man be at one."

When it rained they took their daily exercise on the portico by running races or walking a patrol. If they crisscrossed the porch enough times, they walked a mile. Sometimes Payne trotted at their heels. Afterward, when crystal drops spangled the bushes and the Blue Ridge turned a deeper blue, James would dash out to retrieve the tin measuring cup which he kept embedded in the drive to measure how many inches of rain had watered the fields.

It was harder to gauge politics. Certainly part of the United States was happy to ride the mainstream of its history by rededicating itself to the great Revolutionary ideal of what someone has called "aristocratic democracy"—arisocratic because aiming to take account of quality as well as quantity: a nation whose self-government, central and local, singled out and honored merit. But how gauge the strength of opposing forces? Madison did not underestimate Alexander Hamilton. Though by dismissing Hamilton's henchmen in the Cabinet, President Adams had now paid off his rival for constantly intervening and interfering, he had not loosened Hamilton's grip on Federalist leaders. Madison suspected Hamiltonian plots. With the elections of 1800 looming in the distance, the watchword was "Beware." Jefferson too was apprehensive. Meeting Dolley at Enniscorthy, he begged her to help him get James to Monticello for a vital strategy meeting.

In September the two men talked about Madison's imminent tasks in the Assembly and about the coming struggle for the Presidency. Sometimes Monroe, riding over from Highlands, made a triumvirate. Conceding that, if nominated, he might have to run next year, Jefferson swore that, if elected, he absolutely must have James Madison as his Secretary of State; with no one else could he work a fraction as well. Democrat-Republican prospects at the polls looked dark. But the Federalists were weakening themselves with feuds and backbiting.

The war with France which some Federalists hoped for and which, some suspected, acting Army head Hamilton liked to picture himself as winning, along with Florida, Louisiana, and South America—this war John Adams kept stubbornly refusing. Thank God, said Jefferson, Madison, and Dolley.

Jefferson's usual November visit to Montpelier was forgone. If it got out that he and Madison had met on the eve of Madison's work in the Assembly, enemies would charge collusion. Feeling a little like criminals under surveillance, they stopped corresponding by mail; there was evidence that some snooping clerk in the Charlottesville post office had been opening their letters. According to local tradition, they began to hide messages in hollow trees.

In December the Madisons were in Richmond when George Washington died. Although James had rued as tragic misjudgment Washington's mounting federalism, never had he withdrawn his profound esteem, for he knew the man was incorruptible. Light Horse Harry Lee was certainly right when he called him first in war, peace, and the hearts of Americans. It seemed impossible that death could topple him. Dolley and James wept. Madison was remembering many pleasant visits to Mount Vernon through the years, many intimate talks and mutual strivings with Washington, and then, alas, the recent semiestrangement. Dead! The world seemed poorer.

Partly because Washington's nephew was Dolley's brother-in-law, but more particularly out of love and respect, the Madisons decided to offer their condolences to Mrs. Washington in person, and Jefferson joined them on the long drive to Mount Vernon. From head to foot Dolley wore black. (It made her white skin look whiter.)

From Martha Washington they learned the details of her husband's death: how, riding out in freezing weather, he had run into sleet and hail and come home soaked. The next day he had a heavy cold. But he tramped through 3 inches of snow to mark trees. No, he would take no remedy—"Let it go as it came." Waking between two and three the next morning, he found himself choked by what appeared to be quinsy, but forbade her to get up before a servant built a fire at dawn. His doctors prescribed a gargle of molasses, vinegar, and butter; also the breathing of sage fumes; also a drink of calomel mixed with tartar; also a blistering and leaching. That afternoon he asked her to burn an old will and guard a new one. At five o'clock he said, "Doctor, I die hard, but am not afraid to go," and at ten, "I am just going. Have me decently buried. . . . Do you understand?" "Yes, sir." "'Tis well." Ah, that high riderless horse with the stirrups reversed.

But Madison and Jefferson felt that they had no choice. They must continue to struggle against the federalism which Washington had come to espouse.

Madison was writing a "Report" on last year's Virginia Resolutions, defending them point by point. As creators of the federal compact, he said, only the States themselves could judge constitutional violations. People, Constitution, government: that was the line of descent. The phrase "general welfare," he said, covered only enumerated powers, not "implied" ones. Freedom of the press was a basic principle of government by consent; it was vital to the liberties for which patriots had fought and bled. Whatever its abuses, it had preserved reason and humanity: a priceless contribution. By branding it licentious, Congress was punishing a crime of its own creation and turning loose upon the nation malices which would support tyranny of a new kind, debauch morals, shackle religion, and perhaps shed blood.

Bishop Madison congratulated his cousin on having swept the Augean stable clean.

In his Virginia Resolutions Madison's style had been restrained. Whereas Jefferson vented, Madison curbed, emotion. This does not mean he had none, and it is noteworthy that the passionate nature of his political convictions comes out in this follow-up report—this milestone in the evolving theory of free government, "evolving" because understanding is necessarily a process based on the *process* of experience.

The Virginia Assembly adopted the report 2 to 1.

Madison was now stressing state sovereignty, but if the current danger had overweighted the other side of the scale, he would as quickly have stressed nationalism. Balance was, as always, his goal and plea. National like bodily health depended upon a delicate equilibrium. As in the cosmos depicted so memorably by the Rittenhouse orrery, the pull must be both centripetal and centrifugal—a kind of in-out breathing, an interchange. If Hamilton and Jefferson stood more or less at extremes, Madison was a kind of regulator, checking, at times, both Hamilton's "monarchism" and Jefferson's "Jacobinism."

The century had turned, it was 1800, and Montpelier was still watching the wheel of the seasons, sowing, cultivating, slapping mosquitoes, making candles, chopping corn, and the rest. As Payne's legs strengthened, the old Colonel's grew weaker. Between sessions, James farmed and studied; Dolley read novels and wrote verses and acted as deputy mistress of Montpelier; the carriage measured off miles at a trot en route to dinner at a neighbor's. Soon crows would be cawing in stubble left by the harvest, black walnuts dropping. At a certain hour the distant Appalachians looked almost diaphanous. Anna and Nelly, having piled their hair up high for the first time, looked self-conscious at dinner. Ladies stabbed needles through round embroidery frames. Madison, frowning, indulged his "passion for chess." The family knelt in church—"We have erred and strayed from thy ways like lost sheep. . . ." At dinner Jemmy told the story of the Baroness de Riedesel, hefty wife of a Hessian officer confined near Charlottesville during the Revolution—how on horseback she carried a large open umbrella against Albermarle's fierce sun. Meanwhile Canadian geese honked over the frozen pond. Then it was time to go back to Richmond.

The year inched toward the presidential election upon which depended the future of the nation and of Mr. Jefferson and Mr. and Mrs. Madison. President Adams had moved to the new capital-in-the-wilderness, and gossip had it that Abigail was not pleased with her great unfinished "castle" on the Potomac. Was it really so bad?

The presidential campaign dealt in slanders. The Federalist caucus had nominated John Adams and General Charles Cotesworth Pinckney; the Republican caucus, Thomas Jefferson and Aaron Burr. The struggle was on. Newspapers, pamphlets, and New England preachers charged Jefferson with every crime but murder. He was a coward, an ambitious egotist, a French infidel, a wicked Rehoboam who had defrauded a widow and children of £ 10,000 sterling, a licentious begetter of mulatto children who planned, if elected, to burn Bibles. Nor did John Adams go scot-free. Still furious at the President for dismissing his Hamiltonian Cabinet members, Hamilton attacked Adams in a secretly circulated pamphlet. Obtaining a copy, Burr published it in the *Philadelphia Aurora.* Jefferson called the campaign a "bear garden."

Even Madison received some mauling. Wrote Thomas Mason, "The aristocrats . . . have at last got Madison's character upon the anvil, and into what shape they will endeavor to hammer it is not yet . . . ascertained." It galled Mason to see a man of virtue "weighted down." But in Orange County Madison was so popular, he became an elector by a vote of 340 to 7. Though the Democrat-Republicans had nominated Jefferson for President and Burr for Vice President, the rules of the time would give the highest office to the candidate with the most votes, second place to his runner-up, and in case of a tie the decision would go to the House of Representatives.

There was a tie. Both Jefferson and Burr received 73 electoral votes.

When a tense House convened, Jefferson and Madison were convinced that Burr would bow to the plain intent of the people by declining the Presidency. But Burr's long-time rival Hamilton could not pass up power. (Burr had defeated Hamilton's father-in-law in a race for the Senate, then stubbornly opposed Hamilton himself in New York politics.) Hating Burr more than Jefferson, Hamilton swung toward the latter. Fellow Federalists disagreed—what a coup if they could elect and control Burr! The hope was not extravagant; Burr was a born adventurer. When he thought Jefferson a surefire winner, he had felt "insulted" that anyone should fancy him capable of "submitting to be instrumental in counteracting the wishes . . . of the United States," but when he saw a chance to counteract through chicanery and stealing votes, he had no scruple whatsoever against making a deal with the Federalists. For example, Federalist Bayard agreed to support Burr because he had "distinctly stated" that he was willing to consider the Federalists as his friends and accept the Presidency as their gift.

Balloting in the House of Representatives started on February 5 during a snowstorm which turned into a blizzard. The situation was so tight, ambiguous, and dangerous, Congressman Nicholas of Maryland, desperately ill, had himself carried onto the floor on a litter. The first balloting was 8 to 6 for Jefferson, with two states split—far short of the necessary two-thirds. Six days and thirty-four ballots and much anguish later, the vote was still 8 to 6. How could they break the deadlock? Finally, on the thirty-sixth ballot, one member absented himself, and some Burr supporter dropped a blank into the ballot box. The final count—10 to 4 for Jefferson—brought cheers. But the winner had an uncomfortable feeling that without the help of his bitter foe Hamilton, he would not have been elected.

A galloping messenger rushed handbills to Fredericksburg. A copy went on to Montpelier. " . . . Ten for Jefferson," Madison read. "I hope you will have the cannon out. . . ." They rolled the cannon out. The pounding of the Madisons' hearts would have been salute enough. A promise was a promise. Jefferson's election meant the end of four years at home. In a few weeks they would be negotiating the mudholes between Orange and Washington City. Would they like the crude new Capital? Could they find a house? It was very exciting, the opportunity to help bring the Republic back to its original ideals. Moreover, the job of Secretary of State could hardly be more strenuous than Madison's retirement.

Jefferson hoped his friend would reach Washington before the inauguration. No, Madison replied; in spite of temperance and flannels, his rheumatism had increased, also his father's feebleness. And how awkward to walk onto the political stage ahead of cue.

The Madisons were packing hair trunks when on February 27 Colonel James Madison Sr. died, and Orange County felt the shock of losing its foremost citizen. "Yesterday morning rather suddenly, though very gently," wrote his grieving eldest son, "the flame of life went out."

As chief heir and executor James faced new tasks. The estate was complex, legatees numerous. A lawsuit was filed to clarify residuary bequests, a jointly owned mill sold. By purchasing and swapping, James consolidated his inheritance into three farms totaling about 5,000 acres lying between the top of the Southwest Mountain and the Rapidan. Its core was the old homeplace, Montpelier.

Sixty-eight-year-old Nelly Madison would keep the quarters to the right of the front hall which she and her husband had been occupying, and maintain a private staff. Though she got along extremely well with her daughter-in-law Dolley, she prized her independence.

At the inauguration, through no fault of his own, the new Secretary of State was not in Washington City to accompany Jefferson from Conrad's boardinghouse to the Capitol. He did not see the liberty caps in the crowd nor hear John Marshall administer the oath. But he was already familiar with the inaugural address which Jefferson delivered before a

Senate presided over by the now thoroughly distrusted Burr. It was a conciliatory speech. " . . . Let us then, fellow citizens, unite with one heart and one mind; let us restore to social intercourse that harmony and affection without which liberty and even life itself are but dreary things. . . . We are all Republicans, we are [all] Federalists."

Jefferson's effort to calm troubled waters failed. Federalists found inconsistencies, and later the historian Henry Adams would snap, "In no party sense was it true that all were Republicans and all Federalists." But Jefferson did not mean it in a party sense. He was saying that in its revolutionary intention and Constitution the United States embraced both republicanism (government by representation) and federalism (the principle whereby a number of states are drawn into a nation while retaining part of their original sovereignty); therefore every citizen properly bore a double label.

Among the goals of republican government Jefferson named acquiescence in the decisions of the majority; friendship with other nations, though not entangling alliances (a doctrine enunciated by Madison eighteen years earlier); a crack militia; economic frugality; the fostering of agriculture and its "handmaid," commerce; freedom of religion, press, and person; trial by jury; equal justice; and peace. These objectives, he said, formed a bright constellation.

It was Jefferson speaking, but there were ideas which he and Madison had been discussing for years, in living exchange, each giving and taking. In most matters they had always agreed wonderfully well, the main exception being Jefferson's more radical interpretation of states' rights, a doctrine discreetly omitted from this inaugural address.

A month later Jefferson stopped at Montpelier en route to Monticello for a breather. The two men talked late. They were especially indignant over the way John Adams had tried to undermine his successor's administration by appointing federal judges right up to the deadline of his own Presidency. Should they ask Congress to void the law creating new circuit judgeships? And in Virginia add some Republican marshals? As usual the swapping of ideas was fruitful.

Three weeks later heading north, Jefferson again stopped at Montpelier. Though just out of a sickbed, Madison promised that he and Dolley would follow in a few days. Yes, they'd be happy to stay with Jefferson until they found a suitable lease.

Jefferson sent back a warning. Mudholes on the Ravensworth road were deep enough to overturn a carriage—come by Fairfax Courthouse.

Two days of wind and sun would make "immense odds." Mr. Gaines and Mr. Beanspoke had promised to haul him over Bull Run Hill. Dinner would be held until four.

The trip was easier than expected. Madison arrived in Washington feeling better than when he left home, and Dolley was in fine fettle.

After dinner Jefferson showed the Madisons, Anna, and nine-year-old Payne his Great Cheese. The day it was made in the Berkshires, he told them, everyone with a cow donated all the day's milk—"only no Federalist cow must contribute a drop." Men in clean Sunday shirts and women in beribboned gowns sang hymns and prayed while they worked on the gift. Tubs of curds were poured into a huge refitted cider press to solidify. It had taken Elder Leland in his sleigh three weeks to drive the Great Cheese to Washington.

After that marvel, the oath of office administered to the Secretary of State by one of the "midnight judges" may have seemed an anticlimax.

The Madisons found themselves in a town so scattered, it hardly hung together. The huge unfinished presidential mansion of pale sandstone stood a mile and a half away from a hilltop Senate wing of what had been planned as a noble capitol. Round about, a few taverns and shops and houses were strewed among woods and swamps. Though only a few streets had been laid down, Washington's designer, Pierre L'Enfant, and Commissioner William Thornton had projected the city on a scale consistent with a great future—the future the Madisons believed in and had fallen in love with and hoped to serve.

The new regime must pick its way as delicately as the high-stepping quail walking, single file, through the District of Columbia.

❧ VII ❧

WASHINGTON CITY:
A NATION ON THE RISE

DEMOCRATS WHO SAW THE ELECTION of Jefferson as the second American revolution tended to see Washington City as an image of the radically new regime. Its woods had a republican simplicity. Non-streets still existing only on drawing boards had the vagueness of political theories yet to be tried out. Jefferson called the expanding nation containing this expanding town "a chosen country with room enough for all descendants unto the hundredth and thousandth generation." The only thing necessary to "close the circle of their felicities," he said, was a wise and frugal government. This he proposed to supply.

John Adams left with not a little bitterness. After appointing "midnight judges," the ex-President drove out of town in dudgeon, crying that he had been turned out. Abigail was aware of compensations. Though she regretted her husband's rebuff at the polls, personally she was glad to go home to Quincy, Massachusetts. The President's palace, "built for the future and not comfortable living," was not something she grieved to lose. She had been forced to keep fires burning day and night to dry out damp plaster; many rooms were unfinished, bells nonexistent, the East Room good for nothing but hanging out wet wash. Her sojourn there had been a little like living on a frontier. As they headed north, the Adamses derived some satisfaction from the fact that Hamilton had lost his influence on national affairs. He was out. Of course nothing could keep him from intriguing—that was his nature.

Jefferson made light of the rigors of the presidential mansion. With a pioneering zest he conferred with carpenters, installed furniture from

157

Monticello, and organized his servants. Reaching beyond the house, he planted a double row of poplars along Pennsylvania Avenue. Even the raggedy common across the street pleased him. "We find this a very agreeable country residence," he wrote his son-in-law, "we," now, being himself and his houseguests, the Madisons. They enjoyed "good society, and enough of it, and free from the noise, the heat, the stench and the bustle of a close-knit town." Prospects seemed good. Jefferson's administration had taken over a working concern, and though Adams's last-minute Federalist appointments had seized the judiciary, the Republicans now had a majority in both houses of Congress. Moreover, with Madison as his Secretary of State and Gallatin Secretary of the Treasury, the President was well shored up. Madison's presence in particular gave him great satisfaction, for he considered his friend the most capable man available, a genius of government.

Madison lost no time getting down to work in his temporary office in the complex at 21st and Pennsylvania Avenue called the Six Buildings. Also, he was studying the foreign envoys with whom he must deal: Carlos Martinez d'Yrujo, the handsome, foppish, vain, clever Spanish Minister whom Sally McKean had caught; British Chargé d'Affaires Edward Thornton, his firm chin scraped by white starched ruffles; and thirty-one-year-old French Chargé d'Affaires Louis Pichon with a quick eye for the main point. To save money Jefferson had closed some American legations, which meant fewer legations here.

The three diplomats were studying Madison. Probably the best place for taking each other's measure was Jefferson's dining room at three o'clock of an afternoon when a dozen or so guests took their seats to wash down his French cook's culinary concoctions with excellent wine. It loosened the tongue.

Madison's party knew him as a longtime champion of American rights on the Mississippi, American claims to Western territory, and domestic manufacturing and foreign trade, as well as chief framer of the Constitution. Though no notes on the proceedings of the 1787 Convention had been published, members had talked, word had traveled; in spite of his setback in connection with Jay's Treaty, he commanded great respect. "If Madison be Secretary of State," remarked the Federalist Minister to Holland, William Vans Murray," there will be more justice and liberality of opinions on party men. He is the best of them all."

The problem of the Barbary States tested his mettle. Ever since the sixteenth century, the Turkish satellites (Algeria, Tunis, Morocco, and Tripoli) had formed a pirate stronghold to prey upon Mediterranean shipping, and now that old-type galleys were supplemented by frigates with wind-bellied sails, the Barbary corsairs had become even more wickedly successful. Refused a navy by Congress, Washington and Adams had paid protective bribes to the tune of some 2 million dollars. Jefferson, Madison, and Gallatin together decided that war would be cheaper and more honorable, and when the Pasha of Tripoli demanded an increase in America's annual "gift" of $83,000, it was refused. Hoodlums knocked down the flagpole of an American consulate, and the United States sent out a small, stout, determined naval squadron.

While the ships were spoiling for a fight, Dolley was canvassing the Federal City for a house. Her coach dashed along a gridiron of streets, clear enough on Pierre L'Enfant's grand plan but not always so to the horses; a gridiron imposed on a system of circles out from which rayed avenues, New Jersey the most traveled. Sometimes she crossed to the older shops, homes, and boardinghouses of George Town, which Abigail Adams had once uncourteously called the dirtiest hole she had ever seen. Sometimes Dolley drove 2 miles east along partly swampy Pennsylvania Avenue and up a hill so steep it lathered the horses to visit the group of buildings clustered around the Capitol. Whenever she saw a senator or congressman trudging along the stone footwalk, she called to him to jump aboard.

Should they live in the Six Buildings? In the Seven Buildings? On Carroll Row? In a freestanding house? In Thomas Law's block of nine houses on Capitol Hill? Jefferson said why not just stay on as his guests; this mansion was so big, he got lost in it—stay! It would be a kindness! But the Madisons preferred their own roof. (This without knowing that Federalists had begun gossiping about the "fact" that the President was taking in boarders.) At the end of May the Madisons found a makeshift abode for the one month remaining before a summer vacation. Dr. William Thornton—architectural genius, City Commissioner, jack-of-all-trades—had promised to find them a long-term residence by fall.

During June, while Madison put in long hours, Dolley shopped for her household and Jefferson's; in fact, Jefferson in his widowerhood was finding her in many ways indispensable.

Meanwhile the Madisons were being drawn into the city's social life. Though the President had abolished his predecessors' formality—no celebration of his birthday, no levees, no display—he enjoyed entertaining privately and almost always asked his Secretary of State's wife to act as hostess. Theoretically he could conscript the wife of any Cabinet officer, but Dolley had an unmatched ability to make guests feel at home.

Jefferson's clothes were as informal as his dinners. One envoy reported contemptuously that the President had received him in a "blue coat, a thick grey-colored waistcoat, green velveteen breeches with pearl buttons, yarn stockings, and slippers down at the heels." Federalists made a great to-do about those carpet slippers.

The Madisons stood in some contrast sartorially. James (to teach the many nephews he was supporting the lesson of economy) now wore, almost exclusively, a plain black suit with an unfancy white neckerchief. And at home Dolley still dressed as soberly as a dove. But her formal gowns more and more laid the rainbow under contribution.

At the President's dinners, not only Dolley but Madison too (in spite of some Federalist japes) pleased people. His wit sparkled and his anecdotes were often side splitting. George Tucker has said that he showed unfailing good humor and a strong relish for the ludicrous.

The food was laid out in covered dishes, with plenty of servants hovering around to cut, pass, remove, and pour while guests' eyes swiveled from the roast to Dolley. What beauty, what vivacity. Her own eyes, like as not, were fastened on her husband's face.

At fifty-one he was in the prime of life. His hair, pulled forward to a point over a balding spot, Dolley herself powdered each day and tied in a short queue, a style on the way out. He had a healthy color, and his eyes of conservative blue burned in their sockets.

At the moment he was telling a story about patronage. A Republican whose wild attacks on Federalists had boomeranged onto his own party dropped into the State Department to ask for the governorship of a Western territory. Madison replied that he was sorry but other applicants had stronger claims. A collectorship then? inquired the visitor. Unfortunately they had all been taken. Well, how about a post office? That was out of the question. Well, did the Secretary have any old clothes he could spare?

When Dolley laughed, her sky-colored eyes spilled light. Even if she had heard the joke before, she laughed. Jemmy's tales were so good, she always said, they were worth hearing again.

The Madisons were seeing many ex-Philadelphians, among them Albert Gallatin, that attractive, bald-pated, big-nosed prodigy of intellect whose French accent the Federalists ridiculed so cruelly—"foreigner!"— that his well-born wife, Hannah, had begun to hate the town.

Another Philadelphia friend, Anthony Morris, often showed up in Washington. He had served as groomsman for John Todd at his marriage to Dolley Payne: a big, bland, flaxen-haired lawyer, at core a convinced

Quaker but, not unlike Dolley, peripherally a renegade in the sense that he loved color, left off his broadbrim, and enjoyed merry company. Once he had been tried by the Society of Friends for displaying the "world's manners" and for signing—as leader of the Pennsylvania Senate—a "warlike" measure to put down the Whiskey Rebellion. Only barely had he missed Dolley's fate of disownment. It was a bond of sorts.

The William Thorntons were also from Philadelphia. Gilbert Stuart's patrician-nosed portrait of Dr. Thornton images forth a soul supersensitive, quick to take offense, gifted and generous; in his way a genius. His sloe-eyed wife of French blood, Anna Maria, would perform the prodigy of keeping a diary, meager but valuable, for sixty-seven years. The third member of the family was Mrs. Anna Brodeau, "Mama."

The New Yorker Aaron Burr was another person whom James and Dolley had first known in Philadelphia. But since his shady election maneuvering they were seeing him less. Dolley found it astonishing that she had once appointed him to undertake, in case of her death, Payne's entire education and that it was Burr who had brought Jemmy to her home that fateful first evening. Morally he had shriveled, and no amount of social polish—of which he had a great deal—could make up. (In his portrait by James Sharpless, Burr has a cold, fickle face with a receding brow under powdered hair, a drooping bun over each ear, and pony tail.) The Madisons would continue to treat him with politeness but restraint.

Among their new friends were the Samuel Harrison Smiths. Jefferson had recruited Sam Smith to edit the *National Intelligencer*. The bonus was Smith's twenty-two-year-old capable bride, Margaret Bayard. Here is an entry in her journal: "Mrs. Madison is at the President's . . . ; I have become acquainted with her and am highly pleased with her; she has good humor and sprightliness, united to the most affable and agreeable manners." A democrat with the fierce ardor of a convert, Mrs. Smith found many things in the new democratic administration—as in the ragged mushrooming city—quite glamorous.

In contrast to the comfortable Smiths, Mr. Thomas Law seemed a highly exotic bird; an aristocratic Englishman who had enjoyed a fabulous career in Asia, where he begot five Indian-looking sons before marrying Elizabeth Parke Custis (Martha Washington's granddaughter) and investing a fortune in District of Columbia real estate. He was creature of impulses, "one of the strangest," mused Mrs. Smith, "I ever met with."

And so it went. The Madisons understood that without all kinds of people one could not be human.

But James still had difficulties with living that philosophy. While changing slowly under Dolley's influence, he approached strangers cautiously, alert-minded, standing a little away to measure and perhaps test. It was partly a matter of temperament, partly the result of a life experience less protected than Dolley's and somewhat disillusioning. But though more reticent, he liked people when he got to know them, and he was mellowing.

Dolley, on the other hand, loved almost as easily as she breathed. She loved her relatives, her friends, and the 5 million unmet Americans spread throughout sixteen states (Vermont, Kentucky, and Tennessee having now been added), these people with whom she and Jemmy were trying to forge a nation. She had a talent for establishing good relationships.

That was not her whole story. She was growing intellectually as well as socially. But she did not congratulate herself. When she compared her mind with James's, it was to her detriment, for she saw that she had only a fraction of his knowledge and power of reason. She loved him the more for the contrast.

Precisely because husband and wife had started out as near opposites, one mostly heart, the other head, they could learn and were learning a great deal from each other, each moving slowly, slowly, in the direction of better balance. What neither had to learn much about was moral character.

During a July heat wave they drove home by way of Sully in Loudoun County to visit the Richard Bland Lees. There in a big white frame farmhouse Dolley chattered with Eliza—little Betsey—of the enormous shy eyes and uptilted little nose, her bridesmaid at her first wedding and oldest, dearest friend, while the two men, also old friends, talked politics and farming. Then on to Orange.

Though, as always, Montpelier was rich in the simplicities, a three-way courier system between it and Monticello and the Capital complicated this vacation. The Administration was struggling with the problem of the midnight judges, numerous applications for public office, such Federalist carpings as Yale President Dwight's pity for a nation run by "blockheads and knaves," the revolt in French Santo Domingo (what if American slaves took the cue?), and Britain's continuing ruthlessness on the high seas. Often Madison sat pondering American rights under that "strict and honorable neutrality."

One day there came a rumor that by the Treaty of San Ildefonso, signed October 1, 1800, France had regained the old province of Louisiana which she had ceded to Spain during the Seven Years War, a vast territory stretching from the Ohio to the Rockies—a big part of the continent. Was it only a rumor? Was Napoleon Bonaparte's ambition so gargantuan that he was embarking upon a policy of empire building? Would he soon—with a base in the New World—be coveting Cuba, Mexico, and the United States' Northwest? Nearly half of the produce of the United States went down the Mississippi to New Orleans. It mattered tremendously who controlled them.

Near the end of 1802, Madison heard that the United States' right of deposit for transshipping goods to American ocean-going vessels at New Orleans had been canceled. This was grave. Settlers up the river were cut off from their only market.

The Secretary of State wrote instructions for both Minister to France Robert Livingston and Minister to Spain Pinckney. He said that the United States must try to dissuade France and Spain from consummating the deal. His thinking: a common border between French and American territory would threaten the friendship between France and the United States, therefore the peace. Indeed, any increase of French power might force the United States to join its land power with Britain's sea power in an unbeatable combination. Spain should keep Louisiana. Related to this line of argument was Madison's realization that dangers to the United States would be eased if the nation could acquire the strip of territory called West Florida (roughly the present Alabama and Mississippi), which controlled Mobile Bay. The title was unclear. Did it now belong to Spain or France?

On their return to Washington the Madisons moved into the commodious house on F Street which Dr. Thornton—who lived next door—had secured for them. Leasing it unfinished, he had partitioned its third floor into four extra dormered bedrooms, built a coal bin and wine storage in the cellar, given the roof a cupola with a fire escape, and improved the large lot with a stable and coach house. He had borrowed the first year's paid-in-advance rent of £600.

Gratified and grateful, James and Dolley were soon whirling about pleasantly in a social maelstrom, their home a center of hospitality second only to the President's mansion. Dolley was now, without undue stress, giving dinners on a larger scale. She kept up with the latest fashions. Unable, as always, to believe that ugliness had any special virtue and liking to please, she permitted herself more and more range in ornaments on the theory that one had a kind of obligation to look one's best. Bodices and panniers had gone out; slim high-waisted décolleté French gowns were in vogue. Having a beautiful neck and lovely shoulders and arms, she wore the new style superbly. Why not? She hated dullness.

Invitations from the Madisons were prized. Congressmen, senators, newspapermen, businessmen, Maryland and Virginia planters, the diplomatic set, Cabinet members and their wives, and democrats and Federalists crowded into their dining room to consume good food, discuss current events, banter a bit, and laugh discreetly or uproariously. Afterward, like as not, the company played backgammon.

The day after each dinner Dolley returned to her long-sleeved, high-necked grey stuff dress, her only jewelry the ring with rose diamonds which James had given her as an engagement present. It never left her finger.

Apparently Madison himself was now tutoring Payne. If so, it took patience. The ten-year-old preferred to loaf down at the stable with black people. And he could be difficult. Later Sally McKean would recall with amusement how, as a little fellow, he had "pulled off General Van Courtland's wig" at the very moment the gentleman was making her a "flourishing compliment." After eight years of marriage the Madisons had abandoned hope of giving Payne a brother or sister. All their parental dreams now centered in one small boy, and it was hard, especially for Dolley, not to be overindulgent. To think that yellow fever might have snatched him away. And didn't all children go through baffling stages on their way to maturity?

Anna was no problem. At twenty-one she was a lighthearted, fresh-looking near-beauty with pastel eyes, the high Payne forehead, and enough poise to preside over the President's table when Dolley was unavailable. To her, Dolley was sister and mother, Madison brother and father. A bevy of beaux warned them silently that the time must come, perhaps soon, when she would leave their house. Shrinking from the prospect, Dolley scolded herself. The important thing was Anna's happiness. And the mists of 1802 thickened into hoarfrost.

The Madisons and their neighbors the Thorntons grew more intimate. The bond was great intelligence and an appreciation of beauty. The two couples ran back and forth, sharing meals, drinking tea, borrowing each other's servants and sugar, discussing politics and culture and the future of the city. When the ladies talked apart, they tended to concentrate on fashion, the gentlemen on horses. Like Madison, Dr. Thornton was an expert judge of horseflesh, and it was he who had inaugurated Washington City's fall races. The two bought a racehorse together. Unfortunately their companionship was sometimes marred by Dr. Thornton's talent for getting his feelings hurt over nothing.

The races were an annual three-day meet which closed Congress. The Senate offered the excuse that its ceiling needed replastering, the House that no bills were pending. The contests drew a motley mob, "black and white and yellow of all conditions," wrote the Rev. Manasseh Cutler, "from the President of the United States to the beggar in his rags. . . ." One gentleman celebrated the occasion by wearing three cravats.

The oval hilltop racetrack was 50 feet wide and a mile long, its center occupied by a "prodigious number of booths" containing tables on which spectators loved to stand. A crowd milled about and rushed excitedly from one vantage spot to another: buffs afoot and on horseback.

The "most respectable people," Dr. Cutler would write his son, congregated west of the circle, where they sat in hackney coaches. "These, if they were not all *Democrats,* I should call the *Noblesse.* Their carriages were elegant, and their attendants and servants numerous." They included the President, the Gallatins, the Thorntons (as manager the Doctor often gallivanted off), the Yrujos, the Carrolls, the Tayloes, the Lees, the Madisons. On benches atop a 15-foot-high stage east of the turf sat the judges. Pedestrians passed free. The toll for horses and coaches totaled $1,200 (equal to at least $10,000 today). Dr. Cutler considered the whole shebang rather evil. These nabobs were just out to "sport with their money. Vast sums are bet. . . . It is said one member of Congress lost . . . 700 dollars."

The Madisons did not see it that way. While thoroughbreds pounded down the track they watched, fascinated—Madison tense, Dolley clapping her little gloved hands.

Another highlight of the social season was the Dancing Assembly's big night. It was led by Captain Thomas Tingey, a charming bird-brained naval officer with reams of gold lace and impeccable manners. Though Dolley still hung back from learning to dance, she could be counted on to speak, at crucial moments, the gay, right, and always tactful word.

Time after time at parties she threw a bridge across some chasm. She had learned to dip snuff and play cards and was very popular. While men loitered at brag, the ladies amused themselves with the milder game of loo. As Jefferson said, the Federal City was like one big family.

Each of the Administration's hardest workers—Jefferson, Madison, and Gallatin—contributed something vital to the team. They were striving together to strengthen the young nation. The other Cabinet members were General Henry Dearborn, Secretary of War; Robert Smith, Secretary of the Navy; and General Levi Lincoln, Attorney General. One of the distinctive things about the Secretary of State was that he understood the government *as a whole*. For example, he could easily keep up with Gallatin's thinking as the Secretary of the Treasury struggled to pay off the public debt by two reforms: stricter accounting and detailed congressional appropriations. Both Gallatin and Madison strongly disagreed with Hamilton's opinion that a public debt was good because it acted as a cohesive force. And Madison quietly and unobtrusively modified some of Jefferson's more impulsive judgments. As was proper, State Department utterances were always prefixed with the words "The President has decided." Thus Madison's crucial role in foreign affairs was muted, but insiders like Gallatin knew well that Madison was less agent than equal partner in ideas, and sometimes corrector, sometimes initiator. This is not to disparage Jefferson. His devotion to freedom and democracy and his gift for deep thinking, for reaching plain people, and for hanging onto principle even when unsure of method made him a great President. But Jefferson himself called this friend whom he trusted absolutely a great Secretary of State. " . . . Mr. Madison is justly entitled to his full share of all the measures of my administration. Our principles were the same. . . ."

In November of 1801 they heard that England and France, long at war, had made peace. (The following March they would sign the Treaty of Amiens.) So empire-hungry Napoleon was now free—if he chose—to move against the New World.

Chargé d'Affaires Pichon tried to sound out the Administration. Would the United States help starve out the rebel general Toussaint L'Ouverture now holding France's West Indian Island of Santo Domingo? Jefferson and Madison masked their thoughts while considering imponderables such as the extent of Napoleon's ambition, the depth of British hostility, and Spain's secret intent. Doubtless France was thinking of Santo Domingo as a base of operations for defending Louisiana. Two things had to be kept in mind in determining foreign policy, for they were incontestable: America's need to trade freely up and down the Mississippi and to sail the Atlantic unmolested. If at the President's table Madison's eyes glazed over a saddle of veal, he might be trying to figure how to keep France from taking possession of Louisiana.

Toussaint was ambushed, arrested, and immured in the French Alps. Whereupon a more deadly foe fell upon the 12,000 troops which France had sent, under General Leclerc, to win back Santo Domingo: yellow fever. It killed Leclerc and wiped out his army.

People were asking what Madison thought of Napoleon. Well, he answered, he had once admired the man as a curber of the grim excesses under Danton and Marat. But now the Revolution had moved from a king's tyranny to a general's; it had come full circle—tragic end to a promising development. France's defection left America the only theater giving "true liberty" a fair trial. He meant liberty with a sense of responsibility.

After Christmas the social season quickened. Dr. Samuel Latham Mitchill pictures the President at his New Year's reception as "standing near the middle of the room to salute and converse with visitors." Jefferson was assisted by his two visiting daughters, Patsy and Polly, and by Anna Payne and Dolley Madison. Dr. Mitchell's description of a typical meal at the Great House:

> Dined at the President's. . . . Rice, soup, round of beef, turkey, mutton, ham, loin of veal, cutlets of mutton or veal, fried eggs, fried beef. A pie called macaroni, which appeared to be a rich crust filled with the stribbions of onions or shallots . . . tasted very strong and not very agreeable. . . . Icecream very good, crust wholly dried, crumbled into thin flakes . . . very porous and light, covered with cream-sauce—very fine. Many other jimcracks, a great variety of fruit, plenty of wines, and good.

March blew in, and on St. Patrick's Day the city was overrun by "sons of Hibernia" with shamrocks stuck in their hats.

The democrats, having run the country for a year now, had removed the widespread pre-Jeffersonian fear that monarchists would somehow seize power and make a caricature of freedom. Their party seemed too well entrenched for that. Actually Hamilton was politically quiet because hopeless of regaining influence, therefore bitter and pessimistic. "Every day," he wrote, "proves to me more and more that this American world was not made for me." He still wrote articles under pseudonyms, but they no longer cut deep.

The danger to the Administration was less Hamilton than losing a great outlet. "The day that France takes possession of New Orleans," Jefferson told Robert Livingston, " . . . we must marry ourselves to the British fleet and nation." There were two alternatives: control the heart of the American continent or be drawn into European wars. The first way seemed imperative. But how gain control of the mouth of the Mississippi?

British Chargé d'Affaires Edward Thornton found himself overwhelmed with invitations to dine with the President and Secretary of State. He was not loath to accept. For one thing, both hosts were connoisseurs of excellent wines—it seemed that American consuls in Spain, Portugal, Italy, and France augmented their salaries by finding their bosses the best vintages. Madison's favorite wine was Madeira. (He drank only one glassful at dinner—never whiskey, never brandy.)

Also, sometimes, along with wine crates, a brig brought the President and Secretary of State some delicacy like pâte Périgueux made of partridge and truffles. "These pies are in great estimation in Europe," wrote Consul Lee, and so rich they must be eaten sparingly.

There were other small pleasures: the President's pet mockingbird flying about his study and lighting upon his shoulder; the lupinella seed which Philip Mazzei sent from Tuscany; butter-soaked Sally Lunn; a fiddle scraping "Betty Bonnet."

Dolley's coach picked up Pierre L'Enfant in a cloud of dust. She was sorry Jefferson had dismissed this designer of Washington City for extravagance—could geniuses keep track of money? Ah, a squirrel leaping from bough to bough in a pawlonia tree. Not that Dolley needed anything special to make her happy. It was enough, just pulling on her slippers of a morning. Who knew what the day might bring?

When she and James left Washington for Montpelier the summer of 1802, they were exulting that the by-elections had strengthened republicanism. Look! The Blue Ridge. Then the crimson canopy on their fourposter. The days passed quickly. Suddenly it was September, and they were listening for the sound of the Thorntons' coach on the drive. William! Anna Maria! "Mama"!

During the Thorntons' month-long visit Anna Maria kept her diary. A "wild and romantic country," she calls Orange County, "generally covered with fine flourishing timber and forest trees." She describes the house: 80 feet long, with two wings and a "handsome (but unfinished) portico of the Tuscan order, plain but of grand appearance." How unusual to find such "a taste for the arts" in a place so remote. And what a magnificent view. She notes the "constant variation in the appearance of the clouds and consequently of the mountains . . . sometimes appearing very distant, sometimes much separated and distinct and often like rolling waves." As soon as Mr. Madison had carried out all his plans the place would resemble some of the "elegant seats in England."

The morning after Bishop Madison and his son arrived, seven people started for Monticello. They had reached the foot of the Little Mountain when a violent storm broke. Night had fallen. In the darkness there was real danger of plunging down some steep. Their only lamp was the incessant play of lightning. But for that, says Anna Maria, they would have lost their way. Everyone but Mama abandoned the carriage and walked uphill three-quarters of a mile. They had just entered Jefferson's dry bastion when the heavens fell in and tried to wash it away.

The next day the Thorntons saw Jefferson's home in its chronic state of being torn down and rebuilt. Anna Maria found "something grand and awful in the situation"—beautiful, yes, but "far from convenient or in my opinion agreeable." Storms pinned them down a week.

On their way home the travelers spent a night at Mr. Walker's Castle Hill. Madison had to borrow two horses to replace three which had "gone off." The next day the party ate dinner at Madison's Black Meadow Farm and reached Montpelier at dusk.

Back in Washington the Madisons were enchanted with some French furniture shipped by Monroe; also a $500 secondhand monogrammed carriage bought in Philadelphia. The silver-plated harness cost extra.

In the coach house where the beautiful harness hung, long-legged Payne lounged about with the servants. He was a good-looking boy who would make a handsome man. But he was not very obedient. The Madisons worried somewhat. Should they be more severe? more patient? Dolley told herself he had only to learn a little discipline to become a fine adult.

Sometimes when Payne was fooling around the horses, Dolley was out shopping for elegances she had missed during her youth or running errands for others. Two of her customers were Jefferson's daughters. In October 1802 Martha wrote the President, "Dear Papa . . . will you be so good as to send orders to the milliner—Madame Peco, I believe her name is—through Mrs. Madison, who very obligingly offered to execute any little commission for me in Philadelphia, for two wigs of the color of the hair enclosed, and of the most fashionable shapes."

All through the Washington visit of Mrs. Randolph and Mrs. Eppes, Dolley acted as duenna. Martha charmed people with her conversation and kindness; the slender, golden, shy Maria simply by being there to look at. In a town where a British Minister had remarked on the large number of extraordinarily pretty girls, Maria—Polly—drew all eyes. Thwarted in her desire for a daughter, Dolley was touched by this young woman clinging to her for dear life. Jefferson's daughters were presented to the diplomatic set, including the lovely American Marchioness and the gor-geously vain Marquis. Coming from a simpler life, the visitors could hardly believe they were seeing this swaggering grandee with hair powdered to a snowdrift, striped silk coat, hat tipped with feathers, and bejewelled smallsword. What a world their country-bred father now inhabited!

For many Americans Yrujo had lost his glitter the day Spain withdrew America's right of deposit at New Orleans, thus stopping an annual million dollars' worth of trade. The public was furious; without that port the nation would choke to death. Madison, who considered it America's destiny to expand, wrote indignantly, "The Floridas and New Orleans command the only outlets to the sea and . . . must become a part of the United States either by purchase or conquest." Must. All over the country anxiety was rising. The President appointed Monroe Minister Plenipotentiary to France to help Livingston.

Chief Justice John Marshall, Jefferson's Federalist kinsman and foe, now rendered a verdict technically against Madison but actually against the Administration for refusing to deliver a Justice of Peace commission to one of Adams's midnight appointees, Marbury. The Republicans resented it, some violently. It was now party war to the bone.

On New Year's Day 1803 the Madisons skipped the President's open house. They had just heard of Nelly Madison Hite's death the day before Christmas. Already she lay under snow. James and Dolley remembered sorrowfully how she had looked and moved and spoken and laughed there at Belle Grove. She had left, besides her husband, thirteen-year-old Nelly and ten-year-old James Madison Hite. The Madisons sent Isaac a sorrowing letter of condolence and refused the British Minister's dinner invitation. Forty-two years old—too young to die.

But life could not be arrested. When Monroe had difficulty financing his trip to France, Madison helped by purchasing, with several thousand borrowed dollars, 200 pieces of solid silver which the Monroes had bought on their previous trip to Paris, some gold-banded china, and three dozen of Marie Antoinette's Sèvres plates.

Monroe sailed with Secretary of State Madison's detailed instructions. He was to offer Napoleon 50 million francs for New Orleans and the Floridas; or three-quarters of that sum for New Orleans alone; or, in a pinch, a lesser sum for either a left-bank port site or perpetual rights of navigation and deposit. If he failed to obtain anything at all, he must (this was firm) establish closer relations with Great Britain. On the upshot of the negotiations, Madison was convinced, hung the "future destinies of this Republic." He had great hope. Napoleon was probably more vulnerable than he cared to admit.

Besides the written instructions, there may have been secret ones.

Meanwhile, in Paris, Minister Livingston was striving to persuade Talleyrand that New Orleans and the Floridas were of less value to France than friendship with the United States. Having just heard of the Santo Domingo debacle, Livingston shared Madison's suspicion about Napoleon's weak position. With the island lost, of what value was all that American real estate? It could not be protected. If France and Britain went back to war, Great Britain might pluck off Louisiana like a ripe plum. Or the United States might. Besides, Napoleon must be nearly bankrupt.

Cannily, Livingston showed Talleyrand a clipping from the *New York Chronicle* mentioning Senator Rose's proposal that Congress appropriate $5 million and raise 50,000 troops to seize New Orleans. When this was reported to Napoleon, he made no reply. Even when Livingston quoted Madison as saying that in case of renewed war the United States would push westward, the First Consul remained inscrutable. Livingston's hope began to seep away. Apparently Napoleon was no man to sacrifice control of a continent.

Chargé d'Affaires Pichon wrote his government that this morning when Mr. Madison "combed out the prospect," it had been "impossible to answer him." The Secretary was backed by the American public. The nation was in ferment, expanding and feeling its strength.

The Easter Sunday before Monroe's arrival, Talleyrand startled Livingston by asking, "What would you give for Louisiana?" The *whole* of it? Yes, all the territory from the Ohio to the Rockies, from Canada to the Gulf, including the Mississippi. "Perhaps twenty million francs," said the dazed Livingston. "Too low," said Talleyrand; "reflect and see me tomorrow."

Actually Napoleon's mind was made up. That morning he had said to his Finance Minister, Barbé-Marbois, "I renounce Louisiana. . . . I direct you to negotiate the affair." Then irritably, "I need a lot of money for the war"—the new one with England. She must be forced to her knees. Besides, the New World was too primitive for his taste and talents; he craved to dominate the Old. On half a continent Marbois put a price tag of 100 million francs.

Shocked on getting wind of their brother's decision to sell, Joseph and Lucien Bonaparte accosted him in his bath. How dare he act against the Constitution, cried Joseph, and without the consent of the Chambers? Napoleon spewed sarcasm. Enraged, Joseph threatened to denounce him from the tribune. "You are insolent!" shouted the Conqueror, half rising from the tub. By throwing himself violently backward he deluged his hecklers with perfumed water. Laughter; then the quarrel was renewed. "If I were not your brother, I'd be your enemy!" shouted Lucien. Napoleon moved as if to strike him. "My enemy! I'd break you—look—like this!"—smashing a snuffbox to the floor.

By dickering, by horse trading, Livingston and Monroe slowly backed Marbois down to 80 million francs, with 20 million subtracted for American claims. The treaty was signed May 13, 1803. Louisiana had been bought for about $12 million.

The deal had been achieved by fortunate circumstances, by two envoys, and, most important, by a President and Secretary of State who had worked together, and would continue to work together, more closely than any other President and Secretary of State in American history.

At dawn on the Fourth of July, 1803, Washington City shot off an eighteen-gun salute, followed by an exuberant parade. Jefferson had just proclaimed that this nation had, overnight, doubled in size. Thousands of spectators, including the Madisons, milled about, excited and exulting. At eleven there was an oration. At noon a crowd poured through the south door of the Great House to shake hands with the beaming President, who was serving punch, wine, and cakes "in profusion." A band played:

> Hail Columbia, happy land,
> Hail, ye patriots, heavenborn band. . . .
> Firm united let us be,
> Rallying round our liberty!

The next day Samuel Harrison Smith would write his wife about a gay party. "By the by, what do you think of my going to such an extent as to win 2 Doll. at Loo the first time I ever played the game, and being the most successful at the table? I confess I felt some mortification at putting the money of Mrs. Madison and Mrs. Duval into my pocket." But who cared about losing a little money? Not Dolley. The whole nation was in a holiday mood.

If the sun cast any shadow at this time it was because Dolley and James were about to send eleven-year-old Payne off to school in Alexandria. Eleven: just the age at which Madison had been put into the hands of Mr. Donald Robertson. Fortunately Alexandria was not far; they could visit him and he could sometimes come home. The Alexandria Academy had been chosen because it was rather special. Eighteen years ago the cornerstone of the one-story brick school on Washington Street had been laid by the Worshipful Master of Lodge No. 39 of the Ancient York

Masons. One of the institution's fourteen trustees, George Washington, had enrolled first his stepson and then his nephews Lawrence and George Steptoe Washington (George was now Dolley's brother-in-law) to give them a good classical foundation. He contributed $50 a year for scholarships and later willed the Academy $1,000. Moreover, the Madisons had Alexandrian relatives and friends who would keep an eye on the boy—in particular, perhaps, Dolley's cousin Dr. Isaac Winston IV, whom she had known from childhood, the eldest son of Aunt Lucy and the Judge. With hope and misgivings Payne's parents took him across the Potomac.

Meanwhile the celebration over Louisiana was still running like a prairie fire. Some Federalists, unwilling to give the Administration credit for its coup, argued that it was neither Jefferson's nor Madison's diplomacy but, rather, the sheer luck of a European war which had procured the prize. Others said the vast tract was worthless, or cost too much (4 cents an acre), or came with such a faulty title it could only cause trouble. This went on while the rest of the country was reeling with joy. Madison wrote Monroe: " . . . It is a noble acquisition."

Quibbles over the title were not without point. Napoleon had promised Spain that France would never cede Lousiana to a third power; the Marquis d'Yrujo was filing Spain's protest. Also the French constitution forbade alienation of French territory except by vote of the French legislature. And no less a person than James Madison had declared that the American Constitution gave the federal government no powers beyond those enumerated. The power to buy land was not enumerated.

Yet why worry? people said. It was Secretary of State Madison himself who had directed the negotiations for Louisiana—and crowds went right on celebrating with bands, bonfires, cotillions, wordy toasts, and spectacular fireworks. They were praising America's acquisition of a fitting geographic base for its great governmental experiment. Euphoric citizens asked each other what could stop the nation now. Though they could not foresee that thirteen states would be carved from the new territory, they felt on their faces the fresh wind of the future.

Ratify the treaty before Napoleon changed his mind, urged Jefferson and Madison. The Senate did. And on December 20, 1803, an official ran the Stars and Stripes up a pole to float high, wide, and gallant, landward and seaward, over the American city of New Orleans.

~ VIII ~

DOLLEY'S KNEE
AND THE PROBLEM
OF EVIL

JAMES MADISON HAD LONG WRESTLED with the problem of
evil: its metaphysical basis, relation to good, and grip on mankind. Writers
such as Plato, Aristotle, and Aquinas had helped him ponder the nature
of man, and that nature, obviously, included some evil. Indeed it was
precisely because he recognized that every man has a lower as well as
higher self that Madison had taken a middle position in politics, advocating more government than Jefferson, less than Hamilton. If man's capacity to govern himself depends upon what he is and might become,
Madison said, trust him to govern himself in a republic, yes, but erect
safeguards against the evil to which he is all too prone.

To Dolley, evil was less presence than rumor. Though she had
encountered unethical conduct, she tended to see human shortcomings as
a negation or paucity of love rather than as evidence of any positive thing
called evil; she believed stubbornly in people's good intentions. Thus she
was little prepared for certain unhappy events.

They started small; they started, one might say, with the displeasure,
one evening, of British Minister Anthony Merry—*"Toujours Gai."* When
at the President's house dinner was announced, Jefferson gave his arm to
Mrs. Madison. Dolley, knowing the protocol under Washington and
Adams, whispered, "Take Mrs. Merry!" But Jefferson escorted Dolley to
the seat of honor on his right and put Spanish Minister Yrujo's wife on his
left. Mrs. Merry found herself "below the salt." She and her husband were

174

furious. They picked at their food, rose early, and ordered their coach. As they swept out, the Marchioness de Casa-Yrujo joked under her breath, "This will cause a war!"

In a sense it did. Mrs. Merry protested all over town, and Mr. Merry wrote His Majesty's government about the "insult." Yrujo, already disgruntled by the Louisiana Purchase, joined forces. A snub? Nonsense! said Jefferson; protocol had no place in a democracy. And at a dinner of his own Madison upheld the President by escorting Mrs. Gallatin. Because of Mr. Madison's lesser station, Mr. Merry wrote his government, this was an even greater slight. But then everything in the United States was "equally as perfectly savage."

The fire would have smoldered out, French Chargé Louis Pichon thought, if the Marquis Yrujo, that "vanity personified," had not fanned the blaze. Merry and Yrujo together demanded that henceforth their wives be given, alternately, the seat of honor. Most Federalists and a few Republicans agreed. "Diplomatic superstition," said Madison, who understood that Jefferson was deliberately trying to destroy what he considered the unrepublican pomposities permitted by Washington and Adams; "a farce." When Napoleon's youngest brother, Jerome, arrived with his American bride, Elizabeth Patterson, the President underlined his lesson by escorting eighteen-year-old Betsey to the chair of honor. The Merrys recoiled. Exalting France, humiliating Great Britain!

Mrs. Merry saw Secretary of the Navy Robert Smith's ball for his niece Betsey Bonaparte as an opportunity to reassert her grandeur. Bursting upon the scene in a brilliant blue and white gown with a train and floating draperies, a diamond headband, and a fortune in diamonds on her chest, the big blond woman asked for all eyes.

But young Betsey outdid her, even if few "dared to look at her but by stealth." What a beautiful little creature! What classic features! So that was the auburn hair in which Jerome's watch chain had caught the night they danced together for the first time. But not everyone in Washington City was dazzled. "She has made a great noise here," Margaret Smith wrote. "Mobs of boys . . . crowded round her splendid equipage to see . . . an almost naked woman. . . . Her dress was the thinnest sarcinet. . . . Her back, her bosom, part of her waist and her arms were uncovered and the rest of her form was visible." A group of ladies sent word that if she wished to see them at Mme. Pichon's tomorrow, she must wear more clothes. Mrs. Merry fumed. To lose to that chit!

It was a tempest in a coffee cup. Unfortunately the brunt of the battle, Jefferson wrote Martha, was being borne by Dolley and her sister

Anna, "dragged in the dirt of every Federalist newspaper." But he felt that he could not capitulate; a nation had a right to decide its own customs. When Merry asked for a clear statement on American protocol, Jefferson summed it up in one word: pell-mell.

Madison tried to soothe the Merrys. The British Minister snapped that a policy of no precedence might put him below his own secretary of legation. Well, said Mr. Madison dryly, that labyrinth he refused to enter. To forestall repercussions in London, he had to write Minister Monroe about the imbroglio, but blushed, he said, at having "put so much trash on paper."

To make peace Jefferson sent out invitations to a stag dinner—no wives. Mr. Merry replied that while awaiting instructions from the Crown, he could not attend unless promised former "usages of distinction." The Marquis d'Yrujo and Dr. William Thornton also declined. Jefferson and Madison, Pichon wrote Talleyrand, "couldn't be more hurt." "I shall be highly honored," remarked Jefferson, "when the King of England is good enough to let Mr. Merry come and eat my soup." And he made out an egalitarian code of etiquette for his Administration.

Amid this grim comedy of manners Anna Payne became engaged to Congressman Richard Cutts from Massachusetts' district of Maine. For the Madisons it was both happy and sad news. Cutts was a handsome lawyer, educated at Harvard and in Europe, the wealthy owner of lands and ships. The couple would spend their summers in Maine and winters in Washington. Dolley told herself that Anna's happiness was the important thing. But to lose her sister-child!

About this time Dr. Manasseh Cutler, dining at the Madisons' on F Street, found Dolley "exceedingly pleasant and sensible in conversation." But he did not realize she was teasing him when she agreed that democrats were dishonest. "All democrats?" he asked. "All!" she said impishly, "every one of them!" After another meal there the rabid Federalist wrote even more appreciatively:

> An excellent dinner. The round of beef of which the soup is made is called *bouilli*. It had in the dish spices and something of the sweet herb [basil] and garlic kind, and a rich gravy. It is very much boiled, and is still very good. We had a dish with what appeared to be cabbage, much boiled, then cut in long strips, and somewhat mashed; in the middle a large ham. . . . The dessert . . . like apple pie in the form of half of a musk-melon, the flat side down, tops creased deep, and the color a dark brown.

Mrs. Merry demurred. She called such splendors at the Madison table "more like a harvest home supper than the entertainment of a Secretary of State." Hearing this, Dolley agreed, adding without rancor, "But abundance is preferable to elegance. Circumstances form customs, and customs taste; and as the profusion so repugnant to foreign customs rises from the happy circumstances of the abundance and prosperity of our country, I don't hesitate to sacrifice the delicacy of European taste for the less elegant but more liberal fashion of Virginia." It turned the barb. She was becoming less naïve; against pettiness and worse was learning to defend herself.

Then her sympathy was rushing toward Jefferson. After the birth of a child, his daughter Maria had steadily declined in health, and here he was, painfully anchored to Washington by his Presidential duties, troubled and fretting.

Dolley also felt sorry for the Thomas Laws. Not that she and James believed the gossip that Washington's stepgranddaughter "dashed in a very high military state," meaning with officers, while her husband was in Europe on business. Mr. Law himself had paid tribute to her purity of conduct. No, the two just bored each other.

While the Laws were struggling to separate, the Jerome Bonapartes struggled to stay together, for in spite of the Administration's attempts to pacify him, Napoleon refused to recognize what he called the fake marriage of a nineteen-year-old minor—Jerome had not received his mother's consent nor published banns. Ordering him back home, the First Consul forbade Elizabeth Patterson to set foot on French soil. But, though a Protestant, her rich merchant father had guarded against a papal annulment by insisting that the wedding be performed by the Catholic Archbishop of Baltimore. Would the child whom Betsey was carrying reconcile Napoleon? The fragile girl with the heart of a lioness was eager to meet him.

She did not know that because Napoleon was about to proclaim himself Emperor, this was the worst possible time to plead the case of a commoner sister-in-law; that, forced to create a noble court out of his marshals, he looked to royal sisters-in-law to offset such unlikely duchesses as, for instance, an ex-washerwoman. No, he could not use Miss Patterson.

On March 20, while Jerome's marriage hung in balance, Parson McCormick married Anna Payne and Richard Cutts in the Madisons' drawing room. As with Mary, Madison gave away the bride. At the reception which followed, the bride opened wedding gifts, mostly home-made, knitted, embroidered, painted, and composed in verse. Russian Consul General and Mme. Daschkov had sent Russia's traditional wine coolers, one filled with bread, the staff of life, the other with salt, its essence.

The bride and groom lingered several weeks before taking the "flying machine" north. When the coach had rolled out of sight, Dolley shut herself up in her room and wept. Payne and Anna gone, and Jemmy at the office all day—she felt an emptiness. She went driving alone in the rain. When friends came to offer sympathy, she refused to receive them. But she was glad to see her young cousin Dolley Winston.

Later she scolded Aunt Lucy "for not knowing my heart better" than to suppose the girl stayed too long—the visit was a favor. Dolley's letter ran on. Never had public business been "thicker." She was saving Aunt Lucy some of her best prunes and figs. "Farewell, Aunt, I have nothing new to tell you as you must know all about Burr. Ever your devoted Dolley."

The allusion was to Vice President Burr's campaign for the Gover-norship of New York. After his attempt to steal the Presidency, Burr had been cut by Jefferson, and though he presided over the Senate with dignity, and though most Republicans treated him politely, he was consid-ered a snake in the brush and could get no more patronage. It angered him. He could not accept oblivion. Holding his head high and living in splendor, he began to scheme with New England Federalists to gain power by sabotaging his own party.

More and more New England Federalists were muttering that Jeffer-son had destroyed the Constitution, that the acquisition of Louisiana had weakened their party, and that the only way New England could save itself commercially was to secede from the Union.

Hamilton refused to support the sectional movement. He spoke out against secession, saying it would cure nothing. But his rival Burr knew that if he could deliver New York to the Northern alliance by getting himself elected Governor, he could demand almost any reward, and against formidable opposition set out to swing the election by using his well-known organizational genius. The Madisons were watching the turn-coat from afar. The enigmatic, chameleonlike nature of her erstwhile friend depressed Dolley. Yes, she had to agree with James: it was despica-ble. What was his game now?

One day Burr called on Jefferson. A log fire was flickering in the study as the President asked his mission. Burr said he knew the Republicans would like him to go back to his law practice, but that would look as if he were shrinking from obloquy. His New York enemies were flaying him with Jefferson's name. What he needed was some mark of favor. Would the President consider it? Jefferson said no.

Burr's fury smoldered. It was less against Jefferson than against Alexander Hamilton, who had deprived him (as he thought) of the Presidency in 1800, and who kept calling him such names as Catiline. The two handsome lawyers, roughly the same age, had been concealed enemies for two decades—ever since Burr's defeat of General Schuyler. Three years ago a Federalist had sized up Burr this way: "In every sense a profligate; a voluptuary in the extreme. . . . His friends do not insist on his integrity. . . . A dangerous man with inordinate ambition." The Madisons hung back from going that far. Chicaneries, yes, but wasn't there some good in the man?

While the lion and lynx were glowering at each other, Jefferson finally got away to see his ailing daughter Maria. He found her at the Randolphs' Edgehill in a state of extreme debility. The sherry he had recommended had not helped, nor the more stomachic Pedro Ximenes. Stout fellows bore her to Monticello on a litter. But its bracing air worked no miracle. In good weather she was trundled around the lawn in a jinrikisha, her little niece Ellen running alongside. The April days were cloudless, her family adoring. One day her breath started to come in short, hard gasps. Martha found their father clutching a Bible. When Polly died they covered her body with a white cloth and heaped around her the broken branches of the spring—syringa and spirea, apple, pear, and plum.

The Madisons grieved over Maria. Dolley was downright ill the day the Marquis de Casa Yrujo and his wife in full pomp, on the eve of moving to Philadelphia, paid farewell calls on all of Washington's official set except the Madisons. Sally had to sneak back, later, to apologize to Dolley. Politics!

Meanwhile Madison kept on overworking. At this moment he was hard up against the problem of the Canadian boundary, the Barbary War, Britain's ever bolder theft of sailors, and the increasing opposition of a member of his own party, Representative John Randolph of Roanoke. It was rest and joy, each evening, to go home to Dolley.

She was enchanted when Anna wrote from Baltimore and Philadelphia. To receive her sister's affection and trace her to "that regretted city where we spent our early years," she wrote back, relieved a somberness. And she mentioned "the death of poor Maria, and the consequent misery it has occasioned us all. This is among the many proofs of the uncertainty of life. A girl so young, so lovely!" Remember her to Sally d'Yrujo, for she felt "a tenderness of her and her husband independent of circumstances"—independent of political backbiting.

Two days later (if my dating is correct) she was telling Anna about seeing her in a dream "dressed in beautiful and shining blue."

Her letters were lighter now. She would like to have kept some personal gifts from the Barbary Coast government, but her husband had made her send the patent office the burnous which she had "cabbaged so *snug*." He was "playing inquisitive" about some other things which she expected, yet, to have to refund. She was laughing as she wrote. Even so, the reference seems to point to a weakness in her nature. Between her lines Jemmy wrote a letter to Cutts about Monroe's reception in England. He too jested a little. "You can't expect me to dwell long on the subject . . . pinched between the words of my wife. As you are not . . . in the same situation, I shall expect something from you less cramped."

The following month, at Burr's New York defeat, political bad blood reached fever pitch. For the first time in fourteen years he was out of office. This brilliant erratic man burned with hatred against Alexander Hamilton.

While his star was sinking, another's was rising. On May 18, 1804, in the Cathedral of Notre Dame, Napoleon Bonaparte, diked out in a robe embroidered with golden bees, took a crown into his own hands, set it on his own head, and proclaimed himself Emperor. Both changes of state were destined to affect the Madisons.

Dolley wrote Anna, lamenting again her sister's absence. "I reflect on my selfishness and strive to be reconciled." Like Madame de Sévigné wooing her daughter, she fed Anna odd, interesting facts. The Laws, though separated, live under the same roof. Mama has given John the Kentucky land so that he can sell it and go into business. Tomorrow they visit the Fitzhughs in Alexandria (and of course Payne). Cutts Island in the Saco, so far away! "O, my dear sister, that I were with you, who have always been accustomed to accompany you wherever you went. . . . What are you about? . . . Tell me all you possibly can—I am absolutely crying to hear from you again. . . ." But feeling sorry for herself very long at a time was unlike Dolley. She began to write more matter-of-factly.

Though most of official Washington had left, the Madisons stayed in town until July, breaking the monotony by posing for Gilbert Stuart. He told wonderful anecdotes to divert his sitters. "Stuart is all the rage," Dolley wrote, and "worked to death." She sat quiet while he painted her in a dark dress with white ruching, a shawl, and an exotic turban with tassels. Madison's portrait looks like that of a well-centered man who knows who he is and where he is going.

Dolley was a little happier. Anna had sent her messages and a beautiful bonnet and Mama was expected soon. "Oh, Anna," she wrote, "you little know the triumph I feel when I hear of you and your beloved husband . . . —if Payne were a man married and gone from me I could not feel more sensibly everything that regarded him." Five days later she wrote that their mother was quite ill from dancing attendance on Mary's little daughter Dolley, "whose eyes are in great danger—lovely blossom!" She had mailed money to keep them at White Sulphur Springs, and would send a carriage to fetch them. Brother George, racked by the old consumption, was going to the West Indies. John was too lazy to write. Payne had written but so badly she had insisted he do it over again.

Anna replied, "How I miss you it would not be possible to say." Maine was delightful, but Boston had stifled her. On General Knox's princely estate his wife had turned out to be not haughty but "pleasant and sensible." Still, it was tiresome being dragged into endless games of chess; Madame showed no mercy. "Always, my dearest sister, much love."

Thus the summer dragged on. Stuart was departing, but the Prussian naturalist Alexander von Humboldt had arrived with a "train of philosophers," and all the ladies were in love with him. "He is the most polite, modest, well-informed and interesting traveler we have ever met," Dolley wrote. He was going to France to write a book and the summer doldrums would settle down again—except, of course, for the Fourth of July "grand doings."

The Jerome Bonapartes sailed for France on Mr. Patterson's *Erin*. When the ship slid out to sea Jerome was nervous, the Madisons heard, but Betsey was in fine fettle, standing on deck with her hair blowing. Pichon had frowned on the trip but Betsey didn't care—she'd face the Emperor. People waving her off wondered what troops Napoleon could deploy against such beauty.

Then the British graduated from stealing cargoes and seamen to violating American harbors. The impudence! Jefferson and Madison saw it as evidence of Britain's contempt for her former colonies.

When Payne, vacationing in Washington, came down with fever, the Madisons blamed the city's bad air. Oh, for the high pure air of Montpelier and geese on the mill pond! Payne tossed and turned on his bed.

Mary wrote that little Lucy's dark hair curled like Dolley's. The Jacksons would be returning soon to the "dissipation of Washington."

This was just before horror shot through the nation as it learned the fearful story of Hamilton and Burr.

Six weeks after his New York defeat, Burr had protested Hamilton's "despicable" opinion of him as expressed in a certain letter referred to in a newspaper. Communications were exchanged. Then Burr challenged Hamilton to a duel. Hamilton picked up the gauntlet which Burr had thrown down. Their seconds chose July 11 on the New Jersey dueling ground on the Weehawken heights above the Hudson River (where Hamilton's eldest son had recently died in a duel). At Richmond Hill, Burr was target shooting on a plaster head. Hamilton kept the imminent event from his wife Betsey and their six children. Meeting Burr at a party for the Order of the Cincinnati, he bowed to him, betraying no emotion except perhaps by a deepening of his rich voice as he sang, on request, the *Drum Song*.

Early in the morning of the 11th the antagonists met. Their seconds measured off ten paces. Burr and Hamilton faced each other. Burr took careful aim. A shot, and Hamilton—who had withheld his fire—fell. It had all happened very fast. Friends rowed Hamilton across the river to die at his leisure.

The Madisons were stunned. The news seemed unreal. Alexander Hamilton, "an host"! Madison's friend and collaborator before he became a political opponent—brilliant, desperately wrongheaded, honest Hamilton!

On July 16 Dolley wrote Anna: "Payne continues weak and sick. My prospects rise and fall to sadness as this precious child recovers or declines. . . . You have heard, no doubt, of the terrible duel and of poor Hamilton."

She had the imagination to see everything just as it had happened, a little myth: birds singing, then blood on the grass at Weehawken.

The Madisons read about the funeral: how the procession wound along Broadway to Trinity Church, a grey horse carrying Hamilton's reversed boots and spurs. The great concourse that followed the grieving family included black servants in white suits trimmed with black, a delegation of Cincinnati, a militia regiment, state officials, and a contingent of Columbia students in mourning. A meteor streaking across the American sky had disappeared into a dark void.

While public business forced the postponement of a trip to Montpelier, Dolley heard from the daughter of her old black nurse Mother Amy. But nothing could lift her spirits. She was experiencing, harshly, the wrongnesses in the world. And, indeed, there was a new inexplicable evil.

For the first time someone had set fire to Mount Vernon. "It's suspected some malicious persons are determined to reduce it to ashes." With this thought Dolley seems to have reached a saturation point. "Oh, the wickedness of men and women!" she cried to Anna in disillusionment. "I'm afraid to accept their invitations!"

For one who had always believed in the goodness of mankind this plunge into suspicion showed a certain loss of innocence. She was acquiring, painfully, the knowledge of man's double nature which Jemmy had long ago, as a simple matter of realism, taken into account. Far from turning him cynical, it had helped make him wise and compassionate. What would it do to Dolley?

An example of Madison's scrupulosity in trying to balance all elements before judging is his appraisal of Alexander Hamilton written twenty-seven years after the bloody transaction at Weehawken. He speaks of his party's old adversary as having "intellectual powers of the first order" and "integrity and honour in a captivating degree," and notes that though Hamilton's theory of government deviated from the republican standard, he had had the "candour to avow it" and the "greater merit of co-operating faithfully." Madison was giving a dead man the benefit of a doubt.

As if the problem of evil had settled into her body that summer of Hamilton's death, Dolley went to bed with inflammatory rheumatism, and though Dr. Willis bled her and Mother Madison tended her with kindness and her husband with great devotion, visitors became an intolerable burden. On the day she suffered most, fifteen or twenty kinsmen dined at Montpelier without seeing her or being seen. The dog days passed; not the soreness in her joints. James stood by the tester bed with the crimson hangings, baffled. Payne recovered from fever to find his mother worse off than he had ever been. He was concerned, for he loved her, but more interested in frolicking and getting his way. What school should they send him to, his parents were asking themselves, now that he had finished in Alexandria?

Mama reported that George was worse, and Mary that little Dolley's ears were so inflamed she must go back to the Springs. Then erratic "immense rains."

Dolley recovered in time to welcome her mother and niece. Again Montpelier was alive with voices. Jefferson came for two days. And Dolley put up peaches. Then the family rode off to Monticello. Madison was exuberant over a crop of the "finest tobacco ever seen"; it ought to bring $30,000. And October's tulip poplars were raining gold, and the maples burning. Persimmons dropped and squashed. If you peeled back their skin, the pulp tasted sweet, not puckery, right down to the nest of little slippery black seeds. And it was almost time for the big election: Jefferson for President against Charles Cotesworth Pinckney, George Clinton for Vice President against Rufus King.

Jefferson had three reasons for seeking a second term: to obtain vindication, to consolidate his policies, and to blunt the grief of Maria's death by hard work. But this campaign was more bruising than the one in 1800. Press, pulpit, and soapbox orators let out all stops to call Jefferson a monster of iniquity, and some Republicans perfected their own style of vilification while praising themselves extravagantly for reducing taxes, also the army, navy, and public debt; for licking the Barbary pirates; and for doubling the country's size. Jefferson and Clinton won all but fourteen of the electoral votes.

That victory would keep the Madisons on F Street four more years. Then what? Jefferson had sworn that, like Washington, he would not consider a third term. In drawing rooms and taverns Madison's succession was being taken for granted. But James and Dolley refused to think that far ahead.

A more immediate problem was Payne's need of a scaffolding to support him whenever he had to apply himself to a job.

In November the new French Minister, General Louis Marie Turreau de Garambonville, arrived in all his elegance. Let him explain if he could France's stepped-up spoliations.

Men of peace, Jefferson and Madison—back in Washington—knew that a policy of peace at any price would jeopardize both peace and the national honor. But they also knew that a fresh war following close on the Revolution might overtax a country with no more than a token army and navy. If only they could concentrate on building the nation. Wasn't there a better way than war to settle international disputes? Said Dolley on many occasions and in many ways, "I do not admire contention."

Because she was still weak from her illness, the Madisons were entertaining very little. But they felt duty-bound to give a party for Turreau. He was an extraordinary apparition. When, loaded with lace, he swept into a room, or when, imitating Louis XVI, he drove out in a gold coach, he impressed, terrified, sometimes amused: a tall man with snow hair, bristling black moustaches, and a smear of cruelty spoiling a handsome red face. A confidential report from John Armstrong, the American Minister to France, painted this "butcher of Vendée" as a crude rake merciless in war, and in public service "atrocious." Though Turreau professed great devotion to the Emperor, cautioned Armstrong, he had probably been sent out of France as a bad risk. In view of this report, the Administration could not but eye him askance. His carriage, clattering through the red-light district, hauled berouged girls back to the French legation. Oh, yes, poor man, said his apologists; his lady would not arrive until spring. And even his coldest critics had to admit that he bowed with enormous style. So the Madisons were shining their silver. Dolley planned to dress to the teeth.

Turreau tried to heal the breach between Madison and Yrujo. But a three-cornered meeting at Madison's house fizzled. The French Minister reported to Talleyrand that though the Spaniard had been wrong to join Mr. Merry's wretched dispute over etiquette, then stomp off to Philadelphia to sulk, Madison was also at fault. He had thwarted a reconciliation by being *"sec, haineux, passioné"*—abrupt, ill-humored, passionate. In other words, he spoke forcefully, resolved not to countenance any more of Yrujo's outrageous conduct.

Continuing his efforts as a peacemaker at a dinner served on magnificent gold plates, Turreau found Madison still adamant against sacrificing principle. Later, to explain his lack of success as a broker, the Frenchman wrote Paris that Yrujo would have consented, but the Secretary of State just did not know how to forgive. Actually the Administration had already asked Spain for Yrujo's recall.

Madison discussed diplomatic snarls with Dolley. She possessed what no school could teach: an understanding heart. And she identified herself completely with her husband's interests.

They watched John Randolph conduct the impeachment trial of Supreme Court Justice Samuel Chase. The charge was malfeasance and misfeasance in office. An example of misconduct: a sentence of death for treason against a man who had dared to criticize President Adams. The Madisons called Chase's acquittal a gross miscarriage of justice.

They were also following the odyssey of Betsey Bonaparte. When the *Erin* docked at Lisbon, the French troops who arrested Jerome forbade his wife to land. At Amsterdam Betsey looked into gun muzzles. Expecting her child soon, she sought refuge in Great Britain. There was no message from Jerome. Eventually she accepted the Emperor's bribe of about $60,000 a year to return to America.

In his second inaugural address Jefferson spelled out some facts about a country feeling its strength and said that his Administration was trying to foster friendship with all nations. Unfortunately he spoke in so low a voice few heard him.

Thus the counterpoint of the Madisons' public and private lives went on; the weighty and the comparatively trivial. Mama, who was visiting, had—against Quaker custom—bought a lottery ticket, but drawn a blank. Lucy had "been goose enough to get into Anna's camp" and would accept baby clothes. Then it got around that Madame Turreau had left the rickety old *Shepherdess* at the Azores, whereupon it had sunk to the bottom of the sea. When the loud, likable Frenchwoman reached Washington, rumor made her a jailer's daughter who had saved the "butcher" from the guillotine. Or just from poverty. In any case the General now got her pregnant.

And Dolley Madison injured her knee.

While nursing it, she wrote Anna about these odd French people, a "vast addition." She and Madame, who saw each other almost every day, communicated mostly by gesture. "She is good-natured and intelligent, generous, plain and curious—we ride, walk together and visit *sans* ceremony. I never visit in her chamber but I crack my sides laughing—I wish I could tell you on paper at what. She shows me everything she has and would fain give me everything." On Dolley chattered. She's sending some Olsen lace for "darling Julia or yourself." (Had Anna spoken of calling her baby, if a daughter, by the name Dolley would have preferred for herself?) She is also making a christening cap. "Oh, Anna, I am dying to come to your country—"

Two days later she went to bed in great pain. The "tumor" on her knee threatened gangrene. Two physicians, conferring, decided to use caustic. James, Mama, John, and Payne stood around, apprehensive.

Dolley tried to stay cheerful. She kept culling news for Anna. One evening, while visiting, Mrs. Merry had looked through a window and noticed General Turreau and his family walking near the house. Seizing her shawl, the Englishwoman had "marched off with great dignity and more passion." George had promised to bring Lucy and the boys to Montpelier. He "coughs continually and is hoarse . . . but has no idea of dying." Turreau whipped his wife in front of servants—how odious. Then a shocker: "Alas, it seems as if I should walk no more!"

Madison wanted to take his wife to the University of Pennsylvania's famous chief surgeon, Dr. Philip Physick. But how could he get away from his public duties? Of course he could take her there and leave her, but neither of them liked that idea. "I dread the separation," Dolley wrote Anna.

One day when Dr. Thornton, George Steptoe Washington, and George's brother Lawrence were spending the day with her brother John,

Dolley, lying upstairs, "enjoyed the sound of Virginia hilarity echoing through the house." But George's cough was bad. And she kept remembering how little Dolley Jackson had cried her heart out when her mama had to take her back to Clarksburg. Oh, the pain in her knee was monstrous.

Another day pandemonium broke loose at the French legation. When Madame Turreau protested against the loose women her lord brought home, he stepped up his beatings. She hit him with a flatiron, and he clubbed her. To drown out her screams Turreau's secretary hastily closed the window and played loudly on his French horn. Neighbors called Justice of the Peace William Thornton. "Dr. Thornton," cried the terrible-tempered General, "you do not know ze law of ze nation!" "I know the laws of humanity," replied the officer, "and mean to enforce them." Madame Turreau and her children fled the house. It took Secretary Madison's best diplomacy to get the whole family back under the same roof.

At the President's open house on the Fourth, Dolley sat "quite still . . . amusing myself with the mob." She wished John wouldn't drink so much.

The summer seemed "dull and vacant" to the crippled one. Under Dr. Eldry's treatment her knee was not improving. "I feel very impatient to be in Montpelier," Dolley wrote Anna, "and have confidence in the change of air." She had been asked to select wedding clothes for Mr. Jefferson's granddaughter Virginia, and would try to shop in George Town from the carriage. "I must do the best for them." Impossible to head home until Turreau left for Baltimore.

Meanwhile the United States and France were at loggerheads over Louisiana's eastern boundary. Using old maps of the territory Spain had ceded to France, Madison argued that France had sold everything up to the Perdido River which emptied into the Gulf of Mexico (including present-day lower Mississippi and Alabama). No, replied Turreau; the deal did not include this "West Florida"—and please explain the private, armed American ships violating Dominican ports. The President had asked Congress to restrain them, said Madison quietly. Turreau could not be mollified. He had it on good authority, he stormed, that the flotilla carried 700 men and 80 cannon.

Over in Paris, Napoleon had read in a New York newspaper clipping that a Mr. Samuel H. Ogden had given a banquet for a hundred guests aboard the 22-gun *Indostan* to celebrate the safe return from Santo Domingo of a "little navy nearly or quite equal to the whole force sent by Jefferson to blockade Tripoli." It seemed that the party's ninth toast had run this way: "To the government of Haiti, founded upon the only legitimate basis of all authority—the people's choice!"

One day Turreau sharpened his protests. Madison, refusing to go on the defensive, mentioned a certain marauding French privateer. Yes, admitted Turreau disarmingly, it was violating the laws of humanity and the nations, but did that excuse the Santo Domingo excursion? In the midst of this "warm dispute" the door opened, a hand popped in, and barber Dixon announced he had come to shave the Secretary of State. The high-level talk dissolved in laughter. But Madison had been worn out by eight months of General Louis Marie Turreau de Garambonville. Thank God that bird of prey was finally taking his "cruel and sanguinary" beak to Baltimore.

Dolley's knee was so much worse the Madisons wondered about the wisdom of going to Montpelier. It was July, and they must decide what to do. In the midst of their dilemma they received a shock, and Dolley wrote Anna the stunning news:

> Alas, my beloved Anna, I have just received a heart-rending letter from poor Jackson—our darling little Dolley is dead; our dear Mary and little Lucy very ill—oh Heaven in mercy spare them! I can scarcely write you, so sick with grief, apprehension, is my whole frame. Our mother will feel it so sensibly. Never can I forget the piteous reluctance with which the precious lamb was borne away from us! . . . But who can look into futurity?—it was done for the best.

They had decided to go to Orange within ten days.

They did not. Their hope had been an illusion. The tumor or ulcer hurt dreadfully. Moreover, the calomel taken to eliminate poisons had weakened Dolley down to a thin ghost. Suddenly Madison—thoroughly alarmed—resolved to consult Dr. Physick. They left for Philadelphia on July 25 in the carriage, Peter driving.

Strangely enough, as they traveled in wilting weather, Dolley revived. Somehow riding made her leg feel easier. But James frightened her with a severe bilious attack. "I thought all was over with me," she would write. "I could not fly to him as I used to do. But heaven in its mercy restored him the next morning." The fourth day they breakfasted at the well-remembered resort Gray's Ferry.

A year ago Dolley had written the honeymooning Anna, "I hope [both] are now about entering Philadelphia. I should like vastly to enter it with thee. Yes, I think if I could come within view of the waterworks my heart would bound a little—heigh ho—" And now her heart bounded a little, heigh ho.

They drove straight to Dr. Physick. Yes, it was a bad infection, he said, but there would be no amputation—not even surgery. He believed he could cure this ulcer within a month by splints, leg elevation, diet, and rest.

Dolley wrote Anna from temporary quarters about her reaction. "I feel as if my heart were bursting—no mother, no sister—but, fool that I am! here is my husband sitting anxiously by me . . . my unremitting nurse. But you know how delicate he is—I tremble for him [and she describes his recent attack]. . . . He would not pause until he heard my fate. . . ."

Two days later when they found "excellent lodgings" on Sansom Street, she turned into "another being," her spirits high.

To keep her leg in a fixed position Dr. Physick bound it tightly to a yard-long board. Raised up, it poked at an angle out from the bed, making it quite impossible for her to sit up. All invitations to the homes of the gentry she refused, to "be at ease." But "the world" came to call.

One day two Quakers, Nancy Mifflin and Sally Zane, criticized her for entertaining such a crowd. Their lecture recalled "the times when our Society used to control me entirely and debar me from so many advantages and pleasures, and, although so entirely from their clutches, I really felt my ancient terror . . . revive. . . ." But these zealots could not change her love for gentler Quakers like Betsey Pemberton. For kindness, she wrote, Betsey "bore off the palm." She wrote Anna that the longer she stays in Philadelphia the less she "cares for the vanities," though she suspects—smiling—that she will again love the routs all too well. The press of callers was growing tiresome, "nor can all my vanity make it more than tolerable." Still, she and Jemmy were getting more rest than they had had since their marriage eleven years ago. He was trying not to worry unduly about duties elsewhere—Orange and Washington must shift for themselves.

For three months James Madison watched over his wife, conferring with Jefferson only by letter. Merry and Yrujo he could see here in the city to which they had peevishly fled. Callers without appointments he dodged, for he had set himself the leisure-time task of writing a treatise on the rights and obligations of neutral nations, hoping that, in America's quarrel with Britain, logic might yet prevail. But his first concern was Dolley.

One of their chief topics of conversation was where to send Payne to prepare him for Princeton: a major problem. They were anxious to do the best by him. It was all-imperative.

A letter from Maine announced that Anna had given birth to James Madison Cutts. Mother and child were doing well. The Madisons were relieved and delighted. The news broke the boredom of the slow nonsurgical treatment which would keep them away from Montpelier's corn tasseling and tobacco drying.

So Envoys James Monroe and Charles Pinckney had failed to convince the King of Spain that he no longer owned West Florida or Texas or ought to sell them, and they were advising their government to seize both territories by force. But Madison thought seizure of lands unspecified in the Louisiana Treaty too great a gamble. The King's haughty refusal made a "strong appeal to the honor and sensibility of this country." But with no navy to speak of, the United States must not invite war by threatening what it could not carry out.

Agreeing, Gallatin, erstwhile champion of naval economy, called for naval expansion. Jefferson's small gunboats were inadequate; the nation needed *ships*. Commented Madison, "I have long been of the opinion that it would be a wise and dignified course to take . . . measures for a naval force." This crisis increased the urgency.

Jefferson began to argue for an alliance with Great Britain which would operate when and if the United States clashed with either Spain or France—for Spain was not the only threat. When Napoleon had subjugated Europe, he just might turn and attack America.

Madison wrote back that a treaty of alliance works two ways. How could the United States lay Britain under obligations without assuming some itself? And how could the nation fulfill them? Of course an *eventual* alliance (he was being tactful) would be a good thing. Fortunately Pinckney's latest dispatches suggested that Napoleon-backed Spain did not want war—a conclusion confirmed by Yrujo's sudden issuing of dinner invitations and by his gifts of South American wheat seed and Spanish barley. Madison wondered if the wheat had been green or ripe when Argentine weevils laid eggs in the cracks.

August did not bring the yellow fever outbreak they had feared. With her leg sticking straight out from her hip, Dolley had plenty of time to savor old memories of Philadelphia—Penn's town, the one which she had discovered at the age of fifteen, fresh from Virginia's piny woods. Here walked the ghosts of Papa, Walter, Temple, and Isaac; here her young and lovely mother. While James worked on his treatise, long-past events, bright and dark, crowded her mind. They haunted her while she turned the pages of a book or did needlework or stared out the window at the gigs on Sansom Street. Papa was making white starch. John Todd staggered in, mortally ill. Then one evening Aaron Burr brought the great little Madison.

James was dressing for another of the Yrujos' dinners. Unwilling to recall the Marquis, Spain had asked permission for him to come home "on leave." Agreeing, Madison had been tricked into attending this dinner by an invitation which coupled his name with his old friend Governor McKean. It had turned him angry, and going without Dolley made the whole thing worse. Separated, each felt like little more than half a person.

There were spells of drizzle between humid, stifling, mosquito-ridden days before Dolley was rushed off for the second time in her life to Gray's Inn to escape an epidemic of yellow fever. Time swiveled; she was holding a dying child.

James used this exile from an exile to write a policy statement for the next Cabinet meeting. Luckily frost came early; they could go back to Sansom Street.

The talk in Philadelphia, now, was often of North Africa. Last spring former Consul William Eaton had sent motley troops marching 600 miles from Alexandria in Egypt to Derna in Tripoli to reinstate Pasha Ahmet, who had been promising America the cooperation which his usurper brother Yussuf had refused. This brilliant maneuver, oddly aborted, had led to a treaty not with Ahmet at all but with Yussuf, who pocketed $60,000. Now General Eaton was roasting the Administration for buying a peace which he said he could have enforced by arms. Exactly, said the Federalists to whom the Administration was always wrong. No, wrote Madison; Eaton would have been wiped out in Derna, and Ahmet was even less reliable than Yussuf.

St. Mary's Seminary in Baltimore—would that be the best preparatory school for Payne? Founded in 1802 by the Catholic Bishop of Maryland, John Carroll, and run by the Sulpician Order, it was patronized by many Protestants for its excellent teaching and discipline.

While pondering, the Madisons heard that Anna's "little charmer"— Madison Cutts—had John Payne's "beautiful nose." His mother was looking after him herself. Dolley hoped Anna wasn't overdoing. The other good news was that Mary had given birth to a little namesake who was comforting her for the child who had died.

In October a letter arrived on Sansom Street from President Jefferson. It said that Prime Minister William Pitt was forming an anti-Napoleon coalition, but the Cabinet considered a British alliance too vital a question to be settled without Madison's "aid and council"—could he come back at once?

Madison welcomed the idea of a coalition. For one thing, a besieged France and its ally Spain might grow desperate enough to sell West Florida to the United States. Minister to France Armstrong had suggested offering them $10 million, but considering the United States' strong claim to the territory, surely $5 million was enough. Texas would make a nice bonus. As for a British alliance, well, though not enthusiastic, he was willing to drop that seed into Mr. Merry's mind.

Jefferson kept pressing him to come. The Cabinet meeting would take place on November 12, and the Secretary of State would be sorely needed. Nearly three months had passed—couldn't Dolley travel yet?

Dr. Physick said no. Though almost healed, her knee was still so tender it might be damaged by the shaking up of a long coach trip. The Madisons saw what they must do. Though since marriage they had never, except for the briefest intervals, been separated, and though they dreaded the thought, if duty required Madison's presence in Washington they would resign themselves. The Cuttses could collect Dolley several weeks from now when passing through Philadelphia en route to Washington. Meanwhile Betsey Pemberton and Mother Amy's daughter would nurse her.

On Monday, October 23, Peter drove Madison out of town to catch a stagecoach farther down the road. On his return the black servant would put himself at Miss Dolley's disposal.

When the carriage had driven out of sight, Dolley collapsed. To cheer her, Betsey put on Madison's hat and clowned a little. It did not work. Nothing worked. Dolley was desolate.

During their month-long separation—even though the post went out only irregularly—Dolley wrote James every day. Because letters between this seldom-separated husband and wife are very few, the extant ones from this period in the twelfth year of their marriage are precious evidence of the quality of their relationship. Dolley to James:

> A few hours only have passed since you left me, my beloved, and
> I find nothing can relieve the oppression of my mind but speak-
> ing to you in this the only way. . . .

Betsey Pemberton and Amy seem to "respect the grief" they know she feels. She'll be better when Peter comes back with news, she says. Not that any length of time could lessen her first regret, but it will help to be assured that her husband is "well and easy." Betsey puts on his hat, "but I cannot look at her."

During a restless night Dolley tried to think of the good side. This way Jemmy could not only serve their country but also visit St. Mary's, see Payne, and give her a firsthand report of her child.

> *October 24.* What a sad day! The watchman announced a cloudy morning at one o'clock, and from that moment I found myself unable to sleep from anxiety for thee, my dearest husband. Detention, cold and accident seem to menace thee.

Betsey, who lies beside her, gave her some laudanum. It had only a "partial effect." Everyone is "most kind and attentive." In fancy she is following her husband on his long journey south.

Dolley's next letter might have been written by a bride:

> *October 25.* This clean cold morning . . . my darling. . . . The knee is mending. I eat very little, and sit precisely as you left me. The doctor . . . talks of you. He regards you more than any man he knows, and nothing could please him so much as a prospect of passing his life near you; sentiments so congenial to my own, like dewdrops on flowers, exhilarate as they fall. . . . Adieu my beloved, our hearts understand each other. In fond affection thine,
>
> > Dolley.

This was followed quickly by a headlong communication:

> *October 26.* . . . My dearest Husband, Peter returned safe with your dear letter, and cheered me with a favorable account. . . . I was sorry you could not ride further in our carriage, as it might have spared you fatigue.
>
> In my dreams of last night I saw you in your chamber, unable to move from riding so far and so fast. I pray that an early letter from you may chase away the painful impression of this vision. . . .

She is improving and will observe his advice "strictly."

In view of Dolley's dream, it is perhaps of interest that Madison's library contained Samuel F. Connover's *Dissertation on Sleep and Dreams* (1791), which upholds the possibility of prophetic dreams. Later Dolley would speak of herself as "always the dreamer" (though of course that could have two meanings). As for Madison's inability to move, in the dream related, it may be connected with the early paralyzing illness whose return they still somewhat feared.

Reaching Washington within three days, Madison wrote to assure his wife that he was home safe and in good health, and to give her other news for which he knew she was waiting.

> My dearest, . . . Payne arrived about an hour after I did. I enclose a letter from him. . . . During my halt at Baltimore, I made two efforts to see Bishop Carroll, but without success. . . . I could do nothing therefore towards getting a berth for Payne in the seminary of Mr. Dubourg. I have lost no time, however, in making . . . a request . . . in a letter to Bishop Carroll. . . .
> . . . Let me know that I shall soon have you with me, which is most anxiously desired by your ever affectionate
>
> James Madison.

Dolley was relieved. Her love rushed to meet him.

> *October 28.* . . . I rejoice to hear you are there, and shall await the next post with impatience. . . . I am getting well as fast as I can, for I have the reward in view of seeing my beloved. . . .

Then, because her husband wanted to hear everything, she indulged in some small talk. She writes every day but is so shut up she fears she can say nothing amusing; she hopes to do better when at last she begins to drive out. "Did you see the Bishop, or engage a place at school for Payne? . . . Farewell until tomorrow, my best friend; think of thy wife, who thinks and dreams of thee."

What Madison replied in a lost letter is reflected, as in a mirror, by Dolley's response:

> *October 30.* I have at this moment perused with delight thy letter, my darling husband. . . . The knee is acquiring strength every day but my nerves are often weak. The doctor ordered me some drops . . . [and] directed me to eat meat and drink porter. I take but a morsel of each, having no appetite. I walk about the room. . . . No inflammation, and the little incision nearly fast, so that you may expect me to fly to you as soon—oh! I wish I could say how soon! . . . To find you love me, have my child safe, and that my mother is well, seem to comprise all my happiness.

She chatters on. Madame Pichon has sent her some earrings. Betsey is adding a secret postscript. The President has asked her to bring Martha a "fashionable wig." She will drive to a shop door and do business from the carriage. She has had many callers and invitations. Tell Mrs. Thornton she is seeing about the bonnet. Then, having circled, she comes back to her starting point. "It is now past nine o'clock, and I cease to write only to dream of thee. . . . Write soon to thy devoted Dolley."

Time dragged. But her letter of November 1 carried an announcement she had been longing to make and James to hear:

> I have great pleasure in repeating to you, my beloved, what the doctor has just told me—that I may reasonably hope to leave this place in a fortnight. . . . I am so impatient to be restored to you.

Aware that she will be reentering a political milieu and is "behind," she asks modestly:

> I wish you would indulge me with some information respecting the way with Spain, and the disagreement with England. . . . You know I am not much of a politician, but I am extremely anxious to hear (as far as you think proper) what is going forward in the Cabinet. On this subject I believe you would not desire your wife to be the active partisan that our neighbor is, Mrs. L.; nor will there be the slightest danger while she is conscious of her want of talents. . . .

Madison's next letter, though masculine and a little dry, is in its way just as tender. "Yours of the 1st instant, my dearest, gives me much happiness but it cannot be complete till I have you again with me. . . ." He has sold his tobacco, but there are payment difficulties. He didn't expect her to get much from her Fourth Street tenants. The buildings should be insured. He is puzzled by her question about Spain and England. While one country is slipping into ill humor, the other may grow more amenable. Perhaps a European war would lessen Spain's insults, increase England's. It would be imprudent to force the issue. The power of declaring and propagating war, of course, lies with Congress—"that is always our answer to the newspapers."

This answer to Dolley's question about politics shows him quite willing to take her into his confidence.

Another day he wrote of his pleasure on hearing that she could walk about and his hope that Dr. Physick would soon let her travel. Payne is well. He is trying to keep the boy "at some sort of attention" to his books. "All my affection embraces you." He enclosed $300.

Dolley's letter of November 1 had ended with a lyrical burst:

> Kiss my child for me, and remember me to my friends. Adieu, my dear husband. Peter brings me no letter from you, which really unfits me from writing more to anyone.
>
>   Your ever affectionate
>   Dolley.

Her days were a love letter.

James reported Bishop Carroll's assurance that by December Father Dubourg would find a place for Payne at St. Mary's Seminary—he was sending a copy of the regulations. Dolley was overjoyed.

When their grey horse took sick, she hurried to tell her husband. He suggested that she consult Colonel Patton. She replied that Colonel Patton advised her to sell the tandem team, since the grey horse now put to pasture was incurable; sell and buy a certain handsome pair of sorrels. She added that she had dreamed again of her husband, that a short drive had exhausted her, and that General Turreau had forgotten a lot of his English. She was writing this letter down in the parlor surrounded by visitors, and must leave him.

But not for long. "I received yours containing Payne's letter . . . my best beloved, which gave me much pleasure." Brother John had arrived "in the mail" after three sleepless nights en route from Norfolk; what a surprise. Because Colonel Patton was sure a delay would lose her the opportunity, she had bought the sorrels, paying the $350 difference. All was ready now, the knee "perfectly healed." "No tongue can express my anxiety to be with you at home. I would risk everything to join you." Fearing to overtax her strength, she had declined to spend several days with Molly and Anthony Morris, "much as I love these old and dear friends." A newspaper had announced Spain's declaration of war against the United States. (It would prove false). Yrujo had applied for a passport, but when Mrs. Stewart asked about it he became "terribly angry." Turreau, stumbling around ill, was notorious here in Philadelphia as the cruel commander of La Vendée and a fighting husband. In this letter Dolley's words run uphill; they are all happily out of breath. After four months bereft of Jemmy, she was going home!

Two days later, on November 17, she must write fast:

. . . Mr. Cutts and Anna arrived last evening, my beloved, and so pleased and agitated was I that I could not sleep. We will leave on Monday if I am quite strong enough, but I must await a little your commands. . . . Farewell, my beloved one.

James also wrote in great excitement—"the last mail, my dearest, that will be likely to find you in Philadelphia, and I am not without some hope that this will be too late"; that already she had left Philadelphia for Washington.

The trip was an ordeal. The mud on the rutted roads had frozen, the carriage was unheated. If the usual wrapped hot foot bricks were used, they could do little against such cold. But conversation generated a kind of warmth, and the two bundled-up sisters sitting with Representative Richard Cutts—doubtless hunched over in a greatcoat—had to catch up with questions and reports. The three-month-old little "Madison" had been left behind with Richard's family in Maine. Dolley wanted to know how he looked, and if he smiled and slept well. The carriage jogged, jounced, stopped at inns, and then again took the seemingly endless road. Peter held the spanking new sorrels to a steady pace. At last Washington City—they were clattering along F Street. If the world was full of sickness, death, and heartache, it was also full of joy.

A lady who had feared she would never walk again ran into her husband's arms.

❦ IX ❧

THE ROAD
TO POWER

DURING THE NEXT THREE YEARS, while Madison traveled a rough road to power, Dolley was with him every mile of the way.

Treachery came to the nation and so to them the fall of 1805. Having long brooded over his New York defeat, loss of the Vice Presidency, and general ostracism following his shooting of Hamilton, Aaron Burr had fallen into a reckless mood. A month after the duel he used an agent to offer his services to Great Britain. The feeling out was ignored.

He waited a year, then approached Mr. Merry. Lend him £100,000, he said, and he would see that Louisiana pulled out of the United States. While warning his government against Burr's "known profligacy," Merry reported the proposition. Burr wrote from the Ohio that his scheme had been launched and was going well, and sent an accomplice—ex-Senator Jonathan Dayton—back East with missions and messages. Then last summer while Dolley's knee was mending, a newspaper printed these words: "How long will it be before we shall hear of *Col. Burr* being at the head of a *revolution* party on the western waters?"

That blew the lid off.

But when Burr arrived back in Washington about the same time as Dolley, the Madisons' attention was elsewhere. Dolley was readying Payne's clothes for St. Mary's, Madison embroiled in foreign affairs. Rumors were a copper penny a dozen—why listen to so wild a one?

As if to make up for her long confinement, Dolley gave larger parties. After coffee, the card tables were brought out, and those who wanted to gambled. A servant carried around baskets of raisins, almonds, and candied fruit. Around each sweet was wrapped a little verse, probably of

Dolley's composing. Then a "dish of chocolate." Sometimes Anna Maria Thornton played the piano. At dinner parties Dolley, like Jefferson, used covered silver dishes and often served the new fad, baked Alaska. It was quite a trick to keep the ice cream from melting.

Though Dolley had brought Payne up a Quaker, she was not troubled by Father Dubourg's Catholicism. By all reports he taught pure French along with the humanities. And he would enforce a discipline much needed by a lad with a capable mind and artistic bent but lackadaisical habits who was preparing for Princeton.

Presumably the Madisons accompanied Payne to Baltimore to see St. Mary's and introduce him to his new life.

A friend of theirs has described it. She admired the scientific apparatus, especially an electrical machine. The botanical garden and three courts were beautiful with trees. The Gothic chapel held an almost life-size statue of Christ suspended on a cross, and two other figures were planned—the Virgin Mary and John. In the chapel the guide showed great awe, and no conversation was allowed. Behind the chapel a cross had been erected on a man-made hill representing Mount Calvary. The Catholic priest told visitors that Protestant students were left free to believe as they wished. Academic standards were high.

So Payne stayed, and a wagon brought his trunk and rumbled off, and Dolley had to adjust.

Soon afterward some curious characters converged on Washington. General Francisco Miranda came seeking aid for a Venezuelan revolt, and General William Eaton, brave in a Turkish sash, turned up to be fawned upon and feted. The Tunisian "Ambassador," Sidi Suliman Mellimelli, arrived collect. And Creek, Osage, Sac, Sioux, and Missouri Indians were parading down Pennsylvania Avenue.

The splendidly mounted Creek wore blue coats with red collars, gold-laced hats, and bead moccasins. But some of the other Indians had only ambling nags; they were naked to the waist, their faces brilliantly painted, their shaved heads erupting in feather topknots. They shook gourd rattles while letting out weird yells.

One day the redskins trooped into the Madisons' parlor. There they met the oversized, stately, magnificently turbaned envoy from Tunis, Mellimelli, who demanded to know whom they believed in, Abraham, Mohammed, or Jesus. Through an interpreter they answered, "We worship the Great Spirit without an agent." "Vile heretics!" sneered Mellimelli, and the ladies who always surrounded him closed in happily around his ferocity.

Later, at the funeral of an Osage chief who had danced himself to death, an Indian said, "God being God, it was His work," and Mellimelli was so impressed he softened a bit. Still, he doubted that these savages had descended from Ham, Shem, or Japheth; there must be another explanation.

Mellimelli himself needed explaining. When Jefferson refused Tunis's demand for tribute equal to that paid Algiers, the Dey had dispatched, at American expense, this huge fifty-year-old envoy with an eleven-man retinue and Italian band. Greeted with a salute of guns, the Turk had set out at once to visit Secretary of State Madison, a servant tagging behind to carry his 4-foot pipe. The household on F Street was startled by the sight of the bearded Mellimelli's crimson robe and 20-yard white turban. The scarlet velvet caftan he presented to Dolley was weighted down with 30 pounds of gold bullion. Yes, he conceded, he liked his quarters at Stelle's (the bankrupt hotel rented for the deputation); all the arrangements were fine except one thing. There were no concubines. So Madison charged the State Department with "Georgia a Greek," and listed her fee under "appropriations to foreign intercourse."

But the Administration firmly turned down Mellimelli's plea for more tribute. No, certainly not. Undaunted, he and his suite kept on running up bills at Stelle's. How go home without a promise of more "gifts"?—the Dey would kill him. To illustrate, Mellimelli drew a finger across his throat. Twittering ladies begged to examine his muslin turban. This one turned out to be plaster of Paris.

Inasmuch as three of the four stud horses sent by the Dey had survived the trip, Jefferson and Madison decided it was only right to make the royal pedigreed gifts pay for the embassy's board and rooms. Representative Bryan of Georgia wrote the Secretary of State. "I applied to the President for permission to put a couple of mares to the Barbary horse. . . . He told me I might . . . but the groom refused . . . without an order . . . from you."

Then there was a scare the night the Madisons gave Mellimelli a reception. Opening a door on a "large fat negress" who was preparing coffee, the delighted Turk threw his arms around her, crying in Turkish, "You are the handsomest woman in America! You look like one of my wives, the high-priced one—a load for a camel!" On getting a translation, the beauty and fashion of Washington doubled up with laughter.

That winter a crowd attended the President's New Year reception— even Minister Merry (fresh from secret negotiations with Burr) put in an appearance. But Mellimelli, insulted by Mr. Jefferson's attention to some Creek and Osage, departed in dudgeon.

The President and Secretary of State could not be bothered by such trivialities. They had graver problems on their hands, such as their continuing attempt to force France to settle the Florida controversy and John Randolph's wish to split the Republican party. Then one day they received this anonymous warning: "You admit him at your table . . . at the very moment he is conspiring against the state. . . . Watch his connections with Mr. M—-y and you will find him a British pensioner and agent." Was Burr a traitor?

To that man's annoyance the answer was "not yet." All he possessed was schemes. But they were vigorous. When he and Miranda, rivals for secret British money, met by chance in Philadelphia, they had performed a kind of slow ceremonial dance, circling each other and bowing politely, so to speak, without ever touching.

Though Jefferson and Madison refused to give Miranda money for filibustering, they continued, rather inconsistently, to offer him hospitality. It gave him a sought-for opportunity of which he promptly took advantage. He swore, where it counted, that they had winked at his game for high stakes. The lie raised troops and money for use against Spain.

Chagrined, the Administration pressed Spain to do two things: indemnify the United States for certain sea crimes and sell it the Floridas. Its efforts were scotched by John Randolph of Roanoke.

Last fall House Leader Randolph had told Gallatin his cherished plan to spend several years in Europe. "On my return a king of the Romans will have been elected," he said, meaning not Madison but Monroe. This sally was accompanied by broad hints that he would like to be Minister to the Court of St. James's. When he failed to secure the appointment, he reacted angrily, and when he heard that Madison had called him unfit for the position—worse, that the Administration was so weary of his eccentricities it would prefer a new agent, say, Bidwell of Massachusetts—his boundless pride suffered. Madison, he said, was a damned sneaking villain. As a first step in his malicious feud with the Administration, he fought its request for a $2 million initial appropriation for the purchase of the Floridas, but he lost.

That same day Madison's 60,000-word anonymous pamphlet on the rights and obligations of neutrals was distributed in Congress, together with a staggering tabulation of Britain's impressments. Congressman Andrew Gregg leaped to his feet with a resolution to prohibit, until

Britain reformed, all British importations. Others were for barring only specified goods. Debate was postponed.

In 1789 and again in 1794 Madison had proposed commercial retaliation as the best defense against unfair trade practices. It was his brainchild, and now that Britain deserved such punishment even more richly, he was for inflicting it. He was very sure of himself in this matter (not stumbling as on the night he sprained an ankle falling down the front steps), and he looked forward eagerly to the debate on Gregg's now modified resolution.

It did not go well. John Randolph began his barrage by saying sarcastically that Gregg's nonimportation bill was based on the illusion that the American Navy could outfight Britain's. "After shrinking from the Spanish jackal, do you presume to bully the British lion?" He charged that the Cabinet backing the resolution was no "open declared Cabinet, but an invisible, unconstitutional Cabinet, without responsibility. . . . I speak of a back-stairs influence—of men who bring messages to this House which . . . govern its decisions. . . . I shrink instinctively from this left-handed, invisible, irresponsible influence which defies the touch but pervades and decides everything. . . . *I assert that there is no Cabinet.*" The "back-stairs influence," of course, was James Madison. On Randolph rushed: "Some time ago a book was laid on our tables which, like some other bantlings, did not bear the name of its father. . . . Has any gentleman got the work?" Someone thrust Madison's pamphlet on neutrality into his hands. Randolph read aloud and ridiculed some passages, then flung the pamphlet onto the floor and praised extravagantly an Englishman's tract—*War in Disguise*—whose thesis was the opposite of Madison's. For three hours he railed against the President and Secretary of State. The House sat stunned.

The next day John Smilie answered Randolph forthrightly: "Notwithstanding the contempt with which a certain book was yesterday treated by the gentleman from Virginia, I will venture to predict that, when the mortal part of that gentleman and myself shall be in ashes, the author of that work will be considered a great man." But damage had been done, and the long thin pole of a man with huge hands and feet and the flashing, immense coal-black eyes of his (and Dolley's) forebear Powhatan kept hurling contumely. The first puff of wind, he cried, would demolish Madison's "miserable card-house of an argument." On and on Jack Randolph raved. Finally he completely lost control. "Sit down, sir, pray sit down, sir," he screamed at General Thomas. "Learn to keep your proper level!"

Macon's modified nonimportation resolution passed the House 87 to 35.

As Senator John Quincy Adams, son of old John, observed, Randolph's tantrum was aimed "to prevent Mr. Jefferson from consenting to serve again, and Mr. Madison from being his successor." Missing the target, the speech had boomeranged; it returned upon itself to destroy Randolph's leadership. Thereafter he and his "Old Republicans" or "Quids," as they liked to call themselves in contradistinction to "upstart" Republicans, would fight Madison without quarter, ever disrupting: a kind of palace rebellion.

In April John Randolph, trying a new gambit, accused Madison of advocating that the United States bribe France to help it acquire the Floridas. On discovering this fact, he told Congress, "all the objections I originally had . . . were aggravated to the highest possible degree . . . and from that moment, to the last moment of my life, my confidence in the principles of the man entertaining these sentiments died, never to live again." With an "indignant gesture," he pitched his hat across the room—this legislator who three years ago had begged Congress for funds with which to buy France the empire he now accused her of "bullying out of Spain."

Though Jefferson did not publicly take sides as to choice of a successor, he warned Randolph-backed Monroe against new friends attacking old ones "in a way to tender you" (not Madison) great injury. He agreed with those party members who held that Madison's decency would refute all "malignant calumnies."

The Madisons saw Randolph as a man whose ambition had betrayed him into prostituting a great talent. How sad his treachery against people and principles; sometimes it seemed coeval (co-evil) with Burr's.

James and Dolley did not let it depress them unduly. Visiting—just after one of Randolph's attacks—the Samuel Harrison Smiths' new country home, Sidney, they chatted and laughed happily, swung in a hammock, and admired Margaret's butter pots immersed in cool water in the dairy. "Mrs. Madison was all that was tender, affectionate as usual," wrote Mrs. Smith afterward, and "Mr. Madison . . . in one of his most sportive moods."

Meanwhile the evidence against Burr had been increasing. General Eaton swore that Burr had tried to persuade him to help foment a war against Florida and Mexico, then help break off the Western states from the Union, and, finally, help recruit the Marine Corps to capture Washington, kill the President, "turn Congress neck and heels out of doors," seize the Treasury and declare himself "protector of an energetic government."

Though history has reduced Eaton to a swaggering adventurer with liquor on his breath, it does corroborate his deposition. Burr had made the same pitch to Yrujo, and Yrujo's report was even then on its way to Spanish files in Madrid. Moreover, Burr had recruited General James Wilkinson, Commander in Chief of the Army and Governor of Upper Louisiana, as an accomplice. (Wilkinson was later unmasked as a traitorous rogue long in the pay of Spain.) It now seems clear that Burr's ambitious scheme was to form, with British aid, an empire embracing the two Floridas, Louisiana, the Western states, and Mexico; if that failed, to capture Washington with the help of dissident naval officers and establish a "Cromwellian" dictatorship. If no help was forthcoming but Wilkinson's, Burr planned to go as far as the West's mood would permit. If even the West balked, he could always cut his conspiracy down "in fact to what it was in appearance—a filibustering expedition against the Spanish colonies." Indeed, if all his schemes blew up in his face, he could settle for residence on the "Bastrop grant" on the Ouachita River in Louisiana, to which he held a suspect Spanish deed.

As a spider web allows mobility for the spinner but none for his victims, most of Burr's recruits had no idea what they were getting into. The man was foxy. If a come-on to the effect that "Federal lands in the West are over-priced" triggered resentment against the government, his prospect was caught. Another lure was cheap land: "Mexico should be seized."

In February Jefferson showed Madison a letter from Joseph H. Daveiss, United States Attorney for Kentucky:

> We have traitors among us. A separation of the Union in favor of Spain is the object. . . . Mention the subject to no man from the western country however high in office he may be; some of them are deeply tainted with this treason.

But to proceed against Burr, Jefferson needed proof. That posed a problem. Though the Administration was troubled about Napoleon's mounting land victories, Britain's multiplying sea victories, and John Randolph's rabid newspaper attacks signed "Decius," always it returned to the thorny need to prove Burr's conspiracy.

The Madisons talked it over between them. On a personal level the man's conduct seemed to represent a real fall into corruption; on the national level, a sinister plot. That a onetime senator, Vice President, and almost-President should conspire against the United States was unspeakable; it must be untrue. Yet the growing evidence tallied with his known attempt to steal the Presidency and with his deliberate destruction of Hamilton.

While the Madisons struggled to disentangle fact and rumor, John Payne was drinking too much. Alarmed, they urged him to join the staff of George Davis of Norfolk who was going as Minister to Tunis. New scenes, they told themselves, would bring Dolley's brother a new viewpoint. Jackson and Mary, Cutts and Anna, agreed.

After John had left for Norfolk in July, Dolley was glad to receive this letter from Mr. Davis:

> I received John as a brother, and feel most confident that his new situation . . . will at least call forth those energies of mind which have been cramped by want of action, and open an extensive field for advancement. You may rest assured his interest and happiness are very dear to me. . . .

But the family had not long to be tranquil. Little Lucy Jackson sickened and died, and Mary, wrote Jackson, had "been on the confines of eternity. . . . Oh, God! what is the happiness of man? His life is a dream of pleasure on the bed of torture." Dolley's world had reeled and she wrote her mother in great distress. "Expressions are wanting, my dearest mother, to convey to thee my feelings! I have not been well . . . so deep is the sorrow. . . . Dolley, Lucy, both gone! They are now angels! and can never know evil or misery. . . ." She added that she had received no answer to her letters to John. He must have sailed.

By September 1806 there was hard evidence against Burr. Congressman Williams wrote that the once impoverished Comfort Tyler had returned from the West "full of cash" and was trying to recruit hundreds of young men for a voyage down the Ohio to a mysterious destination, and in October General Nevill and Judge Roberts of Pittsburgh wrote about Burr's enthusiasm for founding a separate nation in the West. Also, General Eaton had forwarded an oddly come-by letter about Burr's boatbuilding. It named General Wilkinson co-plotter.

The President and his Cabinet met in extraordinary session, adopted military measures, canceled them, took further stock, then authorized the Secretary of Orleans Territory, John Graham, to investigate and, if the evidence indicated villainy, arrest Burr.

In the middle of the fracas, Madison received a letter of "gloom and distress" from Jackson. Fever was raging in Clarksburg. Last evening after visiting his ill father, mother, and two sisters, Mary had shown the deadly symptoms.

As if these tidings were not harsh enough, "Querist," writing in a Marietta, Ohio, newspaper, openly advocated Western secession, and Madison's cousin Colonel James Taylor of Kentucky pinned the authorship on an Irishman, Harman Blennerhassett, owner of an island in the Ohio and reportedly the builder of Burr's "gunboats" (actually transports).

A courier brought a message from General Wilkinson on the Texas border. The general reported that in New Orleans 8,000 to 10,000 armed men would soon be massing for an expedition against Mexico. Ignorant of the goal and "prime mover," he was ready to thwart the scheme. Meanwhile he proposed to sue for slander the publisher who had called him an intriguing "pensioner of Spain" and associate of Aaron Burr. "It is the highest ambition of my soul . . . to spend my last breath," said Wilkinson, "in the cause of my country."

This was the man who had recently opened a coded letter from Burr beginning "Your letter, postmarked thirteenth May, is received" and announcing that all was prepared; in November he would move down the Ohio to Natchez with a vanguard of 500 or 1,000 men to meet his second-in-command: Wilkinson. (To Wilkinson, Burr had made no mention of an independent West for the simple reason that, by then, Western patriotism had quashed that part of his plan. Now he was talking only about the glory to be won in Mexico.)

Having warned the President, Wilkinson warned the Viceroy of Mexico. He was willing to throw himself "like a Leonidas" into the breach "to defend it or perish," he said. But Mexico would have to refund the $121,000 he had spent on the project, on her behalf, out of his own pocket (or so he pretended).

In November, Jefferson—ignorant of Wilkinson's perfidy—issued a proclamation ordering the general to arrest the leaders of the conspiracy. The public's reaction was so quick and decisive it sent Burr's "settlers" fleeing toward the Ouachita.

And it was time for the Madisons—before being drawn toward new shapes of horror—to celebrate the birth of Anna's second son, Thomas.

John Randolph of Roanoke demanded further facts about Burr. Releasing some, Jefferson improperly said he had no doubt about Burr's guilt. Because Wilkinson had whitewashed himself with a false decoding of Burr's letter, Jefferson praised him for behaving with the "honor of a soldier and fidelity of a good citizen." A fresh dispatch from Wilkinson invoked the spirit of Thermopylae. General Wilkinson's tiny force—to do or die—was ready to take on Burr's 7,000 (actually 60) desperadoes. Wilkinson was shipping the President two of Burr's lieutenants.

They were charged with treason, and in the House—against logic—Randolph blamed Secretary Madison for the Senate's attempt to suspend the right of habeas corpus. He insinuated that Madison was a malignant force working against human liberty.

The Secretary of State, unperturbed, weighed the facts. Burr had written bad checks and sailed from Nashville with two boats. Treason could not be measured by such things, he wrote, knowing its definition in the Constitution, but Burr's enterprise had "probably received its death blow. Every additional development . . . increases the wonder at his infatuation."

In March 1807 the *Intelligencer* published a letter from the town of Cowitah, Alabama. "Yesterday Colonel Aaron Burr passed here, conducted by a guard of ten men." "I suppose you have heard," Dolley wrote Anna, "that Colonel Burr is retaken and on his way to Richmond for trial." It seemed that, late one stormy night, Burr had roused suspicion by refusing to pause at a tavern before pressing on across a dangerously rain-swollen stream. His pursuer, John Graham, thought it might well have translated him into the next world.

In Richmond (Virginia had claimed Ohio) the charge against Burr was not, as expected, treason. It was only high misdemeanor for organizing an expedition against Mexico. The presiding Chief Justice—John Marshall (a Federalist)—astonished everyone by saying publicly that the Administration's "hand of malignity" was dragging the trial into politics. Moreover, he dined with Burr at the home of Burr's lawyer. Suspicion of a prepossession in favor of the defendant, on Marshall's part, ran through the government. Could the plot's ringleaders be persuaded or forced to testify? It was a nervous spring. In American flesh stuck a burr.

There were other aggravations. In February, in Washington, a hurricane had blown out windows, unroofed houses, overturned coaches. In March, Madison discovered that the commercial treaty with Britain negotiated by William Pinkney and Monroe said nothing whatsoever about Britain's promise to end her hateful impressments—the sine qua non of negotiations. Madison told the new British Minister, David Erskine, that the United States would never, but never—it was a point of honor—accept the insult. Grimly he laid the matter before President Jefferson. It did not mitigate Jefferson's migraines. On the heels of this irritation they heard about Napoleon's Berlin Decree (so called because made in his Berlin camp). It laid a total French blockade on British importations.

A close study of the British treaty strengthened the Administration's conviction that ratification would put American trade completely at Britain's mercy. It would be suicidal. Better war. Why fool with paper arrangements if the British refused to stop their atrocious behavior on the Atlantic?

That spring the Madisons' many happy guests at Montpelier included Dolley's young cousin Dolley Winston, who, on her return home, made Dolley a cap and wrote affectionately. She often sat thinking of Montpelier, she said; her visit was a dream. She could almost see Mrs. Duval "shuffling her cards with her turban and frizet slipped to the back of her head and her false jaws working. . . . Give my love to Payne"—the handsome fifteen-year-old.

But Montpelier's pleasant atmosphere was ruined one day by another flagrant British provocation. When the 36-gun American *Chesapeake* refused to let a delegation from the 50-gun *Leopard* search her for deserters, the British had fired broadside, killing three American sailors and wounding eighteen before they boarded and stole four seamen. Outraged, Jefferson drafted a proclamation excluding British warships from United States waters. Madison's revision stiffened the wording. He called the action an "enormity" of "lawless and bloody purpose." Thus the possibility of war increased. So close was it, that summer of 1807, the President mobilized 100,000 militiamen. Secretary of State Madison sent instructions to Monroe in London: no discussion; the only way Britain could make amends was by apology, "honorable reparation," and the ending of impressments. Then France was told that the United States must withdraw its offer to buy the Floridas. In case of war it would need the money.

Though the crisis was grave, a portion of the Administration's mind remained fixed on Aaron Burr's trial. The Chief Justice had sent a subpoena to the President of the United States. Jefferson had rejected it scornfully, saying the Court could command all pertinent papers, not himself. "Burr's party fights hard," Dolley wrote, "but it is the general conviction that he will be convicted."

She was suffering from a severe neuralgia in her face. But a letter to Anna was full of tenderness. "Tell my dear boy [Mad, aged two] that I . . . will give him another lesson to learn: 'Aunt Dolley will come and take me, her little son, to see the seals dance on the rocks, and then carry me to her home to go gunning with Cousin Payne. . . .' Ah, Anna, 'tis a sad thing to feel myself so far from you." All are well except sister Polly (Mary). "Mama says she is as thin as possible and complains of a pain in her side. I am very uneasy. . . ." John is doing well in North Africa. Cousin Isaac is violently in love with Miss Beardly and seems to have "caught the detestable manners of that stiff set." Dolley Winston is "frantic" to return. Father Dubourg came to dinner. "He says Payne"—Dolley was proud—"does us honor." She has never had the courage to leave Madison long enough to visit St. Mary's (this seems extraordinary), but Payne will spend five weeks with them in August.

Back in the city, the Madisons heard that the imprisoned Burr had sued Dolley's brother-in-law J. G. Jackson in criminal court for "improper practices" while collecting Ohio Valley affidavits, then dropped the charge. Jackson accused Chief Justice Marshall of "dishonest partiality." For example, instead of jailing the accused, Marshall had let him stay in his lawyer's home, guarded but sleeping soft, eating like a king, and entertaining lavishly.

The trial was a circus. While the nation waited, opposing lawyers competed brilliantly—not for the favor of the jury but for that of Chief Justice Marshall. They showed off like acrobats on high trapezes.

Suddenly, when only 14 of 140 witnesses had been examined, Marshall ruled that the government must prove by at least two witnesses that Burr had assembled a force for the *express* purpose of war. The jury had no choice but to bring in the verdict "Not guilty by any evidence submitted to us." The Republicans were aghast. Attorney General Rodney wrote Madison, "Every lawyer with whom I have conversed is of a different opinion."

While a follow-up trial for misdemeanors moved toward another acquittal, the Administration groped for a way to bring hidden evidence to light. Jefferson had no sense of defeat; he said Marshall had heaped coals of fire on his own head. And the Cabinet voted not to drop the charges. Congress, it decided, should publish the court proceedings—all used and unused testimony. Perhaps, for lack of an army, Burr's adventure had stopped short of an overt act of treason, but his intentions had been strictly dishonorable.

Though John Randolph called Wilkinson a "mammoth of iniquity," Jefferson continued to defend him. Thus he escaped indictment. Later, when investigation had revealed his Spanish pension, he would demand and get a court-martial to answer what he called the "foul slander," and the Spanish Governor of West Florida, Folch, would testify that his archives contained not one word to support a charge of bribery. No, they did not. The ugly secret lay elsewhere. Here is Folch's letter to Wilkinson, written just before the trial:

> I have sent to the archives of Havana all that pertains to the ancient history, persuaded that before the United States are in a situation to conquer that capital, you and I, Jefferson, Madison . . . and even the prophet Daniel himself will have made many days' journey into the other world.

Madison had been suspicious of Wilkinson from the start. Though years would be required for the seed of distrust to flower, now in 1807 he was mulling over certain discrepancies, shiftings, slynesses.

He should have been more suspicious of Jacob Wagner, Chief Clerk of the State Department, whom he had held over from Adams's Administration instead of firing. Honor and delicacy, he had said, could make up for political nonconformity. Thereafter, during six years as virtual Undersecretary, Wagner had often praised Madison's "goodness." But when refused the sinecure of a collectorship, he had resigned in a huff, and was now flaying Madison alive in the public prints. But then the whole of Washington City, that autumn of 1807, seemed a hive of malignancy. Few people had Dolley's abiding goodwill.

A small example of her kindness is this note to a friend: "May the horoscope of your young daughter be the most happy; may the bright aspect of her destiny be chronicled in unerring lines"—meaning the chart of the heavens at birth. "Adieu, kiss parent and child." And Dolley sent a gift and jingle:

> 'Twere fair—to thee I send
> The offering, humble, of a tender friend,
> With many pious wishes for thy house
> From husband, children, to the *little mouse*.

Now she was expecting the Cuttses on F Street. She would have fires laid in their room, she wrote, and receive them with "sparkling bottle and a warm heart." William Madison's son Alfred was there "in deep decline," about to set sail for the West Indies. No, she hadn't attended the races; without their handsome grey horse (it had died) they couldn't go in good style. Please—in New York or Philadelphia—please buy her a "shining black frizet."

One day Dolley received word of her mother's death by a "violent stroke of the dead palsy." Grief felled her. To think that already the body of sixty-two-year-old Molly Coles Payne—still with remnants of her beauty—had been buried in Clarksburg. Two weeks later Dolley wrote:

> Deep affliction, my dear friend, has for some time past arrested my pen. My beloved and tender mother left me forever. . . . She was in Virginia with my youngest sister where she died without suffering or regret. . . .

Dolley's religious beliefs held her steady. "The loss is only ours, and for that only ought we her children to mourn."

Uncle Isaac Winston wrote his niece about her "excellent parent." Molly Payne had taught her children the "sublime principles of purity and virtue," said the old Quaker, and Dolley should remember that her mother's death was in accordance with the "unerring wisdom of the infinitely beneficent parent" of them all. Old Isaac spoke of Molly's sweetness and gallantry, her kindness and sense of duty. Dolley herself should work toward the same "eternal weight of glory."

And back and forth between Molly's four daughters—Dolley, Anna, Lucy, and Mary—flowed happy and sad reminiscences of Coles Hill, Scotchtown, Philadelphia.

Mary's emaciated condition deepened the gloom. The family feared she was dying of tuberculosis. Because she longed to see her sisters, and because Jackson was due in Congress, he bought a light wagon in which she could rest full-length while crossing the Appalachians. But one night when Jackson left the Clarksburg Courthouse after prosecuting a criminal, hoodlums clubbed him so savagely they fractured his skull. This news reached the Madisons while the country's relations with Spain, France, and Britain were deteriorating. Britain's new Orders in Council had prompted France to extend her Berlin Decree. It all seemed too much. But the Madisons tried to hold steady.

Retaliation, reprisal, seemed the one hope. That meant prohibiting any and all commercial intercourse. It would hurt the United States, but hurt Britain worse. The former would lose luxuries; the latter, necessities. And there were other good aspects of an embargo. It would, willy-nilly, foster United States manufacturing, open new trade channels, hasten the development of Louisiana, and make Europeans correct their picture of a weakling America whom they could push around.

In mid-December 1807, Jefferson had signed the Embargo Act. People were asking anxiously if it would bring war. "Certainly not,"

Madison replied, "if war be not predetermined against us." In itself it was an impartial measure for peace. He trusted that citizens would be willing to sacrifice private gain for the public good.

More and more Madison was spoken of as the man best qualified to be the next President. In January 1808 Jefferson announced what had been bruited about: he would not consider a third term. James Monroe, home now and embittered by rejection of the treaty he had negotiated in London, was open to the beguilements of John Randolph who wanted him to take the nomination away from Madison. Abruptly Monroe left for Richmond to start a subtle campaign.

George Rose, whom Britain had sent to patch up the *Chesapeake* affair, described Secretary of State Madison as the next President and reported his demands, adding, "It is but justice due to this minister to observe that these considerations were urged in a temper and tone calculated to provide a dispassionate discussion." Unfortunately the talks foundered on the rock of some tardily disclosed instructions: Britain, far from showing remorse, demanded impossible disavowals and *mutual* reparations. Madison was outraged. Looking Rose in the eye, he upbraided him for not laying all his cards on the table from the start. It would have saved them both a lot of time—Rose could just have picked up his hat and gone home.

Madison, Monroe, Clinton: these three names were in people's mouths. Though Jefferson remained officially neutral, his choice of successor was no secret. Old George Clinton was befuddled; Monroe less experienced than Madison and still young enough to wait his turn; Madison would carry on the Administration's policies. Yet how gauge the damage done by Randolph's charge that Madison was "visionary," would drag them into war, and was without principles?

Standing on principle, Madison refused to defend himself—as if remembering a remark by the Abbé du Bos copied into his notebook thirty-five years ago:

> People who are too tender of their reputations, and too deeply piqued by slander are conscious . . . of some inward infirmity. . . .
> A reputation grounded on true virtue is like the sun that may be clouded but not extinguished. Plato, being slandered, said, "I shall behave so as nobody shall believe it."

Late in January 1808 a caucus of the Republican members of Congress—forebear of the latter-day party convention—enthusiastically and unanimously nominated James Madison for President.

Dolley felt that Madison had more than earned the highest honor within the gift of the United States. Personally she was pulled two ways. Because she enjoyed people and a great stir and loved to see her husband receive his due, she hoped he would win the election; but because she enjoyed nature's quiet and knew he did, shrank from the maelstrom of prominence. Slowly the struggle drew her in. She resented Monroe's rivalry; indeed, earlier, she who hated contention had so forgotten herself in talking about Monroe's electioneering, she spoke of him "very slightingly."

For her the ordeal of the campaign came at the worst possible time— so close on the deaths of two nieces and her mother, and while Jackson was fighting to survive and Mary dying. Ah, Mary, Mary. She could remember the day that Mary—little Polly—was born at Coles Hill. And the day James had given her away at Montpelier. Dolley and Anna supported each other, or tried to, when the dreaded news arrived that Polly had died of a hemorrhage. The honor of nomination which had fallen to James could not ease the Madisons' sorrow. Jackson's lament: "Miseries . . . past endurance . . . incalculable and unparalleled misfortune." Seven years of happiness had preceded his three terrible losses, his wife the "dearest of all." Now he had only two-year-old Mary.

Another post brought the news that Uncle's Auburn had burned. The Isaac Winston family was moving from Hanover to Culpeper County. Their new home near Stephensburg had a strange name: Zhe-Hol.

When the Madisons drove home in May, intending to deliver Dolley Winston at Zhe-Hol, their boat barely managed to cross the flooded Rappahannock. They reached Zhe-Hol exhausted and stayed three days, rain-bound, unable to ford the raging Rapidan. "I got home Friday night," Madison would write Jefferson, "by taking my carriage to pieces and making three trips . . . over Porter's mill pond in something like a boat, swimming my horses." But Dolley's mysterious account after the event suggests some unspelled-out tragedy: "My limbs yet tremble with the terror and fatigue of our journey. . . . But Anna—no language can give you an idea of the poignancy of my misery when I recollected the loss of my dearest friends after fainting in the arms of strangers—for at that time Madison had rode out."

Chilled through, she took to bed with inflammatory rheumatism. Dr. Willis bled her, and Mother Madison and Nelly nursed her "with great attention and kindness." "What in this world," she wrote Anna, "can compensate for the sympathy and confidence of a mother and sister?" She answered herself, "Nothing but the tie that binds us to a good husband. Such are ours and we ought to be satisfied."

As usual, Montpelier was like a hostelry. A wagonload of hay for guests' horses disappeared like magic.

Jefferson had met the Federalist whispering campaign against Madison by having his entire foreign affairs record, a file of letters totaling 100,000 words, read before Congress. During the six days it took to plough through the record, the Secretary of State rose in the nation's esteem.

A year-old letter from John Payne told them he had been appointed secretary to the Consul in Tripoli. Dolley just hoped that under the intemperate Mediterranean sun he could master his intemperate fondness for liquor.

In June Jefferson and his secretary Isaac Coles stopped at Montpelier. The household had scarcely settled to sleep when it was four o'clock and time to get up. Blacks and whites stumbled out of bed; candles gleamed; breakfast was washed down; horses led out and hitched up; and the travelers started off briskly, hoping to reach Fauquier Courthouse before nightfall. The Madisons would follow shortly.

The campaign was heating up now, political enemies trying to change the truth of James Madison into a lie, some attempts formidable, others ludicrous. As an example of the latter, the *Virginia Gazette* revealed that the gentleman who bought Madison's wheat had, on being dunned, retorted, "Go . . . tell Mr. Madison if he'll take off the embargo I'll pay him for his crop." In the next issue John Strode stated that though he bought wheat from all three of Mr. Madison's plantations, never once had he been dunned; indeed, after the Embargo had cut prices, Mr. Madison had said he'd be among the very last to demand payment.

Madison was accused of erring in the Yazoo compromise, plotting war, exhibiting both indecision and overboldness, contributing nothing and running the entire Jeffersonian show. Also of being Napoleon's stooge.

But masterly treaty instructions and brilliant sparring with Napoleon, as shown by state papers, continued to stir widespread admiration. Thousands laughed at the propaganda that said the father of the Constitution, champion of freedom, could toady to anyone; his record was that of a patriot.

Two charges were difficult to deny: one, that he was from Virginia (Senator Pickering said Virginia was trying to run the Union); the other, that he had masterminded the Embargo.

That legislation was growing more and more unpopular, especially with New England manufacturers. They made so many protests, the Administration saw that it had overestimated the number of citizens who would cheerfully suffer financial loss for the public good, and it recalled Hamilton's notion that men are moved by nothing but self-interest and greed. Jefferson and Madison, themselves suffering because of plunging wheat, corn, and tobacco prices, were scornful of the complaints of fellow farmers. With Britain, by her Order in Council, and France, by her Berlin and Milan Decrees, making relentless war on American trade, why couldn't they put the honor of the nation first?

The nation's honor was a concept which Dolley could rise to. Hearing a roll of drums on the Fourth of July, she flew out of the house to meet a splendid troop of cavalry parading along F Street. It drew up, horses champing at the bit. Standing tall, Dolley made a little speech before presenting the men with an "elegant standard." They applauded the "Lady President Elect"—or so they hoped.

Having polled the nation's Fourth of July toasts, the *Democratic Press* announced that these "spontaneous effusions of the American people" forecast Madison's election.

Assuming it, foreign ministers began to leapfrog over the President to his Secretary of State. And Turreau wrote Talleyrand's successor, in the Foreign Ministry, Champagny: "The secret but well assured and very constant influence of Madison develops and becomes more powerful as the time of his election draws near. . . . It seems to me that it is necessary to act from now on as if he were President." Would Madison increase his advantage by some spectacular stroke of diplomacy? "The acquisition of the Floridas," wrote Turreau, "is the object of all of Mr. Madison's prayers." Actually Napoleon, master of Spain, had already offered the United States both Floridas for an American declaration of war against Great Britain. No, said Madison sharply; the United States would hew to its "fair and sincere neutrality"—no bribes acceptable.

Then Napoleon's Bayonne Decree set his jaw. So the French proposed to capture American ships anywhere they could *to help enforce the Embargo Act!* How despicable! What hypocrisy!

Late in July he and Dolley drove home for two months of their "deep shade." He was keeping his resolve not to campaign. His campaign was his record.

But world events penetrated to Montpelier. When Napoleon had made his brother Joseph King of Spain, there was rioting in Madrid. New England merchants were petitioning for a special Embargo-removing session of Congress. Month-old London papers carried a defense of Foreign Minister Canning's harsh American policy. The British still insisted that Presidential obduracy had doomed the Rose mission.

The Democrat-Republicans were disgusted. "From the disgraceful animadversions with which the Federal prints abound," said a *National Intelligencer* article written in part by Madison, one would think they had forgotten the "black outrage" of the *Chesapeake*.

> Will anyone, then, dare to say . . . that Britain had a right . . . to refuse making atonement for a *wrong act* committed by her until we rescind a *rightful* act of ours? Will he dare to say that the aggressor has a right to demand redress, instead of the aggrieved?

As Gallatin remarked, there was nothing wrong with the Administration's Embargo policy; because it hurt British interests it should have worked. If it was failing, it was for one outstanding reason: American "violations bordering on insurrection." Vessels kept stealing out of New England ports to traffic with the enemy. The Administration rued the lack of patience, the myopia. As Madison had predicted, the Embargo really was fostering manufacturing; more and more congressmen wore suits of American cloth. Yet businessmen seemed not to value this opportunity for building industries which might, in the long run, prove more remunerative than shipping.

John Randolph wielded the longest knife against Madison. Ill, and furious at voters choosing Madison instead of Monroe, he said he wished he could help Federalists "hunt the polecat."

The hunted and his family were together the day news arrived of the birth of Anna's third son, little Walter. "All clapped their hands in triumph."

On a trip to Monticello they saw Martha Randolph's newborn third little son, and driving on to Enniscorthy, were delighted with nineteen-year-old Sally of the gypsy-brown face.

With a white housekeeper, now, Dolley had gone back to entertaining. Among the new crop of visitors were Henry Clay (a tall, young, raw-boned, talented, Virginian-turned-Kentuckian senator) and Jackson and his three-year-old daughter, Mary. Crowded coaches stopped on their way to and from watering holes: "Bath," the White, the Sweet, Botetourt. As the presidential election neared, the days grew hectic and exhausting. Dolley wrote Anna, "We had expected Mr. and Mrs. Barbour for a week past, and now I begin to hope they will not come as it grows preserving and pickling time." She finished sealing bottles just before they junketed back to Washington late in September. It was almost election time.

Jefferson sent a draft of his Annual Message to Madison for suggestions. He received a Sunday note: "JM . . . was prevented last night by company and has but just got up for breakfast." Madison's comment would be worth waiting for. Cut pussyfooting, he advised; say frankly that the "candid and liberal experiment" of a limited embargo had failed, and there remained only three possible courses: extend the Embargo, submit to Great Britain, or declare war.

Such straight talk was possible because the two men were "extremely intimate; in fact, two brothers could not have been more so."

He still thought the Embargo, if faithfully adhered to, would bring Britain to heel. Special Envoy William Pinkney had reported from England that already, every single day, it was being more "deeply felt." But Madison had to recognize that—especially in New England and New York—the Embargo was being systematically violated and, worse, was promoting national disunion. Increased and arbitrary executive powers, if granted by Congress promptly for enforcement, would be hateful and perhaps dangerous. Repeal the Embargo, swallow insult? Go to war? It was a terrible dilemma.

When Jefferson's last Message made public Madison's 1808 diplomatic correspondence, approval thundered across the land. The *Aurora:* " . . . A manly and honorable vindication of the national rights and independence." But Federalist papers would not concede it. They grumbled and cried out.

Madison awaited his country's verdict. While the November election returns were piling up, no one doubted he had won, but it would be February 1809 before Congress could announce the electoral count.

Mrs. Catherine Mitchill, wife of Madison's friend Dr. Samuel Latham Mitchill, was one of those who greatly admired Dolley, and she noted that the Secretary of State's wife was indulging less often in her favorite amusement: cardplaying. But the crowds at the house on F Street had not diminished—"they are worshipping the rising sun." The Madisons' dinners were delightful. When guests departed, they were "all in fine spirits, which was as much owing to the agreeable society of the master and mistress of the house as to the lively quality of their wine." Dolley enjoyed paying calls and also listening to debates in the House, where, when John Randolph was raving, the argument threatened to go on all night—"it was as good as a play." And there was the fun of shopping. Ladies swarmed into a George Town milliner's back room, where they frantically put on and pulled off hats: a "comic scene." Once Mrs. Mitchill saw Mrs. Madison there. Ah, who else had such taste, such style?

Some Patawatomy Indian chiefs came to town rigged out in their finery. One night a great strapping brave walked into the Mitchill home and asked for whiskey, though he had "already had too much." Others lay out in the rain all night. But most of them turned up at Mr. Jefferson's New Year levee with their bright paint and earrings and nose rings to eat macaroons and listen—baffled but too proud to show it—to an "exquisite band of music . . . reverberating through the spacious halls."

On February 12 the House gallery was jammed with spectators for the ceremony of counting the electoral votes for President and Vice President. Into the handsome hall marched the senators. The representatives received them formally. The reading took two hours, and the President of the Senate announced the results in a loud voice: Clinton, 6; Pinckney, 47; Madison, 122. Madison had taken the South and West solidly; also New York, New Jersey, and Pennsylvania. These states were saying, We believe in the Administration and in the outstanding ability of James Madison.

The next day Dolley was being called the "Queen elect." "There is so much majesty in her appearance," said her friend Mrs. Mitchill, "that I really think she deserves the appellation."

Ironically, at this hour of electoral endorsement, there was a rising tidal wave for war as against the Embargo which Madison had espoused. Congressional "war hawks" led by Henry Clay and John Calhoun were gaining strength. Madison's own position: Though he loved peace, he was not afraid of war, and if that proved the only honorable course, so be it; meanwhile—he stuck to it—the best preparation for any eventuality was retaliation for insults.

But how convince doubters? How keep them from splitting the country? Even Jefferson was calling the Embargo too expensive. The shout of disapproval in Congress grew louder as the election returns were coming in: Repeal! Repeal! David Williams of South Carolina jumped up. "Yes, repeal it!" he mocked—what a fool he had been to think that here in the United States there was patriotism enough, pride enough, to make free men "willing to abstain from making money for the good of the nation."

Few congressmen agreed. The repealers had it, and on February 2, 1809, just a month before Madison's inauguration, the Embargo on which he had hung so much hope was scotched. The effective date of repeal was

March 4. Earlier the country might have passed from embargo to war. Not now. Now many people wanted Madison's idea of the least honorable of Jefferson's three alternatives: submission to British injustice.

To avert national disgrace there was substituted for the Embargo a softer measure, a compromise measure, aimed equally at England and France. While excluding foreign armed ships and banning French and British imports, starting May 30, it gave the President the power to renew trade with either nation when and if it wiped out its unjust decrees. That was better than nothing. Madison hoped the world would not decide that Americans were so spineless they willingly suffered themselves, in any degree, to be insulted.

Thus, on becoming President, Madison would face a situation far worse than the one Jefferson had encountered in 1801. From the three previous administrations he was inheriting horrendous problems, and he would be heading a Federalist-baited, demoralized party, some of whose members resented the financial losses they had suffered and were likely to suffer.

How persuade people that their purses had been flattened—basically—not by America's foreign policy but by the long savage war between England and France which had spawned the hateful decrees; that no Secretary of State or President, however wise, could change certain stubborn facts; that, caught between pincers, the United States should act in its own best long-term interests, whatever the costs?

For years the Madisons had witnessed different kinds of disloyalty such as Burr's disloyalty to the government (he was now an exile in Europe), John Randolph's to old allies (he was mounting new assaults), and that of some Americans to principle for the sake of cold cash. The spectacle was turning some people cynical. Not the Madisons. Seeing the bad, they looked instinctively for the good, for they knew it was there. Visible or hidden, it existed.

But James Madison would enter the Presidency of the United States with few illusions.

X

A BUFF-COLORED INAUGURATION

THE INAUGURATION OF JAMES MADISON on March 4, 1809, would be remembered in the image of a buff-colored gown. It was not that Dolley outranked her husband; it was just that on this day she seemed, in a sense, her self-effacing husband's face to the world.

Just before the historic event she was congratulated by Eliza Lee. "I feel no small degree of exultation in knowing that the mind, temper and manners of my Philadelphia Quaker friend are peculiarly fitted for the station." And Eliza, like hundreds of others, sent the President-elect her felicitations and respect.

The day started with a salute of cannon from the Navy Yard and Fort Warburton. Troops in dress uniform escorted the Madisons' coach-and-four to the Capitol. By eleven o'clock thousands of excited people, wearing their Sunday best on a Saturday, were swarming along Pennsylvania Avenue. Madison had invited Jefferson to ride with him, but the retiring President had said no, the honors of the day belonged to his friend. Shortly before noon Madison—troop-guarded, pale, self-possessed, and followed by a throng traveling on horseback, wheels, and feet—rode forth as to a democratic anointing. His greys began the long hard pull up Capitol Hill. Ahead sat an unfinished Capitol consisting of two marble wings with as yet no domes, and only a colonnade to hold them together.

The House of Representatives was packed to its walls. Jefferson had taken a place among the people. An attempt to seize choice seats for the wives of "public characters" had failed because the "sovereign people would not resign their privileges." On the floor and in the galleries, high and low jostled elbow to elbow—members of Congress, justices of the Supreme Court, foreign diplomats, blue bloods, members of the middle class, and "ragtag." Chief Justice John Marshall, the Federalist who had tried to humiliate Jefferson's Administration, was waiting to swear in the new President. Madison entered and was immediately center and focus, the cynosure of all eyes.

As he stepped forward to take the oath of office, he understood perfectly the responsibility that goes with freedom—in particular, his new responsibilities; Dolley, looking on, understood too. He laid his right hand on the Bible and in a low voice repeated, "I, James Madison. . . ." The crowd took everything in: the voice, the stance, the "full suit of cloth of American manufacture"—a suit made from the wool of American-raised Merinos, no hateful British import; it was a reminder of the international situation Madison had inherited and must deal with. He was wearing a carnelian seal.

Margaret Bayard Smith, who rather resented anyone displacing her idol, Mr. Jefferson, has recorded that Mr. Madison was very pale and trembled when he began to speak but "soon gained confidence and spoke audibly." Another witness describes the ceremony somewhat differently: "Mr. Madison appeared to great advantage, the excitement of the occasion lending color to his pale student face, and dignity to his slender figure." One report of his address: " . . . In point of style it [was] chaste and nervous [forcible], and in point of principle worthy of the man, so honorable, called upon to preside over the affairs of a free and enlightened people."

A boisterous crowd followed the new President's carriage to the Madisons' home on F Street. Guests who had waited more than an hour to get in found the entry, parlor, drawing room, and downstairs bedroom jammed with well-wishers and devotees of free punch. It was quite impossible to move.

The President and his lady stood by the drawing room door receiving guests. Madison was a figure of dignity. But Dolley reigned. It was as if all her life she had been preparing to preside as First Lady. Mrs. Smith, in her journal, remembers proudly that Mr. Madison shook her hand "with all the cordiality of an old acquaintance." As for Mrs. Madison, Mrs. Smith says she

> looked extremely beautiful; was dressed in a plain cambric dress with a very long train, plain around the neck without any hand-

kerchief, and beautiful bonnet of purple velvet and white satin
with white plumes. She was all dignity, grace and affability.

And became at once the toast of Washington.

Running into Jefferson, Mrs. Smith said, "You've resigned a heavy
burden." "Yes indeed!" he smiled, "and am much happier at this moment
than my friend."

It was true. Jackknifing by bowing from the waist to each well-wisher
was murderous on Madison's back.

Between this reception and the inaugural ball there was no time to lie
down. It was a test of stamina.

The ball initiated by George Washington but renounced by Adams
and Jefferson was being revived by the Madisons, doubtless because
Dolley wanted it that way. The *National Intelligencer* had said, "A Dancing
Assembly will be held on the 4th inst. at Mr. Long's Hotel" opposite the
Capitol. The twelve sponsors included Captain Thomas Tingey, John
Tayloe, and John Law. A ticket cost $4. "N.B.," said the newspaper. "The
Dancing will commence at 7 o'clock precisely."

More than 400 people from near and far—as far afield as Orange
Courthouse, Richmond, and Philadelphia—converged on Long's Hotel
(the site of today's Library of Congress) to the sound of hooves, wheels,
and merriment. Some Federalists boycotted the affair, others came out of
a modicum of goodwill or just curiosity. Republicans attended en masse,
their electoral triumph sweet in their mouths. The scene was enlivened by
"female fashion and beauty." Among other attractions, people pointed
out President Madison's stepson, Payne Todd, who was on special leave
from St. Mary's in Baltimore: a leggy, handsome seventeen-year-old with
deep blue eyes. The torchlit ballroom was filling up fast. When Jefferson
entered, he was greeted with "Mr. Jefferson's March." Then there fell an
expectant hush—and the band struck up a new composition, "Mr. Madison's March." Guests craned their necks in excitement.

Mrs. Madison entered on the arm of the ball's manager, Captain
Tingey. Then the new President appeared. Mr. Madison was escorting
Mrs. Cutts. The crowd had a sense of history being enacted before their
eyes. All time seemed to focus on this hour.

The Madisons were swallowed up by a press of people. Guests twisted
and peeped over familiar or strange shoulders to catch a glimpse of the
First Gentleman and Lady. Dolley was radiant, she was incandescent. The
few who got close enough to speak to her were "happy indeed."

Strategically located, Mrs. Smith took in every detail of Mrs. Madison's dress and demeanor.

> She looked like a queen. She had on a pale buff-colored velvet, made plain, with a very long train, but not the least trimming, and a beautiful pearl necklace, earrings and bracelet; her head-dress a turban of the same colored velvet and white satin (from Paris)—with two superb plumes of the bird of paradise feathers. It would be *absolutely impossible* for any one to behave with more perfect propriety ... unassuming dignity, sweetness, grace. It seems to me that such manners would disarm envy itself and conciliate even enemies.

Manager Tingey presented Mrs. Madison with the cotillion's first number.

"What shall I do with it?—I don't dance."

"Give it to a neighbor."

"Oh, no, it would look like partiality."

"Then I will," said the resourceful Captain, passing it to Mrs. Cutts, who, as everyone knew, *did* dance.

Here Mrs. Smith, having remarked on Dolley's perfect propriety, asks her diary a curious question: "I really admired this in Mrs. Madison. Ah, why does she not in all things act with the same propriety? She would be too much beloved if she added all the virtues to all the graces." The contradiction cannot be explained by the cruel Federalist canard, launched during the presidential campaign, that because Madison was impotent, Dolley had had an affair with un unnamed man; Mrs. Smith knew that charge for a lie. Perhaps her question refers to the way Dolley pushed forward her sister Anna; or perhaps it reflects a homely woman's suspicion that Dolley's vivacity sometimes crossed the border of flirtation. One had to understand that Dolley's benevolence fell equally—like the rain—on the just and the unjust.

It was difficult to dance on 1 square foot of floor, but young and old, thick and thin, graceful and heavy-footed—all accepted the handicap. The mood throughout the hall was happy. After a while, however, the milling company began to suffer from bad air. Finding herself next to the President, Mrs. Smith saw how exhausted he was.

"I wish with all my heart I had a little bit of seat to offer you."

"I wish so too," he said, slightly woebegone. But when the manager, afraid he would go, urged President Madison to stay for supper, he cheerfully agreed. But to Mrs. Smith, in an aside: "I would much rather be in bed."

Then he was poking fun at his weariness, making his "old kind of mischievous allusions." Mrs. Smith told him his elevation to the highest place in the land hadn't changed him.

The closely shut-up air was getting staler and staler. The room had become dangerously stifling and oppressive. Volunteers tugged at the upper window sashes which paint had stuck. In vain. Several guests were so faint they had to be taken out. Suddenly a crash of glass and then another—silvery sounds. Someone was knocking out windowpanes. How invigorating the cold pure rush of air!

Servants had brought in tables and were spreading cloths when Mr. Jefferson took his leave. But Dolley was still there. Clear across the room, high above all heads, two birds of paradise were swaying and nodding.

The bemedaled, ceremonious French Minister, General Turreau de Garambonville, led Dolley to supper. Mrs. Cutts, flushed from dancing, leaned on the arm of Merry's successor, British Minister the Honorable David Erskine. At the crescent-shaped head table President Madison locked eyes with his wife. He was smiling. "How stands the glass."

Mrs. Smith continued her dedicated scrutiny. Mrs. Madison "really, in manner and appearance, answered all my ideas of royalty. She was so equally gracious to both French and English, and so affable to all," there with her luminous face and wearing that simple but elegant buff-colored gown. (Certain reminiscences call the velvet pale yellow, but it was buff or champagne with just a whisper of gold, for it still exists.) Her pearl bracelet, necklace, and earrings—gifts of her husband—flattered a skin which needed no flattering. James Madison was quite obviously proud of his wife. They smiled at each other.

Margaret Smith noticed the look on the face of Mrs. Robert Smith of Baltimore. Madison, under heavy political pressure from a congressional clique, was appointing her husband Secretary of State. "I suspect Mrs. Smith could not like the superiority of Mrs. Cutts; and if I am not mistaken, Mrs. Madison's . . . causes her some heart burning."

To the seated guests the collation menu hardly mattered. They were eating and drinking history.

Many thoughtful Americans sympathized with the man who was taking the helm at a peculiarly difficult time, now that the Embargo which he considered the best remedy against outrages had failed for lack of support. Madison's virtues were not the obvious ones dear to the masses.

Could he steer the ship of state through dangerous shoals? Whatever the answer, glasses were raised and clicked. "Your health!"

Wine had a way of loosening up Madison's repertoire of anecdotes, and right here at hand, to remind him, sat Minister Erskine whose father, Lord Chancellor of England, had furnished one of his favorites. When at some dinner a bottle of Cape wine ran out, the Baron had looked at his stingy host. "Well," he said, "if we can't double the Cape, I suppose we must return to port." Madison's jokes were good, but even if they were bad, they would have been laughed at tonight—a privilege and penalty accorded presidents.

After supper Madison stood up smiling, said good-night to the company, bowed, took his wife's arm, and began to withdraw. Dolley had picked up her train and was carrying it. The crowd, loath to give them up, parted like the Red Sea. At the door the Madisons turned for a last smile: James in formal black, Dolley in her beautiful buff-colored creation under the birds of paradise. Then they were gone.

The first year of Madison's administration was the long shadow of this inaugural day: complicated, tiring, but pleasant. Though he was a governmental expert, and Dolley no ingenue in difficult situations, many things about their new position had still to be mastered.

It was a tremendous challenge.

They continued packing to move into a larger house as soon as the current tenant found it convenient to leave. Mrs. Thornton's diary for March 1: "Mr. and Mrs. Madison dined with us for the last time I suppose. . . ." But Anna Maria did not lose her next-door neighbor for fully ten more days. "March 11. Mr. and Mrs. M. went to the *Great House*. Mr. M. came in after dinner for a few minutes." The Thorntons paid $50 for the Madisons' old tables. They were soon invited to dine at the mansion. And one night they rolled along in Mrs. Duval's carriage to the President's first levee. Relations were so informal, Mrs. Thornton sometimes sent a Negro runner to the President's to borrow ice. And it was a familiar sight, a servant drawing water for the first family from the pump at 21st and Pennsylvania. Old friends could rest easy; the Madisons were not putting on airs.

Meanwhile the President, with little aid from Secretary of State Smith, wrestled with foreign affairs. Some said it was his own fault for not having resisted the pressures to appoint Smith when his real choice was Albert Gallatin—though of course Gallatin was making a fine Secretary of the Treasury. Fortunately for Madison, he had a good private secretary in twenty-three-year-old Edward Coles. Dolley's little cousin Ned had grown up.

In substituting the less sweeping Non-Intercourse Act for the Embargo and authorizing the President to lift it for Britain or France *if either repealed its anti-American policy*, Congress had hoped to make peace with one of the country's two commercial foes, even if it meant war with the other. As Jefferson wrote Minister to France Armstrong about the Embargo, after relinquishing power:

> The belligerent Edicts rendered our Embargo necessary, to call home our ships, our seamen, and property. We expected some effects, too, from the coercion of interest. Some it has had; but much less on account of evasions and domestic opposition. . . . After fifteen months . . . it is now discontinued because losing $50,000,000 of exports annually by it; it costs more than war. . . . War therefore must follow if the Edicts are not repealed before the [next] meeting of Congress.

Napoleon was now proving even more difficult than British Foreign Minister George Canning. Madison talked over his double dilemma with Minister Erskine and in April succeeded wonderfully well in his efforts. Erskine agreed that on June 10 Great Britain would exempt the United States from the hated Orders in Council. Delighted, Madison immediately—in conformity with the terms of the Non-Intercourse Act—proclaimed American trade open to Britain, closed to France. He had won his fight.

Though the Federalists would never admit it, the prologue to this action and the action itself were a complete refutation of the Federalist charge that the Republican policy was pro-French.

Most Americans cheered. Of course, Napoleon in his wrath might now declare war against the United States, but the risk seemed worth taking. Six weeks after his inauguration James Madison became immensely popular. He was hailed as a great and glorious peacemaker.

But the bubble burst. In his eagerness to come to terms with the United States, Minister Erskine had violated his government's instructions—instructions naming conditions not divulged to Madison—and when Canning heard about it, he repudiated (against some editorial advice) the Erskine-Madison agreement. So the Orders in Council still stood. When news of this reversal reached America, there was anger and revulsion. Men cursed, and the outraged President reinvoked nonintercourse against Great Britain.

To Madison, playing for high stakes, the episode was aggravation beyond words. Dolley as usual was his anchor in storm. Though certain aspects of government still eluded her, she continued to learn. She seldom faltered in cheerfulness, and never in loyalty.

She was also helping James in practical ways. She took entire charge of their social life, planning official dinners, deciding which invitations to accept and which to reject, seeing that their clothes and new home were kept in order. Her Wednesday night levees became an institution.

When Jefferson moved his furniture back to Monticello, Congress had appropriated $6,000 for furnishing the Presidential Mansion, and Dolley's good taste and enthusiasm made her a worthy partner of the architect-decorator Benjamin Latrobe. Their conferences claimed a great deal of her time.

Though none of the furnishings chosen survive (the crimson "Dolley Madison sofa" in today's White House was not a *White House* sofa), old catalog lists and a Hudson River facsimile of the State Room speak of space-multiplying mirrors, Directoire chairs, valances with drop fringe looped into formal festoons, brass candelabra, mahogany bottlestands, a dumbwaiter, eggshell china, a $458 pianoforte, and, fluted above the sideboard, a yellow damask "sunburst." Gilbert Stuart's full-length, majestic portrait of General Washington wearing a lace-flattered black velvet suit hung in the dining room—his mouth clenched. Not as fond of bright colors as Dolley, Latrobe wrote her from Philadelphia, "The curtains! Oh the terrible velvet curtains! Their effect will ruin me entirely so brilliant will they be. . . ."

The great house now furnished in high style had so many rooms, the Madisons could invite houseguests in battalions. The irrepressible Lucy Payne Washington was one of those who came often. With her husband roving from spa to spa seeking a cure, she often brought her children (George, Willie, and Sam, aged three, nine, and ten, respectively) to sister Dolley's. But when at thirty-six the husband and father found his death on a Georgia roadside, she lost her laughter and ceased to attend levees.

But the social life of the fast-growing capital-in-the-woods could not be stopped. For Dolley it was obligatory: private and state dinners, assemblies, theater parties. When the First Lady swept to her seat in the crude theater, her face, hairstyle, and jewels excited more interest than those of any actress who walked the boards. An old program announces that the play *Point of Honor* will be preceded by "Mrs. Madison's Minuet."

Young people, especially, loved her. A covey of them often surrounded her like sons and daughters. At forty-one she was fresh-spirited and enchanted with life. Often she seemed little more than their age.

After Anthony Morris's motherless daughter Phoebe had reluctantly given up her big cold bedroom in the President's House to go home, Dolley responded to her plea for a portrait by sending a copy of a Stuart. Phoebe was delighted.

Spring passed. A soberer Lucy went back to Harewood to try to raise corn, tobacco, and boys, and the Madisons took Payne to Orange. The President was planning to carry the remodeling of Montpelier further, now with the help of some Latrobe drawings.

Indeed the building of 2 one-story wings that would increase the frontage from 80 to 120 feet had already started. Mother Madison would keep her old quarters. Dolley and James would move their four-poster into a first-floor master bedroom to the left of the complex made up of dining room, study, and "tearoom."

One day in August the Samuel Harrison Smiths arrived from Monticello. Though Margaret had parted dejectedly from her hero, the cure was at hand. In her own words, "The sadness which all day hung on my spirits was instantly dispelled by the cheering smile of Mrs. Madison, and the friendly greeting of our good President." Meeting the Smiths at the door, Madison led them into the dining room, where some gentlemen were drinking wine and puffing away on cigars. Dolley ran in and embraced Margaret, crying, "I'll take you out of this smoke!" She piloted her guest through the fashionable new tearoom to the master chamber, where "everything bespoke comfort." When Margaret sat down on a sofa Dolley cried no! she'd rest better on the bed. Dolley herself took off Margaret's bonnet and loosened her riding habit. A servant brought wine, iced punch, and "delightful" pineapples. "No restraint, no ceremony," Mrs. Smith would report; "hospitality is the presiding genius of this house, and Mrs. M. is kindness personified." Her diary reports part of the conversation:

"Why didn't you bring the little girls?"

"Fear of incommoding my friends."

"Oh," laughed Dolley, "I shouldn't have known they were here among all the children—we have twenty-three."

Amazed, "Where do you store them?"

"Oh, we have house-room a-plenty."

When Anna Cutts entered with little four-year-old Madison, Thomas (aged almost three now), and the baby Walter (who was learning to walk), Dolley beamed.

Later when Madison, Cutts, and Smith came in search of the ladies, they quickly shut the door to adjust their dresses, then joined the gentlemen on the piazza, where everyone strolled until called to a supper of hot breads and cold meats.

On this visit the Smiths met many of Madison's relatives, "all plain country people," Mrs. Smith says, "but frank, kind warm-hearted Virginians." William Madison and his wife, Frances, drove over from their home, Woodbury, 6 miles away. Among relatives the President dropped his reserve to be "plain, friendly, communicative, and unceremonious," and Dolley was her frank warm self.

That evening when the gentlemen adjourned to the piazza and mothers went off to put their children to bed, Mrs. Smith and Dolley sat talking about Washington City until a servant brought candles, and Dolley went upstairs with Margaret to help her undress and stayed to chat. "How unassuming, how kind is this woman," Mrs. Smith would write. "How can any human being be her enemy?"

When Dolley had gone downstairs she said to a black maid, "Nanny, you have a good mistress."

"Yes, the best in the world—I wouldn't change her for any [other] in the whole country."

The next morning Nanny brought water and some ice from the icehouse out under the little "Greek temple" gazebo. By the time Mrs. Smith came downstairs, fifteen or twenty people had started on a "most excellent Virginia breakfast" of tea, coffee, hot wheat bread, corn pone, "light cakes," cold ham, chicken, and "nice hashes." Blacks ran relays between the kitchen and dining room.

Before she left, Mrs. Smith had decided that one word described life at Montpelier: "freedom."

That August Madison was forced to make a trip to Washington, not knowing how long he would be detained there. He and Ned Coles faced a mountain of paperwork from two newly arrived British vessels. Homesick, he wrote Dolley:

> My dearest. . . . The period, you may be sure, will be shortened as much as possible. Everything around and within reminds me that you are absent and makes me anxious to quit the solitude. . . .
> God bless you, and be assured of my constant affection.

Dolley had Payne. Tall for his years, he fascinated the girls and, in a sense, his mother. But she missed her husband severely.

One piece of news that Madison brought home was Britain's decision to replace Erskine with an envoy notorious for bullying neutrals: Francis James Jackson, known as "Copenhagen" Jackson because of the way he once threatened to blow up Copenhagen if it did not capitulate at once. A drought, settling down, threatened to destroy Montpelier's corn and tobacco. Would Copenhagen Jackson help?

Dolley's letters to her sisters were unselfconscious outpourings. But when Benjamin Latrobe cited an anonymous letter, she bared a knife edge. How happy if he had refused to react to falsehoods, she wrote. It was sad to think that her unfailing contradiction of adverse remarks about him had not taught him incredulity. How could she have spoken as Mrs. Sweeny reported? She had always known she had no right to criticize the conduct of a public servant. Besides, she was not interested in other people's business, and did not doubt his taste or sense of honor. She would examine the staff to find out who was "taking the liberty to misrepresent her." If enemies tried to stir up trouble, she would enjoy "counteracting their designs." This letter is that of a strong person. No nonsense. Since marrying Madison, Dolley had learned as much from him as he from her.

So ended the summer of their content. Quail were picking paths through sagebrush and burning leaves throwing off an acrid smell when Madison drove back to Washington to confront Copenhagen Jackson.

The envoy regarded American self-respect as insolence. But Madison was determined to hold his own. Their talks sometimes degenerated into elaborate exchanges of diplomatic insults. Between bouts, the high-handed negotiator went partridge shooting with Federalists. Then the same old sparring. Jackson refused to explain his government's catastrophic repudiation of the Erskine agreement, made no new offer, and stuck to it that revocation of the Orders in Council hinged upon the three conditions laid out by Canning and already rejected by Madison.

One morning after being politely entertained at the "palace," Jackson received a 4,000-word analysis of the situation. Though sent over Smith's signature, like many other foreign affairs communications it had been composed by the President himself. "Obstinate as a mule!" snorted Jackson. Impudent! Madison had let it be known that he saw plainly Britain's true purpose: to throttle—by keeping America from growing commercially—a potential rival.

One day Jackson again accused the President of something previously denied: conniving with Erskine with regard to that Minister's violation of instructions. The President had had enough. He replied with asperity. Jackson flared up, and Madison informed him in a few short words that because of his "gross insinuations," further talks were out of the question.

Traveling north, Jackson used Federalist newspapers to broadcast insulting charges against the Administration.

Most of the country, informed of the breakup, cheered its President. Representative Bacon, for instance, scorched the behavior of this "audacious Minister." In truth, he wrote, "I think that James Madison's Administration is now as strongly entrenched in the public confidence as Thomas Jefferson's ever was at its fullest tide."

Two days later Madison delivered his first Message to Congress. It had the tone and power of a person who believes in the inevitability of what he is doing. He said he regretted that Britain had refused to endorse the step taken by Minister Erskine. Since no ratification had been reserved by Britain, nor notice of broken instructions given, nor principle of equity cited, the United States could not possibly have expected disavowal of the agreement. With American trade crippled by depredations on the high seas, outgo exceeded income. Fortunately a budget surplus had taken care of the deficit. But the militia—"great bulwark of our security"—must be reorganized. He felt sure Congress would act "in a spirit worthy of a nation conscious . . . of its rectitude and . . . rights."

Even John Randolph spoke well of the Message. There was some cant in it, yes, but all politicians, said this politician, canted. Frankly he liked the Message better than "Jefferson's productions."

Madison's keynote was honor. Identifying with the United States, he refused to be kicked around. A nation of consequence was being created; witness its increased manufacturing, prosperity, happiness. Unless older nations could be taught esteem, its position would become intolerable. Loss of ships, seamen, and trade was bad enough; loss of honor would be worse. So war must be risked. The implication: what was a man or nation worth without self-respect?

Dolley was standing at his side; in a sense she was an integral part of his Presidency—"the greatest blessing of my life." Seeing the health-jeopardizing pressures on him, she did what she could to shield him; for instance, arranged her Wednesday evening levees so that he could slip out anytime, and relieved him of responsibility at dinner by placing him in the middle of a side of the table. Sitting at one end, with Ned at the other to pour wine, she led the conversation. Friends knew that Madison's silences were not a sign of misanthropy. Sometimes, especially during dessert, he joined a discussion or fell to jesting in his own dry way.

When Isaac Coles horsewhipped Congressman Nelson, dinner guests did not broach the subject. And when brother-in-law Jackson took a duelist's bullet in his hip, the scandal furnished no table talk.

Dolley's understanding of the burdens her husband bore was an incalculable boon. Sometimes he sat with her awhile an hour or so before dinner just for the pleasure of her company. "My dear," he would say on leaving, "you have rested me and helped me to go on."

A guest at the Madisons' first New Year party thought he saw the President "bending under the weight of cares of office." Another saw "many more wrinkles . . . this winter than last summer"—he looked all of his sixty-three years. These observers might have been surprised to see him, an hour later, romping with the three Cutts boys.

A Quaker begged him to work for peace. "Your anxiety that our country may be kept out of the vortex of war," answered Madison, "is honorable to your judgment as a patriot and your feelings as a man." The nation, Congress, and himself desired peace, but if attacked they would have to choose between war and disgrace, and might not overpatience under affronts invite that very dilemma? Remember, Erskine had been replaced by Jackson. "A worse plaster could not have been devised for the wound."

Though idealistic, Madison was also hardheaded and practical. The United States must prepare for a war which he earnestly hoped to avoid. In January 1810 he asked Congress for defense funds and for an extension of the law requiring the States to arm 100,000 militiamen. He also advised whatever naval repairs Secretary Paul Hamilton might recommend. His proposals set off six weeks of congressional bickering.

The Non-Intercourse (No Trading) Act was about to expire. Macon's bill to replace it with one which would keep out British and French vessels while yet permitting imports languished through congressional indecision. There was simply no agreement on policy.

To darken counsel, John Randolph had returned from a half year in Great Britain to fulminate against Jefferson, Secretary of State Smith (not without cause), and all military expenditures. His hatred of Smith, the growing feud between Smith and Gallatin, and Cabinet scorn of the "young War Hawks" aggravated Madison's problems just when he was striving to unite all factions. They overbrimmed his cup of anxiety. If only all parties would fight fairly and openly. A friction of honest minds might generate light.

In April 1810, a ship brought London papers containing the Regent's "peace speech" in Parliament and ex-Envoy Jackson's assurance that "we will have no war." The news jettisoned Madison's defense program.

Congress cut the budget—why waste money organizing militia and regulars and repairing frigates? Why borrow $4,800,000, ran the argument, if there wasn't going to be any war?

So Macon's bill lost, and he had to frame a weaker one. President Madison, hoping to salvage something, showed the Cabinet a substitute plan of his own: reenact the non-intercourse law, but postpone its effective date, and give the President power to set the time forward against one of the countries if the other revoked its edicts. His idea never reached Congress. On its last day in session that tumultuous body passed Macon's compromise Bill No. 2, which ruled that if France or Britain called off its dogs of commercial restrictions before March 5, 1811—a year from now—the United States would give the other country three months to reconsider before reviving the old Non-Intercourse Act.

In vain did die-hard Federalists like Senator Pickering attack Madison politically and personally. Most of the nation thought Congress had stuffed its ears against the recommendations of a wise President.

Beaten on his front, Madison determined to try a flank movement.

How he would react when galvanized by a crucial issue had been foretold twenty-three years ago in the Constitutional Convention. Wanting to express a conviction but fearing to grow so excited he would rush on to the point of exhaustion, he had asked a gentleman to tug at his coattails before he went too far. As he talked, language flowed more and more rapidly, and at last, sinking into his seat from fatigue, he reproached his friend. "Why didn't you pull me when you heard me going on like that?" "I would rather have laid a finger on the lightning."

Just as the wine laid up behind the piazza cornice at Montpelier had mellowed, so James Madison had improved with time. By the end of his first year in office, he was no longer an apprentice President or journeyman President, he was close to master craftsman.

His Administration had started with two birds of paradise riding high above a lady's buff-colored gown. But in most minds, now, the replacing image was that of a gentleman in a plain black suit, with powdered hair and a destiny-locked face.

Any doubt about his and his party's popularity was settled by the November elections. In the Federalist stronghold of New England the Republicans made an almost clean sweep.

~ XI ~

TOBOGGAN

AT THE BEGINNING OF his second year in the Presidency, Madison, the old chess player, knew he had to checkmate three kings: Joseph Bonaparte of Spain, Napoleon I of France, and George III of Great Britain. His country had a minuscule army, and for a navy only a few little gunboats. His Secretary of State was proving inept, and the hostility of the Pickering-led Federalists and Randolph-led Quids relentless. Facing the odds, Madison proposed to win by outthinking the opposition. Move the rook here? Zigzag the knight? The stakes were high, being the security, prosperity, and honor of the United States.

He had concerns over and beyond freedom of the seas and the acquisition of the Floridas. There was the need to end slavery, to establish a national university, and to deal with the Indians. But these considerations had been dwarfed. He would play his international game—really three games, a tourney—move by move.

Sometimes Robert Smith seemed the worst hazard. This Baltimore lawyer with the grandiose airs could spell, but beyond that, someone had asked, what? With foreign affairs growing ever more complex and the need to delegate responsibilities ever more pressing, Madison had for Secretary of State an obstructionist and dolt. As he studied the chessboard Dolley leaned over his shoulder. Every day she had a better understanding of his goal.

The problem was Hamlet's: to trap a king—three kings.

Some people who had seen Dolley as a charming woman of limited education were reassessing her. A penchant for feeling rather than thinking her way into a situation was being modified. During sixteen years of marriage she had been learning through osmosis, through an intense identification with her husband's interests, through esteem, through love,

234

and was gaining that touchstone of intelligence, the power to make fine distinctions. Politics being Jemmy's controlled passion, she was, inevitably, a political apprentice. Years later Harriet Martineau would call her a "strong-minded woman," adding that there was little doubt Madison "owed much to her intellectual companionship." By 1810 the process was well started.

Madison, and to some extent Dolley, saw the ugliness of the political situation. The British Foreign Minister, Lord Wellesley, was recalling Copenhagen Jackson as requested—but not in disgrace; on the contrary, and incredibly, with praise for his "integrity, zeal and ability." He was replaced by a chargé d'affaires who could only receive, not offer, proposals. To Madison this was proof of a hostility deep in the British Cabinet. Meanwhile France was offering fresh affronts. Napoleon's latest confiscations, said Madison bitterly, "comprise robbery, theft, and breach of trust, and exceed in turpitude any of his enormities not wasting human blood."

In June the President invoked public opinion by printing outrageous foreign dispatches in a *National Intelligencer* extra. People seethed with anger—a pox on France! But the "original sin against neutrals," the Order that spawned all later evils, had been Great Britain's—a pox on Britain! The *Intelligencer,* voice of the Administration, made a powerful plea. Why should anyone feel partiality toward England *or* France? Neither promised justice.

One day Madison got the opening for which he had been looking. Napoleon's Foreign Minister Champagny, le Duc de Cadore, agreed that France would stop molesting American ships if the United States would refuse to submit to Britain's Orders in Council. The President immediately decided to play one nation against the other. Do better, he urged Cadore, and under the Macon law the United States would resist Britain's Orders by reviving the Non-Intercourse Act against her. Of course, France's repeal would have to guarantee the restoration of all seized American property. It was a large bold play.

At about the same time there rose a question about the third king. Should the United States defy Spain by occupying West Florida? From the first Jefferson and Madison had considered this territory part of the Louisiana Purchase, and had held back from forcibly taking possession because they hoped Spain would hand it over peaceably. But ever since Napoleon had seized Spain for his brother Joseph, there had been two Spanish governments, both weak. The Spanish empire was crumbling. If the Florida fruit was ripe for plucking, would France or Britain invade that orchard? Nine-tenths of the inhabitants west of the Pearl River were

Americans, and except for a few Tory runaways, all were hoping for annexation.

East Florida (the present Florida) was a large question mark. The stretch between the Pearl and Perdido was only sparsely settled, but the Perdido emptied into highly strategic Mobile Bay, and though much of the peninsula was swamp, possession by a hostile power would pose a real threat to American security. Spain's "soldiers" at Pensacola were no protection; they were shiftless ruffians.

Years ago Madison had copied this passage from Cardinal de Retz: "There is a critical moment in everything, and the masterpiece of good conduct is to perceive it and take hold of it." Was this the moment?

While the Floridas waited in the sun, the Indians beyond the Ohio were spilling more and more white men's blood, and William Henry Harrison, Governor of the Indian Territory, reported that Canadians were using Chief Tecumseh and his famous brother, "the Prophet," to stir up the tribes.

As if these problems were not enough, the British sloop *Moselle* fired two shots at the American brig *Vixen*. Lieutenant John Trippe cleared his decks, demanded an apology and got it. But a protest must be lodged—the British were getting bolder.

These problems could not altogether spoil the Madisons' summer at Montpelier. Visiting children were racing down the lawn and gorging peaches, the weather was delightful, and the double crop of wheat that year brought a double price. "Our farmers have never experienced such prosperity."

The scene was jolted by news that adventurers had organized a filibuster against Mobile and Pensacola. And a London magazine confirmed that Burr had offered to sell Britain a scheme whereby she and France could carve up the United States. When there were no takers, he had proposed that a French army under his command seize Louisiana and the Floridas. On top of this, General Harrison thought the Sac and Fox were about to go on the warpath. And the long-smoldering Smith-Gallatin feud had burst into flame.

Madison coud not spare Gallatin's financial genius. But with whom could he replace the Secretary of State? Was Monroe still sulking? The President felt crossed up and hedged in.

Contrary to Federalist scuttlebutt, he did not take his problems to Monticello for solution. Though President Jefferson had had Madison's help, President Madison did not, to any appreciable extent, have Jefferson's. The squire of Monticello had bowed out of politics. During the last crucial year and a half, Madison had not once asked Jefferson's views, and had sometimes ignored volunteered advice. Typically, twelve letters to Jefferson between April and August 1810 discuss not politics but the seven-year increase of their Merino sheep and a cure for scab.

Recently James Monroe had been making "great exertions to propitiate a certain gentleman." Jefferson did what he could to help. One day Madison decided to feel out his old friend. They dined together at Monroe's Highlands, near Monticello. John Randolph, riding up just after the "royal birds" had flown, wondered what it all meant.

The next London papers carried a letter from Champagny—now le Duc de Cadore—to Armstrong saying that on November 1 France would revoke her Berlin and Milan Decrees and release much American property. "His Majesty loves the Americans." Madison was elated. By cornering the French "king," he had gained the leverage needed to force Great Britain to repeal her hated Orders in Council. Good, he was ready to make his move! The rule in chess was keep your opponent on the defensive.

News of the French policy shift and a rumor about Monroe ran through Washington like fire through dry sage.

But on October 19 chess player Madison frowned. He had just heard about Britain's reaction to the French repeal. Far from capitulating, she had issued a new decree. Over Smith's signature, Madison wrote Pickering that on November 1 he would issue a proclamation reviving nonintercourse. Wellesley's conduct had betrayed "consciousness of a debt, with a wish to discharge it in false coin." Dispatches from Minister William Pinkney brought Wellesley's statement that His Majesty would end a system forced upon him *whenever the French repeal actually took effect.* Madison scoffed. The British Foreign Minister was crawdabbing.

In the meantime West Florida had held a convention which imagined it was a government, and Baton Rouge adventurers had seized a Spanish fort. Madison wrote Jefferson that he saw merit in the argument that the land to the Perdido, "being our own, may be fairly taken possession of, if it can be done without violence; above all, if there be danger of its passing into the hands of a third and dangerous party." At this point West Florida petitioned to join the United States. Fine, but Madison thought it should acknowledge the United States' rights under the Louisiana Treaty, not pretend autonomy.

To put the matter straight he issued a secret proclamation. The United States was taking possession of territory rightly its own, the order to be executed by Governor William C. C. Claiborne of the Orleans

Territory. And he cautioned Great Obdurate Britain. The sense of this
warning: Don't make the mistake of judging the future of America's
nonintercourse policy—framed to punish the flouting of international
law—by its past.

Again a month-long Atlantic crossing slowed down a conversation
between Europe and America. The waiting was irksome. Would France's
official notice of her repeal—the legal foundation for Madison's November announcement—come too late? Arriving just in the nick of time, it
caused wild jubilation. Beginning November 1, it said, France would
admit any American vessel to her ports.

Promptly on November 2 Madison informed the world that because
France had bowed to the Macon Act, three months hence the Non-
Intercourse Act of 1809 would be reinvoked against Great Britain unless
she too ended her commercial tyranny.

Turreau praised America's "new act of emancipation," and Madison—feeling the catharsis of action—congratulated his "Great and Good
Friend" Napoleon on his marriage to Archduchess Marie Louise.

Cadore's follow-up note destroyed the illusion that the French would
restore all American property. France was keeping cargo ships—"the law
of reprisal must govern." Moreover, there was a condition. To be
returned, vessels had to be French-licensed. Madison was outraged. Fan-
tastic! Never would a French agent wield power in an American port!

Still he clung to France as the only weapon Congress had permitted
him against British insults. A game of chess must be played realistically.
He did not know that Napoleon, out of meanness and rapacity and by
secret decree, had ordered the sale of all seized American vessels and that
Minister John Armstrong, desiring to return home in glory, had been
fooling the President of the United States.

Snow fell softly on the crisis. The great mansion where Madison
worked late every night, by candlelight, lay bedded deep in silence. Dolley
worried about Jemmy's insomnia.

The December 1810 Annual Message included his two proclama-
tions: the secret one authorizing the occupation of West Florida and the
public one reviving the Non-Intercourse Act against Britain. The country
saw that on two fronts its President had acted boldly, imaginatively,
cannily, firmly—and at risk of war. Most citizens approved.

Not all. In some quarters citizens harangued stridently against Madison the "Francophile," the warmonger "too weak to be wicked," that sneak
with an oily tongue. "He is a lost statesman. . . . Ambition has buried his
talents and smothered his patriotism, if he ever had any." On three points

they could hardly fault the Message. He had called for a suppression of slave traffic and, again, for a national university, and he had announced, as proof of a fast recovery from the Embargo, a Treasury balance of $2 million. Nevertheless, the *Federal Republican* called the Message a "masterpiece of art and deception." Never mind, said Dolley; heckling was one of the penalities for being President.

So the Baton Rouge filibusterers marched on Mobile. An *Intelligencer* extra called the action criminal even though the Spanish Governor, Folch, had declared that if by New Year's no Spanish help arrived, he would welcome American troops. His position contrasted with the Governor of East Florida's expressed hope that his province would be taken over by *Britain.*

The President reported these events to Congress. He said he favored a declaration that the nation could not watch, without grave inquietude, any neighboring territory fall into foreign hands, and asked for authority to take temporary possession. Congress's answer: If a local officer delivered it, take it; if a foreign power tried to invade, seize it! The sum of $100,000 was appropriated for the Army and Navy, and Madison appointed commissioners. Having stopped the French head of state, he seemed about to checkmate the Spanish one. That would leave only George III.

Meanwhile a decision hung fire. Should Louisiana Territory be made a state? During the framing of the Constitution Madison had called enlargement of the sphere of government a shield against tyranny, and he was now for expanding the Union. But some congressmen opposed the admission of any state beyond the Mississippi on the ground that it would upset the balance of power in the East. Once a westward push began, how stop short of the Pacific? They denounced the bill as a "death-blow to the Constitution."

Amid these tensions, Dolley opened a brilliant winter season. Past forty and a little plump, she remained persistently youthful, her skin milk white, her eyes gentian blue, her nature capable of arousing the best in people. Madison knew how to value her contribution to his Administration. When her South American macaw, stern as a Supreme Court justice, screamed an irreverence, she laughed out loud with pleasure. It was a beautiful world—or would be if the British behaved.

Her pride in Payne increased. At nineteen he was doing well in natural philosophy and spoke French like a Frenchman. Many people spoke of his "beauty." From time to time he came over from Baltimore, a 6-foot young buck with eyes like his mother's and not a little of her charm.

She and his stepfather continued to plan on some years or months for him at Princeton. And afterward? Dolley looked forward to a pretty daughter-in-law and a troop of grandchildren.

She also cherished her nieces and nephews, especially Anna's children. Mary's daughter Mary—Jackson had retired and rewed—lived in Clarksburg the year round. Lucy's sons were off at school. But the First Lady saw a great deal of Anna's Mad, Tom, and Wat. She often ran over to her former house on F Street to play games, spin yarns, or nurse a sick child. This was not the grand lady of the Wednesday night levees.

There she dressed to the nines in silk, flowers, feathers, and jewels—the aesthetically starved little Quaker girl grown up. A natural good taste made her a kind of fashion arbiter. More sophisticated now, she dipped snuff from a cloisonné box, using a bandanna for "the dirty work," as she said, and a little lace handkerchief as "polisher." And she played cards oftener. Why not? She could not see why not.

Washington Irving has described one of her soirées. Graciously received at the Presidential Mansion, the twenty-seven-year-old future novelist entered a crowd "of great and little men, of ugly old women and beautiful young ones." Mrs. Madison was the cynosure. He found her and her sisters Mrs. Cutts and Mrs. Washington as spirited as the "merry wives of Windsor." Partial to drama, he was not impressed by the tired President, and called him "a withered little apple-john"—which biographers have made the most of.

There is contrary testimony. John Vanderlyn's portrait of Madison at near-sixty, when the President was bearing burdens enough to wither anyone, shows a strong chin and nose, lucid eyes, and a brow stamped with vitality. And Baron de Montlezun, who visited Montpelier five years after Irving saw Madison, which is to say when the President might have been expected to look more "withered," has left this description:

> But when he can disengage himself for a moment from the cares attached to the painful honor of being the Chief of a republican government, the wrinkles smooth out of his face, his countenance lights up; it shines then with all the fire of the spirit and with a gentle gayety; and one is surprised to find in the conversation of the great statesman . . . as much sprightliness as strength.

"When he can disengage himself. . . ." But these days he seldom disengaged himself. The strain of trying constantly to anticipate his adversaries' moves gave him an air of abstraction. The Emperor Napoleon had stopped seizing American vessels, and Joseph Bonaparte was slowly losing the Floridas to the United States, but George III's agents were still agile, still arrogant. To win the tourney Madison must checkmate Great Britain.

On February 11, at the end of the three months of grace granted Britain, the President reinvoked the Non-Intercourse Act against her and recalled Minister Pinkney with the satisfaction of a man raking up last fall's leaves. Now for spring growth. Dolley's smiles, if not as gay as usual, were not forced. She too had confidence.

Washington Irving's letters picture the social whirl. Since the first levee he has been in a "constant round of banqueting, reveling and dancing. . . . I am in clover—happy dog!"

> . . . My time is passed delightfully. . . . In the evening at Mrs. Madison's levee, which was brilliant and crowded with interesting men and fine women. On Thursday a dinner at Latrobe's. On Friday a dinner at the Secretary of the Navy's, and in the evening a ball at the Mayor's.

February brought Louis Sérurier to replace the "magnificent butcher." The new French Minister was a thin, personable, thirty-five-year-old man with a "rather dark melancholy countenance." The Madisons liked him at once. In exchange the United States would send France, on the *Essex* as soon as it returned, the Madisons' poet-friend Joel Barlow.

Meanwhile Secretary Robert Smith's campaign to undermine Secretary of the Treasury Albert Gallatin had quickened. As a young man the President had once copied this maxim by the Cardinal de Retz: "One is oftener deceived by mistrusting people than by confiding in them." In Smith's case had he trusted too much? The man was a liability.

The situation ripened. Saying that Cabinet strife had destroyed his usefulness, Gallatin offered his resignation. It was rejected. Instead, Madison asked for Smith's, offering him the post of Minister to Russia. Smith agreed, and Monroe joined the Cabinet ("Judas," muttered John Randolph) as Secretary of State. It was a smart move. Madison could now buckle down to hounding that third king back across the chessboard. Near the ivory chess pieces shone Dolley's ivory face.

It was the end of Madison's second year in the Presidency. As the third began, he felt encouraged about curbing the maritime arrogance of Great Britain against which Presidents Washington, Adams, and Jefferson had struggled. How could that nation stand very long the punishment

Congress had resolved to mete out, namely, loss of the American trade on which she counted for vital commodities? Her knees must buckle. The news that the British were stoical about the reinvoking of America's Non-Intercourse Act did not faze Madison. Of course they would pretend indifference. That was to be expected.

No one could have foreseen the actual train of events.

Robert Smith had grown sullen about his dismissal. One night he reversed his acceptance of a presidential dinner invitation, and when Dolley, Lucy, and Anna called at his home, he was less than cordial. In March the *Aurora* blamed Gallatin for the "base and detestable" switch at the State Department, and many Federalist papers took up the hue and cry.

The Madisons' private and public lives continued to make a sweet-sorrowful counterpoint.

In May the President—anxious to get back to Montpelier—still worked at his desk, awaiting the *Essex*. Five months since it was to have sailed! Dolley wrote Consul Lee of their "cheerful tranquility" in spite of all, and quoted,

> Though the mast bows beneath the wind
> We make no mercenary prayers,
> Nor with the Gods a bargain bind
> With future vows and streaming tears.

Aware of Smith's malevolence moving behind his back, Madison chose to ignore it. The former Secretary, having developed a "mortification," now swore to his brother Senator Samuel Smith that he would publish the "real circumstances" of his dismissal; Madison must pay. "His humiliation I will effect. . . . His overthrow is my object." And the defecting Republican went so far as to write a friend about the "enfeebled mind of our panic-struck President." At the same time Duane's *Aurora* turned against Madison:

> We are authorized to state that the rupture which has taken place
> between Mr. Madison and Mr. R. Smith has been produced by
> conflicting opinions in relation to certain great public measures

—meaning the Macon and Non-Intercourse Acts—and by the President's habit of making secret recommendations.

When Federalists embellished the theme, Republicans countered with the real reason for Smith's discharge: gross incompetence. But in the case of turncoat Duane, Madison tried to balance good against bad: "I have always regarded Duane, and still regard him, as a sincere friend of liberty, and as ready to make every sacrifice to its cause but that of his passions." Smith must have given the *Aurora* its buckshot.

While memory was fresh, Madison wrote out the circumstances of the dismissal. The main points: He had long suffered from discord in his Cabinet. Smith often agreed with some proposition, only to weaken confidence in the Administration by reversing himself. As President he had been forced to confront him with this fact. When it was denied, he had cited the example of Smith's statement to British Chargé d'Affaires Morier that he disapproved of the United States' "whole course of policy." Such disloyalty was payment for the extra labor he had assumed because, whatever Smith's talents, they were frankly not those of a Secretary of State. Increased public business made it impossible to continue to add Smith's work to his own. To be lenient he had offered the Russian post.

But Madison did not publish the memorandum. Practically everyone in his party was sticking by him, and Federalists, remembering Burr, distrusted a defector. Smith became a man without a party.

There the matter hung while public attention shifted back to the French situation. Why go easy on Napoleon, people were asking, when, in spite of his repeal of the Berlin and Milan Decrees, he kept on confiscating American vessels? Dissatisfaction swelled. But Minister Sérurier, putting his ear to the ground, became convinced that if England did not change her policy, the Americans would fight to defend their interest and honor. And something else was reported to Paris. Mrs. Madison's influence had converted a possible pistol duel between Congressmen Eppes and Randolph into an "accommodation"—all credit belonged to the First Lady.

John Randolph was still stirring up rows. On the first day of the new session he brought two pointers into the Chamber. Every time a Member rose to speak the dogs barked, but no one dared protest. On the last day they almost knocked down Congressman Alston of South Carolina. He struck back. Their master brandished his sword cane. Its sheath fell off, exposing the blade. A Member wrestled it away, and a court fined Randolph $10.

Though amused by such antics, Louis Sérurier took the United States very seriously. Chargé Russell had told him that Americans "feared no one but God," and he agreed. But he was still sizing up the President. Federalists had confided that he was only a front for others, notably Gallatin. Was this true? His first talks with Madison had failed to answer

that question. The President seemed to prefer to discuss French literature, "which he is fond of," the Minister wrote his government, "and
knows well." Of course Madison was hobbled, he added, by having to
answer to public opinion.

After a few months the French Minister firmed up his judgment.
Though without great boldness, the Administration was "honorable and
reliable." France could woo it profitably. When a Federalist paper upset
Sérurier by calling him the "Minister of Rapine and Murder," Monroe
soothed him by saying never mind, that sheet regularly called the President a traitor. By May Sérurier was getting used to the roughnesses of a
two-party system. But there still stood an unanswered question: Was
Madison his own man?

An incident helped resolve it. When officers from the British frigate
Guerrière boarded an American brig to seize an apprentice seaman, Madison ordered Commodore Rodgers of the *President* to sail forth and stop
impressments or *fight*. His instruction: "Be . . . determined at every hazard to vindicate the injured honor of our Navy." Sérurier's report to
Napoleon: "Mr. Madison governs by himself." In other words, he initiated
and implemented policy; he was no yes-man. The French Minister went
on to say that Madison had more intelligence and knowledge of affairs
than any member of his Cabinet with the possible exception of Gallatin, to
whom he showed moderate deference—*"deference sans abandon."* With all
his good qualities Madison combined "proper and decided ideas of Government." His order to Rodgers proved "some toughness of character
when he thinks the national honor is involved."

The President's naval order brought startling results. One night
Norfolk heard cannonading. Where? Why? When Commodore Rodgers
finally reached Sandy Hook, he told his story. For hours the *Little Belt* had
approached the *President* flying signals which meant she was looking for a
fellow warship. Overtaken by night he had called, "What ship is that?"
The answer was a mocking echo: "What ship is that?" Again he asked,
"What ship is that?"—whereupon shot ripped his mainmast. Returning
the fire, he drew a broadside. His all-out barrage silenced the *Little Belt*'s
guns. Only his foremast was damaged. Too late and to his great chagrin
he discovered that he had been firing on not a frigate but a sloop of war of
lesser equipment. In the morning, after lying to all night, he offered help
but was refused. The fact that he had killed or wounded twenty or thirty
Englishmen would have pained him the rest of his life, he stated, if the
alternative had not been to watch supinely an insult to the American flag.
The *Little Belt* was a pooped corvette which, in a stern chase, looked like a

frigate. By the time he saw her broadside it was too dark to distinguish her single tier of guns. He would welcome an investigation.

When the *Intelligencer* printed this report, Federalists raised a ruckus. Dastardly! No, replied Republicans, the British had got precisely what was coming to them for firing first. And the President refused to order an investigation.

But where was the *Essex*? Dolley referred to it as the "provoking" *Essex,* and people talked about the delay at teas and balls, in carriages, and on street corners. Could it be that Britain's Orders in Council had already been repealed? Though hurt by them, some Federalists almost hoped not. Repeal would prove the President right.

On May 25 the *Intelligencer* published a Madison-inspired article signed "Americanus." It declared that commercial greed had formed a noisy lobby against public policy, damaging trade and embarrassing state-craft. What did these malcontents want? War? No. Nonintercourse? No. Submission? No. Yet *these were the only alternatives.* Critics of the Administration refused to deal in particulars; they had no plan, only a talent for carping. "Protect commerce!" was their cry, but when they got protection, they raged against it. Americanus repeated that trade trials would yet prove a boon to trade:

> We have only to turn our attention to the manufacture of raw materials which we grow in abundance, and to cease repining at what we cannot remedy. When commerce is once more unrestricted by France and Great Britain, we cannot fail to . . . enjoy our full share. Meanwhile let us not maintain intercourse with those who have injured us . . . and if compelled to fight, go to it with calmness, like men of true resolution.

Madison's "with calmness" chimed in with Dolley's earlier reference to their "cheerful tranquility."

But in a letter to Cutts, Madison dropped his guard. The results of the by-elections were gratifying; however, on the subject of commerce there was "ignorance and instability." Because France was subordinating American trade to her "grand object of destroying Great Britain's," the United States must expect a continuation of "obstructions and vexations." This clog was bound to cause inconvenience, particularly in New England. He had received more denunciations from New Haven. Though the baggage of the new British Minister, Augustus Foster, had arrived, many doubted that Foster himself would follow or that Britain would leave nonintercourse unavenged.

In the meantime Robert Smith had kept strangely silent. What was brewing? After Ned Coles had stopped off in Baltimore to see a relative of Mrs. Smith's, Dolley asked about his reception. Friendly, he reported through Payne, but the Smiths' displeasure with the President and herself was "very apparent." Masking his spleen, Smith was egging on others to protest his dismissal. And he was whipping up a pamphlet called *Address to the People of the United States.*

Unruffled, Dolley wrote Anna one of her casual, loving letters. She had recovered from an illness and received the bacon and beaten biscuits. She and James were giving a large dinner party. "How I long to be with you and your dear boys. . . . Keep up your spirits." Unspoken was the wish that this time Anna would produce a girl.

A week later she dictated a letter to her "amiable cousin" Ned Coles who was on a trip to New York with his brother John. She suspects both are in danger of getting married. Give her advance notice so she can "strew roses on our mountain path." She's glad the Smiths have "full indemnification" for their malice. Dear brother John is at Cape Henry—she's watching the stagecoaches. She and James enjoyed breakfast at the French Minister's. "Farewell, dear Cousin."

When word came that Anna had indeed borne a daughter, she was ecstatic. That night at a full drawing room she announced "in great triumph" the arrival of her new niece and "daughter." The lyrical letter she shot to Anna is Dolley incarnate:

> Joy! Joy! to you my beloved brother and to you my dearest Anna—but are you sure it is a girl? Now do not deceive me! for you know I have set my heart on having a girl—and I tell you that I shall be sick if in your haste to write you have mistaken. Every one of your little rascals is knocked up now. Why did you not tell the color of her eyes, or has she any? Yes, Mad, Tom, Dick and Wat, stand aside that I may kiss and squeeze the cherub. Dolley, Lucy, Anna, Mary, Julia . . . I claim her as my pet, my darling daughter—I wish Payne could marry her at once to put it out of doubt her being my own.

She appended a snippet of news: "We look for Pinkney and Foster every hour" on the *Essex* with crucial word.

Thus Dolley kept in close touch with her sisters. Anna's letters were affectionate; Lucy's were a loving, high-spirited, delightful hodgepodge of foolishness and gravity, the quoting at length of which must be resisted. They run to gossip and jokes. Laughing about Ned Coles seeing new sights: "I expect he is like a gosling let loose out of a pen, and so wonder-struck by all he sees that he thinks of nothing. Jack too with his scallop nose and wide mouth. . . ." On she prattles. Seriously, she still hopes there won't be war—"fighting is as much my aversion as ever it was Jefferson's." (She does not say Madison's, knowing that her brother-in-law chose middle ground.) Give her "all the scandal." She sends love to Payne, who should pick her up after the Fourth. "Give much love to my dear brother James. Tell him I expect to make twenty barrels of corn to the acre, and the worms have not meddled with it. . . ." Finally: "Take care, my darling sister, of your precious self, and write often and long long letters"— Harewood is lonely. "Your own Washington," a curious signature.

Ex-Secretary Robert Smith's forty-page *Address to the People of the United States,* designed to undermine the President, was published in June and widely copied. Offering the Russian post, Smith claimed, had proved the President's confidence. But Madison's embarrassment during an interview had raised a doubt, the ex-Secretary went on, as to the "*real* object." Rising from his chair, he had declared that some time ago, owing to conflicting views, he had decided to resign. The pamphlet charged Madison with a bitter hostility born of disapproval over some of Smith's instructions to Armstrong.

Smith's! Madison felt the irony, for the words cited as Smith's had been lifted out of a penciled presidential draft. Far from resenting them, Madison had written them!

Smith's disgruntled version of the rupture fell flat. "But St. Thomas of Cantingbury," cried John Randolph, no friend of Madison these days. "does not he outcant all his outcantings?" And Henry St. George Tucker, no Madison-lover either: "Singular, I call it because it is one of the rare instances of a man's giving the finishing stroke to his own character in his eagerness to ruin his enemy. I hear but one opinion of Smith: he has signed his death-warrant. . . . I trust his conduct will be universally and cordially despised. . . ." The general verdict: betrayal of trust. "Malignity." "Weak, wicked and ill-judged." The *National Intelligencer,* cold as January, called the pamphlet "a shameful breach of . . . confidence . . ., an under-hand and insidious recurrence to circumstances in which he cannot be chastised by contradiction, the facts being known only to the party attacked, whose official position forbids a reply even for the refutation of calumny." Later, Barlow and Lee's four-part "Review of Robert Smith's Address" found Smith guilty of incompetence, loss of integrity, and misuse of confidential papers. Even so, some extreme Federalists clasped Mr. Smith to their bosoms as the minority's man.

Then British Captain Bingham challenged Commodore Rodgers's account of the *President*'s encounter with the *Little Belt*. He swore that in broad daylight Rodgers had recognized him perfectly, hoisted colors, and fired the first shot: serious contradiction. If this was true, Commodore Rodgers had deliberately attacked a vessel of half his force, then lied about it.

On Saturaday, June 29, 1811, amid this controversy, H.M.S. *Minerva* landed the new British Minister, Augustus Foster, and a few hours later the long-awaited U.S.S. *Essex* brought retiring Minister Pinkney and some long-expected Paris dispatches. Good or bad news?

All day Sunday Madison and Monroe pored over new intelligence. Yes, Napoleon had kept his promise to repeal the Berlin and Milan Decrees, but not the French licensing system; nor had he restored any American ship. The Emperor's surprise: He was "willing that the United States should proceed in . . . the Floridas as they thought fit."

Monday Sérurier found Monroe "icy." For the "tenth time" the Secretary of State repeated the threat of revolt from American merchants. Sérurier countered with a complaint about diplomat Barlow's delayed departure. Monroe said he would sail as soon as Foster divulged Britain's attitude.

The next day Foster presented his credentials. Any offer of *Chesapeake* reparations, he said, must wait on a clearing up of the "wanton slaughter" of *Little Belt* sailors. He requested a court of inquiry.

A Fourth of July banquet was held under tents pitched along the Potomac. The President seemed preoccupied. A toast to Commodore Rodgers was so sharp it had to be postponed until certain guests had departed: "*Suavitur in modo, fortitur in re.*" What did it mean? General John Mason explained: "Speak when you're spoken to or God damn you I'll sink you." That night there was a brilliant display of fireworks.

Unlike Merry, Minister Foster found no need to protest about protocol. At a Presidential dinner he was allowed to escort Dolley. A greater privilege could not be conferred. But parleys were less cordial. Far from giving in, Britain declared that her Orders in Council must stand until France had *proved* her repeal of the Berlin and Milan Decrees, and until the United States had reopened Europe's ports to British trade. She also protested the occupation of West Florida. The answer to the pressing question, What has Foster brought? was nothing—precisely nothing.

To tangle the skein, Governor Folch had not delivered West Florida after all. He was finding it easier to take orders and money from Havana.

Disgusted Americans urged Madison to seize Mobile and Pensacola. No, he said; he preferred trying to get it without bloodshed.

Chained to his desk, the President gave up his usual vacation at Montpelier. If his crops were neglected, it could not be helped. Which was the slipperiest—Britain, France, or Spain? It seemed a toss-up.

One day Sérurier came over from rented Kalorama (Barlow's home) to suggest that it would seem more appropriate for the President to call the anointed Empeor Napoleon "Sire" instead of "Great and Good Friend." The President spoke dryly. If established protocol were changed, the opposition would charge vassalage. Disappointed, Sérurier took heart. After all, the President did not use "Sire" for His Britannic Majesty or the Emperor of All Russians.

If Dolley found the Little Corporal's aspirations and gyrations funny, Robert Smith's did not strike her so. She wrote Anna, "You ask if we laughed over the Smith pamphlet. Mr. Madison did, but I did not; it was too impertinent to excite any other feeling than anger." But she could see the humor of a mishap the night she and James attended *King Lear*. "It was well acted," Dolley wrote. "Great riot and confusion." After the show they started home. A frightened horse jumped out of harness, and they walked home at one o'clock in the morning.

Dolley's sociable brother John was proving an asset to the Presidential circle. The great surprise to him, after years abroad, was Payne's rapid French (it came in handy with Sérurier) and social ease. Good! He liked his nephew.

The next ship brought word that the new French Foreign Minister, Maret, Duke of Bassano, had actually released sixteen sequestered American vessels. Now Barlow and Lee could sail. Sérurier's report about the President: "I have never seen him more triumphant."

It was an exaggeration. Madison understood what Napoleon wished to conceal: that "sequestered" did not cover "captured at sea." Moreover, the President objected to exorbitant French duties and the demand that two-thirds of a return cargo must be silk, one-third wine (luxuries of uncertain sale). The promised "fair French market" seemed as oppressive as the discarded licensing system; niggardly.

But France's lifting of her blockade did furnish the legal basis for economic pressures which might force maritime justice from Great Britain. The impetus behind Madison's use of this leverage was not love of France but love of his own country. During the Terror he had ceased to admire France—that champion of democracy was democratic no longer.

If Britain had been the first to revoke her unjust decrees, he would have clamped nonintercourse down on France fast and hard. Stiff protests sailed with Barlow. The back-and-forth with England and France had been going on for years. The Administration was worn out with it (as, probably, the reader).

Dolley was busying herself with dress fittings, calls, parties, thank-yous for gifts (a handworked counterpane from a Miss Wilder; a silver fox muff and tippet from John Jacob Astor who hoped she would advertise his fur company), requests for advice, favors, interviews. A Barbara Peters asked protection from a shyster lawyer. Being First Lady had its hazards.

She worried about John's drinking. Hot, boring North Africa had increased it. At twenty-nine, here he was off on another binge. Lucy wrote Anna, "Sister Dolley no doubt has informed you on the state of affairs with our poor dear brother. . . . I know not what to say or do, but greatly fear for him. It seems to me impossible his sisters can render him any essential service without ruin to themselves; and then perhaps it may answer no good and—heaven help him I pray." Lucy added that Dolley said the Federalists "abuse us all in the lump," but lies "seldom injury much." The boys don't want her to leave—William "bawls at it"—but she's going to Orange anyway.

The Baltimore *Federal Republican* gave the Orange-bound Madisons a royal send-off:

> The opinion is gaining ground rapidly that Mr. Madison will be impeached. . . . A doubt nowhere exists that it is in the power of [Robert Smith] to disclose further high crimes and misdemeanors . . . throwing far into the shade the crimes of Charles II. . . .

As if to refute the libel, Captain Mandeville's cavalry met the Madisons at the Potomac bridge and paraded them through Alexandria with great éclat. Fredericksburg too turned out in force, Republicans and Federalists joining to give a big dinner with bursts of cannonading for "their beloved fellow citizen, the Chief Magistrate." Dolley was honored with a ball.

A Presidential proclamation summoned Congress to a special session two months hence.

With so much hanging fire the Madisons' August-September vacation suffered somewhat. The hot wet weather encouraged wheat, corn, and gangs of guests. But one visitor canceled. French-American relations were too precarious for Sérurier to hobnob with the Madisons. When the family moved into the four rooms of the new wings, Payne—the handsome young scion, the prince, 6 inches taller, now, than his stepfather, and with an eye for art—helped arrange the furniture, hang pictures, and place statuary. Madison wrote Cutts that though "the hostile effusions from Baltimore" had fallen off, he expected them to be renewed with deadly hatred. The past recoil had made Smith all the more vindictive. Meanwhile the weather had turned "delightfully cool."

Dolley was not too busy to write Anna that she must take the milk and bread cure for sore breasts. The house is so crammed she has scarcely a moment to breathe. Lucy is mad at John for not fetching her. "He . . . lingers I know not where." She can't dissemble—"my head is turned, my heart oppressed—I am miserable for John and anxious for you. . . ."

Monroe arrived and closeted himself with Madison. Then Jefferson came for three days, his auburn hair turning white, his face crisscrossed by time. For thirty-five years this friendship had endured. As they sat talking in the salon, the dining room, and summerhouse, there was a real meeting of minds. " . . . And Foster said. . . ." Monroe thought it might be best if the Madisons skipped a planned visit to Monticello; enemies might charge that governmental problems were being settled there. Madison said nonsense. He and Dolley would make their usual pilgrimage. Friendship came first.

Thus, in September, at Monticello, the Madisons, Ned Coles, and Payne watched an annular eclipse: darkness biting into the bright wafer of the sun. Payne was so fascinated, Jefferson promised him a split-second chronicle of his observations. What beautiful Michaelmas weather!

While the men talked, Dolley enjoyed Jefferson's grandchildren. "Mrs. Madison helped the older girls with their darning and fancy work," says a Randolph memoir, "made clothes for the dolls, told such lovely fairy stories and was so sympathetic and kind."

Back at Montpelier, Madison received the Naval Board's verdict in the special inquiry. Fifty officers of the *President* had sworn under oath that the *Little Belt* had fired the first shot. Commodore Rodgers—the devil take Bingham—had been exonerated.

In contrast, the verdict in the Wilkinson trial was a "Scotch" one. Though fellow officers saw a "violent presumption" that the General had accepted a $42,000 Spanish pension and four muleloads of extra money, legally the seven charges stood "not proven." With grave misgivings Madison ordered the Army to return the General's sword.

So Cutts had slipped on ice and broken his shoulder. The Madisons were sad as they returned to the house with a lordly view of the Potomac, and an epidemic. It was a "sick and afflicted city," Dolley wrote. Had the Tiber Creek canal under construction caused the sickness?

Week after week Madison kept his bloodied nose to the grindstone, while Dolley launched a new social season. However much hung in the balance, she said, glum faces would not help.

A letter to Phoebe Morris, whom Dolley fancied as her future daughter-in-law, apologizes: "My own beloved Phoebe, your letters have been . . . prized beyond expression. . . . You can readily imagine my preoccupation, curtseying, kissing, etc., etc. . . . I am impatient to enquire whether you will not visit me this winter? Tell dear Papa to . . . perform his promise. . . . *I am in earnest, Phoebe.* . . ." No, Mr. Madison hasn't been hurt; another "silly report." For Phoebe's concern, she sends a kiss from the President. Yes, she accepts the offer to find her "a *fascinating* headdress. I enclose you 20$, my darling, and you will add to the bonnet or turban some artificial flower or fruit."

Autumn again, and Britain—although pressed economically—had not budged. Actually her Orders had been tightened. But the Madisons hoped stubbornly on. However bold her front, the cutting off of her American market must be hurting. Madison! jeered the Federalists. He couldn't be "kicked into a fight."

Foster agreed. Coached by wrongheads, he wrote his government, "How very little it is to be dreaded that this country will originate measures of hostility against us." For one thing, the States had "miserable fortifications." He could not see that Madison was neither war-hungry nor war-shy. His down-the-middle attitude had from the start taken the subjunctive. If Britain remained obdurate, war must ensue; two things would demand it: commerce and the national honor.

If a country let another abuse her, she deserved a reputation for weakness, and its bitter results. As Cardinal de Retz had written, "The reputation of power is power."

In October—past the midpoint in Madison's conditional clause— racing buffs defied a fever epidemic to watch the horses. Wrote an Englishman who had driven up with the British Minister in a smart curricle:

> . . . Mr. Foster . . . had the best equipage on the ground. His horses are very fine ones, and his grooms sported their best liveries. Mrs. Madison was present, with grays in a chariot, and

Mrs. Tayloe in a coach and four, which were the only equipages deserving notice.

Madame Bonaparte, first wife of the King of Westphalia, had only a single pair, and the French Minister—how shocking—came on foot.

While Washington was placing bets, Governor Harrision was deciding that Chief Tecumseh and the "Prophet," allies of the British, were trying to bind into a confederacy all the tribes between the Ohio and the Great Lakes and that Tecumseh, known for his exceptional self-control, eloquence, and ability, had become a grim menace. In November, with these provocations or pretexts, American troops, falling upon the Prophet's town, reddened the Tippecanoe River. "War, savage war," muttered Andrew Jackson; and hawks in Congress approved it as the first skirmish in an inevitable war with Great Britain—thank God the United States had shown no pusillanimity.

By-elections brought changes. The Senate was still 3-to-1 Republican, with Pickering purged. The House, turned topsy-turvy by a flood of new members, was also, now, 3-to-1 Republican. Henry Clay of Kentucky and John Calhoun of South Carolina led the "War Hawks." And there was secret lobbying. "The intrigues for President and Vice President go on," Dolley wrote, "but I think it may terminate as the last did."

Madison's third Annual Message was evenhanded. Condemning Britain's "war on our lawful commerce," he stressed the fact that she had only to change her policy to obtain friendship. The United States had strengthened its harbor fortifications, repaired its gunboats, and built a new frigate. He recommended an increase in the army.

Reactions fell along party lines. But former President John Adams— that honest Federalist—called the Message a "great honor" to Madison, and the country's unanimity the greatest "ever known in America for fifty years." Sérurier thought the Message foretold war, but Foster, who had been listening to Anglophile Federalists, decided that the President, vassal to Congress and an unstable populace, was just doing anything and everything to get reelected—there'd be no war.

About this time Britain offered, for the *Chesapeake,* a settlement almost identical—ironically—with the reparations which Erskine had negotiated in 1809. It took "one splinter out of our wounds," Madison mused, but only one. The Orders in Council remained.

Dolley retailed the news to the Barlows. Cold weather killed the epidemic. She has not yet "begun my journal" (would she had). Mr. R S is "down"; even his brother and Mme. B[onaparte] are now on Madison's side. For the first time she is finding entertaining "oppressive." She wishes she were in Paris. And she would like to import a little of it:

> As you have everything that is beautiful and we nothing, I will ask the favor of you to send me by safe vessels large headdresses, a few flowers, feathers, gloves and stockings, black and white, and any other pretty things suitable to an economist, and draw upon my husband for the amount.

Meanwhile Foster had grown troubled. He found the President absolutely convinced that the nation supported his determination never to acquiesce to the Orders in Council. Indeed Madison had "darkly hinted" at the real British motive, meaning, as Foster well knew, trade monopoly. On hearing France criticized, he had refused to let American-British relations hinge on French offenses; wrong was wrong. But no final decision would be made until the *Hornet* returned in April or May. In other words, Madison was offering a respite during which Britain could, without sacrifice of face, so alter her policies as to avoid the threatened conflict. Thus jarred into reality, Foster wrote the Marquis of Wellesley bluntly, "Unless we change our system, this country is disposed to go to war with us notwithstanding they have few resources. . . ."

Two weeks later he flipflopped. Some Federalists had lulled him into reversing his reversal:

> It is the opinion of most of the sensible men here that this Government will not be pushed into a war with us, but that their object is to secure the support of their party at the next election. . . . To judge from present indications there never was a more favorable moment for Great Britain to impose almost what terms she pleases . . . provided an appearance of conciliation be exhibited.

In this crisis the Federalists responsible for misleading Foster were rendering their country a terrible disservice. With a few it went even further; they actually hoped the Orders in Council would stand so that they might see Madison ruined by the consequences. They were willing to buy his downfall with war, death, and suffering.

Two observers had clearer eyes than Foster's. Sérurier wrote the Duc de Bassano: "Only the recall of the Orders in Council can now prevent war. I do not doubt that Mr. Foster has advised his Government of this."

The other person was Dolley. On December 20 she wrote Anna, "I believe there will be war. Mr. Madison sees no end to our perplexities without it. . . ." Anna's letter has raised her spirits. She longs to kiss the children and finds it gratifying "to be loved and remembered by your precious boys whom I love as my own. . . . Tell Madison, Thomas, Walter and Richard that I send them a thousand kisses, and that I have taken care of their wagon cradle and all their little things. . . . The *Hornet* went to take dispatches and to *let them know* our determination to fight for our rights." She expects little from its and the *Constitution*'s return but won't despair. She has sent Mr. Lee $2,000 for the $3,600 French purchases—"as much as I could." She'll make Anna a cap, and she has rescued the shoes from the tenant. Jemmy's tobacco hasn't sold. Her own new dress is of Lyons silk, but the black velvet and two bonnets are "very smart and becoming." They went to Alexandria in the Tayloes' sleigh—Foster, Miss Caton, Phoebe, Lucy, John, and a "whole dozen more." (How did they cram in?) Very cold weather—she's glad Anna dresses warmly. Everybody but herself attended Foster's ball, and she won't attend Sérurier's. "All go again—not I." Then the prophecy already quoted: "I believe there will be war. Mr. Madison sees no end to our perplexities without it." General Dearborn has been picked to command. More earthquake shocks on Wednesday night and Thursday morning were as frightening as the realization that war is now all but inevitable. She fights off melancholy. John will go into the Army if he can get a commission; he has listened when she "dressed him and pressed him" to forsake bad society. A congressional adjournment seems unlikely. Dr. Thornton is improving after his stroke.

Thus the counterpoint of the music of their lives.

Though Dolley agreed with Madison that a nation struck must retaliate, deep within her Quaker heart raged a war of conscience. Oh those mulish British!

This year of 1812 the President's New Year reception was not the usual feast of goodwill. When the French Minister protested an outrage to his country's flag at Savannah, Madison replied with "heat and irritation" that he deplored the incident, but it was not worse than the indignities France heaped upon America *every day of the world.* The cause of his spleen is clear. He could no more accept an insult to his country than to himself. How live without self-respect?

Returning from London, William Pinkney stirred up great public admiration by saying that his country's resistance to injustice had struck him as fruit of an "unmixed American spirit." Though Federalists sneered at the former Minister and referred to him as the "most noble Marquis of Whitewash," Madison had now acquired a top-notch lawyer as Attorney General.

Congress applauded the President's last Message, and the House Foreign Affairs Committee's report recommended not only a stern defense against international rapine but also the drafting of 20,000 troops and the calling up of 50,000 volunteers. At the same time it was against declaring war before the *Hornet* returned in May—that vessel just might bring news of lawless Britain's capitulation. The nation was likened to a young man who, if he did not resist an unmerited flogging, must expect to be abused the rest of his life.

A fiery speech by John Calhoun defied both Quids and Federalists. There were two alternatives, Calhoun said, a disgraceful peace or armed conflict. The tide of patriotism was running strong.

The last six months had slid like a toboggan. The nation was plunging down a hill toward—what? Wind whistled, and sharp blades cut deeper.

That January 1812 a thick-set, balding, swarthy man with "monstrous thick legs" and a bulbous nose groping through whiskers burst into town and was introduced widely by the Governor of Massachusetts as the son of the "celebrated duke who besieged Gibraltar." Comte Edouard de Crillon cut a wide swath. It was whispered that he had ridiculed the 10-dollar-a-week price for his boardinghouse and insisted on paying 25. He was invited everywhere. At the President's House he dazzled ladies old and young.

That place had never enjoyed a greater whirl. Phoebe Morris wrote home that it was "crowded with company from *top to bottom*." Her brother had just "set off with Mr. Payne to ride over the city." It must have been rather clear to Phoebe that Mrs. Madison fancied her for Payne, and she herself may already have set her heart on the young man. Her father called her "Dolley's daughter."

There were other incipient, thriving, or failed romances. Writing Anna, Lucy spoke of the belles gathering—Phoebe, Betsey Caton, and little Bonaparte. "I name these because they ring the loudest." The last two "are at daggers' claws about Foster. Mrs. Custis swears no one shall take the Frenchman [Crillon] from her with impunity, . . . indeed, it is as good as a farce . . . watching, peeping and snarling. They remind me of two or three dogs with a bone. . . ." The dreadful Richmond theater fire brought gloom, but it is wearing off, "as all things do." Foster has invited nearly four hundred to his "grand ball" and "I fear we shall pull the old house down."

Surprisingly, Lucy neglected to tell Anna that she herself—one of the most attractive belles—was being courted by Supreme Court Justice Thomas Todd. He was a widower twelve years Lucy's senior, with grown children; a man of kindness, learning, wit, and quiet charm who would make a good father for the three Washington boys. But Lucy was hesitating. Was he the man?

While she wavered, there was a feverish quality in part of Washington's social life. Little Betsey Bonaparte, flanked by her sharp-tongued relative Miss Spear, ran about scantily clothed in thinly veiling, low-cut gowns and loaded with diamonds and pearls, talking incessantly, says Mrs. Mitchill, and "wholly devoted to the pleasures of this life." As were others. Cotillions were the rage. Turreau's young son loved dancing so much "his legs [were] half the time in the air." Foster's ball was a smashing success. Then Sérurier tried to outtop him.

But there crept shadows. Mrs. Mitchill had put a growing apprehension into words when she wrote: "A war with England seems almost inevitable. . . . I do indeed dread a war . . . but if there is no other way to maintain the honor and dignity of our nation, let us resort to it at once. . . ."

Though the Madisons felt the seriousness of the hour, they did not alter their way of life. At a "genteel squeeze" the "two great personages"—"their majesties"—stood in the middle of the room receiving congratulations. After two hours Mrs. Mitchill told Mrs. Madison she ought to rejoice when they all went home—she must be worn out from standing so long. No, Dolley answered, she regretted their going so early. "I never saw a lady who enjoyed society more than she does. The more she has around her the happier she appears to be." Mr. Madison had less relish for the "exhibition."

Amid these social doings, Washington heard that the reopened British Parliament had refused to repeal the Orders in Council, and Madison sent 2,500 Army nominations to the Senate. The United States must gird up its loins.

Though Betsey Bonaparte was increasingly criticized, Phoebe admired her thinly veiled figure to excess. She had "never beheld a human form so faultless," she said; it was "impossible to look at anyone else" in her presence.

Except Mrs. Madison—for this still handsome woman of forty-four had the extra attraction of a genuine interest in other people. According to Benjamin Ogle Tayloe, she had an unsurpassable bonhomie and was loved alike by rich and poor. She "never forgot a face or name." In a war-threatened city she continued to move through crowded levees, using her wonderful tact to rest the weary, spark the dull, calm the nervous: a kind of national insurance.

One day a frightened young stranger dropped a saucer and thrust a teacup into his pocket. "The crowd is so great," sympathized Dolley, "that no one can avoid being jostled," and she chatted casually until he felt at ease.

With all her new friends, Dolley was faithful to the old ones. Eliza still came first, that little mouse of a homebody, mother of three sons. Her husband, now Judge of the Orphan's Court, maintained a house at 6th and M. The two women kept in touch.

Young people delighted and delighted in Dolley. At receptions a bevy of girls usually formed a guard of honor.

One day she wrote Anthony Morris to comfort him about an indiscretion committed by "our beloved Phoebe." He feels too acutely the incident at Mr. Tayloe's ball, she said. "Everybody . . . understood that she had danced too much and, though the incident was unpleasant, I am perfectly convinced that her uncommon understanding and sweet disposition are guarantees for the propriety of her conduct through life." Lucy—capable of jealousy—hinted at other matters. "Miss Phoebe is still here and intends staying until April. I will say nothing on the subject till we meet, though I could write a volume." (About Phoebe's preference for Payne?)

One day there came the first sprinkle of snow. It fell so softly on the war threat it seemed unreal.

A farce involving the Comte de Crillon was now the talk of the town. Lucy wrote Anna about the "considerable noise" he had made at O'Neale's Franklin House where, for some time, his identity had been doubted. At a ball on Washington's Birthday he spat in a Mr. Darby's face. Asked if he submitted to that, Darby "very quietly took his snuff and said, 'O it may be his way of spitting!'" But that night Mr. Darby lay awake terrified, and at daybreak he seized his pistols and fired through the door. "Help, gentlemen! for God's sake!" Other guests ran about screaming, and the Duchess of Baltimore threw up a sash and "bawled out, 'Murder! murder!'" But Crillon was found asleep; Darby had only imagined an attempt on his life. Or had he? Catherine Mitchill thought it was a "vile stratagem" to get Crillon thrown out. In any case O'Neale cried, "Darby of Boston, leave my house!" "I'm going, landlord, I'm going."

While the town was having a good laugh, Crillon confided a strange story to Sérurier, who told Monroe, who told the President. Enroute to America, he said, a Captain John Henry had shown him letters proving that three years ago Britain had sent Henry to foment a Massachusetts rebellion. Henry would part with the letters for a consideration. Madison promptly prepared a report for Congress. Getting wind of it, Foster sent his secretary of legation to the Capitol to investigate.

Running into Coles (Madison's secretary), St. John Baker pointed to the documents, asking, "What's it about?"

"Nothing," came the cool answer, "just the correspondence of a man named Henry."

"With whom?" asked Baker, horrified. "Sir James Craig?"—the Governor of Canada.

"There you are!" said Ned Coles, smiling and bowing.

Congress listened round-eyed to this alleged British plot to destroy the Union. It seemed that Governor Craig had instructed John Henry to find out whether or not, in the event of New England's secession, the Federalists would like to rejoin the "mother country"; communications could travel to London via himself. Henry's 1809 reports had denigrated Madison and described New England as about to pull loose. Congress also examined letters showing Henry's inability to collect a promised reward. Angry, he had resolved to punish Britain by exposing her crime.

During the recital to Congress, Federalist Pitkin squirmed, "Quincy" walked the floor, Davenport sweated. "You may know the wounded pigeons," a Republican remarked, "by their fluttering."

But why had Henry failed to name a single American turncoat? And why had the Administration paid $50,000 for the documents? Forgery! swindle! shouted the Federalists. Senator Bayard: "Is not this a fearful prostitution of the first office in our country?" Congressman Tallmadge hoped the nation would see through the President's "pitiful and mean attempt" to vilify honorable men and get himself reelected. A "poor shabby shallow dirty electioneering trick," cried John Randolph's high-pitched voice. It was like a girl's.

But the Administration was convinced that the papers stood up under scrutiny. Henry had received the government's consent to erase all American names because the President preferred to pin the guilt on foreigners. Uncharged guilty citizens, he said, should take warning and help the country unite. Promised immunity, Henry sailed for France. But how, Congress was asking, had the informer Crillon extracted his information on shipboard? It seemed extraordinary.

The Frenchman said he had been made a confidant because he had known John Henry earlier, in London, while exiled for a youthful indiscretion. Yes, on being urged, he had sold Henry his palatial estate, St. Martial. His great hope was so to serve Napoleon, he'd be welcomed back to his native France.

Then Crillon, too, sailed for France, leaving Mrs. Custis in despair. He carried Sérurier's recommendation that, in view of his "thoroughly French conduct," the Emperor forgive and forget. Bassano's tart reply would come later: the Count de Crillon was a gambler and con man named Soubiron who had swindled the spy Henry out of $50,000 for a nonexistent St. Martial.

Recovering aplomb, the Federalists reviled Madison. Never would they attend another of Mrs. Madison's levees. They became still more strident on hearing about Madison's secret recommendation for an embargo of "say 30 days," to be followed—if the *Hornet* brought no news of a British reversal of policy—by war. If they had guessed that in East Florida ex-Governor Mathews had exceeded instructions by seizing St. Augustine, rushing in "patriots," and issuing a declaration of independence before ceding East Florida to the United States, they would have howled like banshees.

Madison's reaction was quiet. That was not the way to get East Florida. He ordered it given back to Spain, thus depriving the Federalists of the pleasure of keeping themselves wonderfully wrought up.

Dolley wrote that all was battle and electioneering, "the Federalists affronted to a man"; only one of their congressmen would enter Madison's door. Then a very special bulletin:

> My beloved sister, ere this reaches you Lucy will be married to Judge Todd of Kentucky . . . a man of the most estimable character . . . [His] residence [is] in Lexington . . . where there is fine society. Though it breaks my heart to find myself left far from my sisters, I rejoice at the husband she will have and the brother we shall acquire. As a Supreme Judge he is obliged to come here for two months every winter.

Actually Judge Todd had been rejected. Disconsolate, he had started home to Kentucky when a fast rider caught up with him at Lancaster, Pennsylvania. Lucy had changed her mind; he could turn his carriage around. It was so difficult a decision, Dolley wrote Anna, "Lucy is in deep distress," and she herself hardly less so. "My nights are miserable and so are my days."

Lucy's coming exile was not the only trouble. The Smith faction was threatening to join the Federalists in an effort to block defense measures. "I still think," she wrote, "we shall have war with England unless she changes her conduct, but how soon I cannot say; probably before Congress adjourns, which is expected in May, and a few begin to talk of June."

To force a British repeal or wage war—either one—Madison needed national unity. He had tried for it with the gentle treatment accorded the sabotaging Federalists in the Henry plot; perhaps too gentle. At the levee of March 25, these Federalists, exonerated from complicity, had come sheepishly back to the "palace" to counter the rallying and solidarity of the Republicans. But they failed to achieve unity. "Nothing," said Congressman Harper, "has mortified the Federalists so much as finding that their own conduct had taught the Republicans to pay respects to the President almost to a man." Then they got an ace in the hole. France had burned some American ships.

Madison still favored a showdown embargo. In the midst of preparations for Lucy's wedding—the first in the presidential mansion—Dolley warned Anna. "Where are Mr. Cutts' vessels? And why does he not get them in?" The toboggan was halfway down the hill. It was streaking.

That did not stop electioneering for the office of the dying Vice President. Dolley shook her head. "The world seems running mad, what with one thing and another. . . . The war business goes on slowly, but I fear it will be sure." Could Anna accompany them to Orange? Lucy could still be gay. To Anna: "I beg you will . . . spend the summer among us— only think what fine strawberries and cherries . . . !" But Dolley's time for chitchat had passed. She understood the peril.

"The most delightful and strange agitation possible," Phoebe reported to Papa. Miss Hamilton, Miss Hay, and herself would be Mrs. Washington's bridesmaids; Ned Coles, John Payne, and Payne Todd, the groomsmen. The ladies had shed so many tears they were beginning to smile in reaction. The forty-seven-year-old Judge was amiable, rich, and very handsome. Lucy's postscript spoke of depression over leaving: "all my heart has been *accustomed* to love . . . but we must *yield to fate*."

On Sunday, March 29, Madison gave away Lucy as he had given away Mary and Anna. But the case was different. The bride and groom whom Mr. Andrew T. McCormick joined in holy wedlock were older and widowed, and a nation trembled on the verge of war. The *Intelligencer*'s announcement was brief. "At the residence of the President of the United States" Justice Thomas Todd of the United States Supreme Court had married Mrs. Madison's sister Mrs. Lucy Washington. The next morning the couple left to spend a week at Harewood, where they would pick up Lucy's boys to drive to Pittsburgh and start the great adventure of floating down the great Ohio River to Kentucky.

They were scarcely out of sight before Monroe reported to the Foreign Affairs Committee, in secret session, that the President's position had not changed since the opening of Congress five months ago: "Without an accommodation with Great Britain, Congress ought to declare war before adjourning"—*before adjourning*. The Administration recommended a sixty-day embargo, during which the country could prepare itself militarily and the *Hornet* have time to get back with its hope-vindicating or hope-destroying news.

Just at this juncture a London newspaper encouraged the embargo by announcing that the Prince Regent had retained, under Prime Minister Perceval, a Cabinet which Madison immediately recognized as one of deadly conservatism, Lord Wellesley being replaced as Foreign Secretary by Lord Castlereagh. Castlereagh! Britain seemed to be saying loud and clear that she preferred war to altering her sea policy.

Madison's confidential message asked Congress for the embargo as a logical step toward the war which, in all likelihood, they could not honorably avoid. The bill passed the House 70 to 41. The Senate increased sixty days to ninety, the House concurred, and Madison signed the bill. It had all taken just three days. The bottom of the hill was flying up to meet the toboggan.

Foster asked if the bill meant preparation for war. "Oh, no," replied the President, "embargo is not war." But of course the United States had enough provocation to declare war, he added—"Great Britain is actually waging war upon us." Her seizure of eighteen more American ships, so richly laden they were worth $1,500,000—was that not justification?

But Foster, still a victim of misinformation and wishful thinking, clung to the idea that war talk was a bluff, the Embargo an election maneuver. He could not see that the President was jeopardizing his chance of reelection by adding "fuel to party discontent"; he could not understand that the Embargo would rob Virginia farmers, including Madison—wheat and tobacco lay moldering in their barns. Federalist fantasies crested in Pickering. He said Madison aimed at war as the best way to serve Napoleon. The Federalist *New York Post* took another tack. "The whole war fire evaporates in smoke," it said; at tonight's levee "Mr. Madison and Mr. Foster were in very familiar chit-chat."

Amid alarms and absurdities Dolley wrote Anna tenderly: "Everything that disturbs you never fails to vibrate through all my heart. . . . Did you get my child's necklace?" Lucy was wise to choose the amiable judge over "gay flirts." John has followed them to Kentucky. "It is not worthwhile to tell you the particulars of his last frolic, or the sum he spent on it. I re-fixed him with my *all, even my credit,* and sent him off in a hack with his friend Green, whose expenses I also paid in order to secure his retreat from *this den of thieves.*" She advised weak French brandy for Anna's watering eyes—Dr. Honymen had used it to cure her own. The political situation is "a little more calm . . . or rather I hear less about it."

But at night, when all guests had departed and the great doors were locked, an unwarlike man and peace-loving woman tried to fathom the ambiguous situation. Was war in the offing? Mercifully nightmares grew dim the next day.

From Pittsburgh, after seven days in the saddle, Lucy wrote with characteristic exuberance. "We have just arrived, my best darling, at this smoky place after a delightful trip," the roads (laughing) "a thousand times better than yours from Washington to Montpelier." The children bore up well; they found good beds and food. John has "behaved quite correctly," though on the road he amused them by complaints of the loss of his *hide.* She hopes kindness will restore him to reason. She veers off to rejoice over a letter from Dolley. "O my best beloved sister . . . tears blind me." The very good verses enclosed made them laugh. Her dear husband says the wine will be kept sacred to Dolley, and he will bring her out next spring. "O that we could . . . I'm in ecstasy at the idea." After some more chatter, she wishes Dolley could be relieved of Anthony and Phoebe Morris's *agreeable* company—Cousin Edward and Phoebe could scarcely part without blows. She felt provoked at "that old hag Mrs. Duval. . . . Everybody knows her disposition, the venom, and nobody loves or respects her, though if I had her head here I'd box her ears. . . ." Then an odd admission about Anna:

> I hope when she arrives you may find comfort in her society—
> *yet, I hope, still, she may scarcely fill the void I have left.* Don't think me
> selfish, dear sister. You know I always was jealous of you because
> I wish to be first in your affections.

And she hopes "my dear brother James" misses her at meals. Then some bantering: when he kissed Dolley he was always afraid of making her mouth water; well, she gets kisses now that would make *his* water. Leaping from topic to topic like a gazelle, Lucy thinks to please a mother: "I suppose Payne has returned to Baltimore. Phoebe says he is a gallant of the *first water*." She sends him much love. And begs for news and wishes Dolley would send her a "handsome fashionable spring hat or bonnet." Her happiness, now, is running in a new channel. "Phoebe's comparing the Judge to still champagne was an error in judgment. . . ." Only now does Lucy's breath give out. "Ever thine with constancy and truth"—Lucy Washington Todd, uncontrollably herself.

While Dolley was reading this marathon letter, the *Hornet* was still overdue, shipowners were cursing the Embargo, and Vice President Clinton dying.

But she held the Wednesday levee, playing her role of catalyst, disarming people and welding them together. Americans must keep up their spirits. "She had the gift of making everyone who left her presence feel he were the better for [it] . . . and that the world was better." No amount of worry about war kept her from dressing with careful elegance. She chose clear colors, usually warm ones such as the rose red of a still extant square-necked, velvet, starkly simple Empire ball gown with a train. But her favorite color was no color. She loved white.

And she never tired of jewelry. Vanderlyn painted her wearing a looped gold chain and amethyst-pearl breastpin. An auction list of some of her treasures during Madison's Presidency includes a headdress studded with twenty-three sapphires and a matching necklace; another necklace of twenty-two white topazes; a gold one featuring Arabian sweet gum and a double-headed eagle; a taupe cameo carved with a bacchante; and a pearl-studded, heart-shaped locket holding a miniature of her husband. James gave her everything; he felt that he could never give her enough. His engagement ring, never removed, had become part of her finger.

But that crucial spring of 1812 there developed a little crisis over Dolley's clothes. Through Mrs. Barlow, Dolley thanked Mr. Lee for the "valuable collection."

> His bill was paid immediately. . . . Duties, two thousand dollars. I am afraid I shall never send for any more. The dresses and every other article indeed are beautiful. The heads [wigs] decorated I could not get on. . . . Their price was so high the ladies of my acquaintance would neither buy nor exchange one, so that I shall lay them aside for next winter and then enlarge and make them fit. My shoes were just a size too short, but the flowers, trimmings and ornaments were enchanting.

Such extravagance while their grain and tobacco rotted in warehouses! Regretting her open order, Dolley reproached herself for naïveté. Madison could not reproach her; it was not in him.

The rest of her letter, dashed off to catch a boat, reveals her thoughts in mid-April. The Embargo will be followed by war. No British amendment, just more arrogance—"Yes! that terrible event is at hand." Henry Dearborn and Thomas Pinckney have been promoted to Major General, and recruiting goes forward. If Congress adjourns before July, it will give the President the power to declare war. She was "filled with selfish regret" over Lucy's marriage, but Judge Todd is all she could wish in a brother. In this political crisis she is the "very shadow" of her husband.

They saw eye to eye about France as well as Britain. To think that in spite of the President's demand for an across-the-board justice, Napoleon still refused to import American cotton or tobacco, while importing mountains of goods from his Britannic foe! It was niggardly, it was intolerable.

One April day when Sérurier came to see Mrs. Madison, he found himself face-to-face with a President irate against French privateers preying on American ships in the Baltic and off Lisbon. Sérurier called them "floating warehouses of the British army." Nonsense, snapped Madison.

When Vice President Clinton kept his appointment with death, the scrambling for place increased.

A few days later Foster invited all the Federalists in Congress to a Sunday-dinner "grand council." How could they force a congressional recess? Only by preventing a quorum. And how after calling the Embargo the first link in the chain with which Madison planned to strangle New England's economy, how after calling Madison's "war preparations" the hoax of a man who couldn't be kicked into a war—how could they explain his stepped-up military measures? The answer hatched up: young hotheads were pushing a reluctant Madison into war; it was the only way he could get renominated.

Honest Federalists knew this line was preposterous. During Jefferson's administration, war had seemed imminent. During Madison's first month as President, he had notified Britain that if she did not revoke her Orders in Council, the United States would declare war, and never once, since then, by word or act, had he swerved a hairbreadth. But now the feeling against the prewar embargo Madison wanted was so strong, Republicans began to fear that the Federalists might get their pious wish to destroy the President politically.

People were out enjoying the spring. They went up to the Great Falls of the Potomac, not so much to see the canal and locks as to see the grandeur of torrents of water, and beauty of dogwood, redbud, phlox, and May apples. Fishermen were catching shad with scoop nets and eating them in a nearby tavern. How beautiful, May.

Early that month Foster called on Madison and Monroe. What he heard hit like a bolt of lightning. At long last he realized that the President meant every word he had been saying. Foster rushed to tell his government that if the Orders in Council were not repealed, the United States would not hesitate to declare war; Madison was openly charging that the real purpose of the Orders in Council was to destroy American trade. But he still clung to a dying hope.

The next day a Madison-inspired article by Monroe warned (this was aimed particularly at Massachusetts) that the Administration would not be intimidated by any state legislature; only the strong, industrious, intelligent American people could plot the country's course. Everyone would rejoice if war could be honorably avoided. If not, woe to slanderers of honest government. As for the upcoming presidential election:

What has [it] to do with avenging our wrongs? If they call for energetic measures, and if energetic measures require united councils, let us without dissension take the attitude the times demand, and settle afterwards, as we please, who shall be our next President.

This call for decisions above politics embarrassed some Federalists. Here was Madison saying he would continue war measures even if it cost him defeat at the polls. They hated him for his decency and statesmanship.

The next day Congress began a vituperative debate. Emboldened by a petition signed by 800 citizens of Albany, long John Randolph demanded repeal of the Embargo. Federalists joined forces with the Quids. It would be impossible to wage war at the end of the Embargo, argued Bleecker—"where are your armies, your navy, your money?" Thereafter foes of the Embargo multiplied as fast as Caesar's assassins, cutting, slashing. Randolph probed for the heart. Madison's Embargo was like Jefferson's infamous one, he said. There was no excuse for embargo *or* war. None whatever!

The Madisonians rallied. Johnson charged Randolph with having once opposed every single measure he now urged, and Calhoun blasted him for saying the Embargo had been "engendered from a fortuitous concourse" between Madison and the Foreign Affairs Committee. "No, sir, it was . . . adopted by both the Executive and the Committee from its manifest propriety as a prelude to war!" Discussion of Albany's petition was derisively postponed until *the Fourth of July.*

Dolley wrote Anna about the quarrelsome Quids. "John Randolph has been firing away . . . against the declaration of war, but we think it will have little effect." Her remark was detritus from a distracted mind. Her husband was "overpowered with business" but very well. Yesterday at dinner they had entertained—among others—the heads of departments and their wives. An extraordinary session of Congress had been called to vote for or against war. "I . . . will prepare a room and pay sisterly attention to your good husband; he will be here, I hope, in time to give his vote for war."

The "shadow" of James Madison was suffering not a little inner turmoil. Though she supported his judgment in this matter as in others, she was not entirely free of her war-decrying Quaker upbringing. Also, would war damage Payne—the son she was so proud of? "Payne is in Baltimore yet, and as much admired and respected as you could wish. He writes me that Mrs. Patterson and Mrs. Bonaparte are very attentive to him, and he is invited to all their great houses there—except the Smiths. We intend to send him in a few months to Princeton." The end of her letter to Anna is an outpouring of love and faith in this hour of peril. "Kiss the sweet girl and boys for me, and sleep in peace, my dear sister. Heaven will preserve you and yours as you trust in its great Power." She was a woman anchored in the spirit.

She wanted to see her husband vindicated by reelection. It would set a seal on thirty-five years of public service. Not that she disliked her role as First Lady. There were opportunities to help; and the routs (she was quick to confess) she loved all too well. Still, Montpelier also offered opportunities to serve, and the pleasures of nature, and human warmth. But at this time any personal choice went down before other considerations. The nation owed James Madison this final honor. De Witt Clinton, Mayor of New York and promoter of the Erie Canal, wanted so desperately to be President he was willing to split the Republican party. And the Federalists were counting on discontent with the Embargo and war preparations to sweep them back into power.

The Republicans in Congress, caucusing on May 18, nominated James Madison—82 to 0—to succeed himself. The *National Intelligencer* saw this unanimity as proof that "honesty, patriotism and plain dealing will forever triumph over duplicity, interest and intrigue." Elbridge Gerry, the sixty-seven-year-old former Governor of Massachusetts, was nominated for Vice President.

A day later the *Hornet* arrived with nothing. Though France still called her Berlin and Milan Decrees revoked, she refused commercial justice. And Britain's Orders stood. Would the *Wasp* bring better news? There were cynical hoots.

The toboggan was flying faster down the hill.

The *Hornet*'s news was three weeks stale. It knew nothing and could say nothing about the fact that eight days earlier Prime Minister Perceval, staunch champion of the British Orders in Council, had been assassinated. Nor about British merchants railing more and more loudly against the ruinous American Embargo. Nor about English politicians who, realizing at last—at long last—that America really meant what she had been crying: repeal the Orders or fight. If transatlantic cables had existed in 1812, a dying American hope would have taken on new life.

A declaration of war in June seemed all but certain. The toboggan rushed on.

Madison pressed military preparations all he could. The new Quartermaster's office seethed. The War Department's eight clerks and two assistant secretaries did not walk from job to job; they ran. But Secretary of War Eustis's department was understaffed, and the Army painfully short of officers. Should old low-ranking Revolutionary veterans or vigorous young men without battle experience be promoted? It was decided to elevate the old gaffers. Unfortunately some of them were chosen for geographic or political reasons. For instance, Brigadier General William Hull, originally of war-resisting Massachusetts, was promoted largely to mollify that state.

Madison did not underestimate the difficulty of arming a nation disarmed for a generation; he just resolved, come hell or high water, to arm it. Foster had said the Americans were unequipped to fight a war. Well, they'd show Mr. Foster!

Dolley's May and June letters—which could have told us so much— have not survived. "Burn this." "Destroy this." But a chatty one from Lucy spills a few facts. She grieves over Cutts's shipping losses. "I scarcely expect you will have the felicity of embracing [the Madison family] this summer"—a war reference. She hopes Dolley will "bear it like a Christian."

This same letter says John left three weeks ago for the Blue Licks to stay a week. "I feel very uneasy." Lucy begs for a "flaming account" of the social news. She sends "love and good wishes to our dear brother Jemmy." To Dolley, "We love you dearly." A postscript says John has come home from the Licks. "I hope he has been well employed"—not drinking. The Judge wants Dolley to "inform brother James that he has got the apple in this discipline" (marriage), knowing how strenuously Madison would disagree. And Lucy has said not a word about war.

The President and his "shadow" could not so easily forget. Together they lived with the threat of war every day of their lives. Senator Pope said sarcastically, "Mrs. Madison makes a very good President, and must not be turned out."

When, late in May, Foster asked Secretary Monroe for an interview, Madison hoped he was bringing news of repeal. He brought the opposite. Viscount Castlereagh no longer bothered to defend the Orders in Council on the ground that France had not yet *proved* the rescinding of her Decrees; instead, he declared in writing that Britain would keep her edicts until France repealed hers in respect to *all nations*. This was a shocking stepping up of Britain's demands. It killed hope. Dispatch No. 9 of the same date (now produced)—and Monroe orally—offered a few concessions, but such unreasonable ones, Madison was outraged. *Never*, he swore, would the United States bargain away its rights.

He wrote out a War Message.

Though some citizens wanted to fight both Britain and France, Madison said the country was not strong enough for a triangular war. Nor was there any necessity. For eighteen months, he pointed out, the French Decrees had not been invoked against any American vessel, and though France had refused to pay indemnity for burned ships, this offense did not cancel Britain's much grosser ones. The two matters were unconnected. Let the country take arms against Britain and afterward, if necessary, deal with France.

On June 1—sixty days after Madison had recommended a sixty-day embargo—Congress, in secret session, listened to a clerk read the President's War Message.

Countless times on that highway of nations, the sea, it said, the British had violated the American flag, kidnapped American seamen, plundered American property, violated American harbors, and spilled American blood. Britain's real purpose was not to cut off supplies to her foes but to set up a commercial monopoly. She was fighting a friend the better to traffic with her archenemy. Hoping to avoid war, the United States had laid an embargo. *At any time* Britain could have shifted the burden from her own shoulders to France's, but no! She had refused to repeal unjust Orders. The President ticked off recent history: Wellesley's disavowal of the Erskine pact, John Henry's spying, Canada's incitement of Indians, Castlereagh's brutal cutting off of hope by the enlargement of his demands. Anxious for peace, Americans had met injuries with "unexampled forbearance and conciliation." It was useless. A war was being waged against the United States. Meet it with war? The decision was up to Congress.

The debate took place behind massive closed doors.

Two days later the Committee on Foreign Affairs submitted a war manifesto. Citing seven years of British aggression, it urged America's "free-born sons" to strike a second blow for freedom. Their cause was just. Looking to the Lord of Hosts, they must do the only thing left to do: *fight*.

The next day Foster thought the President looked "very pale and extremely agitated."

That night at a levee crowds stood about discussing rumors that the Prince Regent was giving ground. If France would authentically repeal her Berlin and Milan Decrees, ran the report, Britain would rescind her Orders in Council—the old tack. The reaction: why in God's name hadn't he said so sooner? Or was this only another ploy? Did the Prince of Wales mean "repeal as applied to all nations"—that very different matter?

On June 4 the House voted 79 to 49 for war. Now the great question: What would the Senate do?

Would-be buyers examined Foster's horses, and Secretary Eustis asked if the Minister would care to sell his marquee. No, he said stoutly, he was staying right here; he had just purchased an icehouse for next winter. His diary for June 7: "Met Mr. Madison coming from church in a coach and four. . . . He wants to show he is not afraid."

Two days later Mr. Augustus Foster received a terrible shock. He discovered that the secret bill passed by the House was no "shuffling" authorization of letters of marque to postpone action until after the election; it was a declaration of war. Federalists ridiculed the notion. The bill would never pass the Senate, they said; not four senators north of the Potomac would agree. Indeed, Madison was probably *counting on resistance*.

The Senate quashed by a tie vote a bill for the strictly maritime war which Monroe favored. Convinced, now, that war was the lesser of two evils, therefore righteous, Madison was ready to go all out. Patriots, rising to defend their rights, interests, and honor, he held, could perform prodigies.

While the issue was hanging fire, William C. Preston described a visit to the President's House.

Taken there in a hack, the eighteen-year-old found a "very grand" mansion. Crowds, including "gaudy regimentals," came and went, and people stood about drinking a hot spiced wine called negus. The general who had brought him approached the President: "My young kinsman Mr. Preston has come to pay his respects to you and Mrs. Madison." The short man with powdered hair seemed abstracted. Preston noted some marvelous mirrors and saw a "portly elegant lady" enter the room wearing a turban and holding a book. Mrs. Madison put out an informal left hand. "Aren't you William Campbell Preston, son of my old friend and beloved kinswoman Sally Campbell?" Yes, he was. "Sit down, my son, for you *are* my son—I was the first one to see you in this world." She explained their degree of cousinship, and the President cordially shook his hand. "General Wilkinson," called Mrs. Madison, "I must present this young gentleman to our distinguished men. Captain Decatur. . . . Yet, after all"— smiling—"you'd probably just as soon be presented to some young ladies." Turning to three who had entered: "Miss Maria Mayo, Miss Worthington, Miss Sally Coles, this young gentleman, if not my son, is my protégé—I commend him to your cares. As long as he's in the city he'll be my guest." She said it with "an easy grace and benignity which no woman in the world could have exceeded," says the diary. Young Preston was shedding his awkwardness. He calls Dolley a "magnificent woman."

Moving into the mansion, he was "translated into a new and fairy sort of existence." Soon he knew everyone under its roof. His cousin Edward Coles struck him as a "thorough gentleman and one of the best-natured. . . ." The reigning belles, Miss Mayo and Miss Coles, were amused by his greenness and soon "turned him to account." He rode and danced and joined their game of writing "thread paper verses."

The President's labors, Preston thought, showed on his "pale set face." Though he left all social arrangements to his wife, he was too harassed to relax except toward the end of a long dinner with friends and wine. Then he grew facetious and anecdotal, his humor sometimes rather broad "after the manner of the old school."

While his confidant Mr. Richard Cutts recounted the day's "news, gossip and *on dits*," Madison would ask "dry keen" questions. "What does General Marshall"—the Chief Justice—"say?" He seemed to feel some contempt for the diplomatic corps. And when snide criticism was reported he could, if very tired, become testy. "The damned rascal! I wonder how he would conduct the government. It is easy for them to make speeches."

Mrs. Madison, too, was "wearied to exhaustion." One day, seeing her with a book, Preston asked, "You still have time to read?" "Oh, no, not a word," she smiled; she just carried *Don Quixote* to be able to say "something not ungraceful." Bill Preston noted that when in private Madison called his wife "Dolley," she relaxed her "somewhat stately demeanor." His final comment: "She is universally loved and admired."

Her greatest worry was her husband's heavy burdens. "The necessities of society," she said, "made sad inroads" on him. He slept little, going to bed late and often getting up during the night to read or write. A candle was kept burning.

The testing time had come. The Senate was preparing to vote for or against war. On June 17, 1812, there was roll call after secret roll call. The question was crucial, the atmosphere tense. At last the vote stood 19 to 13. The Senate had agreed with the House. *War!*

When Foster came to Dolley's drawing room that evening, he was still in the dark about the great decision. Madison bowed three times, then conversed with the British Minister, quite civilly, about the Red River settlement, the Spanish dilemma, and Napoleon's General Bernadotte. Foster would report the President "ghastly pale." Other guests saw him quite differently. The *New York Post:* "The President was all life and spirits."

Like Foster, the country could only guess at what was going on. In fact its clues were fewer and its ignorance deeper, for during the three years Madison had been asking Britain for redress, calming "hot-spurs," rousing sluggards and shaming cowards in an effort to achieve national unity, he had not—on the theory that their nerves were not strong enough for so desperate a balancing on the edge of a chasm—taken the citizens wholly into his confidence. Never had they been told about his ultimatum to Britain and France just after his 1809 inauguration; never had they heard about his firm statement that each must *choose between sea hooliganism and peace.* As a result the public did not know that from the beginning, and in spite of others' foot dragging, the President had acted with absolute consistency. His policy of non-sharing had been a great mistake; he had worked against himself.

The nation learned about the fateful congressional vote through Madison's Proclamation of War. "War exists. . . ." The President was calling upon the people, as they valued their heritage and loved their country, to exert themselves to obtain a quick, just, honorable peace.

It is one of the colossal ironies of history that on June 17—*the very day the United States chose war*—the Orders in Council were repealed. For on May 11, the day Perceval was assassinated, the clamor against the economic damage wreaked by the Orders in Council had grown so loud, the British Cabinet had been forced to resign. The rest followed. But there was no transatlantic cable; rather, a hiatus of a month or two, a horrendous "communications gap." Fate mocked.

It has been said that Madison's policy of nonintercourse failed. That is untrue. In a sense nonintercourse succeeded brilliantly, for it did—finally—achieve its purpose of getting the Orders revoked. Madison just trapped his third king too late. The chess table turned over, spilling the counters.

Henry Clay would always hold that, time lapse or no time lapse, knowledge of repeal should not have stopped America's declaration of war; that Britain's long brutal impressment of American seamen, a policy *not* repealed, was a more outrageous insult than the Orders in Council and alone justified war. Twenty years later Madison would only partly agree. He would blame the War of 1812 on two things: Castlereagh's hope-destroying message stepping up the hateful Orders, and the communications time lag.

The lag worked both ways. For two months after the United States' declaration of war—or, as many preferred to call it, America's recognition of a state of war—Britain would know nothing whatever about it.

The eagle on the Great Seal of the Declaration brandishing arrows in one claw while offering an olive branch with the other was a perfect image of Madison's three-year posture: preparing for war while striving for peace.

At the bottom of a long hill (to return to a metaphor) the toboggan crashed.

THE WAR OF 1812

FROM THE BEGINNING Madison understood the need for victories. "It is victories we want." But a penurious Congress had balked at providing money for the substantial army and navy which the President had asked for and victories would require.

Prevented from shouldering a gun or going down to the sea in a ship, Madison had the lonelier task of waiting for news of the first military encounter. His days were crowded with map study, planning, paperwork, appointments, and recommendations to Congress. Dolley gave full support. She too found everything else child's play compared to this onerous waiting. They suffered together.

Small diversions helped a little. One was a letter from Sally, Marchioness de Casa Yrujo, en route from Brazil to Spain: "I . . . press you to my heart." If she could visit Washington, she'd talk for three days and make Dolley laugh, "and your good husband too." She hears that Washington's season was quite "dashing"; that Madame Bonaparte's a duchess with £50,000 a year; that Lucy, "a great belle and as lovely . . . as ever," has remarried; and that Dolley herself never looked as well in her life and gives "universal satisfaction"—a difficult matter, "but you have always . . . made everybody your friend." She sends "love (aye love) to Mr. Madison," bidding him remember old days, and adding that Payne, visiting in Philadelphia, has been twice to see her, but unfortunately she was out. The Marquis says he is a "fine young man, grown very tall and very much improved."

Dolley felt pride, for while the war was getting started—an embryo Navy putting to sea, a little raw Army marching north—another struggle seemed to be ending: Dolley's to bring her son to an honorable manhood.

At twenty Payne was a good horseman and a good shot. Would he soon be fighting in Canada? And after college, a diplomatic career?

Canada was the first order of business. A widespread wish to annex it had not influenced the declaration of war. Madison had never thought that Canada—like West Florida, which he regarded as integral to the Louisiana Purchase and the national defense—must at all hazards be acquired, if necessary by seizure. He had always thought that Canada would join the Union voluntarily. "When the pear is ripe, it will fall of itself." But now that a war was on, why not seize it? First, it was stirring up the northwest Indians; second, land invasions could be mounted there; third, and most important, it could serve as a means of bringing the war to a swift conclusion—that is, it could be used for bargaining purposes.

"Mr. Madison's war," the Federalist minority called it, as if Madison had created it personally. Wearing a cockade on his round hat in a kind of defiance, he smiled grimly. Having for eighteen years—ever since he first proposed commercial retaliation—labored to stave off war, he felt no guilt. He just regretted the country's disunity. For the bugle had blown. In general, the southern mid-Atlantic and Western states were enthusiastic about the task ahead; New England, that stronghold of Federalism, was sullen. Whereas in Richmond the Declaration of War had made "every man an inch taller," the *Boston Repertory*—rather typically—was asking the citizens of Massachusetts if they wanted to become "slaves of the slaves of Bonaparte." "You must bow to the yoke or break it in pieces." The remedy for such dissidence was a barrel of tar, said Jefferson, and the North might need to use Governor Wright's still stronger 1776 measure: "hemp and confiscation"—hanging.

The plan to invade Canada before it could strengthen its defenses was striking difficulties. When, last November, the President asked Congress for 20,000 trained troops and two Assistant Secretaries of War to speed the job of feeding, clothing, arming, and transporting them, he had received few troops, no secretaries, and a pittance of money. Congress— Madison called it frivolous—thought to prosecute a war with a major power without raising taxes.

But the Canadian plan matured. The army proposed to burst into Canada at four places: Fort Detroit, which controlled the Indian territory; Montreal, center for British reinforcements; and two points between Niagara and Sackett's Harbor on the Great Lakes. Troops were moving up. General William Hull, considered the smartest of the old generals, would first attack Fort Malden near Detroit. Even though he had heard, in July, that Britain had cemented an alliance with Tecumseh's confederacy by seizing the United States garrison at Michilimackinac, he moved up defiantly and crossed the border with 2,500 untrained Americans. A quick occupation of Canada could halt the war before it got started.

The Madisons thought, ate, and breathed Detroit. James, a poor sleeper, sat up later and later writing dispatches by candlelight, weighing contingencies, and considering requests. Anthony Morris, for instance, ailing after the death of his wife, was soliciting a foreign post to give him a total change of scene. In a letter to Cutts, Madison said New England's "rancorous opposition" was crippling operations and encouraging the enemy. The Governors of Massachusetts and Connecticut were refusing his call for militias to man coastal defenses. This virtual revolt "clogged the wheels of the war." The more reason to act quickly and boldly in Canada. Fortunately, from the Canadian border there came Hull's announcement that, having "raised the standard with some éclat," he was preparing to attack Fort Malden.

While they waited for more news, the Madisons entertained two dozen large, well-proportioned Fox, Sac, and Osage chiefs from the Missouri Territory. At the Washington theater and at the President's house they were a sensation. When some "terrific kings and princes" of the Sioux arrived, Dolley invited them all to dinner. In return, forty warriors gave a feast at Greenleaf Point, followed by a war dance which Richard Rush called "the most magnificent, imposing, native human pageantry" on record. In every face he had seen the "loftiest self-consciousness."

One night Dolley saw something else. She had retired and was sitting at her dressing table when an Indian chief stepped into her mirror. She did not panic. After waiting a few minutes she rang a bell for a servant and gently persuaded the intruder to depart.

"President of the Eighteen Fires," Madison asked the Indians to stop their infighting and resist British beguilements. "My Red Children, you have come a long path to see your father . . . a straight clean path kept open." White and red people were made from the same clay and should be friends. Canada had not joined the other Fires—beware of traps. It would be better to graze herds, plow, and spin. The Great Spirit was the father of them all.

The chief of the Big Osage answered, "My great father, I feel new-born." The chief of the Little Osage said all was pleasing to them except being killed; they really didn't like being killed. The Buffalo That Walks, a Sioux, said, "My father, I am a small man, but I am regarded as a man." He praised the Biggest Chief of All. But the Quash-quam-ma of the Sac was blunt: "You have war. It is very well, defend yourselves—we will do the same." Then the Indians grew tired of "rolling about on the floor" and went home.

Meanwhile the text of the June 23 repeal of the British Orders in Council had reached Washington. So commercial losses—as Madison had planned and prophesied—had indeed forced a reversal of policy. But too late.

(Madison's undercover agent, George Joy, had corrected London misconceptions by stressing the President's admiration for British jurisprudence and the fact that the France Madison admired no longer existed.)

Too late, too late. Impossible to suspend hostilities without knowing how Great Britain had taken America's declaration of war. And General Hull might already be occupying Upper Canada.

Even so, the President acted quickly for peace. He authorized Chargé d'Affaires Russell to arrange a face-saving truce without any explicit promise about impressment, only suspension of that nefarious practice. (It could be taken care of by treaty.) He was not too sanguine. He wrote Cutts that in view of the Federalists' conduct and the British Cabinet's known character, the United States should be ready for an angry, malignant British prosecution of the war.

At this point the City of Washington heard rumors of a Detroit defeat. The reaction was disbelief. There must be a mistake.

On August 28 the Madisons, still in bitter suspense, set off for a short visit to Montpelier. "I find myself much worn down," Madison had written General Dearborn. Mountainous work, Monroe's absence, and flooding rivers had delayed the trip. It was good to get started.

At evening, 25 miles out, at Dumfries Tavern, the rider of a lathered horse handed the President a message from Secretary of War Eustis. General Hull had surrendered an army of 2,500 without firing a shot.

The Madisons spent a night of agony. The next day they hastened back to Washington. The President summoned his Cabinet to an extraordinary session. Try to retake Detroit? Build war vessels on the Great Lakes? The answer to both questions was a fierce *Yes*. What folly to have believed General Hull's boast that he would seize control of Lakes Erie and Ontario and the tongue of land called Upper Canada (Ontario). He had surrendered 2,500 troops to a force only half that size.

Madison forbade any public condemnation until he had all the facts. "Do you not tremble with resentment at the treacherous act?" Dolley wrote Ned Coles, then pulled up sharp. "Yet we must not judge the man until we are in possession of his reasons." Comptroller Richard Rush was not so inhibited. He said the nation had been deceived by a "gasconading booby."

Reports on Hull, written before the fiasco, scorched mail pouches. The General had cringed at the sight of a few Indians. He was so incompetent his officers had considered mutiny. The President received this postsurrender report from Ohio:

> Everybody pronounced him a traitor and a coward, and if he was to attempt to pass this way he would be hunted and shot like a mad dog. . . . The poor fellows . . . out with him . . . all say that if Hull had not betrayed them they could have bested the British and the Indians united.

Further facts came in slowly. Hull had suffered no food or ammunition shortage. When General Brock demanded surrender, saying he could not restrain his Indian allies from a war of extermination, the terrified Hull had sat on the ground in an old tent with tobacco spittle dribbling out of his mouth and onto his beard, neckcloth, and vest. And when Britishers marched so close to his 24-pounder that it could have riddled them, he had run up a white flag. Many Americans were so disgusted and ashamed, they wept. Madison's cousin James Taylor of Kentucky called Hull "weak, cowardly and imbecile." (British General Brock's victory report to General Prevost: "Twenty-five hundred troops have this day surrendered without the sacrifice of a drop of British blood. I had not more than 700 troops, including militia, and about 600 Indians. . . . When I detail my good fortune Your Excellency will be astonished.")

The nation would have rued any defeat at all, but one so ignoble! Like the Madisons, it was shocked, mortified, furious. The war had been undertaken to redress a humiliation. How terrible to have to swallow more of the same.

But the pendulum swung. Washington heard that on August 19 the frigate *Constitution* ("Old Ironsides"), commanded by Captain Isaac Hull (the disgraced Hull's nephew), had captured, burned, and sunk the British frigate *Guerrière*. This first sea encounter lifted the nation's spirits. The United States, having a navy of only sixteen vessels, had won a resounding victory over Great Britain with its thousand warships. A wave of patriotism swept the country. Americans went around congratulating each other. What they had done on the sea they would do on land—just give them a chance!

Then Commodore John Rodgers's *President* led into port a scurvy-ridden squadron. For weeks he had been protecting American merchantmen by forcing British warships to travel in herds like whales. He brought back seven captured British prizes. In spite of New England's recalcitrance, a common danger and now these victories were drawing the states closer together.

But Madison felt the blade of criticism. The charge that he had shown a lack of confidence in his countrymen cut deep. Yes, in offering England and France, impartially, alliance or war, he had withheld that information, because he was unsure that they had the intestinal fortitude to press home so stern a choice. On the other hand, the Constitution of the United States—of which he was the chief architect—was a monument to his confidence in the people. So much therein was entrusted to and depended upon not only the will but also the common sense and competence of a majority composed, like the minority, of citizens equal before the law, though not—God knew—equal in abilities. He hoped his critics would remember that, and he told himself and the Cabinet that however small the Army and Navy and however raw the militias, the American people were not a race of William Hulls. When they learned to summon all their latent strength, they would win. A Fourth of July speaker at Ringgold's Rope Walk had toasted the Navy: "An infant Hercules destined . . . to extirpate . . . pirates and freebooters." Madison considered the whole country a young Hercules.

As the presidential election approached, he experienced a natural human desire for the electorate's seal of approval. But that was hardly his main motive for running; he was not in the habit of putting his own interests first. He needed more time to work out policies which he considered vital and to see the war through. Not that reelection would be worth any deviation from principle. He would run on his record.

Ned Coles, suffering from a nonmalignant tumor, was on leave. Though inexperienced as secretaries, Dolley and Payne were trying to set up appointments, placate callers, and answer letters.

Graduating from St. Mary's, Payne Todd had enjoyed the springs that summer of the declaration of war: a young swain probably wearing one of the new green jackets called "lizards," its pointed tails hanging down to calves encased in skin-tight trousers tucked into yellow boots; a young blood with impressively fine manners, quite at ease in society, his eyes as blue and hair as dark as his mother's. He was generally liked.

During the next six months Payne was regarded as Madison's stand-in secretary. Princeton had been postponed, but the hiatus was no hardship. Though smaller, Washington was as socially gay as Baltimore, and to the stepson of the President of the United States every door was open. During off-hours, he rode horseback, bet on the races, danced, and had tête-à-têtes with an assortment of pretty girls. Meanwhile he was seeing at close quarters a President in toils.

Though gratified by the seizure of two British brigs on Lake Erie, Madison worried about lagging enlistments, the hazards of a ship-building race, France's continued refusal to deal a total justice (while Napoleon was amassing an army to invade Russia), the possibility that Britain would seize East Florida, a bungled storming of Queenston Heights, the refusal of the New York militia to fight outside its state, the danger of accepting a British armistice proposal without at least a suspension of impressments (it was refused), and—as elections neared—the increasing malice of Federalists. It had reached a pitch.

Whatever her feelings, Dolley remained calm; in a grey stuff gown with fichu, she ran her household efficiently, and then, dressed up in satins that ransacked the rainbow, presided without guile or peer at state dinners and levees. The Mansion kept up its gaiety or a good imitation thereof. Prominent among its teeming guests were Lucy and Judge Todd (Anna lingered in Maine) and Dolley's gypsy-dark cousin Sally Coles, aged twenty-three. Sally and other bright-mannered young ladies formed a coterie around Dolley.

Mrs. William Seaton has written up a typical Presidential dinner that fall of 1812. She and her husband (coeditor with Joseph Gales of the *Intelligencer*) walked to the end of the great East Room to "pay obeisance to Mrs. Madison, curtsey to his Highness, and take a seat." Guests were amusing themselves much as at any party. The cluster round the Madisons included "Payne Todd their son" and Washington Irving. "Mrs. Madison very handsomely came to me and led me nearest the fire, introduced Mrs. Magruder, and sat down between us, politely conversing on familiar subjects, and by her own ease of manner making her guests feel at home."

At dinner Dolley headed the table. Madison seemed somewhat preoccupied. Their guests enjoyed "French dishes and exquisite . . . sherry and rare old Burgundy and Madeira." After the cloth had been removed, the conversation turned on the quality of wines, a subject on which Madison was an expert. Dessert consisted of ice creams, macaroons, preserves, cakes, almonds, pecans, raisins, apples, and pears. At candlelight, signal for the gentlemen's "social glass," the ladies withdrew to the drawing room, and Mrs. Madison persuaded Mrs. Seaton to play a waltz on an "elegant" grand piano while she herself instructed two young ladies in a dance figure. Later the ladies rejoined the gentlemen in the tearoom, where Mrs. Madison talked interestingly of "books, men and manners, literature in general, and many special branches of knowledge." The President was still rather silent. Mrs. Seaton says she "never spent a more rational or pleasing half hour." And so to her carriage. A postscript:

> I would describe the dignified appearance of Mrs. Madison, but I could not do her justice. 'Tis not her form, 'tis not her face, it is the woman altogether. . . . She wears a crimson cap that almost hides her forehead, but which becomes her extremely, and reminds one of a crown from its brilliant appearance, contrasted with . . . white satin folds and her jet black curls. . . .

During this period Dolley was happy about Payne's presence. For years his vacations had been too short; it was as if she were having a long drink. Payne's height, knowledge, taste in art, and urbanity were sources of pride. If he had a few faults, who was perfect? She was quite philosophical about such lapses as his habitual lateness to appointments. Now that a school schedule no longer scaffolded his days, she thought he needed time to learn to organize himself. Fortunately youth was a handicap which could be outgrown. His polished manners and flawless French suggested that after Princeton, he might become a diplomat helping to mold world events. And the days passed.

The November 3 election was hard-fought. Federalists, Quids, and Clintonian democrats called Madison such complimentary things as Napoleon's agent, Jefferson's puppet, "base wretch," "imbecile," "starver of women and children." His Olympian detachment infuriated them further; a candidate who refused to open his mouth was sinister. He cautioned his friends against retaliating. "The current election," he had written Jefferson, "brings the popularity of the war or of the administration, or both, to the *experimentum crucis.*" The Rev. David Jones was still so indignant against Hull for throwing away an army, he taxed the President with lack of energy. "My dear sir, if you must die politically," he wrote, "die gloriously." And Rush persuaded Charles Ingersoll to send the President a letter pointing out that even friends were prophesying disaster if he kept Secretary of War William Eustis—though Ingersoll wasn't to employ the words "damnation," "infernal," "scabby," or "rotten," or call Eustis a "beast," or the President "Jemmy." Madison refused to make Eustis a scapegoat. Election or no election, he preferred to be his own man.

Meanwhile John Adams was fuming at his Federalists for opposing a "just and necessary" war. The object of all their "spiritual and temporal bluster," he blurted, was to replace the President with some weakling, when of course no substitute could depart essentially or materially from Madison's course. "I own I prefer Madison."

This defense irked the Federalists. *Every* policy of "His Little Majesty," some screamed, should be reversed, especially his corrupt war policy.

As election day drew near, both sides were prophesying victory. Though Madison might have gained a last-minute advantage by publishing the diplomatic papers which proved how long and hard he had striven for peace, he abstained.

Returns came in slowly; it would be January before the final count. But he had been reelected President of the United States by 128 to 89. As reported to Paris, "the honorable and lofty conduct of Mr. Madison rallied to him the minds which his first military reverses had swept away." The only thing about the election which troubled the Madisons was that Richard Cutts—who had lost a fortune in ships to the British—had failed to be reelected. How could the man support a family?

Madison's first wartime Message summarized the national situation. A tribunal would probe Hull's surrender. The Navy, which had performed so gallantly, had two new warships. Relations with France still hung in the balance. Military pay must be higher to compete with civilians'. He recommended stiffer penalties for trafficking with the enemy. Americans, no vassals, would defend their rights. The war was not for vainglory but principle. To shrink from it would be a "degradation blasting our . . . proudest hopes." Afterward, drinking John Jacob Astor's gift of some Canton tea, the Madisons felt comforted.

In December a packet brought word of Napoleon's demand that Barlow meet him in Poland to discuss a treaty. It seemed that Barlow had left at once for Vilna. But Napoleon's Russian campaign was turning into a rout; only a remnant of his Grande Armée was struggling out of the country through incredibly deep snows.

The Madisons were learning to withstand shocks. Again they rallied and closed ranks.

Worn out by the carpings of Congress, Secretary of War Eustis resigned. "Lord!" cried Nancy Spear, looking at the able but alcoholic Secretary of the Navy, "how it will startle poor Mr. Hamilton; it seems like saying 'be ye also ready.'"

Meanwhile the seesaw which had begun with Hull's great defeat and the *Constitution*'s great victory kept rocking back and forth, back and forth.

The Army had not covered itself with glory as expected. After hurling defiance at Canada and exhorting his troops to be strong and brave, General Smyth had turned tail. And General Dearborn's militia, having marched to Plattsburg, where it declined to go further, was ignominiously marched back. The Army's six-month record stood at one victory, five defeats, four doddering old generals cashiered (and high time).

The Navy had done better. Britain's taunt about a few fir-built frigates manned by bastards and outlaws had turned into a proud boast. In twenty-three months the 18-gun sloop *Wasp* had mastered the 22-gun British brig *Frolic* convoying six armed merchantmen. The victory was undimmed by the eventual capture of both disabled vessels by the 74-gun *Poictiers*.

Secretary Hamilton said one 74 was worth three 44-gun frigates—build 74s! But Congress tightened its purse strings.

To soften up the legislators, Captain Charles Steward gave a party at his own expense on the rebuilt *Constellation*. When Madison brought his lady aboard, guns thundered a salute. And there—in spite of the President's efforts to cure him of alcoholism—lay Secretary of the Navy Hamilton, dead drunk. The party was such a hilarious success, the House committee authorized four frigates, four 16s and—praise be—four 74s. But there the matter stuck.

The city was about to repay its social debt with a naval ball when the *Intelligencer* put out a four o'clock edition—"Extra! Extra! Read all about the frigate *United States* and Captain Stephen Decatur!" Near the Canaries, the *United States* had captured Britain's largest frigate, the *Macedonian*. When that night Mrs. Madison left for Tomlinson's Hotel with Ned and some girls—the President had to work—they found themselves driving through lanes of brilliantly lit houses and boisterous, celebrating crowds.

Decatur's dispatches reached the President's House late at night. He sped them on to Tomlinson's. In a ballroom decorated with the captured standards of the *Alert* and *Guerrière,* four captains holding the corners of a captured *Macedonian* flag paraded around the dance floor while the band played "Yankee Doodle" and the crowd went wild. Mrs. Seaton would deny the gossip that Dolley rouged on the ground that as Lieutenant Hamilton laid the flag at Dolley's feet, the First Lady's color had *come and gone*.

After the affair there were the usual distortions. One rumor had it that Washington ladies had stamped on the Union Jack with their slippers and cut out blood spots to wear in breastpins.

Exultant over Decatur's victory, Congress ordered the Navy increased by four ships of the line and six frigates. But not everyone was pleased. Jefferson shook his head over this financial "sacrifice." Madison was elated; ever since 1783 he had pulled and hauled and argued for a bigger Navy.

But Secretary Hamilton, widely praised for his zeal and integrity, now fell so deep into his cups, afternoon work became impossible, and Madison had to ask for his resignation. Now two Cabinet posts stood vacant, War and Navy: in wartime an impossible situation.

Guests at the President's New Year reception were agog over Decatur's victory. But they were not so absorbed in the subject that they failed to admire Mrs. Madison's robe of pink satin trimmed with ermine and gold chains, and worn with a turban topped by nodding ostrich plumes.

The seesaw kept sawing. Again and again that winter the plank's American end rose only to plunge. Monroe, Dearborn, and Crawford refused the War office. Secretary of the Treasury Gallatin accused them of being frightened of responsibility, and when Madison wondered whether to offer the spurned position to New York's Governor Tompkins or to former Minister to France John Armstrong, Gallatin backed Armstrong. The man was indolent and capable of intrigue, Gallatin said, but as General and Minister, he had shown enormous ability. Yes, he was the better qualified. Not without misgivings Madison appointed John Armstrong Secretary of War.

And suddenly the Administration heard that Ohio troops heading for Detroit had met defeat at Frenchtown on the Raisin River, the wounded scalped by Britain's Indian auxiliaries. It gave America a new battle cry: "Remember the Raisin!" Horrified by the debacle, Congress voted money for a larger Army, and Madison appointed younger, more vigorous officers.

While this was going on, Commodore Isaac Chauncey—in snow, sleet, and rain—was building a freshwater Navy on the strategic Great Lakes. American men-of-war crouched in blockaded harbors waiting for spring and their great chance. The new Secretary of the Navy, William Jones, worked tirelessly.

One day the Madisons heard that Minister Barlow had, on his 1,200-league command journey to meet Napoleon, died at Cracow of inflammation of the lungs. It was a cold day; it was a very bleak day. Joel Barlow: poet, diplomat, friend—personally as well as governmentally it was a blow.

But on February 29 there came a happier event. Payne reached his majority and inherited the money and property his mother had set aside and saved for him. Dolley marveled that her little boy had become a man.

Because Madison's second inauguration was taking place in wartime, he sent out no invitations. It was all very simple. He just put his hand on the Bible again and swore to uphold the Constitution. Later the Federalists would insist he was unnerved by Chief Justice Marshall's scornful gaze. One paper said the staring down had happened during the delivery of the inaugural address; another, during the administering of the oath of office.

Happily ignorant of the canard, President Madison rode home from the Capitol, trailed by a festive mob, "every creature that could afford twenty-five cents for hack-hire." At the Presidential Mansion the people "offered their congratulations, ate his ice creams and bonbons, drank his Madeira, made their bow and retired, leaving him fatigued beyond measure with the incessant bowing to which his politeness urged him, and in which he never allows himself to be eclipsed." At the inaugural ball he kept his good humor. How gratifying that the public had given him a vote of confidence.

Gallatin warned that the government had barely enough money to last until the end of this month of March. The crisis could be met only if the $16 million loan were successfully floated. Only a third had been subscribed. Bankers would have to come to the rescue.

To heighten the tension, March brought tales of a British plot to kidnap the President and his Cabinet. Mrs. Seaton wrote in trepidation, "You will see by the *Federal Republican* that the plan might be carried into execution ... with fifty or a hundred men, rendering this nation a laughingstock...."

The *Intelligencer* announced that Alexander I of Russia had offered to mediate between the United States and Britain. Madison liked the idea. "It is to be presumed that our government ... will not hesitate to accede to a measure which, having peace solely and simply for its object, may be beneficial, and cannot be injurious." Actually the offer had been broached informally six weeks ago, and Madison had had time to warm to the idea. He was helped in this by Napoleon's defeat at Waterloo. It had released thousands of British troops for service in America. Also, Russia was the only power in Europe which could command the respect of both France and England. The President decided to appoint a special commission to join Minister John Quincy Adams in St. Petersburg.

His first choice, if the Treasury could spare him, was Albert Gallatin. To make the commission bipartisan, some Federalist should go as well.

But who? He settled on Senator James A. Bayard, the only prominent Federalist who had dared avow on the floor of the Senate that there was "cause enough for war."

Meanwhile there were fresh naval victories. Small armed American ships were eluding the British blockade, privateers ranging widely. Near Brazil the *Constitution* had ruined the *Java*. In fifteen minutes the sloop *Hornet* had sunk the brig *Peacock*. Rumor had it that Britain was throwing into the fight nineteen ships of the line, fifteen frigates, and twenty brigs and that Admiral Cockburn was enlarging his fleet in the Chesapeake. But America's will to win was mounting like spring sap. Secretary Jones went right on building his not-yet-authorized 74-gun man-of-war. Oh, for ice to melt on Erie and Ontario! Mastery of the Lakes might bring about the conquest of Canada botched by General Hull. By April, Lake Ontario ought to be open. Get moving! Work!

About now some Federalists forged letters purportedly written by Barlow to transmit from Cadore an offer to make Madison President for life with a salary of a million francs if he would declare war on Great Britain. An article in the *Federal Republican*—"TREMBLE THOU WRETCH"—announced that America had been "basely betrayed into the hands of France." But the plotters had overlooked one little fact. Before the earliest-dated letter, Cadore had been replaced by Bassano as France's Foreign Minister. Monstrous, charged the *Intelligencer*. Madison thought it all too ridiculous. What young men should he send with the Peace Commission as attachés?

Someone suggested that Payne Todd's French would be highly useful in a country where French was the Court language. Payne did not relish the idea of his going abroad. Dolley did; she thought the trip was a great cultural opportunity—perhaps the opening wedge for a diplomatic career. If it meant a further postponement of Princeton, well, all right; travel was a form of education.

Undoubtedly there were three-sided family discussions. The Commission would be gone about six months. Though Payne would be sorely missed, Dolley wanted the best for him. Young Christopher Hughes and George Dallas had accepted assignments, and Gallatin was taking his son James. Why not Payne?

So it was decided. Hughes would go as Bayard's secretary, Dallas and Todd as Gallatin's. Commissioned as unpaid third lieutenants of cavalry, they would get uniforms almost as splendid as Gallatin's own specially designed, yellow-buttoned, grandly embroidered blue jacket worn with a fancy buff waistcoat. Minister Daschkov was writing Chancellor Count

Romanzov to suggest that the Czar make the goodwill gesture of decorating the three attachés.

While the Commission was preparing and the 1813 compaign getting under way, there came spectacular news. A brigade transported across Lake Ontario by Chauncey's flotilla had seized the village of York (later Toronto), capital of Upper Canada, together with several vessels and 700 prisoners. Unfortunately an explosion had killed a number of Americans. If the fuse had been longer, "the whole column would have been in the air." On the fourth day of occupation a fire of unknown but not American origin had consumed Canada's small frame Parliament building. Later tremendous storms broke. Chauncey had taken Fort George, a splendid beginning for the hoped-for land comeback.

During this period, supply departments were being reorganized. Madison relieved Anna's and Dolley's anxiety and risked a charge of nepotism by appointing war-impoverished Richard Cutts as Superintendent General of Military Supplies. He offered no apology; Cutts would make a fine public servant.

Never had there been so many questions, guesses, rumors, and accusations. The country was awash with them. Fresh war tidings arrived by mailcoach, horseback, grapevine, and imagination.

A little diversion was good, and Dolley was glad to receive a sonnet by Mrs. William Lee. It was a new move in their old game of exchanging verses. Mrs. Lee's husband added an expression of joy over Madison's reelection—the "triumph of principle over faction. His Administration will tend more to the formation of a national character, etc., and to the consolidation of our independence than any that has preceded it." He closed with a flourish: "That you may long live the queen of the people's hearts. . . ."

And it was time for the queen to say good-bye to the crown prince.

Minister Daschkov having obtained a safe-conduct for the Commissioners, the *Neptune* was to sail on May 9 from New Castle on the Delaware. In Philadelphia on business, Gallatin already had in hand Madison's instructions on impressment. (Since Congress forbade Britons to sail American waters, the directory pointed out, the two countries should prohibit the naturalization of each other's seamen and surrender deserters. Madison also demanded a guarantee against further impressments.) But Gallatin needed other documents, and Attaché Todd—a 6-footer rather grand in his new uniform—had been picked to carry them to Philadelphia.

His stepfather slipped a secret note into the packet: "I enclose a draft for $800 to be a fund in your hands for J. P. Todd. He has . . . $200 more, which our estimate called for." If more were needed, Madison told Gallatin, draw on him. It was an amazing grant of latitude. The President was not only sending five times the estimate of Payne's expenses (in those days $1,000 was a prodigious sum); he was also laying himself wide open to levies.

Dolley begged Payne to take care of himself and write often. Madison added warm wishes for a young man still reluctant to attempt the vast steppes of the sea and Russia. The last embraces could not have been easy. Dolley would have preferred to wave him off at New Castle, but she could not leave James's side while the British were burning and pillaging along Chesapeake Bay and the Susquehanna River—Frenchtown, Georgetown, Havre de Grace—and drawing ever closer. Also Anna was ill, and her four boys and baby Dolley had come down with the measles. Aunt Dolley ran back and forth between the mansion and F Street, trying indefatigably to help. It tied her down. Thank God Gallatin, now and during the whole trip, would keep a fatherly eye on Payne. On May 9, 1813, when the *Neptune* lifted anchor, she turned her face toward New Castle and the Atlantic. God leash all storms!

Four days later, writing Ned Coles, she mentioned Payne's reluctance to leave America. But he had written from shipboard to express "satisfaction with all around him." Changing the subject, she hoped Ned would stay with the President "to the end." Not for the world would she retard his prosperity, but no one felt more "affectionate interest" than Mr. Madison and herself, more "regard and esteem." Until Ned's recovery, the President would do without a secretary. "The fears and alarms that circulate around me!—For the last week all the city and George Town (except the Cabinet) have expected a visit from the enemy and were not lacking in expressions of terror and reproach." A British frigate lay at the mouth of the Potomac. The city was repairing the fort and stationing 500 militiamen and perhaps as many regulars on the green. "The twenty tents already look well in my eyes, as I have always been an advocate of fighting when assailed, though a Quaker. I therefore keep the old Tunisian sabre within reach." She was half joking, half serious, and thoroughly angry. A General's discovery of a British plot was now confirmed.

> It is to land as many chosen *rogues* as they can about 14 miles below Alexandria, in the night, who may arrive before day and set fire to the offices and President's House, when, if opposed,

> they are to surrender themselves as prisoners. I do not tremble at
> this, but feel *affronted* that the Admiral should send notice that
> he would make his bow at my drawingroom *soon.*

Dolley's letter then jumped away from the Capital's peril. Congressmen
were crowding in for the special session. The Cuttses had rented the less
expensive Pollock house. She was shut up with sick children.

As she wrote, American troops were watching Lake Erie's ice thaw
and crack, and Captain Oliver H. Perry was waiting to venture forth from
Presqu' Isle with a little flotilla made of sturdy green wood. The cordage,
sails, machinery, and supplies had been hauled across the Alleghenies to
Pittsburgh and poled up the French River. The Madisons had followed
every move. "It's victories we want."

They were hard to come by. Back and forth swung the pendulum.
The frigate *Chesapeake* ("Don't give up the ship!" cried dying Captain
Lawrence) was captured by the British *Shannon*; followed by the loss of
two sloops on the Great Lakes. But these setbacks were somewhat balanced out by the U.S.S. *Enterprise*'s brilliant victory over the brig *Boxer* of
equal fighting power.

The President had been holding up well as the Canadian campaign
matured. Secretary of War Armstrong refused to believe that Washington
City was in danger. And whenever Decatur tried to sneak his frigate
through the New London blockade, traitors warned the British by waving
blue lights. Similarly, on the Potomac, boats flying white flags sold meat
and vegetables to the enemy. Madison's eyes glinted with disgust. "The
President looks better than I have ever seen him," wrote Congressman
Jonathan Roberts. In spite of terrible pressures, he looked "cheerful and
affable."

His special message summed up the state of the Union after a year of
war: the capture of York, the sailing of the Peace Commission, the death
of Barlow, and a need for heavier taxes.

Discussion of money inspired the *New York Post* to ask rhetorically,
Where is Secretary of the Treasury Gallatin? Its answer: "Fled from his
station like a coward." During a Senate debate on the Adams, Gallatin,
and Bayard nominations another sour question was asked: How could
Gallatin serve at one and the same time as both Treasury Chief and Peace
Commissioner? Didn't it violate the Constitution? When Madison pointed
out that Navy Secretary Jones was discharging Gallatin's duties under the
authority of a 1792 statute, its pertinency was challenged.

The First Lady was doing her best as substitute secretary. A letter to Ned is pure Dolley. Sorrowing over his tumor, she remarks that a "cheerful spirit" aids recovery. Excitedly she reports a letter from Payne mailed from the first port of call. "He is charmed with his voyage so far, and has escaped sea-sickness. All the party, with the exception of Mr. Bayard and himself, were sufferers." The city is so crowded her head reels. "Adieu! here they come *by dozens.*"

She was frightened when Madison sank down with bilious fever, and she nursed him day and night until she all but dropped with fatigue. Problems everywhere: Anna ailing, Payne lost in the distance, America at war, her husband white as the pillow.

A hostile Senate committee kept clamoring to see him. After several postponed appointments, Dolley dispatched a polite note. "James Madison is sorry that a continuance of his indisposition will not permit him to see the committee of the Senate today"; nor could he at present fix a time. Three days later Sérurier wrote the Duke of Bassano, "The thought of his possible loss strikes everybody with consternation. . . . His death would be a veritable national calamity. . . . All good Americans pray for the recovery of Mr. Madison." But some politicians had no mercy. "Sir," cried Grosvenor of New York, "the President is old and . . . must soon appear at the bar of Immortal Justice." When Daniel Webster called to deliver some carping congressional resolutions, the President was too sick to read them. After six days of touch and go, friends got around to reporting his illness to Congress. Praising his leadership, they hoped fervently for his recovery.

As if a little appreciation had worked curatively, the *Intelligencer* was soon calling Madison convalescent. After three weeks of round-the-clock nursing Dolley wrote Ned that her husband's fever had gone down. He was taking bark—quinine—every hour. "Sometimes I despair! but now that I see he will get well, I feel as if I should die myself from fatigue." But Dolley got a long drench of sleep, and her patient was sipping hot soup.

Vice President Elbridge Gerry, calling with his son, found the President lying on a pillow-heaped couch in a flannel dressing gown. Though pale, he sounded almost like his old self. Monroe and the Cuttses dropped by, and Dolley prepared refreshments for all seven. Young Gerry would record his impressions: "Mrs. Madison is very handsome, of an elegant form and dignified deportment, has a fine complexion high and delicately colored . . . of elegant manners, accomplished and easy." He felt honored when this lady "not rivaled in excellence" claimed him as a second cousin. She always handed food to her husband first. She was "dressed in a yellow silk gown. . . . rather loose and plain," and wore a very plain bonnet or hat made of silk. Her cravat was spangled and she wore cloth shoes.

After Anna Cutts had shown him over the mansion, he would write a description historically invaluable:

Coming down to the north door, they entered a baronial hall with great pillars and lamps. Doors opened into a row of rooms. The dining room at the far right—"twice the height of modern parlors and three times as large"—held massive furniture. Mrs. Cutts said the sideboard would "cover the whole side of a large parlour." At one end hung Stuart's full-length portrait of General Washington. To the left they walked into a chamber furnished with more delicate pieces as well as Stuart's portrait of Mrs. Madison: her private sitting room. Next came the "magnificent" oval drawing room, its tall windows framed by "superb red silk velvet curtains." Four dollars a yard, whispered Anna. Painted chairs in four groups stood around sofas with "worked bottoms" and cushions of red velvet. The "terrace" (south lawn) had a superb view of the rivers. On levee nights all doors were thrown wide open. Beyond the oval room they peeped into the President's sitting room, then stepped into the huge East Room that balanced the dining room at the other end. Young Gerry was dazzled by the tour. A "perfect palace."

Back in the Madisons' private quarters, he studied the convalescent. "He bears the marks of age and a very strong mind." Age is relative of course; the President was sixty-two.

That week Madison's mind fetched up hard against a constitutional issue. Asked to confer with a Senate committee about his nomination for Minister to Sweden, he made his first business act a dictated reply. Dolley took down the first page, brother-in-law Jackson the second. No, he could not confer. For appointments and treaties, the Constitution made the President and *Senate as a whole* independent and coordinate. As Chief Executive he would be glad to receive the committee and give it any pertinent information. That was all.

His letter caused a ruckus. Affronted senators called the Senate the greatest power under the Constitution, citing George Washington's practice. The reference boomeranged. Washington had declared that the time, place, and manner of consultation with the *entire* Senate was strictly up to the President: "The agency of the Senate," as a body, "is purely executive, and they may be summoned to the President." Madison himself had helped Washington draft this clarification.

In the middle of July he acted out the principle for which he felt duty-bound to fight. Still declining to confer, he received the committee courteously. The chairman handed him a resolution declaring Gallatin's nomination as envoy incompatible with his office as Secretary of the Treasury. Madison said he regretted that the Senate's view deprived him of its aid and advice. In silence the committee shuffled, waited, and bowed out. (It has been charged that Madison so loved harmony, he would not stand up against strong opposition. This was one of the many times he did.) The Senate revenged itself by rejecting Gallatin's nomination. How ironical that if Madison had not weakened his party and himself in the Senate by sending his strongest Senate supporter, President pro tem William Crawford, to replace Barlow, or if he had just declared the Treasury post vacant, Gallatin's appointment might have been confirmed. Nevertheless he did well. By repelling an encroachment on the executive power he saved a principle and kept a balance.

During his illness the city's military predicament had worsened. More British warships had anchored in the Potomac. One day (it was symbolic) the Army's Armstrong and the Navy's Jones—busily running against each other for the 1816 presidential nomination—rode off on scouting trips in different directions. In the overgrown President's Square across from the mansion, militiamen were making a racket with drill guns and alarm bells. At night, guards patrolled the city, but not too seriously. One "drank port wine and ate cake until daybreak."

Very seldom, now, did the Madisons enjoy any brightness. But Sally Coles's letter of July 19 pleased them by conveying the relief of those who "know and love the President" on learning of his improvement: "blessed moment." The Chesapeake Bay invasion has transformed all the young men of central Virginia into heroes, she says. In two days Green Mountain alone raised fifty or sixty volunteers—"Brother John had the honor to kill one horse in the service." Richmond's old men and small boys are forming into companies. The British won't find it easy to conquer Virginia; even the ladies are Spartan. "Goodnight, my more than friend."

Artillerymen, celebrating the foe's inability to attack from the tortuous Potomac, hauled six cannons to the Great House to fire a salute to the President.

But there was always that other side. Dolley wrote Hannah Gallatin that the vexations heaped on her husband by party spirit were holding back his full recovery. She watched over him as over a child. The worst aggravation had been the Senate's rejection of Mr. Gallatin as Commissioner.

Would he prefer to be Secretary of the Treasury or Chairman of the Peace Commission? The question seemed answered when Madison heard that Gallatin, before sailing, had prophesied the Senate's rejection of him as Commissioner and foreseen the loss of his Cabinet post.

So France and Russia had signed an armistice! Would Britain, in pique, refuse Russia's mediation? If so, Gallatin would have plenty of time to decide his fate. In August Madison wrote to tell him how the Senate had "mutilated the mission."

And Rush told John Adams: "Mr. Madison rides out and attends to business again. His long illness has pulled him down a good deal, but I hope he is permanently recovered from his attack."

His growing health shattered Federalist plans. The "little booby in the palace," "as much a despot as the Bey of Algiers," had still to be reckoned with.

Let "all . . . piously disposed," ran Madison's proclamation, "give thanks and offer supplications to the Great Parent and Sovereign of the Universe." Nothing but free-will offerings were acceptable to the God "whom no hypocrisy can deceive and no forced sacrifices propitiate." Madison believed that willing sacrifices and a sense of responsibility were the counterparts of freedom, and tried to live his life accordingly.

As the poplars along Pennsylvania Avenue gathered summer dust, mosquitoes increased. During the "dog days" Madison, though not Dolley, had a touch of influenza. They were buoyed up by the probability that Perry had crossed the sandbar. Was he even now searching Lake Erie's inlets for the British squadron's hideout? And had the Peace Commission reached St. Petersburg?

Dolley seized on every reference to Russia which she could find: St. Petersburg's European veneer; the Czar's glittering court in his vast Winter Palace; the poor wretched peasants. For months there had come no word from the Commission. Jolting to Montpelier with Anna and her children, the Madisons in a sense crossed Russia.

For security reasons their trip went unannounced. That fact caused speculation. "I expect the President has gone to Montpelier," wrote a member of the disbanded Congress. "Poor gentleman, his health needed it. I never saw a man I commiserated more, not because I think him unequal to his station, but because it is a spectacle of no uncommon interest to see 'a good man struggling in the forms of fate.' Though he be brave and virtuous he is put to trial."

His political opponents, on the other hand, pictured him living on laudanum, and the *Federal Republican* expressed confidence that illness had played such havoc with his constitution, he had but a few months to live, perhaps only a few days. The editor was certain that "his mind has shared the fate of his body. . . . Not a few . . . have left his chamber under a full conviction of the derangement of his mind." This was about the time Madison wrote that his three-day jaunt had done him good. "I gained strength on the road. . . ."

Home. It was a tonic to see his mother, brother, and sisters; eat at the worn table; walk under the familiar willows; look over the fields; and breathe deep his mountain air. Not that his mind was free of worry. Often it sped toward the Great Lakes. When the mailbag arrived from Orange Courthouse or a courier from Secretary Jones, he tore open the dispatches with hasty hands, as Dolley came running.

One day they heard that while a British officer courted a pretty widow, Perry had slipped eight boats across the Presqu' Isle sandbar on pontoons and taken to open waters. On Lake Ontario, Chauncey too was on the move, spoiling for a fight. "I participate in all your hopes," Commander in Chief Madison wrote Jones, "as well as anxieties."

News that the Peace Commissioners had arrived in Gothenburg completed Madison's cure. Dolley wrote Mrs. Gallatin joyfully about "the safe arrival of our treasures." Her great hope was an early return. Gallatin, she told Hannah who knew it, was one of the best and greatest. Courage!

She needed some herself, for she was troubled about Anna's little son Richard. Following an attack of measles, he had remained unnaturally weak and listless. And the weeks passed over.

One day Madison erupted. How dared Generals Wilkinson and Hampton feud during the national crisis? Armstrong should never have given them a joint task. As for the miserly Congress, it had left no way to make up the Northern Army's million-dollar-a-month payroll—shameful. But it was not Madison's nature to be choleric. The storm subsided.

Late in September an express rider brought not Perry's famous "We have met the enemy and they are ours" (that went to General Harrison) but a more sedate message for the Commander in Chief:

> It has pleased the Almighty to give to the arms of the United States a signal victory over their enemies. . . . The British squadron consisting of two ships, two brigs, one schooner and one sloop has this moment surrendered to the force under my command, after a sharp conflict.

At dawn Perry had sighted the enemy from Put-in-Bay, then pursued, closed, and fought—two hours—until the *Lawrence*'s guns were useless and most of her crew lay dead or wounded. He himself had tossed in an open boat under fire. But a wind had sprung up, and Elliott had brought the *Niagara* alongside. Boarding her, Perry sailed through the heavy fire raking five ships.

The President promoted Perry to Captain while the nation went crazy with joy. "Perry's triumph," wrote crusty old John Adams, "is enough to revive Mr. Madison if he were in the last stages of consumption. May he long continue to live and be well, and to see the good work of the war prospering in his hands, for a more necessary war"—contradicting his fellow Federalists—"was never undertaken."

Perry's victory, though great, did not silence all grumbling. People asked why the war in Canada didn't move faster. William Wirt, writing from Richmond, blamed Congress and stubborn state governments. Nor did he let Madison off scot-free. Yes, the President replied to a letter, he knew that anything except victories sounded like an excuse. They had had some victories, but they needed more.

He got them. Commodore Rodgers's *President* came back from a five-month cruise with twelve prizes. And in October General Harrison captured Fort Malden (at last), subdued five Indian tribes, and defeated the British on the Thames, killing Tecumseh (and, almost, the fleeing General Proctor). On this rising note of success the Madisons returned to Washington in time for the races.

The turnout was enormous. Attended by General Mason and Secretary Monroe, the President ("game as ever") spurred off to the track, "Virginia-like." And it happened that, this year, a Virginia horse won. To cap his pleasure, he heard that American troops had chased the British out of Niagara Peninsula. Michigan Territory was now free of the enemy, white or red—drink up!

But he was a little ambiguous about the new anti-Napoleon coalition between Russia, Prussia, Sweden, and Austria. One day the French Minister remarked to him that the alliance had the advantage of ten heads, whereas France had only one. "What a puissant one!" retorted Madison. Sérurier decided that the President must have spoken sarcastically. But Madison both abhorred and reluctantly admired the conqueror of Europe.

Meanwhile Secretary Armstrong, a Napoleon manqué, was ignoring evidence that the feuding Generals Wilkinson and Hampton were botching the task of cutting Canada's supply lines. At Sackett's Harbor, Wilkinson missed a fine opportunity to surprise the enemy. And by ordering Hampton to build winter quarters on the Chateaugay, Armstrong showed that he supinely expected defeat. Madison was incensed. Big talk, windiness, but little action! Sophistry! Indecision! They were going to Canada, they were not going! Had Armstrong assumed control out of vainglory, only to run like a rabbit? A ten-day silence was followed by heavy tidings. Encountering some 460 militiamen, Hampton's 4,000 soldiers had lost their nerve; and after a skirmish en route to Montreal, Wilkinson had fallen back to Plattsburg. Yet Armstrong spoke of these retreats as brilliant maneuvers. Madison scowled. Hampton and Wilkinson had proved frivolous and incompetent. Armstrong had twisted facts to shore up his reputation.

Madison's growing distrust of the Secretary of War required self-censure, for he had appointed this blunderer. True, he had in vain offered the job to better men; true, Armstrong had, earlier, shown energy, foresight, and organizational power; true, Gallatin and others had recommended him highly; true, the Senate had endorsed him cordially. But these considerations did not let Madison off the hook. As Chief Executive he bore the brunt of responsibility. What should he do? Turn Armstrong out? Who would accept the job and do it well? Monroe preferred to keep the State Department. Henry Clay? As Speaker of the House he was indispensable.

Madison figured that by the end of June the Peace Commission must have arrived in St. Petersburg; they should have heard. He and Dolley were anxious about the delay—also about the visibly failing little Richard Cutts, whose system, the doctor said, had been impaired by the measles. Poor little Dicky.

All in all, said Madison in his Annual Message, 1813 had been more successful than otherwise, and he ticked off the victories at Fort Meigs, Sackett's Harbor, York, Fort George, Erie, and Malden; the recovery of Detroit; the stamping out of Indian sorties; and the partial seizure of Upper Canada. Though the war had hurt commerce, it had stimulated American manufacture, forced the growth of American sea power, taught Americans discipline, and proved the stability of America's free institutions. In short,

> the war, with all its vicissitudes, is illustrating the capacity and destiny of the United States to be a great, a flourishing, and a powerful nation ... authorized by its own example to require from all an observance of the laws of justice and reciprocity.

A separate message asked for an embargo to stop illegal exports and such British imports as woolens, cotton, and rum. Because its inconveniences were to shorten the war, patriots would bear them cheerfully. Eight days later Madison signed a new embargo bill.

"Dictatorship!" charged Federalists; and John Randolph, still furious over being ousted from Congress, used his whiplash. The United States, like Rome under the Caesars, he said, was a "vast *prison-house.*" His attitude was not typical. The country at large wanted to get on with the war at whatever cost. God smite all smugglers!

But recruiting lagged, and Armstrong's talk about conscription was poorly received. It came out that he was bribing young officers with promises of higher rank. Indeed, almost every post brought new evidence of his wrongheadedness. Madison turned grim. Remove him? Many people were afraid of swapping horses in midstream.

Certainly in one matter Armstrong should be exonerated. A general, misunderstanding the Secretary of War's order, had burned the Canadian village of Newark. The British revenged themselves with an orgy of arson, burning such American towns as Buffalo, Lewiston, Black Rock, and Manchester, as well as numerous homesteads. Indians scalped many inhabitants. All but three of Fort Niagara's defenders lay in their blood. "Retaliation," said the British. "Savagery," said Americans. It was not a happy Christmas. It was the first without Payne, and Dolley was bleak with worry about her husband's "cares and confinements."

Work was the best antidote, and she ploughed through a mountain of letters. Wrote Harriet Hackley, typically, "It is with extreme diffidence, my dear Madam, that I venture to ask a favor. . . ." Some of the pleas were for commissions. Dolley loved to help, but certain things were out of her power.

The weather, like the war, was indecisive, by turns rainy, freezing, pleasant, white with sleet. When General Wilkinson reentered Canada with 4,000 troops and again fell back after a skirmish, the President ordered a court-martial. Hampton escaped by resigning. About this time Jones said he could no longer spread himself so thin between Navy and Treasury; impossible to row double-banked.

The cure would be Gallatin's return. Since by now he must have heard about his rejection as Commissioner and reappointment to the Treasury, Madison daily expected the *Neptune* to bring him into port— the one man able to raise millions without the direct taxes the public hated. The three attachés would come too. Considering the European situation, the Madisons found it understandable that not a single letter had been received from the Peace Commission. The President answered Castlereagh's offer of peace negotiations at London or Gothenburg by choosing Gothenburg. He would replace Gallatin with Henry Clay.

But in January Mrs. Gallatin received a letter from her husband saying he might spend the winter in Europe. This meant Madison would be left again—the Attorney General had resigned—with two Cabinet vacancies.

Then a four-month-old letter from Payne warmed January. It has been lost, but Dolley told Mrs. Gallatin that it contained a good account of the whole party. "All were well. No answer from London, yet. . . ." Mr. Gallatin disliked "machinations," Payne said, and apologized for the obscurity of that message. Dolley told Hannah she hoped Mr. Gallatin would be coming back to his Treasury post. "Burn this scrawl."

Some of the things which had happened to Payne but which the Madisons would not learn for a long time: The Commissioners, attachés, and four black servants, having spent six stormy weeks at sea on the 300-ton *Neptune,* too seasick to read their Russian travel books, had arrived safely in Gothenburg, Sweden, and then detoured to Denmark for a few days to enjoy Hamlet's garden at Elsinore and the gaiety of Copenhagen. The hotels in the Baltic provinces were filthy. They reached St. Petersburg late in July. But the Czar was off fighting Napoleon. Minister John Quincy Adams and Russian Chancellor Count Romanzov took them in hand. Everything seemed strange. Strangest of all, the sun rose at nine and set at three. But they were enormously impressed by the city's wide streets and great palaces. Asked if they wished to be presented at Court, they decided to wait for word from Czar Alexander. Meanwhile droshkies took them to his Summer Palace at Czarskelo where they dined with Count Ovarovsky. "The walls [were] entirely of amber . . . the floor and the doors inlaid with mother-of-pearl," the colors "exquisite." They enjoyed a ride on a lake boat through magnificent gardens. The Countess was young and handsome. The Russians as usual drank unbelievable quantities of vodka. During the next month the Americans' social life quickened. Then they got word that Britain had refused the Czar's offer of mediation and suggested, instead, a joint conference in London or Gothenburg. Waiting to hear from President Madison, they feasted at the mansions of Count Romanzov and other nobles and attended elegant balls. As son of the American President, Payne was everywhere treated as an American prince. Gallatin sat in a gallery, looking on, while Payne danced with the ladies of the Court. It was a great experience, hearing on the Czar's birthday the *Te Deum* as led by the Metropolitan Ambrose at the Monastery of St. Alexis Nevsky. Members of the imperial family prostrated themselves before the high altar. Soon after that there was a *Te Deum* at Kazan Cathedral to celebrate the Allied victory over Napoleon at

Leipzig. Late in October the envoys and their aides were presented—the Czar was still absent—to the Empress Mother Elizabeth, the Grand Dukes Nicholas and Michael, and the Imperial Court. Then suddenly, in November, Milligan and Payne Todd departed, via Gothenburg, for three weeks in Paris. In January Gallatin and the others left for London, via Amsterdam.

Ignorant of these events, Madison kept striving to heal the Cabinet's wounds, and Dolley to lessen his burdens. They said good-bye to Russell and to Gallatin's replacement, Henry Clay. By special permit Russell and Clay would pass through the British blockade now extending (to New England's chagrin) all the way from Maine to New Orleans.

Partly because of new $124 bounties, recruiting had picked up. And the young leaders who had replaced superannuated generals were jacking up discipline. What couldn't the Army do if it gave the war everything it had?

The move for a European peace seemed—for the United States—portentous. Britain's reason for impressing American seamen would vanish completely with her French foe. Thereafter any fighting on American soil would be for prestige only. Already veterans of the Napoleonic wars were crossing the Atlantic to accomplish prodigies.

Madison asked Congress to repeal the Embargo. Let friendly nations trade freely. The United States' growing manufactures could be protected and revenues increased by continuing double duties on imports and by stopping the outflow of money. Congress came to a boil over this unexpected message, then simmered down. One reason for Madison's high hopes was dynamic young Major General Jacob Brown at Sackett's Harbor. Dolley shared this enthusiasm. If she had moments of depression, it was because Payne had not written. But never mind—who knew how many letters had been stolen, sunk, or burned?

Rain-washed Montpelier, that spring, was very lovely. When Madison rode out to hunt the Hessian fly in his wheat, he was lord of the whole arc of the sky as well as the fields. Returning home hot and tired, he found Dolley at the door. Mail pouches increased his paperwork, but there were compensations: a dish of cherries . . . a game of chess . . . the sound of dark laughter—who was that fiddling down in the Grove? Today's news was bad and good. British Admiral Yeo, who controlled Lake Ontario, had burned the fort at Oswego, but its garrison, outnumbered 5 to 1, had fought back with "steady discipline"—victory of another kind.

And still the problem of Armstrong. Madison detected more subterfuge on the man's part. Besides, he sometimes usurped Presidential prerogatives. Was he so busy wooing fame that he was rendering himself unworthy of it? Madison decided on an investigation—and how pretty Dolley looked in her big sun hat.

So the *Peacock* had greeted the fleet of the new British naval commander, Vice Admiral Sir Alexander Cochrane, with forty-five shots in the hull of his sloop, *Epervier*. America was always hospitable. The President had such thoughts as he disappeared into the little Greek pavilion built over the icehouse to think and plan. When he heard that the escaped slaves whom people called "Cochrane's Colonials" were fighting with the redcoats, he was contemptuous of Britain's recruiting system. But America's 10-million-dollar loan had been subscribed!

Sometimes when rain prevented a walk, the Madisons got their exercise, as years ago, by running races on the portico. At forty-six Dolley was no longer a sylph, and Jemmy, at sixty-three, no streak of fire. But they had remarkable vitality.

So Napoleon had abdicated—*sic gloria transit*. It was something to ponder.

The British had grown so cocky over their Continental successes, Madison doubted that the Commission could now accomplish anything. The United States would probably have to fight it out. Well, if they had to, they would. There were some good men coming on. Madison promoted militiaman Andrew Jackson, victor over the Creek, to Major General of the Army.

Dogwood had dropped its petals when Hannah Gallatin wrote that Payne had left St. Petersburg ahead of her husband. "I am distressed at Payne's leaving Mr. Gallatin," replied Dolley. "What could have led him to do so? Nothing but anxiety to get home I hope."

On the road in May, she covered her easily inflamed eyes against billowing dust. Good travelers though they were, the journey tired them. When they reached Washington, squads of awkward recruits were drilling on the overgrown common. Cochrane bestrode the Potomac!

Madison's 11 o'clock Cabinet meeting endorsed his idea: If Brown was to gain control of Lake Ontario, he must retake Niagara Peninsula and York; also sever Kingston from Montreal. Wellington's veterans must be met by American veterans, not raw troops. Fortunately, instead of eight Generals averaging sixty years of age, the country now had nine battle-trained young ones averaging thirty-six. There should be action by mid-July.

Then the *Intelligencer* galvanized the city. Napoleon had been exiled to the island of Elba, and France had another Bourbon king: Louis XVIII.

Another day Madison faced his Cabinet. Presumably the Peace Commission had met British envoys at Gothenburg, he said. Though not bound to follow the Cabinet's advice, he would like to hear it. Should the United States make the stopping of impressment an ultimatum? All but one member said yes. Should a peace treaty refer both impressment and trade questions to future negotiations? All but one said yes. It happened that the majority opinion coincided with his own. His instructions: If England demanded that the United States renounce its Newfoundland fishing rights, or West India trade, or Louisiana, the Commission should "treat it as it deserves."

But before the carrier ship sailed, Madison received a two-month-old letter from Gallatin and Bayard, posted in London en route to Gothenburg. It said that Federalist talk had so convinced rank-and-file Britons that their country was absolutely blameless, indeed grossly put upon, the cry was "Punish the United States!" Gallatin had lost hope of obtaining a treaty on American terms. But with Napoleon's fall the impressment issue had become obsolete anyway—why not just leave it out of a treaty? And could Gothenburg be exchanged for the more convenient Flemish port of Ghent?

Recalling the Cabinet, Madison again put the question: Should a peace treaty keep silent about impressment? Yes, the Cabinet said, and again the answer coincided with his own judgment. After writing a new dispatch, he issued a proclamation saying that since British forces were too weak to sustain a blockade, theirs was a paper blockade only, therefore illegal.

But what of the growing threat to Washington?

A year ago, Madison reminded his Cabinet, they had been warned of a British plot to burn the Capital. Now citizens were urging stiffer defense measures, for if the British struck along the coast, this city would be the most inviting target. Supply depots should be set up, and at least 10,000 regulars and militia prepared. But as he made these points, Madison realized that his department heads were cold to the issue. Secretary of the Navy Jones, Secretary of State Monroe, Secretary of the Treasury Campbell, Secretary of War Armstrong, and even Attorney General Rush did not believe in the danger. He was bashing his head against a rock. Inwardly he groaned. Congress by its penury and his Cabinet by blind inertia were crippling the city's war effort. Armstrong's blindness was the hardest to take.

Madison worked at the problem almost single-handed. He sent a circular to each Governor asking him to raise more militias; he instructed

Armstrong to organize seaport defenses; and he wrote his old friend Governor Barbour, who had offered to help, that the first necessity was to discover the size and objective of any invasion force. Then on July 2 he gave a special Baltimore-Washington command to General William Winder.

At last Britain's threat to carve out a slice of the United States began to shake,some Federalists. Not such fanatics as Pickering. At a Fourth of July banquet in Massachusetts a gentleman would offer this toast: "*The President of the United States*—respect for the office, but contempt for the incumbent; an immediate resignation his first duty, the island of Elba his last retreat." But on Lake Ontario, Chauncey was almost ready to advance.

Sally Coles's letter mused on Napoleon's downfall. She thought he should have ended his life gloriously under the walls of Paris. As for the new regime, "Mr. Jefferson was here the other day. . . . He says the King is scarcely one degree removed from idiotism, a perfect child in intellect, and extremely corpulent and unwieldy in his person (his wife was a *great drunkard* but for the honor of France died some years ago). . . ." Sally hopes little Dicky is recovering. Dolley must tell her *honestly* how she likes the ruffles. As for spending next winter with the Madisons, alas, she fears not. And for Madison, "Present my cordial love, for in truth, dear Cousin, I do love him dearly." It was the kind of warm, scrawly letter Dolley herself wrote intimates.

Washington City stood tense, fearing attack. Rear Admiral Sir George Cockburn's Chesapeake depredations had increased. While warning Virginians of worse to come, he was stealing horses, cattle, and pigs and burning houses. But Armstrong scoffed. Why, for God's sake, should the British attack Washington? Baltimore maybe; but not Washington! As if this aggravation were not enough, Dolley carried the burden of Payne's silence. Where was he? What was he doing? What new influences was he under? Bad ones?

Finally Mrs. Gallatin sent news. On leaving St. Petersburg, Payne and Milligan had

> found the coast frozen, and after a long detention came by way of Copenhagen, and joined them [Gallatin and so forth] at Amsterdam the day before they left it [for London]. . . . Payne . . . was to return . . . in three weeks; he set off the 7th of May. . . . He will have a very pleasant jaunt no doubt, and Dallas expected to follow him.

It was puzzling all over again. Why had Payne left Gallatin? Had something unpleasant happened in St. Petersburg? Couldn't he have foreseen the freezing over of the Baltic? Had he shirked any duty? He had now been gone from home twice as long as expected—fourteen months. With his family straining to hear news, why not a few lines? Still, Dolley found excuses. Versed in French, naturally he wanted to go to France. And it was a great cultural opportunity.

Early in July the British were winning the race on Lake Champlain. They had all but completed a warship more powerful than the *Saratoga*. Only a new 20-gun brig could hope to throw the balance of power toward the United States. Secretary Jones said no. In vain had Madison stressed the high peril—it could be fatal—of letting the foe gain supremacy on the Lakes. So he acted. He overruled his Navy Secretary. He ordered a new 20-gun brig built in all possible haste. At Vergennes, a "roar of broad axes."

Seeing the magnitude of the decisions her husband must make, Dolley redoubled her efforts to shield him from inconsequentia. He was the strength, she the grace, of the Administration.

At their Fourth of July reception she crossed the great vestibule flanked by two pretty girls. A diarist who saw her stop to greet people noted the "tasteful simplicity of her white dress" and the heads of green wheat ornamenting one side of a white turban. If she wore jewels, they were "eclipsed."

Her hospitality was not reserved for fashionable people. One day she welcomed two Quaker ladies, Rebekah Hubbs and Sarah Scull. Miss Hubbs's bread-and-butter letter has survived. "Assuredly, dear Dorothy"— assuming Dolley was a nickname—"I think I shall ever remember thee with gratitude of heart, thee and thy beloved companion, your kind and Christian entertainment of us. . . ."

Suddenly, word of two land victories. On the 4th of July, General Jacob Brown had smashed Fort Erie. At Chippewa Creek the next day, the British fell like lions on their prey: General Winfield Scott's parading troops. It was a historic battle: the only time during the War of 1812 when regular troops, roughly equal in numbers, clashed in broad daylight on level, open ground, neither having advantage of position. Never again would the British beat an American army of regulars—I am not speaking of militiamen.

The two lines advanced in close order. Load, fire, load, fire. The British broke and ran. Madison rejoiced that two years of combat had toughened the soldiers.

But valor was not always enough. After sweeping British privateers out of the South Pacific, the American frigate *Essex* was destroyed by His Majesty's warships *Phoebe* and *Cherub* as she waited in a Chilean harbor to have a storm-broken main-topmast replaced; 154 Americans lay wounded. When the captain of the *Essex* came home on parole he was lionized. (He announced that he had taken possession of an island he named "Madison's Island," telling its thirty-one tribes, "Our chief shall be your chief.")

By contrast, there was no news from Canada. The storming of Queenston Heights had been followed by a lull. What was going on? Had Chauncey brought up his field guns? On July 20 Sérurier wrote that "the Executive shows himself calm to maintain confidence." Lake Champlain, Sackett's Harbor, Detroit—what was going on? Anxiety had reached a pitch when Washington heard that Chauncey was down with fever. He did not recover in time to help Brown and Scott at the important battle of Lundy's Lane.

From sundown until midnight it raged back and forth, bloodily, the war's most desperate fighting. Infantrymen charged uphill into British muzzles. "Steady, boys, close up." Cannoneers in the act of loading were bayoneted. Brown and Scott were both wounded. Their staffs were almost wiped out. But in the end General Riall had to surrender his sword. It was a major American victory.

It was tremendous—but what if the Capital were sacked? At the end of July 1814, Dolley wrote Hannah Gallatin that Washington City was in a "state of perturbation." Disaffection in some circles and the nearby British depredations, she wrote bitterly, were making "difficulties for the Government. Such a place as this has become!—I can't describe it. I wish . . . we were at Philadelphia. The people do not deserve that I should prefer it." It was an indignation which had been building up.

> Among other . . . threats they say if Mr. Madison attempts to move from this House, in case of an attack, they will *stop him* and that he *shall fall with it.* I am not in the least alarmed at these things, but entirely disgusted, and determined to stay with him.

Madison worked day and night, Dolley went on, his preparations for defense "constantly retarded." The British force in Chesapeake Bay seemed too small to attack the Capital, but what if it were reinforced? Floating the new loan was hampered by a rumor that Gallatin denied any possibility of peace. Many citizens were "thrown into consternation." The times were "frightful."

Though Madison wanted to take the reins into his own hands, how could he undercut men he had appointed?

Dolley thought Payne was probably safer in Europe. "I was rejoiced," she wrote Mrs. Gallatin, "at your last letter containing the account of my precious Payne's going to France and England. . . . I hope we shall see our sons highly benefited"—little foreseeing.

On August 13 the President faced Armstrong with a list of his encroachments upon Presidential prerogatives. Having come just short of requiring the War Secretary's resignation, then drawn back (a decision he would live to regret), he laid down ten rules for the future.

While Madison suffered from lack of Cabinet support and Dolley watched anxiously over Anna, who was "very large," they were preparing themselves for—what?

The threat to the city was almost tangible. One could smell, hear, almost touch it. According to leaked news in London papers, half of the 18,000 troops assigned to "attack the most important ports in America" had sailed. Indeed, Norfolk had sighted another British squadron, and Cochrane's subordinate, Rear Admiral Cockburn, was scouting the navigable Patuxent River that led toward Washington. Madison still considered that city a better target than Baltimore because more prestigious and less fortified, but Armstrong was scornful. British marines were fanning out from Nominy Creek. Could it be a feint? Washington's mayor complained to Madison about the city's defenseless state. Both were angry. Both had lost all confidence in Armstrong.

Though two years of war had proved the superiority of regulars over even tested militia, the city's defenses leaned heavily on untried militia. Also, General Winder, given no staff, was wearing himself out on minor jobs. Not until August 16 did Armstrong give him an adjutant. By then the situation was tight as a fist. Yet the Secretary of War continued "treating with indifference . . . the idea of an attack by the enemy."

Prospects were not brightened by some transmitted Parliamentary oratory: "Vigorous war with America; we repeat . . . vigorous war! till America accedes to the following demands"—new western and northern boundaries, loss of her Newfoundland fishing rights and of her trade with the East and West Indies, cession of New Orleans. Nor were hopes raised by the American Prisoners' Agent quoting Cockburn: "I believe, Mr. Skinner, that Mr. Madison will have to put on his armor and fight it out; I see nothing else left."

Fight with what? That was the question. Madison had authorized the use of 15,000 militia for the Washington area, but Armstrong's skepticism had so dampened Winder's zeal, he had called up only a fifth of Maryland's militia. And only a fraction of those called up had responded.

Then the worst happened. Fifty-one British transports anchored at the mouth of the Patuxent River.

Fear spread through the city like a flash fire. Taking some dragoons, Monroe rode off to scout. General Winder summoned militiamen from Pennsylvania, Maryland, and Virginia and marines from Pennsylvania and New York. Would they arrive in time? He asked the President about a call for volunteers. It went out, but with misgivings. Armstrong had never established the supply depots Madison had demanded three months ago.

John Van Ness, head of the District Militia, had a run-in with the Secretary of War.

"The strength of the enemy," he said, "points to a serious blow."

"Yes! by God!" cried Armstrong. "They wouldn't bring such a fleet without meaning to strike, but it won't be here. What the devil would they do *here?*"

"The seat of government's the most logical target."

"No, no! *Baltimore's* the place, sir!" shouted Armstrong. "It's of more consequence!"

Winder positioned regulars and militia. Then he thought of Commodore Joshua Barney's gunboat flotilla of North African fame. It had been blockaded in the Patuxent since June. Would its 500 sailors be available for action?

The evening of August 19 the British landed at the village of Benedict and began foraging. Some Americans hung out white sheets. Said Madison, "Pelt the enemy from the start, throw in all sorts of obstructions." It was advice. Later he would wish he had made it an order.

The British advanced up the river in small craft and afoot. Sailors and soldiers kept parallel lines. On August 22 they reached Nottingham, halfway to the Capital. Barney's flotilla had just left there; also—riding a roan horse—scout Monroe had been shadowing them since Benedict, though at some disadvantage because he had forgotten his spyglass. After learning the enemy's direction, Madison issued two orders: move all government papers out of the Capital, and use every spur to concentrate troops.

On that same Monday, Armstrong—passing between the State and War offices—ran into Clerk Pleasonton, who was hastily stuffing state documents into linen sacks.

"Unnecessary alarm," he scoffed. "I see no British intention to converge on Washington."

With his hands full of such papers as treaties, George Washington's letters, the Declaration of Independence, and the Constitution of the

United States, Pleasonton said it seemed prudent to take no chances. Contemptuous, Armstrong strode on.

Washingtonians were fleeing the city. Roads were choked with pedestrians, horses, gigs, wagons. Under a hot sun, dust clouds swirled. They had no time to settle.

People heard distant explosions. Barney's men had scuttled—just as the British came up—all but one gunboat. It was a warning signal for Winder to take his troops 8 miles northeast, from Wood Yard to a camp called Long Old Fields.

Meanwhile a hundred-man guard had been thrown around the President's Mansion. The hour was desperate.

Madison, who had been pacing the floor, told Dolley his duty lay with the troops; his presence might help to hearten them. Darkness was falling. He asked if she had the courage to stay alone until tomorrow or the next day. She replied that her concern would be with him and the Army. General Mason, Secretary of the Navy Jones, and Attorney General Rush had arrived to accompany him. Embracing her, he begged her to take care of herself and the Cabinet papers. Then he said good-bye, mounted his horse, and rode off.

⤙ XIII ⤚

WASHINGTON PUT TO THE TORCH

MENTALLY DOLLEY FOLLOWED HER HUSBAND to the Navy Yard, crossed the Anacostia bridge, and rode 8 miles to Long Old Fields. The camp was too near enemy-held Upper Marlboro for tranquility.

It was time to take stock. She was alone with her maid Sukey; the French steward, John Sióussat; his fifteen-year-old mulatto assistant, Paul Jennings; a cook; a gardener; a coachman; and the responsibility of priceless papers and furnishings. And it was this house on which the enemy had sworn to take revenge. Outside, night had fallen.

Meanwhile President Madison, acutely aware that Washington City was unprepared for the crisis threatening, had reached the Long Old Fields camp. He was considering alternatives. Would the British attack the stronghold of Fort Washington before moving on to the Capital, or approach it directly? Or, assuming that the main bridges would be destroyed, would they swing around by Bladensburg, where the Eastern Branch could be forded? Or head for Annapolis or Baltimore? No, one way or another, they would come to Washington. There was more glory in seizing the capital of the United States.

That night he slept, not well, at the Williams house near camp, probably waking at 2 A.M., if he was asleep, when a sentry's alarm roused the troops to meet a "British attack"—cattle driven in for the commissary.

At daybreak General Winder galloped up. The farmer's letter in his hand quoted a British jibe that they'd soon "have Mr. and Mrs. Madison." At the ensuing war parley it was decided to attack the British at Upper Marlboro—without cavalry the foe couldn't move very fast. After the parley, Madison interrogated two deserters, then went to review troops in the still fresh air. They looked fit to the Commander in Chief. But danger was ripening.

At noon he penciled a note to Dolley:

> My dearest . . . I have passed the forenoon among the troops who are in high spirits and make a good appearance. The reports as to the enemy have varied every hour. The last and probably truest information is that they are not very strong, and are without cavalry or artillery, and of course that they are not in a condition to strike at Washington. It is believed that they are not about to move from Marlboro. . . . It is possible, however, that they . . . have a greater force, or expect one . . . or that their temerity may be greater than their strength.

He hoped to see her by evening. The optimism seems a little forced. He did not wish to increase her anxiety unnecessarily.

Winder sent for General Tobias Stanbury's militia at Bladensburg to help take the offensive at Upper Marlboro. Seeing District Commander Winder in charge set Armstrong to sulking. When Winder passed on Colonel George Minor's request that his 10th Virginia militia be transferred from Alexandria to Washington, the Secretary of War shrugged and refused to give the order, whereupon Madison tightened his mouth and, overruling Armstrong, granted permission. Not all of the situation's difficulties were British-made.

By 2 P.M. battle plans were formed, and the President, with Armstrong and Jones, started back to Washington only 3 miles ahead of General Robert Ross's crack British army. They had gone only a few miles when a courier caught up with them. He said the British had mustered and left Upper Marlboro heading—where? Fort Washington? Bladensburg? New orders must go to Stansbury's militia to return to Bladensburg.

Madison knew he must warn his wife. He dashed off a second note. It has been lost, but an installment of the letter Dolley was writing Lucy calls it "alarming":

> . . . He desires I should be ready at a moment's warning to enter my carriage and leave the city; that the enemy seemed stronger than reported, and that it might happen they would reach the city with intention to destroy it.

Feeling the extremity of these moments, she packed two small trunks with some state papers and a change of clothes. The carriage could hold no more. Pennsylvania Avenue was packed with such a confusion of fleeing people, she could think of no way to commandeer a wagon.

The hundred-soldier Mansion guard had disappeared without a by-your-leave. The crowd of refugees swarming along Pennsylvania Avenue on foot and horseback and in vehicles, carrying possessions, was swelling: a rout. Dolley sat at an upstairs window staring through a spyglass.

Sióussat ran in, agitated, to get permission to spike the cannon at the gate and lay a train of powder to "blow up the British if they cross the threshold." No, said Mrs. Madison. No, even in war there were "advantages not to be taken." And she went back to writing Lucy the undeliverable letter:

> ... Our private property must be sacrificed. ... I am determined not to go myself until I see Mr. Madison safe and he can accompany me, as I hear of much hostility towards him. ... Disaffection stalks. ... My friends and acquaintances are all gone.

At four—unknown to Dolley—an unwarlike President caught in a war dined at the Cutts house on F Street. Before the cloth was removed, he rose and went to meet Secretary of War Armstrong at Monroe's house at 20th and I Streets. There the three discussed grand strategy. Madison was dog-tired when at last he rode home to Dolley. The evening had an air of unreality.

Just after sundown Colonel Minor came by to report that his Northern Virginia militia had reached Washington but must be armed. Good, said the President, and he hurried Minor off to Armstrong's boarding-house in the Seven Buildings.

No guns or ammunition tonight, said Armstrong; it was too late to open the armory; report to Colonel Carberry tomorrow morning. Colonel Minor stood on the doorstep struck dumb. He was full of "chagrin." It was only about eight o'clock—candlelight—and the safety of the Capital might depend upon arming his regiment at once. But a colonel does not argue with the Secretary of War.

A door shut in Minor's face.

An hour later Armstrong received the District Commander. Fresh from seeing the President, Winder talked fast. The British had stopped at the estate called Melwood, but he feared a night attack. That was something his troops could not stand. At night artillery was useless; it couldn't find its mark. So he had shifted camp from Long Old Fields to Dr. Hunter's near the Navy Yard. Already Stanbury's militia was on its way back to Bladensburg. Some 5,000 troops were now split about evenly between the men stationed 6 miles northeast of the city and the Second Columbian Division, south, at Port Washington. Each division commanded a bridge over the Potomac's Eastern Branch—one or the other of which the British were bound to cross en route to Washington. Unfortunately, while the enemy was getting a good sleep, his men had been exhausted by night alarms, marching and countermarching.

Armstrong could no longer avoid it; for the first time he faced up to the question: What if the British attacked Washington?

His first thought was for his own reputation. Since the President had overruled him to order into the Capital its one defending regiment, he had reason to fear. Sending for the remainder of Colonel Minor's Alexandria militia, he joked a bit, then falsified—by predating—an order to bring the regiment to Washington "with the utmost dispatch." It was delivered two hours after he himself had denied arms to militiamen already in the city. This barefaced attempt to rearrange history infuriated Colonel Minor. Purple, he wrote out the receipt demanded. (Of course Armstrong's ploy was naïve. Later, how muzzle the Colonel or the President?)

As night deepened, Dolley did everything possible to help James get some sleep. God knew what tomorrow would bring. But at midnight they were routed out of bed by a communiqué dashed off by Monroe three hours ago. Bluntly, "The enemy are in full march for Washington. Have the materials prepared to destroy the bridges. You had better remove the records." This warning was rushed on to Armstrong.

The troops were not getting much sleep either. Still without arms or ammunition, Minor's militiamen tossed about on the floor among the House of Representatives' Corinthian columns. When Winder's third borrowed horse broke down, he trudged up Capitol Hill afoot, then on to the Eastern Branch to see if the two bridges had been destroyed as ordered. No; the Navy hadn't sent that boatload of explosives. At midnight the harassed man was back in camp arranging to burn the upper bridge and defend the lower one. (Stansbury, seeing the fire from Bladensburg, thought an attack was near.)

The Madisons stood on the roof of the President's house, before dawn, scanning the city with spyglasses. When a dispatch from Winder asking for a council of war arrived, it too was relayed to Armstrong.

Madison could not know that during the night, peril had almost relented and gone away. Rear Admiral Sir George Cockburn and General Robert Ross, asleep in a shed on the Melwood estate, wrapped in their red cloaks, had been waked at 2 A.M. by Colonel James Scott, who brought a dispatch from their superior Admiral Cochrane, anchored at Benedict. They must not advance further, it said; they were too weak to attack the Capital, it was too risky; *return*. Outdoors the two leaders walked up and down, up and down, arguing. Ross was for complying; Cockburn said they had gone 30 miles, too far to retreat—and history waited on the upshot. Cockburn reinforced his argument: to return would mean staining their arms. Ross began to waver. Cockburn—who had already saved the project twice—pressed his advantage. He jeered at the idea that raw American militias could beat disciplined British troops. Suddenly Ross struck his forehead: "So be it!" On to Washington. But Winder would burn the upper and lower bridges—they must go around by Bladensburg.

At daylight, about the time the British were marching out from Melwood, Madison pressed Dolley to his heart. He'd return by three o'clock, and he expected to bring the already-invited Cabinet members and their wives and perhaps some officers for dinner.

Then he was off to the temporary army headquarters near the Navy Yard, where he and Winder, Jones, and some militia officers were joined by Rush and Monroe: all those involved in imminent great decisions, except Armstrong. Where was the Secretary of War?

He came in puffing. His excuse for being so tardy: Winder's note had arrived late—"The moment I received it I hastened out." The trouble was that Rush, to whom he had shown that very note, had reached headquarters an hour ago.

Grimly Madison asked for Armstrong's ideas of strategy. He offered none; just prophesied somberly that in the battle shaping up, veteran regulars would whip untried militia. Others in the party, angered, bet on the Americans.

Before hastening off, Winder ordered Commodore Barney's sailors to guard the Navy Yard bridge and, if necessary, fire it. Barney objected. He told the President he hated to tie up 500 good men on a job a handful—"any damn corporal"—could handle. Right, said Madison, and he ordered all but half a dozen to Bladensburg. The sun was riding high.

With no great military gift and the odds against him, Madison was slowly beginning to become Commander in Chief in fact as well as title.

A few miles away Dolley sat writing another installment to Lucy.

> Wednesday morning, twelve o'clock—Since sunrise I have been turning my spyglass in every direction, and watching with unwearied anxiety, hoping to discover the approach of my dear

husband and his friends; but, alas, I can descry only groups of
military wandering in all directions, as if there were a lack of
arms or of spirit to fight for their own firesides!

When she laid down her pen, it had helped a little to talk to somebody.

Paul Jennings was setting the table for the three-o'clock dinner his
mistress expected to share with the President and some guests. After
toting cider, ale, and Madeira up from the cellar, he put them into coolers.
Then a messenger delivered Mrs. Jones's regrets. Because of "the present
state of alarm and bustle of preparation for the worst that may happen,"
she imagined it would be more convenient to dispense with the pleasure
of today's hospitality, therefore prayed Mrs. Madison to accept this excuse
for Mr. Jones, Lucy, and herself—she was packing with no idea as to
where they could go. Paul removed three plates from the table.

The harried President had forgotten about dinner. Confirmation of
the British march on Bladensburg had driven out all thoughts but one: he
must see the situation firsthand—perhaps he could help in some way. As
he started for Bladensburg, Secretary Campbell reined in close. He said
he was concerned about Armstrong taking no part in this crisis because
Armstrong had been unwilling to voice opinions not specifically requested
by the President. Astonished, Madison rode up to Armstrong and said he
hoped his instructions had not been so misconstrued as to keep him from
exercising his functions as Secretary of War; *of course* he should aid
Winder. If difficulties about authority arose, he would be there to settle
them. Apparently mollified, Armstrong left for Bladensburg, followed by
Madison and Rush.

The President's horse was limping. At the Marine Barracks he
swapped it for Charles Carroll's. The hot noon sun burned down.

Near Bladensburg, the President and Rush cantered past District
regulars and Stansbury's militia, then plunged downhill toward the river,
past an orchard, a tobacco barn, and artillery implanted on an earth-work
with rifle support on its flanks. When the new mount bucked and tried to
bolt, Madison pulled it up. At the bridge a horseman waved them back—
the British vanguard! Caught between two armies, Madison and Rush
(who lost his hat) had the good sense to gallop back. Near the earthwork
they met Monroe, Winder, and the just-arrived Armstrong. Because his
horse skittered again, Madison missed an exchange between Armstrong
and Winder. Controlling his horse, he asked Armstrong if he had suggested better troop positions. No, said the Secretary, they seemed as good
as circumstances permitted.

General Stansbury of the Baltimore Brigade was not happy.

Ordered, earlier, to hold Bladensburg, he had inspected the brick houses and trenches dug by civilian volunteers. It was a strong position *provided he got reinforcements.* Ordered to Washington, then back, he had finally stationed his hungry footsore troops (their salt beef and flour had spoiled) not in town but on the other side of a 90-foot wooden bridge. He had posted riflemen and artillery on the turnpike and hidden his three motley regiments of soldiers—most of them without uniforms—in the apple orchard above; whereupon Monroe had come along and, without a smidgen of authority, moved them 500 yards back up the hill, out of the only natural position of strength. Now the main body of his militia, having lost both rifle and artillery support, stood forth in suicidal view. Worse, Winder's District militia and main-line regulars lay a full mile to the rear. Stansbury's men did not even have the comfort of knowing they were there. It meant three widely separated lines of defense: the first small, with cannon and, presently, some cavalry, but cavalry so lost in a ravine, they could not see out; the second, 2,000 raw militia wide open to the attack of veterans; the third, Barney's seamen holding the center among the preposterously distant D.C. militia and regulars.

This was the troop pattern Madison and Rush found on riding back up the hill from the bridge that Wednesday afternoon, August 24, 1814. British grenadiers were surging into Bladensburg.

A volley mowed the redcoats down like wheat. Almost an entire British company—officers with gold epaulets and gold-lace hats as well as privates—lay bleeding. Survivors ran behind a warehouse and fired Congreve rockets—powder in capped tubes—from tripods. Meanwhile American officers tried to steel their troops—"You're fine fellows. . . ." Incendiaries exploded near Madison. Getting themselves killed would serve no purpose, and they might be obstructing. He and Rush fell back.

There flew a blizzard of bullets. A British officer raised his sword and bugles sounded a charge. "Wellington's Invincibles" stormed the bridge, then the orchard, using trees as the shields which should have guarded the raw, bewildered, and now panicked, wounded, dying, fleeing Baltimore militiamen—"rabble" was the British word. The men were fleeing not toward Washington, where they might regroup, but toward home base: Montgomery Courthouse. Even Colonel Sterett's fashionable young volunteers who had had a real zest for a fight ran. "Cut down the cowards," Stansbury shouted. In vain. It was a debacle. Wreathed in smoke and conceding defeat, Winder dismissed the third line: D.C. militia and regulars. While men raged, he promised to renew the contest elsewhere.

Madison's party spurred toward Washington. Forced to swap his temperamental mount, he caused a wave of excitement at 7th and Pennsylvania when a group by the town pump and a barrel of whiskey spotted his carriage. "There goes the President!"

The battle at Bladensburg continued. Unaware that they were licked, Barney's seamen (over whom Winder felt he had no authority) kept firing 18-pounders. When the onrushing British shielded themselves behind a fence, the navymen charged with raised cutlasses, crying, "Board 'em!" They fought until ammunition ran out and the gallant Commodore, with a bullet in his thigh, lay pressing his body against the ground to keep from bleeding to death. Admiral Cockburn and General Ross, coming up and admiring courage, paroled him.

With help from the unused regulars a mile to the rear Barney might have stopped the British, but Winder's order to retreat had canceled that possibility. The Americans had the advantage of numbers; the British, of *available* numbers, besides superior discipline from long experience fighting Napoleon. It is ironic that the 2,000 United States muskets to the rear never were allowed to fire a shot.

Flotillaman Charles Ball would put it bitterly. "The militia ran like sheep chased by dogs."

During these events Dolley heard a faint thunder of cannon. Mayor James Blake rushed in to urge her to go. She kept packing. There was just an off chance that they'd find a wagon to transport some of the valuables she knew she could not stuff into her carriage. To four cases of state papers and a few clothes she added silver, books, a favorite clock, and, from her sitting room, her beloved crimson velvet draperies.

She was dead-set on saving Gilbert Stuart's full-length portrait of George Washington: that monolithic figure in a black velvet suit with a foam of lace at the throat and wrists, standing by a scarlet-covered table, one hand gripping a sword, the other outstretched. This likeness of the father of his country was irreplaceable. But how pry loose a picture screwed to the wall? And, if successful, how transport the unwieldy canvas on its stretcher?

She was struggling with the problem and Sukey was "lolling out a chamber window," when the free black James Smith galloped up waving his hat and shouting, "Clear out! Clear out! General Armstrong's ordered a retreat!"

Dolley tried to bring her running account for Lucy up to date:

Three o'clock—Will you believe it, my sister? We have had a battle or skirmish near Bladensburg, and I am still here within sound of the cannon! Mr. Madison comes not; may God protect

him! Two messengers covered with dust come to bid me fly, but I
wait for him. . . .

She was interrupted by the sound of wagon wheels. Relieved, she watched
the wagon being loaded, then cautioned the driver and sent the precious
cargo off to what she hoped was safety. She told Lucy about the
conveyance.

> . . . I have had it filled with plate and the most valuable portable
> articles belonging to the house; whether it will reach its destina-
> tion, the Bank of Maryland, or fall into the hands of British
> soldiers, events must determine.

How good that Anna—pregnant—had gone to the Forrests' place in
Maryland yesterday with Mrs. Forrest.

Servants were wrenching at Washington's portrait when Colonel
Charles Carroll dashed in with the President's instructions. Dolley was to
meet him and the Joneses at Bellevue, the Carrolls' house in George
Town. They would all go to Virginia together, crossing the Potomac at the
Little Falls bridge and following the river to Wiley's Tavern on Difficult
Run. Near there he would recross into Maryland to rejoin the troops
mustering for another battle. Dolley refused to leave before securing
Washington's portrait. Calling that foolish, Carroll urged haste and ran
out to try to find the President.

What was that loud cracking? Puzzled, Dolley added a few lines for
Lucy. Kind Mr. Carroll had been in a "very bad humor" about her
lingering to rescue General Washington, she wrote. And indeed, in these
"perilous moments," unscrewing the portrait was too "tedious." She
looked up from the letter to order a rougher method. When Sióussat had
brought an ax, the gardener Tom Magraw climbed a tipsy ladder and
broke the frame. Wrote Dolley in triumph, "It is done!"

The stretched canvas was lying on the floor when two gentlemen
from out of town, Mr. Robert de Peyster and Mr. Jacob Barker, stopped
by to help in any way they could.

Dolley assigned them the responsibility of carrying the portrait out of
the city to a certain humble farm which she named; also the East Room's
eagle ornaments and four other boxes of Presidential papers. "If you can't
save them, destroy them." Such treasures must not fall into the hands of
the enemy. They might "make a great flourish."

(Thirty-six years later, when a controversy broke out over who had
saved the portrait, Dolley recalled her willingness to remain an hour

longer, risking life and liberty. She had acted out of "respect for General Washington—not . . . to gain laurels.")

Back of the house the butler, John Freeman, was poised to drive off in the President's coachee with his family and a feather bed. Dolley told them good-bye.

She looked around at the rooms which she and Latrobe had worked hard to furnish beautifully—this mansion "so justly admired"—and wrote to Lucy:

> It is done . . . the precious portrait placed in the hands of the [two] gentlemen . . . for safe keeping. And now, dear sister, I must leave this house or the retreating army will make me a prisoner in it by filling up the road I am directed to take. When I shall again write to you, or where I shall be tomorrow, I cannot tell.

She indulged in no heroics; she simply ordered her carriage and stood with an overstuffed net reticule, waiting.

When the coachman Joe Bolin drove up in her carriage, she and Sukey stepped in. They wheeled onto turbulent Pennsylvania Avenue, crossed the congested bridge to George Town, and rolled as fast as crowds permitted toward Bellevue. A Miss Brown's mother and sister saw "Mrs. Madison in her carriage flying full speed . . . accompanied by an officer"—dragoon—"carrying a drawn sword."

Her protector was not, as supposed, the Madisons' uniformed major-domo, John Sióussat. After seeing Dolley off, he had prepared buckets of water and bottles of wine for possibly thirsty American soldiers, then locked up and carried the poll parrot three blocks away to the French legation's temporary quarters: Colonel John Tayloe's townhouse, the Octagon. Because of Sérurier's immunity it was considered safe.

He had hardly gone when troopers rescued two 6-pounders from the front door of the President's House. Why leave them for the enemy? One was dropped as too heavy. Flotillamen would push it off with four from the Capitol.

As Dolley traveled toward Bellevue, she had no idea as to the whereabouts of her husband. Somewhere he was trying to make sound decisions. (Actually it had already been decided that the logical place to make a stand was the heights of Tenley Town.)

Meanwhile George Town had sent Mayor Peter to persuade Winder to save it by capitulation. Madison was outraged. To him such talk was absolutely inconceivable. It was anathema.

Arriving at the Presidential House at 4:30, Madison's party heard from Barker and de Peyster—who had lingered for brandies—that Dolley had just left. The exhausted men rested awhile and talked about the unreliability of militias up against trained regulars. Then they headed for Virginia.

Stragglers were rummaging through the Great House—wasn't it theirs? Someone confiscated from a hall table the dueling pistols which Secretary Campbell had loaned the President. Barker and de Peyster were maneuvering the portrait of George Washington on its stretcher out the front door and into a cart.

At Octagon House, the French Minister was training his telescope on the President's Mansion. He saw the horde on Pennsylvania Avenue spew forth Madison, then after an interval reswallow him. Militia! Unknown quantity! To Talleyrand he would write:

> It was then, my Lord, that the President who in the midst of all this disorder had displayed, to stop it, a firmness and constancy worthy of better success, but powerless in regard to militia which more than once, in the War of the Revolution, had drawn after it in flight the illustrious Washington himself, coolly mounted his horse, accompanied by some friends, and slowly gained the bridge that separates Washington from Virginia.

Dolley had reached Bellevue and found Mrs. Jones and her children waiting. Soon after that Secretary Jones—having ordered Captain Tingey to burn the Navy Yard, a sloop, and a frigate—arrived with Navy Clerk Edward Duvall. They were followed by Chief State Department Clerk John Graham. But where was the President?

A further message from Madison asked Jones to bring his family and Mrs. Madison to Foxall's Cannon Foundry. The earlier plan had proved unfeasible. About five o'clock a procession set out from Bellevue a little like the Canterbury pilgrims—except that the travelers rode in carriages, and their stories about past hardships and future dangers had no merriment, only stoicism. The Capital of this United States stood in jeopardy.

At the foundry, Tench Ringgold reined up with another set of instructions from the President. The route to Foxall's was completely blocked. The President would cross the Potomac at Mason's Ferry, take the causeway from Analostan Island, and meet his wife's party at a place a bit closer than Wiley's Tavern: the Rev. John Maffitt's Salona.

It led to a tragicomedy of errors: three groups searching for each other in a growing and terrible darkness.

Monroe and Ringgold came to Rokeby, Richard Love's white frame house near Little Falls, looking for the President. "Am I safe here?" asked Matilda Love anxiously. "Madame, as safe," said Monroe, "as . . . in the Allegheny Mountains." The two men ate supper before moving on.

Madison too was groping among the hills under the handicap of darkness. He stopped first at Wren's Tavern, then at the Minors' home near Falls Church, then pressed on toward the place of rendezvous: Salona.

Behind him, Dolley and her friends were with great difficulty negotiating the August night. Again and again, confronting the stygian terrain, they stumbled and lost their bearings.

They were playing hide-and-seek in the night.

At the same time British troops—flushed by victory and intent on chastising the United States—swarmed into Washington, looking for trouble. Ross's horse was shot out from under him.

A band of Cockburn's redcoats broke into the Capitol, rushed up a little circular staircase, burst into the House of Representatives, and put through some mock legislation, voting unanimously to burn this wicked Capitol. They piled up woodwork for kindling and sprinkled rocket powder, then set great fires. When wind blew sparks, nearby houses burned too. Mrs. Andrew Hunter, who watched from her roof, says, "No drawing room was ever as brilliantly lit as the whole city that night. As flames burst through the roof of the Capitol, there was a roll of thunder."

About nine o'clock Sérurier stopped walking the floor at the Octagon, seized his spyglass, and trained it out a window. Stupendous and awful grandeur! The burning Navy Yard and Capitol were throwing up a feverish glare. It was as if desperate men were trying to prolong day into night. As the Frenchman watched, new blazes exacerbated the horizon. "I have never beheld a spectacle more terrible," he would write Paris, "and at the same time more magnificent. . . . A profound darkness reigned . . . [where] I live, and one was delivered up to conjectures and false reports."

About 10:30 a double column of redcoats marched toward the President's Mansion. Ross stopped at Mrs. Suter's boardinghouse to order a chicken for himself and his staff—they would come back for it later.

Blacks told Sérurier they had overheard the British plotting to burn government buildings. Would the whole city be razed? Sérurier sent to ask British protection on diplomatic grounds.

His messenger found General Ross in the Oval Room of the President's House stacking up elegant furniture to use as kindling. Having just burned the private home from which his horse had been shot and killed, he was in a bad humor. But he answered civilly enough. Yes, the French legation would be as safe as if Louis XVIII himself were in residence. And he went on preparing his bonfire.

Admiral Cockburn was merrier. Having forced young Roger Weightman to accompany him here as hostage and guide, this swashbuckler—his name fitted—had just discovered a table set for some thirty people. He ordered wine poured, enjoyed the sarcasm of drinking Jemmy's health, then snatched up an old hat of the President's as a souvenir. A cushion from Mrs. Madison's chair occasioned "pleasantries too vulgar to repeat." One soldier's booty was a pair of rhinestone buckles, another's a ceremonial sword, another's the President's best shirt. Ross's prize was a packet of James Madison's love letters.

Filing out into the night, troops lit torches, which, at a signal, were pitched through the long windows. Flames shot up and fire raced through the rooms hungrily, brutally, brilliantly.

In Virginia, during this period, James on horseback and Dolley in a crowded carriage were still groping blindly for one another. Sometimes they and their companions turned to watch in horror the District's demonic fires. The city was wrapped in a "winding sheet of flame"—a gale might burn everything down. They could figure out that the most distant conflagration was the Navy Yard; the high majestic one, the Capitol; the closest, the Executive Mansion. The glare could be seen 40 miles away.

Years later Richard Rush would describe the spectacle as seen from Virginia.

> . . . I have indeed, to this hour, the vivid impression upon my eye of columns of flame and smoke ascending throughout the night of the 24th of August from the Capitol, the President's house, and other public edifices, as the whole were on fire, some burning slowly, others with bursts of flame and sparks mounting high up on the dark horizon. This never can be forgiven. . . .
>
> If at intervals the dismal sight was lost to our view, we got it again from some hill-top. . . .

Fortunately there was no wind. With the charred timbers of their world crashing about their heads, the wanderers suffered fear, horror, frustration, rage, grief, despair.

When at last Madison entered the brick house called Salona, Dolley was not there. What could have happened? That night there was no such thing as rest for the President.

Meanwhile Dolley's party had fetched up at Rokeby, where Monroe and Ringgold had eaten supper before departing. When Dolley's friend Matilda Lee Love offered them beds, the little company felt too exhausted physically and emotionally to say no. Dolley sat at an upstairs window a long time watching the inflamed sky.

The next morning—not knowing the fate of Washington City—two groups renewed their game of blindman's buff. Madison and Rush returned to Wren's Tavern, where the President picked up not his wife, alas, but a volunteer guard of a pair of dragoons. Back at Salona he learned that Dolley had just passed en route to Wiley's Tavern—and off he spurred again.

The sky had darkened strangely, and a gale rose howling. The storm was as violent as the British. Was it the skirts of a hurricane? Madison and Rush took refuge—just in the nick of time—at The Crossroads. Suddenly rain fell in a "mighty cataract."

Dolley's party ran into a house. She had gone upstairs when she got what Sukey called a bawling out. "Miz' Madison!" the mistress of the house screamed from below. "If that's you, come down! Your husband's got mine out fighting and, damn you, you shan't stay in my house; *so get out!*"

The hurricane was unloosed. Far and wide in the District of Columbia, Maryland, and Virginia, terrified people crouched under makeshift shelters. Fifteen-year-old Miss Brown had a harrowing experience, and not just because she lost a white bonnet trimmed with pink ribbons. "The Government papers and other valuables were covered with tarpaulins. Into the corners under these we crept, but failed to find protection from the deluge of rain. The boats were lashed together and to the trees on shore, which . . . bent over like hoops, while the clouds seemed to . . . pour down one continuous stream of electricity. . . ."

But to Washington the storm—like the 1588 miraculous shift of wind which had crushed the Spanish Armada on its way to destroy England—was an angel of mercy. "God sent a wind."

To loop back: After burning the Capitol and the President's House, and finishing up the Navy Yard, the British rolled out of bed, the morning of August 25, intent on winning fresh laurels as arsonists. Under ominous skies they burned some snipers' houses and the big State-Army-Navy Building. The flames shot up with a snapping sound. Three rope walks, fired, produced a smoke so dense, it would have hidden the sun if there had been one. Burning hemp and tar smelled to high heaven. At the *National Intelligencer* redcoats gleefully pitched printer's type through a window. Cockburn said to be sure to destroy all the C's.

"Damn it!" said General Ross when he tried to stuff away yesterday's newspaper assuring readers the city was safe, "my pocket's full of old Madison's love letters!" Cockburn, having appropriated a long-maned white mare with a black foal at her heels, rode up Pennsylvania Avenue in style, highly pleased with himself.

The only public quarters which escaped the holocaust was the combination Post Office and Patent Office in Blodgett's Hotel. Here the Director, Dr. Thornton, pleaded for the privately owned art contents of the "Museum," reminding the British that all enlightened nations condemned the Turks for the dastardly barbarism of burning the Alexandria Library.

Then that "most tremendous hurricane," mentioned earlier, swept in. It ripped up trees, unroofed houses, overturned cannon. At one place toppling walls crushed thirty redcoats. The battered British feared that American troops, regathered and reinforced, would counterattack as ruthlessly as their ally this storm. What if they were cut off from their ships? One redcoat has described the tempest with awe:

> Our column was completely dispersed, as if it had received a total defeat; some of the men flying for shelter behind walls and buildings, and others falling flat upon the ground to prevent themselves from being carried away by the tempest; nay, such was the violence of the wind that two pieces of cannon . . . were fairly lifted from the ground and borne several yards. . . .

George Gleig (later Chaplain General) confirms the enormity of what struck. "A hurricane fell on the city which unroofed houses and upset our three-pounder guns. It upset me too. It fairly lifted me out of the saddle, and the horse which I had been riding I never saw again."

While the British were debating whether to stay or go, a mud-spattered President was resuming his bedeviled search for Dolley.

Navy Clerk Mordecai Booth overtook him and Rush on the Old Dominion Road and asked what he should do with the 136 barrels of powder removed from Washington. They discussed it on the way to Wiley's Tavern, where at last Madison found Dolley.

The thirty-six hours of their separation had seemed like thirty-six years, the time lapse having taken on the proportions of the tragedy being enacted. Now they could bring each other up to date on their trials and frustrations while each thanked God the other was safe. How much of Washington had been burned? Were the Capitol and Great Mansion—their home—in ashes? Useless to speculate. There was a country to be saved.

Holding to his plan to cross into Maryland and rejoin troops seeking a return engagement, Madison could allow himself only until midnight. Dolley understood.

At midnight he said good-bye and rode off with Jones, Graham, Mason, and the dragoons toward Conn's ferry above Great Falls. But the ferryman said no one could cross the roaring Potomac, and the President had to spend the night in Mr. Conn's house. Jones returned to Wiley's Tavern to help the women and children. At dawn Madison's party crossed tumultuous waters. They reached Montgomery Courthouse about six that evening. But the army had left for Frederick.

Though Madison had lived in the saddle almost four days, he pressed stubbornly on. Darkness overtook him at the Quaker village of Brookeville, and he found a warm welcome at the white clapboard home of Caleb and Henrietta Bentley. The daughters of Samuel Harrison Smith, who happened to be refugees at the same house, called the situation that night "novel and interesting." When the President arrived,

> "all hands went to work to prepare supper and lodging for him, his companions and guards . . . beds were spread in the parlor, the house was filled and guards placed round the house during the night. A large troop of horse also arrived and encamped for the night. . . . The fires they kindled . . . and the lights within the tents had a beautiful appearance. All the villagers, gentlemen and ladies, . . . thronged to see the President. He was as tranquil as usual, and though much distressed by the dreadful event which had taken place, not dispirited."

After a ten o'clock supper he sent to the army bivouac to ask Monroe if he should follow at once, summoned Campbell and Armstrong from Frederick, then sank into bed.

The next morning brought electrifying news. The invaders had retreated toward their ships. By midnight they had herded sixty head of stolen cattle as far as Bladensburg. Madison passed the news back to Dolley, adding that he and Rush would start for Washington at once. She should do the same. He didn't know where they could lay their heads.

Monroe galloped up to report that Winder had gone to Baltimore; other officers would have to take the District militia home. And Madison spent another day in the saddle.

When he reached Washington about five o'clock in the afternoon, a citizens' committee had just finished burying the 200 dead the British had left behind. A hundred or so British wounded were being cared for. Not more than 50 Americans had died. Madison lost no time inspecting the gutted government buildings. The Presidential Mansion was a smoke-blackened, roofless shell with a gaping hole in its northeast wall. Fortunately the Marine Barracks, Foxall's Foundry, and most private houses still stood.

Later, Madison heard a loud cannonading downriver, followed by an explosion. A British attack on Fort Washington? In Winder's and Armstrong's absence, Madison gave Monroe temporary command of the army. They must be ready for anything.

Sunday morning, August 28, the President met with all available Cabinet members to plan strategy. There was much to do. Arriving late, Secretary Jones reported that he had put Mrs. Madison into the care of Clerk Edward Duvall and some dragoons. She still had her carriage. It was not too unreassuring. Then more bad news. Most of the books belonging to Congress had been destroyed; warships had been sighted near Mount Vernon; and Alexandria wanted to capitulate to avoid being sacked. Madison found that Anna had returned home from the Forrests' farm in Maryland. And he wrote Dolley a new note to say the situation was unclear. If the British reinvaded Washington, she would be forced to retire again, and that would have a "disagreeable effect"—better stay away until further notice. "Ever and affectionately yours."

When Alexandria's white flag did not prevent looting, Washingtonians argued about their own dilemma. Some would throw up their hands, others fight to the death. Mrs. Thornton's diary: "I lent Mr. M. a spyglass. The people are violently irritated at the thought of our attempting to make any more futile resistance. . . . Dr. T. followed the President and party to tell them what the people said."

Near the ruins of the Capitol he had designed, the Doctor, catching up with Madison, told him the people had had enough; they were ready to send a deputation to the British commander to surrender. Madison forbade it. All-out resistance! At his urging, he said, Monroe had chosen artillery positions at the wrecked Navy Yard and on the river path to George Town. Who were "the people" being quoted? A tiny minority! Thornton began to harangue Monroe, who also froze him out. Any deputation that took a step toward the enemy, said the Acting Secretary of War, would be stopped by bayonets. Angry, Dr. Thornton went home, strapped on a sword, and upset Anna Maria by swearing he would "call the people and join them."

Returning to the Cuttses, Madison embraced Dolley. She had not received his second note. On reading the earlier one from Brookeville, she had disguised herself and with Mr. Duvall and the dragoons ridden toward Washington. On finding the long wooden bridge burned at both ends, they had requested ferry passage, but Colonel Fenwick, who was using the one intact barge to transport munitions, had refused until she removed her disguise. He consented quickly.

Later Dolley would write Mrs. Latrobe about her three-day exile and return, saying she cannot express what she felt on seeing the widespread destruction and the British fleet, in plain sight, plundering Alexandria. En route to Anna's she passed her wrecked and soot-smeared home. It was heartbreaking.

Even refinding Jemmy did not cure a deep melancholy. According to Margaret Smith, "Mrs. M. seemed much depressed. She could scarcely speak without tears. . . ." When she was told the full extent of the damage, her words became uncharacteristically bitter. When Mrs. Smith and Mrs. Thornton dropped by after tea, they found her "very violent against the English," and when some troops passed, she cried out that she wished they had "10,000 such men . . . *to sink our enemy to the bottomless pit.*" Mrs. Thornton was suffering her own sour aftertaste. A diary entry: "She had better attribute the loss of her palace to the right cause, viz, want of proper defense in time."

But Monroe agreed instantly with Mrs. Madison. He said the British from highest to lowest were "all damned rascals!" Throughout the city passions were running high.

Dolley's high pitch of anguish was not lowered by an *Intelligencer* report, printed on borrowed presses, that the chicken-serving Mrs. Suter had recognized General Ross as a man who had (this is very hard to believe) called on Mrs. Madison in the disguise of an afflicted woman *the Saturday preceding the invasion.*

Some citizens thought the unhoused government should go back to Philadelphia, but Madison opposed the idea.

Then the fresh mortification of hearing that Captain Dyson had been so afraid armed British ships would take Fort Washington, he had blown it up without firing a shot. Irate citizens swore he should be cashiered. He was.

That night, around the Cutts house, eleven dragoons bedded down on straw to guard the President, and the umbrageous *Federal Republican* got its chance. "Little Jemmy . . . procured respectable citizens of Virginia to lie down like dogs . . . before brother and pensioner Cutts's door." But most people thought the country would be ill served by the capture or assassination of their President. Indeed four Federalists, headed by Hanson of the *Federal Republican,* called to warn him of British designs against his person.

On Monday he called another Cabinet meeting. As the members

discussed the rape of Washington, the British in Alexandria were loading their seventh confiscated vessel with plunder.

The President—just in case—ordered Commodore Rodgers to bring 650 Baltimore seamen to the Potomac above George Town.

Covering his sadness, he rode about the city. There was some show of disaffection, but most citizens gave him enthusiastic support. Sympathy for him was growing, factions uniting. "Our good President," wrote banker John Barnes, "is out animating the troops and encouraging the citizens not to despair." Madison steeled himself to walk through the charred hulk of the Presidential Mansion. It would take a long time for it to be rebuilt; he and Dolley would never live there again. Five years of memories swept through his mind—thirteen, really, for he and Dolley had stayed there a great deal during Jefferson's administration. But they must look to the future.

Next, he visited the military headquarters at Windmill Point to inspect and confer.

He had returned to the Cuttses' when General Walter Smith galloped up to report that every officer had sworn to tear off his epaulets rather than serve an hour longer under Secretary of War John Armstrong, "willing cause" of the town's disaster. Just after the President left Windmill Point, Armstrong had dropped by and offered his hand to Charles Carroll, who had spurned it and denounced him. The episode had triggered a general repudiation. "But under any other member of the Cabinet," said Smith, "the most cheerful duty will be rendered." The President replied that the contingency would not happen.

That night Madison confronted Armstrong. "You cannot be un-aware," he said, "that violent prejudices exist against the administration as having failed in its duty . . . particularly against me and yourself as head of the War Department." There were even threats of personal violence, especially against Armstrong. And the President conveyed Smith's message.

Armstrong called the repudiation the child of intrigue and falsehood. His sole purpose had been to serve the public, he said. He was ready to resign—or else, with permission, to visit his family in Red Hook, New York.

Because it seemed a bad time for a resignation—it could draw fire—Madison agreed to a Red Hook leave, while warning Armstrong that this temporary withdrawal might be made permanent. The General argued back. He said he had defended Washington by every means "enjoined on him." Madison answered dryly that a Secretary of War should devise as well as execute plans. "It is due truth and myself to say that for the defense of the capital you have never proposed . . . a single precaution. Everything along that line I brought forward. Because of the divergency of our views, and to preclude a worse than reluctant execution, I reduced my arrangements to a minimum."

It was a fact. But inwardly Madison excoriated himself for not having overridden his War Secretary more often or, better, dismissed him outright. It was a hard thought that he had appointed this bungler out of respect for talents displayed as a soldier as well as envoy, had treated him as a friend and, to promote harmony, tolerated the intolerable. No question: it had been a wrong course. Vital goals were jeopardized. Trying to maintain peace with everyone was a weakness. He had overruled Armstrong to bring the Virginia militia into Washington, and overruled Winder to send Barney's seamen to Bladensburg, but he knew, now, that he should have done more overruling in the emergency; realized it with sharp regret. Tight-lipped, Madison ordered Armstrong to start north tomorrow.

The situation demanded the President's best efforts, not the weaknesses of his strengths.

Seeing Jemmy reproach himself, Dolley understood out of her own experience. She too had sometimes permitted herself to be imposed on or talked out of something, only to see this fault of oversoftness, overkindness, fall hard on herself and others.

Several days later Armstrong, holed up in Baltimore, published a defiant apologia as full of distortions as Secretary Smith's. He was resigning, he wrote in the *Baltimore Patriot*. After an ultimatum from some Army officers, the President had advised him to take a temporary absence, to which he had replied that he would never yield to an "impulse so vile and profligate" as the humors of a village mob. When he offered his resignation on the spot, the President had refused it, saying he was aware of the Secretary's "zeal, diligence and talent." Since leaving Washington he had learned that previous to that interview, Hanson had procured the President's promise to remove him as director of the District's defenses. "On this fact all commentary is unnecessary," he wrote, as if the uproar were purely political. Afterward a two-sentence resignation went to Madison.

Reprinting Armstrong's statement, editor Hanson wrote after the passage about himself, "FALSE."

Secretary Jones summed up the case against Armstrong: "With much cunning, an insufferable degree of vanity, a caustic pithy pen, and the affectation of military science, this man has imposed himself upon society without one useful or valuable quality. . . . He has gone and has told his story which is as destitute of candor as of truth."

Meanwhile the British had left Alexandria, their ships loaded with such commodities as flour, beef, sugar, tobacco, cotton, and tar. There was no hint as to where they would turn up next. Washington? Norfolk? Philadelphia? Baltimore?

Because Baltimore, the "pirates' nest" whose privateers had done in some 500 British ships, seemed most likely, Acting Secretary of War Monroe sent it Winder's regulars, numerous regiments of militia, and Commodore Rodgers. The burning of Washington and looting of Alexandria had stung the nation into a rage for vengeance. Volunteers were pouring in.

About now Madison heard from Robert, son of his brother General William Madison. For a long time, this intelligent, sensitive youth had been close to his Uncle and Aunt Madison and Cousin Payne. (Once he had written Dolley, who shared his love of poetry, that her kindness had created a feeling which would last until his heart "ceases to throb.") And Madison had put his nephew through Dickinson College in Carlisle, Pennsylvania. Robert's letter said that on learning of the destruction at Washington he and fifteen other students had rushed to volunteer.

The Madisons would hear another gratifying story. In a boat cabin on the Hudson, someone wondered aloud, sarcastically, what Jemmy Madison was saying now. Burst out Washington Irving, "Sir, do you seize on disaster to sneer? . . . The country's . . . disgraced by this barbarous success. Every loyal citizen should feel the ignominy and be eager to avenge it"—and the ring of strangers murmured approval.

But some critics could not be muzzled. They damned Armstrong for bumbling, Jones for ordering the Navy Yard burned, Winder for exhausting his troops before battle with "senseless" countermarching. As for President Madison, he was fit only for impeachment—"resign! resign!" One day a Federalist's wife drove to the Cutts door in an open carriage, stood up, loosened her famous long hair, and prayed loudly for the privilege of cutting it off so that it could be used to make a rope with which to hang the President.

Dispatches from the North increased Madison's burden. At Plattsburg 2,500 were bracing to battle twice their number, and though the American brig which he had ordered built on Lake Champlain was nearing completion, so was a British warship.

Hating the British "rogues and savages" was more popular, these days, than reading Sir Walter Scott or drinking peach brandy. Madison locked his mouth.

Near the end of August Monroe received a letter from Vice Admiral

Cochrane dated several days *before the British invasion.* He wrote that in "retaliation" for American outrages in Canada, it was his duty to lay waste coastal towns and districts; they would be spared only if the President made amends.

Not for a moment was the Administration fooled. Obviously the letter had been held back or left unwritten until now in order to keep the Capital from improving its defenses before the invasion, and in order to blacken Madison for failing to save the city though "warned." Madison replied to the trick with a proclamation denying American outrages in Canada and accusing Britain of destroying precious archives and public buildings out of sheer malice. Let Americans unite to expel the invader.

At the same time, he asked Secretary Monroe to write Cochrane ridiculing his claim that the British attack was retaliatory. In contrast to Cockburn's systematic rapine, Monroe pointed out, the United States had not only disavowed the burning of Newark but actually court-martialed the officers who destroyed Dover. The President had always worked for reciprocal reparations for lawless damage. Cockburn's ravages showed "deep-rooted hostility" and would be met as became a "free people contending in a just cause for their essential rights and their dearest interests."

Madison and Monroe were on solid ground. Britain's deliberate burning of Buffalo, Black Rock, and Lewiston had more than balanced out the unauthorized burning of Dover. As for the firing of the little wooden parliament building at York, no evidence connects it with American troops. To the contrary. On capturing the top United States officer there, the British, far from punishing him for an outrage, had paroled him for protecting British property. And the York citizenry, while praising the Americans for behaving better than expected, had blamed the fire on traitorous *Canadians.* Moreover, in itemizing the edifices he destroyed in Washington, General Ross had boasted of accomplishing the "object of the expedition," of having carried out his orders. Cochrane also confessed as much when he answered Monroe's letter by saying, "Until I *receive instructions from my Government* the measures which I have adopted must be persisted in."

Their motive would be laid bare by the soldier-historian Gleig, who fought at Bladensburg, when he lamented that insufficient troops kept Ross from doing elsewhere what he had done to Washington, such methods being the only way to defeat a democracy, Gleig said—"burn their houses, plunder their property, block up their harbors, and destroy their shipping in a few places. . . ." Behind this will to victory by any means lay a kind of contempt for Britain's erstwhile colonies, trade jealousies, and anger over American sea successes. The British Cabinet and certain members of Parliament would defend the barbarity. Not all. One citizen recalled in shame that the Goths, on conquering Rome, had refrained from harming public buildings.

Meanwhile, Dr. William Thornton had been accused of cowardice. The people he had quoted as wanting to surrender—who were they? The fools who listened to *him?* Amid charges and countercharges, Thornton replied in the *National Intelligencer.* Though he was willing to give his life for his country, he said, facts were facts. What could a loyal citizen do when there were not enough trained soldiers or arms, and no real plan for the city's defense? The next day, after talking with Mrs. Cutts and Mrs. Madison, Anna Maria noted that these old friends were "not pleased."

The doctor's self-defense triggered a free-for-all in the *Intelligencer.* Mayor Blake, Commandant Tingey, Commodore Rodgers, Dr. Ewell, General Winder, Secretary Monroe, and President Madison all pitched in. Thornton turned the accusation of cowardice back onto Mayor Blake for having discovered that he had business outside Washington that fatal day. Blake's *non sequitur:* Thornton's reputation as a poet had been blown up out of nothing.

A jocular anonymous ballad—"The Bladensburg Races"—impugned the President's horsemanship, which was excellent, and courage, which was great.

Confusing facts, the jingle has Dolley fleeing with the Cuttses to Montgomery Courthouse. Here is the start of this mean yet harmless ribbing:

> James Madison a soldier was
>   Of courage and renown. . . .

Then it goes satiric. Screaming for his sword and "shappo-hat"—chapeau, a jab at his "Frenchness"—Madison gallops off ahead of his Cabinet. When a bugler startles his horse, it jumps out of control. Hunching down, Madison hangs onto its mane with both hands, "gall'd in his seat," sword thumping, cloak billowing out behind. When a button burst he loses the cloak. Armstrong, Monroe, and Rush shout, "Stop, there, your Excellency! *stop!*" "Our hero" keeps riding. At Bladensburg he finds Winder's troops beaten and requests that fire be withheld until the Presidential party has gone. At a roar of cannon, his horse bolts again. This time it never stops until—bump, bump—he catches up with his wife at Montgomery Courthouse. On he flies from the guns—on, on to Frederick. . . .

> Now long live *Madison* the brave!
> And *Armstrong*, long live he!
> And *Rush!* and *Cutts! Monroe!* and *Jones!*
> And *Dolley*, long live *She!*

It was a travesty. Most of the country—the great exception was New England—had trusted Madison during the crisis, and still trusted him. Knowledge of this loyalty comforted him as the government struggled to put a roof over its head.

The *Intelligencer* announced new locations. The Congress would move to Blodgett's Hotel, State to Judge Duvall's, Treasury to Foster's old residence in the Seven Buildings, the War Office next to the Bank of the Metropolis, the Navy to Mr. Mechlin's, the Post Office to new construction, and the President and Mrs. Madison—as soon as Sérurier could reclaim Kalorama—to Colonel Tayloe's Octagon House at 18th and New York Avenue.

The resettlements had hardly begun when Washington heard that about fifty British ships had anchored on the Patapsco River below Baltimore. Two days later some 8,000 redcoats disembarked.

The nation suffered acutely. Would Baltimore balk the British or be ravaged and destroyed? There was no rest at the Cutts home. While nursing Anna, who was nearing childbirth, Dolley was trying to cope with five active children: Mad, aged nine; Tom, nearly eight; Wat, six; ailing little Dicky, four and a half; Dolley, three. Superintendent of Military Supplies Cutts labored day and night, and Madison had a war on his hands.

One day Dolley saw the Rev. John Breckenridge passing the house, the Federalist preacher who, before the invasion, had warned that governmental crimes would doom Washington, like Nineveh, to a fiery punishment.

"Little did I think, sir," she called, half serious, half jesting, "when I heard that threatening sermon, that your prophecies would be fulfilled so soon."

"Oh, Madam," he said devoutly, "I trust this chastening of the Lord will not be in vain."

Suddenly news. Fort McHenry had withstood a brutal battering.

Baltimore was "rolling back upon the foe the storm of war." Ross—the General who had never matched Cockburn's savagery—lay dead. American militia under General Sam Smith had routed "Wellington's Invincibles." Cockburn's ships were fleeing down the Patapsco. A disgrace to American arms had been avenged. Britain's Chesapeake campaign had collapsed.

On September 16, amid wild rejoicing, Anna gave birth to Mary Estelle Elizabeth Cutts.

To Dolley the tiny creature was there to "increase their loves." Though, during twenty years, she had gradually lost hope of a child by James, her career as an aunt had burgeoned with multitudinous nieces and nephews. But it was Anna's brood which she regarded as most her own, and the new little daughter need not cry—the British had got their comeuppance.

On the heels of the victory at Baltimore came fabulous news of a victory at Plattsburg. On Lake Champlain, Americans had captured two sloops, one frigate, and one brig and sent General Prevost's army of 14,000 (all but the deserters) fleeing back to Canada. The battle's importance could hardly be overestimated. Defeat would have laid open the entire Hudson River Valley and given the foe a chance to cut off New England.

Madison was privately thankful he had overruled Jones to order the brig *Eagle* built in haste. Within a month its hull had been fashioned from newly cut timbers and it was ready to perform.

Now America had fresh words for the old tune "Anacreon in Heaven."

Approaching the British on a truce boat to plead for a friend's release, a young lawyer—Francis Scott Key—had been held prisoner during the bombardment of Fort McHenry. Until the sun went down he watched the battle, then all night. The success or failure of the whole American war effort might hinge on the outcome. As bombs exploded in nets of brilliance, he prayed that at daybreak the American flag would still be flying, and he scribbled some words on an envelope. Several weeks later a song was being played on pianos, guitars, and fiddles. Rash singers even dared the high notes:

> O say can you see by the dawn's early light
> What so proudly we hailed at the twilight's last gleaming. . . .
> O say does that star-spangled banner yet wave
> O'er the land of the free and the home of the brave?

❧ XIV ❧

OCTAGON HOUSE
AND THE TREATY
OF GHENT

THE OCTAGON HOUSE—not in size but quality—compared favorably with the President's mansion. Designed by Dr. William Thornton as a town place for Colonel John Tayloe, it had been completed in 1800 ahead of the Great House, and it was a gem, a little jewel. The Madisons had long known it socially. Now, while their wrecked house was being repaired, it would serve as a miniature "palace."

Its geometry was unique. Like many beautiful things it had an element of strangeness. Forced to fit the house into a V-shaped "ship's-prow" of a lot, the architect had achieved a rare individuality.

It is not an octagon. The word "eight-sided" fits it only if the semicircular front is by license considered a side, and the wall out of which it swells is counted as two. Actually the structure is a sexagon with a rounded protuberance. Inside, the first floor has a circular foyer, a hall with a wonderfully graceful staircase, a rectangular canted drawing room, and a balancing dining room; on the second floor, a round study above the foyer, and two splayed bedrooms, the gaps between these odd shapes being used for closets, pantries, and a stairway going down to the servants' quarters.

The Madisons brought their few salvaged belongings to this "Executive Annex" and opened its shutters. Because the drawing room and dining room were pygmy-sized compared to those in the big burned

house on Pennsylvania Avenue, Dolley's entertaining had to be cut down.
It was a relief.

(Once at the Octagon a dinner guest was unusually late. Quipped Dr.
William Thornton, always quick with repartee and teasing, "Mr. Magruder, you are an intruder." "You lie," shot back Magruder. "Mr. Magruder," said Thornton, who stuttered when excited, "you are ruder and
ruder!" Getting cruder, Magruder knocked Thornton down. Astonished,
the mercurial doctor picked himself up. "Damn the fellow," he said. "He
doesn't understand wit.")

Madison's problems were multiplying. On September 19 Congress
reconvened in a testy mood to deal with the President's "radical" recom-
mendations: conscription, a double land bounty for soldiers, and a second
United States Bank. He conferred with groups and individuals and
struggled to cope with New England sedition, a financial crisis, the
rebuilding of public edifices, and the threat of a British attack on New
Orleans. Secretary of the Navy Jones was leaving his post. Alexander
Dallas had refused the Treasury, and Armstrong must be replaced as War
Secretary. Another difficult task was to draw up new instructions for the
Commissioners at Ghent. Though the American victories at Baltimore,
Plattsburg, and Lundy's Lane had raised everyone's spirits, James Madi-
son was a badgered man.

Early in October, attaché George Dallas arrived with dispatches from
the Peace Commission. Five weeks of conferring had produced nothing.
The Madisons asked him why Payne had not come too; circumstances
having changed, he should have come. Young Dallas said this had been
the plan, but Payne's three weeks in Paris had stretched to three months,
and when Mr. Gallatin asked him to sail on the *John Adams,* he had said he
couldn't, he was waiting to be presented to the King, but no, the rumor
was wrong, he was not in love with a French lady.

Whether or not Dallas told the Madisons, there was more to the story
of Payne in Paris. Gallatin had received troubling reports from the
American legation. Minister Crawford wrote that Todd was so dissipated,
he was helping no one, least of all himself. Determined that Payne should
go home to America with Dallas, Gallatin got him a passport and wrote
him as follows:

> Permit me . . . to urge the propriety of your leaving Paris where
> you have remained long enough for every useful purpose. . . . I
> would be very sorry that either your property should be injured
> or your time improperly wasted by your trip to Europe; and you

must ascribe my anxiety solely to my attachment to you, your mother, and Mr. Madison.

Payne replied that in a few days he would be presented at Court, then leave. He thanked his mentor for expressions of attachment but confessed that he was pained to perceive "the very bounded confidence you have of my prudence and good sense." Two weeks later he was still enjoying Paris. He had planned to leave tomorrow, he wrote, but had now heard that his presentation to Louis XVIII would be further delayed. Gallatin was outdone.

Even if Dallas used a soft pedal on this story, the Madisons were bound to ask questions. Given the licentiousness of French society, there were unpleasant possibilities they were too intelligent to ignore.

Actually Payne's downward course had started in Russia, and since Dallas had no reason to conceal an earlier chapter which could only evoke sympathy from Payne's parents, he probably enlightened his listeners.

The story as it has come down: Last fall in St. Petersburg, Payne, treated grandly by royalty because of his relation to the President of the United States, had fallen in love with and become betrothed to the Countess Olga. Years later a relative privy to the secret would testify that the young woman "was mysteriously abducted from him and never again heard of, because she was the daughter of a royal father and was about to marry an American citizen. This disappointed and soured the man's life." If true, the rejection would explain his sudden departure from St. Petersburg and perhaps the heavy drinking into which he slid.

As for the word "royal" as applied to the young lady's father, it may simply mean noble or aristocratic. There were so many Olgas at Court, it is hard to get to the bottom of this matter, but it seems unlikely that the story was made up out of whole cloth. Certainly an immense change took place in Payne, and in Paris he drank and gambled recklessly. Another thing is sure. If the Madisons heard about a Russian jilting, they were deeply disturbed.

Whatever his private worries, the President kept working on Troy's battlements. People who had despaired after the burning of Washington were heartened by the rapidity with which he moved to better the situation.

The lack of a peace treaty did not strike him as disadvantageous. "If the English force us to continue the war," he told the new French Chargé, Roth, repeating an earlier prediction, "they will make us do in ten years what we perhaps would not [otherwise] do in half a century." And more and more visibly the conflict was forcing industrial development. Furthermore, by publishing his instructions to Gallatin, Madison juxtaposed black against white, British orneriness against American reasonableness.

Meantime he was keeping an eye on General Andrew Jackson, for a battle loomed at New Orleans. With Britain's Chesapeake campaign aborted at Baltimore and her Lake Champlain one ended at Plattsburg, it seemed that the United States must expect, at the gateway to the Mississippi, the recoil of a great power. A British expedition had set sail from Jamaica.

General Jackson was Scotch-Irish, able, tough, irascible, and, when goaded, violent—this man who commanded 9,000 militiamen from Kentucky, Tennessee, and Georgia. He hated the British with all the strength of his nature, if only because he bore the scar of a saber cut received when, as a fourteen-year-old Revolutionary prisoner, he had refused to black a British officer's boots.

In October he reported that in East Florida the Union Jack was flying alongside the Spanish flag, and the British recruiting Indians. It seemed sinister. Madison forbade him to embroil the United States. But the President was not noticeably displeased when in November Jackson blew up some forts at Pensacola, fought the British to a standstill, and gave the country back to the Spaniards before marching off to Mobile. There he sank a British frigate, then moved on to New Orleans looking for a foe worth his mettle.

The Northern menace was different. In New England smuggling had increased. American cattle were feeding the Canadian army. Massachusetts continued to flout war loans and requisitions, and it stoned law-enforcement officers—this in spite of the fact that Britain had stolen its district of Maine. (Cutts was worried about his Maine property.) Madison wondered if Connecticut's proposal for an independent New England army was prelude to secession. A convention was being called at Hartford to discuss a "radical reform in the national compact."

After he talked with the President about such problems, William Wirt wrote his wife: "He looks miserably shattered and woe-begone. In short . . . broken-hearted. His mind is full of the New England situation." Though he approved of Madison, Wirt was shocked by the "vast crowd of legislators and gentlemen of the turf assembled for the races. . . . The races!—amid the ruins and desolation of Washington." And he grieved over the Presidential Mansion's "unroofed naked walls cracked, defaced and blackened with fire." To think that the House of Representatives was sitting in a "miserable little narrow box."

The harassed President who had defied Britain did not flinch before dissident Federalists. Though Sérurier was probably somewhat biased, this taking of the Administration's measure, as reported to Paris, cannot be dismissed:

> ... It is a just matter for astonishment that a government so badly armed should be able to fight alone, and with success, against a nation as powerful as England, in the midst of continual obstacles of every kind which cramp its resources, and with so active a hostile faction at the heart of the nation. This proves beyond reply the great firmness of the President and the wisdom of the counsel he is given.

Madison never ceased to be astonished at the way Federalists ignored the logic of circumstances. Because New England produced little, he felt certain that its future lay with war-fostered manufacturing, and obviously manufacturing, trade, and transportation required the rest of the country. Yet here were some blind, foolish New England Federalists trying to pull away from the Union—incredible. He blamed pigheaded leaders. As he wrote Wilson Cary Nicholas: "You are not mistaken in viewing the conduct of the Eastern States as the source of our greatest difficulties in carrying on the war, as it certainly is the greatest, if not the sole, inducement with the enemy to persevere in it." But in spite of the indictment, he planned no overt move and was careful not to exacerbate disaffection. However libeled, he permitted himself no personal pique; what mattered was the Union. He must keep awake to all possibilities. "The best may be hoped, but the worst ought to be kept in view."

While he was wrestling with these problems, olive-skinned Sally Coles came to spend her fourth winter with them. Dolley's cousin was not beautiful, but intelligent, witty, loving, fashionable. She was one of the young ladies Dolley liked to pretend were her daughters. Through the Octagon House floated airy conversation and laughter. The older woman and the younger one talked family, embroidered, pored over fashion pictures, and, putting on their bonnets, made rounds of calls in a reddish brown carriage with silver monograms.

Lucy's high-spirited letters were passed around in the family. One to pregnant Anna is typical. "Never, my dear Anna, did I expect you to grow *so big a lady* or so very fashionable a one as to entirely forget your kin and kind." Lamenting her "exile," she rattles on, her love of life not unlike Dolley's, though Dolley was finer-grained. She wishes she were "out of the scrape." If she gets a girl, "Madisonia's nose will be out of joint but we must submit to our fate, so let us do it handsomely." Send her "a little city scandal." The Judge, after his stroke, is beginning to walk "tolerably straight."

In November the Madisons were waiting for news of Lucy's latest child when they had the surprised joy of a "dear Papa" letter from Payne, written October 9 at Ghent. The situation remains "uncertain." Mr. Gallatin had planned to send dispatches by the *Jenny* but decided it might cause a "wavering of opinion" as to the final result of the negotiations. The matter has been "extremely dilatory." The British Commissioners refer every point back to their government, whether from incompetence or a wish to gain time for further judgments or exploits—"you who are well acquainted with their policy can decide." It will be November at least before the parley ends. Payne has gathered that Mr. Gallatin finds it difficult to raise any part of that low-interest loan in Europe. Then a fine personal message to be read and reread (surely its clarity proved that all was well with him?):

> We received ten days ago the very painful intelligence of the destruction of the public buildings in Washington. This barbarous act meets with universal excoriation. It has induced the Paris journals for the first time to come forth against what were supposed to be the inclinations of the British Government. . . . My absence from Washington I most deeply regret if for no other reason [than that] I might at least have been useful to you and my mother. I shall have an opportunity to write her by the *Herald.* . . .
>
> Yours affectionately—

He enclosed French papers and a manuscript article whose author he took to be Germaine de Staël, "who requests me to make known to you her high respect."

The reference to Madame de Staël suggests the outré company in which Payne had been traveling. At forty-eight this daughter of the great financier Necker was a famous author and hostess. Napoleon had exiled her, but Louis XVIII called her back. Having met Payne in St. Petersburg, she had welcomed him to Paris, and Rosco, her twenty-two-year-old second husband, near Payne's age, had helped introduce the tall, sveltely uniformed, French-speaking, dashing Colonel Todd to the cream of French society.

As a man of the world he now wished to be known by a different name (had he always hated "Payne"?), and signed himself to Madison as to Gallatin: "John P. Todd."

His letter delighted Dolley—its intelligence, openness, hint of social successes, loving consideration. She did not know left-out details such as Payne's heavy drinking and all-night card games on the Veldstraat in Ghent, at which he had won big money from Jonathan Russell before his roommate Henry Clay wiped him out.

Ghent, the medieval Flemish capital, was a city of clothspinners and flowers. After Gothenburg, St. Petersburg, Copenhagen, Amsterdam, Liverpool, London, and Paris, Payne was not greatly excited about its quaint houses and renowned fifty-two-bell carillon. Dolley saw and heard vicariously. So her son would soon be sailing on the *Neptune!* At long last!

About this time Vice President Elbridge Gerry died in a coach, and even before his funeral, a fight broke out for his office. Wasting no kindness, the *Winchester Gazette* assured its readers that even democrats wished Madison were "quietly asleep with the late vice president"—lower case.

The last leaves were eddying down. It was almost winter. The Madisons looked through bare branches to Tiber Creek as the first snow began to fall.

Former President John Adams, one of New England's Federalists but out of step, wrote Madison crying, "All I can say is that I would continue this war forever rather than surrender one acre of territory, one iota of the fisheries . . . or one sailor impressed from any ship. . . . It is the decree of Providence, as I believe, that this nation must be purified in the furnace of affliction."

Continue this war the Americans would, but there was no news from General Jackson. Flooding rivers had cut off all communications with New Orleans. What was going on?

One day Dolley wrote Mrs. Latrobe about the destruction of the "house where Mr. Latrobe's elegant taste had been so justly admired, and where you and I"—nostalgically—"so often wandered together." Recalling the bitter invasion, she mentions how she "sent out the silver (nearly all), the velvet curtains and General Washington's picture, the Cabinet papers, a few books, and the small clock—left everything else belonging to the public, our own valuable stores of every description, a part of my clothes, and all my servants' clothes, etc., etc." It would fatigue her friend to read the entire list of their losses. She had not been afraid; she had been "willing to remain in the *Castle*. If I could have had a cannon through every window, but alas! those who should have placed them there fled before me, and my whole heart mourned for my country. . . ." The tragedy was still with Dolley. She could not shake it off.

The Octagon was pleasant, and life in general ran smoothly. She was only sorry that the drainage around the house was so poor, it made the brick-floored basement rather damp for the servants.

All day visitors used the stair to Madison's circular study: smartly clad military men and civilians of all kinds. In the new Cabinet, Alexander Dallas had finally taken the Treasury; Ben W. Crowninshield had the Navy, Monroe the War office, and they all rejoiced that six American squadrons were seriously hurting British trade from Ireland to China. On the other side of the ledger, the December 15 opening of the Hartford Convention's secret deliberations posed a threat. Also, people were grasping for sinecures, and Congress had killed both the conscription bill and Dallas's national bank, and there was a growing financial crisis. But Madison saw such setbacks as challenges. Let the *London Times* call Washington City a "nest of vipers" and the President's attitude "mulish obstinacy." Madison marshaled facts to prove that England's aim was to make—as he wrote—"English navigation and markets the medium through which, alone, the different parts of the world should exchange their superfluities and supply their wants": in other terms, a world monopoly.

Christmas brought neither Payne, Lucy, nor brother John—just a Canadian announcement that Assistant Quartermaster John C. Payne of the Seventh Division had married Clara Wilcox, whose parents hailed from New York. Startled, the Madisons began to long to meet John's wife—as logs crackled and eggnog was ladled out.

They had no inkling that British Foreign Secretary Castlereagh, hearing about Baltimore and Plattsburg and counting Britain's 1,500 lost merchant ships, had already made a decision which, if known in America, would have turned Christmas into a wild boisterous celebration. As it was, thousands of Americans were asking if 1815 would put an end to the war which—against stubborn Federalist opposition—Madison and his party had seen and still saw as obligatory.

At the President's New Year reception Dolley, as usual, stretched out her hand and said the right word at the right moment: foil for a husband who sometimes seemed absent while present. Their fortitude was still being tested.

They understood Mrs. Gallatin's mood when she wrote, "My spirits [are] so much depressed . . . [by] disappointment in not seeing my beloved husband. . . . The prospect of peace appears to get darker." The Hartford junta had denounced Madison as a violator of the Constitution. "The bond of Union is broken." And rumor said Spain might cede the Floridas to America's foe, England. And at New Orleans fifty British warships with 10,000 veteran fighters were crossing Lake Pontchartrain while Jackson's 5,000 regulars and militiamen tensely awaited reinforcements.

For five days the Madisons bore the suspense as best they could. There was no sitting around wringing their hands; they kept busy. But had Jackson received his reinforcements? Had the two armies clashed?

January 13 brought only Baton Rouge's report that it had seen Tennessee and Kentucky militiamen floating down the Mississippi. It had heard that Jackson had clamped New Orleans down under martial law. After this intelligence, again a wall of silence built up, and torrential rains continued to throw the raging Tennessee River out of its banks. At last, on the twentieth, a fillip. There had been skirmishing.

The next evening two dozen guests had gathered in the Octagon's drawing room when a servant called Madison out for the New Orleans post. Twenty-three-year-old George Tichnor would record that when the President returned, he said there was no news, and it was such a letdown, no one spoke.

When the company moved to the dining room, Tichnor edged toward the foot of the table. But Madison promoted him to a seat between himself and Dolley, and during dinner this young Federalist got one of the surprises of his life. The President was not as described in Boston. He was "free and open," initiating topics and, with a straight face as if inwardly chuckling, passing remarks that "savored of humor and levity." He played on the themes of education and internal improvements, then switched to religious sects, telling the young Bostonian he was "curious to know how the cause of liberal Christianity stood with us, and if the Athanasian creed was well received by our Episcopalians." Tichnor— instead of putting this down to a host's tact—thought Madison "pretty distinctly intimated . . . his own regard for the Unitarian doctrines." Because Tichnor's opinion goes against a great weight of testimony it must be attributed to the fact that it was easy and natural for this young emissary from a Unitarian stronghold to read into Madison's courteous respect for all religion what he would like to hear.

For all of Madison's open-minded theological probing, there is no solid evidence that he was other than loyal, in all basic respects, to the church to which he had belonged since baptism.

Though the military situation dominated his thoughts these days, other matters claimed some attention: the democratic county of Maine had decided to pull free from Massachusetts (to free itself from the "base thraldom of *traitors* and *cowards*"); the damaged *President* had been captured; and Hannah Gallatin agreed to sell the Madisons some stored furniture. But their minds went back to New Orleans as to a lodestar.

Five weeks after the battle Madison received an extraordinary dispatch.

All night, General Jackson wrote, the fog was so dense that both sides held their fire. Then from a position behind a 20-foot dry canal he had to drive off a fierce frontal assault. Its failure persuaded the British vanguard to wait for the main army. This delay won the Americans time to fortify the Chalmette canal before the arrival of 10,000 veterans under Major General Sir Edward Pakenham (Wellington's brother-in-law), seasoned troops *including the very redcoats who had burned Washington*. Behind 5-foot earthworks 5,500 American militiamen crouched around a core of regulars. There was also a sprinkling of blacks, creoles, pirates, and French Louisianians. On the other bank 4,500 militia awaited their baptism by fire. The issue would be decided between a cypress swamp and the Mississippi levee.

Jackson's report had been written before the fighting resumed. How had it ended?

A Federalist congressman knew "absolutely" that the government was concealing the capture of New Orleans, and newspapers were like a pack of hunting dogs raising a great hue and cry. Punish Madison! Impeach "this man if he deserves the name of man." Why hadn't the pride of Louisiana been properly defended? shrilled the *Federal Republican,* answering, "Go ask the wind." It said, "You might as well attempt to reanimate the clay cold tenants of a churchyard as to hope to make any impression on Mr. Madison. His heart is petrified and hard as marble. His body is torpid, and he is without feeling." The tirade was interrupted by news of Jackson's great victory.

People went crazy with joy. On a Saturday night bespangled by torches, lanterns, and bonfires, people shouted and danced, and strangers embraced. The nation had a new sense of solidarity—one nation indivisible.

The figures for the January 8 battle of New Orleans: 700 British killed, including three Generals, one of them Pakenham; 1,400 wounded; 500 captured—this in spectacular disparity against 7 Americans killed, 6 wounded. A few green militiamen had run away, but for the most part both sides fought with bold bravery. The Americans had met the enemy, Jackson reported, with a "fire so deliberate and certain as rendered their scaling ladders and fascines perfectly useless." The tidings were cool water for a dry throat. Now America had a new hero: hard-favored, lank, fierce, scraggle-haired Andrew Jackson in a battered cap, an old blue cloth Spanish jacket, and boots whose tall tops flapped, loose, around bony knees.

Madison pardoned Jean Lafitte's pirates of Barataria. An adventurer, the man had rejected a £30,000 bribe and a commission in the British Royal Navy to man artillery in defense of New Orleans. (Unfortunately he would revert to piracy.)

In the midst of the nation's rejoicing General Brown came to Washington to plan an offensive of 30,000 Vermont volunteers against Montreal. Invited out, he said thanks, but no frivolity. So the British had spiked their guns at midnight, at New Orleans, and stolen away! That was smart, said Brown—because from now till the signing of a peace treaty they would be granted no quarter. The army was no longer a brash youngster; it had come of age.

The country was still celebrating when a copy of the Treaty of Ghent reached New York. Immediately speculators streaked south hell-bent on buying up cotton and tobacco at war prices before peace sent prices soaring. But in Washington there were only rumors. The *Intelligencer* advised against listening to what might be false. But on February 14, 1815, a coach-and-four with foaming horses thundered down Pennsylvania Avenue. Inside, Clay's secretary, Henry Carroll, was clutching the greatest news since Yorktown. "Cheers followed the carriage."

Years later the mulatto Paul Jennings would describe the Octagon's heady hour. Upstairs in the round study Madison and his Cabinet were poring over the Ghent papers, "as pleased as any," Paul says, though they were celebrating less liquidly. The peace treaty as ratified by the Prince Regent for his "insane" father, George III, stated that all possessions and rights would revert to what they had been before the war—no gains, no losses.

Of course that was absurd. Everything had altered; nothing would ever be the same again. During the last two years and eight months—after a bad start—a new, despised nation had proved on land and sea that it could hold its own with the strongest. This had been true when the treaty was drawn up; now, after the victory at New Orleans, it was even more ringingly true. Impressment? Harassment of neutral trade? Whatever the treaty said or did not say about the outrages which had caused the war, the issues had been decided once and for all. Great Britain would not risk further humiliation; it would never again kick around its former colonies. Gains from the war were those prophesied by Madison; they ran a gamut from increased manufacturing to increased world respect.

While officials were deliberating upstairs, downstairs Dolley was dispensing the hospitality of the house. Many people, including members of Congress, were hurrying to the President's house. By eight the drawing room was crowded, Mrs. Madison with a grace all her own doing the honors. She was "the observed of all observers," a woman in the "meridian of life and queenly beauty," and "in her person, for the moment, the representative of the feelings of him who was in grave consultation. . . . No one could doubt, who beheld the radiance of joy which . . . diffused its beams around, that . . . the government . . . had in very truth (to use an expression of Mr. Adams . . .) 'passed from gloom to glory.'"

The room was an excited and exciting place. Gentlemen lately pitted against each other in "fierce debate" congratulated each other in high spirits, cordially, thanking God for "the joyful intelligence, which (should the terms prove acceptable) would re-establish peace."

Not that the upsurge of goodwill was entirely new. For months—in spite of some recalcitrance—the "Second War for Independence" had been slowly consolidating the United States, and tonight the Octagon's drawing room was a kind of a cross section of the country.

The First Lady had an extra reason to shine. She could buttonhole Henry Carroll to ask about Payne's part in the historic occasion at Ghent.

At four o'clock on December 24 the United States Commissioners had driven from the Lovendegram Hotel to the Chartreuse Monastery to go over the treaty, page by page, with the British diplomats. In the midst of signing and sealing this "Treaty of Peace and Amity," the bells of St. Bovan had rung out. Lord Gamblier and Mr. John Quincy Adams expressed their hope that this peace would prove permanent. The signing was followed by a thanksgiving service in the great cathedral, then a festive dinner at which they had eaten roast beef and plum pudding and sung "Yankee Doodle." It was a wonderful Christmas eve, and on Christmas day Payne himself gave a party to introduce Ghent to Virginia eggnog.

Dolley was enchanted.

Just after eight o'clock the President emerged. He endorsed the treaty terms as satisfactory. Rushing to the head of the servants' stair, Sally Coles called down, "Peace! Peace!" Break out the wine! Corks flew. Butler John Freeman poured liberally. Paul seized his fiddle and scraped "Mr. Madison's March." John Sióussat and a lot of folks got drunk for two days, "and such another joyful time was never seen in Washington."

That night, on the round table in the round study, President James

Madison signed the Treaty of Ghent. The next day the Senate ratified it without a dissenting vote.

These stirring events having happened within a week, Mrs. Thornton's diary is correspondingly staccato:

Feby 11. Saturday, Rockets fired for the evacuation of New Orleans—
13. Rumors of expresses announcing peace.
14. Mrs. Madison and Miss Coles called—H. Carroll arrived this evening bringing the Treaty.
15. We went to the Drawingroom, a crowd. George Town illuminated.
18. Treaty exchanged in the night of Friday—Cannons, rockets and illuminations tonight.

From Alexandria to Capitol Hill, the District of Columbia was shooting off cascades of stars.

There were different viewpoints. Three Federalists arriving from the Hartford Convention found their demands outmoded. But one thing was always timely: upbraiding the President. Harrison Gray Otis remembered that on their approach the little pygmy in the Octagon "shook in his shoes." But another New Englander offered this toast: "To the Commander-in-Chief of the Army and Navy of the United States: His patriotism and undaunted perseverance in a season of darkness and difficulty have been to his friends in the East like the 'shadow of a great rock in a weary land.'"

As to the President's own feelings, Senator Barry noted that "the glad tidings of peace procured by the glory of the American arms under his management . . . inspired him with new life and vigor." In reporting the treaty's ratification, Madison called the war's end as honorable as its beginning. A young insulted nation forced to claim its rights could review its conduct without regret or self-reproach. The emphasis on right conduct, for the nation with which he identified so closely, was Madisonian. To him the moral order was a living reality to which all social decisions, including the political, must relate.

Congratulations did not stop at the borders. The world marveled. To think that a new nation, starting with no navy, had won two out of every three naval encounters with the greatest sea power on earth, its privateers capturing nearly 2,000 trading vessels; had "stood the contest, single-handed, against the conqueror of Europe" and broken up three campaigns by veterans of the Napoleonic wars. Baltimore, Erie, Plattsburg, Lundy's lane, New Orleans: "splendid roster." The world noted a phenomenon which Sérurier called to the attention of his government: that the war had "given the Americans what they so essentially lacked, a national character founded on a glory common to all."

A national character. The Federalist phrase of reproach, "Mr. Madison's War," had become an accolade, and the President himself would in time make the best summing-up:

> If our first struggle was a war of our infancy, this last was that of our youth; and the issue of both, wisely improved, may long postpone, if not forever prevent, a necessity for exerting the strength of our manhood.

Great Britain itself understood that its former colonies, united, had become a world power. Said the *London Times* before the treaty signing, "Any peace we can now conclude must be disgraceful." After the "deadly instrument" was a fait accompli, it interpreted the Ministry's reference to a "Peace of Necessity" as meaning that "Russia or Prussia has avowed an inclination to support the innovations on public law which Mr. Madison asserts." In other words, Britain could no longer flout the rights of neutrals.

Quietly Madison turned from the problems of war to those of peace. His Special Message of February 18 recommended a regular army, a growing navy, training academies, a well-organized militia, further improvement of harbor defenses, promotion of manufacturing, and a wise handling of the $16 million war-caused deficit.

But the great new peace became a little unpeaceful.

Madison had to remind Congress that ever since 1812 the Dey of Algiers had been molesting United States shipping, and many Americans still lay rotting in African prisons. Enough was enough; Congress declared war on Algiers, and Commodore Stephen Decatur began preparing a squadron for the Mediterranean. By contrast with the late hard-slugging war, this one seemed a scuffle which the country could win with one hand tied behind its back.

Madison shook up his Cabinet. Monroe re-became, exclusively, Secretary of State. Crawford was summoned home to take the War office. Gallatin was appointed Minister to France; Bayard, Minister to Russia; John Quincy Adams to Great Britain.

The President's analysis of the causes of the War of 1812, written during the war, now received an international hearing. As developed by Dallas, leaked with Madison's blessing by Rush, and printed in the Philadelphia *Aurora,* it created a great stir. The *London Times* screamed libel—that scoundrel Madison ought to be hanged! But his indictment of Britain rested on fact. It had falsified nothing.

Madison was a little like the gentle Numa who gave Rome its charter of government before heading up the state. But in one respect this statesman (who, incidentally, knew his Plutarch) outstripped Numa. He shepherded a war which—for all its cruel setbacks and confusions—accomplished for his country vital, far-reaching goals.

✢ XV ✢

PRODIGAL SON

THE MADISONS WERE TIRED OF WAR, guests, and worrying about Payne. As Dolley wrote Mrs. Gallatin, "Ever since the peace my brain has been harried by noise and bustle; such overflowing rooms I never saw before. I wish for repose and . . . to get into the sunshine. . . ." Having for years shortened or cut out their visits to Orange, and for the last eleven months seen it not at all, they were ready to bolt. Having appointed Van Ness, Ringgold, and Richard Bland Lee to a commission for the reconstruction of public buildings, on March 21 Madison drove up the hill at Montpelier.

It was the old story: a large welcome, Mother Madison rooted in old customs, the President on horseback checking fields, Dolley dangling a bunch of keys from her waist as she managed the household. It was too early to set out seedlings; there was still danger of frost. But how beautiful the crushed carnelian soil turned over by the plough.

Their idyl was jarred by Governor Claiborne's news that in New Orleans General Jackson had continued martial law in peacetime; thrown out French nationals, including the Consul; canceled freedom of the press; and, when Federal Judge Hall resisted, banished him. Had the hero of New Orleans lost his mind? Madison tried to suspend judgment while waiting for Jackson's version—what a pity if the fracas destroyed confidence in a great general.

The matter dragged on. After receiving the President's formal notice of peace, Jackson finally rescinded martial law, whereupon Judge Hall cited him for contempt of court and, copying Jackson's own ruthlessness, refused to hear his defense. It was a struggle for power. A thousand Louisianians chipped in to pay the General's $1,000 fine as he left for Nashville to recuperate from "battle exhaustion." His defense, when

348

printed, charged New Orleans with a seditious spirit. In times when every citizen must be a soldier, he snapped, personal liberty must go.

Madison considered both Jackson's defense and Hall's refusal to hear it dead wrong. But he proposed to judge the General with a "liberality proportioned to the greatness of his service, the purity of his intentions, and peculiarity of the situation." And did. During an Army shake-up the only peacetime major generals retained were Brown and Jackson. Brown was put in charge of the northern military district, Jackson of the southern.

The Madisons knew the war was really over when John Coles Payne, mustered-out Assistant Quartermaster, brought his bride Clara to Montpelier. Having long tried to stop her brother's drinking and drifting, Dolley counted on Clary "settling him," and Madison offered them the use of one of his farms. It was a happy solution. But John's return underscored the fact that Payne's "six months" in Europe had stretched to two years.

Meanwhile Napoleon Bonaparte had burst out of Elba, rallied remnants of the Grande Armée, and within three weeks—Louis XVIII had fled—resecured France. The news posed questions. Would the Allies prevail? Would neutral rights suffer? Should Decatur hold back from the Mediterranean? Should the disbanding of troops be halted? Having weighed all factors, Madison decided to dispatch Decatur and continue army reduction. Then he waited for fresh news of Napoleon.

A letter from twenty-six-year-old Sally Coles denies a secret engagement; for once Dolley's "certain sight" has deceived her. About the Madisons' recent visit:

> You might say with Caesar, "I came, I saw, I conquered. . . ."
> No heart has been able to resist you, and every tongue is
> eloquent in your and our dear Mr. Madison's praises. I
> suspect that in the whole world you will not find hearts more
> sincerely and devotedly attached to you than on the Green
> Mountains—they all greet you with a thousand loves.

She rejoices that Dolley will soon have "the society of your beloved son. He will return to you everything that your heart could wish him." She envies his glimpse of Napoleon, the "most extraordinary man the world has ever seen." The letter contains a lot of small talk: Septimia is ill; the Smiths and Nicholases stopped by in "all their splendor." Sally closes with sentiments a little overblown in the manner of the time: "May heaven bless you, my dear and precious friend . . . is the ardent prayer of thine own S. Coles."

Montpelier was watching a procession of flowers. Jonquils gave way to hyacinths, and those to lilacs heavy with rain, and those to dogwood, and the yellow butterflies of Scotch broom. (The handful of Scotch broom seeds which Jefferson brought from the Jardins des Plantes in Paris to stop erosion had spread the plant all over Albemarle.) Now the warm May nights were haunted with the smell of honeysuckle.

Through the magical spring the Madisons kept in touch with Hannah Gallatin. If for health, Dolley wrote, they exchanged the Octagon for Mr. Gerry's corner house at the Seven Buildings, yes, they would love to use the Gallatins' stored furniture. The *Neptune* bringing their "dear voyagers" should dock soon.

When the President and Dolley moved to the Seven Buildings in June, their front windows looked on the charred White House (as the Presidential Mansion was more frequently called now that they had painted its smoked sandstone white) two blocks away. Mr. Gerry's house did not offer a great deal of privacy, but the servants' quarters were dry and the living space adequate. To enter, one walked up a few steps between black iron railings to a door under an elegant fanlight. Twenty-seven windows were flashing hand-blown glass, and four dormers leaned over a fine cornice. The high airy rooms were waiting for Payne to stride in from his voyage.

The next news from Europe was amazing. Louis XVIII had fled to— of all places—Ghent. Indeed, he had taken a house next door to the American Commissioners. Payne would be accompanying Gallatin to Paris to see the great Napoleon. In the hope that they could secure a good commercial treaty with Great Britain the Commissioners were postponing their return.

Dolley was glad and sorry. Cheated again! It was not the Fourth of July she had planned. But she enjoyed—all glasses raised—the toasts to her husband the President.

He had little time for private pleasures; the situation was almost as bad as in wartime. At the moment, for instance, he must negotiate a peace with the Northwest Indians and send ships to fetch the 4,700 American seamen held in Britain's Dartmoor Prison.

On heat-heavy days a breeze sometimes bellied the glass curtains of the upper windows through which, across woods, they could watch boats drowsing on the Potomac and naked boys merrily diving. People on the sidewalk below were going to the public pump at 21st and Pennsylvania.

In July the Madisons drove to Montpelier with Anna and her children, hoping Payne would soon join them. Farmer James, hurt by low wartime prices and the long neglect of his fields, must now struggle for economic recovery. It would be hard. But their cool, low mountains offered what no one could live without: delight.

The weather turned African. As in Joshua's day, the burning noon sun seemed to stand still.

Then at three o'clock one morning the *Neptune* put into Havre de Grace. Minister Crawford disembarked with a dying Bayard but no Gallatin, no Clay, no Payne; only their baggage.

Again Dolley felt defrauded. Gallatin's absence was understandable. As long as there was hope of a commercial treaty, duty kept him. But Payne! Did Gallatin really need him, or was this lagging behind the result of a spree? a whim? indifference to home and family? Weeping, Dolley wrote Hannah Gallatin, "I am so miserable and astonished at the entire silence of Mr. Crawford . . . that I am induced to consult you, my beloved Mrs. Gallatin." Did the servant who brought Mr. Gallatin's baggage know on what vessel he would return? Were those left behind well? What of the commercial treaty? Please ask Captain Jones to send on Payne's clothes and the artwork he collected. "I feel deeply for you, my dear friend, as your trials seem to continue beyond the term of human patience" (like their own).

Anna's children playing about reminded the Madisons of Payne as a child—baby Mary; Dolley, four; ailing little Dicky, five and a half; handsome Wat, seven; Tom, nearly nine; Mad, all of ten. Dear chatterers!

So Napoleon had been defeated at Waterloo! It was impossible but a fact. What did his 60,000 French casualties portend politically? As details came in, the President paced the floor. He cogitated. A letter from Monroe wondered if the Congress of Vienna, eager to wipe out "every vestige of the French Revolution," would repudiate that first revolter against the old order, meaning the United States. This while the Madisons waited for Crawford to stop by Montpelier and explain.

An unexpected source of information was a letter from Payne himself dated just before the *Neptune* sailed. It was addressed to his stepfather. After an interview with the British Commissioners, he wrote, Gallatin, Clay, and Adams had resolved to try to negotiate a commercial treaty (which the Madisons knew). But Bayard was now dangerously ill. Since the Commissioners' proposals had not yet elicited counterproposals, they might have to let the *Neptune* take Bayard home to his family without them. "We are all perfectly well and hope still to embrace you all in July."

The Madisons' suspicions went down before this "precious letter." Poor Bayard—Crowninshield wrote that he "had just time to bless his family, and is dead." Then Crawford arrived to fill in some details. After a postponement of the sailing date, a decision had been made that Crawford, Bayard, and Todd would board the ship in France and the party sail from England the 25th, whether or not the negotiations had been completed and Gallatin released to go home. But Payne had missed the vessel at Havre—Crawford did not know why—and at Plymouth, for Bayard's sake, they had lifted anchor without Gallatin—he hoped it was justified. Certainly, said Madison. How begrudge a man who had sailed for a port more distant?

The vessel which brought Payne's letter carried one to Cutts asking him to honor a thirty-day draft for £250. Please receive the amount, Payne wrote, from his mother. "It gives me extreme sorrow to impose trouble upon you and nothing but the necessity induces me to do so. Your knowledge in transactions of this nature renders your assistance . . . very important to me and my mother." In other words, he did not want his stepfather to know about his borrowing.

It sounds as if this were not a first levy on Dolley. If it is true, she could have quieted doubts by attributing Payne's drafts on her to necessities arising out of his art purchases.

She had no idea that during the last two years Payne had, with Gallatin's help, borrowed £1,200 from Baring Brothers of London (the firm which loaned the United States the money to meet its European debts)—this in addition to his $200 expense money and $800 from his patrimony. On the basis of the $200 originally figured as adequate for a six-month sojourn in Europe, he had in two years spent on high style, gambling, and *objets d'art* ten times the cost of ordinary living—say $10,000, an amount perhaps equal to $200,000 today. But even if Dolley had known these facts, she could hardly have brought herself to censure Payne. It is not so certain about Madison. His sense of fitness, his powerful realization of the need for measure and balance in all things, and his greater objectivity must have caused some shock and—if only secret— criticism.

Now that Payne's purchases were here, the Madisons admired his choice of paintings, sculpture, and metalwork; indeed, they were so pleased, they planned to order more plaster busts from Paris. The young man had taste. Another cause for pride was a Paris application, signed J. P. Todd, Ghent, for a *"brevet d'invention"* on a priming fluid for firearms. It was a simple formula, but Payne had been the first to think of it. Payne's nice letter had set catbirds, thrushes, and wild canaries to outdoing themselves.

The President pored over French newspapers about Napoleon's final defeat. What a nerve he had had, taking on those four strong allied countries; in some ways a man unmatched. Had he erred in his choice of Marshals? Ney and Grouchy? His new island prison, St. Helena, was only a tiny speck on the map. The old fox had been skinned and his hide hung up to dry.

One day a British newspaper told the President about the signing of a commercial treaty. Almost at once Gallatin disembarked in New York and sent Payne off with a report to the President. It omitted any reference to the young man's value as secretary.

You will find Todd in good health; but he has spent a longer time in Europe and more money than I wished. He owes twelve hundred and eighty pounds sterling, with interest from 1st June last, to the Barings, for which I made myself responsible, and which should be remitted as soon as convenient.

Gallatin expressed gratitude for his appointment to France but said he hesitated; the season was far advanced for taking his family overseas.

Then Payne himself walked through the door at Montpelier. For the Madisons it was a superb moment. There he stood, older, changed, yet unmistakably Payne. Dolley could hardly contain herself; Madison was pleased. Some of their highest hopes centered on this tall, good-looking, self-possessed young man. After two years and six countries he was safely home—a thousand loves and welcomes!

But Payne was not entirely present. He walked in a French haze, had picked up French manners, preferred French cuisine, and looked like a French dandy. As people crowded into the house to question this engrafted shoot on the Madison tree about his European adventure, Dolley was proud of his elegant cosmopolitanism. In public and private he talked about places, people, and impressions odd to Virginians. Sometimes as he rambled he was their own Payne, sometimes almost a stranger.

He had much to tell. By lingering in Paris he had missed being presented to the Czar in London—a splendid-looking man, others said, his jacket plastered with jeweled orders. Ah, but Paris! He had met everyone, gone everywhere. Ghent was a poor substitute. Beautiful spires, but what ugly women. He and his roommate Henry Clay had sat up to all hours playing cards. He won, then was wiped out. Mr. Adams disapproved. He and Clay were at swords' points. After the treaty signing he had been lucky enough to go back to Paris. They had all had the honor of an audience with Louis XVIII at the Tuileries. The Duke and Duchess d'Angoulême attended, and Count d'Artois and the Duke de Berri. Afterward the Commissioners visited his friend and Mr. Gallatin's relative Mme. de Staël—not handsome, but fascinating. There were great performances at the Opéra Comique and the Théâtre Français—Talma was ravishing. One day he and Mr. Adams lingered at the State Museum until put out—three hours—looking at the famous Apollo, the Laocoön, the Venus de Medici, Raphael's *Transfiguration,* Reubens's *Descent from the Cross.* He saw stunning women at a reception for 400 at the Palais Royal. When Napoleon escaped from Elba and landed in France, the King proclaimed him a traitor and fled to Beauvais, then Ghent—*Ghent!* In Paris shops closed, a mob burned the King's notices, and the populace was crying *"Vive l'Empereur!"* Napoleon's grand reentry defied description. Once at the theater Payne himself had sat close to that remarkable man; what a scene! The forty-five guests at the dinner the Commissioners gave for Minister Crawford at Grignan's included Lafayette.

The Madisons, listening intently there at Montpelier, had not seen this observation in John Quincy Adams's diary written while he and Payne were in Paris: "The tendency to dissipation at Paris seems to be irresistible. There is a moral incapacity for industry and application."

Sometimes a distant look came into Payne's eyes. It was as if he were still in France. Or Russia.

He was cold on the idea of Princeton—the time seemed overpast, and hadn't Europe been a kind of higher education? He preferred to travel a bit, see old friends, and eventually go into planting or politics or diplomacy or something. He was told that right now he could act as Papa's secretary; Ned had gone to settle in Illinois in order to free his slaves.

Madison hoped his stepson would find himself. The letter from Gallatin about him had not been reassuring. But of course many a youth had scattered some wild oats and lived to do better. John Quincy Adams had been quoted as saying, "It's surprising! He has sufficient talent to succeed in anything he undertakes!"

With no complaints about the hardship of repayment, Madison wrote to thank Gallatin and to say he was "not unprepared for a heavy demand for the expenses of J. P. Todd." He enclosed a $6,500 check on the Bank of Columbia, the debt plus 17 percent interest. Holding it back, Gallatin wrote to ask Baring if payment couldn't wait on a more propitious time.

Madison considered the commercial treaty a good start. Though it did not give the United States equal trade rights throughout Britain's empire, it did concede them in that main market, Europe. A congressional recess would delay the signing until December. But it might be better not to appear too eager.

About this time Napoleon's brother Joseph, ex-King of Naples and Spain, headed incognito with his retinue for the sanctuary of Montpelier. Impossible! cried Madison, getting wind of his intention; the United States had had enough trouble with Spain. What did Joseph's escort, Commodore Jacob Lewis, *mean*? A letter shot off to Rush, who sped Navy Clerk Duvall off to intercept the party. Rain was falling in torrents, and mud dragged at his wheels. Using a whip and slogging it out, he found that Joseph had left Baltimore for Washington by a back road. At last he overtook the "Comte de Survilliere." A letter warned Commodore Lewis against expecting any special treatment for the "conspicuous stranger." Even if the visit was to be a mark of respect only, the President had said he must decline it for the present. Joseph turned back. Later he would be thankful to take the cheapest lodgings in Philadelphia.

Dolley was too anxious about Dicky Cutts to mourn a necessary refusal of hospitality. All summer long the five-year-old had languished, but had seemed to be improving. Why this sudden steep decline? The next post announced his death. Ah, patient little angel—he had been released from pain into what Sally called "the most perfect beatitude."

September was all radiance. The President was gratified by the peace treaty which Commodore Decatur and the American Consul at Algiers had dictated "at the mouth of the cannon." When chicory began to blue the roadsides, the Madisons started back to Washington with Payne, their pride. He was still talking about his European hegira. Some details were volunteered, others had to be pried out of him. Dolley could never get enough, and Madison was deeply interested. A carriage was rocketing along dried mud ruts, cleaving the bright October woods. But neither parent quite knew Payne's thoughts.

When they reached Washington on October 12, 1815, the President was sixty-four, and his Administration had left a year and a half.

There would be no postwar petering out. The situation had an air of dynamism. Madison was elated that, during Napoleon's Hundred Days, Britain had seized no American vessel, impressed no American seaman. Thanks in considerable part to more manufacturing, the economy was booming. There was widespread new construction, including St. John's Episcopal Church, designed by Latrobe, across the square from the White House. Disloyalty had proved to be suicide for the Federalist party. An "era of good feeling" had begun. Madison was sometimes called as popular as President Washington. If not entirely true, the statement had some validity. He wore two feathers in his cap, "Mr. Madison's War" and "Mr. Madison's Peace." He believed that war-hit planters like himself could recoup. Looking ahead, he was almost as high-hearted as Captain John Smith sighting the Virginia capes.

Dolley also had come through a dark wood into a clear, open space. With her popularity higher than ever, she enjoyed society while looking forward to the tranquility toward which their lives were hastening. One of the future's main pleasures would be watching her polished, art-loving son find his right work, marry some lovely girl, and father a raft of grandchildren.

Payne moved through the fall of 1815 an enigmatic figure. Though not a professional man like his father and stepfather, he expected and was expected to become something extraordinary. Washington fell far short of Paris, but life was not without interest. All doors swung open, and many people—because of his family's position and his own suave sophistication—ministered to his ego. Dolley, in particular, indulged him, and he indulged himself. Among his foibles were special cheeses shipped from France. Fastidiousness in many matters combined curiously with a taste for vulgar company. The honorary cavalry officer had become a svelte man-about-town.

Dolley's eyes followed Payne and Phoebe Morris. They had known each other a long time and made a handsome couple. Phoebe was not as naïve as once. After her father went to Cadiz as Minister, she had joined him and traveled in Spain, Italy, France, Switzerland, and England. Moreover, she was a young woman—twenty-three to Payne's twenty-four—of considerable taste and talent; she played the piano and painted in watercolor. Sometimes Dolley teased the lovely looking blond about the swains who drooped and grieved during her long absences—all those Washington conquests. One day Dolley waved a letter from Lucy. "She tells me to say she loves you sincerely and hopes you'll take a Kentucky beau she has in reserve for you—but what then will become of Payne?" Dolley said. She'd send him for sweet Rebecca (Phoebe's older sister)— yes, *Rebecca*. She was teasing her "dear child" and "dearest daughter" again, and not teasing. The badinage sheltered a hope.

Partly to show her son that Paris had no monopoly on elegance, partly to celebrate peace, partly because she loved a rout, Dolley launched her most glittering season. At forty-seven she was still distinctly attractive. But for the moment a little cast down. Sally had said no, alas, she could not leave her family a fifth winter to join Dolley's "enchanting circle. . . . But I give you notice I will indemnify myself hereafter for every self-denial. . . ."

In spite of all her fashionableness, Dolley had not changed much. For every hour of glamour, she still spent three performing household duties in a plain Quaker dress, and she enjoyed doing things with her hands: washing figurines, trying a new recipe, embroidering a furbelow, skimming the cream off milk. She agreed with Jemmy that a well-rounded person used head, heart, and hands.

Feeding their macaw had become a ritual. The large, handsome bird's small eyes blinked inside a continuous curve from beak to head, his paired toes gripping a bar as he fluffed out his Brazilian feathers. Every day outside the corner window a crowd gathered to watch Dolley pet him and talk to him. She was wearing her inevitable turban. "This bird's brilliant plumage was a great attraction to youngsters of both sexes," and "Mrs. Madison was a favorite under all circumstances."

One morning in the Hall of Representatives she met with a group of ladies to form an association to set up an orphan asylum. "A nobler project cannot engage the sympathy of our females," said the *Intelligencer*. As first directress, she spent much of that winter cutting and making children's clothes. Having long sewn for Montpelier slaves, she was no novice. When asked about sores rubbed by scissors, she said oh! this work was delicious. She also donated $20 and a cow.

The social season, meanwhile, was spinning along. Mrs. Ben Crown-inshield from Massachusetts tried to convey something of Dolley's quality in a letter. As wife of the new Secretary of the Navy, Mrs. Crowninshield had hardly arrived in Washington when her husband urged her to go see Mrs. Madison. Gathering up her children, Mary Boardman Crownin-shield walked down the block and rang a doorbell. A servant ushered them into a large room whose blue damasked draperies had red silk fringe. Mrs. Madison entered and received them "very agreeably, noticed the children much, inquired their names, because, she told them, she meant to be much acquainted with them." As they talked, Mary Crownin-shield was taking in Dolley's white cambric dress, buttoned all the way up and with a strip of embroidery along the buttonholes and a ruffled hem. Over her shoulders was "a peach-bloom-colored silk scarf with a rich border." Her satin spencer was the same color, also her gauze turban. But what captivated was a kind of charisma. "You could not but feel at ease in her company."

At a public meeting in November Commodore Rodgers presented

her with a mat woven from flags from twenty-nine ships captured by the frigate *President*. As she accepted the gift, smiling, a Marine band struck up a march.

General Jackson and his wife received an exuberant welcome. But at a ball given in his honor at McKeowen's Hotel, the 6-foot-1 curmudgeon with freckled face, brassy blue eyes, and wild red hair poking in all directions looked desperately pale. His ensuing illness was a bitter loss to the social season. Still, it was a gay winter.

Around Colonel Payne Todd, man of the world, gathered exciting rumors: he was engaged to this girl, that girl, a different girl. Dolley hoped he would soon make his choice. But Payne was restless. He danced, hunted, played cards, vacillated between high and low company, drank heavily in taverns, rode horseback in Maryland and Virginia and around Tiber Creek. Though he had as yet no long-term goal, it did not worry him; and though Dolley's eyes followed him speculatively, she did not worry either—he would find himself. But James Madison, who at Payne's age was close to being elected to the Virginia Constitutional Convention, probably had misgivings.

In his Congressional Message in December the President said he hoped the commercial treaty would lead to further liberalizations. All Indian tribes were quiet except the Creek, whose cruelties should be punished. He recommended aid to disabled veterans, military academies, naval expansion, stockpiling, the improvement of yards and docks. Public credit had revived, revenue had increased. Uniform currency being desirable, another national bank merited consideration. The $120 million war debt, though high, represented an investment in the country's rights and independence. The federal government would make the best builder of roads and canals, but that work would require a constitutional amendment. And he made his usual plea—the time was ripe—for a national university. It was not a crisis message; the focus was now on internal betterment. Such an emphasis was possible since rabid factionalism was dying with the Federalist party; the country was united. Wrote Sérurier, "Federalists and Republicans agree in praising [the President's] wisdom, foresight and moderation." It should "consolidate forever" this people.

Strange, in a way, that the author of the Virginia Resolutions was now stressing nationhood. Yet it was not an inconsistency. In Madison's mind, state power versus national power was not and never had been an either/or propostion. As a man of the balance beam, of equipoise, temperamentally and by conviction, he had championed states' rights when they stood in jeopardy, and now that some states were pulling too hard against the middle, he felt bound to champion federal power. Balance, goal of the Greeks; balance, the principle which alone could give the body politic an enduring form; balance, crux of the Constitution. That document's chief architect, he knew how all-important, in an edifice, is the ridgepole. As always, in the best interests of the nation he wished passionately to hold the scale steady.

But in one matter he had changed. A Bank of the United States such as Hamilton had proposed in 1791 and he and Jefferson fought, he now endorsed. He did not see it as a violation of principle. He now saw that by helping the government exercise its constitutional power to uphold public credit, a central bank filled a need unfillable by state banks; it worked. Didn't situations change? Time had proved something; the issue had been decided pragmatically. People must learn from experience. Madison's object was the good of the nation, and rigidity was death. Not that he criticized Jefferson for remaining adamant; he just agreed with Gallatin and Dallas that the Constitution could be intepreted as implying the power to create a second national bank, QED.

He was smiling a great deal these days; the corners of his smoke-blue eyes pleated. He enjoyed the levees and was more than ever proud of his wife, the idol of Washington.

One day Mrs. Crowninshield again put down her impressions of the First Lady's gown at a drawingroom—a sky-blue striped velvet one with fine lace around the neck, with which Dolley had worn a white lace turban starred in gold and flaunting a white feather. "Oh, Mrs. Crowninshield," she exclaimed, "your butterfly's too hidden!" "What do you mean?" "The ornament in your hair—it's superb!"

Christmas Eve Mrs. Madison had the parrot brought in to amuse the little Crowninshield girls. But the bird ran after Mary, catching at her feet, and the child screamed and jumped onto a chair, clutching the First Lady. "We had quite a frolic," wrote Mrs. Crowninshield. Guns fired all night; Christmas had something in common with the Fourth of July. For the Madisons—with the return of peace and Payne—it was a very happy one. Though Dolley rued her son's growing capacity for liquor, Christmas called for cinnamon-sprinkled eggnog of the kind Payne had served the British and Flemish at Ghent, and they drank it.

Then at the 1816 New Year reception she stood with her finest jewels—her husband and son—greeting guests. Her gown was yellow satin "embroidered all over with sprigs of butterflies," her bonnet a feathered creation. It took ten minutes for a guest to "push and shove" his way through the dining room. The entry and two parlors were cram-jammed also, "servants squeezing through" with waiters laden with wine, punch, and cake.

The yellow colic which Dolley developed matched her best yellow gown. Struggling out of bed one day to meet dinner guests, she could not make it to the dining room. The Wednesday levee had to be canceled.

Gay Lucy arrived, cracking jokes and taking snuff. The first thing she did for callers was to fetch her tin snuff box and pass it around. Sniffers sneezed. On fine evenings Mrs. Todd and the recuperating Mrs. Madison joined the throng strolling up and down in front of the Seven Buildings. Mrs. Madison looked charming in a little tippet. Snowdrops were blooming under dead leaves.

Though the Madisons' favorite Minister, Louis Sérurier, had requested a recall before Louis XVIII could cashier him for supporting Napoleon, he still enlivened Washington society. As for the new British Minister, the Right Honorable Charles Bagot, he was so pleased, he went around beaming upon Britain's late enemies. Never had Washington parties been so congenial.

In other ways the Madisons' world was changing. Ohio and Louisiana having joined the Union as the seventeenth and eighteenth states, homesteaders were surging westward with all their household goods. Nor had Washington City remained a mere scattering in a forest. During the last fifteen years it had grown surprisingly. Politically, all over the world, it had gained weight.

Its "squeeze" *par excellence,* the late winter of 1816, was the Madisons' February reception for Chief Justice Marshall; the Associate Justices; the Peace Commissioners (or Gallatin, Clay, and Russell, for Adams was in Britain and Bayard in his grave); Generals Brown, Gaines, Ripley, and Scott; and the full diplomatic corps. So brilliantly was the house illuminated, it would be remembered as the "house of a thousand candles." Slaves looking like African sculptures held aloft blazing pine torches, and the decorations were "magnificent." The Justices wore staid gowns, the Generals gold-encrusted uniforms, the diplomats ribbons and medals, dandies like Payne ruffled shirts and tails, women their loveliest gowns. Dolley outshone them all. She entered in a rose-colored creation with a floor-sweeping, "mile-long" white velvet train lined with lavender satin and edged with lace ruching. The gold-embroidered crown of her white velvet turban dripped ostrich tips. Sir Charles Bagot, Knight of the Bath, whose wife was a niece of the Duke of Wellington and a raving beauty, said Dolley looked "every inch a queen." In fact everyone but the Quakers approved. Beauty was virtue's ally and added to the gaiety of nations.

Styles change, but hardly true elegance, and Dolley's surviving clothes keep an ineluctable air: her beige second inaugural gown, a rose-red velvet Empire one with square neck, a negligee strewn with flowers and casually tied with pink bows above a ruffled high-slit skirt worn over a tucked petticoat, a wrapper the color of crushed strawberries, a canary-colored "throw."

Old diaries, letters, and auction fliers establish the broad palette of her clothes. Only greens and brown are missing. Dolley preferred clear colors, especially the whole range of pinks and such offshades as magenta and terra-cotta. But white was her favorite. In a young portrait she wears a white frock with a narrow pale blue sash; a red wrap is draped over her arm. Peale's ivory miniature shows her in another white gown, three rosebuds on her white turban. An old catalog lists a low-necked white French muslin embroidered with silver vines. Even in ripe middle age she still loved the innocence of white. Today one can see her narrow white satin slippers, her white feathered fan, her exquisite little ivory-handled white silk parasol.

But at an 1816 Assembly ball she startled everybody by appearing in black velvet, gold-trimmed and worn with a gold lace turban. She "looked brilliant." She was outdoing herself. People stood on benches to get a better view. That was the night Mrs. Crowninshield's dress tangled in General Brown's spurs and she fell over his sword. Socially, this final year of Madison's Presidency would never be forgotten. It was Dolley's last fling. The Quaker girl, grown up and on top of the heap, was wearing her husband's gift of a tiara set with twenty-three sapphires.

When, the spring of 1816, the President got some troublesome squatters off public lands, his success was not sweeter than seeing Dolley in a "little fantastical ribbon." When the Senate confirmed Pinkney as Minister to Russia, Dolley's swaying earrings celebrated. When a democratic congressional caucus nominated Monroe, Madison's choice for successor, Dolley's feathers were all flags flying. If a national debt of $120 million oppressed, Dolley's hand adjusting a red scarf lightened the burden. Much public business was getting done. A Second National Bank had been created, disabled veterans pensioned, a protective tariff put through. Often, as Madison worked, his eyes rested on a Dolley no longer as slim as the day he married her but with eyes still brimful of light, and a richer inner self. She did not look forty-eight.

Disbanded military units marching down Pennsylvania Avenue always paused at 19th Street to give three cheers for Mrs. Madison. They waited until she came out on the step and called "Godspeed."

The Madisons had hoped to go home in April for Emily Coles's marriage to a Richmond lawyer. (Last October Sally had written Dolley, "All the Enniscorthians beg to kiss your hands. Emily has declared that she will not enter in the 'Holy estate of matrimony' until next spring when she says perhaps you will grace her nuptials. . . .") James was overwhelmed with business, and Dolley could not go without him.

In April they gave a dinner—"very handsome, more so than any I have seen"—for the Heads of Departments and foreign officials. The bejewelled Mrs. Bagot, resolved to please and be pleased, contended for first place with a low-backed pale green Italian crepe with white flowers to set off striking black hair and eyes. It was a good try but in vain. Dolley did not have to resolve to please or be pleased; quite naturally she did and was.

Then suddenly Russian Minister Daschkov was making a terrible row. A Philadelphia court had jailed Consul General Koslov on a charge of raping a twelve-year-old girl before it dismissed the case for lack of jurisdiction. It was an insult to Russia! stormed Daschkov, and he demanded Koslov's acquittal. Told that the federal court could try no one for a common-law crime, he threw another tantrum and complained to the Czar.

No, the President told admirers, he would not run again. He approved of the precedent set by Washington and followed by Jefferson. Never had he considered a third term.

Anticipating retirement, he ordered through Gallatin, who was packing for Paris, plaster busts—marble he could not afford—of Washington, Franklin, Jefferson, Lafayette, and Baron von Humboldt. To retire to a beautiful home, family, neighbors, study, farming, and gardening: the prospect was delightful.

But his thoughts ran most often on the future of the United States. As one expression of it, he wrote Minister Russell about his dream of an expanded American diplomatic service. The ultimate greatness of his country he could imagine and envisage. He called the Constitution adequate to meet changing conditions. If someday the geometrically increasing population necessitated any modifications in it, he trusted they would be made by wise and honest men. Meanwhile, from Capitol Hill to the Potomac, Tiber Creek's plain was an enchanted wood starred with violets, azaleas, hawthorn, and wild roses.

In May, to celebrate the launching of Commodore Chauncey's flagship, the new 74-gun *Washington,* the Madisons took a Navy barge to Annapolis. No, the trip was not official, Madison told the boatman, and insisted on paying the $25 fee out of his pocket. Official couples had gathered for a great ball in honor of the President—"everyone was there," and "all fraternized very cordially." For a week the old town rang with festivities. Jemmy was "gay as a lark." Proudly he inspected this first man-of-war for the stronger navy for which he had worked. Magnificent! The Dey of Algiers was threatening war? So much the worse for him.

The latest Algerian threat of "war or tribute," one copy in Turkish, one in Arabic, baffled the Administration. Where to find a translator? But the threat was fully answered when Madison wrote Monroe, "The Bey must distinctly understand that, although we prefer peace, we . . . will make no . . . concessions."

The Paris shopping list which Dolley gave Mrs. Gallatin: three pairs of red or variegated silk draperies with "cornishes" for the Montpelier drawing room, eighteen chairs, two sofas, two "worked" cambric caps, a spencer (short jacket), the "largest and handsomest thread lace veil," and "any other little cheap and beautiful thing."

"Cheap" was not without point. Soon her husband's salary would stop, and he had had to ask Gallatin to ask Baring if he could with honor postpone, further, payments on Payne's large debt. Financially they must draw in their horns.

Chargé Roth tried to sum up the changes he had observed in the United States. A country once devoted to farming and shipping, he wrote the Duc de Richelieu, had developed a third great interest—manufactur-ing—which was fast freeing it from dependence on British goods. The Second National Bank was gaining control of money and credit for the government. And, strangely, the two political parties were fusing, old antagonisms dead or dying. "The government . . . moves with giant strides toward an extension of strength and power which insensibly changes its nature. . . ." Party names might stick, but hereafter interparty strife would center less on different goals than on the best means to the exact same goal. Roth's diagnosis was typical.

As the Madisons prepared for their last vacation before the perma-nent one, they felt fine and free, knowing that only a ghost of the old Federalist party walked; that Madison, who had taken over a nation rent by factionalism, would hand it on to his successor purged, militarily strong, economically independent, and, as never before, united. It was especially gratifying to know that the Constitution, like some great rooted oak, had withstood hard buffeting storms.

One day two timid old Western countrywomen got lost seeking the President's house. Someone escorted them to the Seven Buildings. Rising from the breakfast table, Dolley ran into the drawing room in her plain grey stuff dress. A kerchief was pinned across her breast. The timid visitors felt as if they had known her always. Waxing bold at the end, "Perhaps," one ventured, "you wouldn't mind if I just kissed you for something to tell my girls?" Each got a kiss and an embrace, and now Dolley could finish breakfast and get on with her packing. The total dependence upon servants affected by many Southern ladies she scorned.

It was the same with Anna—which was fortunate, for her husband's business had been ruined and she must do for herself. In June, when the Madisons left for Orange, Dolley begged her to take care, and wrote at once from Montpelier. "My dear Anna, we got home quite well on the third day, to dinner, and found all pleasant. John and Clary joined us the next day ... with their fine little girl [two-month-old Dolley]. John is altered and sober, thin and industrious; his wife is the same way." After a few days, she said, she'd send them home in a carriage. Aunt and Uncle Winston [whose Auburn had burned] were enjoying Culpeper County. Last evening Payne had arrived safely. Anna wasn't to buy the veil; she could have one Dolley had ordered. Dolley wished Anna could enjoy this fine air. "I shall be always anxious about you, and trust heaven will preserve you always, particularly in the absence of your husband whose efforts for his family's good I pray God to smile upon." And off she hastened. "I am all bustle settling my house."

On the Fourth of July she spread a table under an arbor on the back lawn for ninety persons, all men except herself, Jemmy's mother, his sister Sally Macon, and his niece Nelly Willis. The celebration had abundant food, drink, standing toasts, and merriment. Black children shooed off flies with big palmetto fans.

That same day, in Washington, Benjamin Lear eulogized the Second War of Independence by which the Republic had "taken her stand among the nations, her character established, her power respected, her institutions revered." Another orator praised Madison: "His name will descend to posterity with that of our illustrious Washington. One achieved our independence, the other sustained it." He would retire with a people's grateful prayers.

Scarcely had the giant garden table at Montpelier been dismantled when French Minister Hyde de Neuville arrived with his wife and staff of four. Monroe's warning note, which barely beat the visitors there, had mentioned only the Minister. But Dolley was equal to the occasion, and James approved the effort to get Neuville out of the Capital during a fete featuring toasts hostile to Louis XVIII. Madison dodged the

embarrassment of the Napoleonic interlude by talking as if Louis XVIII
had trod on the heels of Louis XVI. The King's Minister ended his visit so
mellowed his bread-and-butter letter called the United States his *seconde
patrie*. Madison the diplomat replied that he hoped the French would soon
enjoy a constitution adapted to their genius.

Affairs were going swimmingly when, in Washington, Hyde de Neuville read Postmaster Skinner's toast to Napoleon's generals, that threw off
on that "imbecile tyrant" Louis XVIII. Infamous! cried the Frenchman.
Punish the wretch! Although Monroe explained that the Constitution
guaranteed freedom of speech, Hyde de Neuville enlarged his complaints. He even tacked on a demand for the recall of "antimonarchic"
Consul William Lee. Madison, who detested high-handedness, became
bored with French genius. Was the Minister trying to hide the degradation of the Bourbons under a "blustering deportment"?

The Russians were just as troublesome. Thanks to Daschkov's lies
about Koslov, Chargé Harris had been dismissed from St. Petersburg.
Disgusted, Madison sent Ned Coles off to Russia to tell the real story. Let
the Czar judge.

Payne's secretarial work was only a stopgap. The Madisons cherished
high aims for him. Politics? Agriculture? In any case he needed land of his
own until the day he would inherit Montpelier—they must look around.

It was the "year without a summer," cold and rainless. The Hessian
fly made the most of his opportunity. A slashing August hailstorm compounded the damage. Madison knew he would be lucky if he harvested a
third of his usual wheat crop. But when Cutts asked for more time on a
loan, he said yes.

In September Attorney General Rush spent a week at Montpelier.
Never had he seen Mr. Madison "so well fixed anywhere"—this excellent
farmer, this model of kindness to slaves, this hospitable host; never had
the President appeared "under so many interesting lights." He added that
every day's fare included French cooking and Madeira purchased in
Philadelphia in '96. Madison plucked the bottles down from the aging
place behind the cornice of his portico. Obviously he found life good.

Young Baron de Montlezun gives similar testimony. During a week's
visit he kept seeing in Madison "new lights," and he would describe him as
joining much modesty with "a precise and quick mind, infinite wisdom, an
excellent tone in conversation, never dogmatic." His openhanded hospitality was never allowed to hurt public business. "Work is easy for him; he
reads and writes almost all day, and often part of the night." Montlezun
also admired Dolley. "Madam his wife is sweetness, honesty and goodness

itself." Indeed, "one could not be in a company more amiable, better versed in good manners, and possessing to a higher degree the . . . rare art of leaving to the persons who pay them a visit the comfort and freedom they enjoy in their own home."

At last rain—a cloudburst. It fell too late for the corn and too hard for the tobacco; it drowned everything. And the summer was nearing its end.

Public responsibilities kept the Madisons from the pleasure of attending the October marriage of Sally Coles to Congressman Andrew Stevenson; Sally who had written Dolley just a year ago, "In spite of all that rumor has said to the contrary I mean to preserve my freedom. . . . Believe me, it is all a bagatelle."

As the President girded for his last six months in Washington, Daschkov again demanded a Koslov whitewash, otherwise Russia might sever diplomatic relations. Again Madison chose to address St. Petersburg directly. When Daschkov resigned in anger, the President scorned his display of "outrageous insolence," saying the Republic would not stoop before the "first potentate of Europe." Daschkov and Koslov were recalled in disgrace. Good riddance, said Madison. His judgment was confirmed by a discovery that Daschkov had proposed a European coalition against the United States for setting an example which threatened every king on his throne.

And now again Washington was streaming to the October races. The President and his lady watched Dr. Thornton's horse, Herod Eclipse, thunder down the track: a beautiful sight. Payne had an appointment with a former fellow aide, but Christopher Hughes wrote Gallatin, "Our friend Todd was *semper* Todd, and came to the race after it was over."

During the presidential contest between Rufus King and James Monroe, the incumbent enjoyed the thought of release. Monroe's victory was widely interpreted as an endorsement of Madison's Administration, which, in effect, it would continue.

This winter the die-hard Federalist Fitz-Greene Halleck, visiting the Capital, called it a "mere desert." Its site was commanding, yes, but that was all. At Bladensburg he had shed a tear of indignation. "Never . . . was a field more shamefully abandoned. The English fought like bloodhounds." A Republican might have remembered some post-Bladensburg American victories; not Halleck. "Caps, shreds of cloth, etc., and now and then an arm or a leg . . . were still discernible when I passed. The Capitol and the President's House were in ruins." Though repairs had started, it would take years to reachieve the "former splendour." But Halleck did not criticize Dolley.

> His Excellency was . . . ill, and I did not see him. . . . I saw Mrs. Madison at the theatre, where a number of gentlemen amateurs were murdering a play or two. She is a very handsome, dignified-looking personage, and I understand presides at her levee in a style not excelled by European courts.

The Attorney General called the President's 1816 Annual Message the "last act of one of the purest and wisest of statesmen" whose genius would furnish bright pages in some "future American Plutarch." Instead of vaunting his own achievements, Madison drew up a chart for future improvements, among them, adoption of the decimal system, a uniform currency, a sound circuit court system, revision of the criminal code, stronger laws against slave traffic, and (stubbornly) a national university. He summed up the state of the Union in its twenty-seventh year: prosperity at home, respect abroad. When the Father of the Constitution went on to call that document the "palladium" of true liberty, everyone knew he meant not license but *responsible* liberty. (Palladium because safeguard and guarantee; the insurer, like the Parthenon's statue of Pallas Athene, of a nation's continuity.) As reconciler of national strength with individual liberty, he went on, the Constitution had met the strains of its expanding territory. The character of the people standing behind it foretold a splendid future. That his program would remain uncompleted for a century was not Madison's fault; it was Congress's. In advocating it the President showed himself ahead of his time.

At the turn of the year he joined others in the House of Representatives to form "The American Society for Colonizing the Free People of Color in the United States" and adopt a charter. His presence was no empty gesture. Soon after the Revolution he had warmly endorsed Dr. Thornton's idea of sending Negroes back to Africa, and he now stood shoulder to shoulder with such men as Clay, Webster, Key, the Lees, and Randolph. The society's wheels were gathering speed while his were slowing down.

Many Washingtonians had recognized the President's worth; others underestimated it until they were about to lose him.

Three more months: the last lap in a long race. During the final months of Madison's eight-year Administration, not one member of the House or Senate criticized him. And if anyone said "Jemmy," it was not, as sometimes in the past, in derision but affection. Even John Randolph of the poisoned darts called him a great man and "sincerely wished him all happiness."

One element of happiness would be to hear that Payne was suitably engaged. Rumor continued to pair him with this and that lady—one so unsuitable Ned jeered. Payne's gaily partying Aunt Lucy shrugged off the criticism that he had no goal and spent money like water. Surely after a long stay in Europe, he needed time to reorient himself. France had just granted him a patent for his gun-priming fluid. *"Brevet d'invention. Manu-facture d'Armes a feu,"* read the notice, listing as ingredients a flask of *eau de cologne* and three-fourths flask of *eau de fontaine* (spring water). Dolley wasn't wrong; Payne was clever.

Two days after Christmas, St. John's Episcopal Church, a classically simple structure raising aloft a golden "lantern," held its first service across from the White House. Offered one of the high-backed front pews, President Madison had chosen an ordinary one well back, and on that first Sunday he and Dolley joined a large congregation to kneel, pray, sing, and listen to Gospel readings. Then Dr. William H. Wilmer laid aside his shovel hat and climbed a narrow spiral staircase—his silk gown rustling— to a wineglass pulpit on rollers. Please God it would not glide off. (That adventure was reserved for Bishop Ravencroft.) The main floor was crowded with whites, the balcony with blacks. Together they sang a dedicatory hymn by the church's architect, Benjamin Latrobe, beginning "God of power! God of love!"

All too soon they were back at St. John's for the funeral of former Secretary of the Treasury Dallas. After Madison's Annual Message, the ailing man had said jubilantly, "To be praised by such a man! . . . I am content." And he had written Madison, "For my own day, it will serve as a shield against the assault of the envious, malicious and inimical; and for the days of my children it will not be the least precious portion of their inheritance." Now they had their legacy.

During sharply cold days, servants poked logs and carried out ashes. The wind was trying to blow the Seven Buildings into the Potomac. Because chopping down woods had destroyed a windbreak? In his *Travels* of 1816 and '17, British dragoon Francis Hall laments the deforestation. "It used to be a joke against Washington that next-door neighbors must go through a wood to make their visits," he says. Now there was "scarcely a tree between George Town and the Navy Yard." Naked winds rolled hats down Pennsylvania Avenue like bowling balls.

Lieutenant Hall describes the weekly drawing rooms of the President "or rather his lady." Madison shook all the hands presented to him, "shaking hands being discovered in America to be more natural and manly than kissing them. For the rest, it is much as such things are everywhere, chatting and tea, compliments and ices, a little music (some scandal, I suppose, among the ladies), and to bed." The outsider Hall could not understand the excitements of Americans; he probably could not see that the President had lived up to his earlier advice to John Rhea: conduct yourself so as to "put your enemies in the wrong."

This was the winter Madison's nephew Robert wrote that he was giving them for breeding purposes (since they wanted to improve their poultry) the wild male and female turkeys he'd been gentling. Dear Robert—how nice that, after marrying a girl from Lynchburg he had settled near Montpelier.

Madison's last act as President was, appropriately, an effort to save the Constitution from too loose an interpretation. He vetoed the Bonus Bill setting aside money for the roads and canals he strongly favored— vetoed it though committed to some federal aid for internal improvements. Calhoun had supported the appropriation as coming under the "general welfare" clause, but Madison replied that no such power was *enumerated,* and any such latitude of construction would permit future Congresses to legislate practically anything anytime, a manifest impossibility. He said the success of the Constitution depended upon a clear division of state and federal powers. No, such activities would require a constitutional amendment. His veto stood.

March 4, 1817, end and beginning, was a day of mild clear sunshine. Because the Senate and House had quarreled over which hall should be used for his inauguration, Monroe took the presidential oath-swearing outdoors. Standing in a crowd of some 8,000, Madison heard him praise his predecessor's "exalted talents" and "faithful services."

Now he and Dolley had ceased to be public characters. Having moved in with the Cuttses so that the Monroes could give a reception in the Seven Buildings, the Madisons attended the inaugural ball just long enough to say God bless you and farewell.

Among the stacks of letters reaching Dolley that day was one from Eliza Collins Lee:

> My dear Friend . . . Eight years ago I wrote . . . to congratulate you on the joyful event that placed you in the highest station our country can bestow. I then enjoyed the proudest feelings that . . . the friend of my youth, who never had forsaken me,

should be thus distinguished and so peculiarly fitted for it.

How much greater cause have I to congratulate you . . . for having so filled it as to render yourself more enviable this day. . . . It is more difficult to deserve . . . [the] thanks of the community than their congratulations. . . .

Eliza regrets she cannot join the multitude paying respects. "My heart clings to you, my beloved friend." "Principles and manners not to be put off with the robe of state" will be carried to Montpelier. Dolley's talents will live on as the "chief felicity" of her husband and descend in perfection to her son. She recalls how Dolley's uncle once said, "She will hold out to the end; she was a dutiful daughter, and never turned her back on an old friend, and was charitable to the poor." Eliza begs Dolley to say something for her to James Madison—"it is near my heart that you should." And she apologizes for an overlong letter. It grows dark, and she wants her friend to receive it "this momentous evening."

Two days later at a mass meeting, Mayor Blake congratulated ex-President Madison on his "untarnished glory." In 1809 he had inherited chaos. Violent insults forced a declaration of war. The fruits are "a solid peace, a name among the nations of the earth, a self-respect founded upon justice and common strength." Such things had been said before, but this time James Madison was *going*.

He had been a strong President within his conception of the nature of the Presidency, holding that the executive should stay in good balance with the legislative and judiciary branches and be more than a politician: a statesman acting with firmness when he had the prerogative, and exercising, always, a sure integrity.

James Madison was not sorry to say farewell to the pomp and power of the Presidency. Except for a growing anxiety about Payne—the prodigal son returned but not penitentially—he would have been the happiest of men.

~§ XVI §~

ADAM AND EVE
IN PARADISE

WHEN THE MADISONS CAME HOME to Montpelier in April 1817, they were Adam and Eve expelled not out of but into an earthly paradise. Washington had been neither hell nor purgatory, but a kind of limbo, the abode of souls barred from bliss. Now they could settle in, tranquil as Eden's first couple, and watch the seasons—spring, summer, fall, and winter—wheel round the pole. In the distance the Blue Ridge mountains stood guard.

For a full month following Monroe's inauguration, they had attended dinners and balls given in their honor. At a George Town reception a typical message of love was spelled out in transparencies, paintings, and verses "executed on white velvet and most richly framed."

When at last they left Washington they entered the modern world at a leap, traveling on that recent invention, the steamboat. J. K. Paulding, who accompanied them down the Potomac to Aquia Creek, where their coach waited, has described Madison's mood. " . . . If ever man rejoiced sincerely in being freed from the cares of public life it was he. During the voyage he was as playful as a child; talked and joked with everybody on board, and reminded me of a schoolboy on a long vacation."

Home. If loss of his presidential salary required retrenching, well, a simple life was best. Already they had discharged their French cook, Pierre Roux (Madison loaned him $150 to start a restaurant), but what could taste better than Virginia ham, black-eyed peas, and spoon bread? Washington friends had promised to visit them, and Jefferson was only 30 miles away. They had lost little, gained much.

371

Perhaps best of all, the transplanting should benefit Payne. No longer tempted by the taverns along Pennsylvania Avenue, he must soon, like his Uncle John, marry and settle down to raising tobacco and children and experimenting, like his stepfather, with horticulture and the breeding of sheep, cattle, horses, fowl. He had enjoyed riding and hunting, and the library was full of French literature.

When the Madisons arrived, Montpelier's 5,000 acres were smelling of honeysuckle. It was the world in miniature and they were content.

Not Lucy. She was bewailing her fate. "I am almost in despair of ever quitting Kentucky," she wrote, "a place I do not love." Apparently Congress was never going to require the Supreme Court Justices to live in Washington. Kentucky would be her doom. Also her children had whooping cough.

Dolley sent Eliza a pair of oil portraits painted by Joseph Wood. The sixty-six-year-old Madison's face is as concentrated as a blow, yet calm, the eyes looking beyond the beholder; the hands are folded. It is a strong presence. A plump forty-nine, Dolley wears a white dress and rose-red shawl. The portrait suggests a subtle increase of intelligence.

But Eliza's pleasure had reservations. "My beloved friend," she wrote of these so acceptable "precious testimonies of your friendship and confidence," Madison's likeness "almost breathes, and expresses much of the serenity of his feelings . . . ; in short it is himself." She cannot honestly say as much for the other.

> Your likeness, my dear friend, is not so satisfactory *to me*. To a common observer it is sufficient and instantly recognized—but I lament the absence of that expression of your eyes which speaks *from* and *to* the heart, the want of which robs your countenance of its richest treasure.

For herself she can supply the missing element, but not for her children. Happily Mr. Wood has promised to try to capture that quality. "Adieu. God bless you all."

The arrival of Anna's brood, now aged twelve to three, increased the light in Dolley's eyes—"her children" were running, riding, hollering, and stuffing gooseberries. They loved to listen to Aunt Dolley, Uncle Jemmy, and the black people tell stories. When the troop left, there fell a deafening silence.

The great news was that Richard Cutts was planning to build a brick house on the northeast corner of the President's Square, looking across at the White House, two stories with a double parlor and—in back and to the right—a large garden with fruit trees and berry and currant bushes. It sounded very nice.

When James K. Paulding visited in 1817, Mr. Madison and his wife were a picture of contentment. Their life seemed an overbrimming cup. Every morning after breakfast he and Madison sat on the portico looking far away at 90 miles of the rolling Blue Ridge while discussing literature, politics, and philosophy. Paulding enjoyed the ex-President as a "man of wit" relishing wit in others. When struck by some whimsical thought his "small bright blue" eyes shone in the light; they twinkled wickedly. He had always had this side to his nature, but now at sixty-seven he was further mellowed.

Later the two rode around checking the farm's threshing, mowing, milling. With "matchless dexterity" Madison swung a crooked stick to open gates. Once, in a wheat field, he asked grizzled old black Tony how he liked the beer substituted for whiskey at harvest time. "O very fine; very fine, Massa—but I b'lieves a glass of whiskey am very good to make it wholesome." Another day, after a flash flood had strewn a meadow with gravel, Madison said, "Tony, this is bad business!" "Yes, Mass' Jemmy, very bad. I tell you what," he added confidentially, "I believes Gor Almighty, by 'n' large He do most as much harm as good."

Paulding accompanied his hosts on their two o'clock daily visit to Nelly Madison. At eighty-five she was thin and spry as a bird, and, reading without glasses, she kept abreast of the times. Her ancient majordomo Sam's one duty was to pass his mistress, from time to time, a shaky glass of water. Up from her private basement kitchen came meals cooked without any newfangled notions. But in spite of her outmoded way of life, she got along perfectly with her up-to-date daughter-in-law. And with Payne. Because she had loved the little fellow in his growing up, "Grandmama" took a great interest in the young man who had reemerged from three years in Europe somewhat changed; if he seemed lazy, he could yet make something fine of himself.

On that subject, Dolley thought slow starts meant little. Not everybody, in his youth, was as single-minded as Jemmy, and if Payne liked to travel about to springs and dances, well, so did other young men. Look at Isaac Coles. At thirty-seven he had not yet settled down. Sometimes his family had no idea where he was in his mysterious wanderings; right now, for instance, he had the memento of a dirk wound in his hand. There was even an advantage to Payne's migrations. How else look over the field before choosing the future mistress of Montpelier? How risky to marry by default.

Her own favorite candidate was still Quaker-raised pretty Phoebe

Morris. Thrown together, off and on, the two young people had developed a certain fondness. Or certainly Phoebe had. In the early 1800s letter writing was a serious occupation at which the Madisons spent many hours, James setting down well-organized thoughts in a neat hand, Dolley ardent feelings in a script leaning so eagerly forward, it seemed about to fall on its face. And Dolley corresponded with Phoebe.

Newspapers also took much time. They were featuring President Monroe's summerlong northern tour. By fall Dolley said she was travel-weary.

The river flow of guests continued: relatives, friends, strangers. The Madisons let them shift for themselves most of the day, walking, riding, reading, napping, playing parlor games, whatever they pleased. At dinner they came together for wide-ranging discussions seasoned with the *fines herbes* and condiment of wit. Then, like as not, someone played the fortepiano, or Anna her guitar, or black musicians their fiddles, and singing broke out. On hot nights Sukey and Paul, who were married now, passed drinks with ice from the icehouse, and sometimes sherbet. Guests felt so at home they stayed on and on. The Madisons were naturally hospitable, but it increased the cost of living.

And that was hard. Madison was rich in land and slaves but not in money, having been unable to save a nickel from his $25,000-a-year presidential salary; having indeed, like Washington and Jefferson, spent more in his high office than he earned. Bad weather and overseers' mismanagement had for years reduced crops, and the blockades reduced prices; and there was Payne's European debt. Madison promised himself to recoup. If out of love, respect, curiosity, or a wish to save a tavern bill, strangers crowded in, they must be welcomed, made comfortable, fed, and entertained, and their horses given hay and oats and bedded down on clean straw. The Madisons took their life as it came; those in paradise can afford to be generous. So far no visitor had been as rude as the woman who poked her parasol through a window at Monticello.

Deep down, of course, they knew that they could not be living this way without slavery, and slavery seemed to them a dreadful evil; it was the cloud overhanging Eden. Not wanting anything to do with it, they did not know how to get rid of it and remain at Montpelier. Madison did not consider Ned's action, selling his farm and moving to a place where he could free inherited blacks. To him it was no real solution. Freed slaves, he was convinced, were worse off than Montpelier's well-fed, well-clothed, well-taught, and not overworked slaves. How could they support themselves and manage in sickness and old age under present conditions?

As a life member of the American Colonization Society, Madison labored for the resettling of freed slaves near Cape Mesurado in West Africa. It would take huge sums to transport all of them to Liberia, stake them, and reimburse former owners. No matter, he said; if will joined principle, a way could be found. The fact that blacks had been imported through Northern ports and used in the North until found ill-suited to its climate and industries spread the moral responsibility. The cost of emancipation, therefore, should be borne by the whole nation.

Sometimes visitors argued back, asking why freed blacks could not be allowed to stay in America. Undaunted, Madison, like Jefferson, replied; rightly or wrongly, white people would never consent to mixing the two bloodstreams, and without assimilation how do them justice or make them content? No, the only way to undo this sin was to ship freed slaves back to Africa, and the sooner the better.

On chilly evenings, by log fires, Madison and Sir Charles Bagot sat talking. Except for slavery, Sir Charles said, Orange County customs were , very English. And again Madison said, for the whole thing troubled him, without one cent from taxation the government could foot the bill for colonization by selling its vast uninhabited western lands—why not? And it grew late to the barking of little lonely foxes and somewhere the howling of a wolf.

For a long time, first as a Congressman, then as President, Madison had pressed for a national university. Having failed to get it, he was glad to collaborate with Jefferson in building an institution nearer the heart of Virginia than Tidewater's William and Mary. Recently the Virginia Assembly had turned Albemarle Academy near Charlottesville—chartered but existing only on paper—into Central College and appointed six "Visitors," including Jefferson and himself. Could Central College be molded into a state university? During Madison's first spring out of harness, the two friends rode horseback from Monticello to a hill west of Charlottesville for the laying of a cornerstone by Masonic Lodge No. 90.

> Whereupon the Lodge, having formed their procession, marched to the Central College, where they were joined . . . by James Monroe, James Madison, Thomas Jefferson, John H. Cocke, Joseph C. Cabell and David Watson, Visitors of the Central College . . . and did lay . . . the cornerstone . . . in ancient form—

the robed gentlemen well aware that the success of the American political experiment depended in great part upon education.

Farming and education: when Jefferson and Madison got together these two subjects usually dominated the conversation. "They were extremely intimate; in fact, two brothers could not have been more so."

That spring of 1817 they helped found the Albemarle Agricultural Society. Though centered in Charlottesville, it had a five-county membership, its purposes being to exchange knowledge, to experiment, and to hold yearly exhibitions of products. Madison—ex-president of the American Board of Agriculture—was unanimously elected president, and as such he became the target of thick-flying questions. The cure for black rot? The best soil for muskmelons? Granted that Scotch broom held back erosion, how prevent it from seeding itself like mad? And how keep squirrels out of corn? (Jefferson's brother Randolph had come up with the classic solution. Rushing in, "Tom!" he had cried, "squirrels allays eat the outside rows—so don't *plant* any outside row!")

At the same time people continued to ask Madison for political advice, for the squire of Montpelier stayed abreast of public affairs. Acting Secretary of State Rush, for instance, wrote to ask what to do about the Portuguese blockade of Pernambuco. Whereas Jefferson subscribed only to the Richmond *Enquirer* and often left that unread, Madison took many newspapers, all of which he read with intense interest. But though he answered questions from various people, including President Monroe and members of the Cabinet and Congress, he still cared little for credit.

Betweentimes he and Dolley rolled off in a coach-and-four, sometimes with outriders, to dine with friends and relatives, and often Madison was the spearhead of gaiety. Mary Cutts, who lived at Montpelier for several months every summer during her growing up, called him a "lover of fun." He was wrinkled and sunburned, now, with his out-of-style club queue tied with a strip of eelskin, and his grey-blue eyes glinting with mischief. He had shed the weight of worlds; he was free.

Children loved the chuckler. There were so many now, including a recent recruit, the little substitute Richard *Dominicus* Cutts. When Frances Arnett Stevenson was born, Sally sent Dolley a swatch of silken hair, "something from my daughter—who seems by her quiet placid looks to be conscious to whom the gift is to be made. I regret that it does not resemble more the raven locks of the beloved friend. . . ." Sally hopes to see the Madisons soon. It's painful to write more by candle. "Offer Mr. Madison my affectionate love. . . . Goodnight, my ever dear cousin." The parade of births continued. In November John and Clary, who had ordered a boy, got a second little girl, Lucy. Madison was as pleased with the children as Dolley; her family was his; his, hers.

This first Christmas spent at Montpelier in many years was probably typically Virginian: candlelight, holly, running cedar and eggnog. Christmas trees were not yet used.

January turned icy. Log toters and ash removers tracked up the floor, and jabbing pokers raised sparks while faces burned and backs froze.

Then Hamilton was rising from his grave to be contradicted, for in 1810 the editor of his collected works had assigned the eighty-five essays in *The Federalist Papers* to Hamilton, Madison, and Jay in accordance with a list which Hamilton—just before the duel—had clipped into his copy, attributing only fourteen articles and a few extra passages to Madison. At the time Madison had offered no rebuttal. But eight years later the situation had changed. From the flyleaf of Jefferson's copy of *The Federalist Papers,* now in the Library of Congress, the *Gazette* had published quite different attributions, and a controversy had broken out. Jacob Gideon, planning a new edition, asked Madison for the truth. Hamilton, Jay, Madison—who wrote which?

Madison confirmed the memorandum he had given Jefferson. Out of eighty-five essays, Jay had written five, Hamilton fifty-one, he himself (with Hamilton contributing some material for three) not fourteen but twenty-nine. During the next century this assignment of some of the most brilliant and fundamental writing in the historic series would be roundly but never successfully challenged.

The past held interest, but Madison was absorbed in the present. The spring of 1818 he wrote his inaugural address as president of the five-county Agricultural Society. Delivered at Charlottesville in May, it sounded the tocsin for a wiser approach to nature, anticipating by 150 years ecological truths only today getting a countrywide hearing. Behind the scientific language lay a passionate concern. It was an extraordinary paper.

Though, through reason and agriculture, man can do what no animal can through instinct, that is, increase his food supply beyond what nature offers, wrote Madison, he must, if he is to keep the earth unruined and survive, preserve nature's complex interdependence between plants, microscopic organisms, insects, fish, reptiles, and quadrupeds. By over-multiplying some and decimating others he was courting disaster. Since plants restore the oxygen which man and animals steal from the vital air, changing the proportion between plants and animals could so alter the atmosphere, it would no longer support life. That must not happen. To help maintain nature's symmetry, Madison advocated such practices as "horizontal" (contour) plowing, a longer lying-fallow of poor acreage, rotation of crops, scientific breeding of livestock, better methods of fire prevention, the planting of windbreaks, the preservation of species, and reforestation. His great point: maintain nature's own balance.

Printed as a pamphlet, his speech brought letters from all over the United States and Europe. If followed world wide, it might have later forestalled a crisis of pollution and hunger.

Payne showed some interest in the pamphlet—this young man of twenty-six playing the same role of heir to Montpelier which his stepfather had played from birth to fifty years of age. Yes, like the young Madison, he needed property of his own to give him a base for voting and possible running for office—perhaps, even, for learning to take responsibility. Certainly he was intelligent. What he needed was concern, energy, the willpower to see a task through. At the moment, and it seemed a good sign, he was talking about importing France's silk industry. It was a further reason for acquiring property. They must look for a small estate near Montpelier.

Some of Madison's incidental problems: How stop great horned owls from killing Admiral Coffin's gift of pheasants? How cage a return gift of wild turkeys for crossing the Atlantic? How thwart the Holy Alliance? How advise Monroe about South America's effort to throw off the Spanish yoke? How meet Russia's truculence? Should his black walnut trees be cut down to make gunstocks for the War Department at a profit of $1,691.75? Could Jackson's brutal treatment of Florida's Seminole Indians be punished or condoned? Private and public problems jostled together in Madison's mind like hailstones.

No, he was not so financially bedeviled, he decided, that he must deny Cutts's request for a $10,000 loan to take advantage of some fine speculative opportunities. Cutts promised to pay it back soon and at a higher rate of interest than banks offered. Hearing about it, Payne wanted in. Together they made it up: Madison $6,000, Payne $4,000.

In August twenty-one commissioners appointed by Governor Thomas Mann Randolph, including Jefferson and Madison, rode up to a squat stone inn at Rockfish Gap to choose a site for a state university; plan its construction, curriculum, and professorships; and frame a legislative bill for its upkeep.

In a low-ceilinged, whitewashed room the commissioners sat around a big deal table on split-bottom chairs. Their first act was to pick, for seniority and ability, Thomas Jefferson as President of the Board of Visitors. As the tall, rangy, white-haired, seventy-five-year-old gentleman took the chair, he was counting heavily on Madison as his chief lieutenant. How good to work together, again, for a large cause. They wanted to merge the projected state university with Charlottesville's Central College. When some of the commissioners urged other sites, the resulting argument rocked the hall. At last it was put to a vote: three for Lexington, two for Staunton, sixteen for Charlottesville.

The group emerged with a sense of accomplishment into the high clean invigorating mountain air. What a splendid prospect!

Now Jefferson and Madison could get down to specifics about the college buildings. Jefferson was gifted architecturally and had had the experience of designing Monticello and making plans for other structures. Nor was Madison wholly without architectural talent. In 1917 he had loaned Jefferson his copy of a treatise on proportions by Andrea Palladio. (Jefferson kept it a year.) Madison's enlargement of Montpelier, including its handsome Doric portico, had been done on his own, and well. Palladio's theories had simply borne out, in another field, his belief in the need for symmetry in everything.

After the Rockfish conference, Dolley joyfully welcomed her husband back. They had been separated so little during twenty-five years of marriage, and were so close, even a short absence seemed catastrophic. She had some nice news for him. Lucy and the Judge had named their second son James Madison Todd.

The summer stayed cruelly hot and dry. They could water the gardens with buckets, but not the fields. Moths, butterflies, horseflies, and bugs floated through screenless windows. But there was a procession of cool drinks such as orgeat, arrack punch, shrub, and caudle. Then chestnut leaves turned brown and shrivelled.

One day Richard Chapman offered to sell 104 hilly acres on the road to Gordonsville, a few miles from Montpelier. Was this the right property for Payne? The family walked thoughtfully over the tract. A stream, a rock ledge, fairish soil, and the small house which had replaced a burned-down bigger one. Though Payne had squandered a great deal, he still possessed, at the least, a small income from Philadelphia real estate and the Cutts loan, and he was planning a silk experiment. Why not at Toddsberth? The name seemed to mark the land as his own; it was an old name meaning "Todd's Camp," this being one of the sites where in 1716 the Knights of the Golden Horseshoe, explorers including a Todd, had spent a night on their way to that first white-man's view of the Shenandoah Valley.

On October 18, 1818, John Payne Todd paid Richard M. Chapman and his wife, Maria, $540 for 104 acres bounded as follows:

> to wit, beginning at a white oak and gum bush on the east side of Mallory's road . . . thence south . . . to three pines . . . thence south [west] . . . to two white oaks and one hickory sprout. . . .

It was so recorded: "Teste." Now Payne was not only heir apparent to Montpelier; he was also a Virginia landowner able to vote, run for office, and raise mulberry leaves as fodder for silkworms.

Madison was pleased but not blind. Highly educated, he could not but consider Payne's education inadequate; disciplined, he could not but rue Payne's self-indulgence; scrupulous in the handling of money, he could not but worry about Payne's talent for letting it go. But work, marriage, children, and responsibilities had settled many a young man. Brother John seemed a good example.

The new master of Toddsberth sent to France for silk workers before planting any mulberry trees. He said sericulture was so complex he needed expert advice, but once he had an ounce of tiny eggs and a dry, warm, well-ventilated worm shed with clean trays, he could start his project. Papa's white mulberry by Montpelier's Greek temple had enough young leaves to feed an army of horn-tailed caterpillars. Later he'd move everything to Toddsberth. Intensely interested in the experiment and Payne's future, Madison cooperated. The question was, could Payne run a business so exacting? Could he keep larvae clean while they molted four times? Could he supply, after each had spun half a mile of raw thread into a cocoon, just enough heat to kill the insects without injuring their silken shrouds? Could he seal the thread to ensure first-quality silk? Sell to some mill for throwing and weaving, then select the best fat fuzzy moths to repeat the cycle? The answer, in time, would be no. But Payne's failure as a silkman may not have been his fault, at least not altogether. One factor working against him could have been climate. Cortez's effort to bring sericulture to Mexico had failed; a British company in Ireland backed by a million pounds in capital had failed; Franklin in Pennsylvania, and James I's workers and many others in Virginia—all had tried and failed with silk. Only certain countries have ever succeeded.

While Payne's larvae were dying, a new public problem was being born, for Missouri tried to enter the Union as a slave state (the second to be carved from the Louisiana Purchase), and the North, fearing an upset of the delicate balance of power between North and South, objected. The South-controlled Senate said yes, the North-controlled House, no, and Missouri's application for statehood hung fire. A swap was proposed: admit Maine as a free state, Missouri as a slave state, and henceforth prohibit slavery north of the 36°30′ line forming Missouri's southern border.

A balance, but for how long? And when it toppled, what then? The country was growing fast; in twenty years it had gone from four million to nine million. Following the admission of Vermont, Kentucky, Tennessee, Ohio, Louisiana, Indiana, Mississippi, Illinois, and Alabama, the new states of Maine and Missouri would make twenty-four.

And there were other changes. Pioneers were moving west in ever greater numbers; tariffs had been raised to finance public works; the Erie Canal was being built; and just this year the first lake steamboat, "Walk-in-the-Water," had been launched in Detroit. A constant metamorphosis. But could slavery be killed out before the issue exploded? Madison's mind was boomeranging back to the Colonization Society's African plan—the only hope.

Worn out with the North's taunts, he wrote a little parable called "Jonathan and Mary Bull." Southern Mary was trying to rid her arm of the mortifying "African hue" on which northern Jonathan frowned. During courtship and marriage he had not objected—but at that time he himself had been disfigured by "spots and specks." For all his scrubbing, they still showed.

Answering a stranger's plea for a description of Virginia ethics, education, and slavery, Madison wrote that the last problem was now less difficult than before the Revolution. Slaves were better housed, clothed, fed, and treated for two reasons: an increased concern for human suffering (fostered by new political institutions) and, thanks to the abolition of entail and primogeniture, a decreasing ratio of slaves to freemen.

Slavery-abhoring visitors had to admit that the situation at Montpelier was exemplary. The master treated his slaves with a "consideration bordering upon indulgence"; he saw them as human beings, not chattels, and in an effort to be just, often leaned over backward.

Visitors, visitors—they came in greater numbers now that the host was an ex-President; came like hummingbirds to a trumpet flower. At the sound of a stick gig or carriage, Madison lifted his telescope. Who was arriving? Uncle Isaac Winston? A Taylor cousin? Col. Rives? The Randolphs? Strangers? Welcome! Montpelier was like a wayside inn. A stew-

ard has described Jefferson's dilemma, and his thumbnail portrait fits
Madison's situation perfectly:

> They traveled . . . with carriages and riding horses and servants
> . . . sometimes three or four of such gangs at a time. We had
> thirty-six stalls for horses, and only used about ten. . . . Very
> often all the rest were full and I had to send horses off to another
> place. I have often sent a wagon-load of hay up to the stable, and
> the next morning there would not be enough left to make a
> bird's nest. I have killed a fine beef and it would be eaten in a day
> or two.

Once Martha Jefferson Randolph was asked, "What is the largest number
of *uninvited* guests you ever put up?" Fifty, she said. Dolley matched her
or ran a close second. "Everything that came beneath her . . . sway," said a
guest at Montpelier, "the care and entertainment of visitors, the government of the menials, the whole policy of the interior, was admirably
managed." And again, "Few houses in Virginia gave a larger welcome."

The spring of 1819 Eliza passed on a report of the Madisons as seen
by a guest two years after the couple's retirement:

> My beloved friend,
>
> . . . Do you know? or do you now know, my beloved Dolley,
> that your absence from this city is more and more lamented; that
> [your] urbanity, benevolence and cheerfulness . . . will be long
> sought for *in vain.* But you are happier and oh! that I could
> witness that superior happiness . . . painted by Mrs. [Thomas]
> Miller. . . . She says, "I spent two days with Mr. and Mrs. Madi-
> son. . . . Her soul is as big as ever and her body has not
> decreased. Mr. M. is the picture of happiness. They look like
> Adam and Eve in Paradise."

But the first Eden harbored a snake, and that is what William C. Rives
would call Payne—"the snake in Eden."

At first he seemed a harmless garden variety. If the Madisons worried
about him floating from this or that resort to Richmond, to some friend's
plantation, to Philadelphia, to New York, to Williamsburg, gaming, roistering, playing the lotteries, wenching, they could assure themselves it was
only a temporary phase; it would pass. Maybe not even a garden snake—a
tremble of green light among the leaves.

Dolley hoped Payne would marry Phoebe Morris, not for Phoebe's
sake but for a new Payne, an energetic, purposeful head of a household,

the father of sons and daughters. Dolley was a very good hoper; she could put all she had into an act of faith.

In April Clary bore another little girl instead of the boy desired. Having a Dolley and a Lucy, she and John named this one Anna, thus duplicating a sisterhood. When Dolley held the baby in her arms, in Jemmy's presence, she had no inkling of the special blessing this one would bring into their life together.

Drought, alas, was beginning to be a habit. By August of 1819 the ground was hard as granite. When at last a few drops fell, they ran off. Madison would not harvest much tobacco. But watermelons and muskmelons rolled out of their cooler; ice tinkled. As usual Anna brought her brood. The oldest, Madison—Mad—was now fourteen. He and Tom, Wat, and even the second Dick could outrun their sisters Dolley and Mary.

The children's noise was counterpoint to a drawing room debate as to the *location* of sovereignty in the American system. Some Democratic-Republican guests defended extreme states' rights. Not James Madison, the balance-beam man. Tip the scale too far in either direction, he said, and the nation as originally conceived would fall. Like marriage, it had been formed on the principle of give-and-take. One-sidedness was a barbarism.

In September he wrote Ned Coles, whom Monroe had appointed Registrar of the Land Office at Edwardsville, Illinois, a sportive letter:

> . . . The first step on the deck of your bark—pardon me, of that noble structure your ark—makes you a pilot. The name pilot is scarcely pronounced before you are a Captain, and in less than a twinkling of an eye . . . Commodore. On land . . . a ploughman, a railsplitter, a fence builder, a corn planter, a haymaker, and soon-to-be wheat sower. . . . Which leaves but a single defect in your title as husband-man. . . .

He was saying, Bachelor, marry. On two days the thermometer in the coolest part of the house, Madison went on, rose to 92°. Springs and wells were about to dry up. Whereupon he raised a small dust cloud as to the wisdom of freeing slaves under present conditions.

> With the habits of the slave, but without the instruction, property or employment of freemen, the manumitted blacks, instead of deriving advantage from the partial benevolence of their masters, furnish arguments against [it]. . . . I wish your philanthropy could complete its object by changing their color. . . . Without

this they seem destined to a privation of that moral rank and those social blessings which give freedom more than half its value.

Then Madison returned to Ned's bachelorhood. When he came back to Albemarle, Dolley would help him get rid of the thorn in his side—"putting a young rib in its place. She very justly remarks, however, that with your own exertions hers will not be wanted and, without them, not deserved."

Dolley wrote a potpourri postscript. Lucy is spending the winter in Frankfort. Monroe looks better. An odd visitor, Captain O'Brien, has thrown around "a lot of sea phrases." Seriously, she's afraid that while she and Ned deliberate on which to take they'll lose "some of the finest girls now grown." Payne still says he'll write. "I suspect he begins to feel with you that a good wife would add to his happiness."

Suspected or hoped. In any case her gadabout son now returned for at least a visit to Orange.

The Madisons made another trip to Monticello, the two men concentrating on University plans, the two women on domestic subjects. Dolley enjoyed encounters with the children—like the time little Benjamin, unable to cope with a muffin, called on his friend Mrs. Madison for help. She was cutting it when Ben said earnestly, "No, no, not that way." "How then, Master Ben?"—amused. "Why, you must tear him open and put butter inside and stick holes in his back and then pat and squeeze him till the juice runs out."

Back at Montpelier the Madisons received a letter from George Divers of Farmington thanking them for the Hautboy strawberry plants and offering some Hudson Bay strawberries and dwarf roses. He said he was sorry about Jefferson's attack of bilious colic. "For two days, I am told, his life was despaired of." The Madisons were stunned.

Then Jefferson's granddaughter Ellen wrote that she and Mama must give up their visit to Montpelier; Grandfather had had violent colic. It lasted thirty hours. Though out of danger now, he must be carefully tended. He didn't know how to watch his diet and avoid fatigue in exercising.

Madison was anxious about his friend of forty years. No one was getting younger: Dolley was fifty-one, he sixty-eight, Jefferson seventy-six. Yet with luck they could enjoy many more years of friendship. The next world might be better, but this one was worth staying around to observe.

One of the nation's interesting developments was the Potomac ("River of Swans") Steamboat Company. Steam was working such a revolution, Madison looked to the day when steam-driven ships would shorten the Atlantic crossing.

It was not just science; the arts were bringing forth innovations too. Once, in his love for the arts, Madison had copied such quotations as "The fine arts of poetry and painting are never more applauded than when . . . moving us to pity." Now for a long time Dolley had been helping to broaden his appreciations. Though her own poetry was only pleasantly minor, she had the authentic feelings of a poet; it was part of her quality. Sometimes when they plucked poetry off a shelf perhaps to read aloud— Shakespeare, Milton, Goethe, Pope, that new man Wordsworth—there opened out a glory.

This winter Jefferson was too weak to write. The Madisons kept in touch with him through Martha and the granddaughters. A letter from Ellen apologizes for keeping overlong Mr. Todd's loan of La Harpe's *Cours de littérature* and says that Charlottesville's Thespian Society admired the turban Dolley made for Mama. Montpelier had been so "renovating," Mama isn't going to Richmond. The Madisons must come to Monticello again and Mr. Todd keep his promise to stop on his next trip. The multiflora Mama stuck is flourishing.

But not Jefferson's finances. They were in such terrible shape Madison signed a note for Jefferson, then worked hard to get one of the Randolph grandsons a job.

This growing poverty was far from unique. After years of poor crops, following a hurtful blockade, many farmers found themselves compelled to borrow heavily. Indeed, Madison was one of them. In the earthly paradise of Montpelier darkness was impinging on light: a chiaroscuro.

The spring of 1820 Payne—he was now twenty-eight—talked of visiting the Morrises at Bolton Farm in Pennsylvania. He may well have visited there before, and certainly Phoebe had more than once visited Montpelier. Now Phoebe wrote Mrs. Madison that she could trace her friend's hand in all the most important events of her life. Once when "gaiety and fashion and perhaps folly" were her favorite pursuits, Mrs. Madison had guided her steps through the "giddy dance," and she hoped she might be selected to "smoothe the pillow of sickness" or help any other way any time—signing herself "faithful and most affectionate." Dolley was open to such tenderness. Yes, Phoebe could be the solution to a problem.

But April, May, and June passed without Payne showing up at Bolton. For a mother counting grandchildren the delay must have seemed interminable. Dolley knew that Payne liked Phoebe and that Phoebe, at the very least, liked Payne. Something had held him up?

Late in July Dolley received a letter from Anthony Morris, acting as his daughter's "secretary." Phoebe had delayed answering Dolley's welcome letter because she was in "daily expectation of seeing Mr. Todd." She was

> about concluding him a false knight, and was actually preparing a denunciation of him to you, when he suddenly appeared at Bolton to speak for himself, which he has done so amiably and satisfactorily that he has silenced all censure, and made the most favorable impression on our hearts, indeed, my excellent friend, I can't convey to you the pleasure his company afforded to us all.

This good news could be interpreted as telling Dolley that her old Quaker friend joined her in hoping. Phoebe was too busy to write, her father added. At this moment she and Payne were preparing to ride over to Bristol.

The next day Phoebe dealt her matchmaking "dearest Mrs. Madison" a hard blow. After a four-day visit Payne had departed. Skirting the issue, she says something without, perhaps, meaning to confess so much. It is as if a flouted young woman were trying to cover herself against any suspicion that she might have had some design or at least a hope.

> I dare say he has been sufficiently wearied of my questions, for I was so glad to see him and to know everything about you, how you looked, what you did, what you put on, &c, &c, all the minute details which I thought my long absence would make reasonable. However, I think I have extracted this satisfaction from him, that you are still my own Mrs. Madison, blooming, gay, and affectionate as ever. . . . My dear father is in very good health and tolerable spirits. . . . It is a long time since I have seen him so much gratified as by the visit of Mr. Todd, who, he says, he admires for his own sake and loves for yours.

Was Phoebe protesting too much? pretending? She goes on to praise and apologize for a home probably overquiet for a man fond of city excitement. Bolton is so "retired," it has little gaiety, but still—staunchly—the family has its pleasures, including the sweet prattle of her sister Rebecca's children. "They are *(in our eyes, I mean)* beautiful as cherubs and full of intelligence." Her brother-in-law, Major Nourse, tried in vain to induce Payne to stay longer, but "all our united attractions failed," and he had proceeded on his journey. Then, as if against unspoken criticism, she redefends the "tranquil uniformity" of Bolton. "Properly considered," their way of life is really a "happier one than the turbulent varieties of the gay world"—Payne's world. She is sorry not to see Mrs. Madison and quotes as if against her spinsterhood:

> Oft in the stilly night
>> When slumber's chain has bound me
> Fond mem'ry brings the light
>> Of other days around me.

So died a dream. With all circumstances conducive to romance, Payne had walked out and away. Dolley could not have been other than immensely sorry. But she was not giving up. Somewhere some other pretty and eligible young lady must be waiting for her son.

A certain unidentified oil portrait shows an elegant, dark-haired dandy in a pleated shirt, gold-buttoned coat, and black satin cravat, holding a high silk hat and leaning carelessly on a parapet—as if about to leave some girl who considers him a great catch. It may be Payne.

A composite Cain-and-Abel could have stood, just so, in Eden, beyond the flaming sword, for Adam and Eve had two children, and Cain rose up against Abel—one might say the lower self slew the higher—and the Lord said, "How art thou cursed, a fugitive and a vagabond."

←§ XVII §→

LAFAYETTE, JEFFERSON, AND A GOLD-HEADED CANE

WHEN IN 1821 Madison reached the age of seventy, he was more robust than in his youth. Often through the years when he and Jefferson—older by eight years—were talking about, say, the Holy Alliance or the wilt on tomatoes, suddenly they had jumped back nearly half a century to discuss their old friend, that extraordinary Frenchman, that aristocratic democrat, Marie Joseph Paul Yves Roch Gilbert du Motier, the Marquis de Lafayette. Many times they had wondered how he fared. They were wondering about it, again, this year of 1821.

At thirteen he had inherited a fortune; at sixteen married; at nineteen as a captain of dragoons, offered his sword to the American Colonies. At the first news of the quarrel with England, he said, his heart was enrolled in their struggle for freedom. He had suffered a wound at Brandywine, and later maneuvered back and forth across Virginia, turned Cornwallis back at the Mechunk, and shared in the victory at Yorktown. The memory of his exploits sharpened Jefferson's and Madison's delight when they heard that Congress and the President were planning to invite the Marquis to tour the United States as a guest of the nation.

Madison recalled, vividly, his trip with Lafayette to a parley with the

Six Nations: the head winds on the Hudson, the rich loam of the Mohawk Valley, their lugging of rations across rivers and through dense forests, Lafayette's raincoat stuck with shredded Paris newspaper, the cold cabin at Fort Stanwix, the way the Iroquois bucks fondled "Kayewla," and plunging downriver in bright fall weather. That fabulous adventure was a bond.

Had the intervening years changed him? Since leaving America he had served in the French army and Assembly of Notables; proposed social reforms, including the abolition of titles; joined the French Revolution; languished in a vile dungeon at Olmutz (where, it was rumored, he had lost his hair); opposed Napoleon's becoming, first, life Consul, then Emperor; and worked (ironically) for a restoration of the monarchy. Today, under Louis XVIII, he was a Deputy from Sarthe. Oh, he must have changed a great deal—but who had not?

The invitation which the now reelected President Monroe sent across the ocean bore the Great Seal of the United States.

Waiting, Madison busied himself making copies of his notes on the Constitutional Convention of 1787. The task seemed obligatory. Recently Robert Yates, on publishing his shorter notes, had quoted Madison as belittling state sovereignty there in Philadelphia—Madison, author of the Virginia Resolutions! Questioned, Madison had charged Yates with bias and "extreme incorrectness." His notes held the proof.

Actually it was a touchy matter. He had been more of a nationalist during the framing of the Constitution than he was after watching President Adams's nationalistic excesses. The change was not just the growth in thinking of a person who understood a man's obligation to observe, learn, and adjust, since not all wisdom springs full grown and at a bound, like Athena. Madison had had to lean first one way and then the other, strategically, when the delicate balance between federal and state sovereignty—which at the framing of the Constitution was as yet only a brilliant concept—had been thrown out and needed to be reestablished. Now times had altered, the aristocracy-loving Federalists had lost out, and the republic was running on an even keel, without the old danger of shipwreck; heroic adjustments were no longer necessary. And all Americans could profit from experience.

Madison could not help knowing that his notes on the Convention were historically important, but he wanted them published only after his death. Meanwhile he would make them readable. (A hundred years later an accusation that, in transcribing, he altered his original notes would—with one very minor exception—be refuted by watermarks.) It was such an exacting job, he often lost count of time until the dinner bell rang. Sometimes he laid off to write some letter—perhaps to answer a query from Jefferson about the University's faculty, perhaps to enlarge his booklist for the University's library, or give political advice, or file an application for another loan. Thomas Mann Randolph had gone bankrupt; would other friends follow? would he?

The family was celebrating John's first son, William Temple Payne II, when some servants and visiting children were struck down by typhus. It scared everyone, and Dolley wrote Payne to come and take her away. She received no answer. But the disease did not spread.

After many months there came word. In May 1821 Dolley wrote in relief, "I was glad to receive the few lines from you in Baltimore, my dearest Payne, and can have no doubt"—loyally—"you have good reasons for remaining there." She regrets to learn that her letters addressed to Washington, Philadelphia, and Baltimore have miscarried. The epidemic has blown over; he mustn't on her account leave his business unfinished— "though I cannot express my anxiety to see you. Adieu, my son. May heaven bless you. Your Papa sends his love."

If she or Jemmy doubted the reality of Payne's business, they concealed it from themselves and each other, trying to emphasize not his restlessness, extravagance, or neglect but his good qualities, for they existed. Madison often tried to comfort his wife with these lines:

> Errors like straws upon the surface float,
> Those who would seek for pearls must dive below.

If the old defense, Payne's youth, had worn thin with time—he was touching thirty—others could be found: he had obligations and was popular. "I was highly flattered and gratified," wrote Martha Randolph, "by your son's friendly visit." And why should he stay at Toddsberth or Montpelier, Dolley could tell herself, if he enjoyed traveling?

But they were hurt by his preference for New York, Philadelphia, Baltimore, Washington, Annapolis, Richmond, spas, almost any distant place. During the last few years they had shaped Montpelier closer and closer to their hearts' desire. The mountains, birds, and wild flowers for which they could take no credit were supplemented by beauty of their own devising. Mary Cutts has described Montpelier at this period:

The salon contained two sofas upholstered in crimson damask, Madison's "campeachy" chair, Parisian statuary, Persian rugs, and walls "entirely covered with mirrors and pictures," including Stuart's portraits of Washington, Jefferson, and Adams, and a framed copy of the Declaration of Independence.

The halls were highly polished, the one to the Old Lady's quarters hung with many original oils, some copies of old masters, and a fine collection of engravings.

The dining room contained pictures of Confucius, an African king, favorite servants, Louis XIV, an ermine-robed Napoleon; a watercolor of Mr. Jefferson by Kosciusco; views of Constantinople and St. Petersburg; and "testimonials of respect and admiration from crowned heads and simple citizens." In the middle stood a large mahogany table; against the walls, two sideboards loaded with silver, and tables on which stood chests of cutlery, alabaster vases, brown-and-white sugar bowls, wine glasses, and coolers. The marble mantel bore a glass ship under proud full sail. Silk draperies stirred at the windows.

Madison's study, behind the dining room, contained a desk, an armchair, and a crimson-canopied, high-posted iron bed from the Tuileries; also some of Marie Antoinette's china. Here the master kept souvenirs from the farewell George Town ball.

A sculpture-crammed "clock room" flanked the study, so named for an old household-regulating English clock which ticked to the

> marble ears of Washington, Jefferson, Adams, Paul Jones, the Emperor Alexander and his Empress, Lafayette, Baldwin, Barlow, Gallatin, Clay, etc., besides Guido's *Hours*, Cupids, Psyches and—what Mrs. Madison valued most—a profile of Mr. Madison in marble, one of the most successful efforts of Caracci.

A carved staircase led up to Madison's library. There bookcases marching around the walls and down the middle left "just sufficient room to pass." Mary says that Madison had collected "books, pamphlets, paper, all, everything, of interest to our country before and since the Revolution"; also the celebrated library of Lord Dunmore. The library was a scholarly haven strong on the classics, science, philosophy, poetry, and curious memorabilia, with some travel books thrown in.

Outdoors the Blue Ridge formed a backdrop for a landscape varying "from the wildest to the most cultivated; immense waving fields of grain, tobacco." Pet Durhams and Angola sheep grazed near the house. Madison's favorite horse, Liberty, had been put to pasture. "Petted, fed and stalled alone, he was so good at opening gates he well deserved his name," but sometimes he was scolded for felonies committed by the cattle. It amused Madison to repeat these "generally false tales."

The Doric veranda looked out on an immense mulberry guarded by silver pines. In hot weather, sawdust-covered winter iceblocks cut from the pond kept the little Greek temple above them cool. Baffled children loved to listen to it echo. On the other side willows, locusts, tulip poplars, and rare imported trees screened the house and its outbuildings: toolhouse, henhouse, storehouse. The trees were beautiful.

A path led to the Walnut Grove's cabins and small gardens. Old Sawney, now retired, raised yams, cabbages, and chickens whose eggs Miss Dolley bought. One of the children's favorites among the old black folk was hundred-and-four-year-old Granny Milly. Her youngest granddaughter was seventy, and her pride was a copy of *Telemachus* given her, along with French lessons, by the wife of the former gardener Beazée. Granny would rummage around in a chest to find and display her keepsake. Master Jemmy clothed, fed, and doctored the retired as well as active slaves. And nieces and nephews saved tidbits—a herring, fish eggs, a melon—to carry down to the Walnut Grove. Like as not they returned with a tomato or a squash.

Montpelier's back porch was festooned with roses and cape jasmine. It looked out on a lawn surrounded by ha-ha. Behind it stood Madison's "twins," two fine tulip trees; also sweetbrier, Osage orange, and lavender-flowering Pride of China. Beyond, Beazée had laid out a garden horseshoe-shaped like the House of Representatives. Madison liked to walk out to look over his apples, pears, and plums, his strawberry beds, his two-crop figs, and arbor grapes. He preferred to gather the ripe fruit himself. And sometimes stood watching a cardinal—his favorite bird. Visitors coming through the French doors of rear bedrooms onto a terrace above the back porch admired the "Italian" scenery.

Each summer morning Dolley paused on the back porch to enjoy the cape jasmine. She sometimes christened buds with the names of her husband, son, sisters, brother, and friends. When a flower faded before maturing, she was unhappy. Culling roses on sunny days she protected her sensitive skin and weak eyes with a "hideous" contraption she called her "Beazée bonnet."

Returning, she stopped in the hall to speak to the old macaw. Though his once splendid tail was bedraggled by age, he still spread its feathers and screamed out French phrases learned from John Sióussat. Permitted to fly about the house all day, at evening he was brought to his cage and set on his perch. If anyone said "Polly's coming" (never mind the gender), children fled in real or mock (usually real) terror.

The summer of 1822 a mob of them—John and Clary's four, Anna's six, Lucy's three, and assorted great-nieces and great-nephews on Madison's side—were coasting down haymows, trying out the pianoforte, rifling currant bushes, playing ball, following Uncle around fields, and watching him at his cabinetry (two of his best pieces were a candlestand and bureau-secretary). On rainy days children tailed him as he paced the portico, and when the downpour stopped, scampered to retrieve Uncle's measuring cup. They understood the benevolence behind his browned and wrinkled face.

Neighborhood gatherings, says Mary, were "well attended by the first families." Pitching tents, they stayed several days enjoying friends, some of them unseen since the last get-together. There were huge barbecues with sumptuous boards spread under forest oaks and pigs roasted whole. Servants passed wine and punch, and the mountain air smelled good.

> At these feasts the woods were alive with carriages, horses, servants and children—all went—often more than 100 guests . . . happy at the prospect of . . . pleasure and hilarity; the laugh with hearty goodwill, the jest after the crops, farm topics and politics. . . . If not too late, these meetings were terminated by a dance . . . [to] violins. . . . The Negroes like the birds . . . had sweet wild notes filled with melody. . . .

Departure was regulated by the number of miles horses had to jog before nightfall. Sometimes at Montpelier, afterward, the Walnut Grove fiddled and danced until sunup.

One day, this pleasant if droughty summer, the Madisons heard that Ned Coles had been elected the second Governor of Illinois. Dear Ned— they missed him. But late in September, horror. Sally Stevenson's four-year-old Fanny had fallen into a fireplace and burned to death. The accident shook several counties. The Madisons went at once to Enniscorthy. Fourteen years later Sally would write Dolley: "Can I ever forget how in my hour of darkness and bitter anguish you came to me like a ministering angel. He too . . . came with words of love and pity to pour balm into my wounded heart. . . ."

Then life that had paused went on. Fall was followed by the whistling winds of winter, a time for study and reflection. Dolley hoped John would not keep his threat to move west. How support five children, he was complaining, when every summer brought a killing drought?

Spring found Madison at Monticello conferring with Jefferson about the University. It being difficult to find first-rate professors, why not recruit them from Europe—wouldn't it be easier, cheaper, better? They rode over to inspect the new, classical, handsome buildings. When Lafayette came they would have something worth showing—a Southern university which they hoped to make a peer of the great Northern ones.

Lafayette was coming to Montpelier, that was sure, but how about Payne? Dolley's last letter hid a raw heart:

> I am impatient to hear from you, my dearest Payne, and had I known where to direct I should have written you before this; not that there is anything particular to communicate, but for the pleasure of repeating how much I love you, and to hear of your happiness.
>
> Your father received the journal of "*Las Casas*" with your name in it, from Philadelphia, which is an indication that you are there, and I write accordingly. . . .
>
> Adieu, my dear son; your Papa joins me in affectionate wishes for you.

The news that Isaac Coles had married a Norfolk lady was received as a message of hope—Isaac was forty-three to Payne's thirty-one. Dolley and James went back to the notes of the Constitutional Convention debates more contented. James was deciphering his personal shorthand, Dolley copying.

Czar Alexander colonizing California? As long ago as 1783 Madison had opposed any European meddling in the Western Hemisphere. Long ago the Continental Congress had adopted his resolution "that the true interest of these states requires that they should be as little as possible entangled in the politics and controversies of European nations." When, therefore, Monroe asked Jefferson and Madison their opinions as to America mixing in Europe's quarrels, Madison replied promptly yes, mix, but only to the limited extent of joining Britain in condemning French aggression in Spain; make no separate protest.

Why come in as a cockboat (as Adams had said) in the wake of the British man-of-war?

When Cadiz surrendered, Madison was Monroe's first choice for a special envoy to Europe. From the first moment, wrote Secretary of State John Quincy Adams, "I thought of no other person." But Madison preferred to stay in Virginia.

When, later, Monroe formulated his "Monroe Doctrine" against European intervention in the Western Hemisphere, he would perform a national service by stating clearly a preexisting concept. A truer name might have been the Madison-Jefferson-Monroe Doctrine. But Madison, as usual, was all but indifferent to credit. Let Metternich and the other "partisans of despotism," he would tell Monroe, "rage"; the stand taken by the United States was "just and lofty."

Power corrupts some, not all, human beings.

The work of John Taylor of Caroline seemed to Madison unmeasured and lopsided. Three years ago the *Construction Construed* of this champion of extreme states' rights had challenged the Supreme Court's authority to issue writs of error to state courts. But Madison knew that if each state could settle federal-state disputes on its own, the Constitution would receive so many different interpretations, chaos would come again: an inequality of sovereignty which might lead to a trial of strength between part and whole. Impossible! By saying so forthrightly, three years ago, he had risked the disfavor of his beloved state of Virginia. Now Taylor's *New View of the Constitution*—brilliant but blind—was bringing up the old issue. Some people cheered state sovereignty, others federal, when in Madison's view (could he ever say it enough?) the secret of the country's strength lay in *shared* sovereignty. Balance, equilibrium, counterpoise: that was the principle which held the universe—God's and Rittenhouse's—together.

At Montpelier wind found the smallest crack. While Madison worked by the fire, Dolley huddled in shawls, worrying about fifteen-year-old Walter—imagine the gales on the water! To Wat, in November, as he went to sea, she had something very serious to say: "May you make for yourself a shield of religion and honor." And still the wind swept round and badgered the house.

But the news that Lafayette had chosen next summer for his tour was heartwarming. Would he come this way? The Madisons in their retirement had long doubted that they would ever again set eyes on Washington City except in memory and imagination. (How changed the society must be; they'd feel like strangers.) Their great hope was that Lafayette would visit Montpelier.

One day Dolley heard from her daughter-in-law manqué. So much joy and sorrow had passed by, Phoebe wrote, "I often think of you and my dear Mr. Madison alone at Montpelier. . . . I know all your motions and ways so well that at any hour of the day I can represent to myself what you are doing." She believes that the first place Lafayette will "fly to" is Montpelier. And she adds a description of Mrs. John Quincy Adams's reception for General Jackson. His hostess took his arm to parade him about, and ladies "climbed chairs and benches", to see him better. Sadly, "Adieu, my dearest and best friend; believe me, as ever, your own affectionate Phoebe Morris." It was a letter to stir dead hopes.

Troubled by lack of money, Payne's prolonged absence, and Jeffer-

son's decline, but not without substantial compensations, the Madisons
lived, if not in paradise any more, on its outskirts. At seventy-three James
still rode his horse daily; Dolley, at fifty-six, had energy to run the house
and help with her husband's notes. Long ago in the mystery of relationship they had, without losing individuality, come to act almost as one; a
head-heart, fully aware double person with no inner contradictions, no
premonition of disaster.

The blow fell the spring of 1824. Richard Cutts, who had borrowed
$6,000 from Madison and $4,000 from Payne, was tottering on the brink
of bankruptcy.

Terrified for Anna and her children and not a little for themselves,
Dolley wrote her speculator brother-in-law:

> Secret.
>
> It is with inexpressible grief, my dear brother, that I under-
> stand (in confidence) the threatening situation of your affairs! I
> will not insult your sensibility by descanting on the devoted
> friendship and affection for you and yours ever felt by Mr.
> Madison and myself because you know it! But if ever you recip-
> rocated—which we never doubted—I entreat you to secure to
> me the amount of *all the money lent you* in a house, lots or some
> other property, in case you have at this unlucky moment to part
> with what you possess in Washington. It is only in such a case,
> where other creditors may take *all*, that I would ever remind you
> of the *debt*. Yes, it is more for your sake than mine that I now
> write to ask you, for God's sake, to do this just thing that you and
> your children may profit from it, for be assured that you may
> afterwards command this sum with all that could be desired
> from every source to rescue or to enrich you for more fortunate
> speculations. I will . . . simply add that you must preserve the
> confidence of a *ready and efficient friend* [Madison] by acting as I
> suggest. Write me a few lines directly and receive the heart of
> your affectionate and anxious sister
>
> D.P.M.

Cutts's situation worsened rapidly. The mortgage on the house built
largely with Madison's and Payne's money was foreclosed by the Bank of
the United States, and Cutts's creditors clapped the defaulter into debtor's
prison—to him and his family a terrible humiliation. He regained his
freedom by declaring bankruptcy, which threw his property into the
hands of an administrator.

Madison, pinched by a series of crop failures, faced a sizable new loss. He might make up Payne's, but how his own? He and Dolley agonized over the possibility of Anna sinking into destitution. Though many good men had fallen and were falling into bankruptcy—Robert Morris, Light Horse Harry Lee, Thomas Mann Randolph—that fact did not remove the stigma nor solve Cutts's problem of paying off his debts and supporting his large family.

In June, to cushion the fall, the Madisons joined a legal agreement to hold in trust for Anna P. Cutts or her survivors $1,200 furnished by Lucy P. Todd and "others of her kindred and friends."

Madison salvaged something by arranging to buy the Cutts house on the President's Square at a price—"between $5,000 and $6,000—fixed by bank-appointed appraisers, with Cutts undertaking, as partial payment of his debt, to meet monthly installments out of his salary as reinstated Second Comptroller of the Treasury. A memo by Madison says he reluctantly agreed to absentee ownership to keep a roof over Anna and her children.

It was startling to receive a letter from Dr. Thornton, one of Cutts's creditors, quoting a rumor that the real owner, Mrs. Cutts, desiring to continue to live in elegance, was guilty of collusion—was this true? Answering his old friend, Madison said that the house was his own "bonafide and absolute property."

In the midst of strain, the Madisons heard the gossip that Payne Todd was wooing the reigning Williamsburg beauty, Miss Anne Cole. Was it true? If so, how would she respond? Was Anne Cole their son's destiny?

The Cutts tumult lessening, James and Dolley went back to work. They even smiled. Lafayette and the son he had named after George Washington were on the high seas!

On August 21 Madison sat down at his mahogany desk inlaid with silver and mother-of-pearl to write the famous Frenchman.

> I this instant learn, my dear friend, that you have safely reached the shores where you will be hailed by every voice of a free people. That of no one . . . springs more from the heart than mine. May I not hope that the course of your movements will give me an opportunity of proving it by the warmth of my embrace on my own threshold?

After a short wait, he received Lafayette's reply. Yes, in November it would be his pleasure to go from Monticello to Montpelier. That promise was part, if not complete, indemnity for the Madisons' troubles.

Frosts had built a conflagration in the woods as five men struggled for the Presidency—John Quincy Adams, William Crawford, Henry Clay, General Andrew Jackson, John C. Calhoun. When Calhoun was nominated for Vice President, the fight between the remaining four waxed more bitter. Though Madison avoided the campaign, he felt some of its pressures. They mingled with his anxiety over Dolley's anxiety over Payne.

Payne—what did he propose to do with his life? Throw it away? The three oldest Cutts boys, though much younger, had all chosen careers: Mad held a government job, Tom was entering West Point, Wat a midshipman under Commodore Isaac Hull. In contrast, their thirty-two-year-old cousin was loafing, gaming, and (the evidence will be cited later) living loosely. Moreover, his neglect of his mother, whom he professed to love and did love in his curious way, was toppling his own record.

Early in November, Madison rode toward Monticello and his old friend Lafayette. It was probably no accident that he arrived after the General. A natural-born tact could have told him not to risk intruding on the meeting of Lafayette and Jefferson.

While Madison was riding horseback through stripped woods, Lafayette's triumphant progress from New York had brought hin to a delirious welcome in Charlottesville, Virginia. Banners waved, trumpets blew, and a guard of honor escorted him to Monticello. As he stepped from his barouche, a white-haired and stooped Jefferson hastened forward to greet him. Lafayette had changed too! Since his long imprisonment at Olmutz in Austria, the once dapper young revolutionary had grown fat. "Ah, Jefferson!" "Ah, Lafayette!" Embracing, they started to choke up. Four hundred spectators had uncovered; not a few had to wipe their eyes. And at sundown the Jefferson family and Lafayette and his entourage sat down to dinner with much to eat and more to say.

The company was finishing the main course when it heard a noise in the hall. The gentlemen rose respectfully as James Madison entered the dining room. He and General Lafayette converged like a conjunction of planets.

Never had Monticello heard richer conversation than that night. Time dissolved as old friends spoke of George Washington and the hard-beset Continental Army. Lafayette, Jefferson, and Madison were back amid the brotherhood of the Revolution with their fortunes wavering. Jefferson was seeing the fiery friend of his five years in Paris, Madison the volatile Frenchman with whom he had battled head winds, slept under stars, and swum horses across a river while holding abovestream five kegs of "breasts of milk." They had been younger, then, and the United States still younger, just born, and that November night of reunion at Monticello—with the lightning of a heroic past flashing brightly episodic—something in them longed for vanished days.

Before he went to bed Madison wrote Dolley about arriving just in time for dessert. Lafayette would probably reach Montpelier by midweek. "My old friend embraced me with great warmth," ran the report. "He is in fine health and spirits, and so much increased in bulk and changed in aspect I should not have known him." But the meeting was less outward than inward.

The next morning Charlottesville entertained Lafayette at a reception at the Central Hotel. There were flags and bugles and a crowd of girls in white dresses waving white handkerchiefs. At three o'clock, in the rotunda of the not-yet-opened University, 400 citizens sat down to a dinner in honor of the one remaining great military man of the Revolution. The tables were arranged in three concentric circles. Lafayette had an easy way with strangers. "Married, Sir?" he would ask. "Yes." "Happy man!" "Married, Sir?" "No." "Lucky dog!" Toasts piled up to and by Lafayette, to and by the ex-Presidents, some a little wordy, all intensely sincere. Jefferson looked old and tired, but Madison had never been in finer fettle. At one point, lifting his glass, he said, "Happy the people with virtue for their guest and gratitude for their feast." That night Lafayette's secretary, Levasseur, would write in his journal, "Mr. Madison stood out among all of them for the originality of his mind and the delicacy of his allusions."

Several days later the Madisons drove a long distance to meet the Orange County Volunteer Guard escorting Lafayette's carriage to Montpelier. *Bon jour,* and a thousand welcomes!

It was a splendid visit. Lafayette was charmed by his reception, by his old friend Madison, by Dolley, and by the Montpelier plantation. For long hours he and Madison talked about old times and present political and economic trends and their mutual love, horticulture. That subject could hardly be exhausted. Several evenings they called on neighboring farmers, to talk some more. And one day Madison took Lafayette on a visit to Granny Milly in the Walnut Grove. The Frenchman enjoyed himself hugely. He expressed surprise that Montpelier's black people were so well dressed and that some of them actually spoke French, and he regretted all over again that illness had kept his two slavery-hating English "adopted daughters," Fanny and Camilla Wright, from joining him here; they'd have to recognize, here, some mitigating factors. Madison readily agreed that slavery was wrong. (Later Levasseur would speak of his host's noble sentiments on emancipation.) The problem was the *modus operandi,* Madison said earnestly. How give black people genuine instead of just token help?

Though work and reflection and the passing years had lent Madison's face a certain severity, Levasseur says, his "well-preserved frame contains a youthful soul full of gentle sensibility and gaiety."

There is an interesting fourteen-line poem about Lafayette in Dolley's handwriting which she seems to have composed from impressions and judgments formed during the Marquis's 1824 visit.

> He hears in joyous youth a wild report
> Swelling the murmurs of the western gale
> Of a young people struggling to be free. . . .
> And shares the glories of its victory.

The lines turn to address Lafayette directly.

> . . . Crowned at the last with hope and wide applause,
> Champion of freedom! well thy race was run!
> All time shall hail thee, Europe's noblest son!

At the end of the visit Orange County gave the Frenchman a banquet at its Courthouse. When Madison escorted in the honor guest, the pair ran the gauntlet of a double line of 200 welcomers. One of the ex-President's nine toasts: "To love liberty a nation need but know it." Someone jumped up to praise Madison himself as "pure in private life, illustrious in public life; we love the man and venerate the statesman." Apparently the ex-President was embarrassed. In any case he quickly turned the praise away from himself. How speak of gratitude, he remarked, without recalling what the entire nation owed this Frenchman so devoted to the principles of the American Revolution? His final ringing accolade: "To the divine right of self-government and its immortal champions!"—not the divine right of kings but the divine right of self-government based on *the nature of man.*

The banquet was too short, the whole visit too short. It was time for Lafayette to start for Fredericksburg. Hand grasped hand. Hail and farewell; a long farewell.

Lafayette's last glimpse of his host would stay printed on his eye for months. As his barouche rolled away toward new entertainments (none as stimulating as at Montpelier), he and his companions turned to look back for one last glimpse. They saw seventy-three-year-old James Madison mount his horse—as Levasseur would record—"nimbly," to ride back through the forest.

It seems peculiarly fitting that the great Frenchman's last view of his friend in 1824 was of the man on horseback. Madison was an expert rider. In youth he had regained his health on horseback, and he had taken pleasure riding in Williamsburg, Philadelphia, New England, New York, Richmond, and Washington, as well as—for more than three score years and ten—through the fields and woods of Montpelier. Moreover, a man astride a horse is an ancient symbol of reason triumphant over instinct. James Madison was, in truth, man-on-horse.

So, OF COURSE, WAS JEFFERSON, and that was, basically, the reason for their great congeniality. For half a century they had shared problems and pleasures, and were now, with mutual and absolute trust, collaborating in new ways, knowing that in the nature of things their alliance must, all too soon, end. The thought was like a dissonance in music.

Whereas Madison's health remained good, Jefferson's had deteriorated further. After a crumbling step threw him to the ground in 1823, his right hand had stiffened; he could use it very little, and an old digestive disorder—grown more severe—was seriously weakening his constitution. Though he still rode old Eagle every day, he could no longer hoist himself into the saddle; he had to be lowered onto it from a bank. It was a good world, he said; gladly would he relive his last seventy years, but age could reach a point of tedium.

Creditors pursued him. On retiring from the Presidency he had found himself $20,000 in debt. The drop in farm prices during the War of 1812 had compounded his financial embarrassment. The sale to Congress of his 10,000-volume library had brought roughly $24,000, but during the depression of 1819 and '20 ex-Governor Nicholas, his grandson Jeff's father-in-law, whose $25,000 note Jefferson had countersigned, had gone bankrupt. The squire of Monticello met the obligation cheerfully, hoping to recoup by selling land. It was no solution. Fertile Western territories, competing against exhausted Eastern soil, were attracting speculators in ever-growing numbers. Virginia land prices plummeted to one-fifth their former level. And visitors to Monticello (as to Montpelier) kept arriving in droves.

Fortunately Jefferson was "mounted on a hobby." Not only had he designed the University, this "Athenaeum of our country in embryo"; he had also superintended its construction, and now that he could no longer ride horseback to inspect the range's pavilions, he watched their progress through a telescope.

Understanding each other perfectly and in full accord, Jefferson and Madison talked over new problems in the establishment of the institution. When possible they conferred face-to-face, otherwise by letter, about faculty, curriculum, textbooks. As scholars who believed profoundly in disciplined education, they saw the task as intimately theirs. The challenge warmed old blood. It was a burden and a joy. From the beginning Madison had wished to help in every way possible his friend's great project. In a very real sense he was co-founder.

The time came when Jefferson could no longer rise from bed. His long freckled hands shook. The Madisons grew increasingly apprehensive. They could hardly have been more concerned about a member of their family. Spiritually he was of their blood.

At the same time they were painfully perplexed about Payne's rumored courtship—was there anything substantial between him and Anne Cole of Williamsburg? They knew so little about him these days, nothing really. Notice of the marriage of nineteen-year-old Mary Jackson underscored Payne's bachelorhood. They had hoped that the story about his being in love—if the lady was suitable and reciprocated—would prove true and have a happy end, but why the long delay? There had been no announcement, and Payne had not written.

The presidential election of 1824 having given no candidate a majority, the decision was now up to the House of Representatives. One afternoon Henry Clay and a pair of companions reached Montpelier for a two-day visit. If they had come for political help, they left disappointed. Regarding all four candidates as friends—Jackson, Adams, Crawford, and Clay—Madison was resolved to remain strictly neutral.

As Clay departed, a letter from Payne, mailed in Philadelphia, arrived. It contained a baffling allusion. Had the lady refused or encouraged him? He said nothing about coming home.

In her reply to this lost letter Dolley grasps a bull by sharp horns. Mr. Clay, like all of Payne's old acquaintances, she says, has inquired after him affectionately.

> But, my dear son, it seems to be the wonder of them all that you should stay so long from us, and now I am ashamed to tell, when asked, how long my only child has been absent from the home of his mother! Your Papa and myself entreat you to come to us; to

arrange your business with those concerned to return to them when necessary, and let us see you here as soon as possible with your interest-convenience. Your Papa thinks as I do that it would be best for your reputation and happiness, as well as ours, that you should have the appearance of consulting your parents on subjects of deep account to you, and that you should find it so on *returning* to Philadelphia. . . . I have said in my late letters, as well as this, all that I *thought sufficient* to influence you—I must now put my trust in God alone! If the young lady you have followed so long has not yet been won, I fear she declines the chance, Son, to favor your happiness hereafter, though others might be found who would.

Though he asked for $20, she is sending $30. She knows " 'tis insufficient for the journey" but isn't able to send more. With the funds left in her hands, she has paid $200 on Holloway's note, plus two years' interest, also some of his smaller debts, and she hopes to hear, soon, about his plans. Judge Todd is near death. Then back to Payne's mysterious remark.

The "— — occurrence" you allude to I hope is propitious. If it were for your good we might rejoice in your immediate union, provided it brought you speedily to our arms who love you with inexpressible tenderness and constancy.

Your own Mother.

It was not Payne; it was the Federalists Mr. and Mrs. George Tichnor and Daniel Webster, stamping snow off their feet. If Madison remembered how Webster had once baited him cruelly while he lay critically ill in the White House, he gave no sign, nor did Dolley; they were all courtesy. Tichnor says their reception smacked a little of ceremony which quickly gave way to informality. They enjoyed a tour of the house, good food, and great crackling fires. That first day Webster whispered to Tichnor, *"Stare hic."* "He was afraid," the diarist explains, "I might say something about going away the next day, but I had no such intention."

They breakfasted at nine, ate dinner at four, drank tea at seven, and went to bed at ten; "that is, we went to our rooms, where we were furnished with everything we wanted, and where Mrs. Madison sent us a nice supper every night and a nice luncheon every forenoon . . . a hospitality which becomes one who has been at the head of the nation." Madison's vast repertoire of stories amused them greatly, and the New Englanders were struck by the "degree of good sense in his conversation which we had not anticipated from his school of politics and course of life."

In the midst of their visit Payne came home. His arrival startled his parents. It seemed incredible. Here he was, eating in the dining room, talking in the salon, galloping off with the two male guests on long horseback rides in cold brisk air! It was a luxury for the Madisons just to watch him.

During the Christmas season following the New Englanders' departure, the prodigal son ate of the fatted calf and presumably explained about the mysterious lady. Whatever he said or did, he could still be charming; a Cutts cousin has called him the most fascinating of men. (As a boy this witness was taken by Payne to eat strawberries and cream at the Boulanger Restaurant on G Street in Washington. Payne's coffee was spiked with brandy, and so, apparently, were the strawberries eaten by young James Madison Cutts II, for he went home inebriated. On the other hand a girl cousin has said that Payne filled her with fear.) Charming and scattered and dubious.

Sometimes at Montpelier the talk swung to the political Gordian knot now being cut in the House of Representatives. At last the Madisons and Payne heard that Clay had swung to Adams on the first ballot, thus securing John Quincy Adams's election and Jackson's lasting enmity. Bargain and corruption, the Jacksonians charged, since in the original election the hero of New Orleans had received 99 votes to Adams's 87. Nonsense, retorted Madison; Clay and Adams were straight as dies, and there was no harm in Adams offering Clay the State portfolio—after all, Clay was the best man for the job. But no good talk, no topic, no plea, no consideration could hold Payne, this man of weak will, frustrated passions, and hazy objectives.

Perhaps during his visit Payne's parents attempted a heart-to-heart discussion of his drinking, gaming, roving, and imperiled future. If so, it made little impression. And as suddenly as he had come he was gone.

Again Dolley would try to make the best of a deplored separation. Payne's visit had been precious. Thereafter she was to be kept largely in ignorance of his increasingly spendthrift ways. When some odd detail of misconduct got through to her, she said, "My poor boy. Forgive his eccentricities—his heart is right." And indeed his faults seem to have been great weakness before temptation and a certain willfulness rather than any overt evil. His later journal would record a constant making and breaking of good resolutions. Perhaps nothing implies more eloquently what Dolley suffered over his deterioration than his still-extant cradle and a black leather trunk full of baby clothes, including an embroidered christening robe and a child's time-yellowed apron which Dolley saved into his years of manhood.

A letter from Dolley to Mary Cutts shows her picking herself up after the disappointment of his latest departure:

> . . . My sweetest of daughters! . . . Your Uncle and cousins are all
> well and think highly of you. . . . Kiss Dolley for me and tell her I
> hope and trust she yields implicit obedience to her dear mother.
> I hope to hear good news from my favorite Walter and hope to
> see him a good man and great captain. . . . We have had two
> weeks of springlike weather, when the birds came out with their
> summer song and I went to gardening. . . . I go but little from
> home except to ride for exercise—

presumably sidesaddle. " . . . And when you write me, my darling, get a large paper and recollect . . . my old acquaintances as well as the new people, what they say and do." Would the girls go to the "coronation"? To Dolley, relationships were vital. She needed people as the lungs need oxygen.

Her husband, meanwhile, was preoccupied with the University's planned opening on February first. When its motto, John's "Ye shall know the truth, and the truth shall make you free," was announced, critics who had charged the institution with irreligion because it lacked a school of divinity were pulled up sharp. (Actually, ministers from all denominations were invited to preach on campus.) But the University did not open on time. All was ready. The carpenters had stopped hammering on the five classically simple pavilions punctuating a double row of student rooms. And a student body was lined up. But it was not enough. To open they required a faculty. Professor of Ancient Languages George Long had arrived, drawn lots for his pavilion, got Number 5, and settled in. But storms on the Atlantic had delayed the European professors. To start without them, Jefferson wrote Madison, would bring "ridicule and disgrace." It meant a further delay. When at last the savants debarked at Norfolk, students were told to arrive March 7. They streamed toward Charlottesville by horseback, stagecoach, carriage, and wagon, joking about the mud on the roads. Not bad, not bad at all, they said; *never* higher than above the wheel hubs.

In Washington, March 4 inaugurated President John Quincy Adams; in Charlottesville, March 7 began a courageous essay into higher education. Six faculty members, forty students, Rector Jefferson, and six other Visitors, including Madison, took part in a Masonic ceremony. Dolley sat in the audience.

For Jefferson, the assembled students brought back memories of his life at William and Mary; for Madison, his years at Princeton under Dr.

Witherspoon—ah, Dr. Witherspoon, dead these twenty years. Both knew that college can bend the shoot that determines the shape of the full-grown tree.

Madison returned home exhilarated. The great project was off to a fine start. Now if they could just fill the Chair of Law! But the sight of all those earnest young men building toward settled lives must have brought to the mind of both Madisons, by contrast, the dilemma of Payne. What of him? Major McKenney of Philadelphia had written Dolley that Mr. Todd looked well. That was good—but he had again broken off all contact with Montpelier.

Meanwhile Jefferson was fast losing ground. When in 1825 Lafayette (whom Congress had granted $200,000 and a Florida township) came to bid a final good-bye before returning to France, he found Jefferson lying on a couch, racked by rheumatism. In Charlottesville, Madison and Monroe attended a second banquet for the nation's guest. But the chair of the third ex-President stood empty. Mr. Southall read Mr. Jefferson's speech. "My friends, I am old. . . ."

There seemed no end to troubles. For the sixth year in a row, at both Monticello and Montpelier, the harvest was meager. Jefferson tried but could not rally. And Madison—who kept the fact from Dolley—had to bail Payne out of a $500 debt at Washington's lottery.

That was the summer of Phoebe's death. Dolley knew that during a year-long tubercular decline this lovely young woman of thirty-two had been giving her days to poetry, painting, music, and meditation. Now the Madisons heard that her death had been worthy of her Quaker upbringing. During a short interval from severe pain, she called her sister and her brother's children to join her in singing

> There is a land of pure delight
>   Where saints immortal reign.
> Infinite day excludes the night
>   And pleasures banish pain.

That was just before her "happy change." Phoebe had said over and over that she didn't want her loved ones to mourn. But Dolley with her affection and memories and failed hope was hard put to stop grieving. So Phoebe had gone—blond, pretty, loving Phoebe Morris, spinster—the girl who had danced so blithely and who might have become their daughter-in-law. They sent the Anthony Morris family their condolences.

Two months later, in August, Dolley entertained the New England "poetess" Lydia Sigourney (and may have plucked up courage to show some of her own verses). Mrs. Sigourney wrote an adjective-loaded eulogy of Montpelier. Though meretricious as poetry, the tribute holds some interest as a record of what impressed one visitor. We hear of "bright-eyed pheasants," purple-spiked Pride of China, books, paintings, music. "Splendid deeds . . . of hospitality" is clear enough. The "benignant" and "serene" soul mentioned is Dolley. And the final accolade, to James Madison, however florid, is not without truth.

> Here Wisdom rests in sylvan shade
> Which once an empire's counsels swayed,
> And Goodness whose persuasive art
> So justly won that empire's heart,
> And Piety with hoary hair . . .
> Rising from this Eden fair.

Eden: it is Mrs. Miller's word of eight years ago.

In September the Madisons drove over to Monticello and, as on innumerable occasions in the past, lingered on the terrace bareheaded of an evening, talking and drinking in matchless views. But it tore their hearts to see Jefferson so feeble. Was it the last time they would visit together?

How pleasant to sit again in the large entrance hall, this virtual museum exhibiting such curiosities as an ancient coat of mail, the jawbone and tusks of a mammoth, Indian paintings on buffalo hides, two hideous Indian busts, and the stuffed head of a giant ram, as well as portraits of Heraclitus, Democritus, Amerigo Vespucci, Walter Raleigh, Bacon, Locke, Washington, and Lafayette.

The two men discussed the University, farm problems, science, the classics, and then the nation, in the founding of which both had played vital parts. Their interests being close, they had now, more than ever, for it was cumulative, a sense of solidarity. Inevitably they got around to the financial chuckholes into which they were sinking. Though their two predicaments were not exactly the same, they were similar. With his head start, Jefferson was just further along the road in the beggaring process.

Then perhaps one of Jefferson's granddaughters with a sweet voice started singing, or a servant brought a bowl of grapes, or the bonfire of an exotic sunset blazed up, and they could forget, if only for a while, their own and the world's problems.

One day a messenger galloped up with word that a student had tossed a smoking stink bomb through a window into Professor Long's pavilion. It was a shock. Jefferson and Madison had hoped, through stiff, screening entrance requirements, to obtain a soberminded student body, and it had seemed that, in spite of occasional outbreaks of class cutting, carousing, and gaming, the founders' ideals, helped by discipline and time, would reform certain wealthy spoiled youths. A stink bomb! Was the student self-government which had been their pride helpless to stop hoolliganism?

The next night a masked mob roiled about the lawn chanting "Down with the European professors!" And when Professors Tucker and Emmet seized a leader swathed in a counterpane, Tucker was hit with a cane, Emmet with a brick—"The rascal tore my shirt!" Sixty-five students signed a protest against the faculty for "manhandling" that draped figure.

The Board of Visitors—having just received the resignations of Professor of Ancient Languages Long and Professor of Mathematics Key, together with the rest of the faculty's warning that if order were not immediately restored, they too would resign—met around a table in the Rotunda, august and stony-faced: Joseph C. Cabell, General John H. Cocke, Chapman Johnson, and three ex-Presidents, Jefferson, Madison, and Monroe. They were confronting the student body head on. Rising slowly, Rector Jefferson called the episode one of the most painful in his life. Then, overcome, he asked the eloquent lawyer Johnson to express his sentiments, and sat down. When Johnson had finished his indictment, the rioters were told to step up and give their names. Nearly all did. A disciplinary plan was worked out, and Professors Long and Key agreed to stay on.

(The fracas highlighted a fundamental need of democratic government: a sense of responsibility, a trait which Madison's life exemplified. He knew well that without it, freedom becomes license and an empty word. Lack of a balance between freedom and responsibility had disrupted the University—could it some day disrupt the nation? Should responsibility, in fact, have been mentioned in the Declaration of Independence and the Constitution as the reverse of the coin of freedom? Should America have been reminded from the start that responsibility is freedom's other face? It was a thought hard to avoid.)

The Madisons reached home emotionally exhausted.

It was not the best time for sculptor John Henri Isaac Browere to arrive for the making of life masks. Nor did it help Dolley and James to know that he had almost suffocated Jefferson, and then almost torn an ear off. But if the Madisons shrank from their ordeal, they suffered it. Browere's bust of the seventy-five-year-old Madison based on the life mask shows a strong face made grim by the fact that quick-hardening plaster becomes hideously uncomfortable: vaulted forehead, faintly Roman nose, longish upper lip, thick eyebrows, sideburns, outmoded queue. Browere's bust of the fifty-seven-year-old Dolley came off less well. No life mask can record an alabaster quality of skin or the light in eyes. Imprisonment behind plaster of Paris has turned her face wooden, and store-bought curls and a tasseled turban are not flattering. Call it Dolley's off day. A picture painted years later is much more attractive.

Madison now borrowed $1,000 to meet another of Payne's board bills and another lottery debt. News of them had reached him accompanied by horrid intimations as to Payne's mode of life. It was clear that he was a compulsive gambler. Jemmy, whose thoughts had for decades been an open book for Dolley, was put to concealment—she was already too worried. Though hiding facts weighed upon him, he could not bring himself to increase her suffering. Payne seemed to have kicked aside all moral considerations. Had some unknown factor entered his life?

On November 13, 1825, Madison, who could have been angry, wrote his stepson a letter notable for kindness.

> My dear P.,
>
> What shall I say to you? It is painful to utter reproaches; yet how can they be avoided? Your last letter to your mother made us confident that we should see you in a few days. Weeks have passed without even a line explaining the disappointment, or soothing the anxieties of the tenderest of mothers, wound up to the highest pitch by this addition to your long and mysterious absence.
>
> As ample remittances were furnished for all known purposes, your continuance where you are under strange appearances necessarily produces distressing apprehensions. Whatever be the cause of it, you owe it to yourself, as well as to us, to withhold them no longer. Let the worst be known, that the best may be made of it. I wish not to dwell on the subject, but I must not conclude without imploring and conjuring you to hasten to the embraces of your parents, and to put an end to the uncertainties that afflict them; giving immediate assurance that you will do so by a line to your mother by the first mail after this gets to hand. You cannot be too quick in affording relief to her present feelings.
>
> > Your affectionate
> > M—

"Let the worst be known, that the best may be made of it"—faults, defaults.

Like other couples with an erring offspring, the Madisons wondered if they had made mistakes, perhaps been too indulgent, or sent him away too early or to the wrong schools, or pushed the trip to Europe unwisely. A youth can fall under bad influences before he is able to cope.

They spent Christmas 1825 without son, daughter-in-law, or grand-child. Dolley's mood comes out in a letter to Sally.

> I cannot express my anxiety to embrace you once more; but a spell rests upon me and withholds me from those I love best in the world! Not a mile can I go from home; and in no way can I account for it, but that my husband is also fixed there. This is the third winter in which he has been engaged in the arrangement of papers, and the business appears to accumulate as he proceeds, so that I calculate its outlasting my patience, and yet I cannot press him to foresake a duty so important, or find it in my heart to leave him during its fulfillment.

Though there's no one they'd rather visit, she says, they can't accept the Stevensons' invitation—please save their "room and little stand." Anna, who writes regularly, "is in a round of pleasant society and, though devoted as ever to her children, takes time to enjoy a dance." Others keep up a "fashion of dissipation"—among them, she might have added, her son Payne.

Jefferson, meanwhile, was like a carriage running downhill. The drugs which Lafayette sent from France had failed to slow his wheels. Even with the help of his trusty gold-headed cane he could take no more walks. His family did not know how much of his diminishment was owing to disease, how much to old age, how much to apprehension over impend-ing financial ruin. One irony was that, unable to break a habit of hospital-ity, this man on the brink of bankruptcy and death continued to invite University professors and students to dinner.

But he hit on a scheme; he petitioned the Virginia Assembly to permit him to sell most of his land—not his home—by lottery. Only thus, he said, could he get a fair price, pay off his debts, and have something left for old age and his family. It would injure no one. Some opposition developed. But his grandson-manager, Thomas Jefferson Randolph, after attending a session of the legislature, assured him that there was still hope.

Though writing was difficult, Jefferson wrote Madison about the main causes of his catastrophe: drought-stunted crops, new taxes for the protection of manufacturing, the drop in land values. "But why afflict you with these details?"—unless it reduced pain to unburden on a friend. Then a crucial message:

> The friendship which has subsisted between us now half a century, and the harmony of our political principles and pursuits, have been sources of constant happiness to me. . . . If I remove beyond the reach of attentions to the University, or beyond the bourne of life itself, as I soon must, it is a comfort to leave that institution under your care. . . .

Indeed he hopes for something else at the end of their long fruitful collaborations:

> It has . . . been a great solace to me to believe that you are engaged in vindicating to posterity the course we have pursued for preserving to them in all their purity the blessings of self-government, which we had assisted, too, in acquiring for them. If ever the earth had beheld a system of administration conducted single and steadfast eye to the general interest and happiness of those committed to it, . . . it is that to which our lives have been devoted.

And finally, in this virtual farewell, he makes explicit what had long been implicit, asking a last favor: "To myself you have been a pillar of support through life. Take care of me when dead, and be assured that I shall leave with you my last affections." *Take care of me when dead.*

Madison's natural reserves crumbled. Deeply touched, he sat down and wrote a letter to his old partner, sending him "the fullest return of affectionate assurances."

Amid all the sadness, it seemed too much that Assemblyman Cabell was foretelling, delicately, the defeat of Jefferson's lottery plan. Could Virginia be so ungrateful?

Jefferson himself, while expressing thanks for his friends' efforts, felt a sting of bitterness. He said he counted on nothing now; he had been taught to know his standard. The death of his lovely granddaughter Anne Bankhead piled Pelion on Ossa; he was overwhelmed by misfortune and braced himself to receive the *coup de grâce* from Richmond.

It did not happen. In February 1826, the Assembly passed the special lottery bill for Mr. Jefferson. Meanwhile people in New York, Philadelphia, and Baltimore had responded to news of Jefferson's "pauperism" with sums of—respectively—$8,500, $5,000, and $3,000; recourse to a lottery seemed unnecessary. Jefferson was exultant. No taxpayer had lost a penny; the money had come unsolicited, a pure gift of love. He did not know that he owed more than the $16,500 offered, that his debt was nearer $100,000. In May he wrote Madison that his health was much better; he had even managed, by stepping from terrace to saddle, to ride old Eagle again—and the Madisons thanked God.

There was little else to cheer. Lucy had lost the good Judge, Sally was ill, money extremely tight, Payne sent no word, and Madison's correspondence with his stepson's latest creditors left him appalled—clearly Payne had said good-bye to his conscience. When they sent stage fare for him to come home, he diverted it to purposes darkly imaginable. Madison wrote ex-Consul Levett Harris, who had loaned Payne a large sum, that it would have been friendlier to refuse. A month later he was telling Payne's Philadelphia landlord that unfortunately he must delay settling the expected board bill. Mr. Bailey replied gruffly that Mr. Todd was risking debtor's prison.

Madison wrote Payne a difficult letter. After a reference to Dolley, "I now hasten to a subject which if disclosed to her would inflict new torture." He hoped Bailey would let him return to Montpelier. Sorrowfully, affectionately,

> Come then, I entreat and conjure you, to the bosom of your parents who are anxious to do everything to save you from tendencies and past errors and provide for comfort and happiness.

Payne made no reply. Madison could only imagine his condition. Then Postmaster Richard Bache of Philadelphia wrote that to prevent "arrest and imprisonment" and enable Payne to go home, he had cashed Payne's draft for $300, only to find that he had skipped to New York. Stunned and heartsick, Madison mortgaged 361 more acres for $2,000 to cover this new debt. Eden was resembling purgatory. Madison believed or was trying to believe that Payne still possessed some good qualities, but it was getting harder and harder. Even if he had come home, how reach him? As a youth he had shown decency and ambition. Had drink, disappointment in love, corrupt companions, and sexual license so completely alienated him from himself? And was the process irreversible?

It was now that Madison heard of an aggravation of Jefferson's digestive disorder. His friend was critically ill. Late in June Dr. Robley Dunglison of the University faculty sent Madison a note to prepare him for the worst.

Jefferson (as the Madisons would hear later) alternated between wakefulness and stupor. Once he likened himself to an old watch with here a pinion and there a wheel worn out. To his grandson he spoke fondly of James Madison, his learning and wisdom, his extraordinary abilities and pure character. The next day it looked as if he would not get his desire to live until the fiftieth anniversary of the Declaration of Independence. Members of his family slipped in, one by one, to say good-bye. No, he said, no more laudanum. Suddenly he started up crying, "Warn the Committee of Safety!" At daybreak the bells of Milton rang out for the Fourth of July, and that day, about one o'clock, Jefferson stopped breathing.

A letter notifying the Madisons of his peaceful end arrived too late for them to attend the funeral, and they were sorry—but wasn't it sacred to Jefferson's family anyway?

Much affected, for in a larger sense he and Dolley were family too, Madison replied in words which would have pleased Jefferson very much.

> I never doubted that the last scene of our illustrious friend would be worthy of the life it closed. . . . But we are more than consoled for the loss by the gain to him, and by the assurance that he lives, and will live, in the memory and gratitude of the wise and good, as a luminary of science, as a votary of liberty, a model of patriotism, and benefactor of the human kind. In these characters I have known him . . . for . . . fifty years, during which there was not an interruption or diminution of mutual confidence and cordial friendship for a single moment. . . .

Madison was the only person, other than relatives and manumitted slaves, mentioned in Jefferson's will. He inherited his friend's horn cane. Its gold head, when he grasped it, seemed still warm from another's hand.

⊰ XVIII ⊱

"LET THE WORST
BE KNOWN"

THOUGH A PILLAR HAD FALLEN, the structure still stood. The Madisons had a good philosophy of death as of life. Also work helped. In his role as head of the University—"the Rector is dead, long live the Rector"—Madison continued his collaboration with Jefferson. And the hot summer moved on, tormented by flies.

A letter from Dolley Madison to Dolley Cutts shows a reviving *joie de vivre*. She is as proud of Dolché's talents as of a daughter's. Come back to Montpelier—everyone wants to see her. Dolley regrets she couldn't send the flounce. "Kiss my little son," the second Richard. No, she wouldn't like Washington's new afternoon calling rules; she'd "break through"—dash out to see people on "cool mornings and dewy evenings." The garden is bursting with grapes and figs, but she can't enjoy them unless Anna's family helps eat them. Thinking of "precious Wat" on the sea, her eyes fill with tears. "Your tender mother and aunt."

But this openhearted letter contains a veiled passage.

I received by the last post a letter from your cousin Payne at New York. He writes in fine health and spirits, and says he will yet be detained 2 or 3 weeks longer in that city. I flatter myself with the hope of seeing him soon. No, it's impossible for him to prefer Virginia . . . to the North—

hiding more than she tells. The most open of women felt a need to dissemble. It is as if, for one single purpose, she must wear a mask.

Though James systematically concealed the way his stepson was

414

dodging the law, Dolley was not entirely unaware of Payne's profligacy. It was simply her nature to try to put the best face possible on the dubious behavior of her only child, refusing to think of him as a scapegrace, striving to protect and cover. *Of course* a well-traveled and sophisticated young man, she was telling the Cuttses, didn't—couldn't—prefer country life to the excitement of a great city; how unreasonable to expect it.

The sufferings Payne cost the Madisons bound them together with still another cord. Together they had raised him and urged him to seize the European opportunity, and were now trying to brace for whatever eventuality, Dolley in partial knowledge, James all too well informed. That Payne was not only drinking and gambling but also, even now, involved in sexual derelictions seems highly probable in the light of a fragmentary journal written, partly in code, some years later, detailing—amid a few aesthetic appreciations—self-abuse and concourse with loose women, black and white, and his study of a book on venereal diseases. "Let the worst be known that the best may be made of it," Madison had written Payne. Now, as then, his wish was to deal constructively with root causes, for Payne's sake and Dolley's. People could alter. He still hoped his stepson could.

This trouble, this question, within a marriage which, starting out unpropitiously, had made him and Dolley warp and woof of the same cloth, white and yolk of the same egg, two eyes focusing for vision. Though they knew they walked toward death, James with a shorter life expectancy than Dolley, neither believed they could be separated—ever— except in body; and Phoebe's death and Jefferson's had warned them to make the best of the years that remained.

No, they wouldn't attend the auction at Monticello; how terrible to hear the hammer knocking down furnishings interwoven with memories of happy meetings with Jefferson. Better to recall the rooms in their heyday, the expression and bastion of a friend's character. Ah, character!

Dolley wrote a niece about one of the most desirable traits. "Decision, my darling Mary, is an excellent trait of character, provided it is not blended with too much obduracy and self-confidence [overconfidence]; then it becomes a dangerous possession." She added that the Cuttses would get a big welcome in September.

And so they did. The girls stained their frocks with peach juice, the older boys rode, and Dick went with Uncle to watch the harvesting of tobacco. The little boy and the man understood each other. Later, whimsical Uncle Jemmy would write "Richard Cutts, Tobacco Planter, Washington," that his entire 3-ounce tobacco crop was ripe for marketing. Did he plan on pigtail, chewing twist, or snuff? Enclosed please find a penny, advance on the current price.

But this jester turned entirely serious the day he received a letter from Jefferson's grandson-in-law, now secretary of the University, Nicholas P. Trist. Having kept an eye out for Mr. Jefferson, Nick proposed to relay his observations to the new Rector. Certain professors were encouraging idleness by shortening or skipping lectures, he said, and announcing arbitrary holidays. Shouldn't they be required to report deviations from assigned duties?

Oh!—it was Dolley's voice. Opening a box, she had found a beautiful amethyst. A note from their old friend Thomas McKenney said that the enclosed stone had been found in the United States. How refuse it without hurting the giver's feelings? Life was teaching her that one possessed something only by loving it; there was no other way. And this present was too valuable to keep. She mustered all her diplomacy.

> I thank you, my kind friend, for the handsome and curious present I have just received. Your having found and conferred on me a native amethyst is not the only proof that our country contains precious jewels—among those of the first water is genuine friendship, and such I must consider your regard for me, which lives after so many years.
> Be assured I value it highly and return it sincerely.
>   D. P. Madison

And snow fell, and then melted, and Rector Madison felt duty-bound to be on hand during the University's December examinations, but no carriage wheel could turn in this mud; leaving Dolley, who usually accompanied him, at home, he must travel 30 miles by horseback.

Jogging through another snowstorm he visited Cabells, Monroes, Cockes, and Carters en route, and reached the house of a Conway cousin in Charlottesville just in time. He felt like one of the students coming up for his ordeal, he wrote Dolley. Chatting along humorously about University events, he made no bones about where he'd prefer to be.

But under any hint of humor, these days, lay the sorrow of seeing his nephew Robert—father of three fine boys and delegate to the Virginia Assembly—suffering from the tuberculosis which had already taken the lives of several of William's children. Robert, his favorite.

On coming home Madison learned about Payne's new debts: $1,300 overdue, $1,000 coming due in George Town in April, $700 due John

Jacob Astor also in April, and $600 in Philadelphia. He sent a bank note to George Town and promised to meet the rest of the $3,600 obligation.

Hearing that Ned Coles planned to visit New York, he appointed Ned his Minister Plenipotentiary. It troubled him, he wrote, that Payne had not acknowledged his $1,300 negotiable note—what if he racked up new debts instead of paying off an old one? Try to persuade him to come home before his career proved "fatal to everything dear to him in life"— Ned would know how to impress upon him "the misery he is inflicting on his parents."

> With all the concealments and alleviations I have been able to effect, his mother has known enough to make her wretched the whole time of his strange absence and mysterious silence; and it is no longer possible to keep from her the results now threatened.

Madison could still feel pity. "A strange and distressing career."

Payne had cashed and misappropriated the $1,300 note, and the Richmond branch of the Bank of the United States now received the $1,000 George Town debt for collection. By desperate tobacco sales and new borrowings Madison met the immediate problem, but the future was ambiguous. Ned Coles, whose appeal Payne had turned down, did not hesitate to call him a snake in the Garden of Eden.

To meet the April payments Madison tried to sell his Kentucky property, only to discover that his title was unclear (eventually he would lose it), then some Orange County land, but the bottom had dropped completely out of Virginia real estate. Financially he was following fast in Jefferson's footsteps. Arriving at Montpelier, Jared Sparks reported in dismay that forsaken Monticello was overrun by wild bushes. It seemed a possible portent for Montpelier.

There were impetuous rains. General John Hartwell Cocke, a member of the Board of Visitors, was stopped on his way to Montpelier by the swollen Rivanna. Madison was disappointed; he had wanted to discuss his plan to give the University four chaplains.

One day his young liaison Nicholas Trist spat blood. The Madisons were appalled—not Nick! But the young man's University reports kept coming. Besides old problems such as new construction and gymnastics, Trist wrote Rector Madison about Innkeeper Gray, there on the Lawn, a barefaced rogue. His rival, Chapman, whom General Cocke had blackballed, seemed much more reliable—though he did woo boarders very extravagantly with turkeys and rich pies.

Wrestling with such problems as they arose, Madison felt an immense irony. Here he was helping to tame hundreds of young Virginians while quite unable to stop Payne's drinking, gambling, roistering, wasting—God knew what else. "Puffed and reckless libertine." Bounder. Rake. Such unpleasant words.

Dolley's next letter to Anna lacked her usual vivacity. Sally Stevenson is critically ill. She herself walks badly from rheumatism in an ankle. The letter containing her dream, her "folly," must be destroyed—she was "always a dreamer." She hopes it's true that Miss Livermore will preach at Barboursville. "I for one would go to listen to her in search of light! But is she of the pure in spirit, filled with true religion without alloy, or does worldly ambition for éclat tarnish the perfection of the soul she possesses?"—which tells something about Dolley Madison. Payne has refused to accompany Ned but promises to come home. She doesn't admire Andrew Jackson's rough crowd:

> I'm afraid the license people talk with their tongues and pens will blast the good of the country. They display all sorts of evil traits of character that can make for a selfish and savage reign. Under the cloak of politics, our countrymen come out, not like Romans, but Goths and vandals—don't you think this, or are you afraid to say so?

Yes, she'd like a half-pound of Evans-Kapper snuff.

Madison's struggle to keep Payne out of jail would stretch over the next year and a half. Ironically, when Nicholas Trist visited Montpelier, he displayed qualities which a blood son of Madison might have possessed but which Payne most notably lacked: high purpose and willpower. And when Captain Hull wrote praising Midshipman Walter Cutts, it pointed up a painful, inescapable contrast. Once sought after, Payne was now rather widely shunned. Inevitably some people wondered if a famous father made a too difficult measuring rod for any but the strongest characters.

The fall of 1827 saw the first recorded public use of a title which had already been tendered privately. A Philadelphia toast: "If General Washington was father of our country, Mr. Madison should be considered father of the Constitution." During his administration, the speaker went on, America's institutions had weathered the severest storm. Lifting a glass, "To the health and happiness of James Madison!"

In December the Board of Visitors held its winter meeting. Trist was explaining that the Rector was running such a high fever he could not attend—it would entail too great a sacrifice—when in walked Mr. Madison. His sense of duty had raised him up and carried him 30 miles. But the effort put him back to bed; for several days his chair stood empty. When he returned to it, his mind dominated all discussions. Happily home again, he worked on his files while Dolley finished *Hope Leslie*.

This trip, shadowed by illness, may well date an undated letter of Dolley to James: "My beloved, I trust in God that you are well again, as your letter assures me you are. How bitterly I regret not going with you. . . . May angels guard thee, my dear best friend!"

On hearing that Madison was burning documents, Trist wrote in consternation: "Every letter you consign to the flames diminishes the means whereby posterity may derive that intimacy with you on which your best title to their affection and gratitude will rest." And the country would lose. "Indulge not . . . those principles of delicacy and tenderness (for in your character I consider them as principles) towards the feelings of others which have always characterized you." In this matter Madison's "conspicuous trait of modesty" could only work harm.

That spring, having borrowed $2,000, Madison—hard pressed—signed a sixty-day note for $1,200 more, then one for $950: sums equal to at least twenty times more today. No, he would rather not be an elector in the presidential contest between Adams and Jackson. He was fighting for Payne, Dolley, and a modicum of peace, and must soon leave for graduation ceremonies at the University.

So Dr. William Thornton was dead. The news stirred old memories of neighborly visits, of Herod Eclipse pounding the racetrack, of long talks on architecture and literature with a civilized intellect, a man of many talents. How strange the passage of time. Thornton's death was followed by Robert Madison's and then Thomas Mann Randolph's. Such announcements seemed to come more often.

In July 1828, while presiding over another board meeting, Madison was sucked into a Virginia convention gathered in Charlottesville to discuss state internal improvements such as roads and canals. Staying at denuded Monticello gave him and Dolley a sharp pang. But a Richmond reporter was impressed. "Mr. Madison, I think, looks very well [though] Mr. Monroe"—younger—"is the most perfect figure of woe I ever beheld—exceedingly wasted away, and manifesting . . . the most fixed melancholy."

This favorable account of Madison was corroborated by Mrs. Margaret Smith, who, in August, after a nineteen-year absence, revisited Montpelier. Arriving fresh from Monticello, with husband and child, she was still in shock at finding that Martha Randolph hadn't saved enough chairs from the auction for them to sit down—thank God Montpelier was intact.

Madison met the Smiths on the front portico, and Mrs. Madison ran into the hall with open arms. Later Dolley pulled up an armchair for Margaret, and drawing little Anna Smith onto the sofa, showed her some pretty books.

> I reclined at my ease [Margaret would write of that afternoon] while we talked—and oh, how we did talk. We went over the last 20 years and talked of scenes long past and of persons far away or dead. These reminiscences were delightful. . . . Time seems to favour her as much as fortune. She looks young and says she feels so. I can believe her, nor do I think she will ever look or feel like an old woman—

this when Dolley was sixty. The conversation swerving, Mrs. Smith remarked on the Madisons' solitariness here in the country. Oh, they were seldom alone, Dolley said, and she spoke entertainingly of three Members of Parliament who had just departed. So absorbed were they that when dinner was announced at four, Mrs. Smith was startled.

Though they sat at the table until six, Mrs. Smith's memoir says nothing whatsoever about food.

> Mr. Madison was chief speaker, and his conversation was a stream of history . . . so rich in sentiments and facts, so enlivened by anecdotes and epigrammatic remarks, so frank and confidential as to opinions on men and measures that it had an interest and charm which the conversation of few men now living could have. He spoke of scenes in which he himself had acted a conspicuous part, and of great men who had been actors in the same theatre. No commonplaces; every sentence he spoke was worthy of being written down. The formation and adoption of the Constitution. The Convention and first Congress, the characters of their members, and secret debates. Franklin, Washington, Hamilton, John Adams, Jefferson, Jay, Patrick Henry, and a host of great men. . . . Living history!

Afterward, they patrolled the portico until twilight. Cried Mrs. Madison to Anna, "Come! Let's run a race! You can't outrun me!" And she really did run briskly, says Mrs. Smith.

At dark the grown-ups drank coffee while Mr. Madison set them laughing over some droll anecdotes. "He retains all the sportiveness . . . he used to reveal now and then to those whom he knew intimately, and Mrs. Madison says that"—at seventy-seven—"he is as fond of a frolic and of romping with the girls as ever." His blue eyes sparkled like stars. But he drank only one glass of wine at dinner—why (as he once said) make yourself hop like a cork?

When they called on Madison's ninety-seven-year-old mother, she said, "I've been a blessed woman . . . all my life and am blessed in my old age." She had no sickness, no pain. She passed her time reading and knitting. When Dolley said something cheerful about the infirmities of age, Nelly Madison looked at her daughter-in-law with affection: "Now you are *my* mother."

On this visit Mrs. Smith—stimulated for years by clever prominent men—had a rare intellectual experience. She says her mind could scarcely contain all the ideas offered. She "feasted to satiety."

Dr. Robley Dunglison throws another sidelight on the life at Montpelier. Once when he and his wife were visiting, he saw nine guest horses being led into stalls for the night and ventured to comment. "Well, while I'm delighted with the society of their owners," replied Mr. Madison smiling, "I confess I have less feeling for the horses."

That fall when University students grumbled about their expensive braided uniforms, the Rector suggested (in vain) the kind of cheap black academic gowns once used at Princeton. When they grumbled about musket drill, he admitted that it ranked below dancing. When they griped about trumpet noise and Professor Blaettermann's "Prussianism," he just looked pleasant. Enrollment had increased, there were fewer disciplinary problems; the mission of educating young Virginians was proceeding apace.

That same autumn Mr. Madison, too ill to attend a board meeting, lay in bed thinking about the election of Andrew Jackson to the Presidency. It would usher in great changes. Unlike the first six Presidents, Jackson was a populist.

In sending board minutes, Nick reported that instead of putting Monticello up for sale, Martha Randolph and her eldest son had decided to run a boarding school. The land auctions there and at Bedford had failed miserably, some acres going for as little as $6. Nick was considering Henry Clay's offer of a clerkship in Washington.

Suddenly, on February 11, 1829, the venerable Nelly Conway Madison of the many blessings died. She was ninety-seven. They buried her in the Montpelier graveyard beside her husband, under trees in which spring sap was beginning to stir, and the family tried to get used to life without one who had always been there.

That spring the Madisons heard that the White House reception following Jackson's inauguration had been a free-for-all at which 10,000 citizens jostled each other, grabbing food. Some of them had secured a better view of the skirmish by standing on damask sofas in muddy boots. The Madisons winced—was democracy turning into mobocracy? And Madison disliked Jackson's "spoils system."

At seventy-eight he was being drawn more and more into political issues: tariffs, roads, canals. Protective tariffs he saw as constitutional but undesirable. Leave them to private initiative, he said, the sole exceptions being duties on war-destroyed articles and those designed to coddle young industries that promised to mature into national assets. To him federal roads and canals were the opposite: desirable but unconstitutional. The difficulty could be cured by a constitutional amendment.

One day Virginia's tariff problem exploded. William B. Giles rammed through the Assembly resolutions embodying an anti-Madisonian philosophy while citing Madison on a *state's duty to interpose against congressional usurpations of power.* Thus Madison's specific for unconstitutionality, as outlined in 1798–1800, was being invoked in a way which he considered inconsistent and wrong—what a mockery! By such dubious means Giles captured the Governor's Mansion.

As always when the Constitution was threatened, its "father and guardian" sprang alert. Madison had not struggled to forge this great sheet anchor of the Union to watch others, however well intentioned, hammer it out of shape. What caused misinterpretation? Chiefly, he thought, a failure to distinguish between the *use of unconstitutional power* and the *abuse of constitutional power,* and he said so, forthrightly, in his first public declaration on the subject: a letter to the *Lynchburg Virginian.*

It was the opening gun in a war which would pull Madison, willy-nilly, into still other political controversies. The most consequential was the one over South Carolina's doctrine of nullification.

Vice President John C. Calhoun, secret author of the "Exposition" issued by the South Carolina Legislature, tried to pin his defiant doctrine on Madison. It was a deliberate distortion. Calhoun knew perfectly well that in his Report of 1800, Madison had defined interposition as a *solemn appeal to public opinion,* no more, and had never held that a state could unilaterally, in convention or otherwise, overturn federal law; in fact he had, as apostle of constitutional balance, specifically disassociated himself from any such rebellious notion.

Madison chafed over the twisting of facts. If at seventy-eight he must reenter the lists to defend principles dearer than life, well, into the saddle; he would joust with the foes of reason. The crusade was made mandatory by long-held convictions, his public service, his country's need, and Jefferson's parting injunction: "Take care of me when dead."

Madison was adamant against the doctrine of nullification. The truth behind the Virginia Resolutions of 1798 was that the parties to the constitutional compact were not state governments but the *people*—a very different matter. It was the *people* who had agreed to a shared sovereignty as between states and nation, under a system the essence of which was a delicate balance between state and nation, and between the legislative, executive, and judiciary branches of the federal government: a balance not unlike that between the solar system's centrifugal and centripetal forces as illustrated by the famous Rittenhouse orrery. Upsetting the equilibrium might destroy the Union, this greatest of political experiments, this hope of the world. The boundaries of power, if questioned, must be settled by the Supreme Court.

Writing from his new job in Washington, Trist joined Madison's campaign by attacking Giles's No. 7 in the *Richmond Enquirer*. To combat this "renowned logician's" ignorance, he proposed to expound the "true principles of interpretation." Some intents behind the Constitution were self-evident; others needed exploration. Whereupon Trist asked Madison for sources—the beginning of a fruitful collaboration between master and disciple.

A month later Madison's Washington outpost sent unwelcome news. The *Telegraph* had announced the replacement, at the Treasury, of public servants Watkins, Lee, and Cutts. *"Le règne du Néros est commencé."*

President Jackson's decision to discharge Richard Cutts beggared Cutts and forced Madison—already cruelly squeezed—to take over the $150 monthly mortgage payments on the Washington house to prevent foreclosure. At which point he heard that Payne was in debtor's prison in Philadelphia.

With Dolley in anguish over the Cutts disaster, Madison strove harder than ever to hide her son's ignominy. "Let the worst be known," yes, but only to himself. His attempt at secrecy foundered when Payne himself wrote Dolley that he was in prison for a debt of about $300. She broke down and wept; she was beside herself and could not get over it or find any philosophy for it. Darling Payne behind bars!

That whole spring was a trial. John was drinking. Anna was ill—" . . . My dear sister. . . . I'm . . . afraid of your being in the night air. . . . It would throw you back into the agues and destroy you. Oh, that I could come for you and take care of you myself." Moreover, all about, people seemed so contentious. "I would rather hear the birds sing than listen to the whirlwind of men's passions." Nature was healing.

About this time Madison's political ally Trist suffered another hemorrhage. But Nick had no intention of collapsing—he believed firmly in the "cracker and dried fig regimen." And he shipped his mentor at Montpelier a crate of oranges. Other news: John and Clary were naming their eighth child and second son James Madison Payne. So many namesakes!

This complex juncture in time at Montpelier is caught like a midge in amber by a letter dated June 6, 1829, from Dolley to Anna.

James is recovering. Yesterday they rode over to see the baby. Lucy is expected in June; a pity Anna can't come too. Then an outburst, strange coming from Dolley. Cutts "must certainly have lost his senses—no effort to get business, and his son's office uncertain." Tensely,

> I would myself rather be my own cook and keep a respectable boarding house than have the Department of State under General Jackson. . . . However can Mr. C. reconcile himself to loiter in his neighborhood?. . . He ought to go to the East [New England] where he has natural friends who might exert themselves to please him in mercantile or other business. All this sort of neglect, however, is not so unworthy as the conduct towards his wife and daughters. Alas, that I could but help and save them! But what am I—a poor one indeed. . . .

Dolley's indignation against President Jackson and Cutts may have been tinctured by her knowledge of Jackson's dinner parties for a woman whom Anna's circle was boycotting on moral grounds, Peggy Eaton. Certainly there was political disillusionment at Montpelier. Since Jackson's defeat of John Quincy Adams, the General had split Madison's Republican party wide open between the old guard and Jacksonian populists leaning heavily on a "spoils system." Like Adams and Clay, Madison thought Jackson's "democracy" leaned so far toward the unthinking and opportunistic, it lowered the quality of American government: an extreme of a different kind than Hamilton's, and one making for a ferocious imbalance. This government was a *republic*.

Thus Dolley was well steamed up before her letter to Anna reached the subject of Payne's imprisonment.

> I inquired lately if you had heard from or of my dear child—you say nothing—and since that letter I received one from him in which he told me that he was boarding within prison bounds for

a debt of 2 or 300$. He has submitted to this horrid institution! It
almost breaks my heart to think of it. Mr. Cutts owed him more
than this of the money Payne entrusted to him to place in the
bank; still *that* is not the purpose. I don't know that I shall send
you this letter; in truth I feel as if I could not write a letter. My
pride, my sensibility and every feeling of my soul is wounded.
Yet we shall do something—what or when depends on Mr.
Madison's health and strength. . . . His anxiety . . . to aid . . .
Payne is as great as a father's but his ability to command money
in this country is no greater than that of others.

There; writing down resentments might cool the fever.

Dolley tells Anna she loathes the idea of Richmond, but if Madison
doesn't go there, she must. Something may let them decline the Stevensons' invitation; she hopes so. (Dolley's coldness may have sprung from a
reported criticism of Payne on the Stevensons' part—what else could so
turn her against Sally?) She begins to dislike the idea of visiting them;
their professions "seem to add to my disgust. Something must be wrong
between us—perhaps on both sides. I must pray without ceasing for
fortitude from above, as well as for the divine gift of humility and charity
toward all." It seems likely that the necessary trip to Richmond was to
borrow money for Payne. Financially the Madisons were plunging down
Jeffersonian steeps.

Two days later Dolley wrote Anna a mysterious postscript: "The past
days are changed," and something illegible. Had she made up with Sally?
On the envelope, "Pray burn this and all such."

At the same time Madison wrote Cutts that though financially desperate, he did not plan to force a sale of the Lafayette Square (now so called)
house and lots, and he hoped it would never be necessary. But because of
his creditors' hold on his landed property in Orange, posing the danger of
forced sales—a "ruinous sacrifice"—he couldn't but keep in mind the
Washington resource "where a sale, tho' an evil, might not be so great a
one." In view of the misfortunes visited upon him by Cutts, Madison's
"friendly respects and salutations" were generous.

During this changeable, dusty, flower-banked, insect-ridden, guest-
complicated summer of 1829, a letter from Nick Trist railing against the
Capital's political "depravity" spoke of the Constitution as Madison's
"masterpiece." Then, at last, rain.

Vicariously the Madisons were eating prison food, breathing prison
air, enduring surly guards and the contempt of acquaintances: a nightmare of humiliation. Work on the Convention notes fell off. Adam and
Eve had eaten of the tree of the knowledge of good and evil and been

expelled from the Garden. As never before, their religious faith was being challenged and tested.

Because some public men, including Jefferson, were avowed deists, and Madison was friendly with them and had fought for separation of church and state, some commentators have assumed that he too was a deist who saw Christ only as an exceptional human being and high example. But primary sources say otherwise.

Madison had of course studied the forerunners and main writers of eighteenth-century deism, that began in England and moved to France: Lord Herbert of Cherbury, whose doctrine of innate ideas set off a chain of skeptical thought; Hobbes, whose work increased religious doubt; Locke, who saw religion as a code of precepts rather than a power; John Toland, who completely ruled out mystery; David Hume, who attacked revelation, prophecy, and miracles; also such sharp-minded French deists as Voltaire, Diderot, the Encyclopedists. But he had also, with the same thoroughness, studied the Christian apologists who worked to rebut deism, such as Bishop Joseph Butler and, of course, John Witherspoon, who saw no clash at all between reason and revelation. Like all deep thinkers, Madison read authors on both sides. He read everything. He had no intension of being a Christian by default. At the same time he disdained to wear his religion on his sleeve; it was a matter strictly between him and God, or perhaps one should say between him, Dolley, and God.

There is much evidence that his early biblical studies, especially those under Witherspoon, threw forward a light which, if occasionally flickering (few escape moments of doubt), was never quenched. Dolley's Quaker faith, a far cry from deism, was Christ-centered and had come into his life as a strong influence when he was forty-three years old. It reinforced his original commitment to what he had once called, to Bradford, "the cause of Christ." Together the Madisons lived Christianity, as a moral striving. In union and the spirit they found strength. Mary Cutts, who visited Montpelier regularly for many years and who knew Madison intimately, would put it this way (to add to a previous quotation):

> Mr. Madison, although no sectarian, was a religious man, as may be seen throughout his career. . . . He . . . had that religion of the Bible and of the heart so visible throughout his . . . life. When possible he attended the Episcopal Church.

Moreover, stern old Bishop William Meade, a fundamentalist, would testify that at Montpelier Madison, before and after his father's death, conducted family prayers. An honest nonbeliever could not have done so; it would have been a hypocrisy, a farce, a blasphemy condemned by the church. Madison could have conducted the trinitarian Episcopal prayers for one reason only: he believed them.

By 1829 then, the deepening which happens to noble natures through experience—problems, griefs, setbacks, and a growing sense of ever shortening time—had taken place in James Madison.

Looking—Dolley certainly, James probably—for spiritual guidance, they struggled through the agonizing summer of 1829. Brother John was so pinched, James gave him a $400 note for some land in western Virginia. The Cuttses were the only guests the Madisons wanted just now—for one thing, Dolché's guitar had always exercised a healing effect. But other people came. Wrote Trist, "Accept my wishes for your future exemption from all such visitants as those you are now getting rid of."

Madison finally raised the money to spring Payne from prison. The worst was known—or was it?—and the best possible was being made of the whole sorry Philadelphia mess. But only Payne could remake himself.

By the time the iron door on Prune Street clanked to let Payne out, Madison had been elected, not unwillingly, a delegate to the Richmond Convention charged with revising the Virginia Constitution.

❦ XIX ❧

THE
LAST GREAT
FIGHT

As THE ONLY SURVIVOR of both the Virginia Constitutional Convention of 1776 and the Federal Constitutional Convention of 1787, James Madison—old and tired—had been quite unable to refuse election to Virginia's Revisionary Convention of 1829. He wanted to help answer two vital questions: Should the franchise be extended beyond freeholders? And in apportioning representation in the Assembly, should slaves still count at three-fifths their number?

Though the fall before the Convention did not bring Payne, it brought Lucy. A widow again, mother of grown sons, mistress of a handsome house, she seemed sobered. On hot afternoons the sisters talked about past, present, and future, and in the cool of evening James joined them. All three had come to know the two faces of experience, happy and menacing. No, the Madisons decided, the changes were superficial only; their guest was still the warmhearted, impetuous Lucy. She joined heartily in neighborhood activities, church services at Orange Courthouse, fish fries, barbecues, camp meetings, and other "frolics," and she was sorely missed when she went home.

The year moved on. Madison met with the University's Board of Visitors, which approved the new student uniform made up of pantaloons, jacket with a braided collar, and round hat or cap; Dolley preserved peaches. And sometimes they discussed the enigma of Governor Giles, this extreme states' righter who, after publicly scoring Madison's "nationalism," was now inviting them to stay at the executive mansion during the Convention. Thank you but no, they answered; they had promised to stop with their old friends Speaker of the House and Mrs. Andrew Stevenson.

A four-county deputation under General William Madison called to ask Madison's position on the issues. Did he stand for a broader franchise? Yes, he said, he favored giving the vote to all tax-paying householders and heads of families; a government resting on a minority was not a republic but an aristocracy, and dangerous. His callers moved to the other question. Eastern Virginians, whose slaves formed 50 percent of the population, wanted to ensure their power by keeping the three-fifths rule, whereas those beyond the mountains, whose slaves formed only about 10 percent, wanted to even matters by apportioning both Houses on a strictly white basis; how did Madison feel about counting black people? Well, he replied, it hardly seemed fair to give the east twice as many delegates—in proportion to qualified voters—as the west, but with Tidewater tempers flaring the question became so divisive, it jeopardized the well-being of Virginia. So he favored mutual concessions; sometimes compromise, a middle way, was the only practical solution. Good, said his callers. Then James and Dolley were bowling through the bright alleys of October toward Richmond.

It seemed strange not to stop at Monticello, the Little Mountain wrapped in blue distance. Though many families were eager to entertain them—Coleses, Paynes, Flemings, Winstons—no other society, for them, matched that of Jefferson and the Randolphs. But people must adjust.

Revolving wheels had their own excitement, and October its beauty. Look! the spires of Richmond burnished by sunlight!

There was an expansive welcome at Retreat; it was as if no shadow had ever passed over the Stevenson-Madison friendship. Andrew's mind was acute, his heart warm; Cousin Sally—now recovered—ardent, imaginative, witty. So much time had flooded by, yet here they were all together again, undrowned.

At the statehouse, Madison declined the Convention's presidency to nominate Monroe, and he and Chief Justice Marshall escorted their friend to the rostrum.

According to Grigsby, Madison had a "gallant bearing."

The first day was hectic. As chairman of the Legislative Committee, Madison voted with the majority in favor of what western Virginia wanted, a "white basis only" for the House; then helped create the tie which rejected that arrangement for the Senate. These committee decisions, though compromises, represented a reform. Would they pass a quarrelsome Convention?

The question of franchise was thornier. On Madison's proposal, the committee voted to extend voting rights to all tax-paying householders and heads of families: midpoint between the extremes of no enlargement and inclusion of all male (no one mentions female) adults. He probably thought of it as another golden mean. The population had increased; new arrangements were in order.

In open session, the committee's recommendations were fought by both factions. Aware that Madison could make or break a proposition, friends and foes pressed him hard. Defenders of the *status quo* hurled at the committee chairman's grey head words like "fatuity," "treason to eastern Virginia," "bungler." And there were the high squeals of John Randolph. Yes, Madison told hecklers, he did certainly favor compromise, but if neither side would give an inch, he must go with the east. A bitter westerner shouted that such vacillation came from "putting old men into active life." Sitting in the rear among ladies in huge white silk befeathered bonnets, Dolley and Sally listened and were outraged.

Actually the seventy-eight-year-old statesman was full of fire. Not only did he attend all sessions; he scarcely ever missed a party. Dolley, who had dressed his hair for years, took particular pains these days. In a city playing host to many distinguished men—Monroe, Marshall, Tyler, Littleton, Tazewell, Philip Barbour, John Randolph—it was Madison's balanced thought, Madison's wit, which people quoted most often. No one could talk with him without realizing "he was no common man."

A famous woman journalist, Mrs. Anne Royall, had been watching him closely. Seventy-eight and not a large man, but what force! She has described him: "A keen vigorous countenance. He was dressed in a plain Quaker-colored coat and his hair was powdered. He was leaning forward and seemed to listen to the delegates with deep attention."

For three months he listened, conferred, advised.

One day someone denied that Madison had written *Federalist* paper No. 54 defending a fractional slave count. He had no choice. Risking a charge of inconsistency, he rose and said he was sorry to speak on an irrelevant subject, but rather than sanction an untruth by silence, he must state that the article in question had been written not by Mr. Hamilton or Mr. Jay but by a "third person concerned in that work." Then he sat down.

Up jumped Benjamin Leigh to say he had intended nothing personal, but only an idiot would sacrifice the protection of the three-fifths rule in House *or* Senate. A convulsive laugh ran round the room. According to Hugh Blair Grigsby who was present, Madison, by elongating his upper lip, managed to look "irresistibly comic."

He knew he was up against incomprehension. Couldn't these saboteurs see that with changing conditions measures must change too? That the time had come—in fairness—to consider the nonslaveowners beyond the mountains?

On December 2, with snow flying like goose feathers, James Madison threw himself into the debate. Though, like Jefferson, he had never had a strong public voice, he wielded immense authority based upon what he had been and still was to the nation.

> No sooner was he upon his feet than members from all parts of the Hall . . . gathered round him to catch the lowest accents from his tongue. . . . His voice was low and weak; but his sentences were rounded and complete; and his enunciation, though tremulous and full of feeling . . . distinct. . . .

The artist George Catlin would paint the circle of eager listeners gathered around that pivotal figure. Considering Madison's age, it was a magnificent performance.

In its function of protecting persons and property, he said, government could not afford to ignore a minority with right on its side. Justice, humanity, truth—all required that slaves be considered as much as possible not as mere property but as *human beings.* Nor was it illogical or wrong to keep, in state as in nation, the 5-3 basis for *one* of the two legislative branches. Under present social conditions, the difference could help the slaves themselves, one house tending to protect them as property, the other as persons.

Not everyone granted him the point. Concerned not for their slaves but themselves, coveting more power for Tidewater and Piedmont—devil take the western counties—many easterners listened stonily. Why shouldn't his arguments for a 5-3 Senate ratio apply to both chambers?

Moreover, the easterners were energetic in their campaign. A dozen horsemen galloped through Orange County warning against a "white basis only" for *either* Senate or House. Western Virginia (present-day West Virginia) would steal eastern Virginia's property, they shouted, to "level their mountains"; and other nonsense. Such people were too myopic to see Madison's vision. Their selfishness seemed to grow with opposition, like weeds in clay.

During all this uproar Dolley had been enjoying Richmond's sights, shops, and people. At sixty-one she was finding it exciting to be back in the swim.

Early one morning Anne Royall—a plain woman who wore green calash and shawls—decided to try for an interview with the former First Lady. She took umbrage when a "ruffian" driver said he'd charge $1 for hitching up his hack and $2 an hour thereafter. Mrs. Royall walked to Retreat. Misdirections stretched the mile and a quarter to three miles. "After walking my very soul out," she would record, she asked a servant for Mrs. Madison. Unfortunately Mrs. Royall was known as a nuisance. "Not at home." Mr. Stevenson then? "Very ill, and his family can't leave him." Mrs. Madison's maidservant? "Out." In a loud voice Mrs. Royall insisted on an announcement that "Mrs. Royall is in the house." Dolley sent word that she'd be down in a moment. Here is the journalist's graphic and valuable account:

> I listened for her step, and never was I more astonished. I expected to have seen a little old dried-up woman; instead of this, a tall, young, active, elegant woman stood before me. "This is Mrs. Madison? Impossible." She was the self-same lady of whom I had heard more anecdotes than any family in Europe or America. No wonder she was the idol of Washington—at once in the possession of everything that could ennoble woman. But chiefly she captivated by her artless though warm affability; affectation and she were farther asunder than the poles; and her fine full eyes and countenance display a majestic brilliancy found in no other face. She is a stout, tall, straight woman, muscular but not fat, and as active on her feet as a girl.

Dolley wore a plain black silk dress, a black-and-white-checked silk turban, and store-bought "black glossy curls" hanging over her ears. Looking closer, Mrs. Royall decided that no, the lady was not precisely handsome. This face suffused with a "slight tinge of red" seemed rather too broad in the middle. No, she decided, it was Mrs. Madison's power to enjoy and give joy, her gaiety, her radiance, the "irresistible grace of her every movement"—"all she says and does"—which made her so uncommonly attractive.

Mrs. Royall would never get over the surprise of her hostess's self-forgetful energy. Dolley ran out to fetch her a glass of water and wiped the mud off her shoes and tied them; then, seeing she was exhausted, pressed her "with much earnestness" to stay for dinner. This trained reporter's memoir gropes for words. "She appears young enough for Mr. Madison's daughter; there is more indulgence in her eye than in any mortal's."

What Mrs. Royall could not know from an interview was Dolley's brooding concern for not only her husband's but also her son's well-being.

Ransomed from prison, Payne had resumed his odyssey. Dolley told herself that on their return he would be waiting at Montpelier; she convinced herself, counted on it, her expectation becoming a kind of advance Christmas present.

And now the three-month Convention was drawing to a close. The constitution adopted in January was too hidebound and heavily "eastern" to please Madison. It seemed unfair to extend suffrage without changing the rate of apportionment. But he had the satisfaction of knowing that without his unremitting efforts, the outcome would have been a disaster.

The adjourning delegates pressed forward en masse to shake his hand. Even Grigsby, who did not see eye to eye with him had become a convert. "I could scarcely refrain from shedding tears when I saw . . . the deeply affected and venerable Mr. Madison. . . ."

The couple meant to waste no time getting home. "My dear brother," Dolley wrote John, "this day the Convention finished its session, and we propose to set off for home tomorrow if . . . the weather . . . permits. It now rains and blows." The storm held them up several days before an exhausting journey. Through forests of leafless trees candid against the sky, their horses strained, slipped, and slid on ribbons of icy frozen ground or in slough. At last they conquered the stubborn distance, reaching home February 5 with a broken-down team. Payne was not waiting, and Dolley realized that she had deluded herself. It was sad.

But the stimulus of Richmond had given her and James a new lease on life. More than ever, now, their minds were set gallantly on making the best of the years that remained.

During the spring of 1830 George Washington's biographer, Jared Sparks, found Mr. Madison's servant waiting at Orange Courthouse with a horse. During his visit to Montpelier, Madison's memory proved diamond clear. No, he said; Washington *did* sometimes laugh; "no man seemed more to enjoy the jokes, good humor and hilarity of his companions"; and he described the first President's first levee and first ball. Yes, Washington was often criticized by Hamilton. Leaving his subject, Sparks inquired about the War of 1812. After years of protest, Madison said, it was Castlereagh's hostile hope-killing letter which had precipitated it. And so forth. At seventy-nine Madison had a mind full of "pristine vigor,"

Sparks has said. "He is cheerful, gay, and full of anecdotes; never a prosing talker, but sprightly, varied, fertile in his topics. . . ." As for Mrs. Madison, she was "an elegant and accomplished lady" with interesting conversation. The guest hated to pack his bag. "Five delightful days."

Madison's "last" public service was followed by one closely related and more important: a fight to keep not only Virginia but the entire country straight on the nullification issue, for a wrangle had broken out between two brilliant Senators, Massachusetts' Daniel Webster and South Carolina's Robert Y. Hayne. A minor debate about Western public lands triggered a major one about a protective tariff which the South, and particularly South Carolina, thought was helping the industrial North while ruining the agricultural South. Hayne spoke as if South Carolina should repeal it within her borders. But no state had such right of nullification, thundered Webster. No? snapped Hayne—what about *New England's* flouting of federal law and near-secession during the War of 1812? And by favoring this federal tariff wasn't Mr. Webster reversing himself? Had he forgotten his earlier statement that Congress had no power to lay a protective tariff?

Webster said that ex-President Madison's published letters had converted him. He found Mr. Madison's arguments impregnable. The United States *did* have protective power.

Not to be cheated of so valuable an ally, Hayne cited, as basis for his *opposite* conviction, Madison's call for interposition in his Report of 1800, "which deserves," said the South Carolinian, "to last as long as the Constitution itself!" But, like Calhoun and Giles before him, Hayne omitted that part of the Report which, by explaining interposition as an expression of opinion only designed to "excite reflection," left his doctrine of nullification in tatters.

Madison received details of the controversy with mounting concern. The "anarchical principle" of nullification, he said, meaning state power to wipe out federal law, could lead to secession (as indeed it did some thirty years later); it was "putting powder under the Constitution" and a match in the hand of every party.

A chief mark of a first-class mind is the power to make or follow fine distinctions, and Daniel Webster saw that Madison had made a pivotal point: that secession in the face of intolerable tyranny, while a *natural right* antecedent to any constitution, was not and never could be a *constitutional* right, the Constitution having been set up for the precise purpose of holding the States together. And in spite of his federalism, Webster saw something else: that a sovereign people had in freedom *chosen* to divide their sovereignty between state and nation. Madison-enlightened, he stressed that point in Congress.

Reading the debate, Madison spotted the weak link in Webster's chain of logic. Those who had chosen to divide the sovereignty were not people in the aggregate but people as organized into states: a very different matter. Fortunately Webster's serious misconception did not void the rest of his argument.

Meanwhile, in the *Richmond Enquirer* and elsewhere, Nick Trist had been pugnaciously taking Madison's side. "But what is to be expected," he would cry, in a letter to his mentor, "of minds that have nothing of that vivifying principle—an abstract love of truth?" After listening to Webster's superb speech, he called the orator a "mammoth . . . treading the cane brake, and crushing obstacles which nature never intended to impede him."

But look! cried nullifiers. The monstrous federal government was chewing up the states! destroying them!

Madison could not remain aloof. The issue was fundamental. He began to fight for his principles with letters on the boundaries of power. A 4,000-word one to Hayne, with a copy for Congressman Everett, carefully rebutted false deductions from the Resolutions of 1798 and his Report of 1800. A letter to Webster corrected the misunderstanding about "we the people" and suggested that the New Englander read Everett's copy of a letter to a "distinguished champion" of South Carolina's false doctrine. Elsewhere he pointed out that the error of the nullifiers had arisen "from a failure to distinguish between what is declaratory of opinion and what is *ipso facto* executory; between the right of the *parties* to the Constitution, and of a *single party*. . . ."

But the revolt spread. South Carolina threatened to use her "right" of resistance to the collection of the hated federally imposed duties which she claimed were undermining her economy: an idea she tried hard to pin on Jefferson and Madison as authors, respectively, of the Kentucky and Virginia Resolutions.

Thus pressures accumulated for Madison to take up the cudgels, publicly, for truths he had long affirmed privately. To spur him on, Trist asked what would happen if Virginia, too, adopted the disruptive doctrine—would it not "decide the fate of the Union"? The *Richmond Whig* hoped Madison would "arrest the deadly poison circulated under the authority of his name," and Joe Cabell pleaded, "The most alarming doctrines are abroad. The adverse Party are using your name to prepare the people of the South for the worst, the most horrible, measures."

Madison's opposite opinions might again "save our country from the most dire calamities."

Madison took the plunge. When Martin Luther Hurlbut of Charleston requested, for the public good, comment on his antinullification pamphlet, the ex-President backed him, strongly, with a letter to the *Charleston Courier* saying the federal government was subject to two checks and only two: state participation in federal elections, and constitutional amendment. The letter created a sensation and was widely quoted. "It is clear as the light of Heaven," wrote Hurlbut ("Plain Truth"), "that in Mr. Madison's mind resistance to the laws of Congress . . . is identified with 'revolution' and 'civil war.' "

That spring of 1830 when Madison turned seventy-nine, other problems had dimmed. Preservation of the Union without loss of liberty seemed to him the all in all.

On March 10 Dolley wrote her namesake Dolley Cutts (now almost nineteen) a letter which she labeled dull—Dolché deserved better. Actually it is quite diverting:

> Imagine if you can a greater trier of patience than seeing the destruction of a radiant patch of green peas by frost! It came last night on the skirts of a storm, and while I was lamenting that our dear midshipman [Walter] should ever be exposed to such wailing winds, my young adventurers were wrecked off their moorings. But away with complaints, other patches will arise, and I will mourn no more over a mess of peas or pottage. . . .

She wishes she could accompany Dolché to a party. In Richmond she had her "quantum sufficit" of gaiety. She would like to spend all her winters there. If her old acquaintances in Washington were as once, that city would be her preference. "But I confess I do not admire the contention of parties, political or civil, though in my quiet retreat I am anxious to know all the maneuverings. . . ." Too bad Dolché had to refuse Vice President Van Buren's invitation. Then her mind veers off—does her niece ever get hold of a clever novel, new or old? Cooper's *Red Rover* is too full of horrors. "Adieu, my precious Dolley."

Two days later she thanked young Dick for some gifts. She and his uncle "expect great things" of him when he grows up. Because she finds no way to send the handsome knife she bought him in Richmond, she encloses a dollar with which to buy one "for my sake." She is "laying up" pleasures for his coming. The inveterate matchmaker: "I think you'll lose your heart with one of your fair [Payne] cousins when you have them all before you to choose from—your Mama's namesake is a sweet one and very sensible. Adieu, my dear Richard."

(Again, Dolley could not know that her partiality for Anna foreshadowed a consequential relationship. "Sweet." "Sensible." Perhaps because she shared these qualities, she felt an affinity.)

Not long after this the Madisons received a shock worse than frost on peas. Anna Cutts was told first: "Dear Madam," wrote Anthony Morris delicately,

> I have to mention to you a most painful subject from a sense of duty to my most valued friend, your excellent sister, to whom, or to Mr. Madison, I cannot write directly without an intimation from you who know many circumstances with which I am unacquainted. You will anticipate that my reference is to Mr. Payne Todd, whose long confinement in Philadelphia you are no doubt apprised of.

According to a reliable source, Payne was anxious to return to Montpelier. For $200 in notes his creditors would unhand him. Mr. Morris wished to help in any way he could.

"Most anxious to return," though after last year's incarceration he had refused to return. Had shame taught him some values?

When this lightning struck Montpelier, it wreaked havoc. A first arrest might be explained away, but a second within a year! Though some excellent men had been banished to the stone building on Prune Street—to its whitewashed rooms, grated windows, and beds stuffed with red cedar shavings—this fact was no comfort. Nor that, as a special dispensation, he received a quarter of a pint of molasses every other day. Dear God! Payne who had dined with royalty! Dolley's eyes were red from weeping.

Again Madison scraped for money. Even if indignation had told him to let the culprit rot in jail, love for Dolley would have counseled further sacrifices. Somehow he managed to settle with Payne's creditors.

That 4th of July Payne emerged, thin as a lathe, from Philadelphia's debtor's prison and went home chastened. If Montpelier had once seemed lackluster, it was now a haven. His mother held out her arms.

The summer of 1830 was a good one. Only later would James, Dolley, Payne, and the visiting Anna Cutts know just how good.

Though Madison was not free of problems, he had never asked for an easy life, only a meaningful one. He was struggling zestfully for a clear title to his Kentucky land, for a living from his heat-baked farm, for defeat of the nullification heresy, and for the well-being of the University of Virginia. The last had a new problem. He attended a board meeting which arraigned Professor Blaettermann, and later found the stiff-necked Prussian on his doorstep "much in the fidgets" for fear of dismissal.

That fall Congressman Everett begged Madison to let the *North American Review* print his letter to Hayne attacking the doctrine of nullification. Instead, Madison embodied his arguments in a 3,500-word letter to Everett, with permission to print. He had entered the lists in full view of all spectators.

His main points: (1) As a compact between the citizens of *all* the states, the Constitution could not be annulled by any *one* state. (2) The Union would fall apart if the federal court, as supreme agent, did not enforce, along with the Constitution, all laws and treaties. (3) The Virginia Resolutions of 1798 had done nothing but explore various constitutional means of exerting state *influence:* witness the fact that the debates preceding their adoption made no reference to any power of nullification; indeed, the word "null" had been stricken out of the first draft of the Kentucky Resolutions to preclude a gloss of the word "interposition" as any more than a declaration of *opinion.*

Madison's letter-article, reverberating all over the United States, was accepted as the definitive statement from the "unclouded intellect" of a governmental genius. Ned Coles called it the clearest exposition of the Constitution he had ever read. The effect, according to J. C. Cabell, was "as great as ever was produced by any document in any age or country." The *Richmond Enquirer* called its argument "luminous," and Chief Justice Marshall cried, "Madison . . . is himself again!" (Of course he had never been otherwise.) Appropriately, summer was crowned by a splendid autumn. Crops were good, Payne stayed home most of the season, Dolley was in fine fettle, and Madison easily threw off an ailment. The "nullies" (Trist's word) had been stopped in their tracks.

Dolley's November letter to Dolley Cutts is a lark soaring. Yes, she'd like to borrow *The Romance of History.* Governor Barbour is with them. Then a little matchmaking fun:

> I find you have no idea, yet, of the improvement love can make, or you would not surmise that another must have had to do the courting for John. After he became acquainted with S. Carter [Sarah Carter of Redlands] his tongue twanged as if sent from a

bow! Last winter when I . . . heard him talk and laugh like Ganymede, I knew it was Cupid's act by the color. She is a sweet girl. . . .

A letter from the Marchioness de Casa Yrujo of Madrid helped put a period to 1830's fine paragraph.

The once democratic Sally McKean, who now loves the Spanish monarchy, makes a joke of the American Minister's little bottle-green uniform with a black cape, "each end of which flaunts a big silver star." She has grown fat and wears spectacles, and nineteen years after leaving Philadelphia, can't recollect its streets. She tells Dolley about her engaged daughter Narcissa and a son who has just been named to the Court of Saxony. (Twenty-five years later this son, the Duke de Sotomayer, ex-Ambassador to France and Britain and ex-Prime Minister, *Chef du Palais,* would commit suicide in a fit of despair over gout.) Though European-ized, Sally remains loyal to her old friend Dolley: "God bless you! keep up your spirits and hope for the best; there is no such thing as real happiness in this world. . . ." Dolley of course did not see it quite that way. There was trouble in the world, yes, but also real happiness—she had experienced it.

But as 1830 was running out, she had more of the first and less of the second, for James was struck by a rheumatism so brutal it put him to bed. She refused to leave his side. And indeed he could not bear to part with her presence.

The following spring Anna developed dropsy. The sac surrounding her heart filled with serous fluid. The waterlogging edema made portions of her body swell alarmingly. Dolley took the news hard. Was Anna dying? But it was impossible to leave James. If only she could be in two places at once! She pleaded with the girls and their father to write her about Anna's condition—if but a line—by every post.

What a marvelous relief to hear that Anna was better. It eased her "oppressed heart," she wrote Mary. The girls must take good care of the mother they had almost lost and remember the importance of smiles. "Keep her room quiet, and herself free from the slightest agitation or uneasiness, the nervousness . . . attended to with all your delicacy of thought and conduct." She is returning *The Oxonians;* she has been too worried to read it.

A month later Anna and Jemmy were still bedridden, and Dolley as strained as a nation fighting on two fronts. She begged Dolché again to nurse her mother devotedly. She loves the sisters "a thousand times more," she says, "because they are dutiful daughters," and she thanks all the friends who have helped; she "could love the blackest Indian who was kind to her; indeed, I feel as if I could bribe the whole world to make her well." A postscript asks the girls to hide all her letters to their mother "under lock and key."

With Anna waterlogged and James stiff as the iron poker, time dragged its feet. Though Dolley did not leave the yard for eight months, she did not repine. Dear thin contorted Jemmy; though she longed to take him to Warm Springs, travel was out of the question.

There were no guests; friends had to be held off. But she hoped to see them "before the winter throws barriers between."

Then cholera killed two of Lucy's tall sons, George and Sam Washington, aged twenty-two and twenty-five. Before they died they turned as yellow as squash. Dolley wrote trying to comfort Lucy, who could not be comforted.

Half-crippled, Madison kept parrying thrusts by the South Carolina nullifiers. Unable to claim him as a partisan, they rallied round Jefferson's name. Madison hated being pitted against his dead friend; it was a dour experience. True, Jefferson's Kentucky Resolutions—before some editing—had gone further than Madison's Virginia ones, but he had not believed in 1798, and did not believe now, that Jefferson really thought a state could, on its own, annul an act of Congress.

One day they heard of James Monroe's death. Though Madison had never been as close to him as to Jefferson, the two old friends had shared many experiences in and out of government. Ah, those desperate days on horseback, together, when the British burned Washington's public buildings. Franklin, Washington, Hamilton, Jefferson, Adams, and now Monroe—all were gone. Of the many "fathers and founders," he alone still walked the earth. It was a sobering thought.

As the weather of 1831 worsened, so did Madison's money problems. His fall crops failed. Payne's debts accumulated. Feeding and clothing a hundred and twenty slaves, most of them too old or too young to work, weighed more heavily. Also, he was supporting many poor relatives, Francis's children, and Robert's. But he did not despair; in pain but intensely alive, he felt the joy of combat.

Meanwhile he and Dolley heard that the Peggy Eaton scandal had matured like tropical fruit, then rotted as fast. The fashionable ladies whom the death of Andrew Jackson's wife, Rachel, had deprived of the pleasure of snubbing her now concentrated on the President's protégé, Mrs. Eaton, charging that she had been intimate with Major Eaton while still married to another man. The ladies of Washington had infuriated

Jackson by cutting sassy, pretty Peggy at parties. Mrs. Smith called their policy "a stand, a *noble* stand"—should they "violate the respect due to virtue"? It split the Cabinet. Secretary Eaton challenged Secretary Ingham to a duel, and the President demanded the recall of the Dutch Minister to punish a wife who had joined the attackers. When the smoke of battle cleared, the dead and wounded lay all about. To the Madisons—looking off at the majestic Blue Ridge—it all seemed very petty.

Madison's health had improved now, and a few friends were coming to visit. The world seemed brighter. Dolley reverted to what she had always been, a child of the sun: "My sweet Mary," she had written feelingly, "I *must and will* have you, your dear Mama and sister, to come with the Séruriers about the first of June, when I shall give you cherries, peas, etc., etc., etc. I like your motto. . . . It is expressive of hope, that sweet spell, that laughing future. . . . Cherish it, my dear Mary. . . . It is said there are no true enjoyments but those which long hope has purchased." Mary's Payne cousins will write; "Anna"—Annie—"is somewhat before the others in her acquirements," again singling out John's third daughter. "But . . . my first nieces are my first loves." Uncle Madison and Payne send affection. Then a touching postscript from a lady who had once led the nation in chic: "We are old-fashioned—please send me a paper pattern of the present sleeve! And describe the width of dress and waist and how turbans are joined up, bonnets worn, as well as how to behave in the fashion."

Sérurier (again the French Ambassador) and his elegant wife were coming. Ah! look! a splendid equipage rolling through the gates!

After the visit a letter from the Séruriers expressed fear that their two rambunctious children had worn out one suffering so cruelly. On the contrary, replied Madison, he had had the double pleasure of sympathy and reminiscence.

The Fourth of July had brought a political ruckus. While guests at a small dinner in Charleston were hearing a "unionist" letter from President Jackson, to whom all nullifiers were damn traitors, a huge States' Rights dinner in that city was featuring a speech by Senator Hayne which grossly misrepresented Virginia's 1800 stand, followed by another guest's declaration that though Madison denied a state's right to nullify federal law, he had himself *admitted a right to secede*.

It was too much. After mulling it over, Madison drew a long bow, took aim, and let fly. Both nullification and secession were false doctrines, he wrote in September. Both sprang from the same "poisonous root." What he feared was not outright secession but a slow breakdown through systematic flouting of the federal judiciary—and he used one of his more telling metaphors: "Take the linch-pins from a carriage and how soon would a wheel be off its axle." So much for the "speedy fate" of the federal system if the states "loosened from the authority which confines them to their spheres"—the old symbol in another guise. The word "spheres" echoed all the way from the planetary orbits marked out on the Rittenhouse orrery.

Thus Madison waged a fight Jefferson could not join. Though he could flex his sticklike fingers only just enough to achieve a cramped, lilliputian script, he stuck doggedly to his political correspondence. There are different kinds of heroism.

To Trist he recalled Jefferson's early recommendation that the Navy be used to *coerce* states defaulting on congressional requisitions. Madison's dry comment:

> It is remarkable how closely the nullifiers, who make the name of Mr. Jefferson the pedestal for their colossal heresy, shut their eyes and lips whenever his authority is . . . emphatically against them.

Trist, lieutenant under Madison's command in the battle for constitutional clarification, fell on this evidence with glee. They were making progress.

Dolley followed every move. Thirty-seven years of living with James Madison had taught her so much about government, she understood the arguments, and when her husband's hand was too rigid to write, her hand wielded the pen. They worked as one.

In her haste to kindle the master's fire this rainy morning Becky had burned Mary's letter but, because it lived in Dolley's memory, it could be answered. "I am grieved that your Mama is unwell," Dolley wrote, "but trust it proceeds from fatigue. Do persuade her . . . not to worry herself with household or any business." Dolley mentions the butchering of some sixty men, women, and children by Nat Turner's band of slaves. Though the "bustle and alarm" is over, everyone should stay on guard. "Tell Mr. Trist I send him a few leaves from the cape jasmine. . . ." Uncle James still wears the bead ring Mary placed on his finger, looking at it from time to time in silence. She writes with very weak eyes. Tomorrow a large party from Tidewater. Payne is "on the wing to his mine with three gentlemen in his train."

She was alluding to the granite ledge running through Toddsberth.

Hoping it could be developed into a lucrative quarry, Payne had begun questioning geologists. The new interest pleased his parents enormously. For the first time since the silkworm fiasco he had an object in life.

This year Ned Coles was running for Congress, and Madison, in spite of rheumatism, driving his quill in a renewed campaign. Once he had told Monroe that the older he grew, the stiffer his fingers and the smaller his writing (as the shorter his steps). His present calligraphy was tortuous.

And the months crept on. By December his ailment had confounded every attempt at treatment, including Trist's suggestion that he wrap his body, tightly, in oiled silk. But he was obstinate, he refused to stop his political correspondence. Dolley, whose often inflamed eyes gave her violent headaches, helped in every way she could. At the moment she was groping for the spectacles she refused to wear in public.

When Walter visited Montpelier on leave, the Madisons' happiness, like a banked-down fire, flared up. "In my last," Dolley wrote Dolché, "I informed you that Walter and Payne had been detained abroad by bad weather, but now they are safe and sound with us, and we have played chess and talked together all this time without the appearance of ennui." Tell her about the parties, she begs. Long confined to a sickroom, she apologizes for being a dull correspondent.

> Your uncle is better now . . . but his poor hands are still . . . so swollen as to be almost useless, so I lend him mine. The music-box [the girls' gift] is playing beside me and seems well adapted to solitude, as I look out at our mountains white with snow, and the winter's wind sounding loud and clear. . . . I wish I could cover you with furs, but ah! if I dared indulge in wishes—

They were sorry Walter had to leave.

Now they could almost hear the silence. The mountains had put on greater grandeur. Whether or not the Madisons knew Blake's "Great things are done when man and mountains meet," they bore witness.

Paul Jennings helped Mistress roll Master out of bed, unbandage his swollen legs, bathe them in tepid salt water while his sheets were being changed, then rebandage, and carefully put him back. And every other day Paul shaved him.

Madison was pondering his will. What was right and just? Should anyone but Dolley inherit? It was a hard question.

He was also—at the request of James K. Paulding—sketching his life. Strangely, he dwelt longer on the 1829 Richmond Convention than on his two terms as President. With Convention opponents so "fixed in their hot opinions," they were casting doubt on man's capacity for self-government, Madison wrote, the only way to break the deadlock was to compromise. So he had put aside personal opinions to placate the turbulent easterners, whose defeat represented the greater danger. His own mature view of the franchise hinged on the basic requirements of a republic. Though well aware of the risks of universal suffrage—the danger of uninformed or dictated voting, and of building up a mob spirit—he would have liked to see the franchise extended far enough

> to secure . . . a majority of people on the side of power. A government resting on a minority is an aristocracy, not a republic, and could not be safe . . . without a standing army, enslaved press, and disarmed populace.

So he only seemed to be emphasizing the Convention of 1829. His deeper concern, now as always, was the Constitution: what it said, and why it said so. Madison was seizing the opportunity of his life sketch to proclaim his faith in enlightened self-government—for what if Virginia's struggle were to be repeated on a nationwide scale? The nagging question of his old age was the perennial one: Could the Union be preserved under stress without forfeiting liberty? It was his great concern.

Liberty! Madison was too profound a thinker, and his remaining time on earth too limited, for him not to reexamine the dichotomy of freedom and order as reconciled in the great central idea of the United States. The nation, like his own adult life, had been founded in liberty. But did it know that liberty can be subverted into license? That liberty demands a sense of responsibility? Upon the answer hinged the future of the United States. As wise people grow older they examine their lives, their values. Looking ever more deeply into the United States' past and confronting its future possibilities came natural to James Madison, for he could not separate himself from his country; he identified with it.

In the midst of such thoughts the old warrior was not too painridden to send a kind letter to the brother-in-law who had cost him thousands of dollars. "Dear Sir . . . I regret sincerely the difficulties you experience. . . . All my good wishes."

The Madisons put their faith in the sun. Dolley hoped warm weather would so ease her husband's rheumatism, the Lears and Cuttses could come down this spring. "We will combine our musical talents," she wrote

Fanny, "to make you happy midst our shades." It was singing in the darkening light of evening.

So Ned had lost the congressional race to a Jacksonite, then on a trip to New York caught, instead of a wife, influenza and scarlet fever. His friends at Montpelier were sorry. Back on the Illinois prairie, now, he was at loose ends, he wrote, but might decide to raise colts, calves, and pigs. Dolley wrote right back that at forty-six he should settle down to raise *children*.

With warm weather Madison's long tedious illness seemed to be petering out. He looked well, had a good appetite, and enjoyed the sunshine. Dolley wrote Ned: "Our peas are green and flourishing, and all our rural treasures are hailed with the freshness of spirit which is brought to the enjoyment of gay assemblies. . . ." Then the effervescent Dolley tried to comfort Ned for his frustrations. Washington would "indemnify" him. "I hear of many fine girls there. . . . You had better come with them and cheat Illinois, the pigs and prairies."

One reason for her high spirits was Payne's continuing desire to quarry rock. Didn't it disprove his reputation for laziness? She was feeling a kind of mother's triumph when, in May, Madison had a setback. Rheumatism only attacks the body, he wrote Everett, bilious fever the mind.

But a little later he sprang alert to Trist's cry that the Union was in imminent danger; that the "very devil" resided in the heart of John C. Calhoun; there seemed little chance of stopping South Carolina from overt acts. Then what would happen?

Dr. Peyton Grymes has testified that at this time Madison suffered from three ailments besides rheumatism, any one of which could have killed him: a nervous affliction, heart trouble, and liver disease.

Rallying a little one day, he studied Jefferson's draft of the Kentucky Resolutions as printed in the *Enquirer*. Yes, they did declare that states had a right to "nullify of their own authority"—a wording which he himself had told Jefferson was perilously wrong and which Breckenridge had then struck out. No draft of his own Virginia Resolutions said anything like "null and void." Obviously Jefferson's original phrasing would give South Carolina ammunition, and if she went through with calling a Southern Convention as threatened, hotheads like Giles and Calhoun would use it for all it was worth. "Take care of me. . . ."

For Trist, Madison outlined a way to defend Jefferson against the charge of endorsing nullification, adding, "Allowances ought . . . to be made for a habit in Mr. Jefferson, as in others of great genius, of expressing in strong and round terms impressions of the moment." He still hoped his suggestions for tariff reductions would arrest South Carolina's "headlong course." Then vehemently,

> The idea that a Constitution which has been so fruitful of blessings, and a Union admitted to be the only guardian of the peace, liberty and happiness of the people of the states comprising it, should be broken up and scattered to the winds without greater than any existing cause, is more painful than words can express.

Tariff was one horn of the dilemma, "general welfare" the other. In June 1832, the *Enquirer* published a two-year-old letter from Madison to Speaker of the House Stevenson denying that the general welfare clause gave Congress carte blanche.

Through the *Intelligencer,* Madison's staunch admirer ex-President John Quincy Adams retorted that the House had frequently invoked Madison to prove the exact opposite. It was ironical.

> If there be one living man to whom this country is indebted for greater or more eminent services than to any other, it is James Madison. . . . His confidence has been among the most precious consolations of my life. The opinions of Mr. Madison are to me, therefore, among the highest of human authorities.

But Adams denied that he had ever held the "latitudinarian" interpretation of general welfare which Stevenson had attributed to him and refuted by publishing Madison's letter. Though he and Madison differed as to spending power, they agreed as to the constitutionality of a protective tariff—see some letters Madison had written Cabell in 1828. "If you appeal to Mr. Madison as authority you must submit to his authority. . . . The *authority* of Mr. Madison upon this question is against you. . . . Not merely the authority of his name but authority . . . by lucid argument—by impregnable demonstration." It was a neat turning of the tables. Madison admired Adams's dexterity. Blow by blow, the hell-for-leather nullifiers were being brought down.

Though still confined to bed, the old statesman had suffered not one whit of intellectual diminishment. Throughout the summer of 1832, this crucial time, James Madison was a power in the land.

Those who loved him marveled at signs of another slow physical comeback. To hasten the process, Trist suggested a decoction of red pepper in brandy—boil and rub in gently. That or something made him quite able to play host, overnight, in July, to Andrew Jackson. He had a suspicion that the President wanted something connected with the coming election, and so it proved. When gaunt, porcupine-haired Old Hickory had gone, up drove Henry Clay. Warned yesterday, near Monticello, of his enemy's whereabouts, he had ridden on down the road to Governor Barbour's for the night, then posted back. How attractively he talked from his oversized mouth.

Payne being absent, Clay could not swap reminiscences of Ghent nor tease him (as once on a Washington street) about the prince of America dancing with Russian grand duchesses while the Commissioners—Gallatin himself—were relegated to a balcony.

As regular as the clock ticking in the clock room, Dolley wrote her son. Once in a long while he reciprocated. "Yours, dearest, came safe," she wrote one day. Mr. Patton and Mr. Rives hope to see him a "Jackson man." His Papa is better. She hopes soon to be able to ride to Orange Courthouse—what an event! Their tobacco sold for $7 instead of the expected $17—"so it goes with planters." Better a pittance than depend on a *plantation* for pin money. Dolché and Mary have told her of his popularity. At Montpelier they "know little of the great world. . . . Adieu, my son—may Heaven preserve and protect you."

Anna's decline chilled Dolley to the bone. Letters flew back and forth in consternation. At last there came the first faint reassurance. She wrote at once:

> Beloved Sister,
>   Mrs. Macon has just written to me to say you are a little better. Your precious daughters (whom I shall ever consider . . . my own children) have often consoled me. . . . Your husband and sons have also written . . . their deep sense of your value.

Grieved to be separated from the sister she had so tenderly helped to raise, Dolley thanks God that Anna is well cared for. James discusses her, says Dolley, with a brother's partiality. "Do, dear sister, strive to get well and strong for my sake and your children's; what should we do without you? . . . Adieu, my dear, ever and always, your loving sister."

Anna received this letter just before she died August 14, 1832, from dropsy of the heart.

The blow felled Dolley. Great sorrow is rhythmic; it comes in waves.

In the troughs between floats merciful disbelief. Dolley wrote Richard Cutts: "Dear Brother, the heart of your miserable sister mourns with you and your precious daughters! with your sons! . . . Mr. Madison partakes in our sorrow. . . . Show this to Dolley and Mary, please, as I cannot write to them at this moment."

Beneath the letter she sketched a faltering, fragmentary obituary:

> She would have parted from her heart's best blood for the happiness of her offspring. One who from the height of worldly prosperity . . . was reduced . . . to a small income, and while [her husband] gazed on, his energies paralyzed . . . this good mother devoted herself to . . . her children. She brought them up in the fear of the Lord, she implanted pure principles . . . , she taught them to listen to the still small voice within. . . . Her daughters she . . . taught . . . a taste for poetry, the classics, her own love of the beautiful and true.

The stark fact of death brought a rush of memories. A towheaded little Anna at Scotchtown. . . . a sixteen-year-old Anna in Philadelphia dancing with the McKean crowd. . . . a blond bride looking back from the stagecoach, bound for Maine. . . . a mother holding her children and then, inexplicably, a dead child. . . . a woman strong in trouble. . . . Oh, Anna, *Anna!*

In Jefferson, Madison had lost his closest friend; in Anna, Dolley lost the person whom, barring husband and son, she loved most in the world. Lucy was wonderful, but Anna more a part of herself. And because Anna had died comparatively young (thirty years younger than Jefferson), the finality was harder to understand. How versatile was death: by yellow fever, by tuberculosis, by paralytic stroke, by inundation of water on the heart.

That summer of 1832 Madison's corn and tobacco looked promising, but his wheat crop fell victim to the Hessian fly. Still, he insisted on stressing the situation's better side. A letter to Isaac sounds cheerful; he is looking forward. As if to confirm his faith, a settlement of $2,850 came through from Kentucky. Perhaps, with half of Montpelier mortgaged, they could squeeze by without selling any more land at cutthroat prices.

About now the first resident Episcopal rector since before the Revolution, the Rev. William Jones, moved to Orange. The tide at St. Thomas Parish, so long at ebb, was beginning to rise. Bishop William Meade came and preached for two days to large crowds. Seventeen were confirmed, and twice that number took Holy Communion: a quickening, he called it, "a deep awakening in the hearts of many . . . a spirit of earnest inquiry."

The vestry was seeking a new site for a church to replace the old torn-down Brick Church.

James Madison took part in this Orange religious revival. After his death the Rev. Mr. Jones and others would assure Bishop Meade that they were certain, from conversations held with him during his last years, that he attributed the Christian religion to divine revelation. As to the purity of his character, adds Bishop Meade, no one who knew him ever doubted it.

In September a government-commissioned London geologist, Mr. Featherstonhaugh, who was making a survey, examined and admired Toddsberth's vein of marble. Beautiful rock! First-quality, both the white and flush-colored! he told Payne enthusiastically. Quarrying it might be profitable. The Englishman enjoyed himself so much at Montpelier, he promised to come back. His comment was the same as that of many others who had arrived as strangers: the Madisons seemed like old friends.

Meanwhile the Virginia Assembly's full-scale debate on slavery was troubling James Madison. Some prominent legislators were actually calling the dreadful practice of owning human beings a benefit to all concerned. To compound his anxiety, President Jackson had just scotched a cherished plan; he had vetoed a bill to finance colonization through the sale of Western lands.

So Dr. James Turner Barclay of Charlottesville had paid the Randolphs $7,500 for Monticello. The Madisons heard the news while ice was breaking noble trees and while, in the presidential campaign, Jackson was using more and more dubious means of fighting Clay, the one so hotheaded, the other so cold. Their chief bone of contention was the Bank of the United States, the rechartering of which Jackson had vetoed. Claws dug in. Madison, as before, held himself apart. He must spend his remaining energy not on personalities but principles.

One day in November, after he had lain in bed a solid year, he wrote to thank the Stevensons for a warm cap and gloves. Mrs. Madison had also provided for his feet. "I am thus equipped cap-a-pie for the campaign against Boreas and his allies the frosts and snows." But there was one covering his friends could not supply, he joked—the flesh falling from his bones.

The last months of 1832 (while Jackson rang up a majority and Calhoun entered the Senate) Madison lay encased in his cocoon of cap, mittens, wool boots, and blankets. It felt very snug, in the morning, when Becky's match sent fire leaping up the chimney. Pine burned fast, oak more slowly, and chestnut went off like a report of guns. It was a kind of presidential salute.

No, some South Carolinians were not fighting fair. And a South

Carolinian convention had gone ahead and "nullified" federal tariffs by
an ordinance prohibiting their collection, then appealed to the Supreme
Court. Any attempt at force, the state warned, would make it secede from
the Union. The authority cited for this radical stance: again, Madison's
writings of 1798–1800 calling nullification—or so South Carolina
claimed—a constitutional right. If the ex-President declared otherwise, it
said, he had changed. "The states *have*," it quoted him. Did not his plural
prove the states supreme?

No, thundered Madison himself; that plural had been used in connection with basic rights which, because shared by all the states, all should
try to secure for each other. South Carolina was guilty of gross distortion
of facts.

Near Christmas, President Jackson issued a proclamation against the
treason of nullification. "Our Union!" he had said and was in effect
reiterating. "It must be preserved." Madison approved. For all the old
General's coonskin democracy and lowering of standards in government
work, he did sometimes get things right. But the confrontation raised
tension. Now the whole nation was comparing federal and state power,
and the twin dangers of overcentralization and a breaking up of the
Union—the issue which, thirty years later, would precipitate the civil war
which Madison even now feared. Jackson ordered two war vessels to
Charleston. Where was it all leading?

The Virginia Assembly discussed making a "peace offering." Madison's name was like a ball thrown from hand to hand. Some delegates
swore Virginia should stand forever on Madison's Resolutions and Report
of 1800; one called Madison's letter to the *North American* "trash"; another
asked rhetorically if Virginia should take the dictum of any single person,
even James Madison's. Shameful! someone else cried—South Carolina,
knowing its movement would fail without Virginia's support, was trying to
gain that support by discrediting Madison. Another shouted in open
hostility, "We do not believe that the fabric raised by a youthful Hercules"—Madison was all of forty-nine in 1800—"can be thrown down by
him in the weakness and decrepitude of old age."

The historic debate ended with resolutions denying that the Assembly's 1798–1800 stand, here reaffirmed, sanctioned South Carolina's
course. The Assembly requested Congress to ease the situation by lowering the hated tariff and begged South Carolina to wipe out or suspend her
"nullification." These were all Madisonian ideas, his position, as usual,
being at dead center, or say at meridian, a pivot between extremes.
Madison had triumphed.

But John Calhoun would not give up. He kept using the Senate as a sounding board for his extreme states'-rights doctrine. The first resolution which he offered denied that the people of the States formed a nation; no, they formed a *league* of nations. Accordingly, any state deciding that the constitutional compact had been violated could, if it desired, nullify federal law or secede: a fundamental challenge to the Constitution. Madison read the words in horror. Cut, he bled.

Of course he had always known that the best-planned statutory union was not enough. Though the Constitution strove for balance between center and periphery, a certain intrinsic imbalance could not be avoided. To guarantee unity the federal government had to have an edge judicially, and judiciary power *could* perpetrate injustice. What was needed to set everything right was something which no government could confer: a sense of moral responsibility, high ethical development. It could never be achieved en masse; just individually, one by one. So that best of constitutions, the American one, had at its throat the knife of human imperfection. Statutory near-balance could be protected only by a higher balance. What the republic cried for was clearheaded, farseeing, selfless individuals, *great human beings.*

Because Madison identified with the nation, its extremity was his own.

Two allies stepped forward: Alexander Rives, author of a couple of pamphlets signed "A Friend of Union and States' Rights," and his brother the former Minister to France, Senator William C. Rives of nearby Castle Hill. Madison showed his neighbor the masterly essay, "On nullification," on which he had been working.

It is interesting that the sun-and-planets metaphor stemming from Rittenhouse's orrery nearly sixty years ago and used in the Constitutional Convention of 1787, still lived in Madison's mind. He wonders, in this paper, "whether experience would prove the centripetal or centrifugal tendency"—where balance was aimed at—stronger. It would depend on the "extent and effect of the powers granted" in this "political system with a divided sovereignty," he says, this "last hope of true liberty on the face of the earth."

A week later William Rives shot his bolt in the Senate; he "demolished the doctrine of nullification, root and branch," said Trist. His report continues: "Mr. Rives has covered himself with glory . . . nailed his flag (and I am confident the flag of *Virginia*) to the mast."

Rives's speech was pure Madison-taught Madisonianism: the doctrine of divided but shared and cooperative sovereignty. As mouthpiece only, he freely acknowledged his debt. Because of Madison's unique relation to the Constitution, he said, no one could be more "thoroughly imbued with its true philosophy." He followed the ex-President with "peculiar confidence."

Calhoun answered in cold fury. Webster—drawing still closer to Madison's position—likened the South Carolinian to a man who, in his efforts to extricate himself, sinks ever deeper into a quagmire. Standing up to his full height, Clay said he adhered to the doctrines of that "ablest, wisest and purest of American statesmen, James Madison."

The upshot pleased all Madisonians: Congress lowered the tariff, and a South Carolinian convention exchanged its ordinance "nullifying" the tariff for one "nullifying" the "force bill," then found implementation impossible. In all but obstinate breasts the issue died.

The power of lucid analysis had prevailed, and Madison, believer in the great central rooftree—ridgepole—of the United States, could breathe better. If ever the nation reached the brink of dismemberment, he felt sure, it would "recoil from its horrors."

Showing George Tucker some letters for the biography of Jefferson which Tucker was writing, Madison pointed out Jefferson's reference to the Constitution as "making us one people and one nation for certain purposes." Yes, that was it.

The spring of 1833 Madison—as if revitalized by victory—escaped the rigor mortis of rheumatism. He felt amazingly well.

⤜ XX ⤛

MISS MARTINEAU
PERCEIVES SOMETHING

IT WAS THE BEGINNING of a long reprieve. More trials would have to be endured but not yet, not yet. For six splendid months, not yet.

Madison felt like Lazarus. Color had seeped back into his face, his stride had the old spring. Almost as eagerly as in his prime he rode out in young green weather. On his return Dolley stood waiting at the door. No need for words; they understood each other.

On their wedding day they had been almost opposites, he predominantly head, she heart. Now the two natures had in large measure, through mutual influence, merged, intermixed, each taking on qualities of the other. As a result, both were better balanced.

What James and Dolley Madison had become would show forth most clearly in the testimony of the famous English economist and sociologist Harriet Martineau, who visited them in the spring of 1835, but that was still two years away. Meanwhile the Madisons were working together, in harmony, copying James's notes on the debates in the Convention of 1787, a tedious work.

The summer of 1833 the household was enlivened by Annie Payne, John's third daughter, who had come to live at Montpelier to help and be helped. Though full of delightful mischief, she had a serious side, too, this unbeautiful but serene and pleasant young girl. She got along well with her cousin Payne. Now it was a family of four.

If Harriet Martineau had not yet taken Madison's measure, his family had; its members, and particularly Dolley, who had lived with him thirty-nine years, knew his quality, his power, and saw what was happening: a mellowing as of fruit before seedtime.

Details of life and mood at Montpelier, at this period, come out in Dolley's letters to the motherless Cuttses. The Riveses have dropped by again. The girls should beware of "'most everybody." No, she doesn't believe the gossip and hopes the treaty of peace between the quarrelers will stand up, "or will it resemble scratches on an agate which a wet sponge apparently wipes away forever, but which will come back when the stone is dry?"—a fine poetic metaphor.

Stones were in the forefront of the Madisons' and Payne's minds these days, the whole family made rock-conscious by the upcropping of limestone and marble at Toddsberth called the "string." It ran 30 feet wide, but how deep? They talked about testing Mr. Featherstonhaugh's high opinion of the granite by chemical analysis.

They tramped along the rock vein, wondering, speculating, figuring, then went home to reconsult geology books. The new interest seemed to have quite made over the now almost middle-aged Payne—he was past forty—who, ever since returning from Europe twenty years ago, had failed conspicuously to fulfill a conspicuous promise, and who had long appeared to be drowning in a sea of inconsequentials. Dolley felt sure the quarry would revolutionize his life.

Examining rocks for grain and color, the family wiped each with a wet cloth or sponge, studying it closely before it could dry. The amount of pressure required to leave a scratch told them whether a stone was a chunk of quartz or granite. Some grey specimens crumbled like shale, but the white and flush-pink seemed as pure and solid as Parian or Carrara marble.

When Payne languished upstairs with a cold, hacking away and dreaming of the fortune he would make on marble, Dolley, playing nurse, found time to write Mary. There'd be no more teasing about a certain gentleman. "My dear Payne has . . . an alarming cough, which makes me melancholy. . . . As I told you, I hear nothing more of his liking to the young lady report gave him for a wife, and I'm sorry for it"—an understatement. She hoped the girls had watched Jackson's second inauguration, then joked about Mary setting her "cap and curls" for the old Russian Minister. At the end her niece was put into the care of "Him who is able to lead us safely through all the allotments of his wisdom."

One "allotment" was the health which enabled Jemmy to ride about the countryside during this renaissance, chatting with neighbors about

politics and crops. Oh, she was not afraid of coming down in the world
financially, or of anything really, except separation from Jemmy. They
would sooner have lost everything than each other.

The Stevensons were among many friends financially pinched. But if
the Madisons go to the springs, Sally wrote, they may too. She is thin and
longs for Green Mountain; it's too hot in Richmond and the flies are
terrible—"they are in my eyes, ears, crawling over my face, fingers, etc.,
until I am as nervous as a fine lady." Richmond remembers the Madisons
affectionately, she adds, and she thanks them for some excellent wine. If
only they could drink it together.

During that unusually hot summer, at Montpelier, Dolché, twenty-
two and grown up, played her guitar, and Mary, almost nineteen, amused
herself painting. It was like old times. Apparently their brothers could not
come. Dolley sent Wat a message: he was "not born for inglorious life."

The girls had just left when Madison's six-month dispensation faltered. He overcame rheumatism, relapsed, then struggled up again, sore
but cheerful.

Hearing about a fortune-teller's prophecy, Dolley revealed some of
her own beliefs about destiny, free will, and the goals of life, and they are
hardly distinguishable from Madison's:

> May your fortune, dearest Mary, be even *better* than the sybil's
> predictions. There is a secret she did not tell you, however; it is
> that we all have a great hand in the formation of our destiny. We
> must press on, on that intricate path leading to perfection and
> happiness, by doing all that is good and handsome, before we
> can be taken under the silver wing of our rewarding angel.

She rambles on. Though surrounded by cholera, their Aunt Lucy is
well. Their Uncle John still threatens to move West, but she trusts he
won't—his house has been enlarged, and last year's crops were encouraging. More company, and she's indisposed. This morning she couldn't join
a party of eight friends at breakfast, but she has taken a ride with her
husband and will go to the dinner table. Payne has some good business
prospects. Mr. Patterson of Baltimore sent her a pair of Holstein calves.
She's glad the girls left Warm Springs, that place of "bad accommodation
and extortion." Their uncle, though never really well these days, is better.
Lately three artists have worked at his portrait.

Welsh's engraving after James B. Longacre's drawing of this period
shows a rather quizzical old gentleman in a silk cap; Sartain's engraving

after John G. Chapman, a genial old codger with wavy white hair around a bald pate: two different moods which guests sometimes saw alternating over Madison's countenance.

"Coming and going," wrote Dolley about the phalanx of guests, "until I am quite nervous."

And with pride, "Payne is at home with us improving his knowledge of geology."

The geology books said that marble, recrystallized limestone, could be found pure or mixed. What was undesirable was a quartz-veined marble. Being harder, quartz could break a drill. Dolley watched Payne bent over his specimens. Were those veins *quartz?*

Autumn turned the world outrageously beautiful—trees, vines, sumac. There was a sadness so gentle, so delicate, it was almost to be desired. The Madisons sat by the fire, Dolley sewing, James making original remarks; or they conversed about ordinary household matters, while over and again touched by a sense of time's betrayal that

> makes thy love more strong
> to love that well which thou must leave ere long.

In November Sally wrote, not because she had anything to say, she explains, but because she wants to put Dolley so deeply in debt she'll "have to make some return." Actually she has important news: her brother Ned's coming marriage to Sally Logan Roberts of Philadelphia. The lady, just half his age, is called handsome, modest, amiable. "Tell cousin Payne, if a grey-headed old fellow can do such things, what ought he to do without a grey hair on his head."

Later, when Ned brought his bride to Montpelier, the Madisons took to her at once. Nor was Dolley blind to this new Sally's elegant silk gown.

Soon another bride was brought to meet them: Mad Cutts's Ellen O'Neale of Maryland. As their coach drew up, Uncle came out onto the portico leaning on Paul Jennings. Too feeble to join the party at dinner, he stood at the door between his room and the dining room to drink their health. Ellen sent back a letter "full of intelligence and amusement," and Mad some court plaster for Uncle's rheumatism. Because Dolley had cut one of her fingers, her return note was brief. " . . . Your cousin Payne offers you love and respect, and I think is inclined to speak for himself. Your affectionate aunt."

Madison now sent the fifteen-year-old English Princess Victoria the autograph she had requested. And he acquired a special rocking chair. If he couldn't race Dolley on the portico or swing up into a saddle, he could—while winter winds howled—exercise back and forth, back and forth. Snow was falling on Peter's Mountain. All over Orange County it lay 2 feet deep. And many hours were whiled away as Dolley read aloud to James both light and heavy books. He looked at her sitting there by the lamp. He had a philosophy for stepping deeper into old age, but how leave this beloved companion?

One of the books they shared was the Bible, and if Dolley's favorite chapter was the same now as later, she lingered on the Gospel according to John. It was natural to fall to discussing the great verities.

One day Madison's body, like Job's, erupted in great welts. It was desperately hard not to scratch; the strain exhausted him. Dolley was beside herself. Could a man of dignity die of an ailment so undignified? She suffered his ordeal vicariously.

During this nightmare visitation in April 1834 Dolley's nerves grew frayed. She wrote sharply to Mary, "Both your uncle and I think it exceedingly careless of you to keep us so long in suspense." But she could not sustain that mood and was soon reporting with glee that thanks to Mr. Featherstonhaugh's instructions, her Holstein calves had grown into fine, beautiful animals, "the admiration of the neighborhood." She longs to hear Mary play the harp. And she asks for some thin "springlike" material suitable for a turban for "ladies of a certain age." But Mary won't have time to read this. "You never answer all my letters"—another little touch of asperity. She is wounded, taut. "Your uncle . . . is in the same painful state . . . the eruption over him is very bad, and when it is at all easy, he is in a restless sleep all day."

His condition forced him to send Governor Tazewell his resignation to the University of Virginia. He had been Rector eight years—eight times longer than Jefferson himself—and had hung on, hoping for a change. Now he must act. The letter was in Dolley's hand except for his tormented signature: "James Madison." It was a hard blow for the institution and the State.

Passing away, saith the world. . . .

Summer came tanned and free, with running blackberries, and Payne went off to Philadelphia on business, his word no longer suspect, the fear that he would revert to former habits no longer lively.

But a midsummer letter from Dolley seems to remember Prune Street:

> Yours, dearest, promising to write me again, came safely. . . .
> You did not tell me whether you had been successful in your
> collections. If not, you will want supplies proportioned to your
> detention; I am anxious that you should have them, and you
> know the little I have in my power is at your command. *

Though Payne was forty-two now and growing stout, she slipped into
thinking of him as a boy. Not that she wished to overprotect him. It was
just hard to loose him and let him go.

About this time she wrote an autobiographical sketch notable for
misinformation:

> . . . My family are all Virginians except myself, who was born in
> North Carolina whilst my parents were there on a visit of one
> year to an uncle,

whereas John Payne, having gone to Carolina to work a farm given him by
his father, Colonel Josias Payne, had remained three years. " . . . They
[her parents] becoming members of the Society of Friends soon after
their marriage," whereas it was only Dolley's father who was a convert, her
mother being a "birth" Quaker; " . . . manumitted their slaves, and left this
state for . . . Pennsylvania . . . I believe my age at the time was 11 or 12
years," whereas it was fifteen. She had a poor memory for dates, it seems,
and no knowledgeable guide nor written records at hand, and certainly
enough anxiety over Jemmy's ordeal to cloud her mind.

Gradually the torture eased. By September, thanks in part to Dr.
Dunglison's lotion, the welts had disappeared, and Madison sat by a
window, free of pain, pondering his country's future. When Trist arrived
to talk politics, he found his mentor's hands so limber, they could write the
old clear, beautiful script.

The doctrine of nullification was burrowing out of sight like a
groundhog. That did not mean it was dead, and Madison was apprehensive. He wrote Ned Coles,

> . . . What [is] more dangerous than nullification, or more evident
> than the progress it continues to make, either in the original
> shape, or in the disguises it assumes? Nullification has the effect
> of putting powder under the Constitution and Union, and a
> match in the hand of every party—

another telling metaphor. When Ned replied that Jackson's misrule was
turning the country's mind away from nullification, Madison said yes, but

with what result? Taking advantage of the President's averted eyes, the idea was "propagating itself under the name of State rights."

To another correspondent he went further. The old East-West chasm had been closed, but because of animosities between slaveholding and nonslaveholding states, he said with remarkable insight, a still more dangerous North-South chasm was opening up.

Brooding over this, and aware that his life expectancy was limited (three years, two?), he wrote in profound concern "Advice to My Country." If these words ever saw the light of day, he said, it would be after he had gone "where truth alone can be respected." He had served his country forty years. (He should have said nearly sixty, counting not from 1776 to 1817, not from his membership in the first Virginia Convention to his retirement from the Presidency, but, rather, from 1774, when he joined the Orange County Committee of Public Safety, to his powerfully influential present.) Having from youth espoused the cause of liberty and union and taken part in most of the great transactions marking the "epochs of its destiny," he wrote, perhaps he could offer some parting advice. "The advice nearest my heart and deepest in my conviction is that the Union of the States be cherished and perpetuated." Consider any frank and open foe a Pandora opening a fatal box. Consider any secret one a "serpent creeping . . . into Paradise."

Only Dolley knew about this final legacy to his country. She put it carefully away.

Though Madison's physical improvement offered Dolley a reprieve, she did not use it for anything but household activities, and she did not quite know why. "There has been a spell upon my fingers," she wrote Dolché, "and even now there rests one upon my eyes." With congressmen and their attachés streaming back into Washington, she remembers the bustle—the girls must be flying about socially. As to the biographical material Mrs. Smith wanted, "I can't give her anything of importance in my own eyes." Yes, she has other letters about the war, "but egotism is so repugnant . . . I shrink from recording my own feelings, acts or doings." She has bought 30 yards of calico to make dresses for John's girls. During December Annie and her sisters went to a dance at the Newmans', but she stayed "quiet at home" with their uncle. Good wishes have gone off to Mad and Ellen's new daughter, Adéle (destined to become a famous beauty). She's been slicing thousands of strips of bacon for her family (four plus a hundred-odd slaves). "How tired I am of it!"

But she was not tired of trying to help nieces. To Mary, one day, she revealed something of her supporting faith:

> You say, darling, that you "do not advance in anything," but I trust you do in knowledge and faith in the great goodness of God. I pray for you and my beloved Dolley that you may advance in all that is desirable in this world, and that to which you are hastening! I feel for you as my daughters.

The climax of Dolley's letter was about her son. "Mr. Long and others have taken Payne off to look for a location for a railroad," as if to say, You see—he's an important person in touch with modern developments. As the Madisons were themselves. Born in frontier days, they had lived long enough to see the "iron horses" which would revolutionize transportation all over the world.

Dolley was recovering from flu when the British Minister, Sir Charles Vaughn, wrote that the English sociologist Harriet Martineau and her friend Miss Jeffries would like to pay their respects at Montpelier. Dolley hurried back an invitation. The keen-minded Miss Martineau might be an interesting diversion for James.

Waiting for her, Dolley asked Dolché not to worry about writing poor letters; "few can write . . . more handsomely." This praise cushioned an objection to her niece impersonating, at a fancy dress party, a sorceress wreathed with reptiles. " . . . I would have persuaded you to appear in a more feminine and congenial character"; better to sustain a "sweet gentle character." No, contrary to rumor, she isn't inviting anyone to spend the summer; "indeed my love, . . . I should be quite unhappy to think I would be confined at home to receive company during the . . . only season of the year when your sick uncle can go out at all." They both hoped to visit some springs, or at least to be free to "travel about for our health's sake." Her husband has requested an engraving made from the miniature of her in a Quaker cap painted forty years ago just after their marriage.

On February 18, 1834, Miss Martineau and Miss Jeffries got stuck at Orange Courthouse. Although Madison had asked the innkeeper to inform him at once of the ladies' arrival so that he could send his carriage, the man rented them a room for a nap, served a noon breakfast, and overcharged for a carriage.

Miss Martineau has recorded in *Retrospect of Western Travel* that it was a "sweet day of early spring" as they drove toward Montpelier. The patches of snow under fences and on hills were melting, and right up to the portico of Madison's "neat and even handsome" dwelling the road was a slough. Mrs. Madison and her niece Annie Payne stood at the top of the steps smiling.

After freshening up, the guests were taken to the study to meet Mr. Madison. Miss Martineau's picture of him is priceless and must be quoted at length. He sat in his chair,

> a pillow behind him, . . . wrapped in a black silk gown; a warm gray and white cap upon his head, which his lady took care should always sit becomingly, and gray worsted gloves, his hands having been rheumatic. His voice was clear and strong, and his manner of speaking particularly lively, often playful.

Taking a chair next to him, the better to converse, the thirty-three-year-old Miss Martineau got a closer look at the elderly American statesman about whom she had heard so much. Though "smaller and . . . older," the face was like a well-known engraving. "He seemed not to have lost his teeth, and the form of the face was . . . preserved without any striking marks of age. It was an uncommonly pleasant countenance."

Dolley sat on a couch across the room sewing. Though she seldom spoke, when she did so it was with sense and sensibility.

> . . . Mrs. Madison is celebrated throughout the country for the grace and dignity with which she discharged the . . . duties which devolve upon the President's lady . . . [having] such discretion, impartiality and kindness it is believed she gratified everyone and offended nobody.

The two Madisons struck Miss Martineau as extraordinarily well matched.

They, on their side, found her an attractive guest, thin but strongly put together, and with fine alert eyes in a plain face. She was interested in everything, spoke seriously, and laughed heartily.

Because she came fresh from familiar places, they plied her with questions, the gist of the conversation running, as she has reported in detail, like this:

How did she like America and Americans? Very much.

What did she think of Philadelphia and Washington? "At Philadelphia I found perpetual difficulty in remembering that I was in a foreign land. . . . At Washington it was very different." That struggling capital with its quick-changing weather, slaves, and plentiful canvasback ducks seemed "singularly compounded from a large variety of elements and unlike that of any other city in the world."

Had she met any members of Congress? Oh, yes, and she knew the outstanding ones—"Mr. Clay, sitting upright . . . with his snuffbox," talking in his "even, soft, deliberate tone on one of the great subjects of American policy." Mr. Webster leaning back comfortably, telling stories and jokes, and rocking the sofa with bursts of laughter. Mr. Calhoun, man of cast iron, who "looks as if he had never been born and never could be extinguished." Calhoun's speech, went on Miss Martineau, returning Mr. Madison's straight gaze,

> abounds in figures truly illustrative if that which they illustrate were but true also. . . . Power . . . but . . . admiration too soon turned into regret, into absolute melancholy. . . . I know of no man who lives in such utter intellectual solitude. . . . I never saw anyone who so completely gave me the idea of possession—

which came close to Madison's evaluation.

And General Jackson? Yes, she had met him at a White House party. She thought his broom-stiff hair gave him a rather formidable look. His slow, quiet way of speaking stood in contrast. The party had been stuffy.

The Madisons asked the Englishwoman if she was tired of signing fashionable albums. "The plague of the day!"

And how about the weather in Washington? Cold. The roads were sheets of ice.

Was she in town when someone shot at Jackson? Yes. Poor madman—he complained that the President had deprived him of the British crown.

What was the General's reaction? It had thrown him into a "tremendous passion. He fears nothing, but his temper is not equal to his courage."

Had she stopped at Mount Vernon? Yes, and what beauty of situation. "The river was nobler, the terrace finer, the swelling hills, around, more varied than I had imaged." But the house had a "painful air of desolation."

After hours of reporting her experiences, it was Miss Martineau's turn to draw out James Madison. Immediately they moved into the world of ideas.

"He appeared perfectly well during my visit," she would write, "and was a wonderful man of eighty-three." He said one ear was deaf and his sight, never perfect, had become so poor, reading was difficult. As a result, his studies "lay in a nutshell." Fortunately he could hear every word when Mrs. Madison read to him—hadn't Miss Martineau noted that he lost none of the conversation?

Ironically, it was his guest who used a trumpet.

Thus two thinkers widely separated in age found themselves highly congenial. The virtuous bluestocking had already demonstrated her energy and intellectual grasp by publishing the 25-volume popularizing *Illustrations of Political Economy,* the 10-volume *Poor Laws and Papers Illustrated,* and the 5-volume *Illustrations of Taxation.* But Madison was the colossus. Acutely aware of this, Miss Martineau treasured his words while trying, because of his physical frailty, to limit them. "His relish for conversation could never have been keener. I was in perpetual fear of his being exhausted." Every few hours, accordingly, she left her seat by his armchair to go over and sit down on the sofa by Mrs. Madison.

It was no good. Following her like a hound his quarry, he sat down between the two ladies, so that the only effect of her migrations was to deprive him of a comfortable chair. After realizing this, she left her station by his chair only to eat or sleep, "glad enough to make the most of any means of intercourse with one whose political philosophy I deeply venerated."

In her memoir she tries to pick out the best part of his splendid endowment and comes to a surprising conclusion. Not logic, she decides, and not intellect, but his faith.

> There is no need to add another to the many eulogies of Madison; I will only mention that the finest of his characteristics appeared to me to be his inexhaustible faith ... that a wellfounded commonwealth may, as our motto declares, be immortal, not only because the people, its constituency, never die, but because the principles of justice in which a commonwealth originates never die out of the people's heart and mind.

This faith "shone brightly" at all times except one: during their discussion of slavery—a word he hated and avoided using.

As the Madisons had known ahead, Miss Martineau was an ardent abolitionist ready to battle for her viewpoint. But in Madison she found no opposition. If not in despair over slavery, he was "almost in despair." He had been entirely so, he said, until the founding of the American Colonization Society, of which he had long been a life member and was now President. Though the condition of slaves had improved, he said, this didn't ease his conscience. Miss Martineau listened fascinated while he talked on this subject longer than on any other—"acknowledging, without limitation or hesitation, all the evils with which it has ever been charged." He said the black population of Virginia had increased much faster than the white, every slave girl being expected to bear a child by fifteen. Africa, he believed, was the blacks' only refuge. This bothered her. She hadn't heard any reason why they shouldn't, after emancipation, she said, remain in America. But Madison said sadly that the two races (this had been Jefferson's view also) were too far apart to mix successfully.

Madison denied forthrightly that slaves were an economic asset. According to the last returns from his estate, one-third of his were under five. He had parted from some of his best land to feed the increasing numbers, yet last week had been forced to sell a dozen. (She might have added what he must have told her: After having refused all his life to sell blacks, he had sold these to a kind Taylor cousin only after making sure that the transfer was wholly satisfactory to the servants themselves.)

Obviously dismayed by the moral dilemma, he spoke of the fact that the whole Bible condemned slavery. The clergy didn't preach this nor laymen see it. Whereupon he became quite animated describing the eagerness of ministers to catch black converts. But of course, he said meditatively, those who have no rights can have no duties. In other words, freedom and responsibility are inseparable.

Yes, he admitted that his black people had a horror of being sent to Liberia in Africa. This appeared to Miss Martineau to prove the unnaturalness of the scheme. Yes, he replied, cast down, there were great difficulties. And he expressed pity for a downtrodden race.

But he also pitied conscientious white women, he said, who could not trust their servants, many of whom had been taught thievery by free blacks, and all of whom, to carry out orders, needed constant supervision. Owners were kept in a constant state of "suspicion, fear and anger," and he spoke feelingly of the helplessness of countries "cursed with a servile population." Civil war over the issue? He ridiculed the notion that the South would ever imagine it could defeat the more populous, manufacturing North, then laughed at certain strangers who, thinking that all masters whipped their black people all day long, were astonished to see his going to church, the women dressed in bright-colored calicoes and, when it rained, shooting up umbrellas. It had thrown those critics to the other extreme; slavery, they now concluded, was a happy state. The truth of course was at neither extreme. To readjust the balance he had had to point out the degradation of minds—how, for instance, slaves often grew indifferent to close kin and cruel to animals. His honest, fair, judicious treatment of the subject increased Miss Martineau's respect.

At dinner the three ladies and Miss Annie were joined by Payne

Todd. Gross of body now and Grandisonian in manner, he was yet, when he chose, and he did choose today, an attractive conversationalist.

When the meal broke up, the talk in the study was eagerly resumed. That first night Mr. Madison and Miss Martineau addressed such diverse topics as Malthus, Godwin, America's abundance of food, Cincinnatus, Roman farms, English grain laws, commerce ("he declared himself in favor of free trade, though believing that freedom cannot be complete in any one country till universal peace shall afford opportunity for universal agreement"), copyrights against literary piracy, the desirability of training one's hands as well as mind, and the equality of women, in which he believed. In Robert Owen's colony, he reminded her, educated women switched between playing harps and milking cows, and why not?

By now Miss Martineau was agreeing with J. K. Paulding, who had called Madison "emphatically the Sage of his time," and with Benjamin Ogle Tayloe, who thought Madison could hold his own with the peers of England. He was all she had expected, and more.

The next morning she was amazed to discover that before she woke, this old gentleman half-crippled by rheumatism had breakfasted in bed, risen, and dressed. For two hours they discussed American Presidents and politicians. When the post arrived at noon, Madison threw it gaily aside, saying he could read newspapers any time; he wanted to make the most of her visit. Did she think it "too vast and anti-republican a privilege" for ex-Presidents to have their mail franked?—it was the "only earthly benefit they carried away." Trumpet lifted, Miss Martineau heard the question and said no, she did not think so.

Now they launched into the subject which, owing to South Carolina's recalcitrance, had for months been preoccupying the whole country and Madison in particular: the doctrine of nullification. Unfortunately, fearing to lose English readers, Miss Martineau omits from her reminiscences Madison's "luminous history of the nullification struggle." It is a loss.

She also leaves out his explanation of the complex questions involved in what he called that "anomalous institution," the American Senate, except to note that he opposed increasing its power.

Finally, like mountain climbers attaining the summit, they discussed religious freedom. To this sociologist from a nation with an established church, Madison declared himself

> perfectly satisfied that there is in the United States a far more
> ample and equal provision for pastors and religious instruction

for the people than could have been secured by a religious establishment . . . and that one of the greatest services which his country will be hereafter perceived to have rendered to the world will be having proved that religion is more cared for the more unreservedly it is committed to the affections of the people.

Give a land one religion, he quoted Voltaire, and there is despotism; two, and they become deadly rivals; fifty, and they live in harmony. It had certainly worked that way in America. Sects which disagreed on tenets could, out of a common Christianity, work together harmoniously for moral elevation. He discussed such thinkers as Hume, Kames, Edwards, Priestley. To Miss Martineau—as February winds bent the trees and fires crackled—it was all very instructive.

The talk was never sterilely intellectual; it was full of heart, Madison proving again and again a quick moral concern.

The only break was for a tour of the house under Dolley's guidance. Miss Martineau enjoyed it. She thought the wealth of busts and prints gave Montpelier an English air. Slaves were omnipresent. The bedrooms had almost constant attendance. Two or three lounged in the study, leaning against doorpost and sofa; others kept coming to Mrs. Madison for her big bunch of keys.

And the evening and the morning were the second day.

The third day Madison again rose in high spirits. On the subject of guests, he described vivaciously certain strangers who had turned up, "some . . . taxes, others bounties." Miss Martineau enjoyed his inexhaustible fund of anecdotes. He chuckled so much over funny situations, she saw that he had a keen edge of appreciation for the ludicrous. Once when he was out riding with a young English geologist, he told her, for example, his guest spurred up to him in a "fit of transport" brandishing a stone in his face. "Graywacke, sir! graywacke! graywacke!"

Miss Martineau would never forget the picture of her host sitting in his chair, his white hair contrasting strongly with the black silk robe, his eyes smiling. "Dull" was the last word she would have used. He was excellent company—the best.

The morning papers railed against France for refusing to reimburse the United States for Napoleon's sea plunderings. Madison outlined for Miss Martineau the history of the relations between France and America. What a shocking spectacle, he said, if these two representative governments, politically in the "van of the world," should fly at each other's throats; it would "squint" toward confirming the charge that popular governments were by nature unstable. Actually there was a big difference between the eagerness for war felt by a potentate who wages it at no personal cost and the reluctance of people who pay in money and lives. For example, George III had gained £1 million a year during the War of 1812 from his share of the droits of Admiralty, whereas the Salem merchants who had wanted the war but came to suffer from it severely now favored reprisals only.

While listening to these discussions Dolley kept quietly sewing, but sometimes she looked up to make a quiet observation.

Well started, Madison discussed with verve the 1812 fight for freedom of the seas, recalling for his faithful audience of two the "humane agreement" between Frederick the Great and Benjamin Franklin that, in war as in peace, merchant ships should go unarmed and scot-free. This sidetracked him to Franklin. When they first became intimate, he said, Franklin was so old and feeble, he had to be carried about on a sedan, but his self-command was extraordinary. Seized by severe pain, he would "rouse himself to converse almost as if it did not exist." (Here Dolley might have said, "Like you.") Disliking argument, Franklin had preferred to hear out an adversary, then "overthrow him with an anecdote."

Thus, all during the third day, Madison moved from topic to topic with the joy of a man with wanderlust traveling from country to country. Darwin's diction, he said surprisingly, put his imagination into a "gay state." This set him off on literature—how could languages remain stable when even terms of classical derivation kept changing their meanings? Then, switching, he expressed "horror of the machinery" of indirect levy; he much preferred direct taxation—look at Pitt's success.

One statement struck Miss Martineau as particularly novel and interesting. Whether or not she had encountered the idea in the *Federalist Papers,* hearing Madison on the subject fascinated her. The federal idea, he insisted, *had no innate limitation*—a view which (as she would be quick to see) could encourage a federation of Europe or the Western Hemisphere or the world.

> He observed that kings, lords and commons might constitute a government which would work a long while in a kingdom no bigger than Great Britain, but that it would soon become an absolute government in a country as large as Russia, from the magnitude of its executive powers; and that it was a common but serious mistake to suppose that a country must be small to be a

republic, since a republican form with a federal head can be extended almost without losing its proportions, becoming all the while less, instead of more, subject to change.

Proportion, balance: key to many of Madison's convictions. In a small republic the fury of factions makes a lot of noise, he told Miss Martineau, whereas in a "spreading but simply working republic like that of the Union the silent influence of the federal head keeps down more quarrels than ever appear."

This third day, while talk was still "in full flow," Miss Martineau had to leave to keep an appointment at the University. She tore herself away with great reluctance. She had partaken of a mental feast. At parting, the Madisons refused to say farewell; the ladies must stop at Montpelier on their return from the South. "We earnestly wished to do so," Harriet Martineau would write, but she never saw Montpelier again.

Her memory would work on, sifting out essentials, until this perceptive woman had reached a final verdict on the Madisons. It emphasizes, or implies an emphasis on, the give-and-take which she had observed between them—which had been going on, of course, ever since their marriage; an exchange, a reciprocity. In both persons, there was an inward continuity of character; in both, development.

Miss Martineau's book describes each in terms which, forty years earlier, applied outstandingly to the *other*—it is remarkable. She speaks of Dolley's *intellect*. Dolley is

a strong-minded woman, fully capable of entering into her husband's occupations and cares; and there is little doubt that he owed much to her intellectual companionship.

Madison is variously described and praised, but especially in terms of morality and *heart*. It is this "virtuous statesman's" active heart which, above all, she says, has turned knowledge into wisdom.

That is not to say she could not have switched her adjectives, calling Dolley warmly virtuous and Madison intellectual; indeed, her memoir implies the suitability of just such a verbal interchange. But she wrote what she wrote, her choice of words more significant for the Madisons' lives, development, and influence on each other, more eloquent of an achieved equilibrium, than she knew.

⚜ XXI ⚜

"ARK OF UNION"

The spring of 1835 James Madison understood by signs and portents that—whatever the surface waves—his tide was running out. He had no fear. He wanted to finish his papers, protect Dolley's future, and make a good death.

The eighty-four-year-old man looked out a window at the land he loved. The sun was uncurling small, pale, fish-shaped willow leaves, less green than gold, to mark a turning point in time.

At sixty-seven Dolley moved with vigor. Able, after three weeks of inflamed eyes, to use a pen once more, she wrote her nieces a rambling letter. Their uncle was better; she hoped spring would complete his recovery. He had enjoyed Miss Martineau's "enlightened conversation and unassuming manners." She was afraid Mrs. Smith hadn't enough material for an interesting biography—"I ought to tremble." It pleased her that Dolché and Mary had refused to learn the new dance (the waltz)—"our sex is ever losers when they stem the torrent of public opinion." The Baron's parties sounded piquant. After long confinement, she and their uncle needed some outdoor exercise.

When she looked up, Jemmy was with level eyes contemplating an imperfect world. It made her happy to see him free of pain.

Near the end of March his health again took a plunge, and by April he had been thrown back into bed.

But they clung to their hope of riding forth together into the quick green world. Perhaps this spring they could visit Old Warm or White Sulphur. Forsythia was in yellow bloom while Madison shivered under blankets. Was this the chill of April or of death?

He revised his will. Though Dolley was his overriding concern, his relatives and some institutions had claims which she heartily endorsed.

The new instrument gave Dolley land, houses, and slaves, subject to a $9,000 legacy to be divided among nieces and nephews. All personal property and papers would go to Dolley also, except that the proceeds from his *Notes on the Debates in the Federal Convention,* worth perhaps $50,000, should furnish five legacies: $2,000 to the American Colonization Society; $6,000 for the education of Robert's three fatherless children, his great-nephews; $1,000 to Princeton; $1,000 to a college named for him at Uniontown, Pennsylvania; and $1,500 to the University of Virginia. After Dolley had chosen 300 books, the rest of his library would go to the University.

Now that he had signed his will, Madison felt freer. A little more work on multitudinous papers and his house would be in order. As for Dolley—there was no separation in love.

He wrote two codicils.

To John Payne of the large family and small future, he bequeathed the farm his brother-in-law had been working. Please God it would keep him from deserting Dolley by moving west.

Payne was a greater problem. For a long time he had been the greatest problem. Though he had improved, largely through his new interest in marble, he was still a spendthrift in danger of becoming again the old compulsive gambler—or so Madison feared. What guarantee that he wouldn't squander a new inheritance as fast as the old? Though Dolley knew her husband had bailed their son out of many scrapes, she had no idea of the total number, or cost of salvage; she was unaware that Payne had already received his legacy many times over. Madison's second codicil gave his stepson a case of rare medallions struck by Napoleon—Payne could appreciate the artistry. Also a gold-collared, ivory-headed walking stick, the shaft of which was a beautifully carved timber from the *Constitution—Old Ironsides.* There, that should keep him from feeling left out, and others from imagining an estrangement.

Entrusting John Payne with vouchers for payments totaling some $20,000 to cover Payne's "ruinous extravagance," Madison asked him to examine and seal the packet and give it to Dolley after his death. The remittances were exclusive of those made with her knowledge, he said, and those he had furnished her with the means of giving. "The sum thus appropriated probably equaled the same amount." (The grand total, some $40,000, would be equal today to at least twenty times that amount.) The packet would tell his wife why he had in equity left Payne comparatively little and tell her also how much he had been willing to sacrifice to reduce her anxiety; in other words, how much he loved her. No reason to worry about Payne going penniless; Dolley had never been able to refuse him anything, and someday—with or without a wife and children—he would, of course, through his mother, inherit Montpelier. Though Madison knew the arrangement irked his brother William's family, this was the way it had to be. The boy he had raised as his own and suffered over beyond calculation would become by indirection, ultimately, his chief heir.

During this period Payne began putting up a gaggle of buildings at Toddsberth. It included a large, round, towerlike structure—seats circling its one room—which he called his ballroom but filled with trunks and boxes and oddments. His home had five rooms which he could add to, in time, and there was a confusion of outbuildings—separate kitchen, guesthouse, servants' quarters. It looked a little like a small eccentric spa minus mineral water.

While amusing himself architecturally, Payne was testing rock, living easy, going off on sprees, and bringing friends home to Montpelier whenever he liked for dinner or the night, or longer.

One visitor had been Mr. Hodgson, whose admiration for Dolché and Mary, Aunt Dolley wrote them, was recommendation enough. He had delivered the beautiful gloves, but not one of the two music boxes, the one she prized most because the girls had given it to her. Perhaps it had been left behind by mistake and would yet play its tune again in "these deep shades." "My days are devoted to nursing and comforting my patient." He walks only from the bed where he breakfasts to the bed in the little chamber. Anna, a sterling girl, stays home with her a great deal and now sleeps beside her bed. Their uncle is better, and if he recovers enough for a trip, they will all meet at Phillips's spa (Warm Springs). "Adieu for the present, my darling."

But the Madisons would drink no healing waters that summer.

It was a varied season. In July John Marshall died. Man—physical man—was as the flower of the field. At the Chief Justice's funeral the Liberty Bell cracked—but the Madisons refused to take that as a symbol. In their ears it kept ringing. They believed too fiercely in America's constitutional liberties for believing they could end. Built on principles embedded in the universe and man, they might someday be suspended, but how destroyed?

Madison, the last architect of the Republic left alive, the last Founding Father, was elected to fill Marshall's place as president of the Washington National Monument Association. He accepted. How right to raise a noble shaft to the first President.

Thomas McKenney, writing Dolley about monuments, dared to refer to her husband's coming death. "Mr. Madison . . . will leave monuments behind him, go when he may . . . as lasting as time." Go when he may. The letter came with a picture of the great Philadelphia botanist Bartram, whom both Madisons had known and whom Dolley had written a poem about. Revisiting Bartram's house, McKenney wrote, he had recalled how one day the old man had taken his Bible and a bit of bread and cheese and gone out saying, "I'll do as the boys do," and been found throwing up blood, a crumb having ruptured a blood vessel. He had walked toward his pear trees, reached the finest, and died.

Yes, no one could foresee the time or manner of a person's death, one's own or another's; it was a veiled thing. Dolley knew that and shivered at what lay ahead.

Though housebound, the Madisons were not alone; the world kept coming to their door.

In late summer the young sportsman Thomas Count D'Orsey spent three weeks at Montpelier. He would borrow some of Payne's warm-weather clothes and go off for several days, returning "as ragged as bushes and mires could make him." Sometimes he lost his way, and once Negroes pulled him out of a river, but always this "elegant young man, sensible and well-informed except on the intricacies of our woods," Dolley wrote, returned laughing. She couldn't remember who had introduced him, but they enjoyed him. All summer and into the autumn other guests came. Ned and his amusing young wife, for instance, stayed four days, the Stevensons a week.

Dolley was very proud when her cow produced a calf. She and Annie stroked the wobbly little creature's coat. It was smooth as satin, she wrote. But when she passed on news like this, she expected some return. "Tell me everything," she begged Mary, " . . . as I [tell you about] the frolics on my lawn." Today she sent a bonus: the news that Uncle was better. "Goodnight; sweet dreams. . . ." An enclosed note said, "You are a generous little girl, my beloved Dolché," and asked for an amusing book. "It is late at night and my eyes close. . . ."

So Richard was moving to Kentucky. She and his uncle hoped he would return not only rich, she wrote, but also "as good as you are now. May the blessings of heaven be showered upon you."

She was silently invoking a similar blessing on Montpelier as hour after hour, good days and bad, she read poetry, philosophy, and the Bible aloud to Jemmy. "In Him was life. . . ."

In November she wrote Mrs. Lear for the loan of papers relating to General Washington's last illness. "Now look and see if I do not follow my letter ... stretching forth my arms to embrace you in the South Room where you made me sigh for 'the impossible to be.'"

They conquered each setback. Madison managed to stay above his four diseases; they did not touch the real man. On the level of the self he exercised an undivested power.

And he was thinking even more, these days, about the ark of union bearing, as he believed, "the hope of the world." There were dangers, yes. For one thing the federal and state governments kept trying to encroach upon each other. But where legislative authority could not reach, he wrote Preston in February, the nation could—if Americans grew calm enough and cool enough in their minds for "that resort"—receive help from a "higher power."

And like all old people in their right minds, he remembered the past. Sometimes, as he traveled backward, it was more vivid than the present. He was riding a horse into the wind. . . . he and Jefferson were discussing the classics. . . . he and Dolley celebrating the victory at New Orleans. . . . he was taking the oath that made him President of the United States. . . . he was marrying Dolley in front of the green marble mantel at Harewood. . . . sharpening quills for the Constitutional Convention. . . . target shooting in the Committee of Safety. . . . a student at Princeton staring at the Rittenhouse orrery. . . . a little boy following his father around the plantation.

Then he roused himself. He was back in the present, weak, but not too weak to sit up writing an introduction to his notes on the Convention of 1787. In this way—having withdrawn at last from active politics—he was bringing full circle a career begun with a deep care for principles. Yes, he now wrote an anti-Jacksonian senator who had asked if it was ever right to vote contrary to instructions. *Yes;* nothing could alter the primacy of conscience, nothing. Its dictates were "paramount."

"It rains like the mischief," Dolché wrote, and the phrase delighted her aunt and uncle. While James dozed, Dolley pinched off a few minutes to write "precious Dolché" that she wished she could act as chaperone at her nieces' parties. But Washington, once so familiar, she might have added, was now an alien world.

At Montpelier the first spring days of 1836 were simple but rather splendid. Dolley and young Annie Payne brought branches of flowering fruit into the house for forcing in bowls, picked the first English peas for the cheerful man in bed, and continued to help him with Convention notes. At a distance, Annie wrote her cousin Mary Cutts, "the green grass looks like a velvet carpet."

Madison could see that carpet and the Greek temple and the mountains through the windows. And sometimes on the lawn there fell the shadows of great trees.

The newspapers said the defenders of the Alamo—every last man — lay dead. "What a terrible massacre," Annie wrote. (But everyone at Montpelier was proud.) Aunt was "incessantly engaged as Uncle's deputy, morning, noon and night," Annie's letter went on. "He is getting better though still feverish. . . . If he could but he recovered . . . how happy Aunt would be." At this moment, as usual, she was reading to him.

Though Madison could not foresee the future of the United States and had never minimized the difficulties lying in ambush, he was not despondent about the American experiment in balanced government. Responsible freedom was still the hope of the world and the theme of his life. He was surer than ever that it was the only climate for the development of mankind.

(Interestingly, Dolley would call the character of this man who loved balance "symmetrical.")

Reading the start of General Armstrong's *Notices of the War of 1812,* he expected a diatribe against himself and Monroe in the yet-to-come second volume. So be it. Though Jefferson would not be around to "take care of him" after death, he was content to rest his case on discoverable facts.

On May 2 his reveries were broken by a clatter of horses' hooves.

The historian Charles J. Ingersoll had sharp eyes. He saw that the Montpelier mansion was "decayed and in need of considerable repairs." But inside he admired the tasteful paintings, statuary, French carpets. It was a home without fashionable pretensions or great elegance, now, "yet in a gentlemanlike style of rural prosperity," and he enjoyed tremendously the food that came steaming up from the kitchen. "The table was not only abundantly but handsomely provided; good soups, fish, flesh, and vegetables well cooked—dessert and excellent wine." At breakfast the Madisons offered not only hash and bacon and eggs but also hot breads, cornbread, biscuits, and butter-soaked Sally Lunn. When Ingersoll looked dubious, Dolley laughed, "Ah, you city people; you think it's unwholesome, but we're like the French, eat heartily and never feel the worse for it."

To the visitor's wonderment Mrs. Madison seemed to have changed not at all during the last twenty years. She still wore a turban and cravat. (If the turban hid graying hair and the cravat a creeping neck, how could he know?) She rose early and stayed active all day, seldom leaving the house, her devotion to her husband unwearying. It showed a singleness of heart. "Madison!" she would cry. "I must go to him!"

During his three-day visit Ingersoll, like Miss Martineau, stayed in the study almost continuously. Sometimes the ex-President was too exhausted to sit up, sometimes difficult breathing affected his speech. Though Dolley insisted that their guest do all the talking, the rule was often violated. "As I wanted to listen, and he appeared to grow better every day," Ingersoll would write, "our conversation animated without fatiguing him." Or so it appeared.

The two men talked about the tragedy of slavery. Total emancipation was what he had hoped for, Madison said, with the nation selling its Western lands to transport all blacks to Liberia, stake them there, and reimburse their former owners, but Jackson had spiked that hope. Because extremism begets extremism—fanaticism—he believed that Northern abolitionists like Garrison were endangering any solution. "The worst effect," he said grimly, " . . . would be to lead . . . Southerners from looking upon slavery as a necessary evil to looking upon it as one of the greatest blessings." Already some were arguing that way. Furthermore, the abolitionists had worsened the slaves' condition by provoking bitter counter laws. Madison told Ingersoll what he had told Harriet Martineau, that in Virginia slaves were unprofitable; two-thirds of his blacks were too young or too old to labor; it was bankrupting him to house, clothe, feed, and doctor them. Benefit, gain? Nonsense—Richard Rush's 10-acre farm near Philadelphia was more profitable than Montpelier's 2,000 acres. Madison felt the fact so intensely, says Ingersoll, he "raised his almost exanimate body from the couch." Ingersoll agreed with Miss Martineau: "Infirm as his body is, his understanding is as bright as ever; his intelligence, recollections, discriminations, and philosophy all delightfully instructive."

On departing the visitor said he hoped Madison's health would improve. Looking back with straight eyes and without losing his "perfect composure and resignation," the ex-President replied that he believed he understood his situation; he was "on the descending, not ascending, line." Ingersoll was all admiration. "A purer, brighter, juster spirit has seldom existed." This is the way he struck all who came: a man concerned with others and the future of his country. There was a kind of majesty.

Dolley saw signs that Jemmy had again overtaxed himself. By May 8 he was unable to write or even think without "oppressive fatigue." But he had fought his way back from the brink so many times, it was not hard to believe him indestructible. Those who loved him watched and waited for the upturn.

Dictating a letter to Ingersoll, he spoke proudly of the United States' growing navy—that navy which, forty-seven years ago, he had urged Congress to found and which, during the War of 1812, he had struggled to build up. Now he prophesied that it would destroy England's mastery of the sea. The trident must pass to this hemisphere, he said. He just hoped it would be "less abased." And when James Maury sent him a case of sherry, he said he wished he could use it to celebrate the big new ships.

Suddenly Dolley's mood changed, and "harum scarum" Annie grew quiet. Their patient had developed grave symptoms. Frightened, Dolley summoned Dr. Dunglison to consult with Dr. Grymes.

Greeting the Scotsman who had seen Jefferson through the door of death, Madison asked for a diagnosis not of his health but his sherry; then wrote Maury that a better judge than he had pronounced it "of the first chop." He apologized for a letter in another's hand. Though Maury could claim more years, his own fingers were "*de facto* older."

He was not giving up. Paul still carried him back and forth between bedroom and study.

By June 20 there seemed a slight improvement. But Dolley knew what was happening slowly, inexorably, and it filled her with a wild grief. One day she burst into tears in her husband's presence. Tenderly he entreated her to try—when the time came—to be, if not cheerful, composed.

His spirit shone through his flesh. John Payne has described him at this period:

> In his views on important subjects, the same soundness, clearness, vigor and felicity of expression now prevail that have ever distinguished his compositions; the same richness and playfulness of imagination, the same draughts from stores of memory.

"Playfulness" is an odd word for a dying man, but all his life Madison had been gay among intimates, and he remained so while tied to a body approaching dissolution. As his life sank, his spirit rose.

A caller found him lying prone. "Strange as it sounds," he said twinkling, "I talk better when I lie."

June 25 was the anniversary of Virginia's ratification of the Constitution of the United States for which he, more than any other man dead or alive, deserved credit. It had been forty-nine years since the framing, nearly half a century. Under great stress it had proved a cohesive force, *aes triplex*. The legislative, executive, and judiciary branches (not unlike man's nervous, vascular, and metabolic systems) practiced, while independent, a mighty cooperation. Madison believed that whatever problems the future might bring, this whole of many parts, this exquisitely balanced system of checks and balances, could—provided it kept an equipoise between center and periphery—function effectively. The thought gave the weakened man a kind of blood transfusion.

Dolley begged James not to compose any more letters; dictation was fatiguing. But George Tucker had written that he was dedicating his Jefferson biography to Madison, and he must be thanked. For hours Madison struggled with the wording. Tucker, he insisted, had given him too much credit for reconstructing the political system. Friendship had caused an overgenerosity; Tucker was biased. Madison's old modesty was overshooting itself. When Dolley had copied the letter out fair, he signed the page with a trembling quill: "James Madison."

It was June 27, a week from the Fourth of July, the date to which Jefferson and Adams ten years ago, and later Monroe, had managed to live, and to which the doctors thought Madison could be kept alive by artificial stimulants.

He refused them, and the household braced itself for an event it shrank from formulating even to itself.

Madison believed that the roots of everything lay in a primal world— why fight it? A change of consciousness, that was all. As a Bible student he knew Paul's words: "Be not conformed to this world, but be ye transformed by the renewing"—the expansion, the changing—"of your minds."

To leave Dolley was bitterly hard. But a man must accept the common lot of men and his own destiny. Fortunately some things were forever.

Waking early on June 28, the Madisons discussed their religious convictions. James's mind was clear; he spoke with "great calmness and self-possession," his viewpoint, like Dolley's, the age-old one which affirms the grandeur and love of God.

About six o'clock Paul Jennings came up from the Grove, followed by Sukey with the usual breakfast tray. They found the master sitting up in bed. Birds were singing in the treetops, the windows were open, as Nelly Willis wandered into the room. Dolley had momentarily stepped away.

Noticing that though the sick man had carried food to his mouth, he was not swallowing, Nelly asked, "What's the matter, Uncle Jeames?"

Smiling he said, "Nothing, my dear, but a change of mind," and his head dropped. He had gone out, according to Paul, who saw it happen, "like a candle snuffed."

THREE DAYS LATER Judge Philip Barbour, ex-Governor James Barbour, and two cousins carried a black walnut oblong box made from beautiful Montpelier trees to the cemetery. They were followed by an immense crowd.

Dolley's despair fought with her faith. She wore the rose-diamond ring James had given her forty-two years ago at Harewood. She still saw his eyes; she still heard his voice. In her agony she had her brother John to lean on, her nieces, and if he was not off wandering again, her son.

The stillness of the woods was broken only by birdsong as the Rev. Mr. Jones began to speak, " . . . Remember thy servant, O Lord. . . ."

When ropes had lowered the coffin into the grave, Mr. Jones threw in a handful of earth. It struck the box with a hollow sound, "ashes to ashes, dust to dust," as from the throats of a hundred slaves there broke— rending the air "in one violent burst"—a great, inconsolable cry.

It was the nation's lament made audible, and more deeply, more deeply, Dolley's.

Method and Source Usages

There is documentary support for all conversations, thoughts, feelings, and weather. Logically certain deductions from known facts are sometimes permitted, but probabilities are not passed off as certainties, and nothing is made up out of whole cloth.

In old letters and related evidence, spelling and punctuation have—except in rare cases, for special reasons—been modernized. When a reader's attention is diverted from the sense of the narrative to quaintness, an essence is lost.

The Papers of James Madison, now in progress under the able editorship of Robert A. Rutland *et al.*, has reached Volume XI (out of a possible fifty), ending with the date March 1, 1789. At that point I had, regrettably, to switch the documentation of Madison quotations from this definitive work to the less adequate *Writings of James Madison* (1900–1910), edited by Gaillard Hunt. The sole exception to the use of the *Papers* up to 1789 is my reliance, during the four-month framing of the Constitution in 1787, on Max Farrand's four-volume, exhaustive *The Records of the Federal Convention of 1787*.

The notes include sources for all quotations and supplementary material whenever, as in controversial matters, the narrative seems to call for information beyond text and bibliography.

Abbreviations are used for the persons, institutions, collections, records, publications, and JM's writings which recur most often.

KEY TO ABBREVIATIONS

AEU	Archives des Affaires Étrangères, correspondance politique, États Unis (photostats in LC)
AG	Albert Gallatin
AH	Alexander Hamilton
Annals	Annals of Congress (House or Senate named)
ASP	American State Papers, III (other divisions specified)
Bath Archives	Selections from the letters and diaries of Sir George Jackson

479

CC	Continental Congress
Cutts coll	Cutts collection (including Mary E. E. Cutts's memoir) owned by George B. Cutts of Brookline, Mass., on microfilm at LC
DM	Dolley (Payne Todd) Madison
EC	Edward (Ned) Coles
ER	Edmund Randolph
FO 5	Papers of British Foreign Office, 5, on microfilm at LC
GW	George Washington
HG	Hannah Gallatin
HS	Historical Society (usually prefixed by a state abbreviation such as MassHS, NYHS)
JCC	Journals of the Continental Congress
JM	James Madison
JM-LC	James Madison papers in Library of Congress (other papers are similarly treated, f.i. Rives-LC)
JVHD	Journals of the Virginia House of Delegates
Kunkel coll.	John B. Kunkel Collection (including Mary Causten Kunkel's notes)
LC	Library of Congress
Letters	*Letters of James Madison*
NA	National Archives
NYPL	New York Public Library
SC (later SCS)	Sarah (Sally) Coles, later Sarah Coles Stevenson
TJ	Thomas Jefferson
UVa	University of Virginia
VMHB	*Virginia Magazine of History and Biography*
WMQ	*William and Mary Quarterly*
Writings	*Writings of James Madison*, ed. Gaillard Hunt

Sometimes there is good reason not to abbreviate: "JM" for James Monroe would be confused for James Madison, and why shorten Nicholas P. Trist when "Trist" is already short?

$\mathcal{NOTES}$

The full names of books and authors will be found in the Bibliography.

I *MARRIAGE OF OPPOSITES*

The chief sources for this chapter: DM and JM papers, LC; DM papers, UVa; records of the New Garden Meeting, Guilford College, N.C., of Cedar Creek Meeting of Hanover County, Richmond, and of Pine Street Meeting of Philadelphia; Hinshaw, *Encyclopedia of American Quaker Genealogy;* letters from DM to Judith Richardson, Valentine Museum, Richmond; Journal of Elizabeth Drinker, PennHS; testimony of Judge Leon Bazile, Hanover County, Va., and of Washington and Cutts descendants; firsthand observations at Guilford, Scotchtown, Payne and Todd houses in Philadelphia, Harewood, and the Shenandoah Valley; wedding clothes, pictures and Kunkel Collection of MSS at Greensboro Historical Museum; portraits; the 1789 Book of Common Prayer; Lucia B. Cutts, *Memoirs and Letters of Dolly* [sic] *Madison;* Maud Wilder Goodwin, *Dolly* [sic] *Madison;* Allen C. Clark, *Life and Letters of Dolley Madison*—the last three containing some original material.

PAGE

1   Wedding: The books by Lucia B. Cutts and Maud Wilder Goodwin, though valuable, blow up this event, and need the correction of DM's letter of Sept. 15, 1794, to Eliza Collins Lee, DM-LC. Fanny Madison may have accompanied her brother to Harewood. She visited her great aunt Frances Madison Beale near Winchester that year (Ketcham, 381), but the evidence (Bowman-Hite papers, IndHS) is not conclusive.

1   Harewood: Dr. John Washington, direct descendant of George Steptoe Washington, and present owner of Harewood, showed me the house and grounds, and told me some family history and traditions. In the Madisons' time the present back door was the front.

1   Lucy's expulsion: Minutes of the Pine Street Monthly Meeting, Aug. 13, 1793.

1   George Steptoe Washington: Son of Anna Steptoe, second of Samuel Washington's four wives. He took a two-year course at the College of Philadelphia.

2   The Rev. Alexander Balmain: JM gave him 15, 4s, 10d. for performing the ceremony. See Balmain account book, LC.

2   DM's birth: New Garden Monthly Meeting records, Vol. I, 29, Guilford College, N.C. The spelling there and on DM's gravestone at Montpelier includes the "e" which she always used but which several generations omitted.

PAGE

2   The Payne log house: The late Eleanor Fox Pearson (wife of N.C.'s poet laureate) showed me some of the original logs. They were built into a cabin in her backyard near Guilford College. The Payne home had stood on a site across presentday Friendly Road. Besides two large rooms, each with a huge rock fireplace and outside door, it had a commodious attic for sleeping quarters. It has now been reconstructed.

3   John and Mary Payne's reception into the Cedar Creek Meeting: May 11, 1765. Hinshaw, 262.

3   John Payne's North Carolina holdings and sales: Register of Deeds, Books VI, VII, Rowan County, N.C.

3   Payne family: Goochland County records; also Elie Weeks, "Hickory Hill," *Goochland County HS Magazine*, Vol. 9, No. 2. Hanover's records have been destroyed.

3   Scotchtown: Cutts, 45. The restored house is now open to the public. Its history was thoroughly researched by the late Judge Leon Bazile, who confirmed my finding that there exists not a scrap of evidence that John Payne ever owned Scotchtown.

4   Cedar Creek Meeting House: Records, Richmond; Hinshaw, 223–262.

5   Lost locket: Cutts, 5, 6; Goodwin, 2.

6   "I cannot think": DM (then D. Payne) to J. Richardson, n.d. [late June 1783], Valentine Museum, Richmond (photostat in State Archives).

7   "Affectionate love": DM to J. Richardson, Mar. 7, 1800, *ibid.*

7   "She came upon our . . . cold hearts": A. Morris to Annie Payne, June 26, 1837, in G. Peter's "Unpublished Letters of Dolley Madison . . . , " ColHS, Vols. 44–45, 219.

10   "I must see her once more": Lucia B. Cutts, 12, 13.

10   "Item. I give and devise": Will of John Todd Jr., in Goodwin, 46. Todd had inherited £5000 from his father; Payne £50, a silver watch, and residuary rights.

10   "Really, Dolley": Cutts, 14.

10   "Thou must come to me": *Ibid.*, 15.

10   Aaron Burr: In May 1794 Burr was 38. He had fought well in the Revolution, practiced law in Albany, married Theodosia Prevost, widow of a British officer, moved to beautiful Richmond Hill near New York, served in the N.Y. Legislature and as N.Y.'s attorney general, and was now for the fourth year a U.S. Senator. In June 1794 his wife would die of cancer. The story that he boarded at Molly Payne's is a mistake. He lived at 130 South Second Street. For Mrs. Payne's several locations, see Clark, 15, 16; also, opp. p. 20, photograph of the last boarding house, 96 (now 150) North Third Street.

10   "Free exercise of religion": Article on religion as redrafted by JM, in the Virginia Bill of Rights, *Papers of JM*, I, 175. For a full discussion of all circumstances connected with the change, *ibid.*, 170–179.

11   "Are you engaged": Cutts, 14.

12   "Sparkling eyes": C. Coles to DM, June 1, 1794, UVa. In old age JM would speak of the help he received from Isaac Coles in his courting of Dolley. This friend was from Pittsylvania County, Virginia, and is not to be confused with his cousin of the same name—Jefferson's secretary—from Albemarle County.

12   "Your precious favor": JM to DM, Aug. 18, 1794, JM-LC; Clark, 20, 21.

13   JM's new coach: JM to father, Dec. 14, 1794, in Brant, III, 411. Cutts (17) and Goodwin (61) are mistaken about JM taking his bride to Montpelier.

PAGE

14　"That could withstand an attack" and other details about Harewood: Naulty, *passim.*

14　Ring with rose diamonds: Davis and Harvey auction catalog, Philadelphia, n.d., Kunkel Collection, Greensboro Historical Museum. At DM's death it passed to her daughter Mary Carvallo Causten Kunkel. Doubtless it is the ring Mrs. Kunkel sold to Mrs. William Dupont of Wilmington, Delaware. See Mary C. Kunkel to William Dupont, Dec. 9, 1918, Kunkel Collection.

15　"That I have not been insensible": W. Wilkins to DM (then D. Todd), Aug. 22, 1794, DM-LC; Clark, 22, 23.

15　JM's wedding gift to DM: A Davis and Harvey auction catalog, Philadelphia, n.d., describes the necklace and earrings and says they were kept in a morocco case.

16　Lucy Taylor: Daughter of James Madison Sr.'s cousin Erasmus Taylor and Nelly Madison's half-sister Jane Moore, thus doubly related to JM Jr.

16　"September the 16th": DM (then D. Todd) to Eliza Collins Lee, Sept. 15, 1794, DM-LC.

16　Marriage service: 1789 (first American) *Book of Common Prayer.*

17　"Evening": Postscript to Sept. 15, 1794, letter, DM-LC. The second "alas" (spelled "alass"), torn off, is shown in an early copy.

II HONEYMOON

The chief sources for this chapter: JM papers, LC; Hite family letters furnished the author by Minnie Hite Moody; observations at the two Belle Groves, Long Meadows, Montpelier, and Nassau Hall, Princeton University; Francis Taylor's diary, Virginia State Library; JM's drawing of his family tree, LC; information from Chester Hazard, manager of Montpelier; portraits of JM's parents by Polk, MdHS; Meade, *Old Churches, Ministers and Families of Virginia;* Scott, *History of Orange County;* Slaughter, *History of St. Mark's Parish;* Carson, *James Innes and His Brothers;* Donald Robertson's account book, VaHS; JM's commonplace book, JM-LC; Witherspoon syllabus and lecture notes by Calhoun; Madison family Bible; and copy of Peale's miniature of JM with important family testimony on back, Princeton University Library; Fithian, *Journal and Letters;* Rice, *The Rittenhouse Orrery;* Collins, *Life of John Witherspoon;* William Bradford's letterbook, PennHS; Read, Jones and McCosh on Scottish School; JM's 1830 autobiographical note in *Writings,* I; *Papers of James Madison,* I; Orange County records; Williamsburg newspapers, 1775, 1776; Burnaby, *Travels.*

PAGE

19　Old Hall: It is frequently assumed that the Madisons honeymooned at the Hites' Belle Grove. That is impossible. In 1794 Old Hall was still Isaac Hite's home; Belle Grove was only in the planning stage.

20　"*Then there was that child*": Hite family letter owned by Minnie Hite Moody.

20　JM's birth, baptism, and ancestry: Recorded in two extant family Bibles (his father possessed four), both printed in London in 1759, with the JM Jr. record written into them, retrospectively and almost identically, in his father's hand: one at Princeton University and the "Macon Bible," VaHS. JM's godparents: Mrs. Rebecca Catlett [Conway] Moore (grandmother), John Moore (step-grandfather), the Misses Judith and Elizabeth Catlett (great aunts), Jonathan Gibson (husband of another great-aunt). JM was born March 5, 1750, Old or Julian Time, but since the new Gregorian calendar went into effect that year, it is translated into New Style as March 16, 1751. Similarly, the recorded baptism dated, March 20, 1750, a Sunday, becomes March 31, 1751.

22 "In both the paternal and maternal line": Meade, II, 97. JM's elementary education: Small payments to the schoolmasters, John Bricky and Kelly Jennings, by JM's father—5 shillings when JM was three, and £2 when he was nine—suggest the possibility that he attended, briefly, some neighborhood school, perhaps at the home of his uncle Richard Beale through whose hands the payments passed. James Madison Sr.'s account book, 1755–1765, Presbyterian HS, Philadelphia. James also had a few dancing lessons.

23 Polk portraits of JM's parents: MdHS.

24 The new house: Judging by orders for the materials, as recorded in James Madison Sr.'s account book (*op. cit.*) the construction went on for nine or ten years before the great move.

24 "Carried over . . . lighter-weight furniture": Scott, 208.

24 Robertson's school: In 1758 the Rev. Donald Robertson, educated at Aberdeen and the University of Edinburgh, set up a school near Dunkirk, north of the Mattapony River, on the estate of the Rev. Robert Innes. Soon he had about 40 pupils. They boarded with the Innes family (Carson, *James Innes and His Brothers of the F.H.C.*). Robertson's account book (VaHS, "Accounts of the Donald Robertson School, VMHB, XXXIII, 194–198, 288–292) lists books in the school library and records financial matters, including the cost of Jamie's hat. Letters from the schoolmaster to JM's father giving "favorable evidence of the conduct and progress of the pupil," according to a statement by John C. Payne which DM sent John Quincy Adams in 1836 (Adams papers, MassHS), are now missing. While President, JM spoke of Robertson as "a man of great learning and an eminent teacher" (three-page autobiographical sketch, about 1816, Princeton University Library).

24 "When I was at an age": JM to Richard Dominicus Cutts, Jan. 4, 1829, Cutts coll. LC.

25 "Book of Logick," 1766. On exhibition, under glass, LC. For full text, see *Papers of JM*, I, 32–42.

25 "All that I have been in life": Gwathmey, 126.

25 JM's brothers and sisters: Nelly Conway Madison bore 12 children, seven of whom reached maturity, four boys, James, Francis, Ambrose, William, and three girls, Sarah (Sally), Nelly, Frances (Fanny). See Madison family tree, *Papers of JM*, I, following 212. The name, if any, of the 12th child—stillborn—has been torn off.

25 The Rev. Thomas Martin (1742–1770): He graduated from the College of New Jersey (his native state) in 1762. His brother Alexander would have a notable career: Governor of North Carolina, Member of the Convention of 1787, United States Senator.

27 Commonplace book, "Dec. 24, 1759": Mary E. E. Cutts made extensive notes from the original. One copy is owned by Charles M. Storey, Boston; another by Mr. and Mrs. George B. Cutts, Brookline. For full text, see *Papers of JM*, I, 7–24.

27 College of New Jersey: Founded in 1746. Though Presbyterian-oriented, it was independent and welcomed students of all denominations.

28 *Ecclesiastical Characteristics, or the Arcana of Church Policy:* Anonymous, it attacked

clergymen lax in their study of the Scriptures; also Scotch liberals, particularly the philosopher David Hume.

28 "Cut his own wood": Jennings, 17.

28 Dr. John Witherspoon (1723–1794): A graduate of the University of Edinburgh, ordained at twenty-two, conservative in religion, radical in American politics, satirist, eminent teacher, Dr. Witherspoon had come to America and the College of New Jersey in 1768. Varnum L. Collins, *Life of John Witherspoon.*

28 "I am perfectly pleased": JM to the Rev. Thomas Martin, Aug. 10, 1769, JM's earliest extant letter, owned by Charles M. Storey, Boston; *Papers of JM,* I, 43.

28 American Whig Society: The Society, a revival of the Plain-Dealing Club, was founded in June 1769, and though Madison has been named as its founder, he was actually— for he did not arrive until July or August—just "an early member" (as he said) who, in time, assumed a measure of leadership. Beam, 32–35. The Cliosophic Society was a revival of the Well-Meaning Club.

29 Acquisition of the Rittenhouse orrery: Dr. Witherspoon purchased the planetarium in April 1770, using funds voted by the trustees for scientific equipment. It was delivered a year later. Rice, *The Rittenhouse Orrery.*

30 "Neck & rists": JM to father, July 23, 1770, JM-LC; *Papers of JM,* I, 50.

30 Commencement 1770: N.J. Archives, 1st Series, XXVII, 275–279.

30 Francis Taylor's diary: Va State Library, Richmond.

30 College routine: Blair, 38.

31 JM's French accent: Randall, II, 192.

31 Paper wars: Beam, 32–35. William Bradford copied satires signed with the names or initials of Freneau, Brackenridge and Madison. Bradford papers, PennHS.

32 Student roguery: Fithian, 253, 254.

32 "Paper contentions": Green, President of Princeton, in an early history of the Whig Society, in Brant, I, 89.

33 "Dry and serious to the last degree": Lodge, 50.

33 Witherspoon's lectures: Syllabus and lecture notes, Princeton University Library.

36 Peale's miniature of JM: Charles Coleman Sellers, author of *Portraits and Miniatures by Charles Willson Peale* (Transactions of the American Philosophical Society, Vol, 42, Part 1, 139), gives the 1783 date, quoting Irving Brant, who follows Gaillard Hunt (1902), who follows Sidney Howard Gay (1884). Did Gay know and consciously reject the family tradition, or was he unaware of it? If he rejected it, did he have a solid reason for so doing, or did he jump to an unwarranted conclusion? I have not found any primary source for Gay's assertion. Peale left no record of painting JM in either 1771– 2 or 1783. He was certainly in Philadelphia in 1772 (Sellers, 30), painting impressions for fifteen shillings apiece. In correspondence with me, Mr. Sellers says he believes that stylistically the miniature fits in with Peale's 1782–1783 work better than the 1771–1772 group—and this, as far as I can judge, is the one good argument to be brought against the Princeton notation. Even so, the difference seems too little to weigh with any certainty against the documentary evidence cited, the fact that JM's miniature does not match Kitty's in size or frame, the "1782" engraved on hers, and, most serious to my mind, the fact the JM depicted looks far too young to be a man of

thirty-two (I thought this long before I knew the Princeton notation existed). Yes, painters often made their subjects (especially old ones) look younger than they were, but hardly twelve years younger. There I must leave a nagging problem.

37 Commencement 1771: *Pennsylvania Journal,* Oct. 3, 1771; N.J. Archives, 1st Series, XXVIII, 582–584.

37 1830 autobiographical note: Dictated by JM. Princeton U. Library, *Writings,* I, 141.

37 "Very acceptable": JM to father, Oct. 9, 1771, JM-LC; *Papers of JM,* I, 68.

37 "A few Half-Jos": Brant (I, note 23, 413) says the Portuguese half-joe was really a full johannes, the joe a double johannes worth about 36 shillings; at that time the most convenient available hard currency. *Papers of JM,* I, 68.

38 "Captivated much": JM to Bradford, Jan. 24, 1774. Bradford copied this and thirty other letters written between himself and JM into a Letterbook now in the PennHS. Several of them exist in the original. The entire exchange, quoted herein, *ibid.* See also *Papers of JM,* I, 71–161, 180, 184, 235.

38 New paper war: Fithian, I, 16.

38 "I leave Nassau Hall": Bradford to JM, Oct. 13, 1772.

38 "Of the nature of epilepsy": John C. Payne notes as dictated by JM, Princeton U. Library.

39 Theory that JM had epilepsy earlier: Ketcham, 51, 52.

39 Theory of epileptoid hysteria: Brant, I, 105–108.

39 Warm Springs: In Berkeley County, Virginia; later Morgan County, West Virginia. In 1776 the Va. Assembly incorporated the town of Bath, there, on fifty acres, named after the English spa.

39 Nassau Hall "chains": Bradford to JM, Oct. 13, 1772.

39 "First entrance on the Theatre of Life": JM to Bradford, Nov. 9, 1772.

40 "Long Island I have bid adieu": Freneau to JM, Nov. 22, 1772, JM-LC; *Papers of JM,* I, 77–79.

40 "You alarm me": Bradford to JM, Mar. 1, 1773.

40 "My health is a little better": JM to Bradford, Apr. 28, 1773.

40 "Exhaustive theological studies": Rives, I, 33, 34.

40 JM's Bible notes: JM-LC; *Papers of JM,* I, 51–60.

41 "Very sedate and philosophic": JM to Bradford, June 10, 1773.

41 "The most sublime of all sciences": JM to Bradford, Sept. 25, 1773.

42 "Read law occasionally": JM to Bradford, Dec. 1, 1773.

42 "I congratulate you": JM to Bradford, Jan. 24, 1774.

43 "I confess if he were gone": JM to Bradford, Apr. 1, 1774.

43 JM's trip north: Bradford's notation at end of JM's letter of Apr. 1.

43 "Would it not be advisable": JM to Bradford, Aug. 23, 1774.

44 JM's first property: Indenture dated Sept. 22, 1774, Orange County Record Office; *Papers of JM,* I, 123, 124.

44 "Debate . . . like philosophers": Bradford to JM, Oct. 17, 1774.

44 "A spirit of liberty and patriotism": JM to Bradford, Nov. 26, 1774.

44   "In case of a sudden invasion": JM to Bradford, Jan. 20, 1775.

44   "*Your* province seems to take the lead": Bradford to JM, Jan. 4, 1775.

44   "It is happy for us": Bradford to JM, early March 1775.

44   The Rev. John Wingate: Dixon and Hunter's *Virginia Gazette,* Jan. 28, Mar. 11, Apr. 15, 1775.

44   Resolutions and thanks to Henry: Purdie's *Evening Gazette,* May 19, 1775. Rives (I, 95) says he took the address from a MS in JM's hand, but the original is missing, and the Rives version differs slightly from the *Gazette's.* A copy of the four resolutions is among the Madison papers, LC, but in another's hand.

45   Dysentery: JM to Bradford, June 19, 1775. Elizabeth was seven, Reuben four.

45   "The strength of this Colony": *Ibid.*

45   "New canonicals": JM to Bradford, July 28, 1775.

45   JM's commission: Dated Oct. 2, 1775. Henry E. Huntington Library, San Marino, Cal., *Papers of JM,* I, 163.

46   "Decisive": JM to father, Oct. 5, 1794, JM-LC.

III *"INNOCENCY WITH HER OPEN FACE"*

The chief sources for this chapter: Hinshaw, II; Orange County records; JM, DM and TJ papers, LC; Kunkel notes, Greensboro Historical Museum; Mary E.E. Cutts, memoir, and other family papers, Cutts coll., containing material owned by George B. Cutts and Charles M. Storey of Boston, LC; Purdie's *Virginia Gazette,* 1776; Dixon and Hunter's *Gazette,* 1776; JVHD; *Writings of JM* (Hunt); *Papers of JM* (Hutchinson, Rachal, Rutland), I-IX; *Writings of Thomas Jefferson* (Ford); *Writings of Thomas Jefferson* (Lipscomb and Bergh); Randolph, *Domestic Life of Thomas Jefferson; Papers of Thomas Jefferson* (Boyd); *Papers of Alexander Hamilton* (Syrett); *Writings of George Washington* (Fitzpatrick); Grigsby, *Virginia Convention of 1776;* Wharton, *The Revolutionary Diplomatic Correspondence of the U.S.;* Levasseur, *Lafayette between the American and French Revolutions;* JCC; Annals of Congress; Schoepf, *Travels;* Burnett, *Letters of the Members of the Continental Congress;* Stokes, *Church and State in the United States.*

48   "Disregarded the wholesome order": Records, Monthly Meeting of the Society of Friends, Philadelphia, Dec. 26, 1794; also Hinshaw, II, 491, 617, 668.

48   "Joys perpetual": TJ to JM, Oct. 30, 1794, LC.

48   "Hold on, then": TJ to JM, Dec. 28, 1794; *Writings,* IX, 296.

49   "Self-created" societies: GW, Annual Message, Nov. 19, House Annals, Nov. 19, Senate Annals, Nov. 20, 1794; GW, *Writings* XXXIV, 29.

49   "Essential and constitutional": JM to TJ, Dec. 21, 1794, JM-LC; *Writings* VI, 228.

49   "Without rigor": AH to R. King, Oct. 30, 1794, Rufus King papers, NYHS; *Papers,* XVII, 348, 349.

50   Deaths of Temple and Isaac Payne: Drinker, Journal, Jan. 5, 1795, PennHS.

50   "Princely child": Mary Kunkel notes, Kunkel coll., Greensboro Historical Museum.

50   "White eyes": Lucy Todd to Anna Cutts, June 14, 1812, Cutts coll., LC.

50   Dolley's recipes: Marshall, 108.

52   "I hold a lodge": John Francis Mercer to JM, JM-LC. On Jan. 24, 1831, JM answered an inquiry from Stephen Bates (*Letters*, 150, 151) by saying he "never was a Mason." Perhaps Mercer translated an intention into an event. JM could have planned to become a Mason in 1795, when close to George Washington, then changed his mind that same year when, for political reasons, a coolness set in between him and his arch-Masonic friend and perhaps proposed sponsor.

52   "Mr. Madison, though no sectarian": Mary E. E. Cutts, Memoir, Cutts coll., LC.

53   "Law of nature": My view of how Madison interpreted human nature, therefore natural rights, is not that of those commentators who see him as a follower of Locke. (For example, Ketcham, 296: "In understanding the nature of man, Madison followed John Locke's *Essay concerning Human Understanding* [which insisted] that sensory impressions were the sole source of human knowledge. . . .") I am convinced that Madison's conception of the nature of man followed that of the Scottish School (and Christianity) taught by Dr. Witherspoon.

53   Scene at Waller's Grove: Purdie's *Gazette*, May 17, 1776.

54   Dr. Price's sermon: Dixon and Hunter's *Gazette*, May 18, 1776. The text was from II Chron. 20:15.

54   Religious toleration: George Mason's draft granted "fullest toleration in the exercise of religion," *Papers of JM*, I, 171.

54   JM's springy step: Grigsby calls it 'bouncing" (*Virginia Federal Convention of 1788*, I, 96).

54   "His diffidence": ER, "History of Virginia" (MS), VaHS; printed version, 235.

55   The Rev. James Madison: This other James Madison, later the first Bishop of the Protestant Episcopal Church in Virginia, was a grandson of John Madison of Augusta County, Ambrose Madison's brother. The two Jameses were thus second cousins.

55   Committee on Religion appointed: Oct. 11, 1776, LC; JVHD.

56   Free gin and rum: JM, sketch, Rives-LC; *Papers of JM*, I, 193. JM calls them "spiritous liquors."

57   "*Practically* you seem to be": S. S. Smith to JM, Nov. [n.d.] 1777 and Aug. 15, 1778, JM-LC. For the full texts of Smith's two letters, see *Papers of JM*, I, 194-211, 253-258. It is highly unlikely that there was, as Smith implies, a split between Madison's theory and everyday viewpoint; all his life, theory and practice marched together. Smith seems to have made the common simplistic mistake of thinking that one must be either *always free* or *never free*. Yet nothing in his rejoinder shows Madison a determinist; his life, lifelong politics and ideas of government argue quite otherwise. But Madison's belief in free will was not as sweeping as his friend's; he was too sharp an observer of inner processes and abilities for over-simplification. He must have been telling Smith that man is not, at all times, wholly free but in *some* degree conditioned; that, whenever he is coerced outwardly or inwardly, whether by authority, instinct, habit or whatever, he loses free will, but that—the point—he *is* free in his choices when functioning on a certain level and *can, if he will*, increase his freedom. Otherwise the free government, the republicanism for which he was beginning to fight, would be a mockery; and there would be no power of growth in character, no responsibility, no praise nor blame, no true morality. In his second letter Smith—doubtless influenced by Madison—admits that free will is not, as he had originally held, absolute. "Inveterate habit," he concedes (and by implication other forms of coercion, inner or outer?)

does induce a "species of necessity," thus cutting down on free will. This realization made him no less, as Madison no less, a champion of free will—that which separates man from instinct-driven beasts.

58   "13 independent States": JM to W. Bradford, March 23, 1778, Bradford papers, PennHS. The letter is addressed to Philadelphia at the time the British occupied it. The mustermaster was probably with Washington's troops.

58   The stolen hat: Randall, II, 326n: JM had told the story to Nicholas Trist, July 17, 1827.

59   "2 Bear Skins": JM to father, Dec. 8, 1779, JM-LC; *Papers of JM,* I, 315, 316.

59   "Whether poligamy": Records of Phi Beta Kappa, Sept. 12, 1780, WMQ, IV, 235, 253. Evidently William had been transferred from Hampden Sidney Academy to grammar school. In December 1799 the latter was abolished, hence the crisis.

59   "Of strong make": Dixon and Hunter's *Virginia Gazette,* Oct. 30, 1779; *Papers of JM,* I, 310.

60   JM's essay on money: Original lost. Text, *National Gazette,* Dec. 19, 22, 1791. Transcript of roughly a third of the article, McGregor Library, UVa. For full text, see *Papers of JM,* I, 302–310.

61   "Defect of adequate statesmen": JM to TJ, March 27, 1780, JM-LC; *ibid.,* II, 5–7.

61   "Oh, my dear!": Martha Dangerfield Bland to Frances Bland Tucker, March 28, 1781, Tucker papers, Williamsburg Restoration.

61   "Oh, Fanny!": *Ibid.*

62   "A gloomy stiff creature": *Ibid.*

62   "Madison is charming": Thomas Lee Shippen to William Shippen, Apr. 22, 1793, Shippen papers, LC.

62   "So rich in sentiments": Smith, 235.

62   "Glory of triumphing": Draft, JM to Rochambeau, Aug. [17?], 1780, PCC, NA, XVIII, no. 78, 319-320; *Papers of JM,* II, 61, 62.

62   "The wather": Aug. 15, 1780, PCC, II, no. 154, 235.

62   "General good of mankind": Draft, JM to John Jay, Oct. 17, 1780, PCC, I, no. 25, 239-249; *Papers of JM,* II, 127-135.

63   "The back lands": Proceedings of the Maryland Convention of 1776, Force, 5th series, III, 178.

63   "Virginia owns": Appendix, PCC.

64   "For God's sake": *Virginia Gazette,* Dec. 30, 1780.

64   "The boy cannot escape me": General Cornwallis to General Henry Clinton, in E. M. Allen, *Lafayette's Second Expedition to Virginia in 1781,* 34.

64   "Precipitately to Williamsburg": Draft, JM to Philip Mazzei, July 7, 1781, JM-LC; *Papers of JM,* III, 176–181.

65   "Salute Congress as a crowned head": Samuel Livermore to the President of N.H., Sept. 4, 1781, and Ezra L'Hommedieu to the Governor of N.H., Sept. 8, 1781, in Brant, II, 161, 162. See also JM to E. Pendleton, Sept. 3, 1781, JM-LC, *ibid.,* 247.

65   "On the wings of speed": GW to R. Morris, Sept. 6, 1781, GW, *Writings,* XXIII, 89. See also Diary of Robert Morris for Sept. 5, 1781.

65   "Irretrievably lost": JM to Pendleton, Oct. 2, 1781, JM-LC; *Papers of JM,* III, 273, 274.

66   "My charity . . . cannot invent": JM to ER, June 4, 1782, JM-LC, *ibid.*, IV, 313.

66   "Stupor of mind": Sarah N. Randolph, 68.

67   Jefferson's eldest daughter: In 1783, Martha (Patsy) was twelve years old. Jefferson had left his other two surviving children (out of six), Maria (Polly), aged five, and Lucy, two, with their Aunt Eppes of Eppington in Bermuda Hundred. The youngest daughter would die that year of whooping cough. In 1787, Jefferson would insist on Maria, now eight, being sent to him in Paris in care of a kindly captain. Her maid and companion was a "bright" (almost white) mulatto slave girl, Sally Hemings.

67   "On the whole extremely liberal": Notes on Debates, Mar. 12-15, 1783, JM-LC; *Papers of JM,* VI, 328, 330n.

67   "We . . . require all governors": JM's Notes on Debates, Apr. 11, 1783, JM-LC; *ibid.,* 450.

68   Excited a "jealousy": ER to JM, Apr. 26, 1783, JM-LC, *ibid.,* 499.

68   JM's "Address to the States." Adopted by Congress Apr. 26, 1783, PCC. The MS is in JM's hand. Though he did not claim authorship, he was chairman of the committee which Congress asked to prepare an address (other members: Oliver Ellsworth and Alexander Hamilton), and nine years later Hamilton (May 26, 1792) confirmed JM's authorship by saying that the address was "planned by [JM] in conformity to his own ideas and without any previous suggestions from the Committee." Letter to Edward Carrington, May 26, 1792, *Papers of Hamilton,* XI, 427.

68   "Respectable and prosperous or contemptible": Circular, GW to the Governors of the States, June 8, 1783. LC.

68   "Be pleased to make my compliments": TJ to JM, from [an inn on?] the Susquehanna River, Apr. 14, 1783, JM-LC; *Papers of JM,* VI, 459.

69   "Your inference . . . was not groundless": JM to TJ, Apr. 22, 1783, JM-LC; *ibid.,* 481.

69   "I rejoice at the information": TJ to JM, May 7, 1783, JM-LC, *ibid.,* VII, 25.

69   "James Madison Junior": Chevalier de la Luzerne, Liste des Membres du Congrès depuis 1779 jusqu'en 1784, *Archives des Affaires Étrangères, États-Unis,* I, 253–287, in Brant, II, 14.

69   "Must study": *Ibid.*

69   "Spiritous drink": JM, Notes on Debates, June 21, 1783, JM-LC; *Papers of JM,* VII, 177.

70   The dab of rye dough: Gay, 45. Information from Nicoll Floyd, great grandson of General Floyd.

70   "Disappointment": JM to ER, July 28, 1783, JM-LC; *Papers of JM,* VII, 257.

70   " . . . The necessity of my visiting": JM to TJ, Aug. 11, 1783, JM-LC; *ibid.,* 268. The inking-out of passages occurred when, years later, JM's letters were returned.

70   "I sincerely lament": TJ to JM, Aug. 31, 1783, JM-LC; *ibid.,* 298.

70   "Hung round her at the harpsichord": Gay, 44. William Clarkson was a medical student at the College of Philadelphia, aiming to become a doctor like his father. Nine years after his graduation and marriage to Kitty, a severe illness led him into the Presbyterian ministry. He died near the end of JM's first term as President.

70   "Obliged to write in a position": JM to TJ, Sept. 20, 1783, LC: *Papers of JM,* VII, 354. See also JM to father, Aug. 30, JM to ER, Aug. 30, 1783, JM-LC; *ibid.,* 284, 296.

71   "At an era so awful": Burnett (*Letters,* VII, 315, n. 3) was the first to suggest the probability that JM wrote the two "North American" articles. Brant (*Madison,* II, 302–305) is even more firmly convinced. But William T. Hutchinson, joint editor of the first seven volumes of the excellent *Papers of James Madison* argues otherwise (editorial note, VII, 319–342). He thinks Congressman Richard Peters (1743–1838) a more likely author. With all due respect, I believe that his arguments can be met, and that the many arguments for JM's authorship add up to an extremely strong case.

73   "His heterodoxy": JM to TJ, Dec. 10, 1783, JM-LC; *ibid.,* 401.

73   "What would I not give": TJ to JM, Feb. 20, 1784, JM-LC; *ibid.,* 427.

73   "Wild geese flying": American Philosophical Society; *ibid.,* VIII, 514–544.

74   "Living [legal] oracle": JM to ER, Mar. 10, 1784, JM-LC; *ibid.,* 3.

74   "He deserves everything": Eliza Trist to TJ, ca. Apr. 13, 1784, Coolidge-Jefferson Papers, as quoted by Brant, II, 17.

74   "Every evening our inn": Schoepf, II, 55-64.

75   "We shall make a strange figure": JM to father, June 15, 1784, JM-LC; *Papers of JM,* VIII, 80. The latter has "sharp figure."

75   "A frivolous economy": JM to TJ, July 3, 1784, JM-LC; *ibid.,* 94.

75   "Immortal example of true glory": JM, June 22, 1784, JVHD; *ibid.,* 85.

76   "Clear": JM, Meteorological Table, *ibid.,* 522, 523.

76   "I cannot altogether renounce": JM to TJ, Mar. 16, 1784, JM-LC; *ibid.,* 13.

76   "Ramble into the Eastern States": JM to TJ, Sept. 7, 1784, JM-LC; *ibid.,* 113.

76   "In consideration of paternal affection": Deed of gift, Aug. 19, 1784, Orange County Court Records; *ibid.,* 99.

76   Trip to the Mohawk Valley: JM to TJ, Sept. 7, 15, Oct. 11, 17, 1784, JM-LC; *ibid.,* 113–121. See also François de Barbé-Marbois, *Letters,* ed. Eugene B. Chase; Levasseur, *Lafayette between the American and French Revolution,* 96–107; Lafayette, *Mémoires, correspondance et manuscrits,* 98–113. I am indebted to Brant for his fine account (II, 325–335), and for calling attention to Marbois, Gottschalk, and Evans as sources.

76   "Tremendous crap'd heads": Griffith Evans, diary, Sept. 14, 1784, Huntington Library, San Marino, California.

78   "The Commissioners were eclipsed": JM to TJ, Oct. 17, 1784, JM-LC; *Papers of JM,* VIII, 120.

78   "The time I have . . . passed": *Ibid.* This is the first of several sentences which JM altered in his old age to protect Lafayette from now regretted references to the Frenchman's vanity. I give them as restored through the discernment of Julian P. Boyd (VI, 451 n.). JM crossed out some words, including "and strong thirst of praise and popularity;" and changed "as vanity will admit" to read "as can be imagined." The only trace of his observation of Lafayette's vanity left intact was a comparatively harmless reference to the Marquis's wish for a "bright column in French gazettes." JM's tampering was highly uncharacteristic. With a thousand chances to alter records to his own advantage he scorned to do so. But hurt a good friend's reputation with posterity? He chose what seemed the lesser of two evils.

78   Houdon statues: According to Brant (II, 336) one was destroyed in the French Revolution. The other stands in the State House in Richmond.

78 "Not for . . . the homage": JM to TJ, Aug. 20, 1785, JM-LC, *Papers of JM,* VIII, 345. This rephrasing shows that JM's better view of Lafayette began within ten months of his first report.

79 "Moderate tax": PH, resolution, JVHD, Nov. 11, 12, 1784.

79 "Is religion necessary?": JM's Outline B for debate, Dec. 23, 24, 1784, JM-LC; *Papers of JM, viii,* 198.

79 "What we have to do": TJ to JM, Dec. 8, 1784, JM-LC; *ibid.,* 178.

79 "Patron of the Prostestant Episcopal Church": ER to JM, July 17, 1785, JM-LC; *ibid.,* 324. Like JM, Randolph was a member of the more liberal wing—not a dissident—of the Episcopal Church.

79 "March 12 fair": *Ibid.,* 528–531.

80 "To depend as little as possible": JM to ER, July 26, 1785, JM-LC; *ibid.,* 328.

80 "My friend as my heart," Lafayette to JM, Dec. 15, 1784, *ibid.,* 185, 186.

80 "Absolutely." JM to TJ, Apr. 27, 1785, JM-LC; *ibid.,* 270.

80 "Our most respectable freeholders": George Nicholas to JM, July 7, 1785, JM-LC; *ibid.,* 316.

80 "What say you to a trip": Monroe to JM, July 12, 1785, postscript, JM-LC; *ibid.,* 319.

80 "Crushed": "Aspects of Monopoly," in Brant, II, 350; *Harper's Magazine,* March 1914, 439; WMQ, Oct. 1946, 535. A different wording but same meaning, "extinguished forever": JM to TJ, Jan. 22, 1786, LC; *Papers of JM,* VIII, 474.

80 "A right toward man": *A Memorial and Remonstrance* (ms), written about June 20, 1785, JM-LC; anonymous broadside, Virginia State Library; *ibid.,* 298–304.

81 "One of the truly epoch-making documents": Stokes, *Church and State in the United States,* I, 391.

81 "Congress has kept the Vessel": JM to TJ, Oct. 3, 1785, JM-LC; *Papers of JM,* VIII, 373.

81 Authorship of resolution for Annapolis Convention: Though John Tyler introduced the motion for this convention of vast consequences, the evidence for JM's authorship is considerable. He had long advocated federal control of trade; he often worked through others; and he would naturally not wish to irritate the Assembly's many opponents of federal power by *again* appearing as its champion—it would have been tactically unwise. Madison told George Tucker he lay low and "did not venture to offer his own resolution, but prevailed upon Mr. Tyler . . . to offer it" (Tucker, I, 343n). This seems conclusive. JM also wrote Noah Webster: "In 1785 I made a proposition with success." And Judge Tyler's son, when questioned later, said that the motion offered by his father was "by adoption as thoroughly and completely his own"—my italics—*"as if he had penned it himself"* (L. G. Tyler, VIII, 471–484). The letters which JM wrote Jan. 22, 1786, the day after the resolution, do not contradict the above evidence. To Jefferson this man who cared so little for credit wrote that the resolution had been proposed—he did not say written—by Mr. Tyler; to Monroe he called it Mr. Tyler's, which it was in the sense of introducer, sponsor; and observed that the plan was open to objections (as what innovation was not in the Assembly?) and would probably miscarry (at this point he did not much trust the states to pull together) but was "better than nothing." This last consideration was, in desperate straits, enough to move JM to action.

PAGE

82   "Bear a worse aspect": JM to Ambrose Madison, Aug. 7, 1786, JM-LC; *Papers of JM,* IX, 89.

82   "You had better yield": Morse, *Hamilton,* I, 167.

82   "And other important matters": AH, address to the Continental Congress, Sept. 20, 1786, JCC.

83   "Smelt a rat": Henry to an unnamed Georgian, Nov. 12, 1790, PH-LC.

83   "Undermine . . . our Union": Resolutions, Nov. 29, 1786, JVHD; *Papers of JM,* IX, 183.

83   "From Princeton to Paulus' Hook": JM to Eliza Trist, Feb. 10, 1787, Emmet papers, NYPL; *ibid.,* 259.

83   "Vices of the Political System": JM-LC; *ibid.,* 348–357.

84   "Forever closed": TJ to JM, April 27, 1795, JM-LC.

84   "I suspect that Jay": JM to TJ, Feb. 15, 1795, *ibid.*

IV *JAY'S TREATY AND THE CONSTITUTION*

PAGE

88   "Gather ye little Knobs": Bullock, 138, quoting E. Smith, *Compleat Housewife.*

89   "Animated": Slaughter, 76, 77.

89   "Much safer with you": Pierce Butler to JM, June 12, 1795, JM-LC.

90   "A large lofty salon": Chastellux, *Travels in North America,* II, 42.

90   "Should it be final": TJ to JM, Aug. 31, 1783, JM-LC; *Papers of JM,* VII, 298.

90   "The best farmer": TJ as quoted by John Quincy Adams, Nov. 3, 1807, *Memoir,* I, 473. In 1803 JM was elected first President of the American Board of Agriculture, and in 1819 first President of the 5-county Albemarle Agricultural Society.

91   "Ruinous bargain": JM to R. Livingston, Aug. 10, 1795, JM-LC; *Writings,* VI, 234.

91   "Colossus": TJ to JM, Sept. 21, 1795, JM-LC; *Writings of TJ* (Bergh), IX, 309, 310.

93   "Useful in the King's service": Grenville to Hammond, in Freeman, *George Washington,* VII, 279n. (This volume was written after Freeman's death by Carroll and Ashworth.)

93   "That man is a traitor"; *Memoirs . . . edited from the Papers of Oliver Wolcott* (Gibbs), I, 243; *Life of Timothy Pickering* (O. Pickering), III, 217.

94   "His greatest enemies": JM to Monroe, Jan. 26, 1796, JM-LC.

95   "Through what official interstice": JM to TJ, Dec. 6, 1795, JM-LC.

95   "There is a vile": P. Butler to JM, Aug. 21, 1795, JM-LC.

95   "Inspire despair": JM to E. Pendleton, Apr. 22, 1787, JM-LC; *Papers of JM,* IX, 395.

96   JM's position and note-taking: " . . . I chose a seat in front of the presiding member, with the other members on my right and left hands. . . . It happened, also, that I was not absent a single day." Preface to Notes, Farrand, *Records,* III, 550. Several other members took notes but JM's were the fullest.

98   The 15 Resolutions of the Virginia Plan: *Ibid.,* I, 20-22.

98   Charles Pinckney's plan: *Ibid.,* III, 595-609. This is one time that JM's notes cannot be followed; he used Pinckney's now discredited text. See Brant, III, 27–30.

PAGE

99   "National government consisting": JM (JM notes), May 30, Farrand, I, 33.

99   "Essential to . . . free government": JM (JM notes), *ibid.,* 49.

99   "Clear principle": JM (JM notes), *ibid.,* 134.

99   "Enlarge the sphere": JM (JM notes), June 6, *ibid.,* 134–136. See also *The Federalist,* No. X, 61; No. XIV, 83. Here the verb is "extend."

99   "Let our [central] government": Dickinson (King notes), June 7, Farrand, I, 159.

100 "The planetary system": JM, "Symmetry of Nature," *The Princeton University Library Chronicle,* Spring 1962, XXIII, No. 3, with introduction by Stewart M. Robinson and Anna Payne Robinson. Printed as pamphlet.

100 " . . . This prerogative": JM (JM notes), June 8, Farrand, I, 165.

100 "Swallowed up": W. Paterson (JM notes), June 9, *ibid.,* 179.

101 "If no state": J. Wilson (Yates notes), June 9, *ibid.,* 183.

101 The "monster" sovereignty: GW to John Jay, Mar. 10, 1787, *Writings* of GW (Fitzpatrick), XXIX, 176.

101 "Blew Coat" and umbrella: GW to John Augustine Washington, June 10, 15, *ibid.,* 233, 235.

101 "Blacks are property": E. Gerry (Yates notes), June 11, Farrand, I, 206.

101 "We are sent here to *consult*": B. Franklin (JM notes), June 11, *ibid.,* 197.

102 The 9 Resolutions of the New Jersey Plan: *Ibid.,* 242–245.

102 "Will a citizen of *Delaware*": J. Wilson (JM notes), *ibid.,* 253.

102 The 11 Resolutions of Hamilton's plan: *Ibid.,* 282–293.

102 "Men love power": AH (JM notes), June 18, *ibid.,* 284.

103 JM's attack on the New Jersey Plan: *Ibid.,* 314–325.

104 "Foreign aid": AH, June 28, according to Jonathan Dayton, *Intelligencer,* Aug. 26, 1826. JM's notes say merely that "Mr. Hamilton and several others expressed their apprehension": *Ibid.,* 452.

104 "Awful and critical moment": William Few, MS autobiography, about 1816, *ibid.,* III, 423.

104 "When a broad table": Franklin (JM notes), *ibid.,* I, 488.

104 "Amphibious monster": J. Dayton (JM notes), June 30, *ibid.,* 490.

104 "They insist": G. Bedford (Yates notes), June 30, *ibid.,* 500.

104 "Gentlemen!": GW, in William Pierce anecdote, *ibid.,* III, 86.

104 "We were on the verge": L. Martin to the Maryland Legislature, Nov. 29, 1787, *ibid.,* 190.

105 " . . . I *almost* despair": GW to AH, July 10, 1787, *Writings of GW,* XXIX, 245.

105 Cutler's visit: Cutler, I, 253–271.

105 "A separate people": Mason, July 11, Farrand, I, 579.

105 *"Threatening contest"*: JM to Martin Van Buren, May 13, 1828, Farrand, III, 477; *Writings,* IX, 314.

106 "Consulting their safety": Pierce Butler (JM notes), Aug. 30, Farrand, II, 469.

107 "Insuperable obstacles": J. Wilson (JM notes), Sept. 10, *ibid.,* 562.

PAGE

107   "End in tyranny": ER (JM notes), Sept. 10, *ibid.,* 564.

107   "Sir, we have now the honor": *Ibid.,* 583.

107   "It would give great quiet": G. Mason (JM notes), Sept. 12, *ibid.,* 587.

107   " . . . Congress shall never restrain": Noah Webster in a N.Y. newspaper, in Bowen, 246.

108   "Thus I consent, Sir": B. Franklin (JM notes), Sept. 17, Farrand, II, 643.

108   "Col. Mason left": JM to TJ, Oct. 24, 1787, JM-LC, *Writings,* V, 34.

108   Franklin and the rising sun: Sept. 17, Farrand, II, 648.

108   "Almost killed": JM to EC, Grigsby, *Virginia Convention of 1788,* I, 95n.

108   "Every person": Pierce, "Character Sketches," n.d., *ibid.,* III, 94.

110   "Momentous work": GW, Sept. 17, *Diaries,* III, 237.

110   *The Federalist Papers:* For a discussion of the controversy as to authorship, see Carl Van Doren, Introduction, *The Federalist, or the New Constitution.*

110   "Actuated by some common impulse": JM, *The Federalist,* No. X, 55.

110   "If [the subjects are] very numerous": J. Witherspoon, syllabus, Princeton University Library.

110   "Experience is the oracle of truth": JM, *The Federalist,* No. XX, 127.

111   "Mixed character": JM, *ibid.,* No. XXXIX, 255.

111   "Made to counteract": JM, *ibid.,* No. LI, 347.

111   "Notwithstanding the equal authority": JM, *ibid.,* No. LVIII, 391.

V *DEFEAT*

PAGE

114   "Compatible with our national honor": Annals of House.

115   "Mrs. Madison is a fine woman": J. Adams, in Goodwin, 72.

115   "Plum pudding": Grigsby, *op. cit.,* I, 79n.

115   "We, the people . . . We the States": PH, *ibid.,* 81.

116   "More convenient time": JM, June 4, 1789, *ibid.,* 99.

116   "All": PH, *ibid.,* 113.

116   "I would with manly firmness": PH, *ibid.,* 114.

116   "Rock of our salvation": ER, June 6, *ibid.,* 129.

116   "Blue and buff": *Ibid.,* 95.

116   "Eloquence has been defined": Marshall on JM, Rives, *James Madison,* II, 612n.

117   "Mr. Madison followed": Bushrod Washington to GW, June 6, 1788, *Writings of GW* (Sparks), IX, 378n.

117   "Partly national": PH, Grigsby, *op. cit.*

117   "I disdain his aspersions": ER, June 9, 1788, Grigsby, *op. cit.* 162.

117   "Our only chance of success": AH to JM, June 27, 1788, *Papers of Alexander Hamilton* (Syrett), V, 91. See also June 25, *ibid.,* 80: "Our chance of success here is infinitely slender, and none at all if you go wrong."

PAGE

118 "They'll free your niggers!": PH, June 9, 1788, Grigsby, *op. cit.*, I, 157n.

118 "So much honor,": J. Witherspoon to JM, Aug. 11, 1788, JM-LC; *Papers of JM, XI,* 231.

118 "Rivulets of blood": PH as quoted by Henry Lee to JM, Nov. 19, 1788, JM-LC; *ibid.,* 356.

118 JM prefers the House: JM to ER, Oct. 17, 1788; *ibid.,* 305.

119 "Friend to the rights of Conscience": JM to George Eve, Jan. 2, 1789, JM-LC; *ibid.,* 404.

119 Frozen nose story: Nicholas Trist, in Hunt, 165.

119 "Celebrated in America": Brissot de Warville, 163, 164.

119 Washington's inauguration: *New York Advertiser,* May 1, 1789; Freeman, VI, 190–197; Maclay, *Journal,* 9.

120 JM's part in GW's address: GW to JM, May 5, 1789, *Writings of GW,* XXX, 310, 311. See also GW's First Inaugural Address, *ibid.,* 291–308.

120 "A frail and worthless fabric": AH to Gouverneur Morris (draft), Feb. 27, 1801, Hamilton Papers, 1st series, LC.

120 "His Higness the President" and rest of discussion: Annals of Senate, Apr. 24, May 11, 14; Annals of House, Apr. 23–25, May 7–9, 14; JM to TJ, May 9, 23; *Writings,* 355n, 370n; Maclay, *Journal,* May 4, 7–9, 1789.

120 "A national disapprobation" and rest of debate: Annals of Senate, Apr. 24, May 11, 14, 1789 Annals of House, Apr. 23–25, May 7–9, 1789.

121 "Sense, reading, address": F. Ames to G. R. Minot, May 3, 1789, *Works of Fisher Ames* (Seth Ames), I, 35.

121 "As nearly central" and rest of debate: Annals of House, Aug. 27, Sept. 3-5; Ames to Minot, Sept. 3; Tench Cox to JM, Sept. 9, 1789, JM-LC.

122 "Court to the President": Maclay, July 1, 1789, *op. cit.,* 94.

122 "Talk together": J. C. Hamilton, *History of the Republic,* IV, 29n.

122 " . . . Send me your thoughts": AH to JM, Oct. 12, 1789, *Works of AH* (Lodge), IX, 462.

123 "A soldier's pay": *Pennsylvania Gazette,* Mar. 24, 1790, in Brant, III, 299.

123 "The assumption still hangs over us": JM to Monroe, June 17, 1790, JM-LC, *Writings,* VI, 16.

124 "I never knew two men": Thomas Lee Shippen to father, Sept. 15, 16, 1790, Shippen papers, LC.

125 "With all the humanity": JM, instructions to overseers Mordecai and Lewis Collins, and Sawney, JM-LC.

125 "Necessary" and rest of debate: Annals of House, Feb. 2, 8, 1791; TJ, *Writings of TJ* (Ford), III, 145-153; JM, *Writings,* VI, 19-42; AH to Carrington, *Works* (Lodge), IX, 513–535.

127 "Health, recreation": JM to TJ, May 12, 1791, JM-LC; *Writings,* VI, 51n.

127 "Pretorian band" *re* crooked brokers: JM to TJ, July 13, Aug. 8, 1791, JM-LC, *Writings,* VI, 54n. See also *ibid.,* 57n, 58n.

128 "Fascinated": S. L. Mitchill to his wife, Jan. 3, 1802, in Clark, 49.

128 "Squinted at monarchy": PH's phrase (Grigsby, *op. cit.,* I, 117) was often re-used.

PAGE

128   "The glory of America": JM (anon.), *National Gazette,* Feb. 20, 1792, *Writings,* VI, 94.

129   "My overthrow": AH to E. Carrington, May 26, 1792, *Works* (Lodge), IV, 522.

129   "*Anti-Republican*. . . . I denounce": JM, "Who Are the Best Keepers of the People's Liberty?": *National Gazette,* Dec. 20, 1792; *Writings,* VI, 120-123.

130   "Mr. Jefferson fears": AH, *Papers of AH* (Syrett), XVIII, 2793-2795.

130   "Gentleman possessed": TJ to GW, Oct. 17, 1792, *Writings of TJ* (Ford), VII, 165. GW's reply (Oct. 18): " . . . I believe the views of both of you are pure and well meant," *Writings of GW,* XXXII, 186.

130   "Virginia moves": F. Ames to Thomas Dwight, Jan. (n.d.) 1793, Ames, *op. cit.,* I, 127.

131   "Conduct friendly": GW, Proclamation of Neutrality, Apr. 22, 1793, *Writings of GW,* XXXII, 430.

131   "It wounds the national honour": JM to TJ, June 19 (misdated June 10), 1793, *Writings,* VI, 127, 128.

131   "Sink the republican interest": TJ to JM, Aug. 3, 1793, *Writings of TJ* (Ford), VII, 464.

132   "For God's sake": TJ to JM, July 7, 1793, *ibid.,* 338.

132   "Most grating": JM to TJ, July 30, 1793, *Writings,* VI, 138n.

132   "Hamilton is ill": TJ to JM, Sept. 8, 1793, TJ-LC, *Works of TJ* (Ford), VIII, 33.

133   "Mr. Madison's Resolutions": *Writings,* VI, 203–206.

134   "Thou must come to me": DM to Eliza Collins, Cutts, 15.

134   JM's speech against Jay's Treaty, Apr. 6, 1796: *Writings,* VI, 263-295.

135   "Devoid of sincerity": Ames to Minot, Apr. 2, 1796, *Works,* I, 191.

136   "Sounding the tocsin": JM to Monroe, Apr. 19, 1796, JM-LC.

136   "We light the savage fires": Ames's speech for Jay's Treaty, Annals of House, Apr. 28, 1796.

136   "Before some were ripe": JM to Monroe, May 14, 1796, JM-LC, *Writings,* VI, 301n.

136   "The progress of this business": JM to TJ, May 1, 9, 1796, JM-LC.

137   "I would rather work": GW as quoted by JM, memorandum, May 5, 1792, JM-LC.

138   "Wrought up": JM to Monroe, Sept. 29, 1796, JM-LC. The passage about GW's Address is in code.

139   "Sublime delights": TJ to J. Adams, dated Dec. 28, 1796 (*Writings of TJ* [Ford], VII, 96), and sent to JM Jan. 1, *ibid.,* 100n–102n) for his approval. JM tactfully thumbed it down (Jan. 15, 1797) saying it betrayed the difficulty of writing such a thing. Might not "storm" reflect on the skipper?—Mr. Adams's temper seemed "rather ticklish." And would Jefferson's friends like to hear that he relished defeat? And if the President made a mistake would not this expression of confidence prove an embarrassment? And so forth. *Writings,* VI, 302–304.

139   "Screw [him] up": JM to TJ, Jan. 22, 1797, *ibid.,* 307.

139   "Yet I would not trust him alone": AH to Sen. Theodore Sedgwick, Feb. 26, 1797, *The Works of Alexander Hamilton* (Lodge), X, 239, 240. See also TJ, *Anas,* Mar. 2, 1797.

139   The French Republic's "The declaration of rights" (Aug. 24, 1792): See JM's letter of acceptance addressed to J. M. Roland, Minister of the Interior, April 1793, *Writings,* VI, 125, 126.

140   "Immense crowd": Goodwin, 75.

PAGE

140   "Are we forever": J. Adams, "Letters to the Boston *Patriot*," 1809, (C. F. Adams), IX, 286.

VI *TIRELESS RETIREMENT*

PAGE

142   "That extraordinary man Bonaparte": TJ to JM, June 22, 1797, TJ-LC.

143   "Mr. Madison's valet .25": TJ's account book, July 11, 1797.

143   "It would give you a fever": TJ to Philip Mazzei, Apr. 24, 1796, *Writings* (Bergh) IX, 336. See also TJ to JM, Aug. 3, 1797, *ibid.*, 413–415; JM to TJ, Aug. 5, 1797, JM-LC.

144   "Perfect Quixote": JM to TJ, Feb. [n.d.], 1798, *Writings*, VI, 310.

144   "Furnish the seed": JM to Monroe, Feb. 5, 1798, Clark, 32.

145   "Mr. Madison himself superintended": Foster, *Notes on the U.S.A.*, II, 82, LC.

145   "He is verifying completely": JM to TJ, June 10, 1798, *Writings*, VI, 325.

146   Virginia Resolutions of 1798 as written by JM, *Writings*, VI, 326–331. See Adrienne Koch and Harry Ammon, "The Virginia and Kentucky Resolutions," WMQ, April 1948, Third Series, V, No. 1, 145-176.

147   "Interpose for arresting": JM, Report on the Resolutions, *Writings*, VI, 349. For the full report, *ibid.*, 341–406.

147   "Have you ever considered": JM to TJ, Dec. 29, 1798, *Writings*, VI, 328n.

147   "Cut deeper . . . than Jefferson's did": Koch, *Jefferson and Madison: The Great Collaboration*, 292.

147   *"Disgusting blackguardism"*: TJ to JM, Feb. 5, 1799, *Writings of TJ* (Bergh), X, 96.

148   "Consider that Virginia": J. Taylor of Caroline to JM, Mar. 18, 1798, Mar. 4, 1799, Rives-LC.

148   "Unadulterated love,": Kunkel, notes, Hist. Museum, Greensboro, N.C.

148   "Give me liberty": PH, March 1775, Second Virginia Convention, St. John's Church, Richmond.

149   "Give me beauty": Socrates, *Phaedrus, Works of Plato* (Jowett), III, 449.

151   "Let it go": Washington's Secretary, Tobias Lear, "Last Illness and Death of Washington," *Writings of George Washington* (Sparks), I, App. II, 556.

152   "Passion for chess": Thornton to JM, Mar. 17, 1802, JM-LC.

152   "We have erred and strayed": General Confession, Episcopal Prayer Book.

152   "Castle": A. Adams, *Letters*, II, 240.

153   "The aristocrats . . . have at last": T. Mason to Norborn Nicholas, June 9, 1800, NYPL.

153   "Insulted": Burr to Smith, Dec. 16, 29, 1800, John S. Pancake, "Aaron Burr: Would-Be Usurper," WMQ, April 1951.

153   "Distinctly stated": Bayard to AH, Jan. 7, 1801, AH, *Works* (J. C. Hamilton), VI, 505.

154   " . . . Ten for Jefferson": Fontaine Maury to JM, 4 o'clock, Feb. 19, 1801, JM-LC.

154   "Yesterday morning rather suddenly": JM to TJ, Feb. 28, 1801, *Writings*, VI, 416. JM Sr. died a month short of 78.

155   "In no party sense": H. Adams, *A History of the United States during the Administrations of Jefferson and Madison,* I, 290, 291.

155   JM on entangling alliances 18 years earlier: His Continental Congress resolve of June 12, 1783 (JCC), "That the true interest of these states requires that they should be as little as possible entangled in the politics and controversies of European nations." Similarly, on June 21, 1786 (*Writings*, II, 255), JM wrote Monroe about the "labyrinth of *European politics* from which we ought religiously to keep ourselves as free as possible." As for the other half of the Monroe Doctrine, the unacceptability of European meddling in this hemisphere, this too JM affirmed ahead of Monroe. For instance, on March 1, 1803 (ASP), JM wrote Monroe that "the wars of Europe should not prolong their ravages" in the New World; one day it would depend largely on Americans to "guarantee this tranquility." And on November 1, 1810, Crawford represented President JM's policy (Crawford to R. Smith, NA) as aiming "to prevent any European nation from obtaining a footing in the new world."

156   "Only no Federalist cow": Cutler, II, 54n. Four years later, remains of the cheese were still being served with cake and hot punch.

VII *WASHINGTON CITY: A NATION ON THE RISE*

157   "A chosen country": TJ, first Inaugural Address, *Writings of TJ* (Bergh), III, 320.

157   "Built for the future": A. Adams to daughter A. Smith, *Letters*, 240.

158   "We find this a very agreeable": TJ to T. M. Randolph, June 4, 1801, TJ-LC.

158   "If Madison be Secretary of State": W. Vans Murray to J. Q. Adams, May 2, 1801, "Letters . . . ," *American Historical Association Report* of 1912, XIV, 695.

160   "Blue coat . . . and slippers down at the heels": Anthony Merry to Lord Hawkesbury, Dec. 6, 1803, transcript, FO 5, LC; Anthony, 122, 123.

161   "Mrs. Madison is at the President's": Smith, 28.

161   "One of the strangest": *Ibid.*, 4.

162   "Blockheads and knaves": Dr. Timothy Dwight, in Brant, IV, 52.

162   "Strict and honorable neutrality": JM, instructions to Livingston, Sept. 28, 1801, NA.

164   "Pulled off General Van Courtland's wig": Sally McKean Yrujo to DM, June 20, 1812, DM-LC; Clark, 132.

165   "Black and white and yellow": Cutler, II, 143.

165   "Prodigious number of booths": Columbia HS *Records*, XXXIII, 120. The D.C. racetrack was near Columbia Road, between 14th and 15th. See also Cutler to son, Cutler, II, 242, 243.

166   " . . . Mr. Madison is justly entitled": TJ on JM, "James Madison," by Charles E. Hill, in *American Secretaries of State and Their Diplomacy* (ed., Samuel F. Bemis), III, 6, 7.

167   "True liberty": JM to TJ, Apr. 14, 1800, *Writings*, VI, 408, 409.

167   "Standing near the middle": Dr. Samuel Latham Mitchill to wife, Jan. 4, 1802, Clark, 50.

167   "Dined at the President's": Feb. 6, 1802, *ibid.*

167   "Every day proves to me": AH to Gouverneur Morris, July 27, 1802, in A. M. Hamilton, *Life of Alexander Hamilton*, 282.

167   "The day that France": TJ to R. R. Livingston, Apr. 18, 1802, *Writings of TJ* (Ford), VIII, 145.

PAGE

168 "These pies": W. Lee to JM, Feb. 12, 1805, JM-LC.

168 "Wild and romantic country": A. M. Thornton, diary, Sept. 5, 1802, LC.

169 "Dear Papa": Martha Randolph to father, Oct. 29, 1802, in Goodwin, 96.

170 "The Floridas and New Orleans": JM, secret committee report requesting an appropriation. Annals of House, Jan. 12, 1803. Congress voted $2,000,000 for an unspeci-
fied purpose.

170 "Future destinies of this Republic": TJ to Monroe, Jan. 13, 1803, *Writings of TJ*
(Bergh), X, 344.

171 "Combed out the prospect," and other messages: Pichon to Talleyrand, Feb. 13, 18,
20, June 3, 1803, AEU.

171 "What would you give for Louisiana?" and other details of negotiations: François
Barbé-Marbois, *Histoire de la Louisiane,* 301-335.

171 "You are insolent!": Th. Jung, *Lucien Bonaparte et ses Mémoires,* II, 121-192, in H.
Adams, II, 33-40.

172 "By the by, what do you think": S. H. Smith to wife, Smith, 38.

172 The Alexandria Academy: A day school. Where, then, did Payne board? With some
relative? Madison had a Conway cousin in Alexandria. Or the boy could have lived
with Dolley's cousin, Dr. Isaac Winston IV, who, in admiration, had named the first of
his 3 children—now near Payne's age—James Madison Winston. (The doctor would
die at ninety-five, leaving some letters from Dolley Madison. Coles, 182, 183.) The
brick Academy had been founded in 1785 on the East side of Washington Street
between Duke and Wolfe, with Masons from Lodge 39 laying the cornerstone. It was
run by a Presbyterian clergyman Mr. Moffat, and "attended by the best class of
Alexandria boys," with a free school for poor boys attached. "Able instructions were
given in the classics, history and elocution." See Mary A. Powell, *The History of
Alexandria,* 153-155.

173 " . . . It is a noble acquisition": JM to Monroe, July 30, 1803, *Writings,* VII, 60n.

173 Yrujo's protest: Laurent St. Cyr, French Ambassador to Spain, had told the Spanish
Government, July 22, 1802, on Spain's retrocession of Louisiana to France, "I am
authorized to declare to you in the name of the First Consul that France will never
alienate it." Ironically Yrujo himself had urged the transfer to create an obstacle to
American expansion toward Spain's more thriving colony, Mexico, and thus to
"strangle Hercules in his cradle." Now (Yrujo to his father-in-law Gov. Thomas
McKean, Nov. 20, 1803, PennHS) he wished Louisiana were "at the bottom of the
sea." JM reminded Yrujo that Napoleon's promise had formed no part of the earlier
Spanish-French Treaty of San Ildefonso, and that, unwarned by Spain, the United
States had bought Louisiana in good faith.

VIII *DOLLEY'S KNEE AND THE PROBLEM OF EVIL*

PAGE

174 "Take Mrs. Merry!" and the rest of the Merry imbroglio: Merry to Lord Hawkesbury,
Dec. 6, 31, to Hammond, Dec. 7, 1803, FO 5; Pichon to Talleyrand, Feb. 5, 16, 1804,
AEU; Yrujo to Cavallo, Feb. 7, 1804, Spanish Archives; JM to Monroe, Dec. 18, 26,
1803, Rives-LC, *Writings,* VII, 76n; Feb. 16, 1804, *ibid.,* 119; TJ to Monroe, Jan. 8,
1804, NA; Cutler, II, 163, 164; Smith, 46; Cutts, 49, 50; J. Adams, *Works,* II, 366–372;
H. Adams, *op. cit.,* 365–376.

PAGE

175 "Dared to look at her": Smith, 46.

176 "Exceedingly pleasant": Cutler, II (as reported by Cutler's son), 154n.

176 "An excellent dinner": Feb. 21, 1804, *ibid.,* 154.

177 "More like a harvest home": Clark, 64.

177 "But abundance": DM, *ibid.,* 65.

177 "Dashed in a very high": *Ibid.,* 75.

178 "For not knowing my heart better": DM to Mrs. Lucy Winston, Apr. 9, 1804, Cutts, 43.

179 "In every sense a profligate": AH to John Rutledge, Jan. 4, 1801 (enclosing "confidential paper" on Burr), A. M. Hamilton, *op. cit.,* 386.

179 "That regretted city": DM to A. Cutts, May 3, 1804, Cutts coll., LC. Dolley's other letters to Anna quoted in this chapter: *Ibid.* The printed versions are somewhat edited.

180 "Dressed in beautiful and shining blue": DM to A. Cutts, May 5 [1804?], UVa.

181 "How I miss you": A. Cutts to DM, May [n.d.], 1804, DM-LC. Cutts (39–41) rewords this letter somewhat.

181 "Dissipation of Washington": M. Jackson to A. Cutts, July 20, 1804, Cutts coll., LC.

182 "Despicable" opinion, and AH's death. A. M. Hamilton, *op. cit.,* 390–404. Bishop Moore gave Hamilton Communion before he died.

182 "Payne continues": DM to A. Cutts, July 16, 1804, Cutts coll., LC.

183 "It's suspected some malicious": *Ibid.*

183 "Intellectual powers": JM to J. K. Paulding, Apr. 1, 1831, *Writings,* IX, 454.

183 "Immense rains": DM to R. D. Cutts, Aug. 12, 1804, Cutts coll., LC.

183 "Finest tobacco": *Ibid.*

184 "I do not admire contention": DM to D. Cutts, Mar. 10, 1830, *ibid.;* Clark, 238.

184 "Butcher of Vendée": J. Armstrong to JM, Oct. 20, 1804, NA.

185 *"Sec, haineux, passione":* Turreau to Talleyrand, Jan. 26, 1805, AEU. By mistranslating *"sec"* and *"haineux"* as "dry" and "spiteful," Henry Adams (*op. cit.,* II, 272–274) clouded the issue. See Brant, IV, 266, 267.

186 "Been goose enough": L. Washington to mother, Mar. 1, 1805, Cutts coll., LC.

186 "Vast addition": DM to A. Cutts, May 22, 1805, *ibid.* L. B. Cutts (46) predates this letter by a year.

186 "Marched off": DM to A. Cutts, June 4, 1805, Cutts coll., LC.

186 "I dread the separation": DM to A. Cutts, *ibid.*

187 "Enjoyed the sound": *Ibid.*

187 "Dr. Thornton, you do not know": Tayloe, 141.

187 "Quite still": DM to A. Cutts, July 8, 1805, Cutts coll., LC.

187 "Little navy": *New York Herald,* June 15, 1805.

188 "Warm dispute": Foster, Journal, LC.

188 "Cruel and sanguinary": Plumer, 345.

188 "Alas, my beloved Anna": DM to A. Cutts, July 20, 1805, Cutts coll., LC.

188 "I thought all was over with me," DM to A. Cutts, July 29, 1805, *ibid.*

188 "I hope [both] are now about entering": DM to A. Cutts, Apr. 26, 1804, *ibid.*

PAGE

189 "I feel as if my heart": DM to A. Cutts, July 29, 1805, *ibid.*

189 "Excellent lodgings": DM to A. Cutts, July 31, 1805, *ibid.*

189 "The times when our Society": *Ibid.*

189 "Cares for the vanities": DM to A. Cutts, Aug. 19, 1805, UVa.

190 "Strong appeal": JM to TJ, Aug. 2, 1805, TJ-LC.

190 "I have long been of the opinion": JM to AG, Aug. 8, 1805, NYHS. See also AG to JM, Aug. 6, 12, 1805, JM-LC.

191 St. Mary's Seminary: Only some business letters from JM to St. Mary's, no Payne Todd scholastic or personal records, are extant.

191 "Little charmer": A. Cutts to mother, Sept. 1, 1805, Cutts coll., LC.

192 "Aid and council": TJ to JM, Oct. 11, 1805, TJ-LC; *Writings of TJ* (Ford), VIII, 380.

192 "A few hours only": DM to JM, Oct. 23, 1805, Cutts coll., LC. All the other letters from DM to her husband quoted in this chapter, those dated Oct. 24, 25, 26, 28, 30, Nov. 1, 17, 1805, *ibid;* all, that is, except the one on p. 329 in which she speaks of looking forward to Payne's manhood when he will honor his guardians. This is in Ketcham, 446, the original being owned by Mrs. Edward Chavalier, Los Angeles.

194 "My dearest, . . . Payne arrived": JM to DM, Oct 26, 1805, Cutts coll., LC.

195 "Yours of the 1st instant": JM to DM, n.d. [about Nov. 3], 1805, misdated 1809, *Writings,* VIII, 76.

196 "All my affection": JM to DM, n.d. [about Nov. 5], 1805, UVa.

197 "The last mail, my dearest": JM to DM, n.d. [about Nov. 22], 1805, MassHS.

IX *THE ROAD TO POWER*

PAGE

198 "Known profligacy": Merry to British Foreign Office, Aug. 5, 1804, FO 5. For the full story of Burr and England, see Merry's letters of Mar. 29, Apr. 29, Aug. 4, Nov. 25, 1805, *ibid.;* also McCaleb, 42–48.

198 "How long will it be": *U.S. Gazette,* Aug. 2, 1805.

199 "Dish of chocolate": C. Mitchill to M. Miller, Apr. 8, 1806, Mitchill-LC.

199 Description of Seminary: *Ibid.*, Nov. 10, 18.

199 "We worship the Great Spirit": Mary E. E. Cutts's MS notes on Mellimelli, Cutts coll., LC. All details about Mellimelli are from this source.

200 "Georgia a Greek" and "appropriations to foreign intercourse": JM to TJ, Sept. 17, 1806, TJ-LC.

200 "I applied to the President": Joseph Bryan to JM, Feb. 3, 1806, JM-LC.

201 "You admit him at your table": Anonymous; received Dec. 1, 1805, TJ-LC.

201 Money and troops for Miranda: Benjamin Rush to JM, Dec. 4, 5, Miranda to JM, Dec. 10, 1805, JM-LC; Robertson, I, 245–247, 291–299, 300, 305, 325; Biggs, *History of . . . Miranda's Attempt. . . . ,* 4–8. When on Feb. 6, 1806, TJ and JM heard that Miranda had violated the U.S. Neutrality Act by sailing from N.Y. on the *Leander* with American money, arms and volunteers for the Venezuelan revolt against Spain, they ordered the criminal prosecution of Miranda's American accomplices, Col. William S. Smith, Surveyor of the port of N.Y., and Samuel G. Ogden, ship-owner and John Adams's

son-in-law. Turreau's account of an interview with JM on the subject has been distorted by Henry Adams's mistranslation. JM was neither shifty-eyed nor prostrated, only regretful (Brant, IV, 330, 331). Federalists tried to use the trials to discredit the Administration. Smith and Ogden were acquitted "for lack of proof." For JM's statement about his strict neutrality in talks with Miranda, see JM to J. Armstrong, Mar. 15, 1806, JM-LC; *Writings,* VII, 202–204.

201   "On my return a king": J. Randolph to AG, Oct. 25, 1805, NYHS. See also Burwell (TJ's new secretary), memoir, LC. And Foster to mother, Mar. 10, 1806, Foster-LC: "He [Randolph] values nobility of birth very highly. . . . We often ride together."

201   *Examination of the British Doctrine Which Subjects to Capture a Neutral Trade Not Open in Time of Peace,* Anonymous (JM), *Writings,* VII, 204–375.

202   "After shrinking from the Spanish jackal": J. Randolph, Annals of House, Mar. 5, 1806.

202   The flinging of the pamphlet: S. Smith to —, Mar. 14, 1806, Smith Letterbook, LC.

202   "Notwithstanding the contempt": J. Smilie, Annals of House, Mar. 6, 1806.

202   Powhatan as Randolph's forebear: Pecquet du Bellet, IV, 301–313. DM was also distantly related to Powhatan and Pocahontas through a Bolling forebear.

202   "Miserable card-house": Annals of House, J. Randolph, Mar. 6, 1806. See also Brant, IV, 315–316.

203   "To prevent Mr. Jefferson": J. Q. Adams, Mar. 6, 1806, *Memoirs,* I, 418.

203   "Quids": J. Randolph, Annals of House, Mar. 18, 1806.

203   "All the objections": *Ibid.,* Apr. 5, 1806.

203   The pitching of the hat: T. Pickering to R. King, *Life and Correspondence of Rufus King,* IV, 509.

203   "In a way to tender you": TJ to Monroe, Mar. 16, 1806, Monroe-LC. See also TJ to Monroe, May 4, 1806, *Writings of TJ* (Ford), VIII, 447, 448.

203   "Mrs. Madison was all": Smith, 51, for April 6, 1806.

203   "Turn Congress neck and heels": Eaton deposition, *Intelligencer,* Jan. 28, 1807. See also TJ, Anas, *Writings of TJ* (Bergh), I, 459 *et seq.;* Annals of Senate, Sept. 26, 1807 (XVII, Appendix, 508).

204   "We have traitors": J. H. Daveiss to TJ, Feb. 10, 13, 1806, TJ-LC. Daveiss suspected many innocent persons. After his public denouncement of the Administration for slowness to indict, Jefferson fired him.

205   "I received John": G. Davis to DM, July 12, 1806, Cutts coll., LC.

205   "Been on the confines of eternity": J. G. Jackson to Mary Coles Payne, July 27, 1806, *ibid.*

205   "Expressions are wanting": DM to mother, Aug. 4, 1806, *ibid.*

205   "Full of cash": Nathan Williams to JM, Sept. 5, 1806, JM-LC. Corroborating testimony: Gen. Presley Nevill and Judge Sam Roberts to JM, Oct. 7, 1806, Burr Conspiracy Papers, LC.

206   "Gloom and distress": J. G. Jackson to JM, Sept. 29, 1806, NYPL.

206   Burr's "gunboats": J. Taylor to JM, Oct. 13, 1806, JM-LC.

206   "Prime mover": Wilkinson to TJ, Oct. 21 (2 letters), 1806, TJ-LC. See also TJ, proclamation, Nov. 27, 1806, *Writings of TJ* (Ford), VIII, 481, 482; McCaleb, 143.

PAGE

206   "Your letter, postmarked": Burr to Wilkinson, July 29, 1807.

206   "Like a Leonidas": Wilkinson to José de Yturrigaray (translation), Nov. 17, 1806, Spanish Archives (copy in LC); Brant, IV, 348. See also McCaleb, 42–135.

207   "Honor of a soldier": TJ, Annals of Senate, Jan. 23; Annals of House, Jan. 26, 1807. See also McCaleb, "Wilkinson's Duplicity," 136–172.

207   "Probably received its death blow": JM to R. R. Livingston, Jan. 28, 1807, NYHS.

207   "Yesterday Colonel Aaron Burr": *Intelligencer,* Mar. 23, 1807.

207   "I suppose you have heard": DM to A. Cutts, Mar. 27, 1807, UVa.

207   Burr's arrest: John Graham to JM, Mar. 18, 23, May 11; Burr Conspiracy Papers, LC; *Richmond Enquirer,* Mar. 27; *Intelligencer,* Apr. 1, 1807.

207   "Hand of malignity": Marshall, Mar. 31, 1807, before grand jury (quoting Blackstone), Beveridge, III, 376. See also Caesar Rodney to JM, Mar. 31 (misdated 21), Apr. 1, 1807, JM-LC.

208   "Shuffling her cards": Dolley Winston to DM, May 7, 1807, Cutts coll., LC.

208   "Enormity": JM, draft of June 29 strengthening TJ's revision of his Chesapeake proclamation issued July 2, 1807, *Writings of TJ* (Ford), X, 443, 448n.

208   "Honorable reparation": JM to Monroe, July 6, 1807, JM-LC; *Writings,* VII, 455.

208   "Burr's party fights hard": DM to A. Cutts (copy), June 18, 1807, Cutts coll., LC.

209   "Improper practices": Jackson to JM, July 5, 1807, JM-LC.

209   "Every lawyer": Rodney to JM, Sept. 16, 1807, JM-LC.

209   "Mammoth of iniquity": J. Randolph, in Wandell, *Aaron Burr,* II, 197.

210   "I have sent to . . . Havana": Folch to Wilkinson, as quoted by I. J. Cox, "General Wilkinson and His Later Intrigues with the Spaniards," in *American Historical Review,* XIX, No. 4, 807.

210   "May the horoscope": DM to "the Forrests'," Sept. 26, 1807, Clark, 89.

210   "Sparkling bottle": DM to A. Cutts, Oct. 27, 1807, Cutts coll., LC.

210   "Violent stroke": J. G. Jackson to JM, Oct. 18, 1807, JM-LC. See also Jackson to JM, Oct. 25, *ibid.*

211   "Deep affliction": DM to ———, Nov. 7, 1807, in Clark, 90.

211   "Excellent parent": Judge Isaac Winston III to DM, Jan. 30, 1808, Cutts coll., LC.

211   "Certainly not if war": JM, anon. article, reprinted from a Dec. *Intelligencer* by *London Chronicle,* Jan. 27, 1808.

212   "It is but justice": Rose to Foreign Minister George Canning, Jan. 18, 1808, FO 5.

213   "Very slightingly": DM as reported by J. H. Nicholson to Monroe, May 5, 1806, Monroe-LC.

213   "Miseries . . . past endurance": Jackson to JM, July 17, 1808, JM-LC.

213   Zhe-Hol had been Totterdownhill, built in 1782, a white clapboard house with two wings and three enormous stone chimneys, WMQ, 2nd series, I, 163. Picture, *ibid.,* opp. 145.

213   "I got home Friday night": JM to TJ, May 15, 1808, JM-LC.

213   "My limbs yet tremble": DM to A. Cutts, June 3, 1808 (if I read correctly a somewhat

PAGE

obscure date). Apparently Dolley delayed telling her sister about the perilous trip (see letter of May 18) because, on arriving home, she received word of Anna's illness.

214 "Go ... tell Mr. Madison": *Virginia Gazette,* May 25, 1808. For Strode's reply see *Gazette,* June 12, 1808.

215 "Elegant standard": *Intelligencer,* July 6, 1808.

215 "Spontaneous effusions": John Binn's *Democratic Press,* July 1808, in Brant, III, 451.

215 "The secret but well assured . . . influence": Turreau to Foreign Minister Champagny, July 28, 1808, AEU, Supplement, V, 255.

215 "Fair and sincere neutrality": JM to J. Armstrong, May 2, 1808, *Writings,* 28.

216 "From the disgraceful animadversions": JM (in part), *Intelligencer,* Aug. 29, 1808.

216 "Violations bordering on insurrection": AG to JM, Sept. 9, 1808, Rives-LC.

216 "Hunt the polecat": J. Randolph to James M. Garnett, Aug. 31, 1808, Randolph-Garnett Letters, LC.

216 "All clapped": DM to A. Cutts, Aug. 28, 1808, Cutts coll., LC.

217 "JM . . . was prevented": JM to TJ, Oct. 30, 1808, TJ-LC.

217 "Candid and liberal": JM's revision of TJ's 8th Annual Message, TJ-LC.

217 "Extremely intimate": Jennings, 19.

217 "Deeply felt": W. Pinkney to JM, Sept. 21, 1808, ASP, III. See also TJ, *Anas,* Nov. 9, 1808.

217 " . . . A manly and honorable vindication": *Aurora,* Nov. 14, 1808.

217 "They are worshipping the rising sun": C. Mitchill to sister Mrs. Margaret Miller, Dec. 11, 1808, Mitchill-LC.

217 "All in fine spirits": *Ibid.,* Apr. 8, 1806.

217 "It was as good as a play": *Ibid.,* Dec. 9, 1808.

218 "Comic scene": *Ibid.,* n.d. [late 1808 or early 1809].

218 "Already had too much": *Ibid.,* Dec. 11, 1808.

218 "Exquisite band of music": Ibid., Jan. 11, 1809.

218 "Queen elect": *Ibid.,* Feb. 12, 1809.

218 "Yes, repeal it!": David Williams, Annals of House, Jan. 30, 1809.

X *A BUFF-COLORED INAUGURATION*

PAGE

220 "I feel no small degree": E. C. Lee to DM, Mar. 2, 1809, Cutts coll., LC.

220 "Public characters": Smith, 59.

221 "Full suit of cloth": Barent Gardenier to E. Foote, Aug. 8, 1809, UVa.

221 "Soon gained confidence": Smith, 59.

221 " . . . In point of style": *Intelligencer*, Mar. 6, 1809.

221 "With all the cordiality": Smith, 58. The details of this inaugural day come largely from Mrs. Smith, 59-64.

224 "How stands the glass": A popular song.

PAGE

225   "If we can't double": Thomas Erskine, in Brant, IV, 370. For other after-dinner stories by JM, see Jared Sparks, *Journal, 1829-1831*, or excerpts from it in "After-Dinner Ancedotes of James Madison" (ed., Proctor), VMHB, Vol. 60, no. 2 (April 1952), 255–256.

225   "Mr. and Mrs. Madison dined with us": A. M. Thornton, diary, Mar. 1, 1809, LC; Clark, 97.

225   "Mr. and Mrs. M went to the Great House": *Ibid.*, 102.

226   "The belligerent Edicts": TJ to J. Armstrong, Mar.5, 1809, Cutts coll., LC.

227   Stuart's portrait of Washington: DM planned to hang it in the East Room but Latrobe considered the diningroom more appropriate.

227   "The curtains!": Latrobe to DM, Apr. 21, 1809, NYPL. See also Latrobe to DM, Mar. 17, 20, May 7, July 10, Sept. 8, Dec. 7, 1809, *ibid.* For Latrobe's expenditures, see Goodwin, 133-135.

227   George Steptoe Washington's death: He was buried in Augusta, Ga.

227   The Washington theater: The temporary theater near the President's House had pit, benches and boxes. Out-of-town troupes and sometimes foreign ones came in the winter. The Madisons sat in a box.

228   "The sadness which all day hung": Smith, 81. The date of the Smiths' arrival was Mar. 2, not 4. The entire description of their visit is taken from Mrs. Smith's journal, 374–376. Some of the recorded talk has been changed back from indirect to direct discourse.

229   "My dearest. . . . The period . . . will be shortened": JM to DM, Aug. 7, 1809, Cutts coll., LC.

230   "Copenhagen" Jackson: *Intelligencer,* Oct. 5, 7, 19, 1807.

230   "Taking the liberty": DM to Latrobe, Sept. 12, 1809, Columbia HS; facsimile in Clark, following 112.

230   "Obstinate as a mule": F. J. Jackson to G. Jackson, Oct. 26, 1809, *Bath Archives,* series 2, I, 28.

231   "Gross insinuations": R. Smith (actually JM) to Jackson, Nov. 8, 1809, ASP, III, 319. For the fuller record, see *ibid.,* 299–323.

231   "Audacious Minister": Ezekiel Bacon to Joseph Story, Nov. 27, 1809, Story Papers, LC.

231   "Great bulwark of our security": JM, First Annual Message to Congress, Nov. 29, 1809; *Writings,* VIII, 83.

231   "Jefferson's productions": J. Randolph to Judge Joseph Nicholson, Dec. 4, 1809, in H. Adams, V, 177.

231   "The greatest blessing of my life": JM *re* DM, Mary E. E. Cutts, memoir, Cutts coll., LC.

232   "My dear, you have rested me": Upton, 212.

232   "Bending under the weight": T. Cruse to J. Hamilton, Jan. 2, 1810, UVa.

232   "Your anxiety": JM to G. Logan, Jan. 19, 1810, PennHS.

232   "We will have no war": F. J. Jackson to J. Treackle, Jan. 10, 1810, Pickering Papers, MassHS. See also F. J. Jackson to Bathhurst, Jan. 23, 1810, FO 5.

233   "Why didn't you pull me": Mary E. E. Cutts, memoir, Cutts coll., LC.

XI *TOBOGGAN*

235 "Strong-minded woman": H. Martineau, *Retrospect of Western Travel,* I, 193.

235 "Integrity, zeal and ability": Lord Wellesley to W. Pinkney, Mar. 14, 1810, ASP., Foreign Relations, III, 355.

235 "Comprise robbery, theft": JM to TJ, May 25, 1810, *Writings,* VIII, 102.

236 "Our farmers have never": JM to AG, Sept. 5, 1810, Gallatin, *Writings,* I, 486.

237 "Great exertions": J. Garnett to J. Randolph, Sept. 17, 1810, Randolph-Garnett Papers, LC.

237 "His Majesty loves the Americans": Cadore to Armstrong, Aug. 5, on repeal of the Berlin and Milan Decrees, *Intelligencer,* Sept. 26, 1810; ASP, III, 387.

237 "Consciousness of a debt": W. Pinkney to JM, Aug. 13, 1810 (received in mid-October), JM-LC. See also JM to Pinkney, Oct. 30, 1810, Rives-LC; *Writings,* VIII, 117–123.

237 "Being our own": JM to TJ, Oct. 19, 1810, *Writings,* VIII, 110.

237 JM, secret Proclamation, Oct. 27, 1810, *Writings,* VIII, 112–114; ASP, III, 397, 398.

238 "New act of emancipation": Turreau to Cadore, Nov. 1, 1810, AEU.

238 "Great and Good Friend": JM to Napoleon, Nov. 3, 1810, *ibid.*

238 "The law of reprisal": Cadore to Armstrong, Sept. 12, 1810 (received Nov. 8), ASP, III, 389.

238 "Too weak to be wicked": *New York Evening Post,* Nov. 17, 1810.

238 "He is a lost statesman": *Federal Republican,* Nov. 13, 1810.

239 "Masterpiece of art and deception": *Ibid.,* Dec. 8, 1810.

239 "Death-blow to the Constitution": Josiah Quincy, Annals of House, Jan. 14, 1811.

240 "Of great and little men": W. Irving, Jan 13, 1811, *Letters to Henry Brevoort,* I, 24.

240 Vanderlyn's portrait of JM: Monroe Museum, Fredericksburg, Virginia.

240 "But when he can disengage himself": Montlezun, *A Frenchman Visits . . . Orange County,* entry for Sept. 16, 1816.

241 "Constant round of banqueting": Irving, *op. cit.,* I, 24.

241 "Judas": J. Randolph, in Bruce, *John Randolph of Roanoke,* I, 348.

242 "Base and detestable": *Aurora,* Mar. 27, 1811.

242 "Cheerful tranquility": DM to William Lee, May 7, 1811, Clark, 119.

242 "Though the mast bows": *Ibid.* This may be an example of Dolley's own verse.

242 "Mortification": R. Smith to brother Sen. Samuel Smith, Mar. 25, 1811, Smith-LC. See also letters of Mar. 23, 25, 28, *ibid.*

242 "Enfeebled mind": R. Smith to J. Bullus, "Monday" [Apr. 8], 1811, MdHS.

242 "We are authorized to state": *Aurora,* Apr. 5, 1811.

243 "I have always regarded Duane": JM to TJ, May 3, 1811, *Writings,* VIII, 151.

243 "Whole course of policy": JM, "Memorandum as to Robert Smith", *ibid.,* 140.

243 "Accommodation" between Eppes and J. Randolph: Sérurier to Cadore, Mar. 5, 1811, AEU.

243 "Feared no one but God": J. Russell to R. Smith (quoting his words to Sérurier), Nov. 17, 1810, NA.

PAGE

244 "Which he is fond of": Sérurier to Cadore, Apr. 11, 1811, AEU.

244 "Honorable and reliable": Sérurier to Cadore, Apr. 26, 1811, *ibid.*

244 "Minister of Rapine and Murder": *Federal Republican,* Apr. 15, 1811.

244 "Be . . . determined": Official orders (at JM's behest) to Com. Rodgers, ASP, III; 496.

244 "Mr. Madison governs by himself": Sérurier to Cadore, May 24, 1811, AEU.

244 "What ship is that?": Com. John Rodgers' report of May 23, 1811, *Intelligencer,* May 28, 1811; ASP, III, 497.

245 "Provoking" Essex: DM to W. Lee, May 7, 1811, Clark; 119.

245 "We have only to turn": "Americanus" (J. Barlow), *Intelligencer,* May 25, 1811.

245 "Ignorance and instability": JM to R. Cutts, May 23, 1811, Cutts coll., LC.

246 "Very apparent": EC to DM, June 10, 1811, NYPL.

246 "How I long": DM to A. Cutts, June 8, 1811, Cutts coll., LC.

246 "Amiable cousin": DM to EC, June 15, 1811, *ibid.*

246 "In great triumph": DM to A. Cutts, June 20, 1811, *ibid.*

246 "Joy! Joy!": DM to A. Cutts, *ibid.*

247 "I expect he is like a gosling": L. Washington to DM, June [n.d.], 1811, *ibid.*

247 Madison's *"real* object": R. Smith, *Address to the People of the United States,* as quoted in the *Intelligencer,* July 2, 1811.

247 "But St. Thomas of Cantingbury": J. Randolph to Garnett, July 7, 1811, Randolph-Garnett Papers, LC.

247 "Singular, I call it": Garnett to J. Randolph, quoting Tucker, July 23, 1811, *ibid.*

247 "Weak, wicked": B. Hawkins to JM, Oct. 13, 1811, JM-LC.

247 "A shameful breach": Editorial preface to reprint of R. Smith's *Address* in the *Intelligencer,* July 2, 1811, widely copied by newspapers, then distributed as a pamphlet.

247 Lee and Barlow's serialized "Review": *Ibid.,* July 4, 6, 9, 11, 1811.

248 "Willing that the United States": J. Russell to R. Smith, Jan. 28, 1811, NA.

248 Monroe "icy": Sérurier to Bassano, July 5, 1811, AEU.

248 "Wanton slaughter": Foster to Monroe, July 3, 1811, ASP, III, 471.

248 *"Suavitur in modo":* Gen. J. Mason, as reported by Sérurier to Bassano, July 5, 1811, AEU.

249 "You ask if we laughed": DM to A. Cutts, July 15, 1811, Cutts coll., LC.

249 "It was well acted": *Ibid.*

249 "I have never seen him": Sérurier to Bassano, July 20, 1811, AEU.

250 "Sister Dolley no doubt": L. Washington to A. Cutts, July 20, 1811, Cutts coll., LC.

250 "The opinion is gaining": *Federal Republican,* July 25, 1811.

250 "Their beloved fellow citizen": *Intelligencer,* Aug. 3, 1811.

251 "The hostile effusions from Baltimore": JM to R. Cutts, Aug. 24, 1811, Cutts coll., LC.

251 "He . . . lingers": DM to A. Cutts, Oct. 19, 1811, *ibid.*

251 "Mrs. Madison helped the older girls": Upton, 203.

251 "Violent presumption": Wilkinson court-martial records, *Intelligencer,* Feb. 25, 1812.

252　"Sick and afflicted city": DM to Barlows, Nov. 15, 1811, Cutts coll., LC.

252　"My own beloved Phoebe": DM to Phoebe Morris, Oct. 6, 1811, Clark, 121.

252　"Kicked into a fight": Clark, 129. Of course the Federalists were not all of one mind in this matter. Some called Madison a war-coward, others a warmonger, some jumped from the one position to the other.

252　"How very little": Foster to Wellesley, Sept. 17, 1811, FO 5.

252　" . . . Mr. Foster . . . had the best": Anthony St. John Baker, Clark, 122.

253　"War, savage war": Maj. Gen. A. Jackson to Brig. Gen. J. Winchester, division orders, Nov. 28, 1811, Jackson-LC.

253　"The intrigues for President": DM to A. Cutts, Dec. 20, 1811, Cutts coll., LC.

253　"War on our lawful commerce": JM, third Annual Message, Nov. 5, 1811, *Writings,* VIII, 161.

253　"Great honor": J. Adams to Monroe, Dec. 19, 1811, Monroe-LC.

253　"One splinter": JM to J. Q. Adams, Nov. 15, 1811; *Writings,* VIII, 167.

253　"Begun my journal": DM to Barlows, Nov. 15, 1811, Cutts coll., LC.

254　"Darkly hinted": Foster to Wellesley, Nov. 29, 1811, FO 5.

254　"Unless we change": Foster to Wellesley, Dec. 11, 1811, *ibid.*

254　"It is the opinion": Foster to Wellesley, Dec. 25, 1811, *ibid.*

254　"Only the recall": Sérurier to Bassano, Dec. 9, 1811, AEU.

255　"I believe there will be war": DM to A. Cutts, Dec. 20, 1811, Cutts coll., LC.

255　"Heat and irritation": Sérurier to Bassano, Jan. 12, 1812, AEU.

255　"Unmixed American spirit": W. Pinkney to Gov. Edward Lloyd, Aug. 13, *Intelligencer,* Aug. 20, 1811.

256　"Most noble Marquis of Whitewash": *Federal Republican,* Dec. 17, 1811.

256　"Monstrous thick legs": Foster to Hamilton, May 5, 1812, in Brant, V, 412.

256　"Crowded with company": P. Morris to sister Rebecca, Jan. [n.d.] 1812, Clark, 125.

256　"I name these": L. Washington to A. Cutts, Jan. 14, 1812, Cutts coll., LC.

257　Lucy as a belle: Vanderlyn's portrait of her in a loose garment and bonnet (owned by Dr. John A. Washington, a direct descendant of Lucy and George Steptoe Washington) does not show great beauty. Her chief charms were vivacity and wit.

257　"Wholly devoted": C. Mitchill to M. Miller, Nov. 21, 1811, Mitchill-LC.

257　"His legs [were] half the time in the air": *Ibid.,* n.d.

257　"A war with England": *Ibid.,* Dec. 7, 1811.

257　"Two great personages": *Ibid.,* Jan. 2, 1811.

257　"Never beheld a human form": P. Morris to sister Rebecca, n.d. [early 1812], Clark, 126.

258　"Never forgot a face": Tayloe, 155.

258　"The crowd is so great": DM to young man, in Clark, 143, quoting Mrs. E. F. Ellett.

258　"Our beloved Phoebe": DM to A. Morris, Mar. 2, 1812, *ibid.,* 126.

258　"Miss Phoebe is still here": L. Washington to A. Cutts, Mar. 8, 1812, Cutts coll., LC.

258　"Considerable noise": *Ibid.*

PAGE

258 "Help, gentlemen!": C. Mitchill to M. Miller, Mar. 9, 1812, Mitchill-LC.

259 "What's it about?" Baker as reported by Sérurier to Bassano, Mar. 12, 1812, AEU. The whole conversation is from this source.

259 "You may know the wounded pigeons": William Widgery, as reported by J. Harper to W. Plumer, Mar. 11, 1812, Plumer-LC. See also Annals of House, Mar. 9, and Annals of Senate, Mar. 9, 10, 1812.

259 "Is not this a fearful prostitution": J. Bayard to C. Rodney, Mar. 22, 1812, DelHS.

259 "Pitiful and mean attempt": B. Talmadge to J. McHenry, Mar. 16, 1812, NYPL.

259 "Poor shabby shallow": J. Randolph to R. K. Randolph, Mar. 10, 1812, Randolph-Garnett Papers, LC.

260 "Thoroughly French conduct": Sérurier to Bassano, Mar. 2, 1812, AEU.

260 Identity of "Crillon": Foster, Journal, May 25, 1812, LC; Foster to Castlereagh, May 23, 1812, FO 5.

260 "Say 30 days": JM, Special Message to Congress, sent with Henry Papers, Mar. 9, 1812; *Writings*, VIII, 183. See also Foster to Wellesley, Apr. 1, FO 5.

260 "The Federalists affronted": DM to A. Cutts, Mar. [27], 1812, Cutts coll., LC.

261 "Nothing has mortified the Federalists": J. Harper to W. Plumer, Apr. 13, 1812, Plumer-LC.

261 "Where are Mr. Cutts' vessels?": DM to A. Cutts, Mar. [27], 1812, Cutts coll., LC.

261 "I beg you will . . . spend the summer": L. Washington to A. Cutts, Mar. 8, 1812, *ibid.*

261 "The most delightful": P. Morris to father, with postscript by L. Washington, Mar. 22, 1812, Anthony, 208.

261 "At the residence of the President": *Intelligencer,* Mar. 31, 1812.

262 "Without an accommodation": Monroe (for JM) to Foreign Relations Committee, Mar. 31, 1812, according to J. Randolph's memorandum, Smith-LC (identification by Brant).

262 "Oh, no, embargo" and rest of the conversation: Foster to Wellesley, Apr. 2 (two letters), 1812, FO 5.

262 "Fuel to party discontent": JM to TJ, Apr. 3, 1812, JM-LC, *Writings*, VIII, 186.

262 "The whole war fire": *New York Post,* Apr. 4, 1812.

262 "Very familiar chit-chat": *Ibid.,* Apr. 7, 1812.

262 "Everything that disturbs you": DM to A. Cutts, Apr. 8, 1812, Cutts coll., LC.

263 "We have just arrived": L. Todd to DM, Apr. 18, 1812, *ibid.*

264 "She had the gift": Mary Kunkel, sketch, Hist. Museum, Greensboro.

264 Dolley's jewelry: Stan. V. Henkel catalog, Philadelphia, 1899, *ibid.*

264 "Valuable collection": DM to Ruth Barlow, Apr. [n.d.], 1812, Cutts coll., LC.

265 "Floating warehouses": Sérurier to Bassano, Apr. 24, 1812, AEU.

265 "Grand council": J. Harper to W. Plumer, Apr. 29, 1812 (two letters), Plumer-LC.

265 Trip to the Great Falls: C. Mitchill to M. Miller, May 3, 1812, Mitchill-LC.

266 Foster sees the light: Foster to Castlereagh, May 5, 1812, FO 5. See also May 3, 1812, *ibid.*

266 "What has [it] to do": *Intelligencer,* May 5, 1812.

266 "Where are your armies": H. Bleecker, Annals of House, May 6, 1812.

266 "Engendered from a fortuitous": *Ibid.,* May 13, 1812.

267 "John Randolph has been firing away": DM to A. Cutts, May [12?], 1812, Cutts coll., LC.

267 "Honesty, patriotism": *Intelligencer,* May 19, 1812.

268 "I scarcely expect": L. Todd to DM, May 29, 1812, Cutts coll., LC.

269 "Mrs. Madison makes": J. Pope, as reported by Foster to Castlereagh, May 23, 1812, FO 5.

269 Foster's decisive showing of Dispatches No. 8 and No. 9 and related matters: Foster to Castlereagh, May 28, June 6, 8, to Monroe, May 30, 1812, *ibid.; Intelligencer,* May 28, 30, 1812.

270 "Unexampled forbearance": JM, War Message, June 1, 1812; *Writings,* VIII, 198, 199.

270 "Free-born sons": Committee on Foreign Relations, war manifesto, June 3, 1812, ASP (1819 ed.), VIII, 399.

270 "Very pale": Foster, Journal, June 4, 1812, LC.

270 House vote: *Intelligencer,* June 4, 1812.

270 "Met Mr. Madison": Foster, Journal, June 7, 1812, LC.

270 "Shuffling": Foster to Castlereagh, June 9, 1812, FO 5.

270 Senate war debate (behind closed doors): Annals of Senate, June 13–17, 1812.

270 The President's House "very grand": Preston, *Reminiscences,* 6–9.

271 "The damned rascal!": *Ibid.,* 170.

272 "Ghastly pale": Foster, Journal, June 17, 1812, LC.

272 "The President was all life": *New York Post,* June 20, 1812.

272 "War exists": JM, Proclamation of War, June 19, 1812, *Writings,* VIII, 200, 201.

XII *THE WAR OF 1812*

274 "It is victories": JM in late Feb. 1812, as reported by Charles Stewart in *New York Courier and Enquirer,* Oct. 10, 1845. The full statement: "It is victories we want; if you give us them and lose your ships afterwards, they can be replaced by others." See Brant, VI, 39, and note, 539.

274 "I . . . press you": Sally, Marquesa de Casa Yrujo, to DM, June 20, 1812, Cutts coll., LC.

275 "When the pear is ripe": JM as quoted by Turreau to Talleyrand, July 9, 1805, AEU.

275 "Every man an inch taller": DM-LC

275 "Slaves of the slaves": *Boston Repertory,* June 26, as quoted by *Intelligencer,* July 2, 1812.

275 "Hemp and confiscation": TJ to JM, June 29, 1812, TJ-LC. In printing this letter both Ford and Bergh blank the passage.

276 "Rancorous opposition": JM to Cutts, Aug. 8, 1812, Cutts coll., LC.

PAGE

276   "Clogged the wheels": JM to TJ, Aug. 17, 1812, *Writings,* VIII, 210.

276   "Raised the standard": Gen. W. Hull to Sec. Eustis, July 13, 19, 1812, NA. See also Hull's proclamation, Aug. 12, 1812, Forbes, App. II, 10, 17.

276   "Terrific kings and princes": R. Rush to C. J. Ingersoll, Aug. 19, 1812, PennHS.

276   "My Red Children": JM, Address, *Letters,* II, 553–556.

276   Indian replies: JM-LC.

277   "Rolling about on the floor": Big Thunder, *ibid.*

277   "I find myself much worn down": JM to Gen. H. Dearborn, Aug. 9, 1812, *Writings,* VIII, 208.

277   "Do you not tremble": DM to EC, Aug. 31, 1812, Cutts coll., LC.

278   "Gasconading booby": R. Rush to C. J. Ingersoll, Sept. 4, 1812, PennHS.

278   "Everybody pronounced" and other information: J. Graham to Monroe, Aug. 28, Sept. 9, 1812, Monroe-LC.

278   "Weak, cowardly and imbecile": Col. J. Taylor to JM, Sept. 23, 1812, JM-LC.

278   "Twenty-five hundred troops": Gen. Isaac Brock to Gen. Sir George Prevost, Aug. 17, 1812, in Richardson, *The War of 1812,* 65. See also Hull to Eustis, Aug. 26, 1812, *ibid.,* 70–76, and (conflicting testimony) Cass to Eustis, Sept. 10, 1812, *ibid.,* 76–82.

279   "An infant Hercules": Toast offered July 4, *Intelligencer,* July 8, 1812.

280   "Pay obeisance": Mrs. Seaton, Nov. 12, 1812, in Seaton, *A Biographical Sketch,* 84.

281   "The current election": JM to TJ, Oct. 14, 1812, *Writings,* VIII, 220.

281   "My dear sir, if you must die": The Rev. D. Jones to JM, Sept. 17, 1812, Rives-LC.

281   Rush's instructions to Ingersoll: Sept. 9, 18, 1812, PennHS.

282   "Just and necessary" war: J. Adams to Dr. Benjamin Rush, July 12, 1812, Princeton University Library.

282   "The honorable and lofty conduct": Sérurier to Bassano, Nov. 28, 1812, AEU.

282   "Degradation blasting": JM, fourth Annual Message, Nov. 4, 1812, *Writings,* VIII, 230.

282   "Lord! how it will startle": N. Spear, in Brant, VI, 121.

283   The ball at Tomlinson's: Seaton, 88, 89; *Intelligencer,* Dec. 10, 1812; EC to AG, Nov. 12, to J. Gallatin, Nov. 22, 1845, NYHS; *Gallatin,* II, 610–621.

285   "Every creature that could afford": Seaton, 99. See also Sérurier to Bassano, Mar. 6, 1813, AEU; *Intelligencer,* Mar. 6, *Gazette,* Mar. 10, *Federal Republican,* Mar. 8, 12, 1813.

285   "It is to be presumed": *Intelligencer,* Mar. 9, 1813.

286   "Cause enough for war": *Ibid.,* Mar. 10, 1812, quoting Bayard.

286   "Basely betrayed" and related attacks: *Federal Republican,* Apr. 12, 14, 21, 1813.

287   "The whole column" and rest of story: *Montreal Gazette* as quoted by the *Intelligencer,* May 1, 11, 13, 1813. British Gen. Sheaffe to Gen. Prevost: "I caus'd our grand magazine to be blown up." Women's Canadian HS *Transactions,* No. 8, p. 7, in Brant, VI, 550n.

287   "Triumph of principle": William Lee to DM, Apr. [n.d.], 1813.

287   "I enclose a draft": JM to AG, Apr. 26, 1813, NYHS.

PAGE

288 "Satisfaction with all around him": DM to EC, May 13, 1813, Cutts coll., LC.

289 "The President looks better": J. Roberts to M. Roberts, May 28, 1813, PennHS.

289 "Fled from his station": *New York Post,* May 29, 1813.

290 "Cheerful spirit": DM to EC, June 10, 1813, Cutts coll., LC.

290 "The thought of his possible loss": Sérurier to Bassano, June 21, 1813, AEU.

290 "Sir, the President is old" (Thomas Grosvenor) and rest of debate: Annals of Senate, June 6–21, 1813.

290 The five resolutions requested more information about France's repeal of her Berlin and Milan decrees—chiefly, why had the decree, dated April 1811, not been reported to the Government until May 1812?

290 "Sometimes I despair!": DM to EC, July 2, 1813, Cutts coll., LC.

290 "Mrs. Madison is very handsome": E. Gerry Jr., *Diary,* entry for July 9, 1813.

291 "The agency of the Senate": GW to Senate Committee, Aug. 10, 1789, *op. cit.,* XXX, 378.

292 "Drank port wine": Gerry Jr., *Diary,* entry for July 19, 1813.

292 "Know and love the President": SC to DM, July 19, 1813, Cutts coll., LC.

293 "Mutilated the mission": JM to AG, Aug. 2, 1813, NYHS.

293 "Mr. Madison rides out": R. Rush to J. Adams, Aug. 2, 1813, *Pennsylvania Magazine of History and Biography,* LX, 442.

293 "The little booby": J. Lovett to S. Van Rensselear, July 27, 1813, in Bonney, I, 306.

293 "All . . . piously disposed": JM, proclamation, *Messages and Papers of the Presidents,* II, 517. See also Annals of House, July 30, 1813.

293 "I expect the President": J. Roberts to Elizabeth Bushby, Aug. 7, 1813, PennHS.

294 "His mind has shared": *Federal Republican,* Aug. 13, 1813.

294 "I gained strength": JM to W. Jones, Aug. 14, 1813, PennHS.

294 "I participate": JM to W. Jones, Aug. 29, 1813, *ibid.*

294 "The safe arrival": DM to HG, Aug. 30, 1813, NYHS.

294 "It has pleased the Almighty": Capt. Perry to Sec. Jones, Sept. 13, 1813, in *Intelligencer,* Sept. 23, 1813.

295 "Perry's triumph": J. Adams to R. Rush, Oct. 8, 1813, *Pennsylvania Magazine of History and Biography,* LX, 452.

295 "Game as ever": R. Rush to C. J. Ingersoll, Oct. 28, 1813, PennHS.

295 "What a puissant one!": JM, as reported by Sérurier to Bassano, Oct. 28, 1813, AEU.

296 " . . . The war, with all its vicissitudes": JM, fifth Annual Message, Dec. 7, 1813; *Writings,* VIII, 274.

296 "Vast *prison-house*": J. Randolph to R. Kidder, Feb. 15, 1814, Randolph-LC.

297 "Cares and confinements": DM to Clara Baldwin, Dec. 28, 1813, Cutts coll., LC.

297 "It is with extreme diffidence": H. Hackley to DM, Dec. 1, 1813, *ibid.*

298 "All were well": DM to HG, Jan 21, 1814, NYHS.

298 "The walls [were] entirely of amber": J. Q. Adams, *Memoir,* II, 507.

300 "I am distressed": DM to HG, May 22, 1814, NYHS.

PAGE

301 "Treat it as it deserves": JM, draft of instructions to Peace Commission, *Writings,* VIII, 280.

302 *"The President of the United States":* Mass. toast, in Brant, VI, 269.

302 "Mr. Jefferson was here": SC to DM, June 28, 1814, Cutts coll., LC.

302 "Found the coast frozen": HG to DM, July 2, 1814, L. B. Cutts, 128.

303 "Roar of broad axes": Sec. Jones to Com. T. Macdonough, July 5, 1814, NA.

303 "Tasteful simplicity": Miss Brown, diary, July 4, 1814, in Wharton, 163.

303 "Assuredly, dear Dorothy": L. B. Cutts, 123.

303 Battles of Fort Erie and Chippewa: *Intelligencer,* July 15, 20, 1814.

304 "Madison's Island": Nooaheevah Island (later France's Nukahiva in the Marquesas). Capt. D. Porter's report to Sec. Jones, *Intelligencer,* July 13, 1814.

304 "The Executive shows himself": Sérurier to Talleyrand, July 20, 1814, AEU.

304 "State of perturbation": DM to HG, July 28, 1814, NYHS.

305 "Treating with indifference": Congressional investigation of the invasion of Washington. Annals of House, XXVIII.

305 "Vigorous war": *London Courier* as quoted by *Intelligencer,* Aug. 15, 1814.

305 "I believe, Mr. Skinner": Adm. Cockburn to J. S. Skinner as reported by Skinner to JM, Aug. 13, 1814, JM-LC.

306 "The strength of the enemy": Gen. J. Armstrong to Van Ness, Nov. 23, 1814. This whole conversation is part of Van Ness's statement to the Committee which the House appointed on Sept. 23 to investigate the causes of the British success in capturing Washington. The Committee's narrative report, submitted Nov. 29, 1814, an invaluable source, was bolstered by the testimony of many government and military officials. See Annals of House, App., 1518–1738.

306 "Pelt the enemy": JM to Monroe, Aug. 21, 1814, Monroe-LC.

306 "Unnecessary alarm": J. Armstrong as reported by Clerk Stephen Pleasonton to Gen. W. Winder, Aug. 7, 1848, in Ingraham, *Sketch of the Events Which Preceded the Capture of Washington,* 48. The state papers were taken by cart to a Virginia grist mill; then, for greater safety, to an empty Leesburg house to be locked up.

XIII *WASHINGTON PUT TO THE TORCH*

PAGE

308 "Have Mr. and Mrs. Madison": B. Oden to Gen. Winder, Aug. 22, 1814, MdHS.

309 "My dearest . . . I have passed": JM to DM, Aug. 23, 1814, DM-LC, *Writings,* VIII, 293, 294.

309 "Alarming": DM to L. Todd, Aug. 23, 1814, DM-LC, Herring and Longacre, *National Portrait Gallery,* III.

310 "Chagrin": G. Minor to T. L. McKenney, Apr. 10, 1847, in Ingraham, 57. Col. Minor's letter was written to refute a statement by Armstrong's son that his father had been slandered. For an earlier statement by Minor, Oct. 30, 1814, see Williams, App., 355–357. Half of the following day Minor spent hunting for Col. Carberry to get an order for arms. They were dealt out so slowly, his militia never reached Bladensburg. It is possible that 700 or 800 fresh troops supporting Barney's artillery could have kept the British out of Washington. See also Gleig, 155–158.

PAGE

311   "With the utmost dispatch": *Ibid.*

311   "The enemy are in full march": Monroe to JM, Aug. 23, 1814, Monroe-LC; Annals of House, XXVIII, App., 1566.

312   "So be it": Gleig, 114.

312   "The moment I received it": J. Armstrong, Winder testimony, Sept. 26, 1814, Annals of House, XXVIII.

313   Preparations for dinner: Jennings, 10; Gleig, 130. Paul Jennings says he laid 40 places.

313   "The present state of alarm": E. Jones to DM, Aug. 24, 1814, Clark, 162.

314   Battle of Bladensburg: Testimony of Stansbury, Winder, Barney, Sterett, and Minor in Annals of House, XXVIII; Armstrong, II, 126–131; Williams, 205–238; Gleig, 114–123.

315   "The militia ran": Ball, 362.

315   "Lolling out a chamber window": Jennings, 10.

315   The rescue of Washington's portrait: DM to L. Todd, Aug. 24–26, 1814; Dr. G. Carroll to J. Barker [n.d.], J. Barker to C. Carroll, Feb. 11, De Peyster to DM, Feb. 3, DM to De Peyster, Feb. 4, 1848, in Clark, 404–407. Anna Maria Thornton (diary) says Stuart denied that he had painted the portrait in the White House; he "bargained for it."—farmed it out.

317   "So justly admired": DM to M. Latrobe, Clark, 166.

317   "Mrs. Madison in her carriage": Miss Brown, diary, in Wharton, 171. Miss Brown was visiting the family of Benjamin Homans, Chief Clerk, State Department.

318   "It was then, my Lord": Sérurier to Talleyrand, Aug. 27, 1814, AEU.

319   "Madam, as safe": Matilda Lee Love's "Recollections," in Casenove Gardner Lee, *Lee Chronicle,* 291.

319   "No drawingroom": Smith, 111.

319   "I have never beheld": Sérurier to Talleyrand, Aug. 27, 1814, AEU.

320   "Pleasantries too vulgar": Smith, 112.

320   The conflagrations in Washington: Gleig, 130–132.

320   "I have indeed, to this hour": R. Rush to John S. Williams, July 10, 1855, in Williams, 274, 275.

321   "Mighty cataract" and other details of the storm: Gleig, 141, 142.

321   "Miz' Madison!": Jennings, 13. Paul says "Miss," but all commentators, knowing he is attempting a phonetic representation, have corrected it to "Miz'."

321   "The Government papers" and the storm: Miss Brown, diary, in Wharton, 174, 175.

321   "Damn it! my pocket's full": Gen. R. Ross, Cockburn-LC; Lord, 170.

322   The white brood mare: H. Adams, *History of the United States,* VIII, 147.

322   "Most tremendous hurricane": Gleig, 136.

322   "Our column was completely": *Ibid.,* 142. See also Anna Maria Thornton, diary, Aug. 25, 1814, LC.

323   "Novel and interesting": Smith, 107.

324   "Disagreeable effect": JM to DM, Aug. 28, 1814, JM-LC, in Clark, 172.

324   "I lent Mr. M.": A. M. Thornton, diary, Aug. 28, 1814, LC.

325   "Mrs. M. seemed much depressed": Smith, 110.

PAGE

325 "Very violent": A. M. Thornton, diary, Aug. 28, 1814, LC.

325 Ross in disguise: Clark, 169 n.

325 "Little Jemmy . . . procured": *Federal Republican,* Sept. 8, 1814.

326 "Our good President": J. Barnes to TJ, Aug. 29, 1814, UVa.

326 "Willing cause": Williams (who questions the adjective), 105. See also McKenney, I, 44–46; JM, memorandum of confrontation, Aug. 29, 1814, JM-LC, *Writings,* VIII, 300–304.

326 "You cannot be unaware": JM, memorandum of discussion with Armstrong, Aug. 29, 1814, JM-LC; *Writings,* VIII, 301. Part of the conversation has been changed from indirect to direct discourse.

327 "Impulse so vile": J. Armstrong, letter to *Baltimore Patriot,* Sept. 5, 1814, Ingraham, 59.

327 "FALSE": Hanson in *Federal Republican,* Sept. 8, 1814.

327 "With much cunning": E. Jones to A. Dallas, Sept. 15, 1814, PennHS.

328 "Pirates' nest": So called by the British.

328 "Ceases to throb": R. L. Madison to DM, July 15, 1813, NYPL.

328 "Sir, do you seize": W. Irving, *op. cit.,* I, 311.

329 "Retaliation": Vice Adm. Cochrane to Monroe, dated Aug. 18 but posted later, and received Aug. 31, 1814, *Intelligencer,* Sept. 10, 1814; ASP, Foreign Relations, III, 693.

329 "Deep-rooted hostility": Monroe to Cochrane, Sept. 6, 1814, *ibid.,* 693. See also Cochrane's retort, *ibid.,* 694.

329 "Object of the expedition": Gen. Ross to Bathurst, Aug. 30, 1814, FO 5.

329 "Until I receive instructions": Cochrane to Monroe, Sept. 19, 1814, *Intelligencer,* Sept. 27, 1814; ASP, III, 694.

329 "Burn their houses": Gleig, 324.

330 "Not pleased," A. M. Thornton, diary, August 28, 1814, LC.

330 Thornton controversy: Clark, 177; "Dr. and Mrs. William Thornton," ColumbiaHS, *Records,* XVIII, 188; Clark, 177.

330 "The Bladensburg Races," Clark, 178–184.

331 "Little did I think, sir": Smith, 17.

332 "Rolling back upon the foe": On Sept. 15, 1814, an editorial in the *Intelligencer* had exhorted the nation to roll back upon this foe the storm of war. The next day it printed details of the victory at Baltimore.

332 "O say can you see": The *Baltimore Patriot* published the *Star-Spangled Banner* anonymously. Reprinting it Sept. 28, 1814, the *Intelligencer* praised the author's principles and talents.

XIV *THE OCTAGON, AND TREATY OF GHENT*

PAGE

333 The "Annex": The Octagon House, furnished in 18th century style, is now the national headquarters of the American Institute of Architects. The round table on which the Treaty of Ghent was signed and the Treaty room's chairs and settee, stand

in their old places. The brick-walled tunnel stretching twenty feet beyond the brick-floored kitchen (with its huge fireplace and ovens) was probably started when a return call by the British, who had vowed to "take the President," seemed a distinct possibility. Or it could have been started for Turreau. Jefferson had once built an escape tunnel at Monticello (1781) against a similar threat.

334   "Mr. Magruder": Tayloe, 99.

334   "Permit me . . . to urge": AG to P. Todd, July 26, 1814, NYHS.

335   "The very bounded confidence": P. Todd to AG, Aug, 3, 1814, NYHS. See also AG to Crawford, July 26, 1814, Crawford Papers, LC, and Crawford to AG, Aug. 4, 1814, NYHS.

335   "Was mysteriously abducted": Mary Kunkel, memorandum, Hist. Museum, Greensboro. Mary Kunkel was the daughter of Annie Payne Causten, DM's niece, "adopted daughter," companion for last sixteen years, and confidante.

335   "If the English force us": JM's words so struck Roth he quoted them two years later (May 5, 1816) to Richelieu, AEU.

336   "Radical reform": committee report signed by H. G. Otis and submitted to Gov. Caleb Strong of Mass., *Intelligencer,* Oct. 22, 1814.

336   "He looks miserably shattered": Wirt to wife, Oct. 14, 1814, MdHS.

337   " . . . It is a just matter": Sérurier to Talleyrand, Nov. 5, 1814, AEU.

337   "You are not mistaken": JM to Gov. Nicholas, Nov. 26, 1814, *Writings,* VIII, 319.

337   "Never, my dear Anna": L. Todd to A. Cutts, Aug. 27, 1814, Cutts coll., LC.

338   "Dear Papa": P. Todd to JM, Oct. 9, 1814, from Ghent, NYPL.

339   "Quietly asleep": *Federal Republican,* Dec. 9, 1814, quoting *Winchester Gazette.*

339   "All I can say is": J. Adams to JM, Nov. 28, 1814, *Life and Works,* X, 106.

339   "House where Mr. Latrobe's": DM to M. Latrobe, Dec. 3, 1814, Clark, 166.

340   Hartford Convention: For its resolutions, see *Intelligencer,* Jan. 12, 1815.

340   "English navigation": JM, outline (Rives-LC) put into the hands of Alexander Dallas to be fleshed out. The brochure (UVa) was printed anonymously as "Notes on the Causes of the War," Dec. 1814.

340   "My spirits": HG to DM, Jan. 18, 1815, UVa.

341   "Free and open": Tichnor, I, 29.

341   "Base thraldom": *Boston Yankee,* Jan. 12, 1815.

342   "This man if he deserves": *Federal Republican,* Feb. 1, 1815.

342   Battle of New Orleans: Jackson to Monroe, Jan. 13, 1815 (the dispatch of Jan. 9 had described only the opening of the battle), Jackson-LC; Gleig, 323–327; Latour, *Historical Memoir,* 154–164; Lambert's report, James, *Military Occurrences,* II, Appendix, 96.

343   Pardon of the pirates: Their "sincere penitence" was short-lived. Within six months JM would have to send a naval force to stop renewed stealing and smuggling.

343   "As pleased as any": Jennings, 16.

344   "The observed of all observers": Goodwin, 186.

344   "Peace! Peace!": Jennings, 15.

344   "And such another joyful time": *Ibid.,* 16.

PAGE

345 "Feby 11. Saturday. Rockets": A. M. Thornton, diary, LC.

345 "Shook in his shoes": H. G. Otis to wife, Feb. 22, 1815, MassHS.

345 "To the Commander-in-Chief" and other toasts: *Intelligencer,* Mar. 18, 22, 24, 27, 1815.

345 "The glad tidings": Sen. W. T. Barry to wife, Feb. 24, 1815, WMQ, XIII, 237.

345 "Stood the contest": J Story to N. Williams, Feb. 22, 1815, in W. W. Story, I, 254.

346 "Given the Americans": Sérurier to Talleyrand, Feb. 21, 1815, AEU.

346 "If our first struggle": JM to Ingersoll, Jan. 4, 1818, PennHS.

346 "Any peace": *London Times,* Dec, 6, 1814.

346 "Russia or Prussia": *Ibid.,* Dec. 30, 1814.

XV *PRODIGAL SON*

PAGE

348 "Ever since the peace": DM to HG, Mar. 5, 1815, NYHS.

348 The Jackson-Hall controversy: Claiborne to JM, Feb. 24, 1815, JM-LC; Sec. Dallas to Gen. Jackson, Apr. 12, July 1; Jackson to Dallas, May 23; Ingersoll, II, 248–260; *Jackson* (Bassett), II, 203–210; *Intelligencer,* Apr. 27, 1815.

349 "Liberality proportioned": JM to Dallas, May 17, 1815, JM-LC.

349 "Certain sight": SC to DM, May 18, 1815, Cutts coll., LC.

350 "Dear voyagers": DM to HG, July 29, 1813, NYHS.

350 The Dartmoor prisoners: When a crowd of the Americans pressed against a wall to see why a British drummer was beating a call to arms, the gate collapsed. Gunfire and bayonets killed seven.

351 "I am so miserable": DM to HG, Aug. 7, 1815, NYHS.

351 "Every vestige": Monroe to JM, Aug. 10, 1815, Rives-LC.

351 "We are all perfectly well": P. Todd as quoted by DM to HG, Aug. 12, 1815, NYHS.

351 "Had just time to bless": B. Crowninshield to JM, Aug. 14, 1815, JM-LC.

352 "It gives me extreme sorrow": P. Todd to R. Cutts, June 8, 1815, DM-LC.

352 Todd's account with Baring Brothers: From Apr. 28, 1814, to May 9, 1815, NYHS.

352 Todd's art purchases: Mary E. E. Cutts says (memoir, Cutts coll., LC), "He spent lavishly in a refined taste; he purchased many gems of art and printings which for nearly half a century adorned Montpelier." His fragmentary journal (LC)—amid much which condemns him—bears some witness to a love of nature and art.

352 Todd's *Brevet d'Invention:* NYPL. Endorsed on the back as issued in "Paris 1816" for J. P. Todd of Ghent.

353 "You will find Todd": AG to JM, Sept. 4, 1815, NYHS.

353 Payne Todd's Paris experience: J. Q. Adams, *Memoirs,* III, 151–191.

354 "The tendency to dissipation": *Ibid.,* II, 154.

354 "It's surprising!": J. Q. Adams as quoted by Mary E. E. Cutts, memoir, Cutts coll., LC.

354 "Not unprepared": JM to AG, Sept. 11, 1815, NYHS.

355 "The most perfect beatitude": SC to DM, Oct. 16, 1815, Cutts coll., LC.

PAGE

355 "At the mouth of the cannon": Com. S. Decatur to Crowninshield, July 5, 1815, ASP, Naval, I, 396.

356 Payne's special French cheeses: Article, *Washington Post,* Jan. 26, 1900. The author had information from the Cutts family.

356 "She tells me to say she loves you": Wharton, 155.

356 "Enchanting circle": SC to DM, Oct. 16, 1815, Cutts coll., LC.

357 "This bird's brilliant plumage": William W. Birth, in Clark, 198.

357 "A nobler project": *Intelligencer,* Oct. 10, 1815.

357 "Very agreeably": M. Crowninshield, Nov. 11, 1815, *op. cit.,* 15–17.

358 Seventh Annual Message to Congress: JM, Dec. 5, 1815, *Writings,* VIII, 335–344.

358 "Federalists and Republicans": Sérurier to Richelieu, Dec. 21, 1815, AEU.

359 "Oh, Mrs. Crowninshield" and rest of the description: Crowninshield, 23–26.

359 "We had quite a frolic": *Ibid.,* 30.

359 "Embroidered all over": *Ibid.,* 35.

360 The "squeeze" of Feb. 1816: Crowninshield, 35, 36; Cutts, 139, 140.

361 DM's still extant clothes: the beige inaugural gown is in the old Smithsonian building in Washington; her Todd wedding dress, panels from her Madison wedding dress, bridal crown, satin slippers, rose-red Empire gown, negligee, wrapper, fan and parasol in His. Museum, Greensboro.

361 "Looked brilliant": Crowninshield, 57, 58.

361 "Little fantastical ribbon": DM to A. Cutts, fragment, n.d., Cutts coll., LC.

362 "All the Enniscorthians": SC to DM, Oct. 16, 1815, Cutts coll., LC.

362 "Very handsome": Crowninshield, 66.

362 The Koslov affair: Daschkov to R. Rush, Mar. 4, 1816, Princeton University Library; Dallas to JM, June 27, JM-LC; Monroe to JM, June 29, 1816, Rives-LC.

363 "Everyone was there": Seaton, 133.

363 "War or tribute": JM to Monroe, June 25, 1816, JM-LC.

363 "Cornishes": DM to HG, May 1816, NYHS. See also HG to DM, June 2, 1816, UVa.

363 "The government . . . moves": Roth to Richelieu, May 5, 1816, AEU.

364 "Perhaps you wouldn't mind": L. B. Cutts, 141.

364 "My dear Anna, we got home": DM to Anna Cutts, n.d. [about June 9], 1816, Cutts coll., LC. The letter is dated by the Madisons' June 5 departure or their three-day trip to Orange, and the Paynes' "fine little girl." Dolley's namesake was two months old.

364 "His name will descend": Oration of Benjamin L. Lear, *Intelligencer,* July 9, 1816.

365 "Imbecile tyrant": Hyde de Neuville to Monroe, July 21, Monroe to Hyde de Neuville, Aug. 15, 1816, NA.

365 "Blustering deportment": JM to Monroe, July 29, 1816, JM-LC.

365 "So well fixed": R. Rush to JM, Sept. 17, to Ingersoll, Oct. 9, 1816, PennHS.

365 "New lights": Montlezun, *Voyage de New-Yorck,* 52 *et seq.* See also Montlezun to JM [Sept. 16], 1816, JM-LC.

366 "In spite of all that rumor": SC to DM, Oct. 16, 1815, Cutts coll., LC.

366 "Our friend Todd": C. Hughes to AG, Dec. 13, 1816, NYHS.

PAGE

366   "Mere desert": Halleck, *Life and Letters,* 170.

367   "His Excellency was . . . ill": *Ibid.,* 172.

367   JM, eighth Annual Message to Congress, Dec. 3, 1816, *Writings,* VIII, 375–385.

367   "Last act of one of the purest": Att. Gen. Rush, of JM, in Brant, VI, 412, 413.

367   "The American Society": See P. J. Staudenraus, *The African Colonization Movement,* 1816–1865.

368   J. Randolph, "Sincerely wished," and other tributes: Annals of House, Feb. 4–9, 1817.

368   "To be praised": Dallas to Rush, Dec. 7, 1816, Rives-LC. See also Dallas to JM, Dec. 5, 1816; *Dallas,* 480–482.

368   "It used to be a joke": Lt. Francis Hall, *Travels,* 198.

369   "Or rather his lady": *Ibid.,* 200.

369   "Exalted talents": Monroe, first Inaugural Address, Mar. 4, 1817, *Writings of Monroe* (Hamilton), VI, 14.

369   "My dear Friend . . . Eight years": Eliza Collins Lee to DM, Mar. 4, 1817, Cutts coll., LC.

370   "Untarnished glory": Mayor James H. Blake, *Intelligencer,* Mar. 10, 1817.

XVI *ADAM AND EVE IN PARADISE*

PAGE

371   "Executed on white velvet": M. Cutts, memoir, Cutts coll., LC.

371   " . . . If ever man rejoiced": J. K. Paulding, sketch of JM, Rives-LC.

372   Payne just after JM's retirement: Harriet Taylor Upton (p. 525) says that, for six months following Madison's retirement, Payne acted as Monroe's private secretary; and that he ran for the Virginia Assembly but was defeated. I have found no primary source or corroborating evidence for the statement. If true, the political defeat would help to explain his growing cynicism and temptation to gamble and drink heavily.

372   "I am almost in despair": L. Todd to A. Cutts, May 11, 1817, Cutts coll., LC.

372   "My beloved friend": Eliza Lee to DM, June 29, 1817, DM-LC. Later the Wood portrait would come into the hands of John Washington Davidge, a Lee connection.

373   "Man of wit": Paulding, *op. cit.*

375   "Whereupon the Lodge": Minutes of Lodge No. 9, Charlottesville, in Denslow, 49.

376   "They were extremely": Jennings, 19.

376   Albemarle Agricultural Society: the five participating counties were Albemarle, Fluvanna, Louisa, Nelson and Orange.

376   "Tom ! squirrels": Albemarle County tradition.

376   "Lover of fun": M. Cutts, memoir, Cutts coll., LC.

376   "Something from my daughter": SC to DM, Nov. 5, 1817, Cutts coll., LC.

377   JM's list of his contributions to *The Federalist Papers:* First published in *City of Washington Gazette,* Dec. 8, 1817. See J. Gideon to JM, Jan 19, Feb. 12, JM to Gideon, Jan. 28, Feb. 20, 1818, JM-LC.

377   JM's inaugural address to the Agricultural Society: Delivered May 12, 1818; printed in N.Y. as pamphlet, UVa.

PAGE

378   The Rockfish Gap meeting: Wood, *Albemarle County,* 91, 92.

380   "To wit, beginning at a white oak": Orange County Record Office.

381   "Jonathan and Mary Bull": JM, *Writings,* IX, 77.

381   "Consideration bordering upon indulgence": M. Kunkel, notes, Hist. Museum, Greensboro, Mary E. E. Cutts gives the same testimony (Cutts coll., LC): "a kind and indulgent master."

382   "They traveled . . . with carriages": Capt. Edmund Bacon in Goodwin, 223, 224.

382   "What is the largest": Dr. Robley Dunglison's memorandum, S. N. Randolph, 403.

382   "Everything that came beneath her": Unnamed visitor quoted by M. Cutts, memoir, Cutts coll., LC.

382   "My beloved friend, . . . Do you know?": Eliza Lee to DM, Mar. 30, 1819, from Washington, DM-LC. Richard Bland Lee was now Judge of the D. C. Orphan's Court.

383   " . . . The first step": JM to EC, Sept. 3, 1819, postscript by DM, dated Sept. 5, Cutts coll., LC.

384   "No, no, not that way": Upton, 203.

384   "For two days": George Divers to JM, n.d. [Oct. 1819], Cutts coll., LC.

385   "Renovating": Ellen Randolph to DM, Oct. 15, 1819, *ibid.,* LC.

385   "Gaiety and fashion": Phoebe Morris to DM, Mar. 22, 1820, DM-LC.

385   Dolley's choice of Phoebe for daughter-in-law: Wharton, 155; Clark, 211.

386   "Daily expectation": A. Morris to DM, July 14, 1820, Clark, 213.

386   "Dearest Mrs. Madison": Phoebe Morris to DM, July 15, 1820, *ibid.,* 214.

387   The unidentified portrait: This large undated oil painting of a fashionable gentleman by Charles Bird King, in the Kunkel collection at the Greensboro Historical Museum, matches one of Annie Payne by the same artist, and has been thought by some to represent Dr. James H. Causten Jr., whom Annie married after Dolley's death. That may be so. But the argument that the artist painted them the same size and in the same style because at the same time, and because his sitters belonged to the same family, would apply equally to a pair of paintings depicting Payne and Annie. And Dr. Causten does not seem to have been a dandy. In any case, the attitude of the rather nonchalant gentleman symbolizes Payne Todd in his role as man-about-town, man-in-society. Unfortunately a recorded terracotta bust of Payne has been lost or destroyed. The one uncontroversial portrait of him was painted on his return from Europe, at 24, by Wood. A picture by Kurtz, based on this miniature, shows a handsome youth with fine eyes and a weak mouth.

XVII *LAFAYETTE, JEFFERSON, AND A GOLD-HEADED CANE*

PAGE

389   "Extreme incorrectness": JM to J. Gales, Aug. 26, 1821, LC, *Writings,* IX, 69. A later accusation that, at times, JM made a spurious copy of his original notes is refuted by watermarks.

390   "I was glad to receive": DM to son, May 24, 1821, Clark, 215.

390   "Errors like straws": M. Cutts, memoir, Cutts coll., LC.

390   "I was highly flattered": Martha Randolph to DM, Sept. 8, 1820, Cutts coll., LC.

390   "Entirely covered with mirrors": M. Cutts, memoir, *ibid.*—source for the detailed description of Montpelier after JM's retirement which follows. The marble relief of JM was by Guiseppi Ceracchi, guillotined in 1801 for complicity in a plot to kill Napoleon.

392   The "temple" or gazebo over the icehouse: A copy of the Temple of Venus at Versailles.

393   JM's cabinetry: All the tools in his small portable chest fitted into one handle.

393   The death of little Fanny Stevenson: Sept. 23, 1822, Coles, 124. Ellen Randolph to DM (n.d., Cutts coll., LC): "It curdles my blood to hear the tale."

393   "Can I ever forget": SCS to DM, July 26, 1836, UVa.

394   "I am impatient": DM to son, Apr. 9, 1823, Clark, 215.

394   "That the true interest": JM in CC, resolution against foreign entanglements, Sept. 12, 1783.

394   "I thought of no other person": J. Q. Adams, Nov. 15, 1823, *Memoirs,* VI, 187.

395   "Partisans of despotism": JM to Monroe, Apr. 13, 1824, JM-LC.

395   "May you make for yourself": DM to W. Cutts, Nov. 21, 1823, Cutts coll., LC.

395   "I often think of you": Phoebe Morris to DM, Jan. 19, 1824, *ibid.*

396   "Secret": DM to R. Cutts, n.d., *ibid.* See also Cutts's promissory note of Apr. 1, 1817, JM-LC: also Payne Todd's statement (DM-LC) that his mother, unknown to him, allowed Cutts to use her son's money—without security—on his promise to double it. Cutts's near-bankruptcy struck just after JM had lost a large sum through failure of the Swift Run Turnpike Company, and liquidation of the James Madison and Company organized by neighbors to promote better roads. When he approached the Bank of the U.S. for a $6000 loan, it was no longer lending money on real estate.

397   "Others of her kindred": Agreement of June 17, 1824, Cutts coll., LC.

397   "Between $5,000 and $6,000": JM's memorandum, JM-LC.

397   "Bonafide and absolute property": JM to Thornton, Sept. 9, 1824, JM-LC.

397   Miss Anne Cole: Mrs. Goodwin (212, 213), who had sources within the Madison-Cutts family, says, "His mother ardently desired him to marry; but he showed no sign of any such intention; though he did have the grace to fall honestly and respectably in love with the beautiful Anne Cole, a Williamsburg belle, who was hard-hearted or far-sighted enough to decline his suit. . . ."

397   "I this instant learn": JM to Lafayette, Aug. 21, 1824, in Clark, 221. In 1820 each had invited the other to discuss farm problems at his home.

398   "Ah, Jefferson" and the rest of the scene as remembered by TJ's grandson Thomas Jefferson Randolph: S. N. Randolph, *op. cit.,* 390, 391.

399   "My old friend embraced me": JM to DM, n.d., [Nov. 5, 1824], *Writings,* IX, 208–210. See also Levasseur, I, 447; *Richmond Enquirer,* Nov. 9, 12, 16, 1824.

399   "Happy the people": This and other toasts by JM, JM-LC; Levasseur, I, 477; Bruce, II, 331.

399   "Well-preserved frame" and other details of visit to Orange: *Ibid.,* 481, 482, 500, 501. See also M. Cutts, memoir, Cutts coll., LC.

400   "He hears in joyous youth": Entry in Mrs. James J. Roosevelt's album, Apr. 25, 1848, Clark, 417.

PAGE

400 "To love liberty" and other toasts and JM's speech: *Richmond Enquirer,* Nov. 30, 1824.

401 "Nimbly": Levasseur, I, 481. The English version translates *lestement* (I, 501) "with activity."

401 "Mounted on a hobby": TJ to J. Adams, Oct. 12, 1823, in S. N. Randolph, *op. cit.,* 387, 388.

402 "But, my dear son": DM to son, Dec. 2, 1824, in Clark, 217.

403 *"Stare hic":* Tichnor to George Bancroft, Dec. 26, 1824, MassHS; Curtis, I, 223, 224. After the two men returned to Washington, Webster told Tichnor that the visit had confirmed his long-held opinion that Mr. Madison was "the wisest of our Presidents except Washington."

404 "My poor boy": L. B. Cutts, 207.

405 " . . . My sweetest of daughters!": DM to M. Cutts, Jan. 22, 1825, Cutts coll., LC.

405 Transportation to the University: A little later many students used passenger flatboats ("packets") on the James River and Kanawha Canal as far as Scottsville, then posted overland.

406 "My friends, I am old": Bruce, II, 298–301.

408 "Down with the European professors!": *Ibid.,* 298.

409 "My dear P.": JM to Todd, Nov. 13, 1825, JM-LC.

410 "I cannot express": DM to SCS, n.d. [early] 1826, Cutts coll., LC.

410 "But why afflict you": TJ to JM, Feb. 17, 1826, TJ-LC, *Writings of TJ* (Ford), X, 377.

411 "The fullest return": JM to TJ, Feb. 24, 1826, JM-LC, *Writings,* IX, 246.

412 "I now hasten": JM to stepson (shorthand draft), Apr. 26, 1826, JM-LC.

412 "Arrest and imprisonment": R. Bache to JM, June 4 [1826], UVa.

413 "Warn the Committee of Safety!" and other details of TJ's death: S. N. Randolph, 365–370. See also Dr. R. Dunglison to JM, July 1, 1826. Doubtless all the circumstances were revealed to the Madisons by Dr. Dunglison when he visited Montpelier soon after TJ's death.

413 "I never doubted": JM to N. Trist, July 6, 1826, JM-LC, *Writings,* IX, 248.

XVIII *"LET THE WORST BE KNOWN"*

PAGE

414 "Kiss my little son": DM to D. Cutts, July 30, 1826, Cutts coll., LC.

415 Payne Todd's journal: Kept sporadically from June 4, 1844, to the summer of 1847, this broken record refers, among other things, to the making and breaking of resolutions to be decisive ("Lethargy"), and sexual derelictions (partly in code). It also refers fragmentarily to crops, sales of slaves, quarrying of marble, handling of JM papers, occasional remittances of money to his increasingly indigent mother, snarl of lawsuits, indigestion, fears about gonorrhea, purchases of food and liquor, visitors to Toddsberth (some disreputable), and occasional appreciations of beauty: " . . . I look at the beautiful prints," "The sun today shining silverly through the clouds."

415 "Decision, my darling Mary": DM to M. Cutts, Aug. 15, 1826, Cutts coll., LC.

415 "Richard Cutts, Tobacco Planter": JM to young Richard D. Cutts, n.d., *ibid.*

PAGE

415 "I thank you, my kind friend": DM to T. McKenney, Nov. 17, 1826, *ibid.*

416 JM's letters to DM from the University: Dec. 4, 14, 1826, NYPL.

417 "Fatal to everything": JM to EC, Feb. 23, 1827, Princeton University Library.

418 "Folly. . . . Always a dreamer": DM to A. Cutts, Apr. 23, 1827, Cutts coll., LC.

418 "If General Washington": Ingersoll toast, Oct. 26, 1827, at a dinner given by Pennsylvania manufacturers for the German economist Friederick List, *Philadelphia Advertiser,* Nov. 9, 1827. See also Ingersoll to JM, Nov. 9, 1827, Rives-LC.

419 "My beloved, I trust": Goodwin, 243, 244.

419 "Every letter you consign": Trist to JM, Jan. 18, 1828, VaHS.

419 "Mr. Madison, I think": *Richmond Enquirer,* July 18, 1828.

420 "I reclined at my ease" and other details of the Smith visit: Smith, 233–237.

421 "Well, while I'm delighted": JM to Dr. R. Dunglison, in S. N. Randolph, 403.

421 University problems: Wood, 93, 94; Bruce, II, 276.

422 "Spoils System": See JM to EC, Aug. 29, 1834, in which he "agree[s] with the odium," *Letters,* IV, 357.

423 "Renowned logician's" ignorance: Trist to JM, from Washington, Feb. 21, 1829, VaHS.

423 "Le règne du Néros": Trist to JM, Mar., n.d., 1829, *ibid.*

423 " . . . My dear sister. . . . I'm . . . afraid": DM to A. Cutts, May 18 [1829], UVa.

424 "Cracker and dried fig": Trist to JM, May 20, 1829, *ibid.*

424 "Must certainly have lost": DM to A. Cutts, June 6, 1829, Cutts coll., LC.

425 "Ruinous sacrifice": JM to R. Cutts, June 13, 1829, *ibid.*

426 "The cause of Christ": JM to Bradford, Sept. 25, 1773, Bradford Letterbook, PennHS.

426 "Mr. Madison, although no sectarian": M. Cutts, memoir, Cutts coll., LC. See also, for JM's religion, Bishop Meade, I, 50n, II, 99, 101.

427 "Accept my wishes": Trist to JM, June 13, 1829, VaHS.

XIX *THE LAST GREAT FIGHT*

PAGE

428 Neighborhood activities: Slaughter, 75–77; M. Cutts, memoir, Cutts coll., LC.

429 "Gallant bearing": Grigsby, "The Virginia Convention of 1776," 83.

430 "Fatuity," "treason," and other details of the Convention's early weeks: *Richmond Enquirer,* Oct. 15, 17, 20, 22, 1829; Grigsby, diary, Oct. 16, 17, Nov. 3, 10, 11, 1829, VaHS; JM, *Writings,* IX, 358n.

430 JM's social life in Richmond: Grigsby, "The Virigina Convention of 1829–1830," a "Discourse Delivered before the VaHS," Dec. 15, 1853; sketch of JM, *VMHB,* vol. 61, no. 1, Jan. 1853; Thomas Green, diary, Oct. 2–Jan. 15, 1829, VaHS.

430 "A keen vigorous countenance" and the rest of the description: Anne Royall, *Southern Tour,* I, 35–38.

430 "Third person": Grigsby, *The Virginia Convention of 1829,* Oct. 18, 19; *Richmond Enquirer,* Nov. 7, 1829.

431 "No sooner was he upon his feet": *Richmond Enquirer,* Dec. 3, 1829.

431 JM's speech: *Writings,* IX, 358–364. See also Grigsby, *The Virginia Convention of 1829,* and JM's memorandum on the question of suffrage, *ibid.,* 358n–360n.

431 Catlin's painting: VaHS. Grigsby (*Virginia Convention of 1776,* 84) calls the portrait "admirable."

431 "Level their mountains": J. A. G. Davis to Trist, Dec. 15, 1829, Trist-LC. See also Nowell to Jesse B. Harrison, Jan. 12, 1830, Harrison-LC. The discord between eastern and western Virginia over the 5/3 basis foretold the future breaking-away of West Virginia.

432 The "ruffian" driver and other details of Mrs. Royall's visit: A. Royall, *op. cit.,* 41, 42. In Washington, Mrs. Royall had been convicted in open court of being a "common scold." If Dolley knew this, it did not stop her from being gracious.

433 "I could scarcely refrain": Grigsby, diary, Jan. 15, 1830, VaHS. See also *Richmond Enquirer,* Jan. 9, 14, 1830; JM, Autobiography, *WMQ,* Apr. 1845, 208.

433 "My dear brother": DM to John C. Payne, Jan. 15, 1830, Cutts coll., LC.

433 "No man seemed more to enjoy": J. Sparks, "After-Dinner Anecdotes of James Madison: Excerpts from Jared Sparks' Journal for 1829–1831," VMHB, LX, 255–265.

434 "Which deserves to last," and rest of debate: *Register of Debates in Congress* (Senate), VI, Jan. 25, 1830.

434 "Anarchical principle": JM to EC, Aug. 29, 1832, *Letters,* IV, 351. See also JM to Trist, Dec. [n.d.] 1831.

434 "Putting powder under the Constitution": *Ibid.,* 357.

435 "But what is to be expected": Trist to JM, May 29, 1830, VaHS.

435 "Mammoth . . . treading the cane brake": Trist to JM, Feb. 6, 1830, *ibid.*

435 "Distinguished champion": JM to D. Webster, May 27, 1830, *Letters,* IV, 85. See also JM to Hayne, Apr. 3–4 (*Writings,* IX, 383n–394n); to Everett, Apr. 8, 17, Aug. 20, 28, Sept. 10, 1830 (*Letters,* IV, 69, 72, 95, 106, 109); to M. L. Hurlbut, discussing the general welfare clause and rules for interpreting the Constitution, "May" 1830 (*ibid.,* 73–76).

435 "From a failure to distinguish": JM to E. Livingston, May 8, 1830, *ibid.,* 80.

435 "Decide the fate": Trist to JM, Mar. 7, 1830, VaHS. See also JM to Trist, June 3, Sept. 23, 1830, *Letters,* IV, 87, 110.

435 "Arrest the deadly poison": *Richmond Whig,* May 21, 1830.

435 "The most alarming": J. C. Cabell to JM, May 26, 1830, JM-LC.

436 "It is clear as the light": Hurlbut to JM, Apr. 25, 1830, JM-LC. See also JM to Hurlbut, May, n.d., *Writings,* IX, 370–375; *Charleston Courier,* June 9, 1830.

436 "Imagine if you can": DM to D. Cutts, Mar. 10, 1830, Cutts coll., LC.

436 "Expect great things": DM to Richard D. Cutts, Mar. 12, 1830, *ibid.*

437 "Dear Madam, I have to mention": A Morris to A. Cutts, May 19, 1830, Clark, 239.

438 "Much in the fidgets": JM to J. C. Cabell, Sept. 12, 1830, JM-LC.

438 "Unclouded intellect": EC to JM, Nov. 4, 1830, *WMQ,* 2nd series, VII, 35. See also *North American Review,* Oct. 1830.

438 "As great as ever was produced": Cabell to JM, Oct. 28, 1830, JM-LC.

438   JM's "luminous" argument: *Richmond Enquirer,* Oct. 15, 1830.

438   "Madison . . . is himself": J. Marshall to J. Story, Oct. 15, 1830, MassHS, *Proceedings,* 34.

438   "I find you have no idea": DM to D. Cutts, Nov., n.d., 1830 (copy), Cutts coll., LC.

439   "Each end of which flaunts": Sally, Marquioness de Casa Yrujo, to DM, Nov. 10, 1830, *ibid.* For death of Sally's son, *Intelligencer,* Dec. 28, 1855, copying a Madrid paper.

439   "Oppressed heart": DM to M. Cutts, Jan. 5, 1831, Cutts coll., LC.

439   "A thousand times more": DM to D. Cutts, Feb. 2, 1831, *ibid.*

440   Lucy's sons turning yellow: a descendant, John Washington, to the author.

441   "A stand, a *noble* stand": Smith, 288.

441   "My sweet Mary": DM to M. Cutts, n.d. [spring], 1831, Cutts coll., LC.

441   "Poisonous root": JM to J. C. Cabell, Sept. 16, 1831, *Letters,* IV, 196.

442   "It is remarkable": JM to Trist, Sept. 23, 1831, Trist-LC.

442   "I am grieved": DM to M. Cutts, Sept. 16, 1831, Cutts coll., LC.

443   "In my last I informed you": DM to D. Cutts, Dec. [n.d.], 1831, *ibid.*

444   "Fixed in their hot opinions": JM, autobiographical sketch written for Paulding, Jan. 1832, *WMQ,* Apr. 1845. See also Paulding to J. P. Todd, May 24, 1837, UVa.

444   "Dear sir . . . I regret": JM to R. Cutts, Jan. 23, 1832, Cutts coll., LC.

444   "We will combine": DM to F. Lear, Feb. 14, 1832, *ibid.*

444   "Our peas are green": DM to EC, Mar. 6, 1832, *ibid.*

445   "Very devil": Trist to JM, May 8, 1832, VaHS.

445   JM's three diseases: "His habitual cheerfulness was the more remarkable as Dr. Grymes, his physician, told me that to his knowledge Mr. Madison had been twenty years afflicted by three diseases, any one of which might at any moment have carried him off." "Autobiography of George Tucker," 1775–1861, Bermuda Historical Quarterly, Autumn and Winter, 1961, vol. 15, nos. 3, 4, p. 142.

445   "Nullify of their own authority": TJ, Kentucky Resolutions, *Writings of TJ* (Bergh), XVII, 386. Ford prints TJ's rough draft, a fair copy, and the text as actually moved by Breckenridge in the Kentucky legislature.

445   "Allowances ought . . . to be made": JM to Trist (dictated), "May," 1832, *Letters,* IV, 218.

446   "If there be one": J. Q. Adams to A. Stevenson, July 11, in *Intelligencer,* July 12, 1832.

447   "Yours, dearest, came safe": DM to son, July 20, 1832, Cutts coll., LC.

447   "Beloved Sister": DM to A. Cutts, Aug. 6, 1832, *ibid.*

448   "Dear Brother, the heart": DM to R. Cutts, Aug. 16, 1832, *ibid.*

448   "She would have parted": DM, draft of obituary of Anna, enclosed in above, *ibid.*

448   "A deep awakening": Bishop Meade, *op. cit.,* 50, 99, 100.

449   Mr. Featherstonhaugh: Mary E. E. Cutts, memoir, Cutts coll., LC. She records a long poem "Montpelier" written by Featherstonhaugh in Sept. 1832. Extracts: "Perhaps this is the last/of all this excellence." "Never two purer hearts." "Each day she lives/but to watch over his precious life. . . . /Never was man more blessed in such a wife./Never was wife more honored in her mate."

449 "I am thus equipped": JM to A. Stevenson, Nov. 20, 1832, *Writings,* IX, 488.

450 "The states *have*": S. C. "nullifying" ordinance, Nov. 24, in *Richmond Enquirer,* Nov. 30, 1832.

450 JM's rebuttal: JM to Trist, Dec. 23, to Cabell, Dec. 27, 1832, JM-LC.

450 "Our Union!": Pres. A. Jackson, proclamation, Dec. 10, 1832.

450 "Peace offering" and debate in Virginia Assembly: *Richmond Enquirer,* Dec. 22, 1832, Jan. 1, 5, 17, 29, 1833.

451 "On Nullification," JM, Jan. 1833, *Letters,* IV, 395–425. The essay went first to Speaker Stevenson.

451 "Whether experience would prove": *Ibid.,* 423.

451 "Demolished the doctrine": Trist to JM, Jan. 20, 1833, VaHS. See also JM to Alexander Rives, January 1833, marked "Confidential," *Writings,* IX, 495–498; to W. C. Rives, Mar. 12, *ibid.,* 511–514; to Webster, Mar. 15, 1833; to Clay, June 1833, *ibid.,* 515–518; to EC, Aug. 29, 1834, *ibid.,* 536–542.

452 "Thoroughly imbued": W. C. Rives, Feb. 14, 1833, *Register of Debates in Congress* (Senate), IX. For the whole debate on nullification, see *ibid.,* Feb. 6 and 14–16, 1833.

452 "Ablest, wisest and purest": Clay, *ibid.,* Mar. 1, 1833.

452 "Recoil from its horrors": JM to Clay, Apr. 2, 1833, JM, *Letters,* IV, 567.

452 "Making us one people": JM to G. Tucker, July 6, 1833, *Letters,* IV, 303.

XX *MISS MARTINEAU PERCEIVES SOMETHING*

454 "'Most everybody": DM to M. Cutts, Mar. 10, 1833, Cutts coll., LC.

454 "My dear Payne": DM to M. Cutts, Mar. 13, 1833, *ibid.*

455 "They are in my eyes": SCS to DM, June 21, 1833, *ibid.*

455 "Not born for inglorious life": DM to Richard Cutts, Aug. 22, 1833, Cutts coll., LC.

455 "May your fortune": DM to M. Cutts, Aug. 1, 1833, Cutts coll. LC.

456 "Coming and going": DM to D. Cutts, Aug. 27, 1833, *ibid.*

456 "Have to make some return": SCS to DM, Nov. 22, 1833, *ibid.*

456 Madison Cutts and his bride's visit to Montpelier: Goodwin (using family sources), 235, 236.

456 "Full of intelligence": DM to Ellen O'Neale Cutts, Jan. 26, 1834, Clark, 261.

457 "Both your uncle and I": DM to M. Cutts, Apr. 20, 1834, *ibid.*

458 "Yours, dearest, promising to write me": DM to son, July 20, 1834, L. B. Cutts, 190.

458 " . . . My family are all Virginians": DM, autobiographical sketch, Smith, 351. Apparently DM's autobiographical letter of Aug. 31, 1834 (351, 352), furnished the basis for Mrs. Smith's sketch published (signed MBS) in Herring and Longacre, National Portrait Gallery, III, 2nd article, 1–10.

458 " . . . What [is] more dangerous": JM to EC, Aug. 29, 1834, *Letters,* IV, 357.

459 "Propagating itself": JM to EC, Oct. 15, 1834, *ibid.,* 367.

459 JM's perception of growing tension between slaveholding and nonslaveholding states: JM to Daniel Drake, Jan. 12, 1835, JM-LC, *Writings,* IX, 546, 547.

PAGE

459   "Where truth alone": JM, "Advice to My Country," JM-LC; facsimile in Dolley's hand in *Writings,* IX, 552.

459   "There has been a spell": DM to D. Cutts, Dec. 2, 1834, Cutts coll., LC.

460   "You say, darling": DM to M. Cutts, Dec. 2–4, 1834, *ibid.*

460   "Few can write": DM to D. Cutts, Feb. 10, 1835, *ibid.*

460   "Sweet day of early spring": H. Martineau, *Retrospect of Western Travel,* I, 193. All details of her visit are drawn from the section entitled "Madison."

463   JM's presidency of the American Colonization Society succeeded that of Charles Carroll of Carrollton, and was followed, on JM's death, by Henry Clay's.

465   Owen's colony: Robert Dale Owen, eldest son of Robert Owen, founder of the New Harmony Colony in Indiana, had visited Montpelier in early 1825, after which Madison, skeptical but interested, had kept himself informed about this socialistic experiment in shaping character through environment and work.

465   "Emphatically the Sage": J. K. Paulding, "An Unpublished Sketch of James Madison," VMHB, Oct. 1959, Vol. 67, no. 4.

468   JM could hold his own with the peers of England: Benjamin Ogle Tayloe, 118.

XXI *ARK OF UNION*

PAGE

469   "Enlightened conversation": DM to M. Cutts, Mar. 10, 1835, Cutts coll., LC.

469   JM's will: Drawn up April 17, signed April 19, 1835, *Writings,* IX, 548–552. His brother William's displeasure over the bequests would find expression in an 1840 lawsuit against DM. Orange County Records.

470   "Ruinous extravagance": John C. Payne to J. M. Cutts, Sept. 1, 1849, JM-Chicago.

471   Payne's buildings at Toddsberth: Mary E. E. Cutts, Cutts coll., LC. None of the buildings are standing today. In 1962 I talked with the owner Mr. Wade Browning, who remembered the ruins of an old eight-sided "ballroom," about 20 by 30 feet, with a dummy elevator in the middle, and trap door at the head of a staircase down to a round stone-lined wine cellar with copper fittings. The benches around the walls were for the convenience of dancers who never came. There were "towers"—plural—on top.

471   "These deep shades": DM to D. Cutts, May 11, 1835, *ibid.*

471   The Liberty Bell: Originally the "Province Bell," it arrived in Pennsylvania in 1753 to celebrate the Colony's 50th anniversary. Engraved around its crown ran words from Leviticus: "Proclaim liberty throughout all the land."

472   "Mr. Madison . . . will leave monuments": T. L. McKenney to DM, July 28, 1835, Cutts coll., LC.

472   "As ragged as bushes": DM to M. Cutts, with enclosure for D. Cutts, Oct. 31, 1835, *ibid.*

472   "Tell me everything": DM to M. Cutts, Oct. 31, 1835, *ibid.*

472   "As good as you are now": DM to R. D. Cutts, Oct. 23, 1835, *ibid.*

472   "Now look and see": DM to F. Lear, Nov. 3, 1835, *ibid.*

473   "The hope of the world": JM to W. C. Preston, Feb. 22, 1836, JM-IC.

PAGE

473 JM on conscience: JM to B. W. Leigh (though the name is withheld in this unsent draft marked "reflections," the first sentence made impersonal), March 1836, JM-LC; *Letters,* IV, 429. "Its paramount dictates must of course be your guide."

473 "It rains like the mischief": D. Cutts, in DM to D. Cutts, Mar. 15, 1836, Cutts coll., LC.

473 "Precious Dolché": *Ibid.*

473 "The green grass": A. Payne to M. Cutts, Apr. 18, 1836, *ibid.*

474 "What a terrible massacre": *Ibid.*

474 "Symmetrical": DM to Pres. Andrew Jackson (who had sent a letter of sympathy along with copies of his letter to Congress on JM's death and Congressional resolutions of praise and sorrow), July 10, 1836, *ibid.* DM's whole phrase: "consistency, symmetry and beauty of character in all its parts."

474 "Decayed and in need": C. J. Ingersoll, *Washington Globe,* Aug. 12, 1836.

475 "Oppressive fatigue": DM to unknown, May 8, 1836, Cutts coll., LC.

476 "Less abased": JM to Ingersoll (dictated to Payne Todd), May 14, 1836, *ibid.*

476 "Harum scarum" Annie: James Buchanan, statement for Annie Payne's album, Nov. 8, 1848, quoted in sale catalog of Stan. V. Henkels, Jr., Philadelphia, Oct. 13, 1933, NYPL. The tribute goes on: "Though gay as a lark . . . yet a deep undercurrent of good sense and strict propriety controls all her conduct."

476 "Of the first chop": JM to J. Maury, May 26, 1836, JM-LC.

476 JM entreats DM to try to stay composed: Annie Payne to F. Lear, July 16, 1836, Henley-Smith Papers, LC; Anthony, 329.

476 "In his views on important subjects": J. C. Payne to J. M. Cutts, June 20, 1836, *Intelligencer,* July 2, 1836.

476 "Strange as it sounds": Goodwin, 246.

477 The last "James Madison" signature: JM to George Tucker, June 27, 1836, *Letters,* IV, 435. See also George Tucker, memoir, Rives-LC.

477 "Great calmness and self-possession": A. Payne to F. Lear, July 16, 1836, Henley-Smith Papers, LC.

477 "What's the matter, Uncle Jeames?" and other details of JM's death: Jennings, 20, 21.

478 "In one violent burst": ex-Gov. James Barbour, eulogy delivered August 1836, at Orange Courthouse, during a memorial service for James Madison; Mary E. E. Cutts, memoir, Cutts coll., LC.

Bibliography

PRIVATE TESTIMONY, WRITTEN AND ORAL

Judge H. P. Baker, Judge Leon Bazile, Mrs. James Madison Cutts III, Brigadier General Richard Malcolm Cutts, Mrs. Minnie Hite Moody, Dr. and Mrs. John A. Washington of Harewood.

CATALOGS AND INVENTORIES OF MADISON EFFECTS

American Art Association Auction Catalog, January 13, 14, 1836 (No. 4289).
American Art Association Catalog, February 26, 1917 (McGuire Collection).
Davis and Harvey Catalog, Philadelphia, n. d.
Stan. V. Henkels, Philadelphia, May 11, 12, 1892 (No. 686).
Stan. V. Henkels, December 6, 7, 1892)No. 694).
Stan. V. Henkels, May 9, 1899 (No. 821).
Stan. V. Henkels, October 13, 1933 (No. 1478).
Montpelier Inventory, July 26, 1802.
Dining Room Inventory, Montpelier, July 1, 1836.

CLIPPINGS ABOUT THE MADISONS

File, District of Columbia Library.

COURTHOUSE SOURCES

Deed Books, Order Books, Will Books and Tax Records in these Virginia counties: Albemarle, Goochland, Hanover, Orange and Rockbridge.

NEWSPAPERS AND MAGAZINES

Albermarle Gazette
American Citizen
American Daily Advertiser
American Historical Association Reports
American Historical Review
Baltimore Evening Post
Baltimore Federal Republican

Baltimore Patriot
Baltimore Whig
Boston Columbian Sentinel
Boston Gazette
Boston Repertory
Boston Yankee
Charleston Courier

City of Washington Gazette
Democratic Press (John Binn's)
Farmer's Register
Federal Republican
Gazette of the United States
George Town Federalist
Greensboro Daily News
Independent Gazetteer
London Chronicle
London Times
National Gazette
National Intelligencer
New York Advertiser
New York American Citizen
New York Commercial Advertiser
New York Courier and Enquirer
New York Evening Post
New York Herald
New York Spectator
Norfolk Public Ledger
North American
The [Orange Court House] Reporter
The Orange Press

Pennsylvania Chronicle
Pennsylvania Gazette
Pennsylvania Herald
Pennsylvania Journal
Pennsylvania Magazine of History and
    Biography
Pennsylvania Packet
Philadelphia Advertiser
Philadelphia Aurora
Philadelphia Independent Gazetteer
Richmond Constitutional Whig
Richmond Enquirer
Tyler's Quarterly
Virginia Advocate
Virginia Gazette (Dixon and Hunter's)
Virginia Gazette (Purdie's)
Virginia Independent Chronicle
Virginia Magazine of History and Biography
Virginia Patriot
Washington Globe
William and Mary Quarterly, 1st, 2nd, and 3rd
    Series
Winchester Gazette

PRIMARY SOURCES IN MANUSCRIPT

American Philosophical Society: Lee papers; John Shippen correspondence, Madison family weather logs.

Chicago Historical Society: Papers of Edward Coles, Elbridge Gerry.

Columbia Historical Society: Records.

Greensboro Historical Museum, Greensboro, North Carolina: Kunkel Collection, including portraits, daguerreotypes, Dolley Madison clothes and memorabilia, James Madison's vest, the memoirs of Mary Causten Kunkel, daughter of Annie Payne Causten and Dolley Madison's great-niece.

Guilford College Library, North Carolina: Records of the New Garden Quaker Settlement, including Dolley Madison's birth notice.

Henry E. Huntington Library, San Marino, California: James Madison's Commission.

Historical Society of Pennsylvania: William Bradford Letterbook; Catherine Drinker Journal; papers of Edward Coles, Charles J. Ingersoll, William Jones, Thomas McKean.

Hite Material: Hite family manuscript history (loaned by Judge H. P. Baker, Cartersville, Virginia); copies of many Hite family letters, including one about the Madison honeymoon (furnished by Mrs. Minnie Hite Moody of Atlanta, Georgia, then Granville, Ohio).

Independence National Historic Park, Philadelphia: Todd family papers.

Library of Congress: Letters connected with Burr's Conspiracy; John Payne Todd's fragmentary journal; photostats of diplomatic dispatches (Britain's Foreign Office 5, France's *Archives des Affaires Étrangères, correspondance politique, États-Unis*); Randolph-Garnett Letterbook; Smith Letterbook; papers of Rear Admiral George Cockburn, Alexander Hamilton, John Henry, Andrew Jackson, Thomas Jefferson, Dolley Madison (an immense amount), James Madison (the largest collection extant, including Notes of Debates in the Federal Convention of 1787, and "Advice to My Country"), George Mason, James Monroe, William Plumer, William C. Preston, William C. Rives, T. S. and

W. Shippen, Samuel Smith, Andrew Stevenson, Joseph Story, Nicholas P. Trist, Daniel Webster; also Cutts collection on microfilm.

Maryland Historical Society: Microfilm of Benjamin Henry Latrobe papers; papers of Elizabeth Patterson Bonaparte, William Plumer, General William Winder.

Massachusetts Historical Society: Thomas Jefferson Account Book; papers of John Adams, John Quincy Adams, Timothy Pickering, other New Englanders.

National Archives: James Madison letter to Rochambeau; papers of the Continental Congress (microfilm).

New Hampshire Historical Society: Papers of William Plumer, Daniel Webster.

New York Historical Society: Papers of Albert Gallatin, Hannah Gallatin, Rufus King, Robert R. Livingston, James Madison, John Randolph.

New York City Public Library: Papers of Edward Coles, J. A. Jackson, Benjamin Henry Latrobe, James Madison, James Monroe, John Payne Todd.

Pierpont Morgan Library, New York City: Papers of Elbridge Gerry, Dolley Madison, James Madison.

Princeton University Library: Papers of Catherine Coles, Edward Coles, Dolley Madison, James Madison (including his Commonplace Book dated "Dec. 24, 1759" and autobiographical sketch dictated to John C. Payne about 1816), William Pinkney, the Shippen family, Dr. John Witherspoon (including syllabus and lecture notes taken down by students).

University of Virginia (Alderman Library), Charlottesville: Papers of Edward Coles, Hannah Gallatin, Dolley Madison, James Madison (including his essay on money), Todd family; Minutes of the Board of Visitors; Nourse collection on microfilm.

Valentine Museum, Richmond, Virginia: Dolley Madison letters to Judith Richardson.

Virginia Historical Society: Genealogical data; diary of Hugh Blair Grigsby; Donald Robertson's Account Book; Trist-Madison letters; Madison-Macon Bible; manuscript of E. Randolph's History of Virginia (published in 1970).

Virginia State Library: Francis Taylor diary; Journals of the Virginia House of Delegates; copies of Dolley Madison letters to Judith Richardson; Madison's anonymous broadside.

Williamsburg Restoration: George Tucker papers.

PRIMARY SOURCES: BOOKS AND ARTICLES

Adams, Abigail, *Letters,* 2 vols. Boston, 1840.

Adams, John, *Life and Works,* ed., C. F. Adams, 10 vols. Boston, 1850–1856.

Adams, John Quincy, *Diary, 1794–1845* (selections), ed., Allan Nevins, New York, 1951.

———, *Memoirs,* ed., C. F. Adams, 12 vols. Philadelphia, 1874–1877 [Reprint, 1969.]

American State Papers, Foreign Relations, Vols. I–IV. Washington.

Ames, Fisher, *Works,* ed., Seth Ames. Boston, 1854.

Annals of Congress (House and Senate), 1789–1817.

Archives des Affaires Étrangères, correspondance politique, États-Unis; photostats in Library of Congress.

Barbé-Marbois, François, Marquis de, *The History of Louisiana,* Philadelphia, 1830. (Paris, 1829.)

Bath Archives (selections from the diaries and letters of Sir George Jackson), ed., Lady Jackson, 2 vols. London, 1873.

Blair, Samuel, *An Account of the College of New Jersey,* Woodbridge, New Jersey, 1764.

Book of Common Prayer, Revised. Philadelphia, 1789 ed.

Brissot de Warville, Jacques Pierre, *New Travels in the United States of America.* New York, 1792. [Reprint, 1970.]

Burnaby, The Rev. Andrew, *Travels through the Middle Settlements in North-America in the Years 1759 and 1760.* Ithaca, New York, 1960 (reprint from 2nd ed., 1775).

Burnett, Edmund Cody, ed., *Letters of the Members of the Continental Congress,* 8 vols. Washington, 1821–1836.

Calhoun, John C., *Works,* ed., R. K. Crallé, 6 vols. New York, 1851–1856. [Reprint, 1968.]

Carson, Jane, *James Innes and His Brothers of the F. H. C.* Williamsburg, 1965.

Chastellux, François Jean, Marquis de, *Travels in North America,* 2 vols. New York, 1827. [Reprint, 1963.]

Clark, Allen C., *Life and Letters of Dolly Madison.* Washington, 1914.

Clay, Henry, *Papers,* ed., J. F. Hopkins, 2 vols. Lexington, Kentucky, 1959–1961.

Cocke, W. Ronald, *Hanover County Chancery Wills and Notes.* Columbia, Virginia, 1940.

Coles, William B., *The Coles Family of Virginia.* New York, 1931.

Commager, Henry, and Allan Nevins, eds., *The Heritage of America.* Boston, 1939.

Crowninshield, Mary Boardman, *Letters, 1815, 1816.* Cambridge, 1905.

Cutler, Rev. Manasseh, *Life, Journals and Correspondence,* 2 vols. Cincinnati, 1888. [Reprint, 1935.]

Cutts, J. Madison, "Dolley Madison," *Records of the Columbia Historical Society,* Vol. 3.

Cutts, Lucia B. ("Her Grand-Niece"), ed., *Memoirs and Letters of Dolly Madison.* Boston, 1886.

Dallas, Alexander J., *Life and Writings,* ed., G. M. Dallas, 2 vols. Philadelphia, 1871.

De Crèvecoeur, M. G. St. John, *Letters of an American Farmer.* Dublin, 1792.

Elliot, Jonathan, ed., *Debates in the Several State Conventions on the Adoption of the Constitution,* 2nd ed., 5 vols. Philadelphia, 1861. [First printing, 1836.]

Farrand, Max, ed., *The Records of the Federal Convention of 1787,* 4 vols. New Haven, 1937.

Featherstonhaugh, George W., *Excursion through the Slave States,* 2 vols. London, 1844.

Federalist, The, or the New Constitution, with an Introduction by Carl Van Doren. New York, 1945.

Fithian, Philip Vickers, *Journal and Letters, 1767–1774,* ed., John R. Williams, 2 vols. Princeton, 1900–1934.

Force, Peter, ed., *American Archives: A Documentary History, 1833–1843,* 4th and 5th Series. Washington, 1837, 1848.

Foster, Sir Augustus J., *Notes on the United States of America, 1805–1812.* London, 1841.

Gallatin, Albert, *Writings,* ed., Henry Adams, 3 vols. Philadelphia, 1879.

Gerry, Elbridge, Jr., *Diary,* ed., G. B. Claude. New York, 1927.

[Gleig, George R.], *A Narrative of the Campaign of the British Army at Washington and New Orleans, by an Officer Who Served in the Expedition.* Philadelphia, 1831.

Golder, Frank A., *Guide to Materials for American History in Russian Archives,* 2 vols. Washington, 1917–1937.

Gouverneur, Marian, *As I Remember: Recollections of American Society during the Nineteenth Century.* New York, 1911.

Grigsby, Hugh Blair, *The History of the Virginia Federal Convention of 1788,* 2 vols. Richmond, 1890, 1891. [Reprint, 2 vols. in 1, 1969.]

———, *The Virginia Convention of 1776, A Discourse Delivered July 3, 1883.* Richmond, 1855.

———, *The Virginia Convention of 1829, 1830, A Discourse.* Richmond, 1854.

Hall, Basil, *Travels in North America,* 2 vols. Philadelphia, 1829.

Hall, Lt. Francis, *Travels in Canada and the United States in 1816 and 1817.* Boston, 1818.

Halleck, Fitz-Greene, *Life and Letters.* New York, 1869.

Hamilton, Alexander, *Papers,* ed., Harold C. Syrett, 23 vols. to date. New York, 1961–1976.

———, *Works,* ed., Henry Cabot Lodge, 12 vols. New York, 1904.

Haswell, John H., ed., *United States: Treaties and Conventions.* Washington, 1889.

Hayden, Horace Edwin, *Virginia Genealogies.* Wilkes-Barre, Pennsylvania, 1891.

Hening, William Waller, *Statutes at Large of Virginia,* 13 vols. New York, 1819–1823. [Reprint, 1931.]

Henry, William Wirt, *Life and Correspondence of Patrick Henry,* 3 vols. New York, 1891.

Hinshaw, William W., *Encyclopedia of American Quaker Genealogy*, 6 vols., VI. Ann Arbor, Michigan, 1936–1940.

Hone, Philip, *Diary, 1828–1851*, ed., Allan Nevins. New York, 1927.

Irving, Washington, *Life and Letters*, ed., P. M. Irving, 4 vols. New York, 1863, 1864.

———, *Letters to Henry Brevoort*, 2 vols. New York, 1915.

Jackson, Andrew, *Correspondence*, ed., John Spencer Bassett, 7 vols. Washington, 1926–1935.

James, William, *Military Occurrences of the Late War between Great Britian and the United States*, 2 vols. London, 1818.

Jefferson, Thomas, *Notes on Virginia*, 2nd ed. Philadelphia, 1788.

———, *Papers*, ed. Julian Boyd, 19 vols. to date. Princeton, 1950–1974.

———, *Works*, ed., Paul Leicester Ford, 12 vols. New York, 1904–1905.

———, *Writings*, ed. Albert Ellery Bergh, 20 vols. Washington, 1907.

Jennings, Paul, *A Colored Man's Reminiscences of James Madison*. Brooklyn, 1865.

Jones, Joseph, *Letters, 1777–1787*. Washington, 1889.

Journals of the Continental Congress.

Journals of the Council of the State of Virginia, ed., H. R. McIlwaine, II. Richmond, 1932.

King, Rufus, *Life and Correspondence*, ed., C. R. King, 6 vols. Boston, 1894–1900.

Lafayette, Marie Joseph, Marquis de, *Mémoires, correspondance et manuscrits*, 6 vols. Paris, 1837–1838.

Lauzun, Armand Louis, Duc de, *Memoirs*. New York, 1912.

Lee, Cazenove Gardner, *Lee Chronicle*. New York, 1957.

Levasseur, Auguste, *Lafayette in America in 1824 and 1825*, 2 vols. Philadelphia, 1829.

Locke, John, *Essay concerning Human Understanding*, 2 vols., 2nd ed. London, 1694.

Lossing, B. J., *Pictorial Field-Book of the War of 1812*. New York, 1868.

Maclay, William, *Journal*, ed., E. S. Maclay. New York, 1890.

McKenney, Thomas L., *Memoirs*. New York, 1846.

Madison, James, *Debates in the Federal Convention of 1787*, ed., Gaillard Hunt. New York, 1920.

———, *Letters and Other Writings*, eds., W. C. Rives and P. R. Fendall, 4 vols. Philadelphia, 1865.

———, *Papers*, Purchased by order of Congress, ed., H. D. Gilpin, 3 vols. Washington, 1840.

———, *Papers*, eds., I–VII, William T. Hutchinson and William M. E. Rachal, VIII–XI (to date), Robert A. Rutland et al. Chicago, and Charlottesville, Virginia.

———, *Selections from the Private Correspondence . . . from 1813 to 1836*, printed by J. C. McGuire. Washington, 1853.

———, *Writings*, ed., Gaillard Hunt, 9 vols. New York, 1900–1910.

———, "After-Dinner Anecdotes," *Virginia Magazine of History and Biography*, LX, No. 2 (1952).

———, "Autobiography," *William and Mary Quarterly*, II (1945).

Marshall, Anne Parks, *Martha Washington Rules for Cooking*. Washington, 1931.

Martin, Joseph, *A New and Comprehensive Gazeteer of Virginia*. Charlottesville, Virginia, 1835.

Martineau, Harriet, *Retrospect of Western Travel*, 2 vols. New York, 1838.

Meade, Bishop William, *Old Churches, Ministers and Families of Virginia*, 2 vols. Philadelphia, 1857.

Monroe, James, *Writings*, ed., S. M. Hamilton, 7 vols. New York, 1898–1903.

Montlezun, Baron de, *Voyage fait dans . . . 1816 et 1817*. Paris, 1818.

Moreau de St. Mery's American Journey, 1793–1798, eds., Kenneth and A. M. Roberts. Garden City, 1947.

National Portrait Gallery of Distinguished Americans, eds., James Herring and J. B. Longacre, 4 vols. 1834–1839.

Niles, Hezekiah, ed., *Weekly Register*. Baltimore, 1811–1836.

Oldschool, Oliver [Nathan Sargent], *The Portfolio*, 8 vols. Philadelphia, 1801–1812.

Otis, Harrison Grey, *Life and Letters,* ed., S. E. Morrison, 2 vols. Boston, 1913.

Paulding, James K., *Letters from the South.* New York, 1817.

Pecquet du Bellet, Louise, *Some Prominent Virginia Families,* 4 vols. Lynchburg, Virginia, 1907. [Reprint, 4 vols. in 2, Baltimore, 1976.]

Plumer, William, *Memoranda of Proceedings in the United States Senate, 1803–1807,* ed., E. S. Brown. New York, 1923.

Poore, Ben: Perley, *Reminiscences of Sixty Years in the National Metropolis,* 2 vols. Philadelphia, 1886.

Preston, William C., *Reminiscences,* ed., Minnie C. Yarborough. Chapel Hill, North Carolina, 1933.

Purple, Edwin R., *Genealogical Notes of the Colden Family in America.* New York, 1873.

Randolph, Edmund, *History of Virginia,* ed., A. H. Shaffer. Charlottesville, Virginia, 1970.

Randolph, Sarah N., *The Domestic Life of Thomas Jefferson.* New York, 1871.

Randolph, Thomas Jefferson, *Memoir, Correspondence and Miscellanies.* Charlottesville, Virginia, 1829.

Register of Debates (House and Senate). Washington, 1924 to date.

Richardson, James D., ed., *A Compilation of the Messages and Papers of the Presidents.* New York, 1912.

Roberts, Chalmers M., *Washington Past and Present: A Pictorial History of the Nation's Capital.* Washington, 1949–1950.

Robertson, Donald, "Accounts . . . ," *The Virginia Magazine of History and Biography,* XXXIII (1925).

Rogers, William Barton, ed., *Reprint of Annual Reports . . . on the Geology of the Virginias.* New York, 1884.

Royall, Anne, *A Southern Tour,* 3 vols. Washington, 1830, 1831.

Safford, William H., *The Blennerhassett Papers.* Cincinnati, 1864. [Reprint, 1971.]

Schoepf, Johann D., *Travels in the Confederation,* 2 vols. Philadelphia, 1811.

Scott, W. W., *A History of Orange County, Virginia.* Richmond, 1907.

Seaton, William Winston, *A Biographical Sketch.* Boston, 1871.

Slaughter, the Rev. Philip, *A History of St. Mark's Parish, Culpeper County, Virginia . . . with Illustrations of the Manners and Customs of the Olden Time.* Baltimore, 1877.

Smith, Margaret Bayard (Mrs. Samuel Harrison Smith), *The First Forty Years of Washington Society* (letters), ed., Gaillard Hunt. New York, 1906.

Sparks, Jared, *Life and Writings of Jared Sparks,* ed., Herbert Baxter Adams, 2 vols. New York, 1893.

State Papers and Public Documents of the United States . . . Including Confidential Documents, 2nd ed., 10 vols. Boston, 1817.

Stewart, John Q., " Madison and Wilson," with Madison's essay, "Symmetry in Nature." Brochure reprinted from the *Princeton University Library Chronicle,* Vol. XXIII, no. 3. Princeton, 1962.

Story, W. W., *Life and Letters of Joseph Story.* Boston, 1851.

Swem, E. G., *Virginia Historical Index.* Roanoke, Virginia, 1934–1936.

Tayloe, Benjamin Ogle, *In Memoriam,* ed., Winslow M. Watson. Washington, 1872.

Tichnor, George, *Life, Letters and Journal,* 2 vols. Boston, 1909.

Washington, George, *Diaries,* ed., J. C. Fitzpatrick, 4 vols. Boston, 1925.

———, *Writings,* ed., Jared Sparks, 12 vols. Boston, 1837–1847.

———, *Writings,* ed., John C. Fitzpatrick, 39 vols. Washington, 1931–1944.

Webster, Daniel, *Works,* ed., J. W. McIntyre, 6 vols., Boston, 1869.

Wharton, Francis, ed., *The Revolutionary Diplomatic Correspondence of the United States,* 6 vols. Washington, 1889.

Wolcott, Oliver, *Memoirs,* ed., Gibbs, 2 vols. Boston, 1876.

Woods, the Rev. Edgar, *History of Albemarle County, Virginia.* Charlottesville, Virginia, 1901.

SECONDARY SOURCES

(Some of these books contain primary material; for example, Goodwin, Hayden, Naulty.)

Abernathy, Thomas P., *Western Lands and the American Revolution*. New York, 1937.

Adams, Henry, *A History of the United States of America*, 9 vols. New York, 1889–1891.

———, *The Life of Albert Gallatin*. Philadelphia, 1879.

Adams, John Quincy, *The Lives of James Madison and James Monroe*. Boston, 1850.

Allen, E. M., *Lafayette's Second Expedition to Virginia in 1781*. Baltimore, 1891.

Ambler, Chester Henry, *Sectionalism in Virginia from 1776 to 1851*. Chicago, 1910.

Ammon, Harry, *James Monroe: The Quest for National Identity*. New York, 1971.

Anthony, Katharine, *Dolley Madison, Her Life and Times*. Garden City, 1949.

Armstrong, John, *Notices of the War of 1812*, 2 vols. New York, 1836–1840.

*Arnett, Ethel Stevens, *Mrs. James Madison: The Incomparable Dolley*. Greensboro, North Carolina, 1972.

Babcock, K. C., *The Rise of American Nationality, 1811–1819*. New York, 1969.

Bagby, Alfred, *King and Queen County, Virginia*. New York, 1908.

Bancroft, George, *History of the Formation of the Constitution*, 2 vols. New York, 1882.

Barnard, Ella Kent, *Dorothy Payne, Quakeress*. Philadelphia, 1909.

Bassett, John Spencer, *Life of Andrew Jackson*, 2 vols. New York, 1925.

Bates, Ernest Sutherland, *The Story of Congress, 1789–1935*. New York, 1936.

Beam, Jacob Newton, *The American Whig Society of Princeton*. Princeton, 1923.

Bean, Robert Bennett, *The Peopling of Virginia*. Boston, 1938.

Beirne, Francis F., *The War of 1812*. New York, 1949. [Reprint, 1965.]

Bemis, Samuel F., ed., *The American Secretaries of State and Their Diplomacy*, 10 vols. (II, Jefferson, III, Madison). New York, 1827–1829.

———, *Jay's Treaty: A Study in Commerce and Diplomacy*. New Haven, 1962.

Beveridge, Albert J., *The Life of John Marshall*, 4 vols. Boston, 1916–1919.

Biggs, James, *History of . . . Miranda's Attempt to Effect a Revolution in South America*. Boston, 1810.

Bishop, Abraham, *Georgia Speculation Unveiled*. Hartford, 1797.

Bonney, C. V. R., *A Legacy of Historical Gleanings*, 2 vols. Albany, 1875.

Bowen, Catherine Drinker, *Miracle at Philadelphia*. Boston, 1966.

Bowers, Claude G., *Jefferson and Hamilton: The Struggle for Democracy in America*. Boston, 1925.

Brady, Joseph P., *The Trial of Aaron Burr*. New York, 1913.

Brandon, Edgar Ewing, *Lafayette, Guest of the Nation*. Oxford, Ohio, 1950.

Brant, Irving, *James Madison*, 6 vols. Indianapolis, 1941–1961.

Brawley, James S., *The Rowan Story, 1753–1953*. Salisbury, North Carolina, 1953.

Brown, Margaret W., *The Dresses of the First Ladies*. Washington, 1952.

Brown, Roger, *1812: The Republic in Peril*. New York, 1964.

Brown, Stuart G., *The First Republicans*. Syracuse, New York, 1954.

Bruce, Philip Alexander, *A History of the University of Virginia*, 5 vols. New York, 1920.

Bruce, William Cabell, *John Randolph of Roanoke*, 2 vols. New York, 1922.

Bryce, James, Viscount, *The American Commonwealth*. London, 1888.

Bullock, Helen, *The Williamsburg Art of Cookery*. Richmond, 1938.

Burnett, Edmund Cody, *The Continental Congress*. New York, 1941. [Reprint, 1964.]

Burns, Edward McNall, *James Madison: Philosopher of the Constitution*. New Brunswick, New Jersey, 1938.

Cartmell, T. K., *Shenandoah Valley Pioneers and Their Descendants*. Winchester, Virginia, 1909.

*This book was not encountered until mine was in process of publication. It contains some interesting material about Dolley Madison's birthplace.

Channing, Edward, *History of the United States,* 6 vols. New York, 1912–1926.

Coit, Margaret, *John C. Calhoun.* Boston, 1950.

Coles, Harry L., *The War of 1812.* Chicago, 1965.

Collins, Varnum L., *Life of John Witherspoon,* 2 vols. Princeton, 1925.

Coombs, J. J., *The Trial of Aaron Burr for High Treason,* 2 vols. Washington, 1864.

Cooke, Jacob E., ed., *The Federalist: America's Greatest Contribution to Political Philosophy.* Middletown, Connecticut, 1922 (6th ed.).

Cox, Isaac J., *The West Florida Controversy, 1798–1813.* Baltimore, 1918.

Curtis, George Tichnor, *Life of Daniel Webster,* 2 vols. New York, 1870.

Denslow, Ray V., *Freemasonry and the Presidency, U. S. A.,* [Trenton?], 1952.

Earle, Alice Morse, *Stage-Coach and Tavern Days.* New York, 1900.

———, *Two Centuries of Costume in America.* New York, 1903.

Eckenrode, H. J., *The Revolution in Virginia.* Hamden, Connecticut, 1964.

———, *Separation of Church and State in Virginia.* Richmond, 1910.

Ecker, Grace D., *A Portrait of Old George Town.* Richmond, 1933.

Ellet, Elizabeth F., *Court Circles of the Republic.* Philadelphia, 1872. [Reprint, 1975.]

Ellis, Richard E., *The Jeffersonian Crisis; Courts and Politics in the Young Republic.* New York, 1975.

Farrand, Max, *The Fathers of the Constitution.* New Haven, 1921.

Faulkner, Harold Underwood, *American Political and Social History.* New York, 1927.

Faÿ, Bernard, and Avery Claflin, *The American Experiment.* New York, 1929.

Ferguson, E. James, *The Power of the Purse.* Chapel Hill, 1961.

Findley, William, *History of the Insurrection.* Philadelphia, 1796.

Flexner, James Thomas, *Washington, the Indispensable Man.* Boston, 1974.

Freeman, Douglas Southall, *George Washington,* 7 vols. New York, 1948–1957.

Fuller, Herbert Bruce, *The Purchase of Florida: Its History and Diplomacy.* Cleveland, 1906.

Gay, Sydney H., *Life of James Madison.* Boston, 1884.

Goodwin, Maud Wilder, *Dolly Madison.* New York, 1896.

Gottschalk, Louis, *Lafayette Comes to America.* Chicago, 1935.

Green, Constance M., *The Church on Lafayette Square.* Washington, 1970.

———, *Washington: Village and Capital, 1800–1878,* 2 vols., II. Princeton, 1962.

Greene, Evarts Boutell, *History of the Virginia Federal Convention of 1788,* 2 vols. Richmond, 1890–1891.

———, *Religion and the State.* New York, 1941.

Gwathmey, John Hastings, *Twelve Virginia Counties.* Richmond, 1937.

Hamilton, A. M., *The Intimate Life of Alexander Hamilton.* New York, 1910.

Hamilton, J. C., *History of the Republic . . . in the Writings of Alexander Hamilton,* 7 vols. New York, 1857–1864.

Hayden, Horace Edwin, *Virginia Genealogies.* Wilkes-Barre, Pennsylvania, 1891.

Hendrick, Burton J., *Bulwark of the Republic: A Biography of the Constitution.* Boston, 1937.

Hockett, Homer C., *Political and Social Growth of the American People, 1492–1865.* New York, 1944.

Horsman, Reginald, *The War of 1812.* New York, 1969.

Howard, Richard C., *The War of 1812.* New York, 1972.

Hunt, Gaillard, *Life of James Madison.* New York, 1902.

Ingersoll, Charles J., *Historical Sketch of the Second War between the United States and Great Britain,* 2 vols. Philadelphia, 1845.

Ingraham, E. D., *Sketch of the Events which Preceded the Capture of Washington.* Philadelphia, 1849.

Jensen, Merrill, *The New Nation: A History of the United States during the Confederation, 1781–1789.* New York, 1950.

Ketcham, Ralph, *James Madison: A Biography.* New York, 1971.

Kimball, Fiske, *Thomas Jefferson, Architect.* Cambridge, 1916.

Koch, Adrienne, *Jefferson and Madison: The Great Collaboration.* New York, 1950.

——, and Harry Ammon, "The Virginia and Kentucky Resolutions," *William and Mary Quarterly,* April, 1948.

Krout, J. A., and D. R. Fox, *The Completion of Independence, 1790–1830.* New York, 1944.

Kurtz, Stephen G., *The Presidency of John Adams.* Philadelphia, 1957.

Lancaster, Robert Bolling, *A Sketch of the Early History of Hanover County, Virginia.* Ashland, Virginia, 1957.

Lippincott, H. M., *Early Philadelphia: Its People, Life and Progress.* Philadelphia, 1917.

Lodge, Henry Cabot, *Historical and Political Essays.* Boston, 1892.

Long, Breckinridge, *Genesis of the Constitution of the United States of America.* New York, 1926.

Lord, Walter, *The Dawn's Early Light,* New York, 1972.

McCaleb, Walter F., *The Aaron Burr Conspiracy.* New York, 1903.

McCormick, John W., "The First Master of Ceremonies of the White House," *Records,* Columbia Historical Society, Vol. 7, 170–194 (1904).

McCosh, James, *The Scottish Philosophy.* New York, 1883.

McLean, John, *History of the College of New Jersey.* Philadelphia, 1877.

Mahan, Alfred Thayer, *Sea Power in Its Relations to the War of 1812,* 2 vols. New York, 1905 [reprint, 1968].

Malone, Dumas, *Jefferson and His Time,* 5 vols. to date. Boston, 1948–1974.

Mayo, Bernard, *Henry Clay, Spokesman for the West* (to 1812). Boston, 1937.

Meade, Robert D., *Patrick Henry,* 2 vols. Philadelphia, 1957–1969.

Miller, John C., *The Federalist Era, 1789–1801.* New York, 1964.

Mitchell, Broadus, *Alexander Hamilton,* 2 vols. New York, 1957–1962.

Morse, Anson Ely, *The Federalist Party in Massachusetts.* Princeton, 1909.

Morse, John Torrey, Jr., *The Life of Hamilton,* 2 vols. Boston, 1876.

Mott, Frank Luther, *American Journalism: A History of Newspapers in the United States, 1690–1950.* New York, 1950.

Naulty, Edwin Fairfax, *History of Harewood.* Philadelphia, 1901.

Nevins, Allan, *The American States during and after the Revolution.* Boston, 1942.

Nugent, Nell Marion, *Cavaliers and Pioneers; Abstracts of Virginia Land Patents and Grants, 1628–1800,* 5 vols., I. Richmond, 1934.

Pancake, J. S. "Aaron Burr: Would-Be Usurper," *William and Mary Quarterly,* April, 1951.

Parrington, Vernon. *Main Currents in American Thought . . . from the Beginning to 1920,* 3 vols. New York, 1927–1930.

Parton, James, *The Life and Times of Aaron Burr.* New York, 1858.

Pearson, Eleanor Fox, "Dolley Madison: She Was a Rose of Rare Beauty," *Greensboro Daily News,* May 24, 1942.

Perkins, Bradford, *The Causes of the War of 1812.* New York, 1962.

Peterson, Merrill D., "Thomas Jefferson and Commercial Policy, 1783–1793," *William and Mary Quarterly,* XXII (1965).

Phillips, Ulrich B., *Life and Labor in the Old South.* Boston, 1963.

Pickering, Octavius, *The Life of Timothy Pickering,* 4 vols. Boston, 1867–1873.

Powell, John H., *Richard Rush, Republican Diplomat.* Philadelphia, 1942.

Powell, Mary A., *The History of Old Alexandria.* Richmond, 1928.

Prentiss, Charles, *Life of General Eaton.* Brookfield, Massachusetts, 1813.

Randall, Henry S., *The Life of Thomas Jefferson,* 3 vols. New York, 1858.

Reardon, John J., *Edmund Randolph: A Biography.* New York, 1974.

Reniers, Perceval, *The Springs of Virginia: Life, Love and Death at the Waters, 1775–1900.* Chapel Hill, 1941.

Rice, Howard, *The Rittenhouse Orrery.* Princeton, 1954.

Richardson, Maj. John, *The War of 1812.* Toronto, 1902.

Rives, William C., *Life and Times of James Madison,* 3 vols. (unfinished). Boston, 1859–1868.

Robertson, James A., ed., *Louisiana under Spain, France and the United States, 1785–1807.* Cleveland, 1911.

Rossiter, Clinton, *Alexander Hamilton and the Constitution.* New York, 1964.

——, *Seedtime of the Republic.* New York, 1953.

Rowland, Kate Mason, *The Life of George Mason,* 2 vols. New York, 1892.

Rutland, Robert A., *George Mason, Reluctant Statesman.* New York, 1961.

Schachner, Nathan, *Aaron Burr.* New York, 1937.

Sellers, Charles Coleman, *Charles Willson Peale,* 2 vols. New York, 1969.

——, *Portraits and Miniatures by Charles Willson Peale.* Philadelphia, 1952.

Singleton, Esther, *The Story of the White House,* 2 vols. New York, 1907.

Sioussat, Annie M., *Old Baltimore.* New York, 1931.

Smelser, Marshall, *The Democratic Republic, 1801–1815.* New York, 1968.

Smith, Abbot E., *James Madison, Builder.* New York, 1937.

Smith, Charles Pope, *James Wilson, Founding Father.* Chapel Hill, 1956.

Sparks, Jared, *Life of George Washington.* Boston, 1839.

Staudenraus, P. J., *The African Colonization Movement, 1816–1865.* New York, 1961.

Stokes, Anson Phelps, *Church and State in the United States,* 3 vols. New York, 1950. [1-vol. ed., 1964.]

Styron, Arthur, *The Last of the Cocked Hats: James Monroe and the Virginia Dynasty.* Lawton, Oklahoma, 1945.

Tatum, George B., *Penn's Great Town.* Philadelphia, 1961.

Thorp, Willard, ed., *Lives of Eighteen from Princeton.* Princeton, 1946.

Tucker, George, "Autobiography," *Bermuda Historical Quarterly,* Autumn-Winter, 1963–1964.

Tucker, Glenn, *Poltroons and Patriots, a Popular Account of the War of 1812,* 2 vols. Indianapolis, 1954.

Upton, Harriet Taylor, *Our Early Presidents: Their Wives and Children from Washington to Jackson.* Boston, 1891.

Van Tyne, Claude H., "Sovereignty in the American Revolution," *American Historical Review,* Vol. XII, no. 3, April, 1907.

Van Steeg, Charles L., *Robert Morris, Revolutionary Financier.* Philadelphia, 1954.

Walters, Raymond, Jr., *Albert Gallatin, Jeffersonian Financier and Diplomat.* New York, 1957.

Wandell, Samuel Henry, and M. M. Minnegerode, *Aaron Burr.* New York, 1925.

Warren, Charles, *The Making of the Constitution.* New York, 1967.

Wertenbaker, Thomas J., *The Old South: the Founding of American Civilization.* New York, 1942.

Wharton, Anne Hollingsworth, *Social Life in the Early Republic.* Philadelphia, 1902.

White, Leonard D., *The Federalists.* New York, 1948.

——, *The Jeffersonians; A Study in Administrative History.* New York, 1951.

Williams, John S., *History of the Invasion and Capture of Washington.* New York, 1857.

Wirt, William, *Life and Character of Patrick Henry.* New York, 1831.

Woody, Thomas, *Early Quaker Education in Pennsylvania.* New York, 1920.

INDEX